THE INTERNATIONAL LAW OF CIVIL WAR

THE INTERNATIONAL LAW
OF CIVIL WAR

Edited by
RICHARD A. FALK

Quincy Wright
Ann Van Wynen Thomas
A. J. Thomas, Jr.
Arnold Fraleigh

Donald W. McNemar
Kathryn Boals
Percy E. Corbett
Edwin B. Firmage

Published under the auspices of
THE AMERICAN SOCIETY OF INTERNATIONAL LAW

The Johns Hopkins Press   **Baltimore and London**

To
QUINCY WRIGHT
1890–1970

CONTENTS

Contents

Contents

PREFACE

The destiny of the modern world is closely tied to the consequences of widespread revolutionary violence. The character of revolutionary violence does not lend itself very easily to the distinction between civil war and international war that has been basic to thinking in international law on the subject of political violence. The distinguishing mark of revolutionary violence is that it is often so interlinked with wider historical and ideological trends that its particular embodiment in geographical space can be misleading, if not distorting. The reality of revolutionary violence—that is, political violence seeking a drastic reordering of the structure of a domestic society—generates counterrevolutionary historical and ideological trends that may make responses to revolutionary challenges also assume global character and significance. The interplay of these revolutionary and counterrevolutionary patterns is central to the dominant international struggle of our time, a struggle between the Western-led forces of democratic liberalism and the Moscow- and Peking-led forces of communism. It is the central significance of revolutionary violence and its resistance to traditional legal analysis that gives focus and depth to any general study at this historical time of the international law of civil war.

The processes of decolonization and the residues of colonialism in southern Africa contribute a distinctive interrelated dimension to this problem. Decolonization has occurred frequently where a society is insufficiently prepared for the tasks and responsibilities of self-government and national autonomy. Residual colonialism (especially in the Portuguese territories) has defied the collective conscience of mankind and represents such an affront to the governing elites of former colonial states in Africa and Asia as to produce demands for regional and community coercion to induce social and political change. These problems centering upon the aftermath of colonialism and upon residual colonialism coincide in varying degrees with the confrontation of revolutionary and counterrevolutionary politics. We look, then, at the problems of civil war as in part an expression of a broader concern with establishing a just and durable international legal order.

Moreover, the entire struggle to substitute persuasion for coercion as

This Preface has been prepared for the Society Panel on the Role of International Law in Civil Wars by the editor of this volume.

the main engine of social and political change is contingent upon the degree to which the institutions of stable, yet progressive, government can be brought to national societies located in all sectors of the globe. As the strife of the 1960s in Indonesia, Ruanda-Urundi, and Nigeria suggests, critical humanitarian issues may also be at stake. Only once before in world history—during the period between 1815 and 1848—has the cause of peace and justice seemed so closely tied to the interactions between the domestic governing process and the wider international setting of conflict and cooperation among the states that dominate the world power process. The prospects for human welfare, if not survival, may be dependent on the extent to which domestic disorder and conflict can be uncoupled or insulated from the larger disorders and conflicts manifest in the relations among the principal sovereign states of international society. It may be helpful, as part of this Preface, to enumerate some of the factors in international society that account for the urgent international importance of civil-war situations.

1) The existence of a large number of unstable governments incapable of consistently providing either internal or external security for their national society.

2) The apparent absence of adequate alternatives to political violence in many of those countries in the world that are experiencing rising popular demands for social and economic justice.

3) The continuation of an intense ideological struggle between the world's most powerful states as to the philosophy, structure, and priorities that should govern the process of building a modern state, a struggle which in some measure is aggravated by the ideological and practical dedication of several communist countries to world revolution and by Western counterrevolutionary responses.

4) The replication of this global struggle between antagonistic ideologies within many weak states throughout Asia, Africa, and Latin America.

5) The natural and unavoidable links of solidarity and support between adverse internal factions and their principle external counterparts, inducing temptations, opportunities, expectations, and requests for competitive intervention.

6) The rise of strong regional and global ideological movements that advocate and rely upon covert military intervention as a justifiable and effective means to overthrow governments.

7) The occurrence of widespread destruction of human life as a consequence of ethnic, ideological, or religious identity, which at least creates some basis for international concern, if not humanitarian intervention, with regard to the commission of genocide.

8) The overriding incentive of nuclear superpowers to avoid direct military confrontation in view of the dangers of nuclear war.

9) The consequent shift in patterns of diplomatic competition for expanded influence in this unstable and dangerous world to arenas of indirect and limited confrontation, most especially to states vulnerable to external intervention and beset by internal conflict and turmoil.

10) The insufficiency of international fact-finding procedures whereby to identify covert forms of intervention and to organize effective defensive measures on behalf of a beleaguered government.

11) The emergence of national governments that are too weak to control the activities of liberation movements directed against foreign societies.

The cumulative effect of this world setting is to make the stability of international society peculiarly subject to those forms of internal violence that are closely interlinked with substantial rival external interventions. The international climate is conditioned by a pervasive and growing ambivalence on the part of many governments toward the legal status and ethical basis of the doctrine of nonintervention. This pervasive ambivalence can be illustrated by a number of quite distinct diplomatic positions that rely upon the legitimacy of military intervention against certain governments:

1) The claims of the black African states directed against the incumbent regimes of southern Africa and endorsed by the Organization of African Unity and, to some extent, by the political organs of the United Nations.

2) The claims of communist states, most stridently China and Cuba, to support guerrilla activities that are carried on within the framework of "wars of national liberation."

3) The claims of the Arab states to support "liberation movements" engaging in terrorism against the state of Israel.

4) The claims of the United States, many Latin American countries, and the Organization of American States, to take coercive action against the Castro regime in Cuba and, indeed, against movements perceived as communist throughout Latin America.

Some of these explicit claims seem quite inconsistent with the principles of order embodied in the United Nations Charter, principles premised upon mutual respect for the legitimacy of constituted governments. Where these claims enjoy the backing of a regional organization, a special legal question is presented about the conditions under which intervention is legitimate or illegitimate when it has been authorized by a duly constituted regional organization. As matters now stand, this question remains unresolved in law and controversial in practice and discussion.

In addition to the categories of explicit interventionary claims, it is necessary to take some account of prevalent patterns of covert intervention carried out through duly (or unduly) constituted instrumentalities of government or on behalf of the private or quasi-private organizations that operate within a state with or without the indulgence of the government.

The subject, then, of civil war is so prominent at the present time because many states are vulnerable to domestic violence and because many other states have the motivation to promote or exploit this vulnerability for reasons of ideological solidarity, political expansion, national security, or human compassion. In this respect, the kind of civil war that is most serious to the maintenance of international order involves an interplay of interventionary diplomacy and domestic instability. If domestic instability erupts into political violence, even of high intensity and long duration, the pattern of international order will not necessarily grow disturbed. Political violence throughout Indonesia during the years 1965–66 and the costly civil wars in the Sudan and Nigeria illustrate the capacity of the international system to reconcile itself to prolonged domestic violence causing great loss of life and physical destruction. In contrast, the Vietnam War, like the Spanish Civil War a generation earlier, illustrates interventionary contexts in which the entire basis of international stability is drawn into serious question.

The Civil War Project was initiated by the American Society of International Law in 1966 against this broad background of urgent concern. The tasks of the project have not been easy to discharge responsibly at a historical moment when the main currents of United States foreign policy are so controversially associated with intervention and civil strife. International lawyers, in common with other Americans, are deeply divided as to the wisdom of these policies, and these divisions naturally exert an influence upon the pattern and structure of legal analysis and appraisal. Difficulties in determining facts relating to alleged covert interventions in foreign civil strife and in providing any authoritative legal construction for these facts complicate greatly the enterprise of bringing into sharp focus the legal issues presented by a particular instance of civil-war intervention. In these circumstances of controversy and ambiguity it was decided by the Board of Review and Development, an organ primarily entrusted with general intellectual oversight of the society's program of research, that a panel of experts be constituted to represent adequately the spectrum of intellectual and policy perspectives present within the international law community. The main outlines of the project were then agreed upon by the collaborative proceedings of panel meetings. The result of these lively initial meetings was to decide upon a two-stage project. The first stage of the project, by now substantially complete, has involved commissioning specific studies of particular civil wars or of patterns of diplomatic practice by particular states. The second stage of the project, already significantly under way, involves the use by the panel of the studies completed during the first stage as a partial basis for evolving a general and comprehensive reinterpretation of the relevance of international law to civil war.

The panel, despite the diversity of its composition, substantially agreed that the following considerations should guide its inquiry:

1) The surprisingly low degree of recent scholarly attention that had been devoted to the relationship between international law and civil war although it is true that, since the initiation of the project, the problems generated by the Vietnam War have encouraged some international lawyers to examine the field, although mainly within a rather restricted substantive framework.

2) The important set of complicating circumstances that make it difficult to sustain the traditional international-law dichotomy between civil war (in the sense of warfare carried on primarily between factions internal to a single sovereign state) and international war (in the sense of warfare between two or more sovereign states): interventionary diplomacy; the creation, guidance, and support of puppet and proxy factions; and the tendencies for sustained civil violence with outside participation to expand beyond the boundaries of the state experiencing a struggle for internal dominance.

3) The desirability of introducing into the substantive study of the international law of civil war the modern, innovative attitude toward the role of law in relation to political violence, which stresses its managerial significance in constructively shaping the behavior of national governments through the exertion of potential influence on the official decision process.

4) The sense of insufficiency arising from lumping all situations of civil strife into a single normative category. Some, at any rate, see a need to differentiate between different kinds of conflict depending on such variables as the stakes of struggle (for example, revolutionary or nonrevolutionary), the significance and overtness of external or third-party participation, the impartiality or partiality of attitude exhibited by regional and global institutions toward the relative merits of the contending factions, and the extent to which incidental or sustained violence has spilled over the boundaries of the original national locus of struggle.

5) The awareness that modern military technology and tactics of large-scale civil war, especially if the insurgent effort relies upon subconventional or guerrilla tactics, place great pressure upon traditional rules governing the conduct of land warfare. As the scale of violence enlarges, counterguerrilla tactics increasingly rely upon indiscriminate applications of force that suggest the need to reexamine the legal limits, if any, that constrain claims of "military necessity" in these settings.

6) The very great difficulty in identifying the contours of permissible participation in the internal affairs of foreign societies so as to be able to characterize certain forms of participation as impermissible. The interdependence of national societies of greatly unequal strength in all phases of their existence suggests the impossibility of insulating weak national societies from strong competitive currents of external influence; the absence of consensus on the substance of constructive influence and the deficiency of centralized procedures for authoritatively identifying impermissible influence deepen the task of effectively proscribing certain kinds of interventionary conduct.

7) The need to explore the relationship between regional and global international institutions concerned with peace and security and the prevention, regulation, termination, and settlement of civil-war types of conflicts. An adequate conception of the international legal order requires a much clearer interpretation of the potential roles of these institutions in civil war circumstances, that is, of the roles they are constitutionally competent and politically capable of playing.

The international lawyer cannot respond to such an international context with any immediately satisfying solutions. It is a context in which the limits of legal control are readily apparent, perhaps so apparent as to obscure the possibilities for the successful discharge of constructive and moderating law tasks. As was indicated at the outset of this Preface, certain international law issues need to be reexplored in light of the altered international environment. The Civil War Project was specifically designed to clarify current patterns of state practice bearing on the relevance of law to civil-war types of situations and to illuminate the policy problems that arise when a particular conflict exhibits an interplay of domestic violence and external participation.

The purpose of these case studies of particular civil wars has been, in part, to fill gaps in the scholarly literature of international law in an area of great substantive interest and concern. An additional function served by these studies was to generate the sources that the panel believed could usefully be drawn upon for later attempts to generalize about the international law of civil war. To promote this end, it was thought useful to organize the studies of particular civil wars around a common framework of inquiry specific enough to facilitate comparisons and general enough to allow an author to give expression to the vagaries of the particular conflict under investigation and to his own conception of the proper mode of legal analysis. The panel drew up a statement of guidelines, which has been substantially adhered to by the authors. These guidelines were primarily a device by which to assure some attention to the substantive issues that the members of the panel considered most important: the facts and law of external participation on behalf of either or both contending factions; the role, if any, of international institutions; patterns of adherence to the laws of war by the parties to the conflict; and finally, the patterns of settlement by which the violence was ended and order restored.

The case studies were commissioned in such a way as to highlight the various essential features of typical civil-war situations. A variety of constraints limited our ability to be even more comprehensive: limited funds, shortage of qualified authors, failure of authors to complete their work, and the panel's sense that some studies it had commissioned did not sufficiently satisfy scholarly standards. Nevertheless, the studies published here do cut across the main dimensions of time and space, ranging from the American Civil War to the Vietnam War; contrast the pre–World War II context of the Spanish Civil War with the post–World War II context of the Algerian War of Independence, the Yemen Civil War, and Vietnam; and deal with the Congo conflict as the main example of United Nations intervention in a civil war. The panel had particularly hoped to include additional case studies of Soviet intervention in eastern Europe to balance the study of United States practice, of Cyprus to cast further light upon the role of the United Nations in civil-war situations, and of Korea to present more clearly the case for and against a sharp distinction between civil-war and international-war situations. In each instance, however, the panel's plans were frustrated by occurrences beyond its control. Nevertheless, we feel that the studies we have assembled in this volume provide students of civil war with the best available basis for generalizations about the relevance of international law.

The views of each study in the series are entirely those of the author. The panel has reviewed the manuscript at its various stages of completion and is satisfied that its publication would be a contribution to the scholarly literature. The panel recommendation has, in turn, been approved by the Society's Board of Review and Development. The author's discretion to arrive at his own interpretations or conclusions was fully respected by the panel.

Richard A. Falk, *Chairman*

Members of the Panel

Thomas Ehrlich

Edwin Brown Firmage

Tom J. Farer

Wolfgang Friedmann

G. W. Haight

Eliot D. Hawkins

Brunson MacChesney

Myres S. McDougal

John Norton Moore

Stephen M. Schwebel

Louis B. Sohn*

Howard J. Taubenfeld

Lawrence R. Velvel

Burns H. Weston

*Louis B. Sohn took part in the work of the panel prior to his appointment to the Department of State.

NOTE OF ACKNOWLEDGMENT

This volume of case studies represents the major work, to date, of the Civil War Panel of the American Society of International Law. The work is the outcome of a genuinely cooperative effort carried on over a number of years and made possible through the help and support of many people. It seems appropriate to acknowledge a few special debts.

The entire project was made possible by a grant from the Carnegie Corporation. Mr. John Stevenson, then President of the Society and now Legal Adviser to the Secretary of State, encouraged this project, served on its panel, and helped actively and decisively in the quest for outside support. The chapter authors also deserve our warm thanks for undertaking these studies along the lines prescribed by the panel and revising initial drafts on the basis of suggestions received from panel members. Professor Firmage, who undertook the difficult task of preparing the summary chapter, has been of immense help to the panel since he was added to its membership in late 1968. The American Society of International Law has provided the auspices, the administration, and the energy that has enabled us to proceed with this project over a period of several years. Stephen Schwebel, both as a member of the panel and as Executive Vice-President of the Society, has played a vital role of stewardship in relation to the work of the panel.

I would, finally, like to thank my colleagues on the Civil War Panel for their support and participation. In the spirit of inquiry, we have carried on our work in serious fashion despite many specific disagreements about the proper treatment of this controversial subject matter. Our panel explored these disagreements openly and vigorously and never sought to maintain a show of harmony by adopting vague declarations of consensus. Having acted as both Chairman and Rapporteur during the period in which these studies were completed, I am pleased to report that the remaining work of the panel will be carried on under the Chairmanship of Wolfgang Friedmann, with John Norton Moore serving as Rapporteur.

Richard A. Falk

Richard A. Falk

INTRODUCTION

Civil war is a dominant characteristic of world affairs, especially in recent decades.[1] The phenomenon of civil war, despite the terminology, is not, and has never been, an entirely domestic affair. The interrelatedness of world economic and political life is such that governments are often deeply concerned with the official policies of and changes of regimes in foreign states; hence, the impulse to intervene, where the capability exists, is often strong, especially where the alternative is to acquiesce in intervention by rivals or in an outcome that brings a hostile elite to power in a strategic state.

In the years since World War II this focus on struggles for control of foreign states has dominated the central rivalry in international society.[2] The ideological dimension of this rivalry has often made it clear that the outcome of an internal struggle would have a psychological and strategic impact on the balance of forces in world and regional affairs. The inhibitions upon large-scale violence caused by a condition of mutual vulnerability to nuclear attack have converted the internal arena of foreign states into the major testing ground of rival ideologies, capabilities, and commitments. Civil-war situations, in a variety of settings, have assumed a symbolic role in the geopolitics of the nuclear age, whether the strategic goal of a government is some sort of international equilibrium or expansionism. And finally, the widespread arousal of political energy in the improverished and suppressed sections of world society as a result of the collapse of the colonial system and the spread of a determination to achieve rapid economic and social development have created a series of national situations in which the foundations of traditional government have been badly shaken, making a local battle

---

[1] Problems of intervention and civil war have been prominent in earlier periods of international history. For discussion, see Henry A. Kissinger, *A World Restored* (New York: Grosset & Dunlop, 1964); Peter J. Fleiss, *Thucydides and the Politics of Bipolarity* (Baton Rouge: Louisiana State University Press, 1966); George A. Kelly and Linda B. Miller, *Internal War and International Systems: Perspectives on Method*, Occasional Papers in International Affairs, No. 21 (Cambridge: Harvard Center of International Affairs, 1969), pp. 1–26.

[2] See, for example, Samuel P. Huntington, "Patterns of Violence in World Politics," in Huntington (ed.), *Changing Patterns of Military Politics* (New York: Free Press, 1962), pp. 17–50. See also Ted Gurr with Charles Ruttenberg, *Cross-National Studies of Civil Violence* (Washington: American University, Center for Research in Social Systems, May 1969).

between forces of revolution and counterrevolution virtually inevitable.[3]
The disappearance of foreign rule has also removed the façade of political
unity in many countries in Asia and Africa, with the result that underlying ethnic, tribal, and religious differences cause tension, conflict, and
on many occasions, a violent struggle for ascendancy.

These conditions are likely to persist for the indefinite future. As a
result, the prevalence of domestic conflict, foreign intervention, and
world concern is not likely to diminish in the years ahead. Part of the
complexity that confronts the analyst arises from the very diversity of
contexts in which civil wars occur.[4] No sweeping generalizations are useful, even with respect to policy objectives. In a world climate influenced
by moral considerations bearing on social justice, there is little disposition to condemn all political violence or even to attack intervention
under all circumstances of civil strife. In southern Africa, for instance,
the choice between interventionary violence and oppressive racism and
colonialism has been made by the overwhelming majority of governments in favor of the militant demands for revolutionary change, although countervailing pressures are beginning to induce some black
African governments, such as Malawi, Malagasy, and even Zambia, to
seek a tacit accommodation with South Africa. International institutions, most especially the political organs of the United Nations, have
not been able to mobilize a coherent world response, especially to those
civil-war situations in which the United States and the Soviet Union find

[3] Among other studies, see Samuel P. Huntington, *Political Order in Changing
Societies* (New Haven: Yale University Press, 1968), pp. 1–92 (esp. the statistical
summary of various categories of military conflict on p. 4). For very different
interpretations of these same phenomena of civil strife, see Eqbal Ahmed, "Revolution and Counter-Revolution," to be published in Roderick Aya and Norman
Miller (eds.), *Revolutions Reconsidered* (New York: Free Press, 1970); Richard
J. Barnet, *Intervention and Revolution* (New York: World Publishing Co., 1968);
and Orlando Fals Borda, *Subversion and Social Change in Colombia* (New York:
Columbia University Press, 1969). For a special Africa perspective, see Ali A.
Mazrui, "Violent Contiguity and the Politics of Retribalization in Africa," *Journal
of International Affairs* 23: 89–105.

[4] There are a variety of efforts at classification of civil war situations. Among
them, see Lincoln P. Bloomfield and Amelia C. Leiss, *Controlling Small Wars: A
Strategy for the 1970's* (New York: Knopf, 1939); Ivo K. and Rosalind L. Feiera-
bend, "Aggressive Behaviors within Politics, 1948–1962: A Cross-National Study,"
Journal of Conflict Resolution 10 (September 1960); and James N. Rosenau, "Internal War as an International Event," in Rosenau (ed.), *International Aspects
of Civil Strife* (Princeton: Princeton University Press, 1964), pp. 45–91, esp. pp.
60–65. For a more legal perspective on the task of classification, consult John
Norton Moore, "The Control of Foreign Intervention in Foreign Conflict," *Virginia Journal of International Law* 9: 205–342, esp. pp. 254–56; and Rosalyn
Higgins, "Internal War and International Law," in Cyril E. Black and Richard
A. Falk (eds.), *The Future of the International Legal Order: Conflict Management* (Princeton: Princeton University Press, forthcoming), vol. 3.

themselves on opposite sides.[5] As a result, there has been no significant United Nations response to many civil war situations, including even such important occurrences as the Vietnam War and the Nigerian Civil War.[6] Governments decide for themselves what to do about a foreign civil war and present a rationalization in normative terms. There is, then, no machinery to obtain a fair interpretation of the facts associated with a variety of claims and counterclaims asserted in relation to civil-war situations. Summarizing world diplomacy since World War I, one usually cautious legal specialist, Erik Castrén, has observed that "states have been inconsistent with regard to the relevant legal questions. What has been consistently borne in mind is their own interest."[7] Legal language has been frequently employed to justify or complain about official behavior, especially in the course of debates about whether assistance to one side or the other is permissible given the circumstances of the struggle—for example, allegations that what other governments are doing amounts to "illegal intervention" or even "aggression." There has been an intense normative debate carried on about prominent civil-war situations, a debate that has been almost oblivious to the reliance by antagonists upon inconsistent normative traditions in many cases and adversary presentations of facts in almost every case.[8] Each intervening government contends that it is acting to offset prior interventions or, at minimum, is giving help to the duly constituted or "legitimate" government.[9]

Concerning actual behavior, Castrén is correct. Governments are guided not by fidelity to norms but by their conception of what their interests are. Interests have been self-defined by governments in light of their capabilities, foreign policy priorities, and their perception of what others will do in response to provocative action and response. Thus the USSR is cautious (after a brief, dramatic "test" in the Cuban missile

---

[5] See articles by Oscar Schachter, Lincoln P. Bloomfield, and Max Gordon, in Richard A. Falk (ed.), *Vietnam and International Law* (Princeton: Princeton University Press, 1969), 2: 273–357 [hereinafter cited as *Vietnam I* and *Vietnam II*]. On the United Nations role, see, generally, Linda B. Miller, *World Order and Local Disorder* (Princeton: Princeton University Press, 1967).

[6] A short analysis of why the United Nations did not play a role in settling the Nigerian Civil War is found in an article by Henry Tanner, "U.N. Did Not Act on War, Terming It Internal Issue," *New York Times*, Jan. 13, 1970, p. 15.

[7] Erik J. S. Castrén, *Civil War* (Helsinki: Suomalainen Tiedeakatemia, 1966), p. 73.

[8] For some discussion along these lines, see Eliot D. Hawkins, "An Approach to Issues of International Law Raised by United States Actions in Vietnam," and Wolfgang Friedmann, "Intervention, Civil War, and the Role of International Law," in *Vietnam I*, pp. 151–59, 163–200.

[9] Cf. many of the contributions to *Vietnam I* and *Vietnam II*, esp. I: 163–540 and II: 89–270.

crisis of 1962) in the Western Hemisphere.[10] Small, easily accessible countries are more attractive targets of intervention than large or inaccessible ones, and hence there is a tendency to moderate the exertion of influence in Indonesia or India, as compared with the Dominican Republic or even Iran. Interventionary diplomacy is largely practiced by large and powerful countries against weak and small, although strategic and symbolic, countries.[11]

The interest of a government, then, is an expression of its overall foreign policy as applied to a concrete situation, or its perception of that situation. Interests are translated into policies carried on over time, building momentum within the structures of government and creating processes and programs that are difficult to reverse despite a subsequent reappraisal of costs, risks, and opportunities. The long involvement of the United States government in the Vietnam War is the most dramatic illustration of "interests" producing a policy that is officially acknowledged as a mistake but one that persists in any event.[12]

In most discussions by nonlawyers of civil-war situations, there is little evidence, especially in recent practice, that governments or their opponents were guided in forming their policies by the rules of international law.[13] In fact, there is considerable reason to suppose that government decisions are made in this area with little advance effort to assess legal consequences. The main concerns of policymakers center around how much effort is needed to achieve a particular objective, including calculations as to the likely reactions of domestic and world public opinion to a given policy and encompassing the counter-measures

[10] For some discussion of these bipolar patterns of intervention, see Richard A. Falk, "The Legitimacy of Zone II as a Structure of Domination," in Vincent Davis, Maurice East, and James N. Rosenau (eds.), *The Analysis of International Politics* (New York: Free Press, forthcoming).

[11] On general patterns of interventionary diplomacy, see Barnet, *Intervention and Revolution,* and George Liska, *Imperial America* (Baltimore: Johns Hopkins Press, 1967). See also Richard W. Cottam, *Competitive Interference and 20th Century Diplomacy* (Pittsburgh: University of Pittsburgh Press, 1967).

[12] Among many useful discussions of the decisional processes involved in developing American policy toward the Vietnam War, see Townsend Hoopes, *The Limits of Intervention* (New York: McKay Co., 1969); and Arthur M. Schlesinger, Jr., *The Bitter Heritage: Vietnam and American Democracy, 1941–1966* (Boston: Houghton Mifflin, 1966). Also relevant to theorizing about government is an article by Graham T. Allison, "Conceptual Models and the Cuban Missile Crisis," *American Political Science Review* 63 (September 1969): 689–718.

[13] See, for example, Bernard B. Fall, *The Two Viet-Nams: A Political and Military Analysis* (2d rev. ed.; New York: Praeger, 1967); Ellen Hammer, *The Struggle for Indo-China* (Stanford: Stanford University Press, 1954); Robert Scigliano, *South Vietnam: Nation under Stress* (Boston: Houghton Mifflin, 1963). Somewhat more attention is given to the legal-diplomatic context in George McT. Kahin and John W. Lewis, *The United States in Vietnam* (New York: Dial, 1967), esp. pp. 43–65; Robert P. Randle, *Geneva 1954: The Settlement of the Indochinese War* (Princeton: Princeton University Press, 1969).

that might be taken by an adversary government and its allies. The main steps along the trail of intervention in a civil-war situation are prudential and political, not legal.[14] No visible effort is made by principal governments to test a proposed course of policy by reference to the impartial assessment of legal experts. Given the complexity of facts and the uncertainty of norms, such legal guidelines may not be available in any specific enough form to be useful.[15]

Under these circumstances, governments tend to use legal arguments to rationalize policy and to establish a verbal position in relation to critics. A defense based on world order is made of every intervention in a civil-war situation. In a law-oriented society such as the United States, legal authorization for controversial policy is very important. Hence, it is not far-fetched to believe the reports of 1965 and 1966 that President Lyndon Johnson carried the Gulf of Tonkin Resolution around with him to rebuff any contention that his Vietnam policies exceeded the authority of the presidency.

The relevance of international law is more significant than this set of comments has so far indicated, even if it is a subtle and often unnoticed relevance. Governments internalize certain restraints on their behavior that are embodied in basic legal instruments of the world community, such as the Kellogg-Briand Pact and the United Nations Charter. These instruments express certain very fundamental ideas about the use of political violence for military purposes that seem to influence the style and content of behavior. There is a discernible effort to limit force to defensive uses, to premise overt intervention upon an invitation from a governmental ally or on a collective determination by a group or community of governments, to deny altogether covert intervention, and to repudiate any selfish territorial or economic motivation for an interventionary role. Such biases of policy formulation express an adherence, in language at least, to the prohibitions against the use of military force in world affairs, except as a last resort in response to prior aggression. These presiding policies for world order allow at least a basis for principled opposition to intervention to arise in democratic societies and engender a debate as to whether the grounds for intervention in civil war exist; these policies also tend to inhibit governments from intervening militarily by unilateral decision except under truly unusual circumstances. Also important for discouraging intervention in a civil war unless some reasonably substantial evidence of intervention on the other

[14] See Graham Allison, Ernest May, and Adam Yarmolinsky, "U.S. Military Policy: Limits to Intervention," *Foreign Affairs* 48 (January 1970): 245–61.

[15] For a perceptive, skeptical account of the potentialities of such a context for legal determination, see Jaro Mayda's essay, "The Vietnam Conflict and International Law," in *Vietnam II*, pp. 260–70.

side exists is endorsement by governments of the policy of self-determination. The failure of the United States to make manifest its support of the Cuban exiles at the Bay of Pigs in 1961 and the high-level domestic opposition to the Dominican intervention of 1965 suggest a certain policy baseline that is influenced by a consideration of world-order values.[16] These values form a part of what most governments deem to be their interests, and therefore, the implicit conflict between adherence to law and pursuit of interests does not necessarily exist. As John Norton Moore has so aptly observed, "The national interest is more than simply barrels of oil per day or military potential; it also includes the kind of world order which we would like to see established."[17] Any legal order that commands respect is based on the generalized coincidence of legal obligation and self-interest, and it is no reflection upon the quality of international law to emphasize the extent to which its effectiveness depends on its capacity to serve the interests of governments. Of course, the time span used to identify the character of national interests, the rationality of threat perception, and the degree to which a governing elite is generous toward others are among the factors that determine the kinds of interests that it regards as vital. Because international law has neither the central guidance apparatus of highly organized domestic states or the sense of community and tradition of primitive societies, it is peculiarly dependent for its effectiveness on voluntary patterns of compliance. The norms of international behavior are secured by considerations of self-interest (the preferred course of action), habits of compliance, and reciprocity (mutuality of rights and duties to achieve stability of expectation—for example, the treatment of ambassadors). In those circumstances in which conditions of self-interest and reciprocity do not exist (and neither do central guidance nor community solidarity), all efforts at legal regulation tend to falter, especially where the stakes are high.

The relationship of international law to civil-war situations seems to present a context in which there is little immediate hope for effective legal regulation. Self-interest of the principal governments may be closely identified with the victory of one side and the defeat of the other, and this pattern of identification cannot be fixed in relation either to the constituted government or to the anti-government faction, nor can it be domesticated by projecting a set of "rules of the game." In a period

16 See Richard A. Falk, *Legal Order in a Violent World* (Princeton: Princeton University Press, 1968), pp. 184–223; Ved P. Nanda, "The United States Action in the 1965 Dominican Crisis: Impact on "World Order," *Denver Law Journal* 43 (1966): 439–79; 44 (1967): 225–74.

17 Moore, *"The Control of Foreign Intervention,"* p. 311. See also Philip C. Jessup, *The Use of International Law* (Ann Arbor: University of Michigan, 1959), pp. 1–29.

of revolutionary ferment any given government (whether revolutionary or counterrevolutionary) will sometimes favor the incumbent and sometimes the insurgent, depending on the setting. In eastern Europe, the Soviet Union favors the stability of constituted elites under most circumstances, whereas the United States favors ferment and challenge.[18] The reverse attitudes exist, by and large, in relation to revolution in the Third World. It is impossible to form a normative consensus that expresses perceived self-interests. A legal document such as the General Assembly's Declaration on the Inadmissibility of Intervention in the Domestic Affairs of States and the Protection of their Independence and Sovereignty is a hypocritical normative assertion since it contradicts the attitudes and policies of many governments.[19] Most flagrantly, it violates a virtually universal consensus in favor of intervening in the internal affairs of the states in southern Africa; more generally, this resolution affirms a principle of absolute endorsement of state sovereignty at a time when conflicting views of political legitimacy make it unrealistic, and probably undesirable, to regulate behavior by an unconditional acceptance of the precepts of nonintervention. A legal norm that operates in such a climate of contradiction is bound to function as mere rhetoric and to erode generally arguments urging for international law.[20]

Civil-war situations also exhibit very weak links of reciprocity under many circumstances. Only the weak and dependent states are susceptible to intervention. Interested third governments have greatly differing access and perceive their geopolitical prerogatives and stakes in distinct ways. There is often no way for the victims of intervention to strike back against the heartland of the intervener. Therefore, the possibility of intervention, if the calculations of prudence are favorable, may provide a relatively powerful government with strong incentives to promote the outcome it prefers in a foreign civil war.[21] Inequality of national size and power makes considerations of reciprocity least relevant where recourse to military or economic power is at issue. The diminished relevance is accentuated if there is a perception of generalized nonadherence to the norms of nonintervention, especially by principal

---

[18] The Soviet occupation of Czechoslovakia in 1968 illustrates an antiregime intervention in eastern Europe; the important issue is the policy orientation of the elite, not whether it holds or is seeking control of the government situated within a sphere of influence. The United States has engaged in antiregime limited interventions in Central America—Cuba (1961) and Guatemala (1954).

[19] United Nations, General Assembly Resolution 2131 (XX), adopted Dec. 21, 1965, 109 to 0, with the United Kingdom abstaining.

[20] See Richard A. Falk, "New States and International Legal Order," *Hague Academy Recueil des Cours*, 1966, 2: 1–103.

[21] Recently the degree of contiguity has been discounted in the analysis of the scope of security concerns. See Albert Wohlstetter, "Illusions of Distance," *Foreign Affairs* 46 (January 1968): 242–55.

7

rivals, and if there is no real hope for an effective alternative to intervention in the form of an international procedure for setting and enforcing a set of civil-war ground rules. The United Nations has attempted to play such a role in several situations both as an alternative to great power interventions and as an actor trying to terminate or confine the violence and seems able to do so when the country is relatively small (for example, Cyprus) and when the purpose of the mission commands a continuing consensus from the governments of the region involved and the general assent to the mission by the United States and the Soviet Union. The limited success (or failure) of the United Nations in the Congo—and the aftermath involving the structure and financing of such a mission—disclosed the fragility of any general move to substitute the United Nations for third-party intervention in sensitive civil-war situations.

The broad humanitarian objectives of the law of war are also beset by difficulty in the context of modern civil war. The law of war rests upon the capacity and willingness of both sides in an armed conflict to distinguish between civilians and combatants and between military and nonmilitary targets.[22] But in civil-war situations both sides often engage in terrorism, either discriminate or random, so as to discourage popular identification with either the government or its challenger. Torture is also often employed to gain information about the apparatus and plans of the revolutionary faction. The revolutionary side often lacks the equipment and manpower for pitched battle or the facilities to take prisoners or to care for wounded soldiers, whereas the government side often lacks the popular support needed to separate the revolutionary cadre from the population as a whole and thus must wage war virtually against the entire civilian population. The military equipment of the modern state also tends to be unable to direct itself in very discriminating fashion against the military capabilities of its insurgent adversary. Colonial wars have often been conflicts of this character, perhaps most dramatically in the Algerian War of Independence and in the long postcolonial war that has been raging in South Vietnam since 1960. The logic of the conflict is to carry the idea of military necessity beyond all civilized boundaries of humanitarian restraint that have been built into the laws of war over several centuries. Late in 1969 the American conscience was touched to some extent by the disclosures of a massacre of civilians including women and children at Mylai in South Vietnam, but such an event is not an isolated incident in war of this kind, duration, or

---

[22] See discussions by Josef L. Kunz, *The Changing Law of Nations* (Columbus: Ohio State University Press, 1968), pp. 831–923.

intensity.[23] As J. Glenn Gray has written, "Every veteran knows how frequently" such incidents occur "and how infrequently they come to light. War, whose language is violence, breeds such criminality as its legitimate offspring. We send boys into situations that overtax immeasurably their powers of judgment; they become casualties of war even when their bodies are unscarred."[24] Gray's comments apply to war in general, but they are most relevant in the context of civil war, where acts of war are so often indistinguishable from what would be the most shocking kind of crime of man against man. In such circumstances of decentralized combat, the professional military organization may lose control over its personnel to such an extent that even ordinary soldiers are led to commit the most vicious acts of barbarism.[25] Also official policies of counterinsurgency warfare, such as heavy bombardment of villages, may be virtually indistinguishable in effect from willful massacre of civilians by foot soldiers acting on their own initiative.

Here again, the norms of restraint, to remain effective, need to be perceived as generally consistent with interests, but interests can be normally conceived broadly and reciprocally enough to encompass humanitarian values. Article 3, common to the four Geneva Conventions on aspects of the law of war, attempts to extend minimum coverage of the laws of war to all armed conflicts. In addition, there are potential areas of reciprocity in relation to prisoners, wounded and sick soldiers, and even to battlefield tactics. Such a possibility of restraint must be based on ideas of mutuality and on the reactions of world conscience if there is to be any prospect of respect for the positive rules during periods of pressure.

It seems possible, then, to summarize the relevance of international law to civil wars along the following lines: (1) There is little evidence that governments shape their response to civil-war adversaries by reference to legal rules and procedures but rather shape policy mainly on the basis of calculations of prudence and military necessity. (2) Most governments and people share certain values that include the minimization of violence and the avoidance of gratuitous suffering and destruction, provided other perceived interests are not too seriously jeopardized. (3) There exist mutual interests in support of limiting both intervention by foreign governments in civil-war situations and regulating the character of permissible tactics of war. (4) A variety of political circum-

---

[23] For some discussion, see Richard A. Falk, "Songmy: War Crimes and Individual Responsibility," *Trans-Action* 7 (January 1970): 33–40; and Zalin B. Grant, "It's That Kind of War," *The New Republic*, Dec. 20, 1969, pp. 9–11.

[24] Gray, *New York Times Book Review*, Dec. 21, 1969, p. 16.

[25] For extensive documentation, see *In the Name of America*, a study commissioned by Clergy and Laymen Concerned about Vietnam (Annandale, Virginia: Turnpike Press, 1968).

stances makes the widespread occurrence of civil wars probable and often creates incentives for various principal governments to intervene on behalf of their favored faction or to make sure that intervention by a rival government is not effective enough to tip the balance of forces involved in the struggle; in some limited situations—where spheres of influence are more or less defined—a particular government enjoys an option to intervene in foreign societies with reasonable assurance of no more serious adverse reaction by antagonistic governments than denunciation and verbal censure. The Soviet Union has successfully tested this tolerance on several occasions despite its minority position in the political organs of the United Nations.

It seems evident that it is important to consider whether international law is doing all that can be done to moderate the magnitude, scope, and duration of civil wars, and to discourage escalation by fixing the conditions of third-party intervention and by defining more clearly the terms of battle so as to disallow certain tactics and weapons. Such roles for law are admittedly minimal and marginal. There is no expectation, given the prevailing conditions of political consciousness and structure of world society, that governments will forego active intervention when they deem vital interests are at issue, nor is there reason to believe that their battle behavior will not continue to be controlled by a mixture of prudence and military necessity. But a conception of world order can come to be increasingly associated with the perception of vital interests if these interests are articulated in such a way as to establish the potential identity between national welfare and world-community welfare. It is not enough to affirm such an identity; it must be demonstrated to exist in the specific settings of foreign policy choice.

It is possible that some legal guidelines can be formulated in such a way as to have influence on governments and international institutions. The creative challenge for international lawyers, then, is to define the content of enlightened self-interest in civil-war situations in a manner that will generate widespread support. These guidelines need to be framed in light of a careful analysis of practice and an appreciation of the actual issues encountered by those who make foreign policy and by military commanders; they also need to take account of the generalized positions of both sides in a civil-war situation. If the guidelines are weighted for or against the established political order, their prospects for influence other than in polemical discussion are minimal. The normative situation calls for mediatory (rather than encompassing) guidelines designed to confine the scope of violence and to spare innocent bystanders to the extent possible. Because the perceived conflict between the pursuit of peace and quest for justice is often at the center of disagreement about what to do, it is necessary that these guidelines avoid absolute prohibitions. Because there are no adequate international fact-finding procedures and because adversary perception of facts tends to be particularly self-serving in the confused settings of civil wars, it is particularly desirable to have as objective, or self-defining, standards of judgment as possible. Therefore, such clear distinctions as exist—for instance, between territory on different sides of a national boundary or nuclear and nonnuclear weapons or conventional and bacteriological weapons—need to be made explicit and thereby reinforced. Because the tendency to rely on discretion is great when pressure exists, it is also desirable to evolve guidelines during periods of relative calm and not by reliance upon ex parte interpretations of particular situations.

To move in this direction, it is necessary to review and appraise the traditional approaches taken by international law to civil-war situations and to appraise these approaches in the setting of representative civil wars. The case studies that constitute the bulk of this volume provide the kind of systematic source material needed as a data base for such an appraisal. In this introductory essay I shall be advancing some thoughts for movement toward a new international law of civil war that have arisen in relation to the project's experience to date. These thoughts are intended to suggest some questions for students of this subject, especially questions that bear on the realistic prospects for strengthening international law in this delicate area.

I. THE TRADITIONAL APPROACH: ITS RATIONALE AND PARTIAL DECAY

The traditional views of the relevance of international law to civil war situations are based on the insulation of domestic society and on the relative degree of success achieved by the insurgent faction. In the event that an uprising against a government is quickly suppressed or sporadic, it is treated as a purely internal event. The established government is fully entitled to treat captured participants as ordinary criminals. Third states are expected to maintain normal relations with the government and can lend it support in the suppression of the rebellion.

The more difficult problems arise if the rebellious group enjoys partial success, in the sense of developing a countergovernment, administering a substantial portion of national territory, and fielding a military force capable of doing battle for a considerable length of time. Under these conditions third states may continue to provide aid to the constituted government. At the same time, the countergovernment may be accorded insurgent status by third states, which are then obliged to take account of the condition of warfare in their relations with the state. Rosalyn Higgins in an important recent study of this subject has written as follows: "The recognition of insurgency—whether implied or express, is an indication that the recognizing state regards the insurgents as legal contestants, and not as mere lawbreakers. Such an acknowledgement does not entail the legal burdens of a neutral—the recognizing state is possibly still free to assist the legal government, and would be illegally intervening if it materially assisted the insurgents."[26] The consequences of conferring an insurgent status are, at best, uncertain and indefinite; governments retain discretion to deal with competing factions despite the change of status.

If the civil war persists, then, according to Lauterpacht-Oppenheim, it is permissible and, possibly, obligatory to recognize a condition of belligerency, provided "certain conditions of fact exist. . . . These conditions of fact are: the existence of a civil war accompanied by a state of general hostilities; occupation and a measure of orderly administration of a substantial part of national territory by the insurgents; observance of the rules of warfare on the part of the insurgent forces acting under a responsible authority; the practical necessity for Third States to define their attitude to the civil war."[27] Lauterpacht-Oppenheim go on to observe that "without the latter requirement recognition of belligerency might be open to abuse for the purpose of a gratuitous manifestation of sympathy with the cause of the insurgents."[28] If a status of belligerency is formally conferred, then a duty of neutrality ensues and each of the sides in the war is able to exercise belligerent rights. Lauterpacht-Oppenheim contend that an improper recognition of belligerency is tantamount to illegal interference in the affairs of a foreign state and that a refusal to recognize belligerency status when the four conditions of fact have been satisfied "must be deemed contrary to sound principle and precedent."[29] Experts disagree, and there is a considerable body of opinion holding it a matter of discretion whether a foreign government need ever recognize the belligerent status of the antigovernment faction.[30]

The specification of conditions as objective bases of a grant of belligerent status is largely misleading, especially given the contemporary world. Governments define their relationship to an insurgent faction largely in accordance with their political preferences and, if necessary, describe this preference in relation to an appropriate status. Procedures for third-party judgment have never existed except in those rare in-

[26] See Higgins, "Internal War and International Law."

[27] Lassa P. Oppenheim, *International Law*, ed. H. Lauterpacht (7th ed., London: Longmans Green, 1952), 2: 249. For a fuller presentation, see H. Lauterpacht, *Recognition in International Law* (Cambridge: Cambridge University Press, 1947).

[28] Oppenheim, *International Law*, 2: 249–50.

[29] *Ibid.*, p. 250.

[30] Cf. *ibid.*, p. 250 n.

stances in which the parties agree to submit their dispute for settlement; the *Alabama* claims controversy in which Great Britain was held liable to compensate the United States government for its unwarranted interference in the American Civil War by outfitting a ship-of-war for the Confederacy is one famous instance.[31]

The basic policies embodied in the traditional approach of international law are quite clear: first, it is essential to rank civil-war situations in terms of the seriousness of the insurgent challenge; second, it is appropriate to respect the sovereign character of a foreign government confronted by an illegal challenge to its control by a portion of its population; third, therefore, the presumptions are in favor of the incumbent government and the challenger can only hope to achieve a position of parity vis-à-vis outside governments by a significant measure of success, exhibited by governmental control over territory; fourth, even then, third states can withhold recognition of a status of belligerency and confine their acknowledgment of the civil-war situation to the minimal grounds arising out of interaction with the insurgent faction.

In a state system, governments have a mutual interest in their security of tenure. Hence, the bias of the system against revolutionary challenge is a logical expression of the basic idea of sovereign states exercising exclusive control over territory.[32] The qualification of this bias rests on a minimum requirement of flexibility in light of special circumstances of civil war extending over time. Commercial and diplomatic interests presuppose some way of regularizing the relationships between governments of third states and partially victorious insurgent causes, for instance, to permit trade with insurgent-held territory. If the insurgency is altogether successful, the old government disappears and a new one is established. Foreign governments can grant or withhold recognition of the new government, signifying their intention and willingness to establish or maintain normal commercial and diplomatic relations. Nonrecognition of governments that are in firm control of a state is a diplomatic instrument used by governments to express disapproval of the revolutionary ideology, to induce a bargain for normalcy, and to organize an international campaign designed to exclude the new government from as wide a sphere of diplomatic activity as possible, including access to international institutions. This use of nonrecognition as a political weapon has been developed by the United States government especially in relation to the outcome of the Soviet revolution (1917–33) and the victory of the Chinese revolution in 1949. It is also relevant to recall that even

---

[31] *Ibid.*, pp. 715–16.

[32] Cf. Richard A. Falk, "The Interplay of Westphalia and Charter Conceptions of the International Legal Order," in Falk and Black (eds.), *The Future of the International Legal Order: Trends and Patterns*, 1: 32–70.

before the Soviet case the United States refused to recognize the governments of Mexico and Costa Rica and blocked their participation in the Paris Peace conference and the League of Nations. Disapproval of the outcome of a civil war, especially if it includes support for the defeated faction, amounts to undermining the state system from the side of conservatism. The objective is to deny new facts and to act as if an earlier political situation persisted. Delayed recognition is equivalent to premature recognition, by which third states give total approval to an insurgent cause prior to its victory in a civil war. Such diplomatic practice in support of the insurgent challenge was very important in the closing months of the Algerian War of Independence, when many states recognized the FLN;[33] today more than twenty states have recognized the Provisional Revolutionary Government as the sole legitimate government of South Vietnam. Some members of the Organization of African Unity have accorded similar status to the liberation groups directing their efforts against the governments in South Africa and South West Africa, although no sustained civil insurrection has yet taken place.

Given the ideological cleavages in world society, then, the concern for correlating status with facts has disappeared, and with this disappearance, has come a lessening of the link between sovereignty and diplomacy. Both revolutionary and counterrevolutionary governments manipulate recognition symbols to accord with political preferences. There is almost no reliance in recent diplomatic practice upon the gradation of civil-war situations implicit in the scale of rebellion, insurgency, and belligerency. These symbols of legal status have themselves been virtually discarded, and governments determine their relations to competing political elites on the basis of their preferences, capabilities, and foreign policy goals, as well as on the basis of what their adversaries are doing or would tolerate. In an interrelated and ideologically competitive world system, behavioral patterns encourage active intervention rather than induce the creation of regimes of impartiality and aloofness. The Spanish Civil War marked the end of any prospect of insulating a civil-war situation from the overall currents of world politics. To refuse intervention on one side out of deference to the earlier ethos was to influence the outcome in a perverse way by clearing the way for intervention on the other side.

System-wide norms also have little relevance for the subject of intervention. Geopolitical zones of partial dominance create special prerogatives for the dominant governments; for example, the Soviet Union in

[33] For discussion, see the study by Arnold Fraleigh in this volume. See also, for comparison, M. Bedjaoui, *Law and the Algerian Revolution* (Brussels: Publications of the International Association of Democratic Lawyers, 1961), esp. pp. 110–80.

relation to eastern Europe or the United States in relation to Central America.[34] These prerogatives contradict global norms. Revolutionary challenges express wider patterns of political conflict, which convert civil-war situations into arenas of great power competition that are governed by certain tacit limitations. As the Vietnam War exhibits, the internal actor—the Saigon government—may be completely overshadowed by its external ally, with the result that the decision center that determines the course and terms of settlement of the civil war is largely in the hands of the intervening third-party government. Under such circumstances, one or both of the internal factions become proxies in a wider conflict. American requests to the Soviet government for assistance in bringing the Vietnam War to a negotiated end further display the belief that the critical locus of decision has been shifted outside the combat area in certain civil wars that have become arenas for wider geopolitical conflict. Soviet assertions of her inability and unwillingness to influence the Hanoi government to end the war represent a denial, on her side, of any capacity or willingness to bring the war to an end merely by reaching a Soviet-American accord. And on a second level of analysis, it has been urged that North Vietnam cannot even impose terms of settlement upon its ally, the Provisional Revolutionary Government in South Vietnam. Nevertheless, the mechanistic image of a civil war as between internal contestants for control is shattered by the complex politics of affiliation that link domestic elites with broader world revolutionary and counterrevolutionary movements. These links are strongest where the boundaries of great power influence are both unstable and contiguous. Hence, it is not surprising that the most sustained political violence since World War II has been in the divided countries of Korea and Vietnam and that grave, persistent threats to peace have been posed by the division of Germany and China, with each sector looking toward a different superpower for ideological and military backing.

Given these political imperatives, it is also not surprising to discover a virtual abandonment of the traditional categories used to regulate outside participation in civil war. There is no pretense of impartiality or neutrality on the part of principal governments and no consistent willingness to endorse either the legitimacy of the constituted government or the legitimacy of revolutionary challenge. The constituted government may be characterized as "a satellite" or as "racist" or "colonialist" in character and therefore as "illegitimate"; on the other hand, the insurgent challenger may be labeled as "an agent of a foreign power," "an indirect aggressor," or "Communist" or "Communist-inspired" and there-

[34] Falk, "The Legitimacy of Zone II."

fore, an "illegitimate" challenge. Each major political grouping in world affairs is dedicated to "law and order" at home and in the societies of closely allied states and to "revolution" in the camp of its rival. Some countercurrents in favor of stability are created by the fragile peace of the nuclear age, at least in the home societies of the nuclear super-powers.

Such a world political setting is confirmed by widely diffused support for "liberation" tactics to produce political change in certain national societies. Most of black Africa openly seeks to stimulate revolution in South Africa. Under such circumstances, it becomes evident that norms based on the state system are unresponsive to both the values and the practices of many governments and certainly have no prospect of serving as guidelines for the conduct of modern diplomacy. And in fact, maintaining the gap between normative and political imperatives creates an atmosphere that discredits the entire enterprise of law in world affairs. Governments talk one way and act another whenever established norms persistently contradict perceived vital interests. It would be desirable, first of all, to abandon the pretense of norms and then to develop a more responsive normative framework that would appeal to most governments under most circumstances and that would tend to promote basic policies relating to the minimization of violence, the enhancement of human dignity, and the promotion of national self-determination.[35]

II. TOWARD A NEW INTERNATIONAL LAW FOR CIVIL WAR

Traditional international law provides governments with little guidance. Its norms are either contradictory (traditions supporting both interventionary and noninterventionary orientations) or empty (traditions abstracted from policy contexts without which actual decisions could not be made).[36] As a result, legal language is employed as a *post hoc* explanation of behavior that is not intended to be convincing and is not taken very seriously by either advocates or critics. It is not difficult to understand the public indifference to the legal debate about the Vietnam War, despite the highly controversial character of the American involvement. Both sides in the controversy generally preferred to rest their case on moral, ideological, and political foundations rather than, given the confusing facts of the conflict, on the international legal right of the United States to do what it was doing in Vietnam. The

[35] Moore, "The Control of Foreign Intervention," pp. 246–53.
[36] Richard A. Falk, *The Status of Law in International Society* (Princeton: Princeton University Press, 1969), pp. 24–32.

legal debate was a specialized discussion carried on largely within the confines of professional forums.

When the legal perspective is so divorced from both the sense of justice and the perception of geopolitical security, it deteriorates into legalism. Injunctions are put in legal language, but there is no expectation or concern with whether or not these injunctions provide real guidance to actors called upon to respond to real-world problems.[37]

What is needed, then, is a reformulation of the international law of civil war in a manner that is more responsive to the specific contexts within which critical choices are now being made by governments. The main objective of international law must now be to influence those choices to some extent by emphasizing the relevance of widely shared and mutually beneficial world-order policies. These policies come into conflict with one another under certain circumstances, as when the policy of minimizing violence comes into conflict with the policy of promoting national self-determination. Such a conflict cannot be resolved by positing a hierarchy of policies—that is, by urging actors to subordinate the ideals of self-determination to the ideals of peace—because such a hierarchy would only create another legalistic approach to civil war, similar in kind to the categorical rules of prohibition and norms of status developed by the traditional approach.

Those who share the assessment that I have made, including such authors as Tom Farer, Rosalyn Higgins, John Norton Moore, and Oran Young, have sought (1) to classify civil-war situations; (2) to classify claims made by governments and others in relation to civil-war situations; and (3) to recommend policy prescriptions that are intermediate between rules of prohibition and rules of discretion—rules, in other words, that authorize limited intervention for limited ends under specific circumstances. The world-order argument is couched in the language of management, confinement, fire-fighting, and break-waters rather than in the more biblical, restraint-oriented language of prohibition. Given the interdependence and decentralization of international life, regulatory enterprises ultimately depend for success on their capacity to satisfy the self-interest of principal governments as perceived by top officials. Such a capacity in the intervention setting depends on compromise, moderation, and the mutual acceptance of limits. In proposing such a revised approach, the legal expert has cast himself in the role of a legislative adviser, the legislative organ being the aggregation of national governments. Each government by itself and in conjunction with other governments, or through the medium of formal and informal

---

[37] I have tried to develop this position at greater length in Falk, "Law, Lawyers, and the Conduct of American Foreign Relations," *Yale Law Journal* 78 (May 1969): 919–34.

international institutions, can advance or endorse a legislative claim. Much international law develops through the assertion by principal governments of unilateral claims in an effective form, supported by a world-order rationale and fully or partly acquiesced in by other governments. The interaction of claims and counterclaims provides legislative energy within international society. By examining the prospects for a new international law of civil war, we are trying to stimulate this legislative process in one critical area of international life.[38]

We need, first of all, to classify the principal types of civil-war situations and to formulate the characteristic world-order *issues* presented by each. These analytical classifications then have to be considered in relation to geopolitical circumstances, in particular to fairly clearly delimited zones of special prerogative or de facto hegemony.[39] On this basis, it may be possible to bring a new clarity and moderation to governmental responses to civil wars. The scope of concern here is with sustained, large-scale violence between two or more factions seeking to challenge, in whole or in part, the maintenance of governmental authority in a particular state. Sporadic, disorganized, apolitical violent strife is not considered to be a civil-war situation, nor does such strife often present serious international legal issues. There are several principal varieties of civil war that need to be distinguished for analytic and policy purposes:

Standard Civil War. Government A is opposed by Countergovernment B in a struggle to gain control over State X. The entire locus of violence is within State X, and foreign governments can enter into a variety of relationships with A and B at different stages of the civil war.

War of Hegemony. Government A of State X imposes by violence its will upon Government B in State Y through either its support of or opposition to a dependent elite in Y. X does not explicitly rule Y, but it will rely on military means to avoid changes in Y that threaten the minimum conditions of its hegemony, whether this requires opposition to a Countergovernment or the elimination of the constituted govern-

---

[38] Myres S. McDougal and his associates have elaborated this process of legal development. Most relevant in this setting is McDougal and Florentino P. Feliciano, *Law and Minimum World Public Order: The Legal Regulation of International Coercion* (New Haven: Yale University Press, 1961).

[39] Falk, "The Legitimacy of Zone II." Other countries may also practice hegemonial diplomacy. For instance, discussing the motivation for France's interventionary role in the civil war going on in the Republic of Chad, Robert Pledge comments as follows: "No doubt the real reasons for French intervention are strategic, with the French wishing to maintain a zone of influence in the center of Africa free from the encroachment by Arab states in the North and East, the British and the Russians in Nigeria to the West and the Americans to the South in the Congo (Kinshasa)." Pledge, "Chad's Guerrilla War," *Africa Report* 14 (November 1969): 12–13.

ment. Soviet relations with eastern Europe illustrate the potentiality for hegemonial war, although the short duration of the conflicts makes it doubtful whether to include these hegemonial interventions within the scope of civil-war situations.

War of Autonomy. Government A is the agent of foreign Government C (located in State W) and is opposed by Countergovernment B in a struggle to exercise control over State X. Such a war seeks to establish the political autonomy of X (vis-à-vis W), is generally based on the principles of self-determination, and involves a repudiation of colonial or imperial patterns of indirect rule. Countergovernment B may operate totally within X or partially within foreign states Y and Z.

War of Separation (or subnational autonomy). Government A is opposed by Countergovernment B, which seeks to establish a new State, Y, in addition to State X. Ethnic, religious, or economic separatism may explain the drive to break off from the central government and establish a new state entity. Wars of secession are common in states that try to impose homogeneous standards upon a heterogeneous social, ethnic, and political tradition.

War of Reunion. Government A in State X seeks to gain control over the affairs of State Y to permit the merger of X and Y into a single state. Here, the opposite situation of a War of Separation, the basic national identity has been fragmented for allegedly extraneous and artificial reasons and the civil war seeks to achieve reunion. "Divided" countries—geopolitical compromises that are imposed upon national communities by world political compromises—are breeding grounds for Wars of Reunion.

There are many variations and combinations, but these five types of conflict identify the basic forms of civil war. Complicating features arise whenever international institutions achieve a consensus and adopt a role in relation to a civil war. Also important is the mix of internal/external and of covert/overt elements of decision, support, and action, which may change greatly the prospects for moderating or terminating a particular conflict. The size of the country experiencing the conflict also has a bearing on the interventionary or mediating roles that can be played by foreign governments and international institutions under a particular set of circumstances. The smaller the country and the further removed it is from a partisan geopolitical identification, the better the prospects for an agreed international policy of moderation.

No general framework of restraint is likely to operate successfully within "spheres of influence," or as I have called them, special zones of acknowledged unilateral prerogative. Such secondary zones are national communities that enjoy diminished sovereignty; this status is implicitly respected (even when it is overtly condemned), and policy is made by a mixture of internal bureaucratic pressures, public opinion, and the expected costs of varying postures of intervention and nonintervention. General normative directives such as the prohibition of nondefensive military force and respect for self-determination may place certain inhibitions along the interventionary path; but if an elite can be "found" or "constituted" to issue an invitation, or if the operation can be conducted relatively covertly or relatively quickly, or if an international institution or arrangement on a regional level will give its blessing, the decision to intervene is likely to be made.[40] The principal point is that reciprocity is not operative in these contexts, and no general regime of moderation is likely to confine the behavior of the hegemonial actor, such as the Soviet Union or the United States. Secondary geopolitical boundaries are well delimited in most instances, even if their legitimacy is explicitly denied. A Soviet intervention in Hungary or Czechoslovakia does not endanger world peace in the way that a comparable intervention in Yugoslavia or, even more so, Austria might. The condemnations of such hegemonial interventions are based on system-wide norms that do not take into account these well-defined tolerances. These interventions obviously contradict the pure logic of both the Westphalia system (sovereignty) and the Charter system (community protection of norms) but conform to the basic arrangement of power and expectations about its use that exists within the world system at the present time.[41] Such an arrangement is only a degree different from the well-acknowledged prerogative of a government to suppress claims to autonomy or secession by an ethnic minority within its boundary. For example, Wars of Separation, such as the Nigerian Civil War, generally start off with an endorsement of the hegemonial prerogatives of the federal government vis-à-vis subnational groups seeking formal separation (or even a more limited enclave of assured autonomy). Therefore, the idea of special prerogatives with respect to political control is not alien to the values of a sovereignty-oriented system, and in fact, the idea of wider zones of community responsibility is, in part, associated with the movement toward a more centralized world community. If, however, the wider control is centered in the national governments of powerful states, it becomes almost indistinguishable from imperial models of partial world order.

At this stage in international society, it is important to identify imperial or quasi-imperial sectors of world society and work for their amelioration by distinct means. Such an enterprise is essentially separate from the overall task of world order. Its success depends on reorienta-

[40] Some instances are Hungary in 1956, Lebanon in 1958, South Vietnam from 1963 to the present, and Dominican Republic in 1965.
[41] Falk, "The Interplay of Westphalia and Charter Conceptions," p. 32–70.

tions in the structures of values and influence within the imperial centers of power, and it involves a partial or total dissolution of imperial relationships. An appeal for wider world-community policies can help to achieve this end, as can an overall relaxation in world political conflict. Such a process of change should not be confused, however, with the effort to evolve forms of order in the nonimperial sectors of international society, and it is in relation to these sectors that we now offer comment.

Within the principal states of the world, all varieties of civil war are likely to be protected from large-scale sustained intervention. India, China, Indonesia, Brazil, the Soviet Union, the United States, and even France seem unlikely to experience intervention despite sustained internal violence. The scale of significant intervention seems to demand too large an effort and the failure of the allied intervention in the Soviet Civil War after World War I is an instructive precedent.

The main areas of concern are secondary countries, especially those situated along the outer periphery of Sino-Soviet influence. Here, the larger struggle between revolution and counterrevolution is intermingled with the domestic conflicts of badly divided national societies. Here also the intervening government may have a sense that intervention will not escalate the conflict to serious proportions and that it will not become a burden in any very major respect. Vietnam has provided a dramatic lesson of the potential costs and burdens of military intervention, and Yemen produces a confirming, if less spectacular, lesson.[42] There are limits to the effectiveness of military means in shaping the outcome of a political struggle between well-entrenched domestic foes. In Wars of Separation, the interventionary calculus may be easier to determine, as the dissenting faction has a clear ethnic or geographical identity. It is more difficult in Standard Civil Wars or Wars of Autonomy, in which "the government" is often, in effect, struggling against "the people." Many of the revolutionary struggles of the Third World have involved competing efforts to capture the allegiance, or at least the subservience,

[42] The costs of such an intervention far exceed initial expectations, entail significant additional burdens in terms of balance of payments position and domestic inflation. By the end of 1969, the Vietnam War was being called the most expensive war (including World War II) that the United States had ever fought; and because such a war is justified as an undertaking that can be discharged without major burden, there is a tendency to avoid internal wartime controls to protect the economy, such as higher taxes, rationing, and price-fixing. Cf. McGeorge Bundy's address at DePauw University on Dec. 12, 1968, for an example of one policy adviser who recanted his earlier optimism about the capacity of the United States to pursue the war in Vietnam full scale and also proceed with domestic welfare programs at a rapid rate. For text, see *Vietnam II*, pp. 964–75. A typical expression of confidence in the capacity of America to provide "guns and butter" is to be found in President Johnson's State of the Union Message of Jan. 12, 1966, 89 Cong. 2 sess.; "I believe that we can continue the Great Society while we fight in Vietnam."

21

of the people. In this kind of endeavor, the main interventionary role of third states may actually precede the civil-war situation by the provision of military training, financing, and equipment to one side or the other in the struggle. Below certain thresholds of involvement, interventionary policies, while quite possibly inconsistent with the promotion of self-determination, are either so nearly invisible or so nearly normal that no regime of limitation is likely to be effective. Minimum tolerances for the pursuit of interventionary policies are an almost inevitable consequence of a factually intermeshed and an ideologically divided, competitive world order in which the main international political stakes are identified with the outcomes of a series of struggles for national dominance.

In areas of competitive interaction, there is no political basis for a comprehensive prohibition of all intervention in civil-war situations. If certain maximum thresholds can be specified with clarity and reasonable mutuality, there is some prospect of confining the scope, magnitude, and duration of violence. It is encouraging to note, in this respect, that the two governments that have been the most militant in their adoption of revolutionary and counterrevolutionary postures have retreated from an endorsement of overt military intervention. Lin Piao's address on the twentieth anniversary of the Chinese resistance against Japan contains the following passage: "The liberation of the masses is accomplished by the masses themselves—this is a basic principle of Marxism-Leninism. Revolution or people's war in any country is the business of the masses in that country and should be carried out primarily by their own efforts; there is no other way."[43] Discussing the successes of the past in China, Lin Piao goes on to say, "The problem of military equipment was solved mainly by relying on the capture of arms from the enemy, though we did turn out some weapons too. . . . Comrade Mao Tse-tung has said that our fundamental policy should rest on the foundation of our own strength. Only by relying on our own efforts can we in all circumstances remain invincible."[44] This emphasis on self-reliance converges somewhat unexpectedly with President Nixon's so-called Nixon Doctrine, which calls upon foreign governments allied with the United States to rely upon their own fighting capabilities in all struggles in which there has been no overt, massive attack within their territory by another state.[45] "No more Vietnams" comes down to establishing a

---

[43] Lin Piao, *Long Live the Victory of People's War* [delivered Sept. 3, 1965] (Peking: Foreign Language Press, 1968), pp. 84–85. See also the general discussion under the heading "Adhere to the Policy of Self-Reliance," pp. 82–92.

[44] *Ibid.*, pp. 90–91.

[45] Richard M. Nixon, "Address to the Nation," Nov. 3, 1969, text reproduced in *New York Times,* Nov. 4, 1969, p. 16. The portion of the speech containing an exposition of what the President himself referred to as "the Nixon Doctrine"

maximum threshold of participation in foreign civil wars. Such a threshold is also the basis of Tom Farer's proposal of a system-wide prohibition on the use of foreign personnel in civil war battlefield operations.[46] Farer's proposal implies the usefulness of system-wide rules and, therefore, collides with the earlier argument that the maintenance of quasi-imperial spheres of influence includes recourse to police prerogatives (the external equivalent of antisecessionist police prerogatives that occur within national boundaries). John Norton Moore has criticized Farer's proposal because of its possible bias against "a widely recognized government" that is being victimized by "a foreign inspired insurgency."[47] This criticism is persuasive if Farer's proposal is treated as a categorical norm rather than as an ingredient in a framework of guidance evolved by and for the benefit of potential intervening governments. The convergence of Lin Piao and Richard Nixon on the idea of military self-reliance is encouraging because it represents a redefinition of policy on the basis of perceived self-interest. It may produce a moderation of claims and behavior that could reinforce other efforts to evolve a limiting framework for competitive intervention.

There are other thresholds related to more or less visible breaks in the continuum of participation and escalation. The boundary of the state is one very important threshold. It confines the scope of military operations and tends to maintain the distinction between civil and international war. The shipment of supplies, military training, and transfers of aid all involve transactions originating in one country and terminating within the country that is the setting of the struggle. Where countries are contiguous and the target government has been successful in suppressing domestic opposition, it is tempting for "liberation movements" to form in foreign countries, to use foreign territory as a staging and base area, and to infiltrate across the boundary to organize mass support and to disrupt the system of public order. Such a situation places the boundary threshold under great, perhaps unendurable, pressure. The target government is likely to strike across the boundary either to re-

---

counsels self-reliance as a way to "help end the war in Vietnam" and as "an essential element in our program to prevent future Vietnams." As President Nixon put it, "We shall look to the nation directly threatened to assume the primary responsibility of providing the manpower for its defense," and further, "The defense of freedom is everybody's business—not just America's business. And it is particularly the responsibility of the people whose freedom is threatened. In the previous Administration, we Americanized the war in Vietnam. In this Administration, we are Vietnamizing the search for peace."

[46] For Farer's original proposal see *Vietnam I*, pp. 509–22; for further elaboration, see *Vietnam II*, pp. 1089–1116; for sympathetic criticism of the proposal, see Moore, "The Control of Foreign Intervention," pp. 320–27.

[47] Moore, "The Control of Foreign Intervention," p. 327.

taliate against the activities of the liberation movement or to punish the foreign government that encourages or tolerates such activities on its own territory. Both the Middle East and southern Africa provide examples of this kind of situation. The relevant legal analysis should focus on the pattern of claim and counterclaim and the claim's reasonableness in context, not on some kind of absolute prohibition or some total suspension of the boundary threshold. The Israeli attack on Arab commercial airliners at the Beirut airport in December 1968 illustrates one kind of retaliatory claim by a target government.[48] The reasonableness of the Israeli claim depends to some extent on an assessment of the degree of control possessed by the Government of Lebanon over the two Arab terrorists operating out of Lebanon who had attacked an Israeli commercial plane two days earlier in the Athens airport. The remoteness of this affiliation and the poorness of the evidence available to sustain the allegation, as well as the magnitude of the Israeli response, help account for the unanimous censure of Israel in the United Nations Security Council.[49] Thresholds create a presumption in their favor, and departures from them must be demonstrated to be reasonable, reactive, necessary, and proportional. Proportionality is significant, as it tends to communicate a specific message rather than to expand the conflict permanently across the boundary.

Nuclear weapons and other weapons of mass destruction provide another threshold relevant for all violent conflict, but especially relevant for civil-war situations. The prohibition against the use of nuclear weapons would seem to be as close to an absolute limit as it is possible to impose in civil-war situations.[50]

In Standard Civil Wars where there is no major geopolitical stake and no strong quasi-imperial prerogative, there are strong potentialities for insulation of the war from outside intervention. Such insulation can take a passive form and consist merely of keeping potential interveners from overt military participation and deferring to the internal dynamics of struggle and negotiation. Or it can take a more active form in which an international institution is given a mission to secure "peace." Such a

[48] For an extended legal analysis, see Richard A. Falk, "The Beirut Raid and the International Law of Retaliation," *American Journal of International Law* 63 (July 1969): 415–43.

[49] For the text of the Security Council resolution, see S/Res/262 (1968), adopted unanimously on Dec. 31, 1968.

[50] It can be maintained, of course, that in light of customary rules of international law and General Assembly Resolution 1653 (XVI), Declaration on the Prohibition of the Use of Nuclear and Thermonuclear Weapons, adopted Nov. 24, 1961, the use of nuclear weapons under any circumstances, except in retaliation against prior use, would violate the law of war. General Assembly Resolution 1653 (XVI) declares that the use of nuclear weapons constitutes an international crime.

role is often difficult to arrange because civil wars are about issues of justice and legitimacy, and to establish peace is to favor one set of claims at the expense of another. Which side was correct in the Nigerian Civil War? in Cyprus? in the Sudan? Who should decide which side should prevail? The criteria of decision are so elusive and the vagaries of world consensus so pronounced that there is reason to distrust interventions in civil wars, even if they occur under the auspices of international institutions.[51] Interventions in Wars of Separation and Wars of Reunion are particularly doubtful since the insurgent claimants are challenging the legitimacy of a widely recognized government. If that government can tip the scales of struggle in its favor merely by requesting United Nations help, then the bias of the world system in favor of duly constituted governments seems inconsistent, under certain circumstances, with the promotion of human rights and with the encouragement of national self-determination. Only in the event of a clear demonstration that foreign military forces are operating in substantial numbers at the combat level would it be appropriate for a political organ of the United Nations to adopt an interventionary role in favor of an incumbent government confronted by a domestic challenge.[52] The invitation of either the government or its opposition is insufficient to authorize the entry of combat troops into a foreign society, even if entry is authorized by action of an international institution. Again, the threshold of external participation is worth protecting, even in relation to institutions encompassing all nonimperial sectors of international society. If there is a clear normative consensus in the world community supported by a particular demand of one of the parties to a civil war, it would be appropriate for the international institution to take sides by adopting a legislative role, in effect, legislating in favor of one of the sides. The struggle against racism and minority rule in southern Africa is an obvious instance wherein the doctrine of legislative intervention might be developed and tested.[53]

Aside from situations in which the government's invitation to the United Nations is based on solid evidence of the presence of foreign military personnel on the battlefield or on a legislative mandate, the

[51] See Stanley Hoffman, "In Search of a Thread: The UN in the Congo Labyrinth," *International Organization* 16 (1962): 331–61.

[52] Cf. conditions used to justify the initial invitation by President Patrice Lumumba to the United Nations, as described by Donald McNemar, in his study of the postindependence war in the Congo in this volume, pp. 244–302.

[53] For one proposal along these lines, see Falk, *Legal Order in a Violent World*, pp. 336–53. Cf. also the Lusaka Manifesto, proclaimed by the fifth Summit Conference of East and Central African States at Lusaka, Zambia, in April 1969, and endorsed by the UN General Assembly on Nov. 20, 1969. For the text of the Lusaka Manifesto, see *Objective: Justice* 2 (January 1970): 46–49.

United Nations should endeavor only to reinforce the exclusion of third parties and to offer its good offices for mediatory, buffering, or settlement roles whenever the parties to a civil war seek a nonviolent resolution. In essence, the United Nations should provide its facilities only to implement the interests of the contesting factions. United Nations aloofness may be tested by prolonged civil wars that expose large portions of the civilian population to hardship. Starvation of large numbers in Iboland during the Nigerian Civil War posed such a challenge to the world community. It may be desirable to encourage specific humanitarian procedures whereby claims that are unconnected with the military dimension of the conflict are made on behalf of the international community and, if necessary, enforced against the parties to the civil war. The Red Cross or some ad hoc group could be entrusted with emergency relief operations on behalf of the international community. Of course, there are ambiguities concerning what is "humanitarian," for example, the controversial rescue of hostages in the Stanleyville operation of 1964, which can also be plausibly interpreted as facilitating Tshombe's capture of the rebel capital in the Congo civil war.[54]

Procedures of accountability would seem to be constructive steps to discourage the grosser forms of intervention in civil wars, even with respect to quasi-imperial claims. The need to explain and justify, even if no adversary stronger than public opinion was available, would tend to strengthen the position of more moderate pressures within the principal governments.[55] A body of precedents and tradition would unfold. If the present world-order system depends on the voluntary adoption of standards in the war/peace area, then anything that facilitates communications is generally desirable. The greatest importance of international institutions may be to provide forums within which adversary communication occurs; standards of accommodation may gradually take shape, often by tacit adjustment of behavior and objectives. Such developments might occur in relation to outside participation in civil wars, but only if participation in the process of norm-creation is virtually universal. The exclusion of principal actors, most especially China, from the United Nations seriously hampers the line of positive development that has been suggested here in ways that are not even predictable.

[54] On Stanleyville, see Kenneth W. Grundy, "The Stanleyville Rescue: American Policy in the Congo," *The Yale Review*, Winter 1967, pp. 242–55; Falk, *Legal Order in a Violent World*, pp. 324–35. See the more general discussion by Richard B. Lillich, "Forcible Self-Help to Protect Human Rights," *Iowa Law Review* 53 (1967): 325–51; and Lillich, "Intervention to Protect Human Rights" (unpublished paper delivered at Queen's University, Kingston, Ontario, Canada, Nov. 22–23, 1968).

[55] Such pressure may induce a government to withdraw from the United Nations, as Indonesia briefly purported to do in 1965 as a consequence of its dissatisfaction with the manner in which the organization responded to its account of its dispute with Malaysia.

The limitation of imperial privilege in relation to external communities depends mainly on internal developments in the imperial centers of authority. The dynamics of national security in the nuclear age makes territorial defense systems increasingly obsolete and so undermines the security argument for contiguous spheres of influence.[56] Immediate prospects for economic integration and cooperation are good, but do not require coincident political control. Therefore, the rationale for quasi-empires may diminish. Furthermore, it may be possible to weave system-wide legal perspectives into the foreign policymaking processes of national governments. In this regard, the idea of a cabinet-level Attorney General for International Affairs or an Ombudsman of World Order might be a creative innovation that would reinforce the identification of national interests with the strengthening of the world order and discourage unilateral governmental claims to use military force abroad, or even at home.[57]

There is reason to associate the domestic suppression by military means of groups seeking ideological, ethnic, or religious autonomy with the military intervention in a foreign society against a secessionist or military subnational insurgency. One way to build world order is to tear down large sovereign states that achieve cohesion by artificial bonds of hostility against an external enemy or by reliance on a militant ideology; the creation of smaller political units in which the bonds of solidarity are strong and self-evident to the citizenry is one of the most pronounced political movements going on in the world today. Partly, this movement reflects the inability of the state to bring security, dignity, and prosperity to its citizens under modern conditions in exchange for its political rulership, and partly it reflects the growing awareness on the part of oppressed peoples that their welfare depends above all upon control over their own destiny. In this sense, domestic revolutionary movements—for example, the Black Panther party—correctly associate themselves with anticolonial and other liberation movements throughout the world. Their quest for group autonomy builds a bridge between the domestic and the international regulation of civil-war situations.

III. PROSPECTS: A CONCLUDING COMMENT

To write optimistically about the role of law in relation to civil warfare is obviously premature. At this stage we need careful, systematic study of civil-war situations to disclose the characteristic issues pre-

---

[56] For one such contention, see Henry A. Kissinger, "Central Issues of American Foreign Policy," in Kermit Gordon (ed.), *Agenda for the Nation* (Washington: Brookings Institution, 1968), pp. 589–90.

[57] I have discussed this idea to some extent in Falk, "Law, Lawyers, and the Conduct of American Foreign Policy," pp. 933–34; it has been criticized by Moore, "The Control of Foreign Intervention," pp. 310–14.

sented. Given the plurality of policy objectives, it is impossible to derive any single set of recommendations for an ideal legal scheme. Quite the contrary. It may become possible to classify civil-war situations in such a manner as to isolate distinct categories of legal problems both with respect to third-party intervention and with respect to rules of conduct. It may also become possible to grasp the influence of the geopolitical setting on normative regulation.

In conceiving of the relevance of international law to civil-war situations, it is important to avoid the twin pitfalls of rule-oriented legalism and policy-oriented reductionism. Rule-oriented legalism tends to associate the task of law with the formulation of system-wide categorical rules, perhaps drawn up in a single legal document or convention; such a collection of rules either incorporates contradictory policy objectives or ignores them. In either eventuality, it tends to be irrelevant as a source of specific guidance for governments called upon to act. Policy-oriented reductionism keeps the context "open," specifies a wide number of variable considerations, and calls upon the decisionmaker to act in behalf of world order; the choice of action is left indeterminate, no fixed guidelines are hazarded, and the only imperative is the rhetorical one that a government explain its policy preferences by reference to world-community values.[58] I am proposing an approach intermediate between legalism and reductionism through the identification of critical thresholds, the advocacy of frameworks of guidance, and the emphasis on obligations to provide a public accounting of action undertaken.[59]

With respect to humanizing the conduct of war, even the partial crystallizations we have suggested cannot be made until there is a better fit between the tactics and doctrine of civil warfare and the normative task. Modern warfare in any form, by the political character of its justification and by the technology of its combat, tends to obliterate all the distinctions embodied in the classical law of war. The failure to maintain these distinctions in the context of major civil wars is thus just a special case of the general failure to rethink the law of war in light of the actualities of modern warfare.[60] At the present time, we need more than anything else, to stimulate a movement to bring together the governments of the world (and perhaps other relevant actors) in a major world conference on the law of war of the sort held at the Hague in 1899 and 1907. Unlike the regulation of intervention in an interrelated world

[58] Such a perspective is set forth in greater detail in Falk, *The Status of Law in International Society*, pp. 41–59.

[59] It would be possible and, I think, useful to construct a comprehensive approach to world order in light of these three points of emphasis.

[60] Such has long been the eloquent plea of Josef Kunz; see *The Changing Law of Nations*, pp. 831–901.

system encompassing contradictory ideologies of government, the achievement of a universal framework of constraint with respect to the conduct of war is possible, provided, of course, that the framework is not biased in favor of either the revolutionary or counterrevolutionary perspective. Both perspectives need to achieve a *locus standi* in the total effort to build a stronger world order for the future.

In conclusion, then, the relevance of international law to civil-war situations needs to be rethought from a variety of intellectual, ideological, regional, and even cultural perspectives. Proposals emanating from partial perspectives can enter into a law-creating dialogue, but their prospects are minimal unless there is a convergence with proposals from many other perspectives. We require a collaborative approach toward issues of world order that corresponds to the decentralization of power and diversity of policy that exists in international society today.

Quincy Wright

THE AMERICAN CIVIL WAR (1861–65)

I. THE CONFLICT: A FACTUAL INTRODUCTION

a. The Participants

Considering its costs and its consequences, the American Civil War
was the most important war in the Western world during the century
from the battle of Waterloo (1815) to the battle of the Marne (1914).[1]
From direct battle losses it cost over two hundred thousand lives, and
from diseases in the armed forces more than twice as many, a total of
nearly seven hundred thousand lives, more than all the wars in Europe
combined during that century. Only the Chinese Taiping rebellion
(1851–64) and the Lopez war in Paraguay (1865–70) were bloodier.
The monetary costs of the war were over $5 billion, small today but un-
paralleled among the wars of this period. The South mobilized nine-
tenths of its military population and lost a third of those mobilized. The
North mobilized a third of its military population and lost a fourth of
those mobilized.[2] Nearly a tenth of the total population of the country
was mobilized. The war lasted four years (April 1861 to April 1865),
nearly twice as long as any European war of the period.

No war during this period was more important in its consequences,
political, social, and military. By eliminating slavery from the continent
and preserving the Union, the American Civil War assured that the
United States would become a "great power" capable of leading the
"free world." By utilizing for military purposes steam transportation on
land and sea, electrical communication, the ironclad and improved fire-
arms, it initiated modern military technology which was followed by
Germany in its wars of unification soon after and was not greatly
changed until the world wars of the twentieth century had introduced the
motor vehicle, the airplane, the missile, and the nuclear warhead.[3]

From the point of view of the South the war was an international war

---

[1] Quincy Wright, "The Historical Circumstances of Enduring Peace," *Annual
Report of the American Historical Association* 3 (1942): 361–73.

[2] The white male population of military age in the South was 1,065,000, of
which 900,000 were mobilized for three years, and nearly 300,000 died in battle
or from disease in the army. The military population of the North was 4,600,000,
of which 1,700,000 were mobilized and 365,000 died. Woodrow Wilson, *History
of the American People* (New York: Harper, 1902), 4: 267.

[3] Quincy Wright, *A Study of War* (rev. ed., Chicago: University of Chicago
Press, 1965), pp. 300 ff., 1518 ff.

as indicated by the name given it, "the war between the states," and the North was the aggressor. From the point of view of the North the war was a civil war and the southerners were traitors, as indicated by the official name given it, "the war of the rebellion." European powers generally accepted the latter opinion and treated it as a civil war within the domestic jurisdiction of the United States. They refrained from intervention on either side and refused to recognize the independence of the Confederacy. They, however, recognized the situation as "belligerency," requiring that they accept the status of "neutrality," including the duty to treat both sides equally in matters concerning military action, rather than as "insurgency," which, as the term was later defined, would have prevented the exercise of belligerent rights at sea against their vessels and might have permitted a differential treatment favorable to the United States, the government they recognized.

(The parties to the war were the North (the Unionists or the United States) actively supported by eighteen states, fourteen north of the Mason and Dixon Line and the Ohio River and four in the West, Iowa, Minnesota, California, and Oregon. To these were added during the war Kansas in 1861 and Nevada in 1864 from the western territories and West Virginia in 1863 by secession from Virginia. The South (the Secessionists or the Confederacy) consisted of eleven seceding states, South Carolina, Georgia, five gulf states—Florida, Alabama, Mississippi, Louisiana, and Texas—and four border states—North Carolina, Virginia, Tennessee, and Arkansas. Three border slave states—Maryland, Kentucky, and Missouri—remained uncommitted, though portions were at first occupied by Confederate forces and they seriously considered secession. Delaware, also a border slave state, supported the Union. The United States before the war possessed vast western territories (later divided into fourteen states) into which settlers were moving mainly from the North. Only the territories which later became Oklahoma and New Mexico were looked upon as possible acquisitions by the Confederacy.

The population of the country on the outbreak of the war was nearly thirty-two million. Twenty-two million were in the North and seven million in the Confederacy, including two and a half million slaves. The population of the uncommitted border states was two million and of the territories, one million.[4] The area of the two sections committed to the war was about equal. The area of the uncommitted states was less than an eighth of either, and that of the territories larger than either.

[4] Wilson, *History*, 4: 249. Henry W. Elson gives figures less unfavorable to the South, pointing out that the original eighteen Unionist states had a population of over 19 million and all the slave states over 12 million, of which nearly 4 million were slaves. *History of the United States of America* (New York: Macmillan, 1910), p. 621.

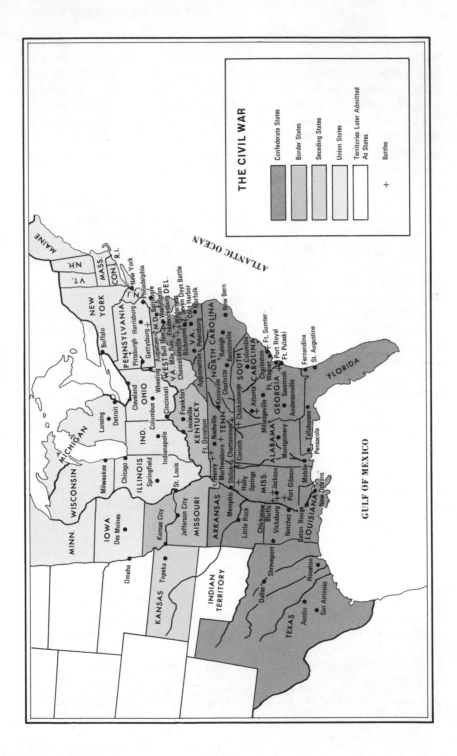

THE CIVIL WAR

Confederate States
Border States
Seceding States
Union States
Territories Later Admitted
As States
+ Battles

In wealth, industrial development, and military production the North was as superior as it was in population. Opinion was not united on either side. In the South, Virginia and North Carolina hesitated to secede and the northern part of Virginia seceded from that State and was admitted to the Union as West Virginia in 1863. In the North there was considerable dissent in southern Indiana and Illinois, requiring the government to declare martial law though the territory was not actually invaded and the Supreme Court later declared the action unconstitutional.[5] The population of the uncommitted states was divided. Although hostilities took place in their territory and as the war went on they tended to support the North, they tried to keep aloof from the war. Slavery remained in all of them until national action in 1862 had eliminated it in all the territories, and the emancipation proclamation of January 1, 1863, had theoretically eliminated it in the Confederacy. Slavery was ended by state action in Maryland and Missouri in 1864 and by national action in Kentucky and Delaware in 1865.[6]

The causes of the war will be analyzed by philosophic, practical, and scientific methods,[7] and its relation to international law will be considered in succeeding sections. It is hoped that the study will contribute to an understanding of war in general and of civil strife in particular, as well as to an understanding of the state of international law in regard to civil strife in the mid–nineteenth century in comparison with later developments.

b. Causes of the Conflict

1. *Philosophical Analysis.* Some historians have considered slavery the sole cause of the Civil War,[8] but most historians recognize that many factors have usually contributed to the outbreak of wars and that the American Civil War was no exception.[9] Philosophical analysts of war have often distinguished ideological, political, economic, and legal factors underlying conflicts which have induced wars.[10]

Slavery was not the only *ideological* and cultural difference between the North and the South in 1861. The North believed in democracy and the

---

[5] *Ex parte Milligan*, 4 Wall. 2 (1866). Earlier in the war Chief Justice Taney had denied the right of the President to suspend the writ of habeas corpus in Maryland, a judgment which the President ignored. *Ex parte Merryman,* Taney's Reports, 246 (1861); Elson, *History*, p. 667.

[6] See map indicating dates of the termination of slavery in the states in Wilson, *History*, 4: 208.

[7] On the meaning of "cause" and the modes of analyzing causes, see Wright, *A Study of War*, pp. 927 ff.

[8] For examples, see Elson, *History*, p. 624.

[9] For example, see James Truslow Adams, *The Epic of America* (New York: Blue Ribbon Books, 1931), pp. 249 ff.

[10] Wright, *A Study of War*, pp. 720 ff., 738, 1236, 1512.

equality of men, manifested in New England town meetings, free labor, and the influence of competitive business. The leaders of opinion in the South, on the other hand, had come to believe in the quasi-feudal system which assumed the inequality of men and white supremacy in the interests of the landowning aristocracy engaged in agriculture with slave labor.

Furthermore, the North had developed primary political loyalty to the nation, because of the abundance of interstate trade, migration, and communication and because of the influence of the increasing flow of migrants from Europe who desired to become Americans, often moving into the western territories, with no attachment to any particular state. The South, on the other hand, with little migration from abroad and with the attachment to the land and the locality characteristic of landowners, continued to feel a primary loyalty to the state.

In the North, moral issues were of great concern to New England Puritanism, even more when liberalized by the Unitarian movement of the early nineteenth century. Pennsylvania Quakers and Mennonites also tended to perceive the basic immorality of slavery. In the South, on the other hand, the less rigid character of the Episcopal religion which prevailed among the upper classes, familiarity with the adaptation of the two races to domestic slavery, and the self-interest of the white population and the illiteracy of the black made it easy for all to ignore the moral issue and some to believe that the slave system was of positive moral value to both races. Both North and South found it easy to quote biblical texts in support of their positions on the moral issue.

The two sections had grown apart in their beliefs—social, political, and moral—since the days when Jefferson and John Adams corresponded on the issues of democracy and aristocracy, states' rights and nationalism, slavery and freedom, with little difference except that the Virginian was more insistent on the virtues and feasibility of democracy than the New Englander.[11] In spite of the unifying influence of the federal government and national political parties, distinct cultures had developed in the two sections. Common language, making communication easy, and common possession of western territories had, in fact, instead of inducing cultural convergence, induced distorted images of each section by the other. The consequence was cultural divergence and rivalry in the effort of each culture to expand in the territories.

Consciousness of cultural distinctiveness, or nationalism, tends to produce an interest in *political* power, whether of the sword, the purse, the word, or the law, adequate to maintain it. Anxiety in the South

[11] L. J. Cappon (ed.), *The Adams-Jefferson Letters* (Chapel Hill: University of North Carolina Press, 1959).

about its power position in the Union played a major part in the Civil War. The balance of political power in the House of Representatives was broken as the North increased more rapidly in population, and the balance in the Senate, carefully maintained since the 1790s by admitting a northern and southern state at the same time, was broken when California was admitted as a free state in 1850. And it became clear, in the controversy over the Kansas-Nebraska Act, that Senator Stephen A. Douglas's conception of popular or squatter sovereignty in the territories, though incorporated in the act, was not acceptable to either section and that a major part of the western territory would eventually be admitted as free states. Furthermore the split of the national political parties reduced the prospect of political compromise. The more rapid increase of population, wealth, and industry in the North deteriorated the relative position of the South in economic and potential military power. In the 1850s it became clear to southern leaders that, in spite of the compromising disposition of the northern presidents Fillmore, Pierce, and Buchanan, the Congress would increasingly support northern positions and that in a contest of military force the South would increasingly be at a disadvantage.

As the southern way of life diverged from the northern, the South's capacity to defend its way of life by political and military means declined. In spite of the Dred Scott decision and the disposition of the North to compromise on threats of secession, the South became less confident that it could defend its position by appeals to law and opinion. Calhoun's concept of "states' rights," of the sanctity of slave property, and of the moral virtues of the slavery system could not long be successful with the increasingly dominant position of northern culture and power in the nation. On the other hand, utilizing Calhoun's conception of the right of secession and the increasing acceptance of the right of distinctive nationalities to independence, as formulated by the American Revolution, the French Revolution, and the Italian Risorgimento, it should be possible to gain the support of foreign nations for southern independence and thus to restore the balance of power between North and South within the society of nations.

Economic and *psychological* factors also played a part in the conflict. The different types of economies, the rural and agricultural economy of the South as compared with the increasingly urban and industrial economy of the North, tended to divergent interests and opinions. As exporters of agricultural products in exchange for British manufactures, free trade was in the interest of the South, whereas Northern industrialists increasingly demanded protection. The tariff debate separated the sections increasingly after the War of 1812, and its importance was indicated by South Carolina's nullification in 1832. Not only did differential rates of economic growth break the political balance of power, but there was increasing realization in the South that slavery might be an uneconomic system compared with free wage labor. Such realization in Virginia, North Carolina, and other border slave states was a factor, along with Union sentiment, in the long hesitation to secede or the final decision in some cases not to secede. Only in the deep South, with its cotton and rice culture, was slavery profitable to the owners of land and slaves. Helper's *Impending Crisis*, published in 1858, suggested that slavery was nowhere in the South profitable to the nonslave-owning majority. Helper's statistics may not have been unimpeachable, but his conclusions stimulated northern criticism of the slave system on economic as well as moral grounds, and though vigorously criticized in the South, it stimulated fear in the deep South, with its large slave and poor white population, that an internal revolt was not beyond the realm of possibility. Nat Turner's rebellion in Virginia in 1831 was remembered, and anxiety was augmented by the aggressiveness which southerners thought they observed in abolitionist activities supported by such figures as William Lloyd Garrison, Wendell Phillips, and Ralph Waldo Emerson, by the misrepresentation and antagonism they thought they detected in such widely circulated books as *Uncle Tom's Cabin* and the *Impending Crisis*, and by the immediate threat they saw in John Brown's raid.[12]

That these fears may have been exaggerated is indicated by the loyalty of both the slaves and the poor whites to the southern cause during the war, but that the fear existed is evidenced by the laws to prevent the circulation of free Negroes in the South, even to the extent in South Carolina of imprisoning free Negro sailors on foreign ships in its ports; by the prolonged effort to prevent congressional consideration of, and consequent publicity to, antislavery petitions; and by the excessive action of the governor of Virginia in summoning state and federal forces before examining the facts on hearing of the raid on the Harper's Ferry arsenal, which it turned out was conducted by sixteen white men and six Negroes led by a fanatic, John Brown.[13] Widespread fear among southerners that their personal welfare and security were threatened by northern propaganda and incitement was added to their fear that the security and autonomy of southern culture were in jeopardy. As secession might restore the balance of political power, so it was hoped it would emancipate the South from northern propaganda and incitement.

Conflict was also supported by the fact that the ambiguities of the federal Constitution made it possible for both North and South to justify in *legal* terms, each to its own satisfaction, the positions which each took

[12] Herman von Holst, *The Constitutional and Political History of the United States*, trans. John J. Laler (Chicago: Callaghan, 1892), 7: 31 ff.
[13] *Ibid.*, 31, 37.

on ideological, political, or economic grounds. The South could argue, with considerable support in the debates of the Constitutional Convention of 1787, the Virginia and Kentucky resolution of 1798, and the Hartford convention of 1811, that the states retained their sovereignty, enjoying full autonomy in their domestic institutions and in the exercise of their reserved powers, and that they could dissolve the constitutional compact when convinced that federal power was encroaching on that autonomy. Furthermore they had full judicial support in the Dred Scott case for their contention that the Constitution forbade the deprivation of property in slaves without due process of law in any state or territory, forbade federal interference with the institution of slavery within the states where it existed, and required the return of fugitive slaves from any state into which they escaped. On the other hand, the North could cite equal support for its contention that the Union was designed to be permanent, especially because the constitutional recognition and definition of the crime of treason against the United States implied, as does international law according to the Nuremburg Tribunal, that an act of a state subject to a superior law, whether by legislation, nullification, or secession, cannot give immunity from prosecution for a crime established by that superior law.[14] The North could also argue cogently against the Dred Scott decision by questioning the priority of "property" over "liberty" in the constitutional clause on due process of law and by citing Mansfield's opinion in Somerset's case, when slavery existed in some parts of the British Empire but not in others. While accepting the incompetence of Congress to interfere with slavery within the states where it existed, the North could argue that the Constitution gave Congress full power to govern the territories, both by the text and by practice since the first Congress reenacted the Northwest Ordinance, first enacted by the Congress under the Confederation.

While the constitutional issues were settled by the Civil War itself and subsequent constitutional amendments, they remained uncertain before the war, and in fact, the Supreme Court, which had supported the northern position on implied powers while John Marshall was chief justice, had so modified its position while his successor Roger Taney was chief justice that by 1860 the South seemed to have the best of the legal argument on the scope of reserved powers of the states. The Court did not directly support secession in the Dred Scott or any other decision, but the South could argue that, since the Court supported much of Calhoun's logical position, it could be assumed that if the issue arose it would support all of it. It was easy for the South to convince itself that secession was legal and constitutional and would not be resisted.

[14] Mountague Bernard, *Historical Account of the Neutrality of Great Britain during the American Civil War* (London: Longmans, 1870), pp. 41 ff.

2. *Practical Analysis*. The immediate causes of the Civil War, as viewed by politicians and the man in the street, were those incidents of the 1850s, manifesting rising tensions on both sides, and the inability of the statesmen of the time to solve the slavery issue by compromises. These incidents culminated in the election of Lincoln in 1860, the secession of most of the southern states on the initiative of South Carolina, the relative inactivity of President Buchanan, the failure of efforts at compromise after secession, the determination of Lincoln to preserve the Union by force if necessary, and the seizure of Fort Sumter by Confederate forces after military resistance.[15]

It has been suggested that the war might have been prevented if the Charleston Convention of 1860 had been successful in keeping the Democratic party together, as hoped by Alexander Stephens of Georgia, who later became vice-president of the Confederacy. This would probably have resulted in the election as president of Stephen A. Douglas, who advocated the policy of "popular sovereignty" in the territories. There might have been no war but the eventual end of slavery as the relative power position of the South declined and the uneconomic character of slavery became evident.[16] It has also been suggested that delay by Georgia and the gulf states to rally to the secessionist initiative of South Carolina, following the example of North Carolina, Virginia, and the border states, might have given time to assure success for the last-minute efforts at compromise. Some have suggested that a firm stand by President Buchanan, threatening military action to oppose secession and to defend federal property in the South, would have stopped the secessionist movement. Others have suggested that if President Lincoln had delayed supplying Fort Sumter, as urged by five members of his cabinet, the Confederacy would have refrained from the fatal attack, as urged by Confederate Secretary of State Toombs, and the compromise, proposed by Congress, might have been accepted.

It seems unlikely that any of these "might-have-beens" would have prevented the war. Tensions had reached such a point before 1860 that, as expressed by Seward, the conflict had become "irrepressible."[17] The

---

[15] According to von Holst, ". . . The three dark powers which unbound the furies of civil war: [were] the doctrine of noncoercion, the slavocratic interpretation of state sovereignty, and slavery," *Constitutional and Political History*, 7: 459.

[16] George Fort Milton, *The Eve of Conflict: Stephen A. Douglas and the Needless War* (New York: Houghton Mifflin, 1934), p. 570; Quincy Wright, "Stephen A. Douglas and the Campaign of 1860," *Vermont History* 28 (October 1960): 250 ff.

[17] Elson, *History*, p. 611; Samuel Eliot Morison, *The Oxford History of the American People* (New York: Oxford University Press, 1965), p. 595; Thornton K. Lothrop, *William Henry Seward* (Boston: Houghton Mifflin, 1899), p. 186. In referring on Oct. 25, 1858, to "an irrepressible conflict between opposing and enduring forces," which meant that "the United States must and will sooner

conviction of the people and politicians of the deep South that they could no longer defend their vital interests in Congress, and that they could not live with the policies which the North would legislate in that body, seems to have crystallized before the Charleston Convention. The rise of the Republican party, the disappearance of the Whigs, the split of the Democrats, the Lincoln and Douglas debates of 1858, and John Brown's raid of 1859 gave them an image of the North which further strengthened this conviction.

At the same time the conviction was widespread in the North that, in spite of the logic of Calhoun and the emotional reaction from Harper's Ferry, the South would not, in final analysis, shatter the Union, founded by the will of all sections in 1776 and 1787, built in its first generation by the Virginia dynasty—Washington, Jefferson, Madison, and Monroe—and developed through half a century by the judicial analyses of Marshall and Storey and the political leadership of Jackson, Webster, and Clay, a Union which in their opinion protected the real interests of all sections of the country. Most northerners agreed with the South that the Constitution guaranteed the states full freedom to deal with slavery internally and were ready to amend the Constitution to underline this guarantee. They recognized the rising opinion in the North that slavery was basically immoral and uneconomic and should not be extended to the territories, but they did not believe that this gave the South any basis, either legal or political, for secession.

The distorted images prevalent on both sides of the Mason and Dixon Line were the product not only of the incidents of the 1850s, which seemed to support them and increased tensions, but of underlying conditions and the course of history during the preceding half century.

Supplementing the conflicting opinions and emotional tensions in each section conducive to war, the calculations of the leaders in the South persuaded them that secession, and war if necessary, would solve their problems, and in the North, that neither secession nor war would occur but that if war did occur it could rapidly be suppressed.[18] Although the South was inferior in industrial resources, it felt better prepared in military leadership and popular morale and also calculated on a favorable attitude, if not actual support, from the industrial countries of Europe, especially Great Britain. The North was aware of its great superiority in

---

or later, become either entirely a slaveholding nation, or entirely a free-labor nation," Seward echoed Lincoln's statement in his debate with Douglas on June 16, 1858, "A House divided against itself can not stand. I believe this government can not endure permanently half slave and half free."

[18] On the "wrong calculations" of both North and South, see von Holst, *Constitutional and Political History*, vol. 7, chaps. 7, 8.

manpower, industry, and military resources and was convinced that foreign intervention could be prevented.

The South was convinced that with victory, the Confederacy could maintain its way of life, extend its influence in the Southwest, and establish mutually advantageous trading relations with Great Britain and other European countries, if unencumbered by a protective tariff demanded by the North. The North, on the other hand, was certain that the speedy victory which it anticipated if the South actually seceded would preserve the Union, eliminate slavery in the territories and ultimately, if not immediately, in the southern states, and promote economic prosperity by the spread of democracy and industrialization throughout the nation.

Each side was convinced of the justice of its cause, the South on grounds of the constitutionality of secession and the political principles, enunciated in the Declaration of Independence, of the right of a people of distinctive character to self-determination and independence, and the North on grounds of the intent of the Constitution to establish a permanent Union and the principle, also enunciated in the Declaration of Independence, of the natural equality, implying the freedom, of all men. With its constitutional interpretation, each side could say that the other started the war and that it was defending a consitutional right.

3. *Scientific Analysis.* In the nuclear age there has been a tendency to attribute international conflict to the increasing gap between the shrinking material world and the disintegrating moral world.[19] The rapid advances in science and technology have made the material world smaller because long-range communication and transport have become rapid and available, and the possibility of rapid and distant military destruction has greatly increased. States have become less self-sufficient, less capable of maintaining empires and spheres of influence, more vulnerable to destruction and more interdependent economically. The moral world, however, has become less integrated because the persistence of old faiths, the dissemination of new knowledge, and the emphasis upon human rights and the self-determination of peoples has developed novel opinions, ideologies, and nationalisms inducing states to demand more self-sufficiency, larger spheres of influence, more armament, and more sovereignty.

Rough measurements of the relations between various pairs of states indicate that if the material distance between two states is shrinking while the moral distance is increasing or shrinking less rapidly, conflicts

---

[19] Wright, *A Study of War*, pp. 403 ff., 1115 ff., 1284 ff., 1502 ff., 1518 ff. Sociologists emphasized the significance of the lag in social adaptation to technological change even before the nuclear age; see W. F. Ogburn, *Social Change* (New York, Huebsch, 1922), pp. 200 ff.

will emerge, tensions will rise, and hostilities will be likely.[20] A lag in the adaptation of moral opinions and institutions to changing material conditions and technologies is almost certain to develop within dynamic societies composed of diverse subsocieties and to induce conflict. Only if the system or society, within which states or subsocieties operate— whether as a balance of power, an empire, an international organization, a confederation, or a federation—is able to adjust the conflicts arising from such a gap can peace be preserved, and the probability of such adjustment is reduced as the advance of science and technology widens the gap, increases the rapidity of change, and narrows the time for adjustment.

If the existing system proves inadequate, a new system is likely to come into operation after a period of war and revolution, as the Roman Empire succeeded to the Hellenistic balance of power, feudalism united by the Christian Church succeeded to the Roman Empire, and a balance of power among territorial nations succeeded to medieval feudal Christendom. Toynbee has indicated a similar succession of systems in many "civilizations."[21] What system will succeed the present "balance of terror" cannot be clearly stated, but many agree that the balance is exceedingly unstable and a new system is the price of enduring peace and escape from human disaster.[22]

This analysis seems applicable to the American Civil War. Little effort has been made to measure the direction and rates of change of moral opinion, material conditions, and political tensions in the period before that war and relations between those rates which would contribute to a scientific analysis of its causes. No such measurements will be attempted here. It seems clear, however, that advancing science and technology, the building of railroads, productive machinery, and systems of postal and telegraphic communication, while favoring the power position of the North had also favored union of the country because of the interest of both sections in the western territories, in economic advance through improved agriculture, industrialization, and trade, and in strengthening the nation in relation to foreign countries. On the other hand, the divergencies of ideology, culture, loyalties, and economic sys-

---

[20] Wright, *A Study of War*, pp. 1257 ff., 1280 ff., 1284 ff., 1492.

[21] Arnold J. Toynbee, *A Study of History* (London: Oxford University Press, 1934), vol. 1; Wright, *A Study of War*, pp. 117 ff.

[22] Kenneth E. Boulding, "The Prevention of World War III," *Virginia Quarterly Review* 38 (Winter 1962): 1 ff.; Herman Kahn, "The Arms Race and World Order," in Morton A. Kaplan (ed.), *The Revolution in World Politics* (New York: Wiley, 1962), pp. 350 ff.; Wright, *A Study of War*, pp. 1502 ff., and *On Predicting International Relations, the Year 2000*, University of Denver Monograph No. 1, 1969–70.

tems induced conflict and favored separation. Furthermore these divergent movements of opinion inducing conflict were proceeding more rapidly than the movements of technology tending to preserve the Union. The gap between material conditions and cultural convictions was widening and the federal system proved incapable of dealing with it. Edward A. Freeman, in his *History of Federal Government from the Foundation of the Achaian League to the Disruption of the United States* published in 1863, when the fortunes of the Union were at their lowest ebb, suggested that such difficulties always disrupted federal systems, replacing them either by a unitary government or empire, or by independent states in balance-of-power relations. Before the Civil War the North tended to favor a more unitary government, the South a looser federation or separation. Both lost hope in compromises under the existing Constitution.

There can be little doubt that the system which emerged after the Civil War was different from the Constitution of 1787. While the same in form, the acceptance of the northern interpretation as a result of the war and the postwar amendments provided for a centralization of federal authority and diminution of "states' rights" not contemplated by the Constitution of 1787. A new system of government had come into being to preserve the nation.[23]

II. THE ROLE OF THE LAW OF WAR IN RELATIONS BETWEEN THE BELLIGERENTS

International law exerted an important influence during the Civil War in determining the relations with each other of the two sections of the country and their armed forces. This influence was important (*a*) in establishing the status of the hostilities and of the Confederacy, (*b*) in guiding the conduct of the hostilities, and (*c*) in terminating hostilities and establishing peace.

a. The Status of the Hostilities

It was clear that war in the material sense existed between the North and the South after the battle at Fort Sumter on April 12, 1861, and it was held by the Supreme Court of the United States in December 1862 that war in the legal sense began at the same time. Evidence for this was found in the magnitude of the hostilities. "However long may have been its previous conception," wrote Justice Grier for the Court, "it nevertheless sprung forth suddenly from the parent brain, a Minerva in the full panoply of *war*. The President was bound to meet it in the shape

[23] Von Holst, *Constitutional and Political History*, 7: 458 ff.

it presented itself, without waiting for Congress to baptize it with a name; and no name given to it by him or them could change the fact."[1]

Prior to this decision, the status of the hostilities was controversial, and international law was invoked to support various positions. This discussion contributed much to clarifying the distinction, in periods of civil strife, (1) between insurgency and belligerency, (2) between belligerency and independence, and (3) between insurgency and piracy.

1. *Insurgency and Belligerency.* The Supreme Court, speaking through Justice Grier in the Prize cases held that large-scale insurrection constitutes war in the legal sense as well as in the material sense.

Insurrection against a government may or may not culminate in an organized rebellion, but a civil war always begins by insurrection against the lawful authority of the government. A civil war is never solemnly declared; it becomes such by its accidents—the number, power and organization of the persons who originate and carry it on. When the party in rebellion occupy and hold in a hostile manner a certain portion of territory; have declared their independence; have cast off their allegiance; have organized armies; have commenced hostilities against their former sovereign, the world acknowledges them as belligerents, and the contest is *war. They* claim to be in arms to establish their liberty and independence in order to become a sovereign state, while the sovereign party treats them as insurgents and rebels who owe allegiance, and who should be punished with death for their treason. ... As a civil war is never publicly proclaimed, *eo nomine* against insurgents, its actual existence is a fact in our domestic history which the court is bound to notice and to know .... Therefore, we are of opinion that the President had a right *jure belli*, to institute a blockade of ports in possession of the states in rebellion, which neutrals are bound to regard.[2]

The opinion also referred to the president's Blockade Proclamation of April 19, notified to foreign states on April 27 and 30; to the British recognition of war by proclaiming neutrality on May 14; to the president's constitutional power to recognize the existence of war, international or civil; and to the confirmation of the president's action by Congress in July 1861. The Confederate Congress had formally recognized the existence of war on May 6, 1861.

Justice Nelson wrote a dissenting opinion in which Chief Justice Taney and Justices Catron and Clifford concurred, distinguishing war in the material sense from war in the legal sense. Referring to the constitutional provision giving Congress sole power to declare war, he thought that war in the legal sense could not exist for the United States until

---

[1] *The Prize Cases,* 2 Black 635, 669 (1862). This was affirmed in *Thorington* v. *Smith,* 8 Wall. 1 (1868); *Williams* v. *Bruffy,* 96 U.S. 176, 189 (1877); *Ford* v. *Surget,* 97 U.S. 594, 605 (1878); and *Baldy* v. *Hunter,* 171 U.S. 388 (1897).

[2] *The Prize Cases,* pp. 667, 671.

Congress had declared or recognized it. Large-scale insurrection may determine the "existence of war in the material sense," but this is not relevant to "what constitutes war in the legal sense of the law of nations and of the Constitution of the United States."[3] To exist in this sense war must be "recognized or declared by the sovereign power of the state," that is, in the United States, by Congress. The president's power conferred by Congress to call forth the militia, the army, or the navy, "to execute the laws of the Union, suppress insurrection and repel invasion," his power as commander in chief to order movements of the armed forces for such purposes, and his responsibility to see that the laws are faithfully executed[4] justified President Lincoln's call for the militia after the Fort Sumter engagement but did not imply, as the majority of the court suggested, a power to recognize war in the legal sense. Only Congress, insisted Justice Nelson, could do that. Insurrection, even if hostilities developed of such large scale as to constitute "war in the material sense" remained *personal*, justifying hostile action only against disloyal citizens. It did not become *territorial* war, permitting treatment of all persons in the Confederate States as enemies, until Congress had recognized it as "civil war." Congress did not do this until July 13, 1861, consequently, said Justice Nelson, prior to that date the hostilities were not war in the legal sense and the blockade could not apply to neutral vessels. Congressional confirmation of past actions of the president could not validate the blockade because this would amount to ex post facto legislation which was prohibited by the Constitution. Consequently the neutral vessels which had been captured on the high seas for breach of blockade should be restored to their owners. Justice Nelson cited by analogy the act of the British Parliament in 1776 which recognized the insurrection of the American colonies as war. The hostilities which had

---

[3] *Ibid.*, p. 690.

[4] U.S. Constitution, art. II, sec. 3; Acts of Congress, May 2, 1794, Feb. 28, 1795, 1 Stat. 264, 424. It has been contended that none of these purposes permit the president to use armed force outside of the territory without express congressional authority, but both practice and legal opinion have recognized the president's power to use the armed forces anywhere to defend the territory, to protect the citizens, and to maintain rights and fulfill obligations under international law and treaties. Furthermore, it has been held that the president can determine the existence of one of these exigencies. *Martin* v. *Mott*, 12 Wheat. 19 (1827); *Luther* v. *Borden*, 7 How. 1 (1848); *Durand* v. *Hollins*, 4 Blatch. 451, 454 (1860); *In re Neagle*, 135 U.S. 1 (1890); Wickersham, Attorney General, 29 Op. 322 (1912). Express congressional authorization, therefore, seems necessary only if the president wishes to use forces abroad for political purposes and can think of no rationalization to bring it under one of these heads. *Flemming* v. *Page*, 9 How. 603 (1850); Quincy Wright, *The Control of American Foreign Relations*, (New York: Macmillan, 1922), pp. 157 ff., 192 ff., 276, 296, 305 ff.; and "The United States Government and the State Militia," *Report of the Efficiency and Economy Commission* (State of Illinois, 1915), pp. 889–906.

been going on for almost a year since the battles of Lexington and Concord were considered insurrection not war.[5]

This argument was difficult to reconcile with Justice Nelson's admission that the president has power to recognize that foreign civil strife, such as that of the Spanish American colonies against Spain in the early nineteenth century, constituted war requiring the United States to proclaim neutrality, as held in the Supreme Court's decision in the case of the *Santissima Trinidad*.[6] If the president could recognize foreign hostilities as war, could he not recognize civil or international hostilities thrust upon the United States as war? The majority of the court answered yes, as did Congress in its action on August 6, 1861, confirming the president's action since March 4, 1861, and half a century later on April 25, 1898, declaring that war with Spain had existed since April 21, when President McKinley had recognized war initiated by the action of Spain and proclaimed a blockade of Cuba.[7] In any case, it would seem that if a foreign country recognized the American civil strife as war, as did Great Britain in its neutrality proclamation of May 13, 1861, Justice Nelson should have admitted that the situation became war in the legal sense in relation to that country and legitimatized the blockade in respect to its ships.

Justice Nelson's argument had been set forth by the attorney appearing in behalf of the Mexican vessel *Brilliant* captured in April for breach of blockade. The attorney also argued that the phraseology of the blockade proclamation of April 19 indicated that it was not intended to be a war blockade because it referred to the existence of "insurrection" not of "war" and was "provisional" until Congress had acted. The closing of the southern ports was not, therefore, a "strict blockade," and neutral vessels could not be accused of "intent" to break a war blockade.[8] A reading of the proclamation indicates the weakness of this argument. The proclamation of April 19 states that the president "deemed it advisable to set on foot a blockade of the ports within the states aforementioned in pursuance of the law of the United States and of the law of nations in such case provided" and added that a competent force would be posted to prevent entrance and exit of vessels, that approaching or departing vessels would be warned and the facts recorded in the vessel's register, and that such vessels if again attempting to enter or depart

[5] *The Prize Cases*, pp. 695 ff.
[6] *The Santissima Trinidad*, 7 Wheat. 283 (1822).
[7] Wright, *Control of American Foreign Relations*, pp. 286 ff.
[8] *The Prize Cases*, p. 665. The *Hiawatha* was captured and condemned for breach of blockade (Blatchford, *Prize Cases* 1 [1861]) before the *Brilliant*, and both condemnations were confirmed by the Supreme Court in the Prize cases.

would be captured and sent into port for prize proceedings.[9] Clearly a war blockade under international law was intended.

The proclamation, like the majority opinion in the Prize cases, indicates both recognition by the president that war in the legal sense existed because of the fact of large-scale hostilities and his desire to conform to the traditional requirements of war blockade under international law.

The Confederate government manifested a similar interpretation of the situation. President Davis's Proclamation of April 17, 1861, asserted the duty of his government "to repel the threatened invasion and defend the rights and liberties of the people by all the means which the laws of nations and usages of civilized warfare place at its disposal" and invited applications for privateering commissions "to aid this government in resisting so wanton and wicked an aggression."[10] The act of the Confederate Congress on May 6, 1861, narrated the effort of the Confederate States to settle all disagreements peacefully and justly, the refusal of the United States to negotiate, its raising of forces to attack forts belonging to the Confederate States, and its setting on foot of a blockade of Confederate ports, and then declared that the acts of "hostility and wanton aggression intended to subjugate the people of the Confederate States" indicates that "war exists between the Confederate States and the Government of the United States and the States and territories thereof except the States of Maryland, North Carolina, Tennessee, Kentucky, Arkansas, Missouri, and Delaware, and the territories of Arizona and New Mexico, and the Indian Territory south of Kansas," thus suggesting its conception of the potential area of the Confederacy. The act then authorized the president of the Confederacy to "use the land and naval force of the Confederate States to meet the war thus commenced," to issue letters of marque and reprisal, and to allow thirty days of grace for vessels of citizens of the United States to leave Confederate ports. It also provided detailed regulations to control privateers, for prize court procedures, and for division of prize money, or bounty in case a captured vessel was "burnt, sunk or destroyed."[11]

The code of land warfare prepared by Francis Lieber and adopted by the United States War Department on April 24, 1863, as General Orders No. 100, "Instructions for the Government of Armies of the United States in the Field,"[12] distinguishes between "insurrection" and

[9] For text, see Mountague Bernard, *Historical Account of the Neutrality of Great Britain during the American Civil War* (London: Longmans, 1870), p. 79.

[10] *Ibid.*, p. 78.

[11] *Ibid.*, pp. 100 ff.

[12] *General Orders Affecting the Volunteer Force, Adjutant General's Office, 1863* (Washington: Government Printing Office, 1864), No. 100, pp. 64 ff.; printed in G. G. Wilson, *International Law* (9th ed.; New York: Silver Burdett, 1935), app. 2 (cited as General Orders No. 100 and Lieber's Code).

"civil war" and implies that insurrection becomes war when of "large extent" and of territorial character in fact, but is not explicit on the criteria for determining the existence of war in the legal sense.

149. Insurrection is the rising of people in arms against their government, or a portion of it, or against one or more of its laws, or against an officer or officers of the government. It may be confined to mere armed resistance, or it may have greater ends in view.

150. Civil war is war between two or more portions of a country or state, each contending for the mastery of the whole, and each claiming to be the legitimate government. The term is also sometimes applied to war of rebellion, when the rebellious provinces or portions of the State are contiguous to those containing the seat of government.

151. The term rebellion is applied to an insurrection of large extent, and is usually a war between the legitimate government of a country and portions or provinces of the same who seek to throw off their allegiance to it, and set up a government of their own.

This code does not declare categorically that "the rules of regular war" must be applied in civil strife[13] but states that if they are, because of "humanity," this does not imply recognition of the independence of the rebel government nor does it give other states a right to recognize such independence.[14] It does not prevent the legitimate government from punishing rebels for treason,[15] and in the interest of both "common justice and plain expediency," the military commander should "protect the manifestly loyal citizens in revolted territories, against the hardships of war, as much as the common misfortune of all war admits" and will "throw the burden of war, as much as lies within his power on the disloyal citizens of the revolted portion or province."[16]

General Orders No. 100, which was issued after the Supreme Court's decision in the Prize cases, adopted elements of both the majority and the minority opinions. It recognized that the rebellion was "civil war,"

---

[13] The four Geneva Conventions of 1949 provide in article 3 that certain humanitarian rules must be applied in all hostilities and this principle is incorporated in *U.S. Army Field Manual: The Law of Land Warfare* (1956), par. 57, U.N. Treaty Series, 75: 31, 135, 287; Raymund T. Yingling and Robert W. Ginnane, "The Geneva Conventions of 1949," *American Journal of International Law* 46 (1952): 393. Writers generally recognize that the "humanitarian" rules of war must be applied by both sides even in situations of "insurgency" and "aggression." Harvard Research on International Law (Philip Jessup, Reporter), "Draft Code on Aggression," *American Journal of International Law*, vol. 33 (1939), supp., p. 897; Josef L. Kunz, *The Changing Law of Nations* (Columbus: Ohio State University Press, 1968), p. 877; Erik Castrén, *Civil War* (Helsinki: Suomalainen Tiedeakatemia, 1966), p. 219.

[14] Art. 152.

[15] Art. 154.

[16] Art. 156.

as did the majority opinion, but it emphasized the distinction between insurgency and belligerency. In either situation it suggested discrimination in the treatment of loyal and disloyal citizens in enemy territory but did not declare explicitly as did Justice Nelson, that when insurrection has not been recognized as war, only disloyal citizens can be treated as enemies. The opinion of the Supreme Court a generation later in the case of *The Three Friends*, which was concerned with civil strife in Cuba in 1896, also distinguished insurgency from belligerency and held that civil strife, even if the hostilities were of great magnitude, remained insurgency until the participants or other states have recognized belligerency.[17]

This case indicated that the existence of either insurgency or belligerency depends on appreciation of the magnitude of the hostilities; that this appreciation belongs to the political organs of the government, particularly in the United States to the president; and that, while the law of war and neutrality applies in the full only in case of belligerency, some obligations of neutrality exist during insurgency. Third states must not permit military expeditions to leave their territory to aid the insurgents. Whether this obligation extends also to such expeditions intended to aid the recognized government was not made clear, though the statute of 1818, which the court applied, says that it does.[18]

The considerations which should control the recognition of belligerency or of insurgency were set forth by President Grant in his message to Congress on December 7, 1875, in connection with the civil strife in Cuba, but obviously with memories of the American Civil War in mind. "Unless justified by necessity it (recognition of belligerency) is always and justly regarded as an unfriendly act and a gratuitous demonstration of moral support to the rebellion."[19]

President Grant refused to recognize belligerency but did recognize insurgency in Cuba. Mountague Bernard writing on the Civil War from an English point of view allows wide discretion to foreign states in recognizing belligerency when insurgency exists in fact.

If it be asked when and how foreign nations may recognize the existence of a state of war, the answer is easy. They may recognize it as soon as it exists, and in whatever way they please. They are at liberty, if they think fit, to wait until their ships are actually detained or captured by either belligerent; they are equally at liberty to anticipate these contingencies by an early notification; and this latter course, which is the more prudent of the two, is com-

[17] *The Three Friends*, 166 U.S. 1 (1896); The Court treated insurgency as a question of fact rather than of recognition, but there has been a tendency for states to recognize insurgency. Castrén, *Civil War*, pp. 207 ff.

[18] 3 Stat. 447, c. 88; Rev. Stat., sec. 5283.

[19] James D. Richardson, *A Compilation of Messages and Papers of the Presidents, 1789–1897* (Washington: Government Printing Office, 1896–99), pp. 336–40.

monly pursued by States which are near to the theatre of hostilities or have a large mercantile marine. If it be further asked what constitutes a state of war—where the line which divides it from a mere insurrection is to be drawn—what amounts to a sustained struggle—what quantity of force is necessary, and what degree of organization?—the answer must be that these terms, though intelligible enough, and not too vague for common use, do not admit of precise definition.[20]

Comparison of this statement with that of President Grant and others quoted in this section indicates that the problem is more difficult than Bernard suggests. This is indicated by the diverse policies of the belligerents and other states during the Civil War, by their opposing positions concerning the legality and the effect of the British recognition of Confederate belligerency, and by the obsolescence of the practice of recognizing belligerency in instances of civil strife after that war.

2. *Belligerency and Independence.* That recognition of belligerency does not imply recognition of independence of the insurgents was indicated in provisions of General Orders No. 100.

152. Neutrals have no right to make the adoption of the rules of war by the assailed government toward rebels the ground of their own acknowledgement of the revolted people as an independent power.

153. Nor does the adoption of the rules of war toward rebels imply an engagement with them extending beyond the limits of these rules. It is victory in the field that ends the strife and settles the future relations between the contending parties.[21]

The same point was emphasized by the Supreme Court in the Prize cases and by the United States government in correspondence with Great Britain.[22]

Judge Treat in an opinion in the Federal District Court in 1862 emphasized the duty of foreign states not to intervene in civil strife by premature recognition of belligerency or recognition of independence and the duty of United States courts to follow United States law exclusively in dealing with rebel persons and property:

The position of foreign nations with respect to this insurrection . . . does not determine its status in American courts. The latter follow exclusively the decision of the political department of the United States government on that question. Even if other governments had recognized the so called Confederate government as an independent power, their recognition would bind themselves and their subjects alone—not the United States. . . . As to all foreign nations, the United States government is absolutely sovereign within its own territorial limits, and over its own subjects. Its internal constitution

[20] Bernard, *Historical Account*, pp. 116–17.
[21] For full citation, see n. 12 above.
[22] *The Prize Cases*, p. 665; Bernard, *Historical Account*, pp. 152 ff., 159 ff.

49

is a subject with which foreign powers have no right to intermeddle. The equality and independence of nations could not otherwise exist.[23]

The question of what conditions will justify the recognition of the independence of a revolting community was discussed by the British government when considering such recognition of the Confederacy, but no action was taken.[24] Secretary of State John Quincy Adams had made a classical statement on this subject in connection with the Latin American republics in 1817, suggesting that recognition of their independence was permissible and might properly be demanded by the insurgents

---

[23] *U.S.* v. *One Hundred Barrels*, 27 Fed. Cas. 292, 297 (1862).

[24] In a letter to the foreign minister, Lord John Russell, on May 5, 1861, the prime minister, Lord Palmerston, referred to pressures for British mediation in the Civil War, the "obvious objections to any step on our part at the present moment," but "the great importance of the matter" which deserved to be fully weighed and considered. "If any step were thought admissible," he added, "perhaps the best mode of feeling our way would be to communicate confidentially with the South by the men who have come over here from thence, and with the North by Dallas (U.S. Minister) who is about to return, is not a political friend of Lincoln, but on the contrary rather leans to the South; but still would be an organ, if it should be deemed prudent to take any step."

In an enclosed letter to a member of Parliament (Edward Ellice) he had written: "The day on which we would succeed in putting an end to this unnatural war between the two sections of our *North American Cousins* would be one of the happiest of our lives, and all that is wanting to induce us to take Steps for that purpose is a belief that any such Steps would lead towards the accomplishment of that purpose and would not do more harm than good. The danger is that in the excited State of Men's Minds in America, the offer of anyone to interpose to arrest their action and disappoint them in their expected Triumph might be resented by both sides; and that jealousy of European and especially of English interference in their internal Affairs might make them still more prone to reject our offer as impertinent. There would moreover be a great Difficulty in suggesting any Basis of arrangement to which both Parties could agree and which it would not be repugnant to English Feelings and Principles to propose. *We* could not well mix ourselves up with the acknowledgement of Slavery and the Principle that a slave escaping to a free soil State, should be followed and claimed and recovered like a Horse or an Ox. We might possibly propose that the North and South should separate amicably.—That they should make some Boundary Line of Separation between them; and that each Confederation should be free to make for its own internal affairs and concerns such Laws as it might think fit.—The two Confederations entering however into certain mutual arrangements as to Trade and Commerce with each other." He then questioned whether "the time is come for any arrangement of such a kind" and whether "it is not in human Nature that the Wing Edge must be taken off this craving Appetite for Conflict of Arms, before any real and wide-spread Desire for Peace by Mutual Concession can be looked for."

Pressure for intervention arose again in August 1862, but Russell wrote to Palmerston on Aug. 24, 1862: "I think that we must allow the President to spend his second batch of 600,000 men before we can hope that he and his Democracy will listen to reason." In the following month the pressure increased. Lee's advance in Maryland threatened the fall of Washington and Baltimore, and on Sept. 14, Palmerston wrote Russell: "If this should happen would it not be time for us to consider whether in such a state of things England and France might not ad-

"when independence is established as a matter of fact so as to leave the chances of the opposite party to recover their dominion utterly desperate." He recognized, however, that the neutral and the belligerent nation may judge of this differently and that this difference may lead to war between them as it did between France and England in 1778.[25] The

---

dress the contending parties and recommend an arrangement on the basis of separation." Russell replied on Sept. 17 that since "the Federal Army has made no progress in subduing the Insurgent States.—I agree with you that the time is come for offering Mediation to the United States Government, with a view to the recognition of the Independence of the Confederates. I agree further than in case of failure, we ought ourselves to recognize the Southern States, as an Independent State."

Gladstone, chancellor of the exchequer, made his famous speech at Newcastle on Oct. 7, saying: "Jefferson Davis and other leaders of the South have made an army, they are making, it appears a Navy; and they have made, what is more than either, they have made a nation." He had on Sept. 25 in a letter to Lord Palmerston referred to his preparations for this speech and indicated his agreement with what he took to be the opinion of Palmerston and Russell that "the time has arrived for coming to an understanding with some other Principal Powers of Europe so as to be in a condition to take part with a view to procuring a cessation of the deadly struggles in America." There were reasons urging action. The progress of their arms would soon prompt the Confederacy "with something like justice to ask of us the highest recognition," but "a friendly offer should first be made to induce the North to recede." Furthermore action should be taken before the population of Lancashire which "have borne their sufferings with a fortitude and patience exceeding all example, and almost all belief" became "excited" and outbreaks occurred which would make action appear to be for "our immediate interests" rather than in the "general interests of humanity and peace."

News of the northern victory at Antietam was received, Palmerston hesitated, and other members of the Cabinet opposed action, especially Argyle, Granville, and Clarendon. After Lincoln's preliminary Emancipation Proclamation had been received, the Cabinet meeting of Oct. 23 "doubted the policy of moving, or moving at that time." Gladstone, however, prepared a long memorandum on Oct. 25 arguing that there was no question of the right of Britain under international law to offer mediation to end the war and that the only issue concerned the advantages of ending the war, of which he had no doubt, and the probability of the success of mediation, which he thought would be enhanced by joint action including France and Russia and by the mobilization of world public opinion, to which he attributed considerable weight. He thought it important that action be taken before the British public became aware that Lincoln had turned the war into one against slavery by the preliminary Emancipation Proclamation. (See Broadlands Archives, Palmerston House, London.) In spite of Gladstone's appeal the Cabinet meeting of Nov. 11, 1862, definitely rejected mediation, recognition, or intervention. Henry Adams, *The Education of Henry Adams* (Boston: Houghton Mifflin, 1918), pp. 152–61; Samuel Eliot Morison, *The Oxford History of the American People* (New York: Oxford University Press, 1965), pp. 652 ff.

[25] J. Q. Adams to the President, Aug. 24, 1818, in J. B. Moore, *Digest of International Law* (Washington, 1906), 1: 78; Wright, *Control of American Foreign Relations*, p. 269. The precise timing of the recognition of independence is discretionary but premature recognition clearly violates the rights of the de jure state. It is controversial whether *long-delayed* recognition of a de facto state violates its rights. See Hersh Lauterpacht, *Recognition in International Law* (Cambridge: Cambridge University Press, 1947), pp. 6 ff., 420 ff.

same opinion was vigorously asserted by British opponents of recognition of the Confederacy during the Civil War.[26]

Although the recognition of belligerency has been almost unknown since the Civil War, the recognition of the independence of insurgents especially in colonial areas, sometimes prematurely, has become common. Respect for the principle of self-determination of peoples, the duty of administering states to develop self-government in their nonself-governing territories called for by the United Nations Charter, and pressures from newly independent states in the United Nations have often induced imperial powers to recognize the independence of their colonies before there is an active revolt.

3. *Insurgency and Piracy.* In his blockade proclamation of April 19, 1861, President Lincoln "proclaimed and declared that if any person, under the pretended authority of the said States, or under any other pretence, shall molest a vessel of the United States, or the Persons or cargo on board of her, such person will be held amenable to the laws of the United States for the prevention and punishment of piracy."[27] The Confederate States had issued letters of marque and reprisal to a number of vessels, and several of these privateers were captured by Union warships and proceeded against for piracy.[28] The United States had tried unsuccessfully to become a party to the Declaration of Paris of 1856, which declared that "privateering is and remains abolished" and which, among the parties, might be interpreted to identify privateering with piracy.[29]

In the case of *United States* v. *Baker* in October 1861 Justice Nelson held that the defendant, an officer of the Confederate privateer *Savannah*, captured early in the war, was not guilty of piracy under inter-

[26] "When a sovereign State, from exhaustion or any other cause, has virtually and substantially abandoned the struggle for supremacy, it has no right to complain if a foreign State treat the independence of its former subjects as de facto established; nor can it prolong its sovereignty by a mere paper assertion of right. When, on the other hand, the contest is not absolutely or permanently decided, a recognition of the inchoate independence of the insurgents by a foreign state is a hostile act towards the sovereign State which the latter is entitled to resent as a breach of neutrality and friendship." Sir Vernon Harcourt *"Historicus" Letters* (London: Macmillan, 1863), p. 9.

[27] For full citation, see n. 9 above.

[28] William Marvin Robinson, Jr., *The Confederate Privateers* (New Haven: Yale University Press, 1928), pp. 133 ff., 148 ff. In the British House of Lords, the Earl of Derby and others expressed the opinion that "privateering was not piracy" (*ibid.,* p. 135), and the lord chancellor was reported to have declared that those who treated a privateersman "as a pirate would be guilty of murder." Jefferson Davis, *The Rise and Fall of the Confederate States Government* (New York: Appleton, 1882), 2: 12.

[29] Charles Francis Adams, Jr., "Seward and the Declaration of Paris," *Proceedings of the Massachusetts Historical Society* 46 (1912): 23 ff.

national law.[30] The indictment, he said, "shows if anything, an intent to depredate upon the vessels and property of one nation only, the United States, which falls far short of the spirit and intent which are said to constitute the essential elements of the crime." On the other hand, an act of Congress of 1820 gave a definition of piracy which went beyond piracy by the law of nations: "It declares the person a pirate punishable by death, who commits the crime of robbery upon the high seas, against any ship or vessel." Baker, might, therefore, be liable under the statutory offense. The jury, however, was divided. In Philadelphia at the same time William Smith and other members of the crew of the privateer *Jeff Davis* were tried and convicted of piracy.[31] These sentences were not carried out, however, because the South threatened retaliation against northern prisoners of war, and on January 31, 1862, Secretary of State Seward ordered the transfer of all prisoners charged with piracy, including those who had been convicted, to military prisons for exchange of prisoners.[32]

In the case of the *Golden Rocket*, captured by the privateer *Sumter* and burnt at sea, the United States District Court held that the owners could not recover on a policy which insured against captures by pirates but not against belligerent captures. The destruction of the *Golden Rocket*, it held, was not an act of piracy under international law, though it might be under United States statutes. The insurance policy, however, must be construed to intend piracy under the law of nations.[33] The courts, therefore, in spite of the president's proclamation and the doubt whether belligerency had been recognized, applied the distinction between piracy and insurgency which became recognized in international law. A vessel not engaged in robbery, or violence, against any vessel on the high seas for private ends but acting against vessels of a particular state for political purposes is an insurgent vessel not a pirate, though its action would be illegal if it interfered with vessels of other states.[34]

Until insurgency was clearly established as a status, American diplomats and courts sometimes failed to make this distinction. The American

[30] *U.S.* v. *Baker*, 5 Blatch. 6 (1861); Robinson, *Confederate Privateers*, pp. 141–47.

[31] Robinson, *Conference Privateers*, p. 147.

[32] *Ibid.*, pp. 133, 148 ff.

[33] *Dole* v. *N.E.M.M. Ins. Co.*, 6 Allen 373 (1863).

[34] League of Nations, Committee of Experts for Progressive Codification of International Law, "Report on Piracy," *American Journal of International Law*, vol. 20 (1926), spec. supp., pp. 222 ff.; Harvard Research on International Law, "Draft Convention on Piracy" (1932), *American Journal of International Law*, vol. 26 supp., pp. 741 ff.; Green Hackworth, *Digest of International Law* (Washington, 1941), 2: 681 ff.; Moore, *Digest*, 2: 1084 ff.; Inter-American Convention on Civil Strife, 1928, in Manley O. Hudson (ed.), *International Legislation* 4: 2418; Lauterpacht, *Recognition*, pp. 296, 327; Castrén, *Civil War*, pp. 127–32.

minister to Spain in 1874 thought that the Cuban insurgent vessel *Virginius* might be a pirate as held by Spain, although the United States and Britain protested against the execution of their nationals in the crew as pirates.[35] Judge Brown in the District Court of New York in 1885 held that a vessel of Colombian insurgents, brought in by a United States naval vessel for condemnation for piracy, was engaged "in an expedition technically piratical" when captured. He, however, subsequently released it under the mistaken impression that the secretary of state had recognized the belligerency of the insurgents.[36] In the Civil War, belligerency had been recognized and members of the Confederate armed forces, whether captured on privateers or elsewhere, were treated as prisoners of war unless found guilty of war crimes in spite of the initial declaration by the United States that Confederate privateers were pirates and Seward's reluctance to recognize that the Confederates had belligerent rights.

b. The Conduct of the Hostilities

Both sides in the Civil War intended to apply the established laws of war during the hostilities, as a natural consequence of the recognition of belligerency, but these laws were not well known. According to Major George B. Davis:

> The Federal Government had succeeded in placing in the field armies of unexampled size, composed in great part of men taken from civil pursuits; most of whom were unfamiliar with military affairs, and so utterly unacquainted with the usages of war. These armies were carrying on hostile operations of every kind, over a wide area, and questions of considerable intricacy and difficulty were constantly arising which required for their decision, a knowledge of international law which was not always possessed by those to whom these questions were submitted for decision. Conflicting decisions and rulings were of frequent occurrence in different armies, and, at times, in different parts of the same field of operations; and great harm not infrequently resulted before decisions could be reversed by competent authority.[37]

The situation induced the War Department to accept Francis Lieber's suggestion that he prepare a code of land warfare. Lieber had already,

[35] *The Virginius,* in *U.S. Foreign Relations* (1876), p. 503, Moore, *Digest,* 2: 967 ff.

[36] *U.S.* v. *Ambrose Light,* 25 Fed. 408 (1885); Moore, *Digest,* 2: 1098: Francis Wharton, "Insurgents and Belligerents," *Albany Law Journal* 33: 125 ff.

[37] George B. Davis, *Outlines of International Law,* quoted by Lewis R. Harley, *Francis Lieber, His Life and Political Philosophy* (New York: Columbia University Press, 1899), p. 148. The Confederate officers seem to have been better informed. See the confidential appraisal by Sir James Fergusson, in a letter of Nov. 11, 1861, transmitted to British Prime Minister Palmerston, Broadlands Archives (described below in pt. 3, n. 16).

with agreement of General H. W. Halleck, who had written a text on international law, prepared a work on "Guerrilla Parties Considered in Reference to the Laws and Usages of War."[38] In a letter to General Halleck, Lieber discusses his difficulty in writing the code.

I had no guide, no groundwork, no textbook. I can assure you, as a friend that no counsellor of Justinian sat down to his task of the Digest with a deeper feeling of the gravity of his labor, than filled my breast in the laying down for the first time such a code, where nearly everything was floating. Usage, history, reason, and conscientiousness, a sincere love of truth, justice and civilization, have been my guides; but of course the whole must be still very imperfect.[39]

The code, after revision by a board of officers, was published by the War Department in April 1863 as General Orders No. 100, "Instructions for the Government of the Armies of the United States in the Field."[40] It was reissued during the Spanish-American War and was utilized in preparing the *U.S. Rules of Land Warfare*, published in 1917 and 1940 but replaced by the *Law of Land Warfare* in 1956. Several European nations utilized Lieber's Code in preparing instructions for their armies. It was also utilized in the preparation of the declaration of the international conference at Brussels in 1874, the manual of the Institute of International Law (Oxford, 1880), and the Hague Regulations of 1899 (revised in 1907) on "Rules of Land Warfare."[41]

Although its observance was obligatory for United States armies during the Civil War, the code suggested that the application of the rules of war, required by international law in wars between states, was required toward rebels less by a sense of legal obligation than by considerations of humanity.[42] This distinction seems to have had little practical importance during the hostilities.

[38] Francis B. Friedel, *Francis Lieber, Nineteenth-Century Liberal* (Baton Rouge: Louisiana State University Press, 1947), pp. 529 ff.; Harley, *Francis Lieber*, p. 93; Richard R. Baxter, "Le première effort Moderne de Codification du droit de la Guerre," *Review Internationale de Croix Rouge*, 1963, p. 14. Lieber, an immigrant from Germany, had been a slave-owner while teaching at South Carolina College, but after going to Columbia College in New York he vigorously opposed slavery and espoused the Union cause. His interest in the law of war was stimulated by the fact that his three sons were in the war. One on the Confederate side was killed at the battle of Williamsburg in 1862, his brother on the Union side survived.

[39] Harley, *Francis Lieber*, p. 150. Friedel presents a very full account of the preparation of the code and its subsequent influence (*Francis Lieber*, pp. 317 ff).

[40] For full citation, see n. 12 above.

[41] W. E. Hall, *A Treatise on International Law* (8th ed.; Oxford: At the Clarendon Press, 1924), p. 469; Harley, *Francis Lieber*, p. 153; Friedel, *Francis Lieber*, p. 340; W. W. Bishop, Jr., *International Law; Cases and Materials* (2d ed.; Boston: Little, Brown, 1962), p. 55.

[42] Art. 152.

The code dealt with military jurisdiction in occupied territory; with military necessity and reprisals; with bombardments; with the treatment of public and private property of the enemy; with the treatment of civilians; with the protection of art, science, religion, and medical services; with prisoners of war, *levées en masse*, hostages, and paroles; with the status of partisans, irregular troops, war traitors in occupied territory, spies, and war criminals; with the use of poison, assassination, and other forbidden methods; and with flags of truce, armistices, capitulations, and other military agreements.

The standards set by the code seem to have been generally observed by both sides during the Civil War and detailed comment is not necessary except on some special problems which arose in connection with (1) enemy persons, (2) enemy territory, (3) bombardments, (4) enemy property, and (5) war crimes.

1. *Enemy Persons.* The white population of the seceding states were, before the war, citizens of the United States and some remained loyal to the United States, although the overwhelming majority transferred their loyalty to the Confederacy. Similarly most of the population of the North remained loyal to the Union during the war although there was some dissent in the border slave states and in southern Indiana and Ohio. In the main, however, personal loyalties conformed to the territorial division between the North and the South.

There was at first a disposition in the North to identify enemy character with disloyalty to the Union, especially because of the hope that the loyal element in the border states might prevent their secession. Justice Nelson in his dissent in the Prize cases thought, as noted (pages 43–44), that until there was a formal recognition of war by Congress, this was necessary. The president's power conferred by Congress to use force to execute the laws of the Union, suppress insurrection, and repel invasion did not, in Justice Nelson's opinion, give him power to convert loyal citizens into enemies. Until Congress recognized war, hostilities were personal not territorial. The majority of the Court, however, recognized that war in the legal sense began with the attack on Fort Sumter and that the seceding states became enemy territory and their inhabitants enemy persons whatever their personal attitudes (page 43). This was explicitly affirmed in the case of Mrs. Alexander's cotton. The confiscation of the cotton, which had been captured, was sustained by the Supreme Court on the ground that, although private property was usually exempt from confiscation if seized on land, cotton was of such importance to the Confederacy that Congress was justified in declaring it confiscable and that Mrs. Alexander, although loyal to the Union, lived in the South and so was an enemy person.[43]

[43] *Mrs. Alexander's Cotton*, 2 Wall. 404, 419 (1864).

Lieber's Code held the same. "The citizen or native of a hostile country is thus an enemy, as one of the constituents of the hostile state or nation, and as such is subjected to the hardships of war."[44] Lieber's Code is remarkable for its effort to justify the rules on moral or philosophical grounds, and this rule was justified because it is a "requisite of civilized existence that men live in political, continuous societies, forming organized units, called states or nations, whose constituents bear, enjoy, and suffer, advance and retrograde together, in peace and war."[45] "Nevertheless, as civilization had advanced, . . . so has likewise steadily advanced, especially in war on land, the distinction between the private individual belonging to the hostile country and the hostile country itself, with its men in arms. The principle has been more and more acknowledged that the unarmed citizen is to be spared in person, property, and honor, as much as the exigencies of war will admit."[46] The exigencies of war were thought by Congress and the Supreme Court to justify the confiscation of privately owned cotton.

The code recognized the difficulty of applying these principles in civil war which may be between two factions, "each contending for the mastery of the whole, and each claiming to be the legitimate government," or may be a rebellion, or "war between the legitimate government of a country and portions or provinces of the same who seek to throw off their allegiance to it, and set up a government of their own."[47] In the latter case the inhabitants of the rebelling area are enemies which are divided into "two general classes: combatants and noncombatants or unarmed citizens of the hostile government."[48] However, the code continues:

155. The military commander of the legitimate government, in a war of rebellion, distinguishes between the loyal citizens in the revolted portion of the country and the disloyal citizen. The disloyal citizens may further be classified into those citizens known to sympathize with the rebellion, without positively aiding it, and those who, without taking up arms, give positive aid and comfort to the rebellious enemy, without being bodily forced thereto.

156. Common justice and plain expediency require that the military commander protect the manifestly loyal citizen, in revolted territories, against the hardships of war, as much as the common misfortune of all war admits.

The Commander will throw the burden of the war, as much as lies within his power, on the disloyal citizens of the revolted portion or province, subjecting them to a stricter police than the noncombatant enemies have to suffer in regular war; and if he deems it appropriate, or if his government demands of him that every citizen shall, by an oath of allegiance or by some other

[44] Art. 21.
[45] Art. 20.
[46] Art. 22; see also art. 38.
[47] Arts. 150, 151.
[48] Art. 155.

manifest act, declare his fidelity to the legitimate government, he may expel, transfer, imprison, or fine the revolted citizens who refuse to pledge themselves anew as citizens obedient to the law and loyal to the government.

Whether it is expedient to do so, and whether reliance can be placed upon such oaths, the commander or his government have the right to decide.

157. Armed or unarmed resistance by citizens of the United States against the lawful movements of their troops is levying war against the United States, and is therefore treason.

These final provisions of the code obviously give the commander suppressing rebellion considerable discretion to depart from the general principle stated in article 22, and also in articles 26 and 33, which limited the requirement of oaths of allegiance to "magistrates and civil officers of the hostile country" under penalty of expulsion and declared it "a serious breach of the law of war to force the subjects of the enemy into the service of the victorious government" until there had been a completed conquest.

What was the status of slaves during the war? A quarter of the southern population were Negro slaves, recognized in the South, and indeed by the United States Supreme Court in the Dred Scott case, as property, not as persons, and incapable of being citizens.[49] There were several hundred thousand free Negroes in the North and some in the South. It is remarkable that the Confederacy was not faced by a slave rebellion. Although most of the white men were in the armies at the front, the slaves continued to operate the plantations and maintain the southern economy under the direction of white women during the war.[50]

There have been many territorial rebellions in modern history of adjacent and overseas territories, and in all there has been considerable opposition to the revolt in the revolting territory; but compared with other situations, the leaders of the Confederacy were faced with little internal trouble. The white population was remarkably loyal, in spite of extraordinary hardships, and only small minorities remained favorable to the Union. The Negro population, whether from ignorance, lethargy, or loyalty to their masters, kept at work as directed by their masters whether in agriculture, industry, or in nonmilitary service in the army. Only when the Union army was in the neighborhood did some desert and seek the protection of that army. It is also remarkable that in spite of internal opposition most revolts in modern history, whether of domestic minorities or overseas colonies, have been in the long run successful in establishing independence, usually with outside assistance

[49] Elson, *History*, p. 596; *Scott* v. *Sanford*, 19 How. 393 (1857), Justice Curtis wrote a dissenting opinion in the Dred Scott case.

[50] See Sir James Fergusson's report, Broadlands Archives, described below in pt. 3, n. 16.

and sometimes after long delay. The Confederacy, on the other hand, without substantial internal opposition but without foreign assistance, failed.[51]

The initial policy of the North was to insist that the war was to preserve the Union and not to disturb the status of slavery in the states where it existed. It was hoped that this policy would persuade the border slave states not to secede. By the summer of 1862, however, it was clear that the border slave states which had not seceded were not likely to do so and that the great problem was to prevent British intervention on the side of the Confederacy. Consequently on September 22, 1862, President Lincoln issued the preliminary Emancipation Proclamation declaring that a final proclamation would be issued on January 1, 1863, liberating all slaves in states still in rebellion. The preliminary proclamation did not induce any of the seceding states to return to the Union, but it did prevent British intervention and assured ultimate northern victory. Missouri and Maryland emancipated their slaves by state action in 1864. Congressional action emancipated them in Delaware and Kentucky in 1865, and the President's final Emancipation Proclamation was enforced in the seceding states after Union victory and was accepted by most of them during the early reconstruction period.[52] Doubts as to the constitutionality of the Emancipation Proclamation were quieted by the passage of the Thirteenth Amendment to the Constitution abolishing slavery in the United States, which came into force on December 18, 1965.[53]

Before the Union government had decided what to do about slavery, northern generals had been forced to deal with slaves in areas they occupied. As early as May 1861 General Butler, in command of Fortress Monroe on the North Carolina coast, refused to return three Negro fugitive slaves to their masters, calling them "contraband of war." Congress in August 1861 passed an act confiscating all property, including slaves employed in the service of the rebellion. Orders of various generals declaring the emancipation of slaves in areas which they did not

[51] According to Morison, *Oxford History*, "The white South almost unanimously, a strong minority in the Northern states, and almost every thinking European, expected the Confederacy to achieve independence. Numbers and wealth, to be sure, were against the South.—But determined secessions had generally been successful against even greater odds" (p. 615). The combination of long union, territorial propinquity, and cultural similarity probably contributed to the defeat of secession, as they did in the revolts of Scotland and Wales from England, of the Ukraine from Russia, and of Biafra from Nigeria.

[52] Woodrow Wilson, *History of the American People* (New York: Harper, 1902), 4: 208; Elson, *History*, p. 794.

[53] John W. Burgess, *The Civil War and the Constitution*, 2: 117; James Ford Rhodes, *History of the United States . . .* (New York: Macmillan, 1907), 4: 70; Wright, *Control of American Foreign Relations*, pp. 86, 300.

occupy were overruled by Lincoln.[54] An act of Congress on July 17, 1862, declared free all slaves that came into the protection of the government if their owners were in rebellion.

General Orders No. 100, issued on April 24, 1863, after the final Emancipation Proclamation, declared that all captured or fugitive slaves in possession of United States forces were free.[55] Lieber, the author of this code, opposed slavery, although during the twenty years he taught at South Carolina College before the war, he owned slaves as the only means for obtaining household service in the state.[56]

At first neither side in the war used Negroes as soldiers because of the opposition of white soldiers to fighting alongside them. In 1862, however, General Butler recruited a Negro army corps in Louisiana, calling it *Le Corps d'Afrique*. In July 1862 Congress authorized the employment of Negroes in camp service and trench digging. In 1863 Negro regiments were recruited in New England, Philadelphia, and St. Louis. That recruited by Colonel Robert Gould Shaw in Boston became so famous for its heroic action at Fort Wagner near Charleston, where Colonel Shaw lost his life, that a monument was erected to it in Boston Common.[57] Lieber's Code sought to protect free Negro soldiers by declaring:

58. The law of nations knows of no distinction of color, and if an enemy of the United States should enslave and sell any captured persons of their army, it would be a case for severest retaliation, if not redressed upon complaint.

The United States can not retaliate by enslavement; therefore death must be the retaliation for this crime against the law of nations.

Both slaves and free Negroes were used in the Confederate armies from the first as cooks, body servants, teamsters, and laborers, and the Tennessee legislature had authorized the enlistment of Negroes by an act of June 28, 1861. The Virginia legislature discussed a similar bill in February 1862, and in November 1862 a regiment of fourteen hundred free Negro troops entered the Confederate service.[58] There was, however, such a strong feeling in the Confederacy that the use of Negro troops against them was an indignity that the Confederate Congress on May 1, 1863, resolved that a white officer of colored troops should be

[54] Elson, *History*, p. 713.

[55] Arts. 42, 43.

[56] John B. McConaughy, "Francis Lieber and the Rules of Land Warfare," *Judge Advocate's Journal*, Bulletin no. 32 (February 1962), p. 56; see also n. 38 above.

[57] Morison, *Oxford History*, p. 675.

[58] Elson, *History*, p. 746, citing Horace Greeley, *The American Conflict* (Hartford: Case; and Chicago: Sherwood, 1866), 2: 522.

executed if captured. Threats of retaliation prevented the carrying out of this resolution.[59]

In spite of this attitude, when southern manpower ebbed, General Robert E. Lee urged President Jefferson Davis in March 1865 to authorize the recruitment of slave soldiers if both the slave and his master volunteered. A bill authorizing such recruitment was passed and signed by the president but with the proviso that such service would not result in emancipation of the slave. Two companies of slaves were organized in Richmond, but neither served before Lee's surrender. Even before this in 1865, President Davis had sent a special envoy to London authorized to offer abolition of slavery in return for British recognition of the independence of the Confederacy. The South was aware of its desperate situation and so was Britain; consequently nothing came of the proposal.[60]

Prisoners of war seem generally to have been treated as required by the law of war and by Lieber's Code, although nearly thirty thousand died out of some two hundred thousand in both northern and southern prisons during the war, in the North from cold weather and disease, and in the South from inadequate food and disease.[61] The South found it difficult to feed its armies as the blockade and the war continued and so was unable to provide proper food for its prisoners. In both North and South medicine and sanitation had not advanced to present-day standards. The treatment of Union prisoners at the Andersonville stockade was a scandal, and after the war the commander, Captain Henry Wirtz, was tried and executed for breach of the law of war.[62]

As already noted, the North threatened to treat officers and crew of Confederate privateers as pirates, and the South threatened to treat Northern officers of slave corps as criminals, but neither of these threats was carried out because of threats of retaliation. Lieber's Code required humane treatment of prisoners and provided for, but did not require, exchange of prisoners.[63] Prisoners were actually exchanged on the initiative of President Lincoln, though the North, aware of the manpower shortage in the South, agreed to exchanges only rarely.[64] Lieber's Code provided that prisoners could be required to work for the benefit of the captors' government according to their rank and condition, they could not be tortured to get information, and their killing was in general pro-

[59] Morison, *Oxford History*, p. 675.
[60] *Ibid.*
[61] Art. 56; Wilson, *History*, pp. 294, 307.
[62] Morison, *Oxford History*, p. 715.
[63] Arts. 56, 75, 76, 109.
[64] James Brown Scott, *Cases in International Law* (St. Paul: West, 1906), p. 350.

hibited.[65] "Modern wars are not internecine wars, in which the killing of the enemy is the object . . . . Unnecessary or revengeful destruction of life is not lawful."[66]

Not only captured enemy soldiers but civilians attached to the enemy army, chief officers of the enemy country, and diplomatic agents without a safe conduct might be made prisoners of war.[67] Hostages if taken, "rare in modern war," must be treated as prisoners of war, but chaplains, doctors, and nurses should be left free unless detained for special reasons, in which case they should be exchanged.[68]

Troops might refuse to give quarter only "if only by the commander in great straits making encumberment by prisoners impossible."[69] Participants in *levées en masse* if captured in invaded territory before actual occupation were to be made prisoners of war.[70]

52. No belligerent has the right to declare that he will treat every captured man in arms of a *levée en masse* as a brigand or bandit.

If, however, the people of a country or any portion of the same, already occupied by an army rise against it, they are violators of the law of war, and are not entitled to their protection.

59. A prisoner of war remains answerable for his crimes committed against the captor's army or people, committed before he was captured, and for which he has not been punished by his own authorities.

All prisoners of war are liable to the infliction of retaliatory measures.

2. *Enemy Territory.* Territory of the seceding states was recognized by the North as enemy territory and when occupied by the northern forces was automatically subject to martial law.[71] According to General Orders No. 100, "Martial law is the immediate and direct effect and consequence of occupation or conquest. The presence of a hostile army proclaims its martial law"[72] Northern Virginia was an exception. It seceded from Virginia and was admitted to the Union in 1863 as the

[65] Arts. 76, 80.

[66] Art. 68; see also art. 44. Lieber's Code recognizes that irregular forces of the enemy do not enjoy the protection of the rules of war (art. 82) unless they constitute a *levée en masse* in invaded but unoccupied territory (arts. 49, 51, 52, 81). In such situations "military necessity" prevails (art. 14). It is difficult to justify the use of napalm and bombing targets in civilian areas against guerrillas in South Vietnam in 1966 by these rules, though Sherman's action in Georgia seems to have been similar; see page 64 below.

[67] Arts. 49, 50.

[68] Arts. 53, 54, 55.

[69] Art. 60.

[70] Art. 51.

[71] Art. 1.

[72] In considering recognition of the Confederacy, Lord Palmerston was aware that it would be difficult to determine its boundary with the North, but Gladstone did not hesistate to make concrete proposals on the question, in his letter of Sept. 25, 1862, to Palmerston; see n. 24 above.

state of West Virginia. Early in the war the South was in control of portions of Missouri, Kentucky, Maryland, and the western territories which much later became Oklahoma, Arizona, and New Mexico. It invaded Pennsylvania in 1863 before the battle of Gettysburg. These controls were, however, short lived and were treated as "invasion" rather than "occupation."

Lieber's Code recognized the distinction between "invaded" and "occupied" territory. In the latter case a person who resists the occupying authority or disobeys its decrees is described as a "war rebel," and if he gives information of military value to the enemy, as a "war traitor," in either case punishable by death.[73] The occupant should, however, be "strictly guided by the principles of justice, honor and humanity— virtues adorning a soldier even more than other men, for the very reason that he possesses the power of his arms against the unarmed."[74] He should respect the "person, property and honor" of the unarmed citizen "as much as the exigencies of war will admit."[75] Civil and penal law continue in occupied territory "unless interrupted by orders of the occupying military power" and are administered by the judges and administrative and police officers who remain in the territory and who are paid from its revenues.[76] Such officers might be obliged to take an oath of temporary allegiance to the occupant or an oath of fidelity to their own victorious government and might be expelled if they declined to do so.[77]

In invaded territory, not yet occupied, participants in *levées en masse* and irregular forces or partisans if wearing the uniform of their army were to be treated as prisoners of war if captured.[78] During an invasion, military necessity permits "measures indispensable for securing the end of war," including destruction of property, obstruction of communications, withdrawing of means of life from the enemy, and utilization of whatever is needed for the invading army.[79] It does not, however, permit cruelty, torture, or perfidy or "wanton devastation of a district."[80]

---

[73] Arts. 26, 52, 85, 90, 91. The Hague Regulations (1907) and the Geneva Conventions (1909) have qualified the occupant's authority and made these terms obsolete. Richard R. Baxter, "The Duty of Obedience to the Belligerent Occupant," *British Year Book of International Law*, 1950, pp. 235 ff.; Quincy Wright, "The Value of International Law in Occupied Territory," *American Journal of International Law* 39 (1945): 775 ff.

[74] Art. 4.

[75] Art. 22.

[76] Arts. 6, 39.

[77] Art. 26.

[78] Arts. 49 (2), 51, 52, 81. See also text accompanying n. 66 above.

[79] Arts. 14, 15.

[80] Art. 16.

Whether these principles were observed by General Sherman's armies in their invasion of the South in 1864, and especially in the march from Atlanta to Savannah on the sea, has been controversial. Wilson and Elson are uncritical,[81] but Morison says: "Sherman glimpsed the concept of total war—war on the enemy's will to fight and capacity to support fighting men, as much as the soldiers themselves. Robert E. Lee was the finest general of a Napoleonic age that was passing; Sherman was the first general of an age that was coming, and whose end we have not yet seen." He quotes Sherman's letter of June 26, 1864, during the march to Atlanta: "We have devoured the land and our animals eat up the wheat and cornfields close. All the people retire before us and desolation is behind. To realize what war is one should follow our tracks." "The March to the sea," continues Morison, "like Sheridan's Shenandoah campaign, was one of deliberate destruction, in order to ruin a main source of provisions for Lee's and Hood's armies."[82]

The humanitarian solicitude of Francis Lieber for enemy territory gave way in the last months of the Civil War, as it did in the wars of the twentieth century, to "scorched-earth policies" justifying Sherman's assertion that "War is Hell."

3. *Bombardments*. The humanitarian issue arose also in connection with bombardment of cities, especially that of Atlanta. Lieber's Code permitted the bombardment of fortified towns, and states that, while notice of bombardment is generally given, its omission is "no infraction of the common law of war."[83] It contained no rule limiting bombardment to military targets, though works of art, scientific collections, libraries, and hospitals were to be spared.[84]

General Sherman ordered the systematic bombardment of Atlanta, which he considered fortified, in 1864. After surrender of the city, General Hood, the Confederate commander, while agreeing to Sherman's proposal to remove noncombatants, added: ". . . The unprecedented measure you propose transcends, in studied and ingenious cruelty, all acts ever before brought to my attention in the dark history of war. In the name of God and humanity I protest." His objection seems to have been more to the failure to give notice in advance of the bombardment than to the bombardment itself. Sherman replied: "I was not bound by the laws of war to give notice of the shelling of Atlanta, a fortified city. . . . You were bound to take notice. See the books." His action seems to have conformed to the international law of the time, but

[81] Wilson, *History*, p. 256; Elson, *History*, p. 766.
[82] Morison, *Oxford History*, pp. 687, 696, 699.
[83] Art. 19.
[84] Art. 35.

such action has been criticized by later international lawyers and is forbidden by the Hague Regulations.[85]

In the Civil War there was no question but that the general rules of war applied to bombardments, but the incident at Atlanta indicated the difficulty of determining the circumstances under which the bombardment of a city properly balanced the principles of "humanity" and "military necessity." There was a tendency to accept the thesis, subsequently supported by Italian General Giulio Douhet, that the object of war could best be achieved by attacking the civilian morale of the enemy directly, especially by aerial bombardment of cities.[86]

4. *Enemy Property.* General Orders No. 100, applied to the Civil War, recognized principles of the law of war concerning property. It declared that the belligerent occupant may appropriate movable public property of the enemy and sequestrate revenues of real public property but that title does not pass until complete conquest.[87] The occupying authority may suspend, change, or abolish, as far as the martial power extends, the relations which arise from the services due, according to the existing laws of the invaded country, from one citizen, subject, or native of the same to another. The commander of the army must leave it to the ultimate treaty of peace to settle the permanency of this change.[88] This provision obviously referred to the status of slaves and, although issued after the Emancipation Proclamation, reflected the caution which Lincoln had observed earlier in regard to slavery within the states where it was protected by the Constitution.

[85] Brigadier General Oliver Spaulding, *Ahriman: A Study in Air Bombardment* (Boston: World Peace Foundation, 1939), pp. 4 ff.; W. E. Hall, *A Treatise on International Law* (8th ed.; Oxford: Clarendon Press, 1924), p. 646; Moore, *Digest*, vol. 7, par. 1170. The Hague Regulations of 1899 prohibited the bombardment of undefended towns, and those of 1907 add "by any means whatever" (art. 25), thus forbidding air bombardment of such towns. Air bombardment had been forbidden generally by a special but temporary declaration of the 1899 Hague conference. Differing from Lieber's Code, the 1907 regulations required notification of intention to bomb to the authorities of the town (art. 26). The 1907 convention on naval bombardment introduced the concept of confining bombardment to military targets, and this was emphasized in the draft convention on aerial war of 1923, though both of these conventions added that unavoidable civilian damage does not entail responsibility. Efforts to regulate aerial bombardment by treaty have been unsuccessful, but in the Shimoda case, a Japanese court held that if the weapon used inevitably caused disproportionate civilian damage, as did the atomic bomb, it was illegal. *Shimoda* v. *Japan*, Tokyo District Court, Dec. 7, 1963, cited in Richard A. Falk and Saul H. Mendlovitz (eds.), *The Strategy of World Order* (New York: World Law Fund, 1966), 1: 314 ff. See also Falk, "The Claimants of Hiroshima," *ibid.*, p. 317; and Institute of International Law, *Resolution on the Distinction between Military Objectives and Non-Military Objectives in General and Particularly the Problems Associated with Weapons of Mass Destruction*, Sept. 9, 1969.

[86] Spaulding, *Ahriman*, pp. 17 ff.

[87] Art. 31.

[88] Art. 32.

"Strictly private property" must be protected in occupied territory, but the right is asserted of the "victorious invader" to tax the people or their property, to levy forced loans, to billet soldiers, or to appropriate property, especially houses, land, boats or ships, and churches for temporary and military uses."[89] Requisitions should eventually be paid for.[90] Private property of prisoners of war, including the side arms of officers, should be retained for eventual restoration, except large sums of money found on the person or in the baggage of such persons.[91]

Property of churches, hospitals, charitable and educational institutions, and museums of science or art, even though "as a general rule" public, may not be confiscated or sequestrated though it may be taxed. Works of art, scientific collections, libraries, and hospitals must be protected from injury even in "fortified places whilst besieged or bombarded."[92] They may be removed but not given away or injured. Ultimate ownership is to be decided by the treaty of peace.[93]

United States courts were obliged to deal with many cases after the war involving the status of property and contract during the war and looked to international law to provide the rule of decision. The principle that enemy private property on land was not subject to confiscation was generally accepted, although it had been controversial;[94] enemy private property captured at sea, however, was clearly subject to condemnation by prize courts. The courts held that enemy public property and types of private property held by Congress to be of especial value to the enemy, such as cotton, were confiscable.[95]

It was held by the United States, Great Britain, and arbitral tribunals after the war that the United States was not as a rule responsible to foreign states for property losses or other injuries to their nationals from Confederate action, even if the foreign state had not recognized the belligerency of the South.[96] An exception, however, was recognized if

---

[89] Art. 37.
[90] Fergusson (notes 37, 50 above) states that the Confederate armies paid for requisitions.
[91] Arts. 72, 73.
[92] Art. 35.
[93] Art. 36.
[94] *Brown* v. *U.S.*, 8 Cranch 110 (1814).
[95] *Mrs. Alexander's Cotton*, 2 Wall. 404 (1864).
[96] *U.S. Foreign Affairs* (1863), 2: 742; Moore, *Digest*, 6: 885; H. A. Smith (ed.), *Great Britain and the Law of Nations* (London: King, 1932), 332; British-American Claims Commission, 1871, Hanna Case, Docket, no. 2. Such claims were barred by the US-French convention of June 15, 1880, and the French Claims Commission, 1880–84; see *Report of the French Claims Commission* (Washington, 1884), p. 5. US-Mexican Claims Commission, July 4, 1886, Prats claim, no. 748, and Olivares claim, no. 749; and R. R. Oglesby, "Application of International Law under Conditions of Civil Strife" (Ph.D. dissertation, Duke University, 1949), pp. 192–94, 197.

the United States had inexcusably neglected to take proper and available measures to prevent the injury, and British courts held that when the United States succeeded to Confederate property in British territory after the war the claims of British creditors against the property should be deducted.[97]

Furthermore, the Confederate government, though considered illegitimate, exercised de facto authority during the war, and the courts were faced by the question: To what extent did its acts establish property and contract rights of individuals enforceable after the war? The Supreme Court distinguished between acts directly in aid of rebellion and acts necessary for the maintenance of law and order among the people within the area which it governed during the war. It also distinguished a "general *de facto* government" in complete control of a state from a "partial *de facto* government" in control of a part of a state the remainder of which was controlled by the "*de jure* government." The first type, while in control, could exercise all powers of government within the territory and make treaties with foreign governments even though the de jure government continued to exist in exile. The acts of such a general de facto government affecting property and contract rights within its territory and creating international obligations should generally be considered valid by foreign governments and even by the de jure government if it eventually returned to power. Furthermore the latter should not regard adherents of a general de facto government as traitors. Cromwell's government in England was cited as this type of de facto government.[98]

The Confederacy, on the other hand, was a partial de facto government. Belligerent occupants of enemy territory during international war and rebel governments controlling territory during civil strife illustrated this type of de facto government. Such a government had the rights of a military occupant, suspending the authority of the de jure government in the occupied territory, and its acts affecting private rights, if necessary to maintain civil life in the area and not directly related to the war, remained valid after the war. In accord with this principle the Confederate currency, although illegal and of no value after the war, was valid during the war; consequently contracts made during the war calling for payment in that currency should be enforced, attributing to the currency the value, in terms of United States dollars, which it had at the time the contract was made.[99] The Supreme Court also recognized that trading

[97] *U.S.* v. *Prioleau*, 2 Hemm. and Mil. 559 (1865); *U.S.* v. *McRae*, L.R. 8 Eq. 68 (1869); Moore, *Digest*, 6: 957.

[98] *Thorington* v. *Smith*, 8 Wall. 1 (1868). See also the Tinoca arbitration, *Great Britain* v. *Costa Rica*, *American Journal of International Law* 18 (1924): 147 ff.

[99] *Thorington* v. *Smith*, 8 Wall. 1.

with the enemy was illegal, that contracts made between persons separated by the line of war were unenforceable, and that executory contracts between such persons made before the war were dissolved by the outbreak of war; but it held that executed contracts, including debts, not related to the war were merely suspended and could be enforced after the war, though interest did not run during the war period.[100]

The same principles were applied to acts of the seceding state governments. The Union was designed to be a "permanent Union of permanent States" and the states did not cease to exist during the rebellion, but their governments in rebellion were not de jure but merely de facto governments.[101] Their acts were valid, insofar as necessary for the maintenance of peace and order among the inhabitants of the state and not in aid of rebellion. Thus a corporation formed in Georgia during the war for peaceful purposes was deemed to have a valid existence.[102]

In general, respect for property rights during and after the Civil War seemed to be at a higher level than that shown for private property in the hands of alien property custodians by the United States after the two world wars.[103]

5. *War Crimes.* General Orders No. 100 specifies the nature of martial law and the various acts constituting crimes in areas under its jurisdiction, including occupied enemy territory in civil war. Martial law, it says, is military authority exercised in accord with the laws and usages of war, guided by justice, honor, and humanity and administered by military courts. Sentences of death must normally be approved by the chief executive.[104] Offenses provided by statutory rules, including the articles of war, are tried by courts martial, other offenses by military commissions. Ordinary civil and penal laws continue in occupied territory unless explicitly suspended by the commanding officer, and offenses against them are tried by the existing judges under the supervision of the military government, which may require these judges to take an oath of temporary allegiance or an oath of fidelity to their own government under penalty of expulsion.[105]

---

[100] *Hanger* v. *Abbott,* 6 Wall. 532 (1867); in *Kershaw* v. *Kelsey,* 100 Mass. 561 (1868), an executory contract made during the war by persons separated by the line of war was maintained on the ground that it did not in any way aid the enemy.

[101] *Texas* v. *White,* 7 Wall. 700 (1868).

[102] *The Home Insurance Company Case,* 8 Court of Claims 449 (1872); Scott, *Cases,* p. 59. Scott cites other cases, p. 61.

[103] Bishop, *International Law,* pp. 792–98.

[104] Arts. 4, 12.

[105] Art. 26. Acts by occupying forces of either side in accord with the law of war were held by the United States Supreme Court after the war to be immune from civil liability (*Ford* v. *Surget,* 97 U.S. 594, 606 [1878]; *Dow* v. *Johnson,* 100 U.S. 158 [1879]; *Freeland* v. *Williams,* 131 U.S. 405, 416 [1891]), but criminal acts not adequately dealt with by the occupant could apparently be dealt with

It is a serious breach of the law of war, according to General Orders No. 100, to force subjects of the enemy into service of the occupant unless there has been a completed conquest and annexation of the territory.[106] Wanton violence; unauthorized destruction of property; robbery, pillage, rape, wounding, or killing of inhabitants are prohibited under penalty of death or other severe penalty adequate for the gravity of the offense.[107] If a serious crime is "committed by an American soldier in a hostile country against its inhabitants," it is "not only punishable as at home, but in all cases in which death is not inflicted, the severer punishment shall be preferred."[108] "A soldier, officer or private, in the act of committing such violence, and disobeying a superior ordering him to abstain from it, may be lawfully killed on the spot by such superior."[109]

The use of power for private gain by officers and soldiers is punishable.[110] Deserters if recaptured suffer death.[111] Risings against the occupant by the inhabitants constitute a crime.[112]

Men or squads not part of the enemy army but intermittently acting as civilians, engaged in destruction or plunder or unauthorized raids, are not entitled to be treated as prisoners of war if captured and "shall be treated summarily as highway robbers or pirates."[113] Scouts in disguise, armed prowlers, war rebels in occupied territory; spies, traitors, and war traitors; voluntary guides, and guides proven to have intentionally misled may be punished by death if caught in the act.[114]

Acts of perfidy are punishable, including the use of the enemy's flag in battle, false use of a flag of truce or of a flag of protection for hospitals or museums; breaches of parole, and acts of treachery distinguished from legitimate deception.[115] The intentional killing or wounding of a disabled enemy, or the ordering of such acts, is punishable by death on conviction whether the accused belongs to the United States or enemy army.[116]

---

by state courts, thus modifying the majority opinion in *Coleman* v. *Tennessee* (97 U.S. 509 [1878]). See Moore, *Digest*, 7:177; and Quincy Wright, "War Criminals," *American Journal of International Law* 39 (1945): 270 ff.

[106] Art. 37.

[107] Art. 44. U.S. courts martial received indictments for such offenses by American soldiers and officers in the Vietnam hostilities in 1970.

[108] Art. 47.

[109] Art. 44 (2).

[110] Art. 46.

[111] Art. 48.

[112] Art. 52.

[113] Art. 82.

[114] Arts. 83, 84, 85, 88, 89, 90, 91, 92, 95, 96, 97.

[115] Arts. 15, 16, 65, 101, 114, 117, 118, 124.

[116] Art. 71.

Prisoners of war are liable for war crimes committed before capture,[117] but

104. A successful spy or war traitor, safely returned to his own army, and afterwards captured as an enemy, is not subject to punishment for his acts as a spy or war traitor, but he may be held in closer custody as a person individually dangerous.

An escaped prisoner of war who has not made a pledge is not punishable if recaptured.[118] Attempts of prisoners to escape are not a crime, though the individual may be shot to prevent escape. Initiation of a conspiracy to escape or to rebel is a crime.[119]

Assassination of enemy persons is a crime, and proclamations of outlawry of individuals may be retaliated against. "Civilized nations look with horror upon offers of rewards for the assassination of enemies as relapses into barbarism."[120] Rebels, though treated as belligerents during war, are not exempt from subsequent punishment for treason unless there is a general amnesty.[121] "Armed or unarmed resistance by citizens of the United States against the lawful movements of their troops is levying war against the United States, and is therefore treason."[122]

These provisions seem to have been observed by the United States in dealing with war crimes during the war and were applied in the case of Henry Wirtz, who was tried after the war for brutal treatment of Union prisoners at the Confederate prison at Andersonville.[123]

General Orders No. 100, like other national codes for the instruction of their armies, including United States *Law of Land Warfare*, Basic Field Manual 27-10 (1956);[124] the charters of the international military tribunals of 1945 under which the Nuremburg and Tokyo trials were held following World War II;[125] and the Geneva Conventions of 1949 define individual crimes and punishments, thus differing from the Hague Conventions, which state rules and prohibitions but do not specify individual criminal liabilities. They do, however, declare that a belligerent state which violates the regulations is obliged to pay compensation to the injured belligerent, is responsible for acts of persons in its armed forces, and is required to issue instructions to its armed forces

[117] Art. 59.
[118] Art. 78.
[119] Art. 77.
[120] Art. 148.
[121] Art. 154.
[122] Art. 157.
[123] Morison, *Oxford History*, p. 715.
[124] Printed in part Bishop, *International Law*, pp. 800 ff.
[125] *Ibid.*, pp. 840 ff.

70

in conformity with the regulations.[126] The Nuremburg Tribunal held that violations of the Hague Regulations, which generally codified the customary rules of war, constituted war crimes for which the individual was criminally liable under international law.[127] General Orders No. 100 initiated and would generally conform to the rules of war concerning criminal liability which have subsequently been codified by international conventions and maintained by international and national war crimes tribunals.

c. The Termination of Hostilities

The termination of a civil war normally differs from that of an international war. In the latter case it is assumed that both parties will continue to exist, although there may be a "completed conquest" and annexation, eliminating one of the parties as in the Boer War of 1900. Normally, however, international wars end with a treaty of peace involving some compromises between the victor and the defeated power, both of which survive but perhaps with some transfers of territory. The United States terminated its two wars with Germany by unilateral acts, but they were confirmed by subsequent agreements.[128]

In civil war, however, the state engaged assumes that the insurgents when defeated will cease to exist as a political entity or in any case can be treated at the state's discretion. Although the insurgents assume that their cause is legitimate and that they will survive the war and be recognized as a state, foreign states usually refuse to recognize them unless the de jure state has given up the struggle. If the de jure state wins the war, foreign states usually make no objection to its demand for unconditional surrender of the insurgents. If the insurgents win and establish a new

[126] *Ibid.*, p. 802.
[127] *Ibid.*, p. 857, quoting *Judgment of the Nuremburg Tribunal*, September 30, 1946 (Washington: Government Printing Office, 1947); *American Journal of International Law* 41 (1947): 172 ff., and Q. Wright, "The Law of the Nuremburg Trial," *ibid.*, pp. 59 ff. The *U.S. Rules of Land Warfare*, Basic Field Manual 27-10 (1940), assert to the same effect that the written rules of the Hague and other conventions "are in large part but formal and specific applications of the unwritten rules." Art. 5 (*b*), quoted in Bishop, *International Law*, p. 799.
[128] Quincy Wright, "Some Legal Aspects of the Berlin Crisis," *American Journal of International Law* 55 (October 1961): 959. Prior to these agreements, President Truman had proclaimed on Oct. 24, 1951, that the state of war with Germany declared by Congress on Dec. 11, 1941, was terminated by the Congressional Resolution of Oct. 19, 1951. See Wright, "The Status of Germany and the Peace Proclamation," *ibid.*, 48 (April 1952): 599. The United States terminated the first war with Germany by a similar procedure. After rejecting the Treaty of Versailles, which ended World War I for most of the belligerents, Congress passed a resolution signed by President Harding on July 2, 1921, which declared the war "at an end." It was confirmed by the separate peace treaty with Germany signed on Aug. 25, 1921, and proclaimed by the President on November 14, 1921. See Wright, *Control of American Foreign Relations*, p. 292.

state, the war is usually ended by a peace treaty as was the American Revolution in 1783 or by informal agreement as was the Algerian revolt in 1962.

The American Civil War ended with victory of the United States and application of the usual assumption of the state in civil war, that the insurgents had ceased to exist.[129] The Confederate armies surrendered unconditionally, those under General Lee to General Grant at Appomattox Court House on April 9, 1865, and those under General Johnston to General Sherman on April 26. General Orders No. 100 provides that an armistice concluded by a military commander requires ratification by the superior authority if it goes beyond the district under his command,[130] and it has been the recognized rule that the same is true of armistices and capitulations that include political provisions.[131] General Sherman's acceptance of General Johnston's surrender was not approved in Washington for this reason, but it was revised to accord with General Lee's surrender and approved.[132] It was later held by the United States that the generous conditions of these surrenders, permitting the Confederate soldiers to return home with their horses for spring plowing, did not prevent the treatment of the South "as conquered soil."

Although President Davis tried to continue the struggle after these surrenders, he was captured on May 10 with some members of his cabinet while trying to escape in Georgia. There was fighting near the Rio Grande on May 12, the last battle of the war and a Confederate victory. All Confederate forces west of the Mississippi surrendered on May 26 to General Simon Bolivar Buckner. Some Cherokee and Choctaw Indians, allied to the Confederacy, did not surrender until June 23, and some Confederate warships continued attacks on Yankee whalers in the Pacific in the autumn. The last of these surrendered in England on November 6, 1865.[133]

President Lincoln was assassinated in Washington on April 13, 1865, but President Andrew Johnson, who succeeded him, proceeded with the policy of reconstruction which he had proposed. Lincoln had issued a

---

[129] The Confederacy made unsuccessful efforts near the end of the war to induce Britain to mediate a negotiated settlement on the basis of the elimination of slavery with compensation to the owners. Morison, *Oxford History*, pp. 675, 693, 698; Martin B. Duberman, *Charles Francis Adams, 1807–1866* (Boston: Houghton Mifflin, 1920), pp. 317 ff.

[130] Arts. 135, 140.

[131] As in the capitulation of Napoleon's army in Egypt to British Commodore Sir Sidney Smith at El Arish in 1800, by which the French army would be transported to France with their arms and other property. Hall, *A Treatise on International Law*, p. 667.

[132] Elson, *History*, p. 772.

[133] Morison, *Oxford History*, pp. 701, 702.

proclamation in 1863 that elections could be held in any state after 10 percent of the voting population had taken oaths of allegiance, and in his second inaugural on March 4, 1865, he had called for a policy of "malice toward none," "charity for all," and "firmness in the right," a policy that would "bind up the nation's wounds," and "achieve and cherish a just and lasting peace among ourselves and with all nations."[134]

In this spirit President Johnson proclaimed a general amnesty on May 29, extending pardon to the entire South with the exception of designated leaders of the rebellion.[135] Elections were held for conventions in the southern states. They declared the secession ordinances invalid and accepted the abolition of slavery; and by June 1866 state governments had been reestablished in all the southern states except Texas. Martial law was ended, and on August 20, 1866, President Johnson declared that the insurrection had ended and peace existed throughout the United States.[136]

The South, however, had not abandoned the idea of white supremacy and pursued a policy of keeping the ex-slaves in actual subservience. Large elements in the North, especially after Lincoln's assassination, which became a symbol of southern intransigence, wanted a severe policy. The election of November 1866 brought into power the northern "radicals." Led by Thaddeus Stevens in the House, Charles Sumner in the Senate, and Secretary of War Edwin M. Stanton in the Cabinet, they proceeded to undo the president's reconstruction and to treat the South as "conquered soil." Military governments were set up, the governments in the states were ruled by "carpetbaggers" from the North and freed Negroes, and the South resisted by underground organizations such as the Ku Klux Klan.[137]

As noted, war criminals were tried, including Captain Henry Wirtz for maltreatment of prisoners of war at Andersonville, and treason trials were initiated against major southern leaders. Lieber's Code had insisted that the law of war did not prevent proceeding against rebels for treason after the war,[138] and indictments were issued against Confederate President Jefferson Davis and members of his cabinet who had been captured while trying to escape. Davis was held in Fortress Monroe for two years,

---

[134] *Ibid.*, p. 702.

[135] Elson, *History*, p. 792.

[136] 14 Stat. 817, confirmed by Act of Congress, March 2, 1867, 14 Stat. 421. The Supreme Court held that the war did not end with surrender of the last Confederate general but required a public act or proclamation. *U.S. v. Anderson*, 9 Wall. 50, 70 (1869). See also *Hanger v. Abbott*, pp. 532, 541; Morison, *Oxford History*, pp. 711–12.

[137] Morison, *Oxford History*, pp. 712–20.

[138] Arts. 154, 157.

Vice-President Stephens and a few members of the cabinet were held for shorter periods, but none was tried.[139]

The opposition of President Johnson to the congressional reconstruction policy resulted in his dismissal of Secretary Stanton and his impeachment by the House in February 1868 on various charges, including violation of the tenure of office act, which he considered unconstitutional. In his trial in the Senate he was acquitted by one vote. The southern states were not restored to self-government until 1876, after the Democrats had won control of Congress.[140]

International law was held to determine the circumstances in which the United States was responsible for claims of persons arising from acts of rebel de facto governments during the war, but the law was held to accord a wide discretion to the United States in determining when hostilities with rebels had ended and in the treatment of rebel persons and territory after the war. Some limitations may be imposed by provisions concerning human rights and the self-determination of peoples in treaties, such as are to be found in the United Nations Charter, but in the absence of such treaties, limitations of this character are generally treated as questions of constitutional law and were so treated after the Civil War. If the humane precepts of Francis Lieber and Abraham Lincoln and the liberal reconstruction policy of President Johnson had been sustained by Congress, it is probable that a second President Johnson would have had less difficulty in maintaining constitutional civil liberties in the South a century later.

III. THE ROLE OF INTERNATIONAL LAW IN RELATIONS BETWEEN FOREIGN COUNTRIES AND THE BELLIGERENTS

To understand the role of international law in the relations of foreign countries and the belligerents, it is necessary to examine the policies of the states and the statesmen involved and the attention which they paid to international law in pursuing these policies. The positions of the United States, the Confederacy, and Great Britain are especially important.

a. The Policies of the States Involved in the Situation

1. *United States Policies.* During the first hundred days of the war, from the battle of Fort Sumter to the battle of Bull Run, most northerners considered the war an insurrection, engineered by a minority in

---

[139] Morison, *Oxford History*, p. 705; James C. Bonner, "War Crimes Trials, 1865–67," *Social Science*, April 1947, pp. 128 ff.

[140] Morison, *Oxford History*, pp. 720, 721.

the South, which could be speedily crushed if it were so treated by foreign states, especially by Great Britain.[1] The recognition of southern belligerency by Great Britain and by most other commercial nations was, therefore, a great disappointment. In spite of its relative lack of military success on land for two years after its defeat at Bull Run in July 1861 until its victories at Vicksburg and Gettysburg in July 1863, the North was confident that its tremendous superiority in seapower, manpower, wealth, and industrial equipment assured its eventual victory if the morale of its population could be maintained and if foreign intervention and assistance to the Confederacy could be prevented.[2]

The general policy of the United States in relations with Great Britain and France, the most important of the foreign states, was to persuade them to refrain from any action which would encourage or assist the South, or hamper the North, especially in its naval operations. Four diplomatic problems were presented: (1) These states must be induced to refrain from recognizing the belligerency or independence of the Confederacy, from initiating mediation to stop the war and frustrate Union victory, and especially, from intervening on the side of the South to assure its victory. (2) They must be persuaded to take effective measures to prevent the use of their territory for Confederate naval bases or the preparation or launching of military or naval expeditions. (3) They must be induced to acquiesce in United States naval action to maintain a blockade and stop all trade, even that of neutrals, with the Confederacy insofar as permitted by international law. (4) They must be persuaded to cooperate in United States efforts to protect American and neutral commerce and navigation from depredations by Confederate naval activity and to this end to deny harborage and supplies to Confederate privateers, warships, and prizes and to treat the officers and crews of Confederate privateers as pirates. American statesmen sometimes differed in their interpretations of these policies.

President Lincoln was at first most interested in preventing the border states, especially Virginia, from seceding and in persuading the states that had seceded to return to the Union, but he seems soon to have recognized that the war was serious, that if the Union was to be preserved large military forces must be recruited, and above all, that for-

[1] Charles Francis Adams, Jr., "Seward and the Declaration of Paris," *Proceedings of the Massachusetts Historical Society*, 46 (1912): 23; Henry Adams, *The Education of Henry Adams* (Boston: Houghton Mifflin, 1918), p. 98; letter of Sir James Fergusson, November 11, 1861, to Lord Derby, Broadlands Archives, Palmerston House, London; Herman von Holst, *The Constitutional and Political History of the United States*, trans. John J. Laler (Chicago: Callaghan, 1892), 7: 249 ff.

[2] See pt. 1, pp. 39–40.

eign recognition of the Confederacy or intervention in the war must be prevented.[3]

Secretary of State Seward, who, in view of Lincoln's inexperience, thought he would be the power behind the throne, was early obsessed by the idea that if diplomatic conflicts, or even war, with foreign countries could be induced the national patriotism of all Americans, both North and South, would rally them to the defense of the country and the civil strife would end. Seward expressed this idea even before the inauguration in a memorandum of April 1, 1861, to Lincoln, who quietly rejected it.[4] The idea, however, lurked in Seward's mind and was manifested in the famous Dispatch No. 10 of May 21, 1861, which Minister Charles Francis Adams in London thought sounded as if the United States was "ready to declare war with all the powers of Europe."[5] It convinced his son, Charles Francis Adams, Jr., examining the record fifty years later

[3] Samuel Eliot Morison, *Oxford History of the American People* (New York: Oxford University Press, 1965), pp. 610 ff., comments on Lincoln's policy and also asserts that Lincoln's grasp of military strategy was superior to that of his generals (p. 626). In his circular of March 9, 1861, to all United States missions abroad, Secretary Seward instructed them "to exercise the greatest possible diligence and fidelity" to prevent foreign intervention "in any unfriendly way in the domestic concerns of this country." He wrote: "You will truthfully urge the consideration that the present disturbances have had their origin only in popular passions excited under novel circumstances of very transient character. [No one] with well balanced mind has attempted to show that dissolution of the Union would be permanently conducive to the security and welfare of any state and the people themselves still retain and cherish a profound confidence in our happy Constitution, together with a veneration and affection for it such as no other form of Government ever received at the hands of those for whom it was established."

He suggested that revolt, should it break up the Union, "might tend by its influence to disturb and unsettle the existing system of government in other parts of the world, and arrest the progress of civilization and improvement." Mountague Bernard, *Historical Account of the Neutrality of Great Britain during the American Civil War* (London: Longmans, 1870), p. 124. See also Joint Resolution of Congress, March 1863, to similar effect (described in pt. 4, pp. 101–2), and n. 16 below and pt. 2, n. 25, for a very different image of the situation in Britain.

[4] Martin B. Duberman, *Charles Francis Adams, 1807–1886* (Boston: Houghton Mifflin, 1920), p. 267; John G. Nicolay and John Hay (eds.), *Abraham Lincoln: Complete Works* (New York: Century, 1894), 2: 29; Henry W. Elson, *History of the United States of America* (New York: Macmillan, 1910), p. 641; R. B. Mowat, *The Diplomatic Relations of Great Britain and the United States* (New York: Longmans, 1925), p. 169. Thornton K. Lothrop, *William Henry Seward* (Boston: Houghton Mifflin, 1899), pp. 178 ff., gives an explanation of the memorandum favorable to Seward.

[5] C. F. Adams, Jr., "Declaration of Paris," pp. 45, 75; Duberman, *Charles Francis Adams*, p. 268; Bernard, *Historical Account*, p. 159. The American government's "extreme apprehension lest the revolted states should succeed in obtaining from foreign powers recognition of their independence" was indicated, according to Bernard, by "the elaborate series of separate instructions composed by Mr. Seward for its diplomatic agents in Europe—instructions in which no pains were spared to shape the argument according to the interests or sentiments which he supposed most likely to influence each individual court."

Bernard adds: "The idea of recognizing them immediately, before their independence had been firmly established does not appear to have been entertained by

that, during the first hundred days of the war, Seward's policy was "ill-advised, illogical, contradictory, and incomprehensible."[6] Seward did not accept the recognitions of Confederate belligerency but insisted that Confederate privateers and even warships did not enjoy belligerent rights at sea, should be detained by foreign states if they entered their waters, and could be pursued and captured by United States naval vessels in such waters.[7] Although a lawyer, Seward's knowledge of international law seems to have been very limited, as were his concepts of diplomatic discretion.[8] He sent some diplomatic dispatches without getting the president's consent, and manifested great discontent when the president stopped this activity. His erratic activities aroused apprehension in Secretary of the Navy Gideon Welles and Chairman of the Senate Foreign Relations Committee Charles Sumner.[9]

American foreign policy was therefore in a state of chaos during the hundred days before Bull Run, and foreign governments were in a state of perplexity. After Bull Run Seward calmed down, though he did not wholly abandon his conception of the rebellion; and with the explanations of his ministers abroad, Charles Francis Adams in London and William L. Dayton in Paris, who were more aware of the requirements of international law than the secretary of state, American foreign policy became more comprehensible.[10]

---

any European government. [But compare pt. 2, n. 24.] However, it was certain at this time [when Lincoln took office] that the Confederate States possessed a political organization which would have qualified them for a place among independent nations. It was not certain whether, if a serious effort were made to subdue them, they could maintain their independence. It was uncertain, also, whether such an attempt would be made." He therefore considers that the guarded reply (see n. 29 below) which Lord John Russell made to Seward's note was justified. Bernard, *Historical Account*, pp. 125–27.

[6] C. F. Adams, Jr., "Declaration of Paris," p. 81.

[7] *Ibid.*, p. 47, 50, quoting Seward's note to the Brazilian chargé d'affaires on Dec. 20, 1864. See also Bernard, *Historical Account*, pp. 161, 167; and below, n. 10.

[8] C. F. Adams, Jr., "Declaration of Paris," p. 47.

[9] *Ibid.*

[10] Writing from a British point of view, Bernard characterizes Seward's early positions as "erroneous, unreasonable, flatly opposed to the settled opinion and practice of nations, and especially to the settled opinion and practice of the United States." *Historical Account*, p. 162. Charles Francis Adams, Jr., son of the American minister to England is no less critical of Seward's positions on international law. "Mr. Seward did not possess what is known as a legal mind, much less a judicial cast. . . . The proposition [which he supported in a note to Britain] was certainly 'bold' not to say 'startling' and his position in the note to Brazil [seeking to justify the seizure of the Confederate cruiser Florida in the harbor of Bahia, Brazil, on Oct. 6, 1864] was high handed and in manifest violation of recognized principles of international law." "Declaration of Paris," p. 24. Adams explains Seward's position by his conception (1) that the Southern forces were insurgents not belligerents, (2) that insurgent privateers and warships were "pirates," and (3) that it was wise policy for the United States to exacerbate conflict with foreign states.

2. *Confederate Policies*. In the early stages of the war the South was better prepared and even more confident of speedy victory than the North. The people of the Confederacy were more united in conviction of the righteousness of their cause, their generals were more able, and the morale of their troops was higher. There was a general belief that the North, because of military incompetence, desertions, and reluctance to wage a war of aggression against their southern brethren, would soon abandon the war, and this feeling was increased by the sorry Union performance at Bull Run.[11] In spite of their optimism, however, the southern leaders recognized that the attitude of foreign states was of major importance. If the war continued, success depended on gaining recognition not only of belligerency but of independence. The South believed that the need of foreign countries, especially Britain, for southern cotton and for southern markets for industrial goods would induce such recognition, as would the inconvenience and losses arising from the blockade and maritime war generally. The southern leaders, therefore, anticipated a favorable attitude toward the use of foreign ports and industrial equipment for developing a Confederate navy to break the blockade, toward the extension of credits on cotton stored in the South and development of trade after the war, and toward the sojourn in foreign ports of Confederate warships and privateers with their prizes so long as the blockade prevented their access to southern ports. They seem to have considered these expectations consistent with the obligations of neutral states under international law.[12]

As the prospects of British recognition of Confederate independence receded, and the military superiority of the North became obvious, the southern leaders recognized that their situation was desperate, and even President Jefferson Davis, who professed confidence in victory to the end, was ready to negotiate for the abolition of slavery in the South in exchange for recognition.[13]

3. *British Policies*. The outbreak of the war caught Britain by surprise, and as it proceeded differences of opinion on appropriate policy developed among leading statesmen. There was even more diversity of opinion in both the North and the South on what British policy really was.[14]

The upper classes in England generally felt more congenial to southern than to northern society. It was clear that, if the United States were divided, its power position in the world would be weakened and it would be less menacing to Canada, which sections of American opinion had

[11] Von Holst, *Constitutional and Political History*, 7: 282 ff.; Morison, *Oxford History*, p. 615; n. 16 below.
[12] Morison, *Oxford History*, p. 632.
[13] *Ibid.*, pp. 675, 698, 701.
[14] See pt. 2, n. 24.

always wanted to annex. It was also clear that the South, if independent and free of the protectionist tendencies of the North, would welcome free trade and the opportunity to trade their cotton and tobacco for British industrial products on favorable terms. Furthermore, the principle of national self-determination, which Britain had supported in the revolts of Latin American states from Spain and Portugal, of Belgium from the Netherlands, of Greece from Turkey, and of Italian states from the Hapsburgs, would favor southern independence, if, as many Britishers believed, the South had a distinctive national culture.[15] In addition, the early information received in Britain of the political and military situation in the two sections, together with the early military successes of the Confederacy, induced a strong feeling in Britain that the South was going to win.[16] There was, finally, a considerable sentiment that war was inhumane and detrimental to progress, that the European powers had a moral responsibility to end it by mediation if not intervention, and that the most reasonable basis for such mediation would be the separation of the two sections by a negotiated boundary.[17]

[15] Morison, *Oxford History*, p. 633; Bernard, *Historical Account*, pp. 465 ff.

[16] The interpretation of the situation by the British government is indicated by a long letter from Sir James Fergusson, who had been traveling in the northern, southern, and western states and had conversed with "well-informed persons" on both sides, to Lord Derby on Nov. 11, 1861. It was transmitted by the latter to Lord Palmerston, the Prime Minister. (Broadlands Archives.) Fergusson emphasized the erroneous picture each side had of the other, but especially the poor sources of information utilized by the Union generals and government. He wrote of the superior material resources of the North, the utilization of which was, however, hampered by the political diversities among its people and parties and by the lack of morale, discipline, and good regimental officers in its armies. These conditions contrasted with the high morale and excellent leadership and discipline of both armies and people of the South.

"For England and for the world the question of superlative Moment is the power of the new confederacy to establish its position as a *de facto* Government —to maintain itself against the great armaments of the Federal Government . . . . No man can visit the Southern States with the most careless eye without being persuaded that their feeling is absolutely unanimous in the assertion of their independence and that they have roused themselves to an effort such as Nations make in their Extremity . . . . Crime and Violence were never so rare. The Cities on Sunday present an appearance almost of Scottish Tranquility—the numerous bodies of Slaves, so far from proving the cause of embarrassment or weakness, have continued the Cultivation of the Soil, while the Male Population have joined the Army and the women live with confidence on the plantations. In all ranks of civil and Military life they reign with sternest resolution and absolute confident of success. This conclusion I conceive to be irresistible that although with constancy and perseverence the North may mould its heterogeneous Army into Efficiency and through the lesson of the War may gradually supply that Military Character in which for the present it is defficient—her "Gros Bataillons" and her outpoured treasures will fail like other Armies and more ancient Powers to crush the newly won independence of a resolute and united people." (See also pt. 2, n. 24 above.)

[17] Letters of Lord Palmerston to Lord Russell, May 5, 1861, and Sept. 14, 1862, Broadlands Archives; and pt. 2, n. 24.

These considerations—cultural, political, economic, legal, military, and moral—created in Britain an atmosphere favorable to recognition of the independence of the Confederacy so long as the slavery issue was kept in the background. President Lincoln had declared himself against slavery in principle in his campaign for the Senate in 1858, but in 1861 he did not stress this position in order to induce the border slave states not to secede. As long as the North was fighting solely to preserve the Union, the South seemed to have a good moral case for self-determination, especially because of the nearly unanimous sentiment in that section of loyalty to the Confederacy. However, Britain was aware that slavery was the underlying issue, and early in the war, in response to proposals for mediation, the British prime minister, Lord Palmerston, emphasized the great difficulty of supporting proposals which would perpetuate slavery in a vast area.[18]

Liberals, like Richard Cobden, John Bright, and Monckten Milnes, favored the North because of the slavery issue, and when the preliminary Emancipation Proclamation of September 1862 was issued, this sentiment became overwhelming, although it was after this (October 7, 1862) that William E. Gladstone, chancellor of the exchequer, made his extraordinary speech at Newcastle saying that "Jefferson Davis and other leaders of the South have made an army; they are making a navy; and they have made, what is more than either, they have made a nation."[19]

Northern leaders were aware of the reasons which might induce British recognition of Confederate independence. They also witnessed what they deemed the premature recognition of southern belligerency, the refusal to permit United States accession to the Declaration of Paris in a way to permit the treatment of southern privateering as piracy, and the willingness of Britain to allow construction of Confederate cruisers on its territory. They therefore became convinced that there was a conspiracy in the British Cabinet, led by Prime Minister Palmerston, the foreign minister, Lord John Russell, and Chancellor of the Exchequer W. E. Gladstone, to favor the South and to recognize it as soon as the situation seemed favorable. Henry Adams, serving as his father's private secretary in London, was convinced of this, though his father was more willing to accept the good faith of Russell in his professions of neutrality. Secretary Seward seems also to have been convinced of British hostility and was even ready to augment it, with the expectation, early in the war, that foreign conflict would end civil strife.[20]

Subsequent examination of documents seems to indicate that Ameri-

[18] *Ibid.*
[19] *Ibid*; and Henry Adams, *Education*, p. 156.
[20] *Ibid.*, pp. 145 ff.

can opinion on this matter was not justified. British policy seems to have generally favored strict neutrality. Russell admitted his negligence in permitting the *Alabama* and other vessels to escape, although he had some doubt on the meaning of the Foreign Enlistment Act and its adequacy to meet neutral obligations under international law. He did at times favor mediation to end the war and, if that was unsuccessful, recognition of Confederate independence, but his interest in mediation evaporated when he heard of the preliminary Emancipation Proclamation. Gladstone, in his memoirs written thirty years later, regarded his Newcastle speech as the greatest error of his career, but unpublished letters written to Palmerston in the fall of 1862 indicate that he was the most active in the Cabinet in pressing for British intervention, even outlining in detail appropriate boundaries between the North and South. Palmerston seems to have been convinced in the first years of the war that the South would win and at times favored recognition of the Confederacy, but he was cautious and anxious not to give either side cause for offense. Some members of the Cabinet strongly opposed intervention, and in all important decisions the government seems to have solicited and followed the opinions of the law officers of the crown on international law, though on some occasions, especially in the *Alabama* situation, these opinions seem to have been inadequate.[21]

To summarize, British policy was based on the assumption that the recognition of belligerency was a question of fact and that after the President had proclaimed a war blockade the United States had no grounds for objecting to a British proclamation of neutrality. While the recognition of southern independence was discussed in the Cabinet, the British government was aware that such recognition, or even pressure to accept mediation, would violate the rights of the United States under international law until the independence of the Confederacy had been fully established in fact. Britain attempted, without complete success, to observe its obligations as a neutral in regard to the use of its territory for belligerent purposes. Britain sought to protect the commerce on the high seas against action by either belligerent, but with full recognition of the belligerent rights of visit, search, capture, and condemnation as defined by international law. Finally, Britain tried to protect the rights of

[21] *Ibid.*, pp. 156 ff.; minute of Lord Palmerston, Aug. 15, 1861, Broadlands Archives; Lord Newton, *Lord Lyons: A Record of British Diplomacy* (London: Edward Arnold, 1913), p. 48. See also from Broadlands Archives, Palmerston to Russell, May 5, 1861; Russell to Palmerston, Sept. 13 and Nov. 2, 1862; Gladstone to Palmerston, Sept. 2, 1862 (he thought the time had not come to offer mediation); Granville to Palmerston, Sept. 29, 1862 (he opposed a mediation offer unless it would be successful, which he doubted); and Clarendon to Palmerston, Oct. 16, 1862 (he vigorously criticized Gladstone's Newcastle speech). For additional references concerning the *Alabama*, see n. 56 below.

its nationals in territory of the belligerents and access of its consuls to them in case of trouble.[22]

4. *Policies of Other Neutrals.* The position of France was similar to that of Britain, and there was an effort by the two countries to act in harmony.[23] France was less involved in the maintenance of neutral obligations because the South found Britain more available for the manufacture of warships although an effort was made to build some in France. France also was less involved in controversies over maritime captures because it had less trade with the Confederacy, although it was adversely affected by the blockade.[24] It was, however, more interested in southern independence because the Emperor Louis Napoleon wished to build prestige by establishing an empire in Mexico, hardly possible if the United States should be able to maintain the Monroe Doctrine. To this end, after setting up Maximilian in Mexico, Napoleon initiated a move for mediation, which the United States promptly rejected.[25]

Most states with maritime interests followed Britain and France in proclaiming neutrality in June and July 1861.[26] Some stated in their proclamations that the Declaration of Paris would be observed and that privateers would not be permitted to enter their ports and would be treated as pirates.[27] A number of neutrals, not directly affected, protested against United States action in removing the southern emissaries from the *Trent* on the ground that it was a grave affront to neutral rights.[28]

Russia, the Germanic Confederation, and Austria were most favorable to the North, partly because of the refusal of these absolute monarchies to recognize revolutions, partly because they had little commerce or navigation in the Atlantic and were little affected by the blockade, and, in the case of Russia, because of its recent hostility to Britain and France in the Crimean War and the sympathy of the latter for Polish

[22] Bernard, *Historical Account*, pp. 135, 143, 164, 213 ff., 245, 264, 303, 361.

[23] Lord Lyons, British minister in Washington to Lord John Russell, April 15, 1861, in Newton, *Lord Lyons*, 1: 37. The French declaration of neutrality of June 10, 1861, resembled the British; for the text, see Bernard, *Historical Account*, p. 144.

[24] Bernard, *Historical Account*, p. 361; Duberman, *Charles Francis Adams*, p. 277.

[25] Bernard, *Historical Account*, p. 467; Newton, *Lord Lyons*, pp. 85, 92, 96. A concurrent resolution of Congress in March 1863 rejected all proposals for mediation and announced that the war would be prosecuted "until the rebellion should be overcome." (For a discussion of the resolution, see pp. 101–2 below.) See also Elson, *History*, pp. 778–79.

[26] Proclamations of Prussia, Belgium, Netherlands, Spain, Portugal, Hawaiian Islands, Bremen, and Hamburg are printed in Bernard, *Historical Account*, pp. 145 ff.

[27] Prussia, Belgium, Netherlands, and Hamburg (*ibid.*).

[28] See pt. 4, sec. *b*, below.

revolutionaries.[29] These eastern European countries did not support Napoleon's move for mediation, although they did join in protests in the *Trent* case.[30] The visit of portions of the Russian fleet to New York and San Francisco in 1863 was interpreted in the North as a friendly gesture manifesting a willingness to join the North in war against Britain and France if they should intervene on the side of the Confederacy. The purchase of Alaska in 1867 was said to be a form of compensation to Russia for this action. Later investigations suggest that the visits of the Russian fleet were less to manifest friendliness to the North than to find a place of security for their fleet in case of war with France and England over the Polish problem.[31]

A few issues concerning violation of territorial waters, use of neutral territory as a base, and maritime captures arose with Canada, Latin American countries, Netherlands, and others.[32]

5. *The Diverse Images of the Situation.* A study of the period indicates the wide diversity of the images of the situation and of the interpretations of policy which existed among the statesmen of the period. This point is emphasized by the studies of members of the Adams family, always willing to criticize, even themselves. Charles Francis Adams, Jr., writing in 1912 on the negotiations concerning the Declaration of Paris in 1861 finds that the interpretation by his father while minister to England, that by his brother Henry serving as his father's private secretary, and that by himself in writing his father's biography somewhat later, all of which had attributed duplicity to Lord Palmerston and Lord John Russell, were quite erroneous and that Secretary of State Seward, whom they had defended, was in fact engaged in the "incomprehensible" game of trying to convince the British and himself "that the conflict in which the country was engaged was a war so far as the United States was concerned, and a war or not a war so far as the foreign powers were concerned, as the interests of the United States might dictate."[33] The

[29] In reply to Seward's instructions to all United States missions abroad in March and April 1861 (see Bernard, *Historical Account*, pp. 124–25, and n. 5 above), the British government had merely said that it was "in no hurry to recognize the separation as complete and final" but "it was impossible to tell how and when circumstances might arise which would make a decision necessary." The French government had said that "no hasty or precipitate action would be taken" but "the practice and usage of the present century had fully established the right of *de facto* governments to recognition." Russia, however, replied that, "from the principle of unrelenting opposition to all revolutionary movements [it] would be the last to recognize any *de facto* Government of the disaffected States of the American Union"; Austria said it "was not inclined to recognize *de facto* governments anywhere"; and Spain said it "would have nothing to do with the rebel party in the United States in any sense." Bernard, *Historical Account*, pp. 124–26.

[30] See pt. 4, secs. *b* and *d* below.

[31] Elson, *History*, pp. 779–80.

[32] See sec. *b* (1) and (4) below.

[33] C. F. Adams, Jr., "Declaration of Paris," p. 60.

same critical disposition is illustrated by Henry Adams in his *Education*, written in 1905, privately printed in 1907, and published in 1918, completely revising his own and his father's opinions of the intentions of the British ministers in 1862. Instead of a conspiracy led by Palmerston to recognize southern independence at a suitable moment, he finds that Palmerston was cautious, Russell relatively straightforward, and Gladstone mistaken in facts and indiscreet.[34]

The actual correspondence of British Cabinet members at the time, recently made available, indicates that the truth lay between the contemporary and later interpretations of their attitudes. Palmerston was not "conspiring" and Russell could not be charged with "duplicity," but both did at times, as indicated in the preceding section, seriously consider mediation for peace or recognition of Confederate independence while publicly pursuing a policy of neutrality, and Gladstone was most energetic both publicly and privately in urging such a policy.[35]

The later interpretations by the Adams family in regard both to the British ministers and to Seward were accepted by British commentators at the time as indicated by the detailed study of British neutrality during the war published by Mountague Bernard in 1870.[36] After defending Russell, he writes that Seward argued that the war was not a war because it was an insurrection and that "the President need not have instituted a blockade: foreign nations, therefore, were bound to act as if he had not instituted one." He then comments: "It is impossible to speak respectfully, or even seriously, of an argument conducted in this fashion. It is unworthy of a manly and honest reasoner; it is strangely unsuited to the Government of a great people."[37]

Although the participants often made diverse, and erroneous, interpretations of the situation at various critical periods, the diplomacy of the war indicates how cool judgment in diplomatic action may bridge these difficulties. Peace between the United States and Britain undoubtedly profited by the careful diplomacy of their ministers in London and Washington. Charles Francis Adams, though he may not always have understood the attitude of the members of the British Cabinet, was ready to moderate the tone of his instructions when they manifested the belligerency or confusion of Secretary Seward, and Lord Lyons was also ready to "avoid the slightest semblance of anything which might cause offense to the United States government" and to urge moderation when Lord John Russell seemed to manifest an interventionist disposition.[38]

[34] Henry Adams, *Education*, pp. 144–66.
[35] See n. 21 above and pt. 2, n. 24.
[36] Bernard, *Historical Account*, pp. 159 ff., 172 ff.
[37] *Ibid.*, p. 170.
[38] Duberman, *Charles Francis Adams*, p. 268; Bernard, *Historical Account*, pp. 151 ff.; Newton, *Lord Lyons*, 2: 38, 67 ff., 77, 102, 106, 127, 142.

Special attention will be given to the protests, generally on grounds of international law, by the United States and the Confederacy against actions by neutral states and by Great Britain and other neutral states against actions taken by the United States. Some of these protests manifested confusion over the apparent claim of the United States to enjoy sovereign rights as well as belligerent rights over southern territory, ships, and persons. Issues involving proposals for multilateral action will be considered in the next part on the role of international institutions.

b. Diplomatic Protests

1. *United States Protests.* The United States initially protested against the recognition of the belligerency of the South on the ground that war did not exist de facto and that recognition encouraged the rebellion, and later, on the ground that even though justifiable it had been premature.[39] After President Lincoln's proclamation of a blockade of southern ports on April 19, 1861, claiming belligerent rights against foreign ships on the high seas, the United States could not deny that war existed and that foreign states were justified in proclaiming neutrality, constituting a recognition of southern belligerency. Even after this, however, Secretary Seward threatened war if Britain and other states did not acknowledge the sovereign rights of the United States and had any intercourse with the Confederacy.[40] In spite of the general understanding, confirmed by the United States Supreme Court, that the situation was war in the legal sense, Secretary Seward contended on occasion throughout the war that the United States had sovereign rights and that foreign states should respect its law treating Confederate privateers or even warships as pirates, excluding them from its ports and permitting United States warships to capture them in foreign territorial waters; but this position was not consistently maintained.[41]

Even before the attack on Fort Sumter, the United States had made it clear that recognition of the independence of the Confederacy would be considered an illegal act of intervention in a matter within the domestic jurisdiction of the United States and would be responded to accordingly.[42] This position was reiterated throughout the war and there were no such recognitions, although the matter was discussed in both the British and French cabinets, especially in the spring of 1861 and the summer and autumn of 1862.[43]

The French emperor made a tender of good offices in 1863 proposing mediation to end the war by negotiation. Although it was promptly re-

[39] Bernard, *Historical Account*, p. 155.
[40] Seward's Dispatch No. 10 to Adams, May 21, 1861, cited in n. 5 above.
[41] See pp. 42–43 and n. 10 above.
[42] See n. 3 above.
[43] See pt. 4, sec. *d* below.

jected by the President with full support of Congress, the United States did not contend that such tender violated its rights under international law. Both the administration and Congress made it clear that the United States would reject all such tenders in the future, even if friendly in form, and if persisted in would regard them as unfriendly acts.[44]

Early in the war the United States protested against British admission of Confederate warships to its ports, and in January 1862 the British announced regulations concerning the hospitality to be given in its ports to belligerent vessels.[45] A merchant vessel under the Confederate flag entered a British port for the first time in June 1861, and Minister Adams was informed that there was no objection to such entry.[46] By a regulation of June 1, 1861, belligerent cruisers or privateers were forbidden to bring prizes into British ports, home or colonial, and by a regulation of June 1864 it was made clear that, except in case of stress of weather or conversion of the prize into a bona fide warship, such prizes would be detained.[47] This regulation, however, did not apply to belligerent merchant vessels, which were free to enter and leave. Foreign consuls could not interfere with them, and British authorities should not prevent their taking on cargoes, even arms, unless in violation of the Foreign Enlistment Act.[48] The regulations of January 1862 forbade the stay of foreign warships or privateers in a British port more than twenty-four hours unless such a vessel of the opposing belligerent was there, in which case a twenty-four hour interval should elapse between the departure of vessels of opposing belligerents. Further, detailed rules limited the supplies which could be allowed to such vessels. These regulations seem to have been considered satisfactory by the United States, though it objected on a few occasions that more hospitality was extended to Confederate cruisers than the regulations permitted.[49]

An order of May 11, 1865, notified the authorities in all British ports that the war was over and the regulations ceased. On June 2, 1865, a further notification denied access to British ports by Confederate warships and required departure of all such vessels already there unless the twenty-four-hour interval rule was applicable. If a Confederate war vessel was ready to divest itself of all belligerent character and of the Confederate flag, it might stay in port subject to the risk of legal proceedings against it.[50] The United States claimed title to public property

[44] *Ibid.*
[45] Bernard, *Historical Account*, pp. 136 ff., 263.
[46] *Ibid.,* p. 247.
[47] *Ibid.,* pp. 136, 190.
[48] *Ibid.,* p. 137.
[49] Duberman, *Charles Francis Adams*, p. 316. On application of the twenty-four hour interval rule by Britain and other states, see Bernard, *Historical Account*, pp. 267–82.
[50] Bernard, *Historical Account*, p. 143.

of the Confederacy in foreign ports, and the British courts supported this claim subject to liens of British merchants.[51]

The United States had protested, without justification in the international law of the time and without effect, British tolerance of shipments of arms and ammunition to the South on merchant vessels, but its vigorous protests against the building of Confederate cruisers in British territory, even though veiled as commercial transactions, was more justifiable and eventually more effective.[52] There is no evidence that any Confederate privateers were equipped in neutral ports, but an early incident showed the sensitivity of the United States on the point.[53] In May 1861 Secretary Seward heard that an iron steamer, the *Peerless*, equipped in the Great Lakes, had been bought by the Confederacy and ordered United States naval vessels to seize her. The British protested, and Seward replied that if his information proved to be incorrect he would give full satisfaction, adding that he understood the vessel was to be used as a "privateer," a statement which seems inconsistent with his assertion that it had been bought by the Confederate government. After investigation it turned out that the *Peerless* had in fact been purchased by the United States Navy; communication between the State and Navy departments seems to have been imperfect.[54]

There was no doubt that Confederate cruisers were being built in British territory in 1862. Minister Adams kept a close check with the consul in Liverpool and demanded that the British prevent the departure of the vessels.[55] Having a report from the law officers that departure of "290" (the *Alabama*) would violate the Foreign Enlistment Act, Lord Russell tried to have it detained, but it got away without arms or Confederate crew.[56] It took these on at sea and in the Azores, where Captain

[51] *U.S.* v. *Prioleau*, 35 Law Journal, Chancery, N.S. (1866); *U.S.* v. *McRae*, L.R. 8 Equ. 69 (1866).

[52] Bernard, *Historical Account*, p. 335; pt. 4, sec. *e* below.

[53] C. F. Adams, Jr., "Declaration of Paris," p. 41.

[54] *Ibid.*, p. 40, quoting British Parliamentary Paper, North America No. 1, 1862, pp. 31–33.

[55] Bernard, *Historical Account*, pp. 338 ff. The correspondence concerning the departure of the *Alabama*, including Minister Adams's note of Oct. 23, 1863, proposing arbitration, which was declined by the British in August 1865, is summarized by Bernard, pp. 370–77.

In a letter to Palmerston on March 27, 1863, Russell wrote: "As the fitting out and escape of the Alabama and Oreto was clearly an evasion of War law, I think you now have no difficulty in declaring this evening that the government disapproves of all such attempts to elude our law with a view to assist one of the belligerents. The case is quite different from that of furnishing arms and munitions of war to one of the belligerents. It is an evasion, very subtle—contraveneous of our law of foreign enlistment." (Broadlands Archives.) This seems to support the American claim.

[56] Bernard, *Historical Account*, pp. 344–45; Brunson MacChesney, "The Alabama and the Queen's Advocate—a mystery of History," *Northwestern University Law Review* 62 (1967): 568 ff. In the case of *The Alexandra*, which escaped

Semmes of the Confederate Navy took command.[57] Half a dozen other vessels escaped, but Adams's protest was effective in the case of the armored rams under construction in the Laird yards at Birkenhead after he had threatened war if they left.[58] The issue of British negligence in letting the *Alabama* and other vessels depart was settled after the war by the award of the Geneva Arbitral Tribunal of $15,500,000 to the United States in reparation for the direct damage it had caused to commerce but ruling out the claim for indirect damage resulting from the alleged prolongation of the war for two years because of the encouragement it had given the Confederacy.[59]

The United States also protested against the seizure of United States vessels in Lake Erie and the Atlantic by Confederate marauders from

---

under similar circumstances in March 1863, action was brought against the builders under the Foreign Enlistment Act, and they were found not guilty on the ground that their intent was commercial and they were under no obligation to inquire into the use which the purchaser might make of the vessel. *Attorney General* v. *Sillem*, 2 Hurlstone and Caldman, Exchequer Reports, 431; Bernard, *Historical Account*, pp. 353–54. In a note to Lord Palmerston on April 5, 1863, E. Hammond of the Foreign Office said he had "no doubt that Mr. Adams is right" but doubted whether the courts would convict. (Broadlands Archives.) Five prosecutions were instituted under the Foreign Enlistment Act against persons charged with enlisting or engaging men for service in the Confederate Navy, of which three were successful. Bernard, *Historical Account*, pp. 361–62.

[57] Bernard, *Historical Account*, pp. 337–50.

[58] *Ibid.*, pp. 350–60. Henry Adams devotes a chapter of his *Education* to "The Battle of the Rams" and explains the subtlety of his father's warning to Russell: "It would be superfluous in me to point out to your Lordship that this is war" (pp. 172–73). By delay and ultimate favorable response, Henry Adams writes, "Lord Russell had sacrificed the Lairds: had cost his Ministry the price of two iron clads, besides the Alabama claims—say in round numbers, twenty million dollars—and had put himself in the position of appearing to yield only to a threat of war" (p. 178).

Duberman, however, believes that Russell had decided to seize the rams before receiving Adams's note. *Charles Francis Adams*, p. 312. Bernard devotes a page to the rams, stating that it was originally supposed that they were being built for France or Egypt, but when it appeared that they were being built for Bullock, the Confederate agent, they were seized and purchased by Britain for 500,000 pounds. *Historical Account*, pp. 456–57. Six ships were built for the Confederates in Bordeaux and Nantes, France, two of them ironclad rams, but on complaint of the American Minister Dayton, the French government forbade the transaction, and they were eventually sold to neutral governments, with exception of the *Olinde*, later the *Stonewall*, which eventually got to sea under Confederate command. Bernard, *Historical Account*, p. 361.

[59] See pt. 4, sec. *d* below. Bernard, whose book appeared before the treaty of Washington, discusses at length the United States claim as presented in 1869 and attempts to defend the British position. *Historical Account*, pp. 378–408. He narrates the careers of the Confederate cruisers (pp. 411 ff.) and concludes: "It is true that of the crews which manned them, a large proportion were British subjects. It is true also that they severely harrassed American shipping, and inflicted heavy losses on American trade. All this is true. What is not true, I think, is that for these losses the British nation is justly responsible" (p. 438). But see Russell's statement in n. 55 above.

Canada and against the use of Canadian territory for raids in United States territory, especially in the late stages of the war. The most notorious raid was in St. Albans in northern Vermont in October 1864. The raiders after robbing a bank had returned to Canadian territory and were released, the United States demand for extradition having been refused on the ground that their act was "political" and so not subject to extradition.[60] In retaliation for this incident Secretary Seward instructed Adams to give notice of termination of the Rush-Bagot Agreement of 1817, limiting armaments on the Great Lakes. The Canadian authorities, however, then exercised greater diligence, the raids ceased, and the war ended before the notice regarding the Rush-Bagot Agreement came into effect and it was withdrawn. The agreement was still in effect in 1970, the longest lived disarmament agreement on record.[61]

The United States refused to participate in the joint demand in 1862 by France, Great Britain, and Spain to induce Mexico to pay claims for injuries to their nationals. After arrangements had been made satisfying Britain and Spain, France undertook an individual intervention, ousting President Juarez and setting up the Maximilian empire. The United States mildly protested, but after the war was over, it made it clear that it did not tolerate this action in violation of the Monroe Doctrine and sent an army of observation to the border. France withdrew, Juarez was restored, and Maximilian was executed.[62]

2. *Confederate Protests.* The Confederacy sought to establish formal or informal diplomatic relations with neutrals. It sent a mission of four— William P. Yancey, P. A. Rost, Dudley Mann, and T. Butler King to Britain early in the war, and later James M. Mason and John Slidell went to Britain and France respectively after their adventure on the *Trent.*[63] None of these emissaries was received officially, as this would have constituted recognition of the independence of the Confederacy, but informal discussions were held with them in spite of United States protests. British Consul Bunch in Charleston also held informal conversations with members of the Confederate government in Richmond in regard to Confederate accession to the Declaration of Paris. On learning of this the United States withdrew his exequatur, although the British claimed such communication was legitimate. Consul Bunch remained

[60] Duberman, *Charles Francis Adams,* p. 317; Bernard, *Historical Account,* pp. 463–65; Newton, *Lord Lyons,* 1: 135; Morison, *Oxford History,* p. 667.

[61] Morison, *Oxford History,* p. 667; J. B. Moore, *Digest of International Law* (Washington, 1906), 5: 169; Quincy Wright, *The Control of American Foreign Relations* (New York: Macmillan, 1922), pp. 39, 258.

[62] Elson, *History,* p. 779; Morison, *Oxford History,* pp. 662, 706–7.

[63] C. F. Adams, Jr., "Declaration of Paris," p. 34; Mowat, *Diplomatic Relations,* p. 173; Thomas L. Harris, *The Trent Affair* (Indianapolis: Bowen-Merrill, 1896), p. 71. See also sec. 3 below.

for some time in the South.[64] Mason withdrew from England on September 25, 1863, when it became evident he could not obtain British recognition, and the South in retaliation dismissed British consuls in its territory.[65]

In its first mission to Britain the Confederacy drew attention to the actual discrimination it suffered in the use of British ports. The British regulations were equal in form, but actually Confederate cruisers and privateers, barred from their own ports by the blockade, had great difficulty in keeping at sea when barred from sojourn and supply in British ports. The emissaries did not formally protest, apparently recognizing the legal competence of neutrals to make port regulations.[66]

The Confederacy, through Mason in London, continually asserted that the blockade was not effective, as required by international law and the Declaration of Paris, and that the British should so declare and demand the opening of southern ports to trade. In reply, the British defined the meaning of "effectiveness," holding that it was not jeopardized by the occasional entry or departure of a vessel.[67] At first the blockade undoubtedly lacked effectiveness on some parts of the long southern coastline, but it soon became effective in the meaning of international law.

3. *British Protests.* Great Britain protested vigorously, even threatening war if its demands were not satisfied, in the case of the *Trent.* This British merchant vessel bound for England took the Confederate emissaries, Mason and Slidell, as passengers while in port at Havana, where they had come from the South in a blockade runner. The *Trent* was stopped by the United States war vessel, *San Jacinto,* under Captain Wilkes, who reported he had read Kent, Wheaton, Vattel, and other authorities to assure himself of the legality of his action. Mason and Slidell were removed with two attendants, leaving their families behind.[68]

[64] Bernard, *Historical Account,* pp. 181–86.

[65] *Ibid.,* pp. 471–73.

[66] Adams, "Declaration of Paris," p. 34.

[67] Bernard, *Historical Account,* pp. 292–95; A. D. MacNair, *International Law Opinions* (Cambridge: Cambridge University Press, 1956), 3: 248; Russell to Mason, February 10, 1863, *British and Foreign State Papers,* 55: 737. In the *Hiawatha,* the first vessel condemned for breach of blockade (Blatchford, *Prize Cases,* 1, [1861]) the district court held that the blockade was effective and was sustained by the Supreme Court (*The Prize Cases,* 2 Black 675 [1862]). The *Amy Warwick* captured earlier (July 10, 1861) was condemned as enemy property (2 Sprague 143 [1861]). In the postwar arbitration the tribunal held in the case of the *Springbok* that the blockade was effective. This effectiveness was indicated by the fact that British cotton textiles in the South increased from twenty-four cents to twenty dollars a yard during the war. Roscoe Ralph Oglesby, "*Applications of International Law Under Conditions of Civil Strife*" (Ph.D. dissertation, Duke University, 1949), p. 220.

[68] Moore, *Digest,* 7: 768. Harris, *Trent Affair,* gives a detailed account of the seizure, pp. 97 ff.

The four men were taken to Boston where they were imprisoned. The incident caused great excitement in Britain, where it was looked upon as an indignity to the British flag, and also in the United States, where there was popular rejoicing at the capture. Lord Palmerston, the British prime minister, at first thought the law officers of the crown had advised him that the visit, search, and seizure of the *Trent* would be legitimate if she was carrying dispatches valuable for the Confederacy, provided the vessel was submitted to a prize court. Later, however, he declared the seizure a gross breach of international law and demanded, in a seven-day ultimatum, return of the emissaries and apology, at the same time ordering the movement of armed forces to Canada and the West Indies. After long discussions in the United States Cabinet, Secretary Seward agreed in a long note, and the emissaries were returned.[69]

While visit and search of the *Trent* was certainly permissible, its capture would probably not be permissible on the charge of "unneutral service." Carriage of dispatches or military persons would not usually constitute "unneutral service" unless the vessel was destined directly or indirectly for an enemy port. Proof of such a destination would certainly be necessary if the emissaries were considered analogous to contraband (as Seward contended), though it might not be if the voyage was undertaken to benefit the belligerent by serving as a transport or dispatch carrier. In either case, Seward admitted the vessel should have been brought in and submitted to a prize court, a procedure which, Adams remarked, would have been more onerous to the vessel than taking the emissaries off. Seward referred to the British practice of taking alleged British subjects from United States vessels to impress them into the British Navy before the War of 1812, and it is to be noted that the Declaration of London of 1909 permitted belligerents to take persons destined for the enemy armed forces from neutral vessels on the high seas, a practice also followed in World War I. The discussion in the *Trent* affair did not fully define the belligerent right of dealing with neutral vessels on grounds of unneutral service, a subject which commentators agree was at the time somewhat uncertain.[70]

The British admitted the general belligerent right of visit and search of neutral merchant vessels on the high seas and the right of capture in case there was probable cause from evidence found on the vessel that she was of enemy character, was violating blockade, was carrying contraband, or was engaged in unneutral service. Britain, however, objected to some prize court decisions condemning vessels for breach of blockade

---

[69] Bernard, *Historical Account*, pp. 187–223, quotes much of the correspondence, which is also contained in *Papers Relating to Foreign Affairs, Accompanying the Annual Message of the President* (Washington, 1862).

[70] Bernard, *Historical Account*, p. 224; W. E. Hall, *A Treatise on International Law* (8th ed., Oxford: Clarendon Press, 1924), p. 829.

when the blockade was actually ineffective or when the designated fifteen days of grace to depart for vessels in port when the blockade was proclaimed had not expired.[71] It also questioned extreme applications of the doctrine of continuous voyage to breach of blockade and carriage of contraband.[72] Several of these cases decided by the United States Supreme Court were submitted to arbitration after the war, but the claims were in most cases disallowed. The arbitral tribunal concluded that contraband on a neutral vessel bound for a neutral port could be condemned if there was good evidence that the ultimate destination of the contraband goods was belligerent, but a vessel or its cargo could not be condemned for breach of blockade unless, when captured, it was actually destined for a blockaded port or had actually departed from such a port.[73] The doctrine of continuous voyage was given even greater latitude by the allies during World War I, when statistical and other evidence from sources outside the vessel were utilized to determine the ultimate destination of contraband cargoes.[74]

The British protested a few cases of Union seizure of vessels in their territorial waters, and the United States returned them without hesita-

---

[71] The *Hiawatha*, in *The Prize Cases*, 2 Black 675 (1862); Bernard, *Historical Account*, pp. 235–46.

[72] Bernard, *Historical Account*, pp. 307 ff.; Morison, *Oxford History*, p. 665; Hall, *International Law*, p. 800; Herbert Briggs, *The Doctrine of Continuous Voyage* (Baltimore: Johns Hopkins Press, 1926), pp. 43 ff. The law officers of the crown advised on April 3, 1863, that the seizure of the *Peterhoff* was unjustifiable. In a letter to Palmerston on April 22, 1863, E. Hammond of the Foreign Office enclosed one which he had written on April 13 to Joseph Spence, owner of the *Peterhoff*, saying: "Her Majesty's Government have concluded: The Government of the United States has clearly no right to seize British Vessels *bona fide* bound from this country or from any other British possession, to the Ports of Vera Cruz and Matamoras, or either of them or vice versa, unless such vessels attempt to touch at, or have an intermediate or contingent destination to some blockaded place or port, or are carriers of contraband of War destined for the Confederate States, and in any admitted case of such unlawful capture, Her Majesty's Government would feel it their duty promptly to interfere, with a view to obtain the immediate restitution of the Ship and Cargo, with full compensation, and without delay of a Prize Court."

However, he pointed out that visit and search of neutral vessels is permissible and that evidence might be found indicating liability to capture. According to these criteria, the seizure of the *Peterhoff* seemed wholly unjustifiable, and Lord Lyons was instructed to make immediate representations to the United States government. (Broadlands Archives.) For Lord Lyons's action, see Newton, *Lord Lyons*, 1: 100–106. The vessel was submitted to the United States Prize Court which condemned it for carriage of contraband destined for the Confederacy, but it was released on appeal to the Supreme Court, which, however, sustained condemnation of the contraband cargo, as did the arbitration after the war. Moore, *Digest*, 7: 715, 725.

[73] Moore, *Digest*, 7: 715, 725.

[74] Hall, *International Law*, pp. 804 ff.; *The Kim*, Great Britain, High Court of Justice [1915], p. 215; Bishop, *International Law*, p. 670.

tion.[75] Britain protested against the decision of the United States Prize Court in the case of the *Lilla,* which held that Confederate prize courts could not pass title. It insisted that the Confederacy had the same war powers as the Union.[76]

4. *Protests by Other Neutrals.* The principal discussions concerning belligerent and neutral rights were between the United States and Great Britain, though France complained on the same grounds as Britain of the application of continuous voyage to maritime captures and of the violation of territorial waters. France, Russia, Spain, and other neutrals generally maintained the same positions in regard to belligerent merchant and war vessels entering their ports and liberated prizes captured in their territorial waters.[77] The Dutch minister, in reply to Seward's complaint that the Confederate cruiser *Sumter* had been admitted to Curaçao, said that it was not a privateer, much less a pirate, any more than Paul Jones's frigate was a pirate, although Britain had called it one when it entered a Dutch port in 1779.[78]

There was an interesting controversy with Brazil as late in the war as December 1864 concerning Brazil's permission of Confederate war vessels to enter its ports and seizure by the United States warship *Wachusett* of the Confederate warship *Florida* in the harbor of Bahia. Secretary Seward wrote the Brazilian chargé d'affaires: "This government disallows your assumption that the insurgents of this country are a lawful naval belligerent; and on the contrary it maintains that the ascription of that character by the Government of Brazil to insurgent citizens of the United States who still are destitute of naval forces, ports and courts, is an act of intervention in derogation of the law of nations, and unfriendly and wrongful as it is manifestly injurious to the United States." It appears that Seward never really accepted the belligerency of the Confederacy or the legitimacy of the neutrality of foreign states. He did, however, disavow the action of the *Wachusett,* and he made amends to Brazil.[79]

The position of foreign states during the war, wholeheartedly accepted by the Confederacy and half-heartedly by the Union, was that civil strife

[75] Bernard, *Historical Account,* p. 463; Morison, *Oxford History,* p. 664; Moore, *Digest,* 7: 1089–90; and opinion of the law officers of the crown in the case of *The Chesapeake,* Jan. 25, 1864, Broadlands Archives.

[76] *The Lilla,* 2 Sprague 177, (1862); *British and Foreign State Papers,* 55: 800 ff.; and opinion of law officers of the crown, Jan. 17, 1863, and Sept. 13, 1863, Broadlands Archives; Herbert A. Smith, *Great Britain and the Law of Nations* (London: King, 1932), 1: 305 ff.

[77] Bernard, *Historical Account,* pp. 248–49, 250–53.

[78] *Ibid.,* p. 259; *Papers Relating to Foreign Affairs,* 1861, pp. 357 ff., 371.

[79] Bernard, *Historical Account,* p. 167; C. F. Adams, Jr., "Declaration of Paris," pp. 47, 50, citing Geneva Arbitration, British Case, *Papers Relating to the Treaty of Washington* (Washington, 1872), 1: 304; Moore, *Digest,* 7: 1090.

recognized as civil war should be identified with international war and the international law of war and neutrality should be applied so long as the war lasted. This position was manifested by the opinions of the law officers of the British crown, by the arguments in the diplomatic controversies, and by the arbitrations after the war.

IV. THE ROLE OF INTERNATIONAL INSTITUTIONS DURING THE WAR

There were no organized international institutions at the time of the American Civil War, although the International Telegraphic Union, the Universal Postal Union, and the International Red Cross were about to emerge.

The concept of the community of nations under international law, functioning through the diplomatic system, existed and was the basis and the instrument for the protests made by states when they deemed their rights violated, as indicated in the previous section.

The diplomatic system ordinarily functioned in bilateral relations. A state protested action by another state which it believed had violated its rights under international law or made representations when it believed acts, or preparations to act, impaired an interest, though not a right, or when it wished to open negotiations to effect an agreement. Diplomacy, however, occasionally functioned in behalf of the general interest in law observance, as when the diplomatic corps at a capital protested against an act by the state to which they were accredited that in their view violated the diplomatic immunities of one of their number. Several instances of diplomatic action during the Civil War manifested such a general interest, especially (*a*) the negotiations over the Declaration of Paris, (*b*) the *Trent*, (*c*) General Butler's activities in New Orleans, and (*d*) proposals for joint mediation to end the war. (*e*) The utilization of international arbitration also manifested the emergence of international institutions.

a. International Legislation (The Declaration of Paris)

The Declaration of Paris on naval warfare had been accepted in 1856 by the belligerents in the Crimean War and subsequently had been acceded to by many other states, thus constituting "international legislation." Its application in the Civil War was first suggested by Great Britain,[1] although before and after the Napoleonic Wars Britain had

---

[1] Mountague Bernard, *Historical Account of the Neutrality of Great Britain during the American Civil War* (London: Longmans, 1870), p. 172; Sir Francis Piggott, *The Declaration of Paris* (London: University of London Press, 1916), p. 156, quoting Russell to Cowley, May 6, 1861.

generally opposed the principle that free ships make free goods declared in the declaration. It had claimed the right, advantageous to it as dominant naval belligerent, to capture all enemy goods and ships at sea. As a neutral, however, it would benefit by the liberal principles of the declaration, generally supported in the past by neutral states, with exception of the provision abolishing privateering. The United States treaty with France of 1778 and the "armed neutralities" proclaimed by several European states in 1780 and 1802 had supported these principles.[2] The United States had refused to accept the declaration when invited to do so in 1856, although it favored most of its principles, because, lacking a large navy, it insisted it must utilize privateers—"the militia of the seas"—unless its proposal, the Marcy Amendment, were accepted abolishing the right to capture any enemy private property at sea except contraband of war.[3]

On the outbreak of the Civil War, however, the position of the United States was different. In a circular of April 24, 1861, Secretary of State Seward instructed United States representatives in the principal capitals to indicate the desire of the United States to accede to the declaration and to have it applied during the war.[4] The purpose was to implement the president's blockade proclamation of April 19, which had declared that Confederate privateers would be treated as pirates. It was, therefore, the first article of the declaration, "Privateering is and remains abolished," which Marcy had balked on in 1856, that Seward was now anxious to have implemented, though he had no objection to the other principles which declared that free ships make free goods, neutral goods are free on enemy ships—both with exception of contraband—and blockades to be binding must be effective. Adams in London and Dayton in Paris were instructed to open negotiations on the subject. Before they had acted on these instructions, Britain and France had instructed their representatives in Washington, Lord Lyons and M. Mercier, to negotiate on the subject but had informed them that, since the belligerency of the Confederacy had been recognized and it was not a party, the Declaration of Paris could not apply to it in the present war.[5] Seward, apparently aware of this, refused to receive their instructions on the ground that they assumed the belligerency of the South, which he was not ready to accept. The negotiations were, therefore, transferred to London and Paris, Seward apparently believing that, once the United States had become a party to the Declaration, it could insist that Confederate privateers be treated as pirates by all the parties. In spite of Dayton's conviction that

[2] J. B. Moore, *Digest of International Law* (Washington, 1906), 7: 558–60.
[3] *Ibid.*, pp. 561–68.
[4] *Ibid.*, pp. 570–73.
[5] *Ibid.*, pp. 568–70; Bernard, *Historical Account*, p. 178.

the British and French would not agree to the application of the declaration in respect to privateering during the war, Adams followed his instructions, and a treaty was signed by which the United States would have acceded to the declaration.[6] In signing, however, the British insisted on a formal declaration that they did "not intend, thereby, to undertake any engagement which shall have any bearing direct or indirect on the internal differences now prevailing in the United States." This obviously defeated Seward's purpose, and as a result the negotiations came to nothing.[7]

It is interesting to notice, however, that Belgium, the Netherlands, and other neutrals, in proclaiming neutrality, assumed that the Declaration of Paris was in effect and that under it privateers would not be admitted to their ports and would be treated as pirates.[8] In fact, no southern privateers attempted to enter a British or French port, and Confederate privateering, although at first looked upon with great confidence by the South, resulted in only a few captures early in the war and soon died out. The blockade precluded their operation from southern ports, they could not sojourn, get supplies, or bring prizes into neutral ports, and so they had to sink their prizes, with the result that the incentive to privateering did not exist. Confederate maritime activities were carried on by regular naval vessels.[9] Although the United States authorized privateers for three years by act of Congress on March 3, 1863, over the opposition of Senator Sumner who recognized that the practice, profitable in the Napoleonic period, had ceased to be so with the change from sail to steam, no privateers were commissioned by the United States.[10]

The British and French interest in the last three articles of the Declaration of Paris was manifested in negotiations opened with the Confederacy through British Consul Bunch in Charleston. He was instructed to act with discretion to avoid any suggestion of recognition of Confederate independence. He communicated with President Davis in Richmond through an intermediary, and Davis got a resolution through the Confederate Congress accepting the declaration with exception of the first article. The United States, however, got wind of the matter and

[6] Bernard, *Historical Account*, pp. 176–77.

[7] *Ibid.*, p. 179; Moore, *Digest*, 7: 573–83. See also Charles Francis Adams, Jr., "Seward and the Declaration of Paris," *Proceedings of the Massachusetts Historical Society* 46 (1912): 23–81.

[8] Bernard, *Historical Account*, pp. 145–50.

[9] *Ibid.*, p. 181; C. F. Adams, Jr., "Declaration of Paris," pp. 41 ff.; Martin B. Duberman, *Charles Francis Adams, 1807–1886* (Boston: Houghton Mifflin, 1920), p. 302.

[10] See Senate speech of Senator Charles Sumner, February 17, 1863, *Congressional Globe*, p. 1020. Secretary of the Navy Gideon Welles also opposed the policy, and Secretary Seward seems to have approved it with the purpose of threatening the British in connection with the *Alabama* dispute.

revoked Consul Bunch's exequatur on the curious ground that he had violated the Logan Act, which forbade Americans to deal with foreign governments without authority of the State Department. The British asserted that Consul Bunch had violated no law, either United States law or international law, but since the United States could revoke consular exequaturs at discretion, the British had no grounds for protest. Consul Bunch continued to live in Charleston for some time.[11]

The last three articles of the Declaration of Paris appear to have been generally observed during the war, although some doubts were raised about the effectiveness of the blockade early in the war.[12]

b. Collective Action by Neutrals (The Trent)

The removal of Mason and Slidell from the Trent was a matter primarily of British interest and Britain protested vigorously, as noted in part 3, b (3) above, but the case has relevance here because of the protests by other nations not directly interested.[13] France, Austria, Russia, and Prussia instructed their representatives in Washington to make representations to the United States. The Prussian note said:

The maritime operations undertaken by President Lincoln against the Southern Seceding States could not, from their very commencement, but fill the King's Government with apprehensions lest they should result in possible prejudice to the legitimate interests of neutral Powers. [The apprehensions, it continued, have been fully justified by the forcible seizure of Mason and Slidell from the Trent by the United States warship San Jacinto. This occurrence has produced] throughout Europe the most profound sensation [in governments and public opinion]. For, although at present it is England only which is immediately concerned in the matter, yet, on the other hand, it is one of the most important and universally recognized rights of the neutral flag which has been called into question. . . . Public opinion in Europe has, with singular unanimity, pronounced in the most positive manner for the injured party. [While it is not yet clear that the Captain of the San Jacinto acted under orders from his government, should it be found that he did] to our great regret we should find ourselves constrained to see in it not an isolated fact but a public menace offered to the existing rights of all neutrals. [While lacking full information] we are convinced that no conditions have been put forward by the British Government which could justifiably offend President Lincoln's sense of honour. [Therefore] His Majesty the King, filled with the most ardent wishes for the welfare of the United States of North America, has commanded me to advocate the cause of peace with President Lincoln through your instrumentality, to the utmost of my power.[14]

[11] Bernard, *Historical Account*, pp. 185–86; Lord Newton, *Lord Lyons: A Record of British Diplomacy* (London: Edward Arnold, 1913), 1: 42, 44, 51–52.
[12] Samuel Eliot Morison, *The Oxford History of the American People* (New York: Oxford University Press, 1965), pp. 633, 642; and pt. 3, n. 67, above.
[13] Bernard, *Historical Account*, pp. 196 ff.
[14] *Ibid.*, p. 199.

The other communications were similar.[15] This *démarche* of neutrals, especially those generally favoring the North, doubtless influenced the favorable response of the United States to the British demands. France cooperated with Britain in the matter.[16] What, if any, influence the British exerted in inducing this pressure from other neutrals is not known.

The incident recalls the armed neutralities of 1780 and 1800 in which most of these countries declared principles of neutrality which they proposed to enforce by arms upon the leading naval belligerent of the time, Great Britain, and also the collective declarations of neutrals in World War I, all manifesting a certain solidarity of neutral interests.[17]

c. *Neutral Representations on the Law of War (General Butler's Proclamation)*

The diplomatic system could not function in the relations of the belligerents because the United States considered the war a rebellion excluding even the indirect diplomatic contacts usual between belligerents in international wars. Quasi-diplomatic contacts were limited to military agreements between officers in the field and two conferences for peace before the war and near its end.[18] Consequently, belligerent relations under international law were determined by unilateral proclamations such as those on blockade and piracy, legislation such as Lieber's Code and privateering regulations, judicial decisions mainly in prize cases, mutual threats of retaliation, as in treatment of prisoners of war, and in action respecting persons and property in occupied territory.[19]

There was, however, one instance in which the British made representations concerning the conduct of war between the belligerents. This concerned an aspect of General Benjamin Butler's conduct during the

---

[15] *Ibid.*

[16] Russell to Lyons, Dec. 1, 1861, and Lyons to Russell, Dec. 19 and 23, 1861, in Newton, *Lord Lyons*, 1: 63, 66, 68, 70.

[17] Moore, *Digest*, 7: 558–60; U.S. Naval War College, *International Law Documents, 1916* (Washington: Government Printing Office, 1916).

[18] After secession but before hostilities, a peace conference was held in Washington, initiated by the Virginia legislature; but Virginia had not yet seceded and the states that had were not represented. The Confederates sent an official mission to Washington after Lincoln's inauguration to treat for the handing over of forts in Confederate territory. Secretary Seward refused to receive them but communicated with them indirectly. In the last days of the war, President Davis sent Vice-President Stephens as an envoy of an independent republic to negotiate for peace with President Lincoln, an old friend in Congress. They met on a steamer in Hampton Roads, and Stephens cited as a precedent the negotiations during the English Civil War; but Lincoln would not negotiate on the basis of Confederate independence and said, while disclaiming a wide knowledge of history, "All I distinctly recollect about the case of Charles I is that he lost his head." Morison, *Oxford History*, pp. 609, 698.

[19] Pt. 2 above.

occupation of New Orleans. Lord Palmerston on June 11, 1862, sent a "private and confidential" note to Minister Adams containing a violent attack upon the recent order of General Butler in New Orleans. The general had responded to what he considered humiliating behavior by the ladies in the city toward his soldiers by announcing that women acting in this way would be "regarded and treated as common women plying their vocation." This action, wrote Lord Palmerston, was considered in England as "barbarous and atrocious." He expressed "disgust" at the order and said "no such infamous act could be found in the whole history of civilized nations."[20] Adams feared this note might be a prelude to intervention and asked whether it was a private or an official communication. He got no satisfactory answer but showed the note to Lord Russell, who said it was a "highly irregular, private communication" and did not look toward recognition of the Confederacy. Palmerston finally made a somewhat conciliatory reply, but Adams said in the future he would not receive communications from him except through Lord Russell. The incident occasioned a breach between Adams and the prime minister for some time and indicates the delicacy of such third-party intervention in the relations between belligerents. Such incidents are rare, but there were a few in World War I and more in World War II[21]

d. The Concert of Europe (Mediation Proposals)

While there was no formal organization to maintain peace in the community of nations at the time of the Civil War, the Concert of Europe, composed of the great European powers, had assumed, since the Napoleonic Wars, the responsibility of intervening collectively in situations which they thought threatened "the public law of Europe" or the maintenance of peace. There had been a basis for such action in treaties ending the Napoleonic Wars, under which several conferences were held from 1815 to 1822. But the conservative powers had sought to utilize these conferences to maintain the principle of legitimacy against revolutions in both Europe and Latin America, and after the death of British Foreign Minister Castlereagh and the advent of Canning, Britain had

---

[20] Bernard, *Historical Account*, p. 289; R. B. Mowat, *The Diplomatic Relations of Great Britain and the United States* (New York: Longmans, 1925), pp. 185–86; Duberman, *Charles Francis Adams*, p. 479. The letters of Palmerston to Adams, June 11, 1862; Adams to Palmerston, June 12; Palmerston to Adams, July 15; Adams to Palmerston, June 16; Palmerston to Adams, July 19; Russell to Palmerston, June 13; and Adams to Palmerston, June 20, closing the incident are in the Broadlands Archives, Palmerston House.

[21] Before the United States entered World War I, President Wilson protested to Germany against the transportation of women and girls from occupied territory to Germany, and before World War II President F. D. Roosevelt made declarations against Hitler's atrocities.

withdrawn.[22] Nevertheless, the more informal "Concert" continued and intervened to sanction the Greek revolt from Turkey in the 1820s, the Belgian revolt from the Netherlands in the 1830s, and subsequent revolts in the Balkans.[23]

Such collective intervention has been looked upon by some international lawyers as more justifiable in law than individual interventions,[24] though Sir Vernon Harcourt in his influential letters to the *Times* under the name Historicus, published during the American Civil War, held that like all intervention "its essence is illegality and its justification is its success" and that it is not likely to be successful unless supported by armed force.[25] He also insisted that premature recognition of the independence of a revolting community is an act of intervention.[26]

The United States made it clear that any intervention, individual or collective, in the Civil War would be regarded as both illegal and unfriendly and that recognition of the independence of the Confederacy would be considered such an intervention.[27] Nevertheless there were various proposals in the British cabinet for recognition of the independence of the Confederacy, especially in the autumn of 1862, and the French continually pressed for collective mediation or intervention, culminating in the proposal of November 1862 that France, Russia, and Great Britain tender their good offices to the belligerents to end "the innumerable calamities and immense bloodshed" which attended the war and the evils which it inflicted upon Europe.[28] In his communication to Britain the French ambassador, M. Drouyn de Lhuys, proposed that

[22] W. Alison Phillips, *The Confederation of Europe* (2d ed.; London: Longmans, 1920). Britain's withdrawal was stimulated by its interest, for commercial reasons, in the independence of the Latin American states, and Britain was supported by the United States in maintaining the policy of recognizing de facto states and governments and the Monroe Doctrine.

[23] Thomas Erskine Holland, *The European Concert in the Eastern Question* (Oxford: Clarendon, 1885); H. J. Tobin, *The Termination of Multipartite Treaties* (New York: Columbia University Press, 1933); R. B. Mowat, *The European State System* (2d ed.; London: Oxford University Press, 1929); Quincy Wright, *A Study of War* (2d ed.; Chicago: University of Chicago Press, 1965), pp. 361, 780, 934.

[24] W. E. Hall, *A Treatise on International Law* (8th ed.; Oxford: Clarendon Press, 1924), sec. 95, pp. 347–49; Ellery Stowell, *Intervention in International Law* (Washington: Byrne, 1921), p. 310. The United States generally refused to cooperate in interventions by the Concert of Europe in the nineteenth century, but its policy changed in the twentieth century even before its participation in World Wars I and II, especially in regard to Far Eastern and African questions; see Stowell, *Intervention*, pp. 174 ff.

[25] In *The "Historicus" Letters* (London: Macmillan, 1863), Sir Vernon Harcourt discusses the collective interventions in Greece (1821) and Belgium (1830), pp. 41 ff.

[26] *Ibid.*, pp. 4 ff.

[27] See pt. 3, *a* (1), and pt. 3, n. 3.

[28] Bernard, *Historical Account*, pp. 467–68.

the three powers recommend an armistice of six months during which means might be found for a lasting pacification. The British government rejected the proposal, and Lord Russell said in the House of Lords "that if this war is to cease, it is far better that it should cease by a conviction both on the part of the North and on that of the South, that they can never live together again happily as one community and as one Republic, and that the termination of hostilities can never be brought about by the advice, the mediation, or the interference of any European Power."[29]

Russia, Austria, and Prussia had early in the war made it clear that they, least of all, would recognize revolutionary governments.[30] The French, failing to obtain British cooperation, independently submitted proposals for mediation to the United States in 1862 and again in 1863, but President Lincoln promptly rejected them.[31] Congress on March 3, 1863, passed, by large majorities in both houses, a resolution reciting the facts and, in order to avoid future efforts at mediation or intervention which might embarrass friendly relations, stating its position at some length. Congress noted that the United States in the past had accepted friendly offers of mediation or arbitration by foreign powers to adjust international questions and had recognized the natural and human desire of foreign powers to aid in arresting domestic troubles which afflicted other countries, but in the present "unprovoked and wicked rebellion" seeking to build a new power on the cornerstone of slavery, any proposal of a foreign power seeking to arrest the military effort of the United States would encourage the rebellion, prolong the conflict, and postpone peace. Consequently, "Congress would be obliged to look upon any further attempt in the same direction as an unfriendly act which it earnestly deprecates." The resolution concluded by noting that foreign intervention was the hope of the South and that its leaders thought the need of cotton would result in their recognition and foreign intervention. Congress regretted that foreign powers had not told the chiefs of the rebellion that the work they were engaged in was "hateful" and that the government they sought, built on slavery, was "shocking to civilization and the moral sense of mankind," and must not "expect welcome or recognition in the Commonwealth of Nations." Consequently, in the name of justice, human rights, and peace, the United States announced that "the war will be vigorously prosecuted, according to the humane principles of Christian states until the rebellion shall be overcome." Finally it requested that the resolution be transmitted by the president to

[29] *Ibid.*, p. 468.

[30] *Ibid.*, p. 126. Russia did, however, agree to give France moral support. Lord Newton, *Lord Lyons*, 1: 92.

[31] Newton, *Lord Lyons*, 1: 34.

his representatives abroad to transmit to the governments to which they were accredited.[32]

This resolution, drafted by Charles Sumner, chairman of the Senate Foreign Relations Committee, seems to have ended proposals for mediation or intervention, whether collective or individual.[33]

e. *Arbitration (The* Alabama *Claims)*

The foregoing resolution referred to the approval of proposals for arbitration as well as for mediation by the United States in the past. The United States and Great Britain had in fact initiated arbitration as a means for the peaceful settlement of international disputes in the Jay Treaty of 1794 after it had been dormant for centuries, and there had been many utilizations of this procedure by these and other countries in the succeeding decades. Along with diplomacy and collective intervention, arbitration had become an institution of the community of nations.

The United States rejected proposals for arbitration of political issues along with proposals for mediation and intervention during the war, though it recognized the principle that international law required a belligerent to submit captures to adjudication in its prize courts and proposed in 1863, without immediate success, arbitration of the *Alabama* claims. After the war and prolonged negotiation, further support for arbitration was given in the Treaty of Washington of 1871, which submitted to arbitration the *Alabama* and other claims of the United States against Britain[34] and also British claims against the United States, especially for certain prize court decisions believed not in accord with international law.[35]

These issues had threatened peace, especially because Britain had insisted that its "national honor" was involved in the allegation that it had violated international law by permitting the *Alabama* to escape. Britain's hesitancy to arbitrate claims said to be based on international law was increased by Secretary Seward's insistence that the hasty British recognition of southern belligerency was a breach of international law requiring compensation which might be effected by cession of the Bahamas to the United States and by Senator Sumner's suggestion, later supported by Secretary of State Fish, that no reparation less than the cession of Canada would be acceptable for the direct and indirect dam-

[32] Concurrent Resolution, March 3, 1863 (*Congressional Globe*, pp. 1360, 1497, 1513).

[33] Senator Sumner had his Senate speech of Feb. 17, 1863 (see n. 10 above), opposing the pending bill that would permit the president to commission privateers, printed in a pamphlet with this resolution.

[34] Moore, *Digest*, 6: 999, 7: 1059 ff.; Moore, *A History and Digest of the International Arbitrations to Which the United States Has Been a Party* (Washington: Government Printing Office, 1898), 1: 495 ff., 4: 4057 ff.

[35] Moore, *Digest*, 7: 725 ff.; Moore, *International Arbitrations*, 1: 683 ff., 4: 3902 ff.

age wrought by the *Alabama*, which had, he thought, prolonged the war two years.[36] The Senate rejected the Johnson-Clarendon Treaty negotiated in 1868, which provided for arbitration of the *Alabama* claims, because it did not include the indirect claims. This did not help the situation.[37]

The Treaty of Washington, in providing for the arbitration, left the question of indirect claims open, but when the tribunal met at Geneva in 1871, the British objected to consideration of the indirect claims. The United States, on the other hand, insisted that they were within the scope of the agreement to arbitrate. The problem was solved by the initiative of Charles Francis Adams, one of the arbitrators. He persuaded his colleagues on the tribunal to make a preliminary judgment denying the validity of the indirect claims. The treaty eliminated the British worry about "national honor" by stating the rules concerning neutral duty which the tribunal must apply without identifying them as the rules of international law applicable when the *Alabama* escaped, thus leaving the British free to say, however the award came out, that they had not violated international law.[38]

The tribunal awarded the United States $15,500,000 for direct losses from the activities of the *Alabama* and other Confederate cruisers built in Britain during the war. Its success in settling a dangerous dispute between major powers increased the prestige of international arbitration and international law, led to more frequent resorts to arbitration by governments in the period before World War I, to conferences for the codification and development of international law, and to the establishment of organizations of private jurists for these purposes, such as the Institute of International Law and the International Law Association, both of which remain active a century later.

This review indicates the rudimentary character of international organization in the mid-nineteenth century, though some of the ideas of collective responsibility for applying and maintaining international law, developed in the twentieth century, were to be found in embryonic form.

V. CONCLUSION

This study indicates that international law was continually referred to by belligerent and neutral governments during the American Civil War, especially in respect to the status of the rebels, the conduct of hostilities, and the rights and duties of neutrals.

[36] Henry W. Elson, *History of the United States of America* (New York: Macmillan, 1910), p. 819; Mowat, *Diplomatic Relations*, pp. 209–10; Moore, *Digest*, 1: 582; Moore, *International Arbitrations*, 4: 4057 ff., Charles Francis Adams, Jr., *Lee at Appomattox and Other Papers* (Boston: Houghton Mifflin, 1902), p. 156.

[37] Duberman, *Charles Francis Adams*, pp. 325–26.

[38] *Ibid.*; Bishop, *International Law*, p. 865; and the references given in n. 36 above.

Quincy Wright

Practice, judicial opinion, and official regulations established that when civil strife was of such magnitude as to constitute war in the material sense, now called "insurgency," both rebels and government were obliged to apply the rules of war in their relations with each other[1] and the government or outside states might recognize the situation as war in the legal sense, implying an equal status to both sides during the war and permitting both to exercise belligerent powers at sea over neutral as well as enemy commerce. During the war, therefore, the government should treat rebels or insurgents whom it might capture as prisoners of war and not as pirates, brigands, or traitors. It might, however, punish enemy persons convicted of war crimes, and after the war was over, it might, if it won, treat them as traitors.

Insurgency was distinguished from politically motivated riots, mob violence, or revolt which had not got beyond the control of the government by the magnitude of the hostilities and the consequent uncertainty of the result, and from piracy, brigandage, and other uses of force of considerable magnitude, for private gain, by the political objectives of the rebels or insurgents. It was recognized that these two categories converge in the case of privateers, considered legitimate in time of war until outlawed by the Declaration of Paris of 1856. While ostensibly acting for political purposes of the government whose commission he carried, the privateer was actually seeking to take prizes for private gain and thus resembled the pirate even though his operations were directed only against the enemy state. While it was recognized that the parties to the Declaration of Paris might treat privateers as pirates, such treatment was not considered permissible during the Civil War because the Confederacy was not a party to the declaration and the existing parties insisted that the United States could not apply the provision concerning privateering during the war even if it became a party, as it wished to do.[2]

The United States emphasized that civil strife was within the domestic jurisdiction of the state in which it occurred and that foreign states should not intervene.[3] Foreign states recognized that both sides were free to use armed force against each other, provided they kept within the rules of war, but only if belligerency was recognized could they interfere with the commerce of other states or their nationals on the high seas or in foreign territory.[4]

[1] The Geneva Conventions of 1949 recognized this to a limited extent; see pt. 2, n. 13 above.
[2] Charles Francis Adams, Jr., "Seward and the Declaration of Paris," *Proceedings of the Massachusetts Historical Society* 46 (1912): 32–33.
[3] Whether intervention on invitation of the de jure government is permissible has been controversial; see below notes 9, 10, 11.
[4] This was required by the nonintervention agreement of the powers during the Spanish civil strife, 1936–39. Norman J. Padelford, *International Law and Diplomacy in the Spanish Civil Strife* (New York: Macmillan, 1939), pp. 57, 205 ff.

✳ The line between insurgency and belligerency was not clearly drawn in the Civil War. A minority of the Supreme Court sharply distinguished the two terms, as did the Court itself a generation later in characterizing the civil strife which then existed in Cuba. The majority of the Court in the Civil War cases held that large-scale war in the material sense constituted war in the legal sense by virtue of its magnitude and permitted the president to recognize it as such without congressional authority.[5] British opinion seemed to share this view. Secretary Seward at first contended that insurrection, however large, did not confer belligerent rights on the insurgents, but he could not sustain this position after the president had declared a war blockade intended to impair the peacetime rights of foreign states on the high seas.[6] He had to recognize that the British proclamation of neutrality, manifesting their acquiescence, was permissible, because the United States by its blockade declaration had itself recognized the situation as war and the proclamation was more courteous to the United States than the alternative of protesting against the blockade.

Belligerency was held, on the one hand, to imply that foreign states must assume the obligations of neutrality, involving impartiality as between the recognized government and the rebels, abstention from official aid to either, and as illustrated in the *Alabama* case, prevention of military expeditions from their territory to aid either side. On the other hand, belligerency implied that both the de jure government and the rebels enjoyed the belligerent right to visit, search, and perhaps capture and condemn merchant vessels of all states on the high seas. These consequences of belligerency were generally accepted, but few, if any, of the many situations of civil strife since the Civil War have been recognized as belligerency. They have been treated as insurgency, a status which has been held to arise from the fact of large-scale hostilities.

The de jure government has feared that recognition of belligerency would assist the rebels and might lead to interventions by outside states on their side, as it nearly did in the Civil War. Outside states have feared that such recognition would be considered an unfriendly act by the recognized government, as it was at first by the United States in the Civil War. Furthermore, they have wanted to avoid interferences with their maritime commerce, from which Britain and other neutrals suffered during the Civil War. In a number of cases of civil strife since the Civil War, outside states have intervened, but even then, with the sole exception of the United States intervention in Cuba in 1898, the situation has

---

[5] See pt. 2, *a* (1) above.

[6] Foreign states can take the president's acts on military and foreign affairs as authoritative without consideration of the exclusive power of Congress to declare war. Quincy Wright, *The Control of American Foreign Relations* (New York: Macmillan, 1922), pp. 21 ff., 36, 38.

not been recognized as war in the legal sense, and maritime commerce of outside states has not been interfered with.[7]

The experience of both belligerents and neutrals during the American Civil War, therefore, initiated a development of international law by establishing the status of insurgency during serious civil strife and making recognition of belligerency in such a situation obsolete.[8] This change is intended to maintain the humanitarian rules of war in civil strife, to prevent outside intervention, to contain hostilities, to prevent escalation, and to permit the people of the state freedom to decide by legal, political, or military means, in accord with the principle of self-determination, whether to adopt a new constitution, to remain as one state or to divide.

While it reluctantly accepted the belligerency of the Confederates in the Civil War, the United States made it clear that recognition of the independence of the Confederacy or outside intervention, eagerly sought by the Confederates, would violate international law and would be resented, probably by war. Great Britain seriously considered such action on grounds of national interest, humanity, and self-determination, especially in September 1862, when it was convinced that the South would win, but was deterred by Lincoln's preliminary Emancipation Proclamation issued immediately after the Union victory at Antietam. The objective of the war became not merely preservation of the Union but the abolition of slavery, and British sentiment would not permit support of slavery. France continued to propose mediation even after Britain had refused to concur, but the president and Congress made it clear that although legally permissible this proposal was unacceptable and if pressed would be considered unfriendly.

It has remained controversial whether civil strife of sufficient magnitude to constitute insurgency, but not recognized as belligerency, imposes an obligation upon each foreign state to treat the hostile factions impartially and to refrain from intervention even on request of the government which it recognizes.[9] In spite of a number of interventions, especially as a result of the cold war and of "regional understandings" like the Monroe Doctrine and the Warsaw and NATO alliances, practice and juristic opinion, with some exceptions,[10] have favored impartiality and

[7] *The Three Friends*, 166 U.S. 1 (1896); and pt. 2, n. 17.

[8] The "outlawry of war" in the legal sense and the development of the concepts of collective security and collective self-defense since World War I have also contributed to this obsolescence.

[9] Erik Castrén, *Civil War* (Helsinki: Suomalainen Tiedeakatemia, 1966), pp. 20–21, 110.

[10] Herbert W. Briggs, *The Law of Nations* (2d. ed.; New York: Appleton-Century-Crofts, 1952), p. 1000; Pan-American Convention on Duties and Rights of States in Event of Civil Strife, Havana, 1928, *ibid.*, p. 998; and Manley O. Hudson (ed.), *International Legislation* (Washington: Carnegie Endowment, 1931), 4: 2416; J. W. Garner, "Questions of International Law in the Spanish Civil War," *American Journal of International Law* 31 (1937): 66–73. The United States in the twentieth century has departed from its traditional policy of

nonintervention in the interest of localization of hostilites, nonescalation, and national self-determination.[11] This interpretation identifies belligerency and insurgency in respect to the duty of states to refrain from intervention and to treat the factions impartially during civil strife, but it differentiates them in respect to the rights of foreign states on the high seas. In case of insurgency, neither the government nor the rebels can exercise belligerent rights against vessels of outside states at sea.

In addition to its contributions to the laws of war, neutrality, and insurgency, the Civil War also contributed to the practice of arbitration as a means for settling disputes, even those of political importance, and to the codification of international law, as indicated by the production of Lieber's Code and the discussions on the Declaration of Paris and their influence on subsequent codifications of aspects of international law.

The Civil War discussions stimulated widespread interest in international law, resulting in the creation soon after of the Institute of International Law and the International Law Association for the scientific study of international law among jurists of all countries. In spite of a number of international wars and many insurrections in the next half century, the period was one of juristic optimism with high hopes that international law, arbitration, and disarmament would soon establish peace on earth. This optimism was halted by World War I, somewhat revived by the League of Nations, but more rudely shocked by World War II and the cold war which followed.[12] It remains to be seen whether

---

recognizing de facto governments and has pursued commercial, nonrecognition, and interventionist policies in cases of civil strife in Latin America and elsewhere, ostensibly to assure free elections or other political freedoms rather than to support the incumbent government or discourage revolutionists, though it has sometimes in fact followed the latter policy, asserted by Dr. Carlos Tobar of Ecuador and adopted by the Central American states in 1907; see T. P. Wright, Jr., *American Support of Free Elections Abroad* (Washington: Public Affairs Press, 1964). Roscoe Ralph Oglesby cites H. Lauterpacht as holding that insurgency does not enforce a duty of *impartiality* on foreign states. "Applications of International Law under Conditions of Civil Strife" (Ph.D. dissertation, Duke University, 1949), p. 304.

[11] This conforms to the doctrine asserted by the Mexican Foreign Minister Estrado of nonintervention and recognizing only de facto governments. W. E. Hall, *A Treatise on International Law* (8th ed.; Oxford: Clarendon Press, 1924), sec. 94, p. 346; *The Three Friends*, 166 U.S. 1 (1896); G. G. Wilson, "Insurgency and International Maritime Law," *American Journal of International Law* 1 (1907): 46, 51; J. B. Moore, *A Digest of International Law* (Washington, 1906), 1: 242; Moore, *Collected Papers* (New Haven: Yale University Press, 1945), 6: 355; Quincy Wright, "International Law and Civil Strife," *Proceedings of the American Society of International Law*, 1959, pp. 145 ff. Oglesby cites Weiss, Brierly, J. B. Moore, G. G. Wilson, and Philip Jessup as requiring impartiality by outside states if insurgency is recognized, a view which Oglesby favors. "Applications," pp. 306 ff., 510 ff., 595 ff.

[12] Quincy Wright, *Research in International Law since the War* (Washington: Carnegie Endowment for International Peace, 1930); *The Strengthening of International Law*, Hague Academy of International Law, *Recueil des Cours*, 1959 (Leyden: A. W. Sijthoff, 1960), chap. 1; *Predicting International Relations, the Year 2000* (University of Denver, Monograph No. 1, 1969–70), p. 5.

the high hopes for international law after the Geneva award of 1871 will be revived.

SOURCES

For the causes of the conflict (Part I) I have used mainly secondary materials, especially, Henry W. Elson's *History of the United States of America* reflecting a northern point of view; Woodrow Wilson's *History of the American People* reflecting a southern point of view; Mountague Bernard's *Historical Account of the Neutrality of Great Britain during the American Civil War* reflecting a British point of view; Herman von Holst, *The Constitutional and Political History of the United States* reflecting a continental European point of view; and two recent American histories, James Truslow Adams, *The Epic of America*, and Samuel Eliot Morison, *The Oxford History of the American People*.[1]

For the role of international law in the relations of the belligerents (Part II) I have used Lieber's Code; Francis B. Friedel and Lewis R. Harley's biographies of Francis Lieber;[2] United States Supreme Court Reports; and several international law textbooks and casebooks, as well as the histories referred to above.

For the role of international law and international institutions in the relations between foreign states and the belligerents (Parts III and IV) I have utilized United States diplomatic correspondence (published annually as *United States Foreign Affairs* from 1861 to 1869 and later as *United States Foreign Relations*); *British and Foreign State Papers*; J. B. Moore's *Digest of International Law*; Bernard's book mentioned above which prints much diplomatic material; the "Historicus" Letters to the *Times* (London) by Sir Vernon Harcourt; the biography and letters of William H. Seward, United States secretary of state, of Lord Lyons, the British minister to the United States, and of Charles Francis Adams, American minister to England, together with comments on

[1] Henry W. Elson, *History of the United States of America*, (New York: Macmillan, 1910); Woodrow Wilson, *History of the American People* (New York: Harper, 1902); Mountague Bernard, *Historical Account of the Neutrality of Great Britain during the American Civil War* (London: Longmans, 1870); Herman von Holst, *The Constitutional and Political History of the United States*, trans. John J. Laler (Chicago: Callaghan, 1892); James Truslow Adams, *The Epic of America* (New York: Blue Ribbon Books, 1931); Samuel Eliot Morison, *The Oxford History of the American People* (New York: Oxford University Press, 1965).

[2] United States, War Department, General Orders No. 100, cited as Lieber's Code; Francis B. Friedel, *Francis Lieber, Nineteenth-Century Liberal* (Baton Rouge: Louisiana State University Press, 1947); Lewis R. Harley, *Francis Lieber, His Life and Political Philosophy* (New York: Columbia University Press, 1899).

aspects of British American relations by two of Minister Adams's sons.[3] Especially useful was the well-documented dissertation by Roscoe Ralph Oglesby, over a third of which is devoted to the Civil War.[4]

The quantity of secondary and source materials published about the American Civil War is almost infinite, and I have used only selected examples. I have, however, been especially fortunate in having had the opportunity, through the courtesy of Frank Vandiver of Rice University, to study and utilize unpublished correspondence between Lord Palmerston, the British prime minister, Lord John Russell, the British foreign minister, William C. Gladstone, chancellor of the exchequer, and other members of the British Cabinet during the Civil War. Professor Vandiver had had copies made of the Palmerston Papers by permission of Earl Mountbatten of Burma now in possession of the Broadlands Archives in Palmerston House, London. These papers indicate how near Britain came to intervening in the Civil War on the side of the South, a step which would doubtless have changed the course of history. They also indicate the varied and changing opinions about the expediency of this step by the members of the British Cabinet and the often distorted views about these opinions held by the American minister and the government in Washington.

[3] *Papers Relating to Foreign Affairs, Accompanying the Annual Message of the President* (Washington: Government Printing Office, 1862–69), cited *U.S. Foreign Affairs* (after 1870 the series was entitled *Foreign Relations of the United States*); *British and Foreign State Papers* (London, 1862–65); J. B. Moore, *Digest of International Law* (Washington, 1906); Sir Vernon Harcourt, *The "Historicus" Letters* (London: Macmillan, 1863); Thornton K. Lothrop, *William Henry Seward* (Boston: Houghton Mifflin, 1899); Lord Newton, *Lord Lyons: A Record of British Diplomacy* (London: Edward Arnold, 1913); Martin B. Duberman, *Charles Francis Adams, 1807–1886* (Boston: Houghton Mifflin, 1920); Charles Francis Adams, Jr., *Charles Francis Adams* (Boston: Houghton Mifflin, 1900), *Lee at Appomattox and Other Papers* (Boston: Houghton Mifflin, 1902), and "Seward and the Declaration of Paris," *Proceedings of the Massachusetts Historical Society* 46 (1912): 23–81; Henry Adams, *The Education of Henry Adams* (Boston: Houghton Mifflin, 1918).

[4] Roscoe Ralph Oglesby, "Applications of International Law under Conditions of Civil Strife" (Ph.D. dissertation, Duke University, 1949).

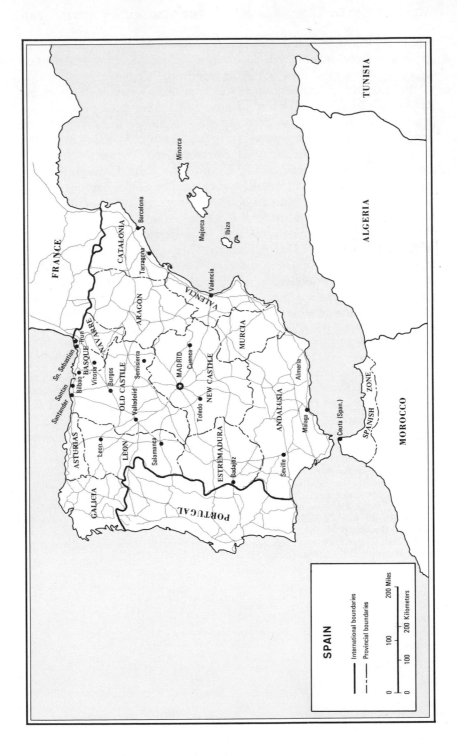

SPAIN

International boundaries
Provincial boundaries

0   100   200 Miles

0   100   200 Kilometers

FRANCE

TUNISIA

ALGERIA

MOROCCO

SPANISH ZONE

Ceuta (Span.)

PORTUGAL

GALICIA

ASTURIAS

LEON

OLD CASTILE

NEW CASTILE

ESTREMADURA

ANDALUSIA

MURCIA

VALENCIA

ARAGON

NAVARRE

BASQUE

CATALONIA

MADRID

Barcelona

Tarragona

Valencia

Cuenca

Toledo

Somosierra

Valladolid

Burgos

Vitoria

Bilbao

Sn. Sebastian

Santan

Santander

Leon

Salamanca

Badajoz

Seville

Malaga

Almeria

Minorca

Majorca

Ibiza

Irun

Ann Van Wynen Thomas and A. J. Thomas, Jr.

INTERNATIONAL LEGAL ASPECTS OF THE CIVIL WAR IN SPAIN, 1936–39

I. THE CONFLICT: A FACTUAL INTRODUCTION

The Conflict Begins

On July 17, 1936, in Spanish Morocco, the Spanish army revolted against the duly elected government of the Spanish Republic—the Popular Front.[1] Within the next two days, similar army revolts took place in garrison towns throughout the nation.[2] The confusion and disorder prevailing in the government, the mutual suspicion among the various political parties of the Popular Front, the hostility between the leaders of the various factions making up that front, the indiscipline of the masses, and the weakness of the government's military supports led the rebels to believe the rebellion would not encounter any serious obstacles and would soon succeed. The movement was led by dissident army generals who had the support of powerful social classes, the backing of two-thirds of the officers of the Spanish army, the assistance of the well-armed and fanatical Carlists, and the control of the elite Spanish combat units, the Moorish troops and Foreign Legion of the Army of Africa. A series of misfortunes among the conspirator generals coupled with the fact that General Francisco Franco commanded the veteran Army of Africa, which was far better equipped and far better trained than the other garrisons, led to his designation as commander-in-chief of the rebel or Nationalist Army and assumption of the title of chief of the Spanish state in October 1936.[3]

[1] For background discussion of the Spanish civil strife, see Antonio Ramos Oliveira, *Politics, Economics, and Men of Modern Spain: 1808–1946* (London: Crown, 1946); Edgar Allison Peers, *The Spanish Tragedy, 1930–1936: Dictatorship, Republic, Chaos* (Oxford: Methuen, 1937); W. Horsfall Carter, "Spain and Her Immaculate Republic," *Contemporary Review*, June 1931, p. 122; Claude G. Bowers, *My Mission to Spain* (New York: Simon & Schuster, 1954); David T. Cattell, *Communism and the Spanish Civil War* (Berkeley: University of California Press, 1955); Frank Edward Manuel, *The Politics of Modern Spain* (New York: McGraw-Hill, 1938); Hugh Thomas, *The Spanish Civil War* (New York: Harper & Row, 1961); Gerald Brenan, *The Spanish Labyrinth: An Account of the Social and Political Background of the Civil War* (2d ed.; Cambridge: Cambridge University Press, 1950).

[2] Henry W. Buckley, *Life and Death of the Spanish Republic* (London: Hamish Hamilton, 1940), p. 195.

[3] E. J. Hughes, *Report from Spain* (New York: Holt, 1947), pp. 24 ff.

111

Throughout the Spanish peninsula during the three days immediately following the revolt in Morocco, garrison after garrison placed the Spanish people under the control of the Spanish army. All was anarchy on the governmental side, for there remained no army, no police, and hence no way to enforce authority. The Nationalists had no intention of launching a civil war. They had assumed that with their military might the Republic would quickly fall. Here they miscalculated, for they failed to take into account the feelings of the Spanish workers and peasants. In Madrid the government, after two days of hesitation, sent trucks loaded with arms into the working-class areas to arm the populace. In other cities, even without government prompting, workers arose in the face of the threat of army control and established their own barricades, militias, and forces.[4] For the next few days absolute terror reigned. Quarrels and enmities dating back for generations found outlet in assassinations and violence. The workers and peasants fought not only to resist the army but also for their own revolution—much as in the French Revolution. The army, industrialists, middle class, landowners, and aristocrats fought back. Each fought for himself. Every organization, social club, union, political party, and religious faction engaged in its own war, armed its own men. Sovereign power ceased to exist except in those few areas where military might was able to maintain some semblance of order. Individuals and communities acted without constraint as if they were beyond the pale of civilization and history.

From the beginning the foreign press tended to characterize the civil strife in Spain as an ideological struggle between two imported non-Spanish ideologies. Actually the conflict originated from strictly internal affairs.[5] The social antagonisms in Spain had not come to the point of civil war overnight; they were of long-standing duration and when they burst forth they did so without the need of outside prompting. As long as the moderate republicans had been in power, the extreme right had managed to sabotage all reforms which sought to curb the power of the industrialists, to bring about agrarian change, to separate church and state, and to democratize the army. But in sabotaging these reforms, the extreme right merely forced many center groups into the camp of the extreme left. With the victory of the Popular Front in February 1936, the extreme right realized that the balance of power had swung leftward—that only military rule could now restore the dominance of the traditional church-state-army system. There was no question in the minds of the Nationalists, therefore, that they were fighting what they considered to be a "communist" influence in Spain; while on the Loyalist

[4] Thomas, *The Spanish Civil War*, pp. 139 ff.
[5] Alfredo Mendizábal, *The Martyrdom of Spain: Origins of a Civil War* (New York: Scribner, 1938), p. 12.

or governmental side, all felt they were fighting what they considered to be a "fascist" influence.[6] As to which side the majority of the Spanish population supported, there can be no absolute answer. The electoral victory of the Popular Front of February 1936 had been by no means a landslide.[7] On the other hand, even though the rebels were backed by most of the military might of the nation and even though they eventually received more aid from abroad than did the Republicans, it took them three years of hard fighting to put down the resistance to their rule. It would seem that the majority of the civilian population did support the Republic.

Intervention and Nonintervention

Notwithstanding the fact that the origins of the rebellion were domestic in nature, once the fighting began the Spanish civil strife was quickly changed from an internal struggle to a conflict in which international elements became predominant. The two major fascist nations in Europe, Germany and Italy, had closely watched the progressive degeneration of the Republic, and although they had little or no direct relationship with the spark that set Spain afire, when aid was requested by the revolutionaries, they were fully prepared to give it. By July 25, Italy had sent a number of military transport planes to Morocco to aid Franco in transporting the Army of Africa to the mainland, and the following day, Hitler agreed to send to Franco, arms and airplanes of all types—transports, fighters, and bombers—and also advisers and technicians to teach the Spanish military how to make the best use of the equipment.[8] In these crucial first ten days, when it appeared that the rebellion might be defeated by the government, the scales were tipped in favor of the revolting generals by this aid from abroad. Once committed, Germany and Italy continued to lend the Nationalists support throughout the war; their aid included entire fighting divisions, as well as armaments, planes, and technicians.[9]

Portugal, sharing the Iberian peninsula with Spain, watched the course

[6] Arnold Toynbee, "The International Repercussions of the War in Spain," *Survey of International Affairs, 1937* (London: Oxford University Press, 1938), 2: 23.

[7] Of the total vote cast, the Popular Front received 4,176,000, the National Front 3,784,000, the Basque nationalists 130,000 and other minor parties 681,000. Thomas, *The Spanish Civil War*, p. 94.

[8] *Ibid.*, pp. 226, 229.

[9] For German and Italian diplomatic interests in Spain and the Spanish Civil War, see a political report of the German ambassador to Italy of December 18, 1936, from the archives of the German foreign ministry of 1950, as contained in U.S. Department of State, *Documents on German Foreign Policy, 1918–1945*, 3: 171–72. See also John Selby Haupert, "German Intervention in Spain, 1936–1943" (M.A. thesis, Southern Methodist University, 1952), pp. 11–18.

of the Spanish government with apprehension. In 1932, under the dictatorship of Antonio Salazar, Portugal had adopted a corporative system modeled on that of Italy, but with more distinct theocratic overtones. Salazar knew that his regime would be in trouble if Spain became a viable democratic republic. He, therefore, permitted much of the early planning of the revolt of the generals to take place on Portuguese soil, seeing in the Nationalists' plans for the future the same type of government he had given to Portugal. Once the revolution began, Portugal not only aided the rebels with "volunteer" troops, arms, and ammunition but, more important, placed Portuguese port facilities at rebel disposal. It was through Portugal that the greater part of the German aid was shipped. Spanish Republicans who escaped into Portuguese territory were usually handed over to the Nationalists, and the controlled Portuguese press and radio served the Nationalist cause exclusively throughout the war.[10]

When the Popular Front of Spain appealed by telegram and money order to the Popular Front of France for arms and airplanes, there was no doubt in the minds of the Spanish Government that such aid would be immediately forthcoming.[11] The traditional policy of France had always favored a friendly Spanish government in Madrid, leaving France free to concentrate on the problem of defending its border with Germany. The Spanish government was certain that France would recognize the danger of having a fascist government in Spain that would side with the other fascist nations of Europe against the democracies and might even give to Italy and Germany certain privileges in Spanish possessions in Morocco, the Atlantic, and the Mediterranean, thereby drastically shifting the balance of power and threatening French communication routes between the mother country and its colonies in Africa and the Far East.[12] Consequently, it was inconceivable to the Spanish government that France would not come to its immediate aid. But in this it miscalculated.

Leon Blum, the head of the French Popular Front government, received the Spanish government's request for aid on the night of July 19, 1936, but he did not immediately act on it. On July 22 he flew to London to participate in a meeting of Belgium, France, and Great Britain pertaining to Germany's violation of the Locarno Pact. At this meeting the Conservative party of Britain intimated that French aid to Loyalist Spain might be detrimental to British-French security arrangements. In

---

[10] See Ramos Oliveira, *Politics, Economics, and Men of Modern Spain*, pp. 585 ff.; Julio Alvarez del Vayo, *Freedom's Battle* (London: William Heinemann, 1940), p. 30. See also U.S. Department of State, *Documents on German Foreign Policy, 1918–1945*, p. 55.

[11] David T. Cattell, *Soviet Diplomacy and the Spanish Civil War* (Berkeley: University of California Press, 1957), p. 10.

[12] Alexander Werth, *Which Way France?* (New York: Harper, 1937), p. 379.

Europe, the only defensive alliance that France could depend upon in the face of a rearming Germany was that with the British. A mere hint that French aid to the legitimate government of Spain might jeopardize British-French relations was sufficient to prevent direct governmental aid.[13] Therefore, the French cabinet decided that the French government would not intervene in any manner in the Spanish conflict. Supply of arms to the Loyalists was refused. Recognizing that this decision would bring about a violent outcry from the left, the government stated that France would not place an embargo on private arms dealers, who would be permitted to furnish the Spanish government with war materials and supplies as condoned by customary international law.[14]

At the outbreak of the Spanish civil strife, public opinion in England was about equally divided in its support of the Loyalists and Nationalists, but both factions were agreed that this was strictly an internal struggle in Spain and that, consequently, the British government should not sell arms to either side. Since customary international law permitted private individuals to sell arms to whomever they pleased, the British government did not immediately place an embargo on the private sale of arms. They merely refused to give or sell government weapons to either side.[15] At this point, British diplomacy appeared to be based on the premise that, if the Spaniards were allowed to fight it out among themselves, neither side would be the victor and some sort of neutral compromise solution between left and right would then magically come into being.

On July 30, two Italian bombers en route to join the Nationalist forces made emergency landings and one Italian bomber crashed in French Morocco.[16] Two days later, after a thorough investigation, there was a meeting of the French cabinet. The leftist parties of the Popular Front demanded that the French government aid the Popular Front of Spain in view of the fact that the Italians were intervening actively on the side of the revolting generals. The moderates eventually agreed that planes, including bombers, fighters, transports, and trainers, should be sent immediately to aid the Loyalists but that, on the other hand, France should appeal urgently to all interested governments, including Britain, Germany, and Italy, to join in a nonintervention pact which would prohibit the direct or indirect imports of arms, munitions, and war materials into Spain.[17]

By August 7, Britain, Belgium, Holland, Poland, Czechoslovakia, and

---

[13] Louis Lévy, *Vérités sur la France* (Middlesex, England: Penguin, 1941), p. 114.

[14] Lassa Oppenheim, *International Law*, ed. H. Lauterpacht (7th ed.; London: Longmans Green, 1952), 2: 739.

[15] Alvarez del Vayo, *Freedom's Battle*, pp. 239, 266.

[16] Cattell, *Soviet Diplomacy and the Spanish Civil War*, p. 14.

[17] Thomas, *The Spanish Civil War*, p. 234. On the Nonintervention agreement,

France had all signed the completed agreement. On August 9, as the first gesture of nonintervention, the French government closed the frontiers of France to all exportation—public and private—of war materials to either side in Spain. And on August 15, the British prohibited all public and private shipment of arms to either side.[18]

On August 13, Portugal had accepted the "thought of nonintervention" in principle, reserving liberty of action direct or indirect if her border should appear threatened by the progress of the war, or if she found it necessary to safeguard Western civilization against any subversive social regimes that might be established in Spain, or if she recognized the belligerency of the contending parties or a new government of Spain. She also declared that if any country sent "volunteers" or raised funds for the war Portugal would consider herself automatically released from the accord.[19] This of course was a far different agreement than had been signed by the six other nations.

Germany signed the three articles of the agreement on August 17 but carefully omitted the preamble, which called for nonintervention in Spain's internal affairs, thus leaving herself free to engage in all forms of interference or intervention not specifically forbidden, such as the sending of volunteers, officers, or financial aid to either side.[20] Even after giving himself this much latitude, Hitler clearly indicated that he considered the pact but a scrap of paper by sending on August 25, one of his leading generals to join the Nationalists in Spain to determine their needs for manpower and war materials and to assure them that such supplies would continue to be forthcoming in spite of the nonintervention agreement.[21]

Italy, on August 21, also signed the agreement without the preamble but indicated in an exchange of notes with the British that the nonintervention pact would be considered worthless by Italy unless there was a commission appointed to supervise its working. Within two weeks of signing the agreement, Italian warships were aiding the Nationalists in defending the Mediterranean island of Majorca and in capturing the neighboring island of Ibiza.[22]

---

see Norman J. Padelford, *International Law and Diplomacy in the Spanish Civil Strife* (New York: Macmillan Co., 1939), p. 57.

[18] Thomas, *The Spanish Civil War*, pp. 258, 260.

[19] Padelford, *International Law and Diplomacy in the Spanish Civil Strife*, p. 59.

[20] *Ibid.*, p. 58.

[21] United Nations, Security Council, *Official Records*, 1st year, 1st series, Special Supplement: Report of the Subcommittee on the Spanish Question (S/76–31, May 1946), p. 7.

[22] U.S. Department of State, *Documents on German Foreign Policy, 1918–1945*, p. 60, contains a statement by the German chargé d'affaires in Italy to the effect that it was obvious that the Italian government did not intend to abide by the declaration.

On August 23, Russia signed the agreement, including the preamble, but at the same time Stalin was establishing diplomatic relations with the Loyalists.[23] The first Soviet ambassador to Spain arrived with his staff on August 27 to open the Russian embassy, which had been closed since 1918. The ambassador was a former revolutionary general, and his staff was composed of trained military men.[24] Stalin did not send Russian aid at this time, but he alerted the Comintern (the international communist organization) to begin setting up subsidiary organizations which could supply arms to the Loyalists if German and Italian intervention on behalf of the Nationalists continued.[25]

In the United States, pacifist sentiment ran high in the early 1930s. Congress had enacted a neutrality law, providing that no belligerent nation could procure arms or ammunition within the United States unless cash were paid for each shipment and unless such shipment were carried in vessels other than those of United States registry.[26] Within days after the commencement of the revolt, the Loyalist government placed orders for arms with various American manufacturers. Inasmuch as the United States neutrality laws applied only to international wars, the Loyalists assumed that, in a case of civil strife in which one of the parties had been duly recognized as the legitimate government by the United States, there would be no problem in the purchase of arms on the American open market. After the European nations had signed the nonintervention accord, the United States Secretary of State announced that, although the president had no authority to inaugurate an arms embargo in a case of civil strife, he hoped nonetheless that American exporters of arms and ammunition would refrain from shipping war materials to either side in Spain. Since the Spanish government paid for its orders in cash, this request was largely ignored.[27] Consequently, in January 1937, at the urging of various pacifist groups and of a number of Catholic organizations whose members had been outraged by the atrocities against the church, most of which took place in Loyalist-held areas, Congress enacted a law prohibiting the export of arms, ammunition, or implements of war to either of the opposing forces in the Spanish civil strife.[28]

The long and bitter struggle of the Mexicans against entrenched in-

---

[23] Cattell, *Soviet Diplomacy and the Spanish Civil War*, p. 18.

[24] Thomas, *The Spanish Civil War*, p. 262.

[25] Burnett Bolloten, *The Grand Camouflage: The Communist Conspiracy in the Spanish Civil War* (New York: Praeger, 1961), p. 100.

[26] Edwin Borchard and William Potter Lage, *Neutrality for the United States* (2d ed.; New Haven: Yale University Press, 1940), p. 324.

[27] Julius William Pratt, *A History of United States Foreign Policy* (2d ed.; New York: Prentice-Hall, 1955), pp. 364–65.

[28] Cordell Hull defended this policy as the only way the United States could keep aloof from the struggle. Hull, *Memoirs* (New York: Macmillan Co., 1948), 2: 491. On the other hand, Sumner Welles called it a cardinal error. Welles, *Time for Decision* (New York: Harper & Bros., 1944), p. 60.

terests and also against a reactionary church made Mexico feel at one with the Loyalist cause in Spain. Hence, Mexico's announcement that it would aid the legitimate government in every way possible was not surprising. Mexico did not base this policy on ideological grounds but on the international law doctrine of nonintervention and international law rules relating to direct aggression. Mexico contended that since the Spanish Republican regime had come into being as a result of a free election it was the legitimate government of the nation; therefore, the European nonintervention agreement was a denial of the international rights of a legitimate government, an indirect way of giving aid and comfort to the insurgents, and thus actually interventionary in character. Furthermore, Mexico alleged, since the Nationalists were receiving aid from Germany and Italy, the legitimate government of Spain was the victim of an aggression, and all signatories of the charter of the League of Nations were legally required to come to the aid of the victim of such an aggression. In accord with this view, Mexico aided the Loyalists through the course of the war by supplying them with arms and foodstuffs and by acting as an intermediary in the purchase of weapons in other nations.[29]

Contrary to the propaganda claims of the Nationalists, the Germans, and the Italians, Russia did not act immediately to supply the Loyalists with materials of war. At the outbreak of the civil strife, Stalin was presented with a dilemma. He had just completed his purge of influential Russians who sided with Trotsky in demanding that immediate communist world revolution take precedence over all else. Stalin held firm to the belief that the industrialization and complete communization of Russia were more important than the cause of the working classes in other parts of the world. If Russia came to the aid of the Loyalist government, Trotsky would appear to be directing Stalin's foreign policy. And yet, if the Soviet Union failed to come to the aid of the Loyalists, whatever merit communism held in the eyes of the working classes elsewhere would be lost. Over and above this problem, Stalin had no desire to enter an undeclared war in Spain against German and Italian troops.[30]

These considerations did not deter Stalin long, however, and he soon turned to the Comintern to organize international brigades of volunteers in various countries of the world. In assembling these international brigades, the Comintern used local communist parties and fellow-traveller organizations as recruiting groups, seeking men of democratic sympathies.[31] Communists, for the most part, were not permitted to join the

---

[29] L. E. Smith, *Mexico and the Spanish Republicans* (Berkeley: University of California Press, 1955), pp. 171, 181, 196.

[30] Julian Gorkin, *Canibales Políticos (Hitler y Stalin en España)* (Mexico: Ediciones "Quetzal," 1941), p. 24.

[31] Louis Fischer, *Men and Politics: An Autobiography* (New York: Duell, Sloan & Pearce, 1941), p. 495.

brigades because that would have depleted the ranks of local communist parties. They maintained control of the brigades, however, although their control was so well concealed that many volunteers never realized that Russian communists and not Spanish Loyalists were supervising their training and equipment and, above all, deciding when and where they were to be used.[32] No Russians were permitted to volunteer; the only manpower contribution made by the Russians to the international brigades was the sending of six hundred foreign communists who had been exiled from their own nations and were living in Russia.[33]

During the first year of the war, the Loyalist government, fearing that Madrid might fall, sent a large part of the Spanish gold reserves to Russia for safekeeping. Russia, in return, sent a vast quantity of non-military supplies (foodstuffs, fertilizers, and clothing).[34] Although the Russian military supplies, such as guns, technicians, tanks, and planes, were not supplied on a very vast scale, they arrived at a crucial moment in October 1936 and helped the Loyalists prevent the Nationalists from capturing Madrid. This fact was a tremendous boost for the small Communist party of Spain. It enabled communists to secure important high-level military posts in the Loyalist army, increased the prestige of the party and hence its numerical strength, and permitted communist dictation of many Loyalist governmental policies.[35]

Nevertheless, direct military aid from the Soviet Union was not as great as the indirect aid given by the agents of the Comintern who used their connections and world-wide subversive organizations to purchase war materials for the Spanish government from Czechoslovakia, France, Japan, Poland, Holland, and even Nazi Germany.[36] It is impossible to assess accurately the amount of communist aid, but it is clear that it did not reach the magnitude of the aid given to the Nationalists by the Germans and Italians. Undoubtedly, during the first year of the war, over half of the military equipment used by the government troops came from communist sources, but what proportion came directly from the Soviet Union and what proportion from other nations has never been determined exactly. That communist aid saved the Republican government during 1936 and 1937 has never been questioned since almost all other

[32] Julian Gorkin, "Spain: First Test of a People's Democracy," *The Strategy of Deception: A Study in World-Wide Communist Tactics*, ed. J. Kirkpatrick (New York: Farrar Straus, 1963), p. 213.

[33] Gorkin points out that the military technicians sent by Russia during the first days of fighting, including the first Soviet ambassador to Spain and the Soviet consul-general at Barcelona, were recalled shortly to Moscow, accused of being traitors, and liquidated. *Ibid.*, p. 205.

[34] Cattell, *Communism and the Spanish Civil War*, p. 70.

[35] Franz Borkenau, *The Spanish Cockpit* (London: Faber & Faber, 1937), pp. 239–40.

[36] Walter G. Krivitsky, *In Stalin's Secret Service* (New York: Harper, 1939), pp. 78–87.

sources of supply had been cut.[37] Franco and his Italian and German benefactors would have conquered Spain much more quickly had it not been for such communist assistance.

The Conflict Ends

From beginning to end, the Spanish Civil War was a war of attrition. With ever increasing aid from Italy and Germany, the Nationalists gained territory slowly but relentlessly, while the Loyalists, in spite of an occasional outstanding victory, continued to retreat. By April 1938, the Russians had apparently realized that, no matter how much aid Italy and Germany sent to the Nationalists, the democracies would not massively aid the Loyalists. The Russian leaders were also aware that Italy and Germany had both committed so many troops and so much materiél to Franco that they would not leave Spain without a Nationalist victory, for to do so would have shattered both Hitler's and Mussolini's image of invincibility. Since Stalin had never been willing to commit the Soviet Union absolutely to a Loyalist victory, he decided at this point to end communist aid to Spain and concentrate Russian defenses against a potential attack from either Germany or Japan. By July 1938 most of the communist aid, whether from Russia or the Comintern, had virtually ceased.[38]

The situation in Republican Spain became desperate; there was no food, no heat, no medical supplies. The army was in rags, but it fought on until overwhelmed on all fronts, finally capitulating on March 31, 1939.[39] Thereafter, the Nationalist government began purging Republican soldiers and political leaders who had not escaped, either killing or placing them in concentration camps. It has been estimated that over twenty thousand Republicans were killed outright within a few months of the end of the war and that over two million were sent to Spanish concentration camps or prisons for periods ranging from a few months to life.[40] It was not until November 11, 1966, thirty years after the commencement of the war, that General Franco decreed a general pardon for all political crimes committed before and during the Civil War.[41]

Five months after the end of the Civil War, the confrontation between the democratic nations and the fascist nations, which Britain, France, and the United States had so carefully avoided in Spain, took place over Hitler's occupation of Poland.

[37] P. A. M. van Esch, *Prelude to War: The International Repercussions of the Spanish Civil War (1936–1939)* (The Hague: M. Nijhoff, 1951), pp. 70 ff.

[38] Cattell, *Communism and the Spanish Civil War*, pp. 90–96.

[39] On the final period of the war, see Alvarez del Vayo, *Freedom's Battle*, pp. 278 ff.; Thomas, *The Spanish Civil War*, pp. 581, 583.

[40] A. V. Phillips, *Spain under Franco* (London: Gollancz, 1940), p. 14.

[41] *New York Times,* November 12, 1966.

II. THE ROLE OF THE LAWS OF WAR IN THE CONDUCT OF THE SPANISH CIVIL WAR

Introduction

As early as the writings of Vattel in the middle of the eighteenth century, it was accepted customary law that both parties in a civil war had an obligation to observe the common laws of war.[1] Even though it took two centuries to reduce this customary law to codification,[2] in the Geneva Conventions of 1949, the obligation was no less valid. It was generally accepted by governments faced with civil war, as well as the parties seeking to overthrow such governments, that it was not legally permissible to murder, mutilate, torture, or otherwise mistreat persons taking no active part in hostilities. Although in many instances of civil war such actions did take place, they did not abrogate the customary law, for the possibility always exists that a legal order—municipal or international—may be violated.

Treatment of Prisoners of War

At the time of the Spanish Civil War, a large number of states, including Spain, were governed in relation to the treatment of prisoners of war by the convention concluded at Geneva on July 27, 1929, "Relative to the Treatment of Prisoners of War."[3] Persons entitled to the protection of this convention and hence to treatment as prisoners of war included regular armed forces personnel, members of the militia and volunteer corps (provided certain conditions were fulfilled), individuals who formed a part of a lawful *levée en masse*, and also noncombatant members of the armed forces, that is, authorized persons accompanying such forces such as war correspondents and contractors. Certain fundamental principles were announced to the effect that prisoners of war were "in the power of the hostile Government" rather than the individuals or corps which captured them, and it was demanded that such prisoners be humanely treated and protected and not be subject to reprisals. Respect for the persons and honor of prisoners of war was required. Women were to be treated with the consideration due to their sex. These and other provisions of a more specific nature concerning various aspects of the treatment to be afforded assured civilized and

---

[1] Emmerich de Vattell, *The Law of Nations or the Principles of International Law*, trans. of 1788 ed. by C. G. Fenwick (Washington, D. C.: Carnegie Institution, 1916), 3: 336, 338, 340.

[2] The Geneva Conventions of 1949 are contained in *Final Record of the Diplomatic Conference of Geneva of 1949* (Berne: Federal Political Department, 1949), 1: 205 ff.

[3] Manley O. Hudson, *International Legislation, 1929–1931* (Washington: Carnegie Endowment, 1936), 5: 20 ff. For discussion of the convention, see James W. Garner, "Recent Conventions for the Regulation of War," *American Journal of International Law* 26 (October 1932): 807.

humane treatment of prisoners of war. Unfortunately, the thousands of prisoners captured during the Spanish Civil War were not considered to be legally protected by this convention because they were not involved in an international war or war of an international character.[4]

To become an international war, civil conflict would at the very least have to ripen into an actual civil war or be identified as a state of belligerency.[5] It has been said that even a de facto civil war does not necessarily bring into operation the laws for the conduct of warfare. Only after belligerency has been recognized either by the legitimate government or possibly by a number of other states do the international rules of war govern.[6] During the Spanish civil strife, there was doubt whether even then the contending sides were actually obligated by international legal principles to apply such rules.[7] The Madrid government announced on August 9, 1936, that the four thousand prisoners which it held would be treated according to the military code for the treatment of war prisoners. It also declared certain areas to be zones of war and subject to blockade.[8] Padelford was of the opinion that such announcements constituted recognition of belligerency and belligerent rights despite the fact that later reports indicated a failure by the government to abide by its announcement.[9]

Although the application of the Geneva rules of 1929 relative to prisoners of war and their treatment may be limited to situations of belligerency, there is authority for the application of basic rules of humanity even in situations of insurgency, so that internal strife is to a degree restricted.[10] In this respect it has been stated:

[4] See Julius Stone, *Legal Control of International Conflicts* (2d ed.; London: Rinehart, 1959), p. 653.

[5] See pt. 3 on belligerency and insurgency, pp. 141–46.

[6] Lassa Oppenheim, *International Law*, ed. H. Lauterpacht (London: Longmans Green, 1952), 2: 209–10, 370 (n. 1).

[7] Padelford recognizes that the parties to a conflict should behave in accord with the rules but only in a war between states. Norman J. Padelford, "International Law and the Spanish Civil War," *American Journal of International Law*, 31 (April 1937): 228. On the other hand, Greenspan is of the opinion that belligerent status brings the rules of war into "full legal effect." Morris Greenspan, *The Modern Law of Land Warfare* (Berkeley: University of California Press, 1959), p. 18. See also Oppenheim, *International Law*, vol. 2, sec. 59.

[8] Padelford, "International Law and the Spanish Civil War," pp. 226–27.

[9] *Ibid.*, pp. 229–30.

[10] See, in accord, Vattell, *The Law of Nations*, 3: 336, 338, 340; Greenspan, *The Modern Law of Land Warfare*, p. 623; James W. Garner, "Questions of International Law in the Spanish Civil Strife," *American Journal of International Law* 31 (January 1937): 66. But note that the League of Nations in considering the Spanish civil strife condemned certain actions as violative of *humanitarian rights* generally. It did not declare such acts as violative of international law. Norman J. Padelford, *International Law and Diplomacy in the Spanish Civil Strife* (New York: Macmillan, 1939), p. 141. But see a later resolution of the League condemning the bombing of open towns during the civil strife and calling such conduct violative of international law. League of Nations, *Official Journal*, 19th Assembly, Plenary meetings, 1938, Special Supplement No. 183, pp. 135–36.

As regards relations of insurgents and parent state, it may be said that they must, so far as possible, observe the rules of civilized warfare. This is expedient for the parent state in order that it may maintain the respect of sister states, as well as give no ground for retaliation by the insurgents, and for the insurgents that they may, if successful, be more readily admitted into the family of nations.[11]

Thus a state of insurgency would require the observance of a bare minimum of humanitarian behavior by the parties in conflict. This is recognized by the later Geneva Convention of 1949, which provides detailed rules for treatment of prisoners in case of war—belligerency—including civil war as war of an international character if belligerency has been recognized.[12] In addition, minimum and fundamental standards of humanitarian conduct are prescribed for a conflict not of an international character, that is, a civil conflict in which the belligerency of the rebels has not been recognized.[13] These standards apply to persons who have taken no active part in the hostilities, including members of the armed forces who have laid down their arms or are incapacitated by sickness, wounds, detention, or any other cause. Such persons must be treated humanely with no adverse distinction based on race, color, religion or faith, sex, birth or wealth, or any similar criteria. In general, the convention prohibits violence to life and person and, in particular, murder, mutilation, cruel treatment, and torture. The taking of hostages is outlawed, as are outrages upon personal dignity and the passing of sentences and carrying out of executions without previous judgment pronounced by a regularly constituted court affording all judicial guarantees recognized by civilized peoples. Further, the convention commands that the sick and wounded be collected and cared for.

If, as Padelford contends, a state of belligerency was recognized by the Republican government, then the 1929 Geneva rules concerning treatment of prisoners of war should have been applicable. If, on the other hand, belligerency was not recognized, then insurgency in Spain should have demanded the observance by the contending factions of minimum customary rules of humanity in the treatment of prisoners of war, perhaps similar to the minimum civilized standards later developed in the 1949 convention.

[11] George Grafton Wilson, *International Law* (3d ed.; St. Paul: West, 1939), p. 41.

[12] Arts. 2 and 3 of the convention, which is contained in *Final Record of the Diplomatic Conference of Geneva of 1949*, 1: 243. For a discussion, see Jean S. Pictet, "The New Geneva Conventions of 1949," *American Journal of International Law* 46 (July 1951): 462.

[13] On the meaning of an armed conflict not of an international character, see Greenspan, *The Modern Law of Land Warfare*, p. 621; Oppenheim, *International Law*, 2: 370 ff.; Raymund T. Yingling and Robert W. Ginnance, "The Geneva Conventions of 1949," *American Journal of International Law* 46 (July 1951): 395–96.

Unfortunately, neither the laws of civilized warfare nor the rules of humanity were observed in Spain to any great extent. As mentioned before, the Republicans stated that they would treat prisoners of war according to the military code and then failed to do so. The Nationalist government declared that it respected and caused "to be respected, with the utmost scrupulousness, the laws and customs of warfare. . . ."[14] But this is obviously an extreme overstatement, contradicted by numerous reports to the contrary. Actually, the hostilities were carried on with ruthlessness by both factions.[15]

The outbreak of the Spanish struggle was particularly marked by terror and violence. Captive military prisoners were treated with savagery. In Madrid, militiamen tried officers captured in rebel barracks in summary courts and executed them. In other instances, officers and the defenders of rebel garrisons were shot without a semblance of trial. The Nationalists did not lack in fervor. Many, including captured officers loyal to the government, were shot arbitrarily, while others were given drumhead trials and then shot. After a battle between seamen loyal to the government and the insurgents on certain naval vessels, the loyal seamen were shot after the surrender of the vessels into insurgent hands.

With the development of actual battles, the ferocity continued. During the war's early period, few prisoners were taken during battle. Most of those who were captured were shot after a summary trial or with no trial at all. This state of affairs existed on both sides. Certain illustrative examples may be mentioned. At the battles of Alto de Leon and Somosierra, all prisoners were killed by both sides, and physicians were hard pressed to prevent wounded men from being shot. Although facts concerning the Battle of Badajoz are still controversial, it was reported that many disarmed Republican militiamen were executed and that their bodies were subjected to mutilation in the form of castration—a Moorish battle custom. Upon defeat of the Republican Catalan expeditionary force in Majorca by the Nationalists, the legionnaires executed most of the prisoners, and the wounded stationed in a convent were shot before the mother superior.

---

[14] As quoted in Padelford, *International Law and Diplomacy in the Spanish Civil Strife*, p. 597.

[15] For accounts and reports of treatment of prisoners by the two sides, accounts upon which the review herein is based, see Claude G. Bowers, *My Mission to Spain* (New York: Simon & Schuster, 1954), pp. 308–10, 349–51; Hugh Thomas, *The Spanish Civil War* (New York: Harper & Row, 1961), pp. 155–56, 160–70, 201–2, 204, 246–49, 253–54, 267–68, 284, 356–57, 471; Arnold J. Toynbee, "The International Repercussions of the War in Spain (1936–1937)," *Survey of International Affairs, 1937* (London: Oxford University Press, 1938), 2: 53, 84–86, 386; Toynbee, "The War in Spain and Its Repercussions," *Survey of International Affairs, 1938* (London: Oxford University Press, 1941), 1: 284–85, 389–91, 391–92.

Some of the terror had subsided by 1937. It was reported that the Republicans still executed prisoners of war who were members of fascist organizations or of the Civil Guard. Prisoners who could convince their Republican captors that they had been forced to fight for the Nationalists against their will were enrolled in the Republican army. In Nationalist Spain, outright execution of prisoners was said to have ceased by 1937 and judicial proceedings to have been instituted which at least created an appearance of justice. Prisoners of war not suspected of political offenses were either brought into the Nationalist army or put to work on public works or for private firms. Payment consisted of a small amount of pocket money and an allowance for dependents. Some three hundred thousand prisoners of war were said to be at work in Catalonia and southern Spain at the end of the war.[16]

In 1938 the Republican government proposed that each side should suspend execution of military prisoners for a month. Although agreement was not reached, the number of executions by both the Nationalists and Republicans seems to have been considerably reduced after this proposal. The Chetwode Commission claimed that it had persuaded the Republicans to stop the execution of prisoners and the Nationalists to remit some four hundred death sentences.[17]

Although international law imposes no obligation upon belligerents to exchange prisoners of war, such exchange may be carried out by special agreement as an act of convenience to the belligerents.[18] The International Red Cross and certain foreign governments sought to effect prisoner exchange in Spain. Some exchanges were secured, but none on a large scale. The Red Cross occasionally arranged for exchanges of individuals or small groups. In early 1938 forty-one Basque officers who had been sentenced to death were exchanged for an equal number of Nationalists held by the Republicans. The Chetwode Commission also made exchange arrangements, one of which involved one hundred British prisoners in Nationalist hands for one hundred Italians in Republican hands. Ambassador Claude G. Bowers of the United States arranged an exchange of certain Americans of the Lincoln Brigade captured by the Nationalists for an equal number of Italians in the hands of the Republic. Such exchanges hardly dented the prisoner problem, however, for military and civilian prisoners held by the two factions numbered many thousands.[19]

---

[16] Toynbee, "The War in Spain and Its Repercussions," 1: 209.

[17] *Ibid.*, p. 285. See also Thomas, *The Spanish War*, p. 559.

[18] Greenspan, *The Modern Law of Land Warfare*, p. 148; Charles Cheney Hyde, *International Law Chiefly as Interpreted and Applied by the United States* (2d rev. ed.; Boston: Little Brown & Co.), 3: 1857.

[19] See Toynbee, "The War in Spain and Its Repercussions," 1: 391–93; Thomas, *The Spanish Civil War*, p. 559; Bowers, *My Mission to Spain*, p. 393; Marcel Junod, *Warrior without Weapons* (New York: The Macmillan Co., 1951), chap. 8.

The Red Cross was never able to obtain from either the Republicans or the Nationalists prisoner lists and regular prison visitation. The Red Cross was permitted by both sides to establish a message service so that families of the fighting men would know whether they were alive or dead.[20]

With the end of the war, captured and surrendering soldiers, guerrillas, and political prisoners were court-martialed for military rebellion by the triumphant Nationalists in groups of twenty to thirty persons per day in the many camps in which they were held and then executed. Thousands of men died during this period, and thousands of others died later in labor camps of disease, lack of food, and overwork.[21]

Protection of Civilians and Property

According to the 1907 Hague Regulations Concerning the Laws and Customs of Land Warfare, which were applicable at the time of the Spanish Civil War, belligerents were to accord certain protection to civilians in the fighting zones and in occupied territory. Such personal protection included respect for family honor and rights, life, and religious convictions and worship. Outright killing, wounding, and maltreating of civilians were prohibited. Compulsion to take part in military operations and military labor or to furnish information concerning the army or means of defense of the other country was banned, as were compelled oaths of allegiance to the hostile power.[22]

The Hague Regulations contained no direct mention of hostages.[23] States have taken hostages at various times and for various purposes: to ensure against certain acts by the enemy, particularly unlawful acts, to ensure proper treatment of the sick and wounded left behind in hostile territory, to protect the lives of prisoners who have fallen into the hands of irregular troops, to protect lines of communications through occupied territory, and to secure compliance with requisition and contributions. With respect to the execution of hostages, the law was subject to some controversy and difference of opinion. The legality of taking hostages

[20] These principles are set forth in arts. 77, 79, and 86 of the 1929 Geneva convention. Hudson, *International Legislation*, vol. 5. For a discussion of their application to Spain, see Gabriel Jackson, *The Spanish Republic and the Civil War, 1931–1939* (Princeton: Princeton University Press, 1965), p. 435.

[21] Jackson, *The Spanish Republic and the Civil War*, pp. 536–39.

[22] Arts. 46, 23(h), 52, 44, and 45 respectively. The Convention Regarding the Laws and Customs of Land Warfare and the Annex to the Convention, Regulations Concerning the Laws and Customs of Land Warfare, are set forth in *American Journal of International Law*, Supplement (1908), 2: 91, 97.

[23] For a discussion of the taking of hostages, see Greenspan, *The Modern Law of Land Warfare*, pp. 413 ff.; Erik Johannes S. Castrén, *The Present Law of War and Neutrality* (Helsinki: Annales Academiae Scientiarum Fenicas, 1954), pp. 76 ff.

was generally founded upon article 43 of the Hague Regulations Concerning the Laws and Customs of Land Warfare, which called upon the military occupant of enemy territory to restore and ensure public order within such territory. To carry out this command, the killing of hostages was permissible as a last resort when all other measures had failed.[24] Other authority condemned the killing of hostages as a violation of rules of humanity and, although possibly recognizing that they could be held captive, advanced the further belief that they should be treated as prisoners of war during their captivity and not executed even in those cases in which the enemy might have violated the laws of war.[25]

As for civilians and their imprisonment by a belligerent in the fighting areas or as occupant of enemy territory, the general rule prohibited the detention of civilians as prisoners of war. In certain instances, however, international law permitted their imprisonment. Thus private enemy persons were subject to detention if the safety of the belligerent's armed forces so demanded or if such persons were causing harm to the belligerent's forces. Interference with the conduct of war in the fighting zone justified imprisonment, as did failure to obey the legal orders of the military authorities designed to preserve order and tranquility of the enemy territory. Persons rising *en masse* to defend their territory could be imprisoned. High civil functionaries of government were subject to imprisonment, as were influential citizens of the enemy state who incited their people to resistance.[26]

The 1907 Hague Regulations also contained principles for the protection of private property in war time. Respect for private property was required of the belligerents and its confiscation was prohibited. Looting was forbidden. Article 23(g) of the rules further forbade the seizure or destruction of enemy property unless it was "imperiously demanded by the necessities of war." Since certain types of property were peculiarly adapted to warlike purposes, their seizure was permitted, provided restoration and compensation were given when peace came. The occupying army could also seize movable property of the enemy government that

[24] Castrén, *The Present Law of War and Neutrality*, p. 78; Hyde, *International Law*, 2: 1903; and *The Hostage Case (U.S. v. List et al.)*, U.S. Military Court, TWC, XI Judgment rendered February, 1948. *The Hostage Case*, which was one of the Nuremberg War Trials, held that hostages taken to guarantee the peaceful conduct of civilians in occupied territory could under certain conditions and as a last resort be shot. But see U.S. Department of the Army Field Manual, *The Law of Land Warfare* (Washington, 1956), sec. 273, which now forbids the taking of hostages.

[25] See, for example, Oppenheim, *International Law*, 2: 591; Greenspan, *The Modern Law of Land Warfare*, pp. 415 ff.; Arthur K. Kuhn, "The Execution of Hostages," *American Journal of International Law* 36 (April 1942): 271.

[26] See Oppenheim, *International Law*, 2: 346–47; Hyde, *International Law*, 2: 1861.

could be used in military operations, but as for real property owned by the enemy government, the occupying authority was regarded as an administrator and usufructuary only. The property of municipalities, as well as that devoted to religion, charity and education, and the arts and sciences, even when owned by the state, was to be treated as private property. Seizure, destruction, or intentional injury of such property, and also of historic monuments and works of art or science, was forbidden.[27]

The Hague Regulations applied only to wars of an international character, and even here the rules were vague concerning the treatment of private enemy persons and their property. Civil strife—at least until it had matured to a state of belligerency—was thus almost unregulated by positive rules of international law. Only the most basic and fundamental humanitarian requirements protected the civilian population from the contending factions. The 1949 Geneva Convention Relative to the Protection of Civilian Persons in Time of War, like the Prisoners of War Convention of the same year, now requires each party to an armed conflict not of an international character to accord the minimum of fundamental rights of humanity to civilians taking no active part in the hostilities. Certain of the proscriptions are similar to the humanitarian requirements of customary international law, such as the bans on murder, cruel treatment, mutilation, torture, outrages upon personal dignity, and executions and sentences unless imposed by a regularly constituted court, acting in accord with civilized judicial procedures. The former Hague rules calling for respect for religious convictions and worship are also included. The treaty's outright prohibition of the taking of hostages can hardly be said to have been based on customary international law or earlier treaties, since the Hague Regulations did not clearly prohibit the practice and there was some authority even for killing hostages in certain circumstances. At the time of the Spanish Civil War the rules of warfare concerning the imprisonment of civilians in time of war probably reflected a bare minimum of humanitarian requirements which may also have been applicable in time of civil strife. Whether this was also true for the treatment of property is a subject for speculation.

Few of the bare requirements of humanity and civilized conduct have been observed in civil wars which, in the twentieth century, have proved to be the most bitter and savage types of armed conflicts. The Spanish Civil War was no exception. The savagery on both sides was based on hatred and fears generated in large degree by the Spanish character itself. "From the very first, the war in Spain became a tragic example of what an English correspondent in Andalusia described as 'the peculiar

---

[27] Arts. 46, 47, 53, 55, and 56 respectively, of the Hague Regulations, as contained in *American Journal of International Law*, Supplement (1908), 2: 97.

attitude—a combination of fatalism, exaltation and delight in all de-struction—which Spaniards have toward death.' "[28]

At various times during the course of the war, appeals were made by third parties to secure greater regard for humanitarian principles by the two sides. The British government, for example, in deploring the treatment of the civilian population, conveyed to both sides a strong disapproval of the use of methods "which have earned public condemnation and are contrary to the rules of international law."[29] The heads of missions of nine other countries also sought to intercede to humanize the conflict.

The idea of the Heads of Diplomatic Missions has been to protect the civil population from suffering, which consists notably in the imprisonment of hostages and other non-combatants, in the danger to public health caused by lack of medicines, water and light, and in the loss of life resulting from the bombardment of undefended towns. They also desire measures to be taken to preserve the monuments and works of art which reflect the grandeur and the glories of the past.[30]

The Nonintervention Committee in 1937 also sought to obtain respect for principles of humanity in the conduct of the conflict in order to lessen "the cruel sufferings inflicted upon the civilian population."[31] These entreaties had little effect, for at the beginning of the civil conflict a wave of violence covered Spain. The revolution started with murder and destruction on a grand scale. Militia units of the various predominant political groups sprang into being and became known as "murder gangs." These units conducted terroristic operations, killing without trial those they considered to be their class enemies. The lives of those suspected of sympathy with the insurgent cause were forfeit.

In the larger towns investigation committees called "Chekas" were set up by various unions and political parties. Their self-imposed duty was to round up, try, and execute or imprison Nationalist suspects. Their methods hardly paralleled those of civilized judicial proceedings. In fact, their sentences of death could be considered as arbitrary murders. The government of Republican Spain eventually set up special tribunals for the administration of law, but the Chekas continued to act against those they considered enemies. The central government was powerless during the early months of the war to prevent these illegal killings, although it

---

[28] As quoted from the *Manchester Guardian* by Toynbee, "The International Repercussions of the War in Spain," 2: 80.

[29] *Ibid.*, p. 377.

[30] *Ibid.*, p. 378.

[31] *Ibid.*, p. 381. This statement is also set forth in Norman J. Padelford, *International Law and Diplomacy in the Spanish Civil Strife* (New York: Macmillan Co., 1939), p. 95, n. 109.

did issue appeals for a cessation of the terrorism. It was not until 1937 that the violent stage, the period of terrorism, was brought under control in Republican Spain.[32]

Much of the fury in Republican Spain vented itself against the church. Some seven thousand Roman Catholic Church officials were killed, accounting for many of the reported atrocities of the war.[33] Church buildings were subjected to looting and burning. Those left standing were closed. The free exercise of religion was proscribed, and this abridgment of religious freedom was to continue in Republican Spain during the course of the conflict. Although some religious toleration eventually reemerged, there was never any general reopening of the churches. Religious services were eventually permitted in private houses by certain government-licensed priests, and the Basque leaders, after their defeat and removal to Barcelona, were permitted to hold religious services in their headquarters. On returning from exile in 1938, many priests were forced to dress as laymen. Despite some measures of relaxation, there was no formal reestablishment of religion.[34]

Large numbers of political prisoners were taken and held by Republican authorities. Captured political leaders of the right were either killed or sent to prison. Some ten thousand persons were held in Barcelona alone in the spring of 1938. Many of them were imprisoned in three ships in the harbor, where they were exposed to Nationalist air raids.[35] Political prisoners numbering three thousand were held in the model prison in Madrid. On August 23, 1936, militiamen stormed the building and massacred some seventy of the most eminent prisoners. Later, during the siege of Madrid, there was a wholesale massacre by the guards of most of the remaining prisoners in the model prison when they were being transferred to another prison. Eventually, nearly all of the political prisoners held in Madrid were executed.[36]

In spite of denials by various governmental authorities, hostages were taken by the Republican side and were subject to reprisals, particularly when passions ran high after air raids by Nationalists or Nationalist victories.[37] At San Sebastián and Irun in August 1936, hostages were

[32] For a description of the revolutionary terror in Republican Spain, see Toynbee, "The International Repercussions of the War in Spain," 2: 80–84; Jackson, *The Spanish Republic and the Civil War*, pp. 276 ff.; Thomas, *The Spanish Civil War*, pp. 171 ff., 184 ff.

[33] For statistics concerning the killing of churchmen, see Thomas, *The Spanish Civil War*, p. 174.

[34] *Ibid.*, p. 495. See also Toynbee, "The War in Spain and Its Repercussions," 1: 281, 282, 286–87.

[35] Toynbee, "The War in Spain and Its Repercussions," 1: 382.

[36] Thomas, *The Spanish Civil War*, p. 268.

[37] The Republican government described the prisoners as political prisoners, not hostages. Toynbee, "The International Repercussions of the War in Spain," 2: 385–86.

held in places likely to be bombed. At a fort near Irun where some two hundred hostages were held, four were reported shot on August 19 and another nine on September 4. Some forty-five to fifty prisoners were shot in Malaga on August 23 after air raids. When Nationalist naval forces threatened to shell San Sebastián, the colonel in charge promised to shoot a certain number of prisoners for each death from the bombardment. The Nationalist ships attacked on August 17, causing the death of four persons and the wounding of others; eight hostages were shot. Later in the year some one hundred hostages who had been moved to Bilbao from San Sebastián and other prisoners were shot after air raids on the city. Another example of the killing of hostages occurred near the end of the war. After the fall of Barcelona, the retreating Republican army murdered a number of hostages who had been taken along from the prisons of Barcelona just before it crossed the French border.[38]

Property rights of class enemies were little respected in Republican Spain. With the outbreak of the civil strife, a revolution within a revolution took place in areas remaining loyal to the Republic, and the properties of the right wing—lands, houses, hotels, newspapers, and factories—were subjected to confiscation by the left wing political groups controlling the municipalities. Those in authority in Madrid took over the properties of persons who favored the Nationalist cause. Not only their residences but also their bank accounts, jewels, and other articles of private wealth were confiscated. According to reports, some 330 million pesetas, or 8 million pounds in money and securities, were confiscated in all Spain, as well as gold and jewels in the amount of 100 million pesetas, or 2½ million pounds.[39] All foreign businesses were taken over by the government, but many were restored to their owners if they had not been incorporated in Spain. The extent of the takeover of private property varied with the locality. The activity in Barcelona and Catalonia was largely subject to the direction of the Anarchists. Here the requisition of hotels, stores, banks, and factories was the rule. In Catalonia and in Republican Aragon, the municipalities appropriated the houses and lands of the middle class. In certain areas of Andalusia, private property was entirely abolished, whereas in Basque territories, a middle class social order continued, with only the properties of capitalists who had taken the Nationalist side in the rebellion being appropriated.[40]

The strong anticlerical feeling in much of Republican Spain caused

[38] On hostages and reprisals against them, see *ibid.*, pp. 86–87; Toynbee, "The War in Spain and Its Repercussions," 1: 394; Jackson, *The Spanish Republic and The Civil War*, pp. 285–86, 342–43; Thomas, *The Spanish Civil War*, p. 249.

[39] Thomas, *The Spanish Civil War*, p. 185.

[40] For a discussion of the confiscation of property, see *ibid.*, pp. 171, 185 ff.; Jackson, *The Spanish Republic and the Civil War*, pp. 278 ff.

widespread destruction of churches and church property at the beginning of the conflict, but the great works of Spanish art and literature were for the most part saved. An exception was the burning of some ten thousand volumes of the library of the Cuenca Cathedral.[41] As the war progressed, the Republican government acted to safeguard the artistic heritage of the nation against the rigors of war. Pictures, tapestries, and other great works were packed and stored in places of safety. When all areas became unsafe, the Republican government and a special committee arranged to remove some of the most valuable works to Geneva. There they were placed under the trusteeship of the secretary-general of the League of Nations and were returned to Spain after the war's end.[42]

The treatment of civilians sympathetic to the Republican cause in Nationalist Spain also departed from norms of civilized conduct. In the territory controlled by the insurgents, violent purges were instituted against those of their fellow Spaniards whom they regarded as the enemy. Freemasons, liberals, members of Popular Front parties, and trade unionists were arrested and many were executed. Governmental officials, if they had been appointed by the Republican government, were almost always shot, as were those who sought to maintain the general strike when the conflict commenced. It was a holy war by the insurgents to wipe out liberal and leftist elements. A Nationalist official gave as an example a town described as "red" in which the whole population had been imprisoned and many executed.[43] These killings were not ordinarily those of revolutionary mobs, like those that had occurred in the early period of the uprising in Republican Spain. They were the work of Nationalist military commanders who believed that ruthless action was requisite to maintain order, destroy the enemy, and cleanse Spain of heretical beliefs. Thomas estimates that the Nationalist executions during the war approximated forty thousand.[44] In the beginning, the enemies of the Nationalist regime were shot without trial. A little later emergency tribunals were constituted which gave the captured some right of defense. By the beginning of 1937, a council of war had been established to try such cases, and it at least created a pretense of justice. Sentences were still given for political reasons, however.[45]

Upon conquest of Republican cities and territories, the Nationalists mercilessly proscribed the Republican sympathizers. Malaga provides a notable example. Upon Republican defeat and Nationalist occupation of that city, Republican sympathizers—whose names had been compiled on

[41] Thomas, *The Spanish Civil War*, p. 185.
[42] Toynbee, "The War in Spain and Its Repercussions," 1: 412–13.
[43] As quoted in Junod, *Warrior without Weapons*, p. 81.
[44] Thomas, *The Spanish Civil War*, p. 168.
[45] For accounts of Nationalist killings, see *ibid.*, pp. 165 ff., 365 ff.; Toynbee, "The War in Spain and Its Repercussions," 2: 84–86, 1: 389–91; Jackson, *The Spanish Republic and the Civil War*, pp. 293 ff.

a long Nationalist list—became subject to the death penalty. Some were shot immediately. Others were imprisoned and then tried under crowded court conditions by the council of war, consisting of three military judges. After being sentenced to death for military rebellion, the convicted were loaded into trucks and carried to the edge of the city, where they were shot by firing squads. Italian authorities present were said to have been "horrified at the number of executions and the mutilations practiced on the corpses. . . ."[46] Some one hundred thousand persons attempted to flee the city along a coastal road to Almería. Nationalist tanks followed them, apprehending many. The men were shot, but the women were permitted to go free. The Nationalist navy and air force fired upon the refugees, as did German warships.[47]

The defeat of the Basques and the pacification of the north of Spain were also accompanied by fierce repression by the Nationalists. Fearing this, the Basque leaders at Santoña sought to surrender to the Italians and received assurance that the lives of Basque fighters would be guaranteed, that Basque authorities would be permitted to leave the country, and that the Basque population would not be subjected to political persecution. But the surrender terms were not honored. Franco gave orders that no one was to leave Santoña, and Basques departing the country were removed from ships in the harbor and imprisoned. Executions then took place.[48] Conquests of other areas in Basque country were also followed by executions. By November 1937 it was said that one thousand persons had been killed and that eleven thousand were under death sentence. Eighty Basques were shot in December without trial, several of them women and churchmen. It was reported that the latter were executed within minutes of the handing down of sentence and were buried without coffins. These and similar examples were all too common.[49] Actually, the Nationalist executions of political offenders during and after the civil war, including not only civilians but soldiers and guerrillas executed after capture or surrender, constituted the greatest single category of deaths in the conflict.[50]

Since the Nationalist movement proclaimed itself the guardian of Spain's conservative tradition and its deliverer from atheism, and since the Catholic church by and large supported the insurgent side, persecution of the church was not a policy of Nationalist Spain, as it was of Republican Spain.[51] There were reports of attacks upon and persecution

[46] As quoted in Jackson, *The Spanish Republic and the Civil War*, p. 343.

[47] *Ibid.*, pp. 343–45; Thomas, *The Spanish Civil War*, p. 373.

[48] See Thomas, *The Spanish Civil War*, p. 471; Bowers, *My Mission to Spain*, pp. 343–45.

[49] Thomas, *The Spanish Civil War*, p. 483.

[50] Jackson, *The Spanish Republic and the Civil War*, p. 538.

[51] Toynbee, "The International Repercussions of the War in Spain," 2: 297–98; Jackson, *The Spanish Republic and the Civil War*, pp. 307–9, 422–23.

of Protestants and Protestant ministers, however, and religious freedom did not exist in Nationalist areas.[52] After the conquest of the Basques, who had remained loyal to the Republic and yet were ardent Catholics, the Nationalists did conduct a campaign of persecution against Basque church officials. Many were imprisoned and others were exiled to other parts of the country. Some sixteen were executed.[53]

Large numbers of civilian adherents to the Republic were imprisoned by the Nationalists. There were mass court-martials of persons charged with complicity in the Popular Front government. Sentences of imprisonment were usually given, although later many of such prisoners were shot.[54] A decree of 1939 provided for imprisonment of persons guilty of subversive activities. It was retroactive to 1934, and subversion was understood to include those who had taken part in the formation of the Popular Front, as well as those on the Republican side during the war. It also applied to Freemasons, regional separatists, and those who had left Spain during the war.[55]

There were thousands of political prisoners in Nationalist prisons and camps at the end of the war, and those not executed were held in labor camps on long prison sentences. The health and food conditions of such camps were apparently far from good, for large numbers died of disease, overwork, and undernourishment.[56]

The Nationalists, like the Republicans, also held prisoners as hostages and indulged in reprisals. The Nationalist defenders of the Alcazar took many persons associated with left wing politics into that fortress when it was under Republican siege. The number taken has been estimated at from twenty to one hundred. In another instance, a civil guard unit loyal to the insurgents was able to hold out for some time against Loyalist units by using wives and children of trade union members as human barricades. In order to assure good behavior by hostile communities, the people were warned that hostages from their community would be executed if anyone aided the enemy. When the Republicans executed the leader of the Falange, the Nationalists put to death the son of Largo Caballero, the Republican prime minister, whom they held in prison.[57]

Revolution did not occur in Nationalist-held territory at the beginning

---

[52] *The Spectator*, November 6, 1936, p. 813; *The New Statesman and Nation*, November 14, 1936, pp. 763–64; Thomas, *The Spanish Civil War*, p. 450.

[53] *Ibid.* See also Jackson, *The Spanish Republic and the Civil War*, pp. 377, 385–87.

[54] Toynbee, "The War in Spain and Its Repercussions," 1: 392; Thomas, *The Spanish Civil War*, pp. 165 ff., 356 ff.

[55] Toynbee, "The War in Spain and Its Repercussions," 1: 290–91.

[56] Jackson, *The Spanish Republic and the Civil War*, pp. 537–38.

[57] On these and other episodes, see *ibid.*, pp. 271, 302; Thomas, *The Spanish Civil War*, pp. 156–57, 205, 353; Toynbee, "The International Repercussions of the War in Spain," 2: 56.

of the conflict, as it did in Republican areas. Thus, there was not the same destruction of property. Arbitrary confiscation of property from those arrested for their leftist views and Popular Front connections did take place, however, from the very beginning. Special sequestration commissions were later set up to carry out the confiscations, and the Nationalist decree of 1939, enacted to punish the opposition for subversion, listed confiscation of property among the punishments.[58]

From this summary, it can be seen that uncivilized and inhuman practices were the order of the day in Spain during the conflict with respect to the treatment of noncombatant civilians. There were only a few bright spots. The care with which the Republicans sought to preserve Spain's art treasures can be mentioned, as well as their admission of the International Red Cross to aid the emigration of noncombatants in the Republican zone and to aid widows of men who were killed in that area during the early period of the conflict. The Red Cross was also able to effect a very limited number of exchanges of noncombatants held as prisoners and hostages by each side.[59]

Avoidance of Nonmilitary Targets

The Hague Regulations Concerning the Laws and Customs of Land Warfare prohibited the attack or bombardment of "undefended cities, villages, dwellings, or buildings, whatever be the means employed," which would include bombardment from aircraft.[60] Naval bombardment was also forbidden.[61] The land warfare regulations further demanded that precaution be taken to spare, as far as possible, buildings devoted to religious worship, to the arts and sciences, to charity, and to hospitals and places where the sick and wounded were collected, and also historical monuments unless they were used for military purposes. The besieged were called upon to designate these places by special visible signs, which were to be previously brought to the attention of the besieger. Further, warning was to be given to the civil population in areas where bombardment was to take place so that noncombatants might take shelter or remove themselves before the bombing began.[62]

The regulations proscribing bombardment of undefended towns, vil-

---

[58] Toynbee, "The International Repercussions of the War in Spain," 2: 85; Toynbee, "The War in Spain and Its Repercussions," 1: 290–91; Thomas, *The Spanish Civil War*, pp. 356 ff.

[59] On the efforts of the Red Cross, see Junod, *Warrior without Weapons*, pp. 93 ff.; Jackson, *The Spanish Republic and the Civil War*, pp. 430 ff.; Toynbee, "The War in Spain and Its Repercussions," 1: 391 ff.

[60] Art. 25, as contained in *American Journal of International Law*, Supplement (1908), 2: 97. See also Greenspan, *The Modern Law of Land Warfare*, p. 332.

[61] Art. 1, Convention Respecting Bombardments by Naval Forces in Time of War, *American Journal of International Law*, Supplement (1908), 2: 146.

[62] Arts. 26 and 27, in *ibid.*, p. 97.

lages, dwellings, or buildings failed to define the word "undefended," which in practice made the prohibition of little value. With the development of long-range artillery and the airplane, areas far beyond the fighting fronts were involved in warfare.[63] With a view to protecting the civilian populations from indiscriminate air bombardment, a commission of jurists drew up the Hague Rules of Air Warfare in 1923.[64] This draft code would have prohibited air bombardment for the purpose of terrorizing the civilian population, destroying nonmilitary property, injuring noncombatants, and enforcing requisitions in kind and contributions. Aerial bombardment was considered legitimate only when it was directed at a military objective, an objective whose destruction would constitute a "distinct military advantage to the belligerent." Certain legitimate objectives were listed, such as military establishments, munitions and military supply factories, and lines of communications or transportation used for military purposes. Even these were excluded if they could not be bombarded without the indiscriminate bombardment of civilians. Bombardment of cities, villages, towns, dwellings, or buildings not in the immediate neighborhood of the operations of land forces was prohibited, and where there was such a military concentration, it had to be sufficiently important to justify such bombardment.[65]

Although this code of aerial warfare was not adopted as a multipartite international agreement, it has had persuasive authority as a guide to rules of aerial combat.[66] Its prohibition of indiscriminate bombing of civilian populations, although not formally adopted, now forms part of international law. At the time of the Spanish Civil War, most jurists considered aerial bombardment of civilian populations exclusively to terrorize them as outlawed unless in reprisal or in connection with the destruction of military objectives located in civilian centers.[67] Although the code was thought to be primarily applicable to international wars, it would also seem to express a principle of humanity and civilized conduct and thus to be applicable in times of civil strife.

There were some reports of attempts to avoid nonmilitary targets and to protect noncombatants from direct attack in the Spanish conflict. A safety zone of a middle class residential area which was not to be shelled was marked out by General Franco upon the occasion of the assault against Madrid by the Nationalists. The Nationalist forces were ordered not to bombard an area where the evacuation by ship of noncombatants

[63] For a discussion of when a town may be considered open or undefended, see Greenspan, *The Modern Law of Land Warfare*, pp. 332 ff.

[64] These rules are contained in *American Journal of International Law*, Supplement (1938), 32: 1.

[65] Arts. 22, 23, and 24, in *ibid.*

[66] See Greenspan, *The Modern Law of Land Warfare*, p. 334; Oppenheim, *International Law*, 2: 519.

[67] Oppenheim, *International Law*, 2: 524–25; Hyde, *International Law*, 3: 1829.

was being effected by foreign consuls in Bilbao. The Nationalists protested against the removal of refugees and offered instead to provide a neutral zone where they could reside; but this offer was rejected by the Basque authorities. Both the Republicans and the Nationalists generally respected the Red Cross emblem on hospitals, although there were some infractions.[68]

On the other hand, there were what appear to be many deliberate and direct attacks on nonmilitary targets in violation of principles of international law and humanity. Such transgressions were ordinarily denied, or an attempt was made to justify them on grounds of military necessity or reprisals. Thus, despite the safety zone which was established in one area of Madrid, the city was, during the siege, a target of Nationalist air and artillery bombardment. During the period of one week, one thousand people were killed. Fires were started in many parts of the city by incendiary bombs. General Franco remarked that he would destroy the city rather than leave it to the Marxists. It was reported that the bombing attacks were conducted in such a way as to cause civilian panic and were mounted in part to satisfy German advisers who were studying the civilian reaction to such attacks. The Nationalists justified their bombardment by stating that barracks and ammunition dumps were located in various spots all around the city and that the Republicans had also bombed towns.[69]

A flagrant violation of the principle barring direct attack on noncombatants occurred when the Nationalists bombarded by air and sea the refugees fleeing Malaga via a coast road after the city fell to Nationalist forces. The German navy assisted in this shelling.[70] German warships also shelled the Spanish port of Almería; nineteen deaths resulted and thirty-five buildings were destroyed. This attack was said to be in reprisal for the bombing of a German cruiser in the Spanish Nationalist port of Ibiza by a Republican aircraft. The German warship was a part of the nonintervention patrol, although the legality of such patrols in Spanish territorial waters had not been recognized by the Spanish Republican government. The Republicans claimed the right to carry out acts of war in Spanish waters and called the German attack on Almería not reprisal but aggression.[71]

[68] On these actions, see Jackson, *The Spanish Republic and the Civil War*, p. 430; Toynbee, "The International Repercussions of the War in Spain," 2: 393–94.

[69] On the bombing of Madrid during the siege, see Toynbee, "The International Repercussions of the War in Spain," 2: 61–62, 66–67; Thomas, *The Spanish Civil War*, pp. 317–18, 329.

[70] See Jackson, *The Spanish Republic and the Civil War*, pp. 344–45.

[71] For the Spanish note charging aggression, see Padelford, *International Law and Diplomacy in the Spanish Civil Strife*, p. 94, n. 104; on the Almería incident itself, see Toynbee, "The International Repercussions of the War in Spain," 2: 226, 312–13.

The Nationalist general in charge of the Basque campaign promised "to raze Viscaya [a Basque province] to the ground, beginning with the industries of war."[72] True to his word, villages along the front line were subjected to dive-bombing attacks, as was the town of Durango, a road and rail junction situated between Bilbao and the front. Durango may have had some military value, but the fact that the town was not only bombed but machine-gunned indicated that the primary objective was to terrorize the civilian population.[73]

German aviators, on April 26, 1937, conducted the world-shocking air raid on Guernica, a small town of seven thousand people celebrated since medieval times as the home of Basque liberties and traditions and the place where Spanish kings swore to respect the ancient laws of the Basques. It is at least conceivable that Guernica might have been regarded as a valid military objective. It did have a barracks and a munitions factory on its outskirts, and it was a communications center not too far from the front. On the other hand, it was said to be without defenses; no troops were concentrated there, and it was not on the Nationalist military line of march to the city of Bilbao. It appears, therefore, that the purpose of the air raid and bombardment was not the destruction of a military target but to terrorize the civilian population. Guernica was a testing ground of the reactions to and results of such attacks. The German airplanes first bombed the town, then machine-gunned the inhabitants as they attempted to escape, and finally set the town afire with incendiary bombs. The center of town was destroyed, 1,654 people were killed, and some 889 were wounded. Ironically, the barracks and the munitions factory were undamaged. Hitler declared that the Nationalist authorities were responsible for the bombing. The Nationalists denied it and accused the Republicans themselves of destroying the town so as to place the blame on the Nationalists. The responsibility of the Nationalists and Germans, however, seems fully verified.[74]

In early 1938, both sides increased their air attacks. Nationalist air raids on Valencia brought retaliatory air raids by the Republicans on Salamanca, Seville, Ceuta, and Valladolid. Nationalist retaliatory raids were increased in turn, particularly against Barcelona. Within the space of a few days, Barcelona suffered several air raids. The two raids of Jan-

---

[72] Statement of General Mola quoted in Thomas, *The Spanish Civil War*, p. 403. The campaign against the Basques is described by George L. Steer, *The Tree of Guernica* (London: Hodder, 1938).

[73] Thomas, *The Spanish Civil War*, p. 403.

[74] For accounts of the attack, see *ibid.*, pp. 419–22; Toynbee, "The International Repercussions of the War in Spain," 2: 68–72; Jackson, *The Spanish Republic and the Civil War*, pp. 381–82. See also Edgar Allison Peers, *Spain in Eclipse, 1937–1943* (2d ed.; London: Methuen, 1945), who takes the Nationalist side and accepts the Nationalist explanations (pp. 3–4).

uary 30 were said to have killed some three hundred fifty people and to have injured seven hundred. Nationalist raids on Republican towns were to continue until the end of the war. Many of them could hardly be justified as being directed against military objectives, and appear to have been deliberately ordered against defenseless populations. For example, destructive raids were directed against Alicante. Some of the raids were conducted against the port and railway station, which were the only conceivable military targets in the town, but at least two of the attacks were deliberately aimed at exclusive residential areas. Some of the attacks on Barcelona and other places were described at the time as deliberately aimed at the civilian population or were, although directed at military targets, impossible to carry out without jeopardizing the civilian population and therefore equivalent to deliberate civilian attacks.[75]

These practices caused considerable condemnation by world opinion and appeals to the combatants to cease such conduct. As early as August 21, 1936, the nine heads of mission who were urging humanitarian measures pleaded for prevention of "the bombardment of undefended towns."[76] In April 1937, after the air attacks on Guernica and other Basque towns, the British suggested that the Nonintervention Committee appeal to the two fighting factions "to abandon the practice of bombing open towns."[77] On June 18 the committee finally made such an appeal.[78] In May 1937 the Council of the League of Nations had condemned the use of methods of warfare violative of international law and singled out particularly the bombing of open towns.[79]

These appeals seem to have had little effect, however, since, as mentioned above, the bombings were later intensified. After the increase in air bombardments in early 1938, particularly after the destructive bombing of Barcelona in February 1938, protests were registered by Britain and France and also by the Pope.[80] In June a statement was issued by the government of the United States, protesting against the bombing of unfortified localities and areas with large populations. Such bombings were described as barbarous and against principles of law and humanity.[81] The British-French appeals drew some response from the Republi-

[75] For accounts of these raids, see Thomas, *The Spanish Civil War*, pp. 513, 523–24; Toynbee, "The War in Spain and Its Repercussions," 1: 271–72, 403–13.

[76] The statement is quoted in Toynbee, "The International Repercussions of the War in Spain," 2: 378–79.

[77] *Ibid.*, p. 380.

[78] *Ibid.*, p. 381.

[79] Resolution of the Council on the Spanish Appeal Against Foreign Intervention, May 29, 1937, League of Nations Official Journal, May-June, 1937, pp. 333–34.

[80] Toynbee, "The War in Spain and Its Repercussions," 1: 404, 406.

[81] Statement of Sumner Welles, acting secretary of state, June 3, 1938, Department of State Press Releases, June 4, 1938, p. 642.

cans. In January, even before these appeals, the Republicans had announced that they would cease bombing open towns if the Nationalists would follow suit. The Nationalists had not replied but instead had bombed Barcelona on January 30.[82] After the British-French appeal, the Republicans agreed to stop their reprisal raids and accepted the British offer of good offices to put an end to bombings of noncombatant areas. In June, however, the Republicans revoked the pledge.[83]

Both Republicans and Nationalists did agree to the establishment of a British commission to visit places that had been subjected to air raids, report upon the damage, and establish whether there were military objectives that might justify the bombing. After investigation, this commission concluded that of a total of fifty-six Nationalist raids conducted between August 19, 1938, and November 24, 1938, nine were not directed against military objectives. The commission refrained from saying that in all nine cases the bombs had been intentionally directed against the civilian population. It did state that a raid on Barcelona on December 31, 1938, was a deliberate attack on civilians conducted at a time when the streets were full and in an area of the city that had previously been immune.[84]

The Council of the League of Nations, following the report of the British commission, passed a resolution on January 20, 1939, that accepted the fact that Nationalist air attacks had been directed against the civilian population and condemned them as contrary "to the conscience of mankind and to the principles of international law."[85]

None of these appeals and condemnations was effective in preventing the Nationalist bombings. The Nationalists stated their regret at the loss of life and injury to noncombatants but justified their actions on the ground that the bombings were directed against legitimate military targets and that the hurt to civilians was merely incidental. They also pointed to attacks conducted by the Republicans as justification for their own and accused the Republicans of deliberately keeping civilians in areas in which there were military objectives, even after prior notification, in order to reap propaganda value after the bombings.[86]

---

[82] Thomas, *The Spanish Civil War*, p. 513; Toynbee, "The War in Spain and Its Repercussions," 1: 406, n. 2. Peers is of the opinion that the Republicans made such a proposal because they were "hopelessly outclassed in aerial warfare" and thus "attempted to make a virtue of necessity by coming to terms over it." Peers, *Spain in Eclipse*, p. 41.

[83] Toynbee, "The War in Spain and Its Repercussions," 1: 406; Peers, *Spain in Eclipse*, p. 62.

[84] For a discussion of the conclusions of this commission, see Toynbee, "The War in Spain and Its Repercussions," 1: 409–10. See also League of Nations, *Official Journal*, 1939, pp. 87–89, 96–97.

[85] League of Nations, *Official Journal*, 1939, p. 97.

[86] On the Nationalist attitude, see Toynbee, "The War in Spain and Its Repercussions," 1: 407–11.

III. THE ROLE OF FOREIGN COUNTRIES

International Law, Civil Strife, and Foreign Governments

At the time of the Spanish Civil War, international law had come to accept the principle that when civil strife becomes all-out civil war (and the parties are recognized as belligerents) the regulation of the activities of third states is based on the principle of neutrality. Three conditions are requisite for granting belligerent rights to insurgents: (1) possession by the insurgents of a portion of the national territory; (2) organization of a government upon this territory that exercises the apparent rights of sovereignty; and (3) existence of an organized army that respects and complies with the laws and customs of war.[1] When these conditions are present, the rights and duties of the law of neutrality govern the belligerents as well as the neutral states.[2]

But as civil unrest may range from street mobs to international wars, it was apparent that additional rules were needed to cover stages below the level of international war. Some jurists contended that, once a government was faced with serious internal disorder, strict impartiality became the duty of foreign states, and aid to the legitimate government or the revolutionaries was prohibited.[3] But another line of authority, which has been accepted by most internationalists, took issue with this view. In this latter view there are various stages in the development of civil strife, and certain kinds of disorder, such as a mob outbreak, a riot, or some other isolated instance of rebellion, in no way change the relations of other states to the government in which the incidents have occurred. If the situation assumes more serious proportions, is organized, has leaders, and offers for a time effective resistance to the established government, then it is generally viewed by other states as an insurgency. An insurgency is an intermediate stage between internal peace and all-

---

[1] J. B. Moore, *Digest of International Law* (Washington: Government Printing Office, 1906), 1: 196 ff.

[2] J. L. Brierly, *The Law of Nations* (6th ed.; New York and Oxford: Oxford University Press, 1963), p. 142; Lassa Oppenheim, *International Law*, ed. H. Lauterpacht (7th ed.; London: Longmans Green, 1952), 2: 659–60, 667; James W. Garner, "Questions of International Law in the Spanish Civil Strife," *American Journal of International Law* 31 (January 1937): 67.

[3] William Edward Hall, *International Law* (6th ed.; Oxford: Clarendon Press, 1909), p. 287; Manuel R. García Mora, "International Law and the Law of Hostile Military Expeditions," *Fordham Law Review* 27 (1958–59): 309; Quincy Wright, "United States Intervention in the Lebanon," *American Journal of International Law* 53 (January 1959): 121–22. For contrary views, see Amos Shartle Hershey, *The Essentials of International Public Law and Organization* (rev. ed.; New York: The Macmillan Co., 1935); Charles Cheney Hyde, *International Law Chiefly as Interpreted and Applied by the United States* (2d rev. ed.; Boston: Little Brown & Co., 1947), vol. 1, sec. 50.

out civil war, not yet calling into play the laws of neutrality.[4] When a foreign state recognizes the existence of an insurgency, it is merely acknowledging the fact of civil strife and not creating a new international relationship between itself and either party to the civil strife. It has been said that recognition of insurgency merely calls the attention of the public to the existence of a factor requiring special care. A status of insurgency, recognized or unrecognized, does not change the obligations owed by a foreign state to the state in which civil strife prevails. It does not place upon the foreign state the obligation of neutrality; hence the obligations which the outside state owes to the state involved in civil strife are owed to the de jure government, and no duty under international law prevents a state from continuing its obligations to the government. The fact of insurgency has no effect on the juridical status of the state. No rule of international law prohibits a foreign state from assisting the government to put down the revolt against its authority. If assistance were rendered to the rebels, however, it would be considered an unlawful intervention.[5]

Situations may arise—economic or humanitarian in character—in which it is impractical for an outside state to act as if there were no civil strife, even if some of the legal conditions for the recognition of belligerency are absent. Thus some authorities believe that certain international legal consequences should follow from the recognition of insurrection.[6] Such recognition should indicate that the rebellious group has established de facto authority in the territory which they actually control and that they are not mere lawbreakers. It should also be considered an acknowledgment that the legitimate government can no longer protect foreign property and foreign persons in areas controlled by the insurgents and hence that responsibility for acts performed within such areas must devolve upon the insurgents. Consequently, if the insurgents should injure the subjects of foreign nations, the foreign nation may hold the insurgent authorities responsible and take appropriate action.

Without doubt, there was an implied recognition of the civil war in Spain as insurgency by many nations, for protests were addressed to the

[4] Hyde, *International Law*, secs. 47, 50; Hershey, *The Essentials of International Public Law*, pp. 201–6; Julius Goebel, "The International Responsibility of States for Injuries Sustained by Aliens on Account of Mob Violence, Insurrections, and Civil War," *American Journal of International Law* 8 (October 1914): 802.

[5] See Ti-Chiang Chen, *The International Law of Recognition*, ed. L. C. Green (New York: Stevens, 1951), chap. 26; Garner, "Questions of International Law in the Spanish Civil Strife," pp. 67–68; Norman J. Padelford, *International Law and Diplomacy in the Spanish Civil Strife* (New York: Macmillan, 1939), pp. 1–8; and Luis A. Podesta Costa, *Derecho Internacional Público* (3rd ed.; Buenos Aires: Tipografica Editora Argentina, 1955), 2: 265; but see also H. Lauterpacht, *Recognition in International Law* (Cambridge: Cambridge University Press, 1948), pp. 232–33.

[6] Lauterpacht, *Recognition in International Law*, chap. 16.

insurgent authorities when foreign rights were ignored or violated, appeals for humanization of the war were made to them, and they were requested to guarantee the safety of foreign lives and property.[7]

Shortly after the initiation of the Spanish Civil War, a group of nations signed a collective nonintervention agreement in which all signatories agreed to prohibit the shipping of arms to either faction in Spain.[8] The legality of this collective agreement is open to question. Under general international law, no state is bound to sell munitions to the government of another state, whether or not that government is involved in civil strife.[9] But international law would also recognize that, during insurgency, the established government is entitled to partial treatment from third powers, which would seemingly include the right to purchase munitions from other states.[10] The parties to the nonintervention pact could have determined unilaterally not to sell or permit their subjects to sell munitions to the lawful government of Spain, but in collectively agreeing by treaty not to supply munitions to a legitimate government, they were in effect attempting to change general international law by denying rights of a nonsignatory state, without that state's consent. This would seem to be interference in the external affairs of a state as well as in its internal affairs, in that rebels were placed on the same footing as the lawful government and the latter denied its right to preferential treatment which might enable it to put down the insurgency.[11] Furthermore, the nonintervention agreement would seem to have been a derogation of the principle of equality before the law, for the legitimate government of Spain was placed on a lower legal level than the legitimate governments of other states.[12]

[7] Wyndham Leigh Walker, "Recognition of Belligerency and Grant of Belligerent Rights," *Transactions of the Grotius Society*, 23 (1938): 207.

[8] Padelford, *International Law and Diplomacy in the Spanish Civil Strife*, pp. 205–30, sets forth the declarations of the governments that were parties to the nonintervention agreement.

[9] Moore, *Digest*, 7: 1080; Louis Jaffe, *Judicial Aspects of Foreign Relations* (Cambridge: Harvard University Press, 1933), p. 120.

[10] See Sir Arnold Duncan McNair, "The Law Relating to the Civil War in Spain," *Law Quarterly Review* 53 (1937): 473, where an opposite point of view is taken.

[11] See Note of the Spanish Government to the Powers Participating in the Non-Intervention Accord, September 15, 1936, as set forth in Padelford, *International Law and Diplomacy in the Spanish Civil Strife*, p. 213; Chen, *The International Law of Recognition*, pp. 348–49; Norman J. Padelford, "The International Non-Intervention Agreement," *American Journal of International Law* 31 (April 1937): 585–86; H. A. Smith, "Some Problems of the Spanish Civil War," *British Yearbook of International Law* 18 (1937): 27–28; and Vernon A. O'Rourke, "Recognition of Belligerency and the Spanish War," *American Journal of International Law* 31 (July, 1937): 409–10; but see also Lauterpacht, *Recognition in International Law*, pp. 233–36.

[12] On the principle of equality in international law, see Ann V. W. Thomas and A. J. Thomas, Jr., "Equality of States in International Law—Fact or Fiction?" *Virginia Law Review* 37 (1951): 791.

If the nonintervention agreement had been authorized by the League of Nations, which was not the case, its character would have been completely different. Article 11 of the Covenant granted the League the power to take any action "it deemed wise" to safeguard international peace when there was a threat of war. Since Spain was a member of the League, any action by or under League authorization would have been legitimate under the theory of prior consent.[13]

Further, if the Spanish nonintervention agreement had been based on a recognition of belligerency, a legal case could have been made for it. The conditions which must precede the recognition of belligerency are established by general international law, and after they have come into existence, certain belligerent rights are accorded the states directly affected. These rights include the neutrality of third parties.[14]

Having recognized belligerency either by words or by deeds, a neutral power is always at liberty to permit or prohibit its private citizens from exporting munitions to the disrupted state, with the provision that both sides must be treated equally.[15] It has long been agreed that direct sale of munitions by the state itself to either side in circumstances of all-out civil war is prohibited. In the words of Phillimore: "If I have wrested my enemy's sword from his hands, the bystander who furnishes him with a fresh weapon can have no pretence to be considered as a neutral in the contest."[16]

It must be emphasized that recognition of belligerency before the legal conditions have come into being is an illegal interference in the internal affairs of the state torn by civil strife. Therefore, each nation must make its own appraisal of the facts to see if the requisite conditions exist as far as its own situation is concerned.[17] Thereafter, nations similarly affected may agree to a common policy toward a particular state, but only after each has characterized the conflict as belligerency individually.

All of the governments signing the nonintervention agreement denied that the agreement implied a recognition of belligerency, which at the

[13] Ann V. W. Thomas and A. J. Thomas, Jr., *Non-Intervention—the Law and Its Import in the Americas* (Dallas: S.M.U. Press, 1956), p. 98.

[14] See Chen, *The International Law of Recognition*, chaps. 21 and 22; Lauterpacht, *Recognition in International Law*, chaps. 12, 13, 14, 15.

[15] James W. Garner, "Some Questions of International Law in the European War," *American Journal of International Law* 10 (October 1916): 751, n. 5. See also Leonard H. Pomeroy, "The International Trade and Traffic in Arms: Its Supervision and Control," *Department of State Bulletin* 20 (February 1950): 187.

[16] Sir Robert Joseph Phillimore, *Commentaries upon International Law* (London: Butterworth, 1888), vol. 3, sec. 229.

[17] See Charles G. Fenwick, "Can Civil Wars Be Brought under the Control of International Law?" *American Journal of International Law* 32 (July 1938): 539; Lauterpacht, *Recognition in International Law*, sec. 68.

time the agreement was drawn up (two weeks after the outbreak of the rebellion) would have been an illegal interference in the internal affairs of Spain. Furthermore, if belligerency had been recognized, both sides to the fighting would have been entitled to exercise full belligerent rights against neutral commerce both at sea and on land.[18] But the signatory nations informed both factions that they would not tolerate interference with their commerce and shipping. Notwithstanding such a declaration, if certain actions by the signatories implied recognition of belligerency,[19] the warning could have been ignored by both sides to the conflict. But the signatory states took active steps to prevent either side from exercising those rights which international law has long recognized as belonging to belligerents. Thus it would seem that the nonintervention agreement was not a common policy based upon recognition of belligerency, implicit or explicit, by each signatory. If it was based upon implied recognition of belligerency, the signatory nations were acting illegally with respect to the rights of belligerents under international law, and such illegal action was an intervention in the affairs of Spain. If it was not based on implied recognition of belligerency by each state, it was illegal *ab initio*.

It might be argued that although the European nations called their collective agreements a "nonintervention" agreement this was a misnomer. Since the agreement bound each signatory nation to prohibit the direct or indirect exportation of war materials to either side, it was, in effect, equivalent to an invocation of the law of neutrality under which both sides to a conflict are treated absolutely as equals. Until a conflict has achieved a status of civil war, the legitimate government has an international legal right to expect a higher standard of treatment by foreign powers than the revolutionaries. When both are placed on the same plane, the implication exists that belligerency has been recognized and the law of neutrality invoked. But in that case, all rights of belligerency should have been granted to both sides. Failure to do so was an illegal intervention in the internal affairs of Spain.

Lauterpacht would reduce the nonintervention agreement to the following anomaly:

... These agreements consisted in an undertaking on the part of certain powers to refrain from committing an international illegality in consideration of the promise of other powers to refrain from action in a manner in which they were entitled—and according to some, legally bound—to act.[20]

[18] Norman J. Padelford, "Foreign Shipping during the Spanish Civil War," *American Journal of International Law* 22 (April 1938): 264.

[19] H. A. Smith, "Some Problems of the Spanish Civil War," p. 29; but see note, "Implied Recognition," *British Yearbook of International Law* 21 (1944): 146, wherein Smith's viewpoint is disputed.

[20] Lassa Oppenheim, *International Law*, ed. H. Lauterpacht (7th ed.; London: Longmans Green, 1948), 1: 273.

A number of European powers defended their policy toward the Spanish conflict on the ground that there was a large-scale involvement of foreign troops on both sides, making it impossible to classify the affair as mere civil strife.[21] But if it was not civil strife, then it must have been a civil war. And if it was a civil war, then the belligerents should have been granted the rights due them from neutral states and should have been subject to the obligations they owed neutrals.

The legal position taken by the United States with reference to the conflict was equally enigmatic. Early in 1937 Congress placed an embargo on monetary aid and armaments to both sides, implying that there was in existence a civil war in which the United States chose to be neutral. Nevertheless, the executive branch refused to recognize the belligerency of the rebels, claiming that the duly constituted government was the legitimate government of Spain. Despite the fact that international law permits a nation to trade with whomever it pleases, its trade policy should not be used as a weapon of intervention. If the Loyalists were the only government of Spain, then the refusal to permit them to obtain loans or buy weapons with which to put down the rebellion, which placed them on a parity with the rebels, could be considered an act of intervention in favor of the rebels. Furthermore, any proclamation of neutrality (and an embargo on money or armaments to both groups certainly was the act of a neutral) should have served as a recognition of belligerency, carrying with it the recognition of belligerent rights. Since this was refused, a strong argument can be made that the United States illegally intervened in the internal affairs of Spain.[22]

Relations of Foreign Governments with the Incumbent Government

Diplomatic Envoys. One of the most well-established principles of international law is the inviolability of the person of diplomatic envoys and of diplomatic correspondence. The receiving states have the duty to protect diplomats from bodily injury and to assure them unfettered communication with their home governments.[23]

By the time the revolution broke out, most of the ambassadors accredited to Spain had taken up residence in San Sebastián, the summer capital for the Spanish government. One of the first acts of the rebel

[21] League of Nations, *Official Journal*, 1938, p. 330.

[22] Edwin Borchard and William Potter Lage, *Neutrality for the United States* (2d ed.; New Haven: Yale University Press, 1940), pp. 355–59. The U.S. Department of State has contended otherwise, for example, with respect to the shipment of arms to the government of Cuba, headed by President Batista, in its fight with the forces of Fidel Castro. See the statement of the Office of the Legal Adviser contained in Marjorie Whiteman, *Digest of International Law* (Washington: Government Printing Office, 1963), 2: 517–18.

[23] Sir Ernest Satow, *A Guide to Diplomatic Practice* (London: Longmans Green, 1922), 1: 251; Raoul Genet, *Traité de Diplomatie et de Droit Diplomatique* (Paris: Perdone, 1931), 1: 487.

generals was the cutting of the road to and all communications with Madrid. Consequently, for the first weeks, it was impossible for the heads of diplomatic missions either to return to their Madrid embassies or to communicate with them. Furthermore, Madrid, being under siege, was dangerous; thus on July 22, 1936, most of the ambassadors moved from Spain across the border into France. The American ambassador, who was staying at the seaport of Fuenterrabia, near San Sebastián, did not join in this move until ordered to do so by the Department of State. The various embassies in Madrid were left in the hands of junior officers. After the successful defense of Madrid, the Spanish government requested the ambassadors to return to Madrid, guaranteeing them safe conduct. But the *corps diplomatique* refused. It was far safer in France, and since the rebels held a portion of Spain along the French border, it was possible for the ambassadors to communicate with their consuls in the rebel-held area and also with rebel leaders. Furthermore, in view of the unsettled conditions, the ambassadors felt the established government might be unable to provide them with adequate facilities for communication. Although this situation was both embarrassing and inconvenient as far as the Madrid government was concerned, it probably did not contravene any rules of international law relating to the conduct of relations between states. The embassies remained open, and the Republicans could have dealt with lesser officials had they so desired; but they continued for the most part to deal with the envoys residing in France throughout the strife for fear that failure to do so might bring about a rupture of diplomatic relations and the recognition of the insurgents as the de jure government of Spain. Only the Mexican, Brazilian, Chilean, and Russian ambassadors returned to Madrid.[24]

On January 7, 1937, the first secretary of the Belgian legation was found murdered in Madrid. It was an open secret in the city that he had persuaded a number of Belgians who had come to serve with the International Brigade to desert. The Belgian government demanded an apology and monetary indemnification. Failure to comply, the Belgian government declared, would mean the breaking of diplomatic relations and referral of the case to the International Court of Justice on grounds of the Spanish government's complicity in the crime. The Madrid government requested the Belgians not to break off relations and agreed to pay indemnity if it were so decided by the court. The case was never decided, for on January 6, 1938, the Belgian government informed the court that it had reached an understanding with the Madrid government, which paid the indemnity and issued the apology. It may well be that some

---

[24] See Claude G. Bowers, *My Mission to Spain* (New York: Simon & Schuster, 1954), pp. 253 ff.; Padelford, *International Law and Diplomacy in the Spanish Civil Strife*, p. 149; Julio Alvarez del Vayo, *Freedom's Battle* (London: 1949), p. 240.

member of the Spanish government was involved in the crime and consequently that there was a breach of international law:

The murder of a diplomat by forces subject to the control of the government to which he is accredited, no matter what his actions may be, is without question contrary to the fundamental principles of international law regarding the inviolability and immunity of diplomatic representatives, and is a violation of Spanish law as well.[25]

Diplomatic Asylum. The concept of diplomatic asylum for political offenders in embassies and legations is an outgrowth of acceptance of the right of people to rebel against oppression, and in the event of failure of the rebellion it has been understood that the refugee in a foreign embassy or legation is to be granted safe-conduct outside the country rather than surrendered to qualified officers of the government in power. The rationale is that political offenders, in such circumstances, could never receive a fair trial from the government against which they had rebelled. Where there has been a propensity toward revolutions as in some states of Latin America, the law of diplomatic asylum has become an accepted part of general international law, but elsewhere it is not universally recognized. Various writers have pointed out that diplomatic asylum is a derogation of sovereign rights over territory and subjects. That is, the law of diplomatic asylum puts beyond the power of the sovereign a person who may have committed a political offense and who, as a national, should be fully subject to the sovereign. Furthermore, this rebuff to sovereignty is administered within the very territory of the sovereign, for, although international law speaks of the extraterritoriality of embassies and legations, in reality embassies and legations are subject to the will of the territorial sovereign and are granted immunity through reciprocity and custom rather than extraterritoriality. It might therefore be said that diplomatic asylum qualifies the modern concept that no one is above the law by providing a means for a person to escape the applition of his country's laws.[26]

With the beginning of the rebellion in July 1936, numerous persons sought asylum in the embassies in Madrid.[27] The Latin American am-

[25] Padelford, *International Law and Diplomacy in the Spanish Civil Strife*, pp. 152–54.

[26] Thomas and Thomas, *Non-Intervention*, pp. 392–93; Carlos Salamanca, "Political Asylum—What and Why," *Bar Bulletin of the New York County Lawyers' Association* 10 (1952): 77; Francisco J. Parra, *El Derecho de Asilo* (Lima, a los estudiantes universitarios del Peru, 1936), p. 6; Armando Fernández Franco, "El Asilo Diplomático," *Revista de Derecho Internacional* 49 (1946): 203.

[27] Burnett Bolloten, in *The Grand Camouflage: The Communist Conspiracy and the Spanish War* (New York: Praeger, 1961), p. 40, estimates that about twenty thousand refugees sought asylum. At the end of the war between two thousand and three thousand refugees were still harbored in various embassies in Madrid.

bassadors, acting as though the right of asylum were accepted customary law binding upon all nations, immediately granted asylum to all who sought it. The American and English embassies granted a temporary safe haven to those attempting to escape death at the hands of the mobs during the first days of terror, but when order was established, they were instructed not to open their embassies to refugees of Spanish nationality on the ground that such actions would constitute intervention in the internal affairs of Spain. When the Soviet Union established diplomatic relations with the incumbent government, it announced that Russia did not recognize any right of asylum in embassies.[28] Other European nations, although refusing to admit any universal right of asylum in their embassies, did permit refugees to enter, viewing this as an act of humanitarianism toward victims of political and religious persecution.[29]

A number of the refugees were members of the Republican center parties fleeing the terrorism of the communists or anarchists, but for the most part, they were pro-Nationalists. Claude Bowers, the American ambassador to Spain, pointed out that

... from the first day of the war, a very large portion of the diplomatic corps was aggressively aligned with the enemies of Spanish democracy. Germany, Italy, Portugal would naturally be expected to denounce the constitutional regime and to sneer at its democratic character. I could even understand how democratic nations, looking upon the struggle as a "civil war" could adopt a policy of neutrality and stand aloof. But when, almost at once, the complicity of Axis powers became notorious, I could not understand how diplomats, presumably representing democratic nations, could earnestly compete with their Fascist colleagues in bitter hostility to the government to which they were accredited.[30]

Because of this hostility, many permitted their embassies to be used as centers of espionage and subversion, placing at the disposal of the refugees the legation radio transmitters as well as the diplomatic pouch. By these two methods, vital military information was sent to the Nationalist forces. This was clearly a breach of international law and would not have been tolerated by a strong government. In a few instances the Madrid government did take action. In January 1937, for example, the Chilean ambassador was declared *persona non grata* and requested to leave Spain immediately. He was accused of smuggling out of Spain in diplomatic pouches money belonging to Nationalist refugees in the

[28] See C. Neale Ronning, *Diplomatic Asylum: Legal Norms and Political Reality in Latin American Relations* (The Hague: M. Nijhoff, 1965), p. 18.

[29] Henry Helfant, *The Trujillo Doctrine of Humanitarian Diplomatic Asylum* (Mexico: Editorial Ofsset Continente, 1947), p. 197.

[30] Bowers, *My Mission to Spain*, p. 290.

Chilean embassy and also of permitting the refugees to engage in political activities.[31]

Early in August 1936, the Argentine government demanded that the Madrid government recognize the right of political asylum and provide safe-conduct for the Spanish refugees in the Argentine embassy. When the government refused, Argentina sent a warship to Spain, and the government, although denying the right of asylum, did provide safe-conduct for those persons harbored by the Argentine embassy.[32]

Although the Republican government never admitted any legal obligation to respect the right of asylum, in order not to antagonize the democratic nations, on October 13, 1936, it laid down the following guidelines:

1. Asylum may be granted only in urgent cases, and only for such time as is necessary for the refugee to find security elsewhere.
2. The diplomatic agent ... shall notify immediately the Minister of Foreign Affairs of the persons to whom he has extended asylum.
3. The government ... may demand that the refugees be removed from the country within the shortest time possible; and the diplomatic agent of the country which granted asylum may demand the necessary guarantee of protection for the safe conduct of the refugee.
4. The refugee may not be disembarked at any point within the national boundaries.
5. During their term of asylum refugees shall not be permitted to engage in any activities detrimental to public order.[33]

These guidelines were largely ignored. Those envoys granting asylum refused to give the minister of foreign affairs either the names or the numbers of persons granted asylum. And illegal fifth-column activities under the protection of foreign flags continued until the end of the war.

The government tried to empty the embassies by signing bilateral treaties with various nations agreeing to grant safe-conduct passes to the refugees if the nation extending asylum would undertake to keep the refugees from returning to the Nationalist-held portions of Spain to fight against the incumbent government. About four thousand persons, one thousand of them of military age, left the embassies under such agreements in 1937. Most of the governments honored their pledges. Belgium was the exception. Once its refugees had crossed the Spanish border,

---

[31] Helfant, *The Trujillo Doctrine*, p. 219; Padelford, *International Law and Diplomacy in the Spanish Civil Strife*, p. 154.
[32] Padelford, *International Law and Diplomacy in the Spanish Civil Strife*, p. 157.
[33] Bowers, *My Mission to Spain*, p. 301.

they were informed that they were free to go where they pleased. In face of such a gross breach of treaty law, the Loyalists refused further evacuations.[34]

While a nebulous right of asylum for humanitarian reasons may be based on the internationally recognized immunity of ambassadors, ministers, and other accredited diplomatic officers and also their offices and official residences from local jurisdiction, it does not rest equally on the immunities of consular officers and their buildings or offices from invasion by local authorities. Thus it is generally held that a consul is bound to hand over any fugitives who have taken refuge in the consulate on the simple request of the local authorities.[35]

During the first days of the revolt, the Peruvian consulate in Madrid granted asylum to a number of refugees. When safe-conduct passes were handed out to the refugees in the Peruvian embassy, they were also given to those in the Peruvian consulate, and all left Spain without hindrance. But in May 1937, asylum again having been granted to a number of Spanish nationals in the Peruvian consulate in Madrid, the Spanish police broke into the consulate and removed them. Peru demanded the return of the refugees, arguing that Spain had accepted the legal principle of diplomatic asylum in embassies and by its previous action had indicated that consulates were also included. The Spanish government rejected the contention, pointing out that from the beginning of the war it had denied that there was a universally accepted legal right of asylum; it had only acceded to asylum in embassies because the territory of embassies was traditionally immune from local jurisdiction. It had previously granted safe-conduct passes to refugees in the Peruvian consulate for humanitarian purposes and in so doing had not intended to establish the immunity of consular offices and residences. Consequently, the Madrid government believed itself free to remove those who sought asylum therein. This attitude, although consistent with international precedent, led to a breach of relations between Spain and Peru on May 17, 1938.[36]

There were no accredited diplomatic missions to the rebels during the first period of the war; therefore, the question of diplomatic asylum did not arise in that portion of Spain. A number of Loyalists sought to obtain asylum in various Latin American consulates but were refused. By the time the Franco government became officially recognized and entered into diplomatic relations with other nations, there was little need

[34] Padelford, *International Law and Diplomacy in the Spanish Civil Strife*, p. 159.
[35] Barry Gilbert, "The Practice of Asylum in Legations and Consulates of the United States," *American Journal of International Law* 3 (July 1909): 562.
[36] Ronning, *Diplomatic Asylum*, p. 135.

for diplomatic asylum. Most Loyalist leaders had been ferreted out and either killed or imprisoned.[37]

Blockade. From the beginning of the conflict, the Loyalist government was faced with far graver economic problems than was the Nationalist group. In an effort to change this economic disadvantage, in August 1936, the government announced that it was establishing a naval blockade of Nationalist-held ports.[38] This immediately brought the Loyalists into conflict with other nations.

The purpose of a blockade is the complete isolation of the blockaded area from all sea communications. It is an established method of direct interference with an area's import and export trade. International law recognizes the right of a belligerent to blockade the coasts and ports of its enemies; but in order to be recognized by other countries, it must be maintained by a belligerent force sufficient to prevent access to or egress from enemy ports, and a warning must have been given in advance to neutral shipping. Once a blockade has been effectively established, ships seized in breach of the blockade are, together with their cargoes, liable to condemnation as good and lawful prize.[39]

There is no question but that the legitimate government of Spain had a right to establish a blockade of ports held by the insurgents. But in so doing, it is probable that it implicitly recognized the belligerency of the insurgent powers. In 1861, for example, after President Lincoln had declared a blockade of Confederate-held ports, the British recognized the belligerency of the Confederate Army. When the United States complained to Great Britain that the recognition was premature, the British replied that Lincoln's declaration of blockade, by implication, had elevated the Confederacy to the position of belligerent.[40] It would therefore seem that the Madrid declaration would have had the same effect, namely, to recognize that a state of war existed between the insurgents, who held a part of the Spanish territory, and the government, which claimed their allegiance and was attempting to subdue them. If the cases are similar, neutral powers, according to the law of nations, may not withdraw their ships and subjects upon the high seas from the operation of the ordinary laws of war by merely declining to acknowledge the existence of war.[41] Yet this is what the European powers did.

[37] Smith points out that after Madrid had fallen to the insurgents the Chileans disputed with Franco concerning Republican refugees sheltered in the Chilean embassy. L. E. Smith, *Mexico and the Spanish Republicans* (Berkeley: University of California Press, 1955), p. 183.

[38] H. A. Smith, "Some Problems of the Spanish Civil War," p. 27.

[39] Moore, *Digest*, 7: 803; Maurice F. Parmelee, *Blockade and Sea Power* (New York: Thomas Y. Crowell Co., 1924), p. 7.

[40] See H. A. Smith, "Some Problems of the Spanish Civil War," p. 20.

[41] Walker, "Recognition of Belligerency and Grant of Belligerent Rights," points this out succinctly on page 200.

The British government informed the Loyalists that since it regarded neither party as a legal belligerent it would permit no interference with its merchant vessels. The British thus implied that belligerent rights under international law depended on British recognition of belligerency. But in truth, belligerent rights are determined by international law, not individual countries' foreign policies. If the facts are such as to constitute a state of war between the contending parties, according to the law of nations neutral powers must submit themselves to the exercise of belligerent rights.[42]

In January 1937, a German warship captured two Spanish government merchant vessels and turned them over to rebel authorities in reprisal for an earlier seizure by the Loyalists of the German freighter *Palos*, which had attempted to run the blockade loaded with contraband goods. Although the goods of the *Palos* had been confiscated, the ship had been released.[43] The Germans claimed that this action on the part of the Loyalists was "an act of piracy." But if there were a civil war in Spain, the actions of belligerents on either side could not be equated with piracy. Furthermore, a reprisal, to be a legal act, can only be taken against international wrongdoer. If the Spanish government's blockade was legal, then the German reprisal had to be illegal.[44]

The reply of the United States to the Loyalist government's blockade announcement did not deny the right of the Loyalists to establish a blockade. Rather, the United States pointed out that, according to international law, an economic and commercial blockade must be based on naval power, for a mere declaration of blockade, unless rendered effective by force, is not binding in international law. Apparently the United States felt that the naval forces of the Spanish government would be insufficient to maintain an effective blockade of the rebel ports and that therefore blockade would not be recognized.[45]

Military Assistance. From the moment the nonintervention agreement was proposed, the Spanish government began a series of protests to the governments concerned. It objected to nonintervention on the ground that a legitimate government ought not to be subjected to the same treatment as those in rebellion against it: it was illegal to sell arms to the

[42] H. A. Smith, in *Great Britain and the Law of Nations* (London: King, 1945), vol. I, states that the law officers of the crown believed the question of war or no war to be one of fact, the effects of which could not be avoided by declining to acknowledge its existence (p. 313).

[43] Arnold Toynbee, "The International Repercussions of the War in Spain (1936–1937)," *Survey of International Affairs, 1937* (London: Oxford University Press, 1938), 2: 281.

[44] A. Pearce Higgins, "Retaliation in Naval Warfare," *British Yearbook of International Law* 8 (1927): 127; O'Rourke, "Recognition of Belligerency and the Spanish War," p. 398.

[45] James W. Garner, "Spanish Civil War—Neutrality Policy of the United States," *British Yearbook of International Law* 18 (1937): 197.

latter and equally illegal for the European nations collectively to refuse to sell arms to the former. The Spanish government objected more strongly as time went by, pointing out that the countries from which they had hoped to procure arms were abiding by the agreement, while the rebellious forces were being copiously supplied by Portugal, Germany, and Italy.[46]

A serious gap was soon found in the agreement. It referred only to arms and implements of war and not to manpower. Thousands of volunteers, attracted in part by desire for employment, or love of adventure, or sympathy for the cause, made their way to help the Republicans. Other volunteers were carefully organized by the Comintern into international brigades and sent into Spain also to aid the incumbent government. On the Nationalist side, there were extensive reinforcements from the armed forces of Italy and Germany, which were also called "volunteers" although they were military units sent into conflict by their governments.[47]

Each state has the general duty in international law to abstain from intervening in the internal affairs of another state. The duty, of course, is attached to states, not private individuals, whose activities cannot impair the independence of a state. Although intervention *qua* intervention can normally only be committed by one sovereign state against another, a state is obligated not to tolerate acts within its territory which would amount to an armed intervention in a situation of civil strife. Failure to exercise due diligence to prevent its territory from being used as a base for hostile armed acts against another state with which it is at peace is an international delict, since such carelesssness and negligence amount to a virtual complicity in the hostile attacks and impute the acts of the private persons to the state. When a state's negligence reaches such proportions as to indicate a disregard of its international obligation, it may be considered as having consented to the attacks on another state; it may even be regarded as assisting in the hostilities by protecting the persons it has allowed to use its territory as a base of operations.[48]

Hostile activity would include the departure from a state's territory of organized hostile military expeditions against an established and recog-

---

[46] On the functions of the nonintervention agreement, see Toynbee, "The International Repercussion of the War in Spain," pp. 222–362; and Padelford, *International Law and Diplomacy in the Spanish Civil Strife*, pp. 53–118.

[47] David T. Cattell, *Soviet Diplomacy and the Spanish Civil War* (Berkeley: University of California Press, 1957), pp. 57–70; Alvarez de Vayo, *Freedom's Battle*, pp. 45–48.

[48] H. Lauterpacht, "Revolutionary Activities by Private Persons against Foreign States," *American Journal of International Law* 22 (January 1928): 105; Manuel R. García Mora, *International Responsibility for Hostile Acts of Private Persons against Foreign States* (The Hague: M. Nijhoff, 1961), chaps. 2, 3; Roy Emerson Curtis, "The Law of Hostile Military Expeditions as Applied by the United States," *American Journal of International Law* 8 (January 1914): 36.

nized government undergoing unrest or insurrection.[49] The majority of authorities would hold that privileged status in international law is granted a legitimate government until the belligerency of the rebels is recognized. Thus, military units formed to support a recognized government would not be considered illegal.[50]

When the belligerency of the rebels has been recognized, articles 4, 5, and 6 of the Hague Convention of 1907 come into play.[51] Article 4 prohibits the setting up of enlistment or recruiting offices on the territory of neutral powers and also the formation of corps of combatants. Article 5 states that a neutral nation must not permit such activities in its territory. The effectiveness of these rules does not depend on whether the activities are carried out by belligerents or private persons or corporations especially established for the purpose; they are all inclusive. Article 6 excludes a neutral state from responsibility for persons crossing "the frontier singly in order to place themselves at the service of one of the belligerents." The article proceeds to draw a line of demarcation between the sphere of government and the sphere of purely private action. Although article 6 definitely speaks in terms of individuals crossing *singly*, from the time of its codification it has been liberally interpreted. As long as there were no bonds or obvious organizations, large groups of individuals could cross frontiers to volunteer with foreign forces without involving the state from which they embarked. It is the lack of organization which prevents volunteer groups from being equated with corps of combatants or hostile military expeditions.[52]

If the Spanish civil conflict is looked upon as an internal affair that had not yet reached the status of all-out civil war, then volunteers crossing the frontier singly or in groups to aid the government would be internationally legal, but military units crossing to aid the rebels would be illegal. If, on the other hand, the Spanish civil strife is recognized, in fact or by implication, as all-out civil war—and if it can be assumed

[49] This view is stated emphatically by many jurists. See, for example, Garner, "Questions of International Law in the Spanish Civil Strife," pp. 67–78; Herbert W. Briggs, *The Law of Nations: Cases, Documents, Notes* (2d ed.; New York: F. S. Crofts & Co., 1952); Clyde Eagleton, *International Government* (3d ed.; New York: Ronald Press Co., 1957), pp. 71–72; Philip C. Jessup, "The Spanish Rebellion and International Law," *Foreign Affairs* 15 (January 1937): 265–68; Padelford, *International Law and Diplomacy in the Spanish Civil Strife*, pp. 1–8; Llewellyn E. Pfankuchen, *A Documentary Textbook of International Law* (New York: Farrar & Rinehart, 1960), p. 54.

[50] Maurice Borquin, "Crimes et Délits contre la Sûreté des Etats Etrangers," *Recueil des Cours*, 16 (1927): 226; Podesta Costa, *Derecho Internacional Público*, 2: 264–65; Luis A. Podesta Costa, *Ensayo sobre las Luchas Civiles y el Derecho Internacional* (Buenos Aires: Tip. A. G. Rezzónico, 1926), p. 166.

[51] A. Pearce Higgins, *The Hague Peace Conference* (London: Longmans Green, 1909), p. 281.

[52] Hackworth, *Digest of International Law* (Washington: Government Printing Office, 1940), 2: 340.

that the Hague conventions referred to civil wars as well as international wars—then unorganized volunteers crossing the frontier in groups to aid either side would not be internationally illegal, but organized military units aiding either side would be a violation of neutrality. In any event, to call regular military units "volunteers" is misleading, and the fact that they are so labelled would not place them within the scope of the Hague regulation concerning volunteers. The nonintervention agreement was eventually extended to prohibit foreign volunteers as well as arms shipments, and the Nonintervention Committee then established a land and sea system of observation around Spain to prevent arms or "volunteers" from being sent to either side.[53]

From the beginning, the Republican government had protested that the ban on shipping arms to it in the nonintervention accord was illegal.[54] In addition, it now pointed out that the nature of its "volunteers" was completely different from those aiding the Nationalists. To treat them as the same, it claimed, was decidedly an illegal act in favor of those in rebellion. Nevertheless, the government was convinced that if neither side received foreign help it could quickly suppress the rebellion; therefore it was hopeful that the patrol system would enforce true nonintervention. Again the Loyalists were bitterly disappointed, for the flow of Italian and German supplies and troops to the rebels was in no way hampered by the patrol whereas Russian aid was drastically reduced and the influx of volunteers reaching Republican Spain sharply curtailed.[55]

Relations of Foreign Governments with the Nationalists

Recognition. In instances of civil strife, the issue of recognition arises not only with respect to belligerency but also with respect to the new government. Jurists taking the constituent view maintain that certain conditions of fact impose a duty on other nations to recognize the new entity and confer a right on it to be recognized. In the declaratory view, on the other hand, recognition is a formal act of political significance only; hence each state may confer recognition at its discretion and as its own policy dictates.[56] But whichever view is held, recognition, through the establishment of diplomatic relations, does have important political, economic, and even legal consequences for a new government, and an

[53] Cattell, *Soviet Diplomacy and the Spanish War*, p. 59; Padelford, *International Law and Diplomacy in the Spanish Civil Strife*, p. 79.

[54] League of Nations, *Official Journal*, 1936, Special Supplement No. 155, pp. 46 ff.

[55] See Hugh Thomas, *The Spanish Civil War* (New York: Harper & Row, 1961), pp. 440–41.

[56] On the two views, see Lauterpacht, *Recognition in International Law*, chaps. 2, 3, 4, 5; Chen, *The International Law of Recognition*, chaps. 4, 5, 6.

arbitrary grant or refusal of recognition for political considerations alone can be equated with intervention.[57]

It can be said that premature recognition of a revolutionary government as the legal government of the whole nation—that is, prior to the time that the parent government's efforts to maintain its rule have become hopeless—is, of course, a violation of the rights of the state. It is intervention, an unwarranted interference in the internal affairs of the country aimed at altering the condition of things within it. By its recognition, the interfering state confers advantages on the rebel government and consequently affects the right of the state to govern internally as it sees fit.[58]

Intervention may also result if recognition is delayed too long, for the withholding of diplomatic relations after a rebellious government has overthrown the legitimate government and met the criteria of international law for recognition also constitutes an attempt to alter the condition of things within the state.[59] This much can be said, but clarity ends here, for there is no agreement on what the international criteria for recognition are.

One view is that the individual or body of individuals seeking recognition as a new government of a state must be competent to act on behalf of the state in relations with other states through effective control of the machinery of government. When this requirement has been fulfilled, the refusal of a foreign state to recognize an established government for any reason whatsoever is a violation of the principle of internal autonomy and an act of intervention. Within this line of reasoning, facts are law, and a refusal to recognize facts constitutes an intervention.

Another view accepts the fact that the new government seeking recognition must be competent to act on behalf of the state in its relations with other states but adds a further condition—the new government must show in some manner a willingness to accept the legal rights and duties imposed on all governments by rules of general international law. Until both requirements are fulfilled, nonrecognition cannot be considered an illegal interference in the affairs of the state.[60]

The whole field of recognition of governments is thus divided into two camps, and to say that nations adopt one viewpoint or another would be to deny historical reality. Confusion, misinterpretation, misunderstanding, and contradictions between words and deeds dot the landscape of recognition by governments.

[57] Chen, *The International Law of Recognition*, pp. 128–29, 133–65. For a definition of intervention, see Thomas and Thomas, *Non-Intervention*, p. 71.

[58] Lauterpacht, *Recognition in International Law*, p. 92.

[59] *Ibid.*, p. 158; Justino Eduardo Jiménez de Arechaga, *Reconocimiento de Gobiernos* (Montevideo: Facultad de Derecho, 1947), chap. 2.

[60] For lists of jurists on one side or the other, see Chen, *The International Law of Recognition*, pp. 13–17.

The subject of recognition is further confused by the introduction of the terms "de facto" and "de jure."[61] The British and French governments refused to recognize the belligerency of the insurgents in Spain for various reasons. Nevertheless, British-Spanish commerce decreased rapidly because most of British trade had been with areas now in the hands of the Nationalists. The British began exploring the possibility of entering into a de facto consular relationship with the Franco government.[62] This was pleasing to the Nationalists, for it would look like a step toward diplomatic recognition however carefully the British government might label the relationship informal or ad hoc or de facto. The arrangement was concluded in December 1937 on a basis of strict reciprocity; the agents of the Spanish Nationalist regime were to be permitted in British territory, and British agents in the Spanish territory occupied by the Nationalists. Though neither would enjoy diplomatic status, they would be allowed to exercise all the normal functions of consuls in relation to matters of commerce and navigation.[63] The British government strenuously denied that it was possible to read into an act which they called purely a matter of expediency the implication that Gerat Britain had or was planning to recognize the Nationalist government or even a status of belligerency.[64]

In 1938 the *Arantzazu Mendi*, a ship belonging to the Republican government of Spain, was handed over in a British harbor by its captain to the Nationalists. The Republican government sought to regain the ship as sovereign of Spain, and the question came before a British court. At issue was the status of the Nationalist government. The British Foreign Office informed the court by letter that the British government, while recognizing the government of the Spanish Republic as the de jure government of Spain, also recognized that the Nationalist government exercized de facto administrative control over the larger portion of Spain. The court decided that recognition had been granted the Nationalists as exercising all the functions of a sovereign government and that therefore sovereign immunity attached as much to the Nationalist government as to the Republican government.

I think that there may be in the eyes of the law, two sovereigns, one *de facto* and one *de jure*, in the same country. It seems to me that the law, based on the reality of facts material to the particular case, must regard as having the essentials of sovereignty a government in effective administrative

[61] V. Cavaré, "La Reconnaissance de l'Etat et le Mandchoukuou," *Revue Générale de Droit International Public* (Paris: Pedone, 1935), 42: 1.

[62] Great Britain, *Parliamentary Debates*, Commons, 5th Series, vol. 328 (Nov. 8, 1937), cols. 1124–25.

[63] Toynbee, "The International Repercussions of the War in Spain," 2: 177.

[64] Herbert W. Briggs, "Relations Officieuses and Intent to Recognize," *American Journal of International Law* 34 (January 1940): 47.

control over the territory in question and not subordinate to any other government, because their decrees are the only legal authority which governs the areas to which the subject matter of the dispute belongs.[65]

Here is presented a confusing, nebulous, and unsettled area of international law. The court pointed out that it was contradictory to think of two sovereign governments in only one state. Jurists are divided as to the meaning of de facto recognition. One line of authority speaks of the distinction between de jure and de facto as merely political, not legal; that the extension of de facto recognition, in the sense of qualified recognition, is merely political expediency, since in law such qualified recognition is not possible. Since no legal distinction exists, it follows, in this view, that the legal effects of de jure or de facto recognition are the same. Spain, therefore, could claim that an international injury had been done the legitimate government, for the insurgents had not established effective control over all Spain and yet were accorded equal legal status. But one cannot be sure, because this line of authority further contends that, although there is no legal distinction between de jure and de facto recognition, there is a legal distinction between de jure and de facto governments. Hence, it is argued that recognition itself is not de jure or de facto but that governments may be recognized as de jure or de facto, the latter being a government exercising effective power over the territory under its control. Because of the element of control, a measure of legality must be granted certain internal acts of insurgents within their territory.

Another line of authority holds that there is a legal distinction between de jure and de facto recognition, the latter being qualified recognition whereby the acts of the de facto authority within the territory subject to its control are acknowledged as valid, although the authority itself is not to be placed on the same plane as the de jure government for all purposes or extended all international rights or treated as the sovereign of the state. Such limited recognition does not violate the prohibition in international law against premature recognition of governments, since that rule is applicable only to recognition de jure.[66]

Although Portugal had broken off diplomatic relations with the Madrid government as early as October 1936, she had not officially

[65] *Law Reports,* 1938, Probate Division, p. 245. The case was affirmed by the Court of Appeals and also by the House of Lords. *Law Times Report,* 55 (Feb. 23, 1939): 454. The House of Lords opinion is also contained in *American Journal of International Law* 33 (July 1939): 583. An excellent discussion of the case is that of Herbert W. Briggs, "De Facto and De Jure Recognition: The Arantzazu Mendi," *American Journal of International Law* 33 (October 1939): 689.

[66] On these various points of view, see Chen, *International Law of Recognition,* chap. 20; Lauterpacht, *Recognition in International Law,* chap. 17.

recognized the Franco régime or granted belligerent recognition thereto. But in December 1937, she followed the British example of appointing an agent to represent her interests in the Nationalist portions of Spain. A similar step was taken by Austria, Hungary, and Switzerland. France raised no objection to the British move but did not follow suit.[67]

The Franco government was recognized de jure simultaneously by the French and British governments on February 27, 1939. The prime minister of Great Britain, Neville Chamberlain, stated: "Moreover, it seems to H. M. Government impossible to regard the Spanish Republican Government, scattered as it is and no longer exercising settled authority, as the Sovereign Government of Spain."[68]

In 1938 the United States consul at Seville (which was in Nationalist hands) reported that the Nationalists had approached him and had assured him that the United States consuls "would be permitted to continue functioning" but proposed that an exchange of agents be arranged between the Nationalist government and the government of the United States. In reply to this proposal, the Department of State instructed the consul that "this government has taken no step which might be in any way construed as recognition of the Franco régime, and that there is no provision in our practice for the exchange of agents with a régime which has not been recognized."[69] Only after the complete disappearance of the previously recognized Republican government did the United States recognize the Nationalist regime as the de jure government of Spain.

Late in October 1936, when the war was barely four months old, the Germans agreed to recognize Franco as the legitimate government of Spain as soon as he captured Madrid.[70] But in spite of such moral support, the Nationalist forces failed to capture Madrid at that time. It was by no means certain who would be the winner in the Spanish civil strife; nevertheless, the Italians and Germans agreed on November 17, 1936, to accord full diplomatic recognition to Franco, skipping over the next legally correct stage, recognition of belligerency.[71] Without doubt, this was premature recognition and an intervention in the affairs of Spain— an internationally illegal act. Although the decision to recognize the Nationalists did not help them capture Madrid, it did have important repercussions on future events. The prestige of the two dictators, their image of invincibility, was clearly placed on the line. Consequently, there was strong motivation to intensify efforts to tip the balance in the Nationalist favor.

The Germans and Italians were not the first to recognize the Franco

[67] Toynbee, "The International Repercussions of the War in Spain," 2: 374.
[68] As quoted by Briggs, "Relations Officieuses and Intent to Recognize," p. 52.
[69] Whiteman, *Digest*, 2: 572.
[70] U.S. Department of State, *Documents on German Foreign Policy 1918– 1945*, vol. 3: *Germany and the Spanish War* (1950), doc. no. 114, p. 123.
[71] *Ibid.*, doc. no. 123, p. 132.

régime as the de jure government of all Spain; on November 10, 1936, General Jorge Ubico, the dictator of Guatemala, and President Maximilian Hernandes Martínez, the strongman of El Salvador, had both accorded full recognition to Franco. In December 1936, another Central American dictator, General Anastacio Somoza, also recognized Franco. Albania, which was virtually an Italian protectorate at this time, extended its recognition to Franco on November 26, 1936.[72]

The Vatican did not immediately extend recognition to the Nationalist régime, as Franco so earnestly desired. After the weeks of anarchy and terror in the Loyalist zone immediately following the revolt of the generals, during which the Catholic church was a prime target, there was a distinct antipathy for the Republican cause at the Holy See.[73] And in July 1937, the Nationalist cause was greatly aided by the publication of a joint letter to "The Bishops of the Whole World," drafted by Cardinal Góma, the archbishop of Toledo, and signed by Spain's prelates with the significant exceptions of Bishop Mugica of Vitoria and Cardinal Vidal of Tarragoña, both of whom championed the cause of the Loyalist Catalans and Basques. In this letter, it was stated that the civil war was theologically just, for the Spanish Nationalists had taken up arms "to save the principles of religion."[74] It was not surprising, therefore, that within a few weeks, the Vatican recognized the Nationalist government, even though the Republicans still held a goodly portion of the territory of Spain, and the outcome of the struggle was by no means as yet assured.[75]

When the forces fighting with the Nationalists defeated the final remnants of the Loyalist army at the end of March 1939, most of the nations of the world extended diplomatic recognition to Franco. An outstanding exception was Mexico. When the war ended, all official diplomatic relations between Mexico and Spain were severed, and to date they have never been resumed. Mexico refused to recognize the Nationalist regime on legal grounds.[76] The war, it believed, had not been a civil war but an aggressive war in which foreign troops, aiding a minority dissident faction, had, through the use of force, denied to the Spanish majority their international, legally protected right of self-determination. Mexico pointed out that she was a signatory of a number of multipartite treaties that obligated her not to recognize territorial acquisitions

[72] See Padelford, *International Law and Diplomacy in the Spanish Civil Strife*, p. 6, n. 18.
[73] See Toynbee, "The International Repercussions of the War in Spain," 2: 219–20; Juan de Iturralde, *El Catolicismo y la Cruzada de Franco* (Bayonne, 1955), 1: 99–104; Georges Bernanos, *Les Grands Cimetières sous la Lune* (Paris: Plon, 1938), p. 141.
[74] Thomas, *The Spanish Civil War*, p. 450.
[75] José Yanguas y Messia, *Beligerencia, No Intervención y Recocimiento* (Bilboa: Artes Graficas "Grijelmo," 1938), pp. 169 ff.
[76] L. E. Smith, *Mexico and the Spanish Republicans*, p. 202.

or special advantages obtained by force or other effective coercive measures but to defend the inviolability of the territory of a state from military occupation or other measures imposed by another state, directly or indirectly, even temporarily for any motive whatever. Any recognition of the Franco régime, which had been brought into power only by the aggressive acts of other nations, would be a breach of international law and would imply that force constituted the basis of right.

If these treaties to which Mexico was a party could be considered codifications of existing general international legal principles, then Mexico's legal stand is unassailable. If, on the other hand, they enunciated new principles of international law, they could only apply among the signatories. Since Spain was not one of the contracting parties, she would then have good grounds to object to such rules being applied in her case.[77]

Mexico also voted for the 1932 resolution of the League of Nations which declared that "it is incumbent upon the Members of the League of Nations not to recognize any situation, treaty or agreement which may be brought about by means contrary to the Covenant of the League of Nations or to the Pact of Paris."[78] Since article 10 of the covenant clearly stated that all signatories agreed to respect and preserve from external aggression the territorial integrity and existing political independence of all member states, and since Franco had taken over the government of Spain with the assistance of Germany and Italy, Mexico strongly implied that it was the duty of all League members not to recognize the régime.

This nonrecognition resolution of the League, however, may not have been an enunciation of a rule of either general or particular international law. The binding nature of league, and later United Nations, resolutions has been open to doubt and controversy. A number of authorities take the position that a mere international resolution or declaration, no matter how strong the language used, does not have the same force of law as a ratified treaty.[79] Resolutions are thought to create at best only moral obligations. On the other hand, there is a strong body of authoritative opinion which declares that resolutions are juridical in nature, have an obligatory force upon adopting nations, and constitute international legislation.[80] Again, if resolutions are truly statements of existing law or have the force of creating law, Mexico's position could not be challenged. The

[77] Treaties do not impose duties upon third parties that are not parties thereto. Georg Schwarzenberger, *A Manual of International Law* (3d ed.; London: Stevens, 1952), p. 68.

[78] As contained in *American Journal of International Law*, Supplement (1933), 27: 132.

[79] "The Binding Force of League Resolutions," *British Yearbook of International Law* 16 (1935): 157.

[80] Podesta Costa, *Derecho Internacional Público*, 1: 367; Charles G. Fenwick, *International Law* (3d ed.; New York: Appleton-Century-Crofts, 1948), p. 205.

covenant of the League does not contain an express provision requiring nonrecognition, although it can be strongly argued that the duty of non-recognition flows from the obligation of the parties to the treaty to condemn resort to force for the solution of international controversies. Such an obligation would be incompatible with approval of the results of the use of force, which would obviously be involved in an act of recognition. But again, some might question whether the Spanish Civil War was an "international" controversy in the sense used by the covenant.

Since Mexico's nonrecognition of Franco withheld from his government the moral and material support it would have derived from being accepted by one of the leading Latin American nations, it has been intimated that such nonrecognition was an interventionary act on the part of Mexico.[81] But if one acknowledges the fact that Franco came into power primarily as a result of German and Italian intervention, it can be said that acts violative of international law do not give rise to new rights and obligations and therefore that nonrecognition by Mexico was a permissible legal sanction. The Mexican stand was endorsed by certain other nations, such as China, New Zealand, and Russia, which have not extended official recognition to the Franco régime.[82]

Blockade. As early as November 1936, the Nationalists had announced a blockade of Republican ports and warned foreign shipping that it would be attacked in Republican harbors if found carrying arms to Spain. This presented the neutral nations with a dilemma. Since they had refused to recognize the belligerency of the rebels, a state of war could not be said to exist. And if a state of war did not exist, then all nations had a right to pursue ordinary peacetime maritime trade with the legitimate government and to receive protection at the docks. The legitimate government could, of course, take internal police measures within its own territory and territorial waters to prevent outside assistance from reaching those in rebellion, but the rebels had no acknowledged international legal right to interfere with neutral trade.[83] Thus foreign ships captured by the rebels could not be considered prizes, nor could foreign ships be made the object of direct attack. If they were, the state of registry could take retaliatory action. This, of course, would involve such states in the civil strife—precisely what all were attempting to avoid.

The neutral nations refused to acknowledge that a war was in progress. The Nationalists paid little heed to this refusal. They behaved as if belligerency had been recognized, even going beyond the internationally

[81] L. E. Smith, *Mexico and the Spanish Republicans*, p. 205.

[82] United Nations, "Report of the Subcommittee on the Spanish Question," *Official Records of the Security Council*, 1st year, 1st series, Special Supplement (rev. ed., 1946), pp. 73, 74, 78–82.

[83] H. A. Smith, "Some Problems of the Spanish Civil War," p. 25.

established rights of search and seizure, sinking neutral merchantmen, and capturing those not engaged in contraband trade. The nations subjected to such indignities limited themselves to protests and requests for compensation.[84]

Early in April 1937, the Nationalists announced an extension of their blockade of Republican ports to include not only ships carrying arms but also foreign relief ships carrying food to Republican Spain, claiming that the Republicans, with the vast sums in their control, could purchase all the food necessary for the feeding of their people and that if foreign humanitarian agencies sent food the Republicans would have more money to spend on armaments.[85] Since food for civilians had never been considered contraband, this brought increased protests from abroad. There was some question whether the Nationalists meant to enforce this blockade. Within a few days, the British navy announced that the blockade was effective, and the British government warned all British merchantmen to remain outside Spanish territorial waters. The liberal parties of Britain were becoming increasingly disenchanted with the Conservative government's conduct of Spanish relations, in view of the open intervention of Italy and Germany on the side of the Nationalists, and this warning created an uproar in Parliament. It was claimed that it was equivalent to an acceptance of the Nationalist blockade and therefore an intervention. A British merchantman, defying the government, tested the effectiveness of the blockade. It entered a Republican port without encountering a Nationalist blockade. The British admiralty then had to admit publicly that it had been in error in announcing that the blockade was effective, and the British government was forced to rescind its warning.[86]

Military Assistance. Although the number of German and Italian troops who went to fight for the Nationalists and the amount of war material from German and Italian sources will probably never be known absolutely, some figures have been published. The Italian War Office revealed in 1939 that between mid-December 1936 and mid-April 1937 the navy had transported to Spain 100,000 men, 4,370 motor vehicles, 40,000 tons of war material, and 750 guns. In addition, units of the Italian fleet had been employed in the first days of the war not only in escorting Italian troop transports from Italy to Spain but also in naval operations against the Republican fleet and coast, as well as against ships bringing cargoes to Republican ports, many of which had been sunk. Italian warships had assisted General Franco's forces in defense of Majorca and with the occupation of the neighboring island of Ibiza in September 1936. With regard to Italian ground forces, the first con-

---

[84] McNair, "The Law Relating to the Civil War in Spain," p. 471.
[85] Toynbee, "The International Repercussions of the War in Spain," 2: 307 ff.
[86] Thomas, *The Spanish Civil War*, pp. 407–10.

tingent of Black Shirts, numbering 3,000, did not leave Italy until December 18, 1936. The first shipment of Italian artillery, anti-aircraft guns, and armored cars, however, reached Spain toward the end of September.

German planes were active on the side of General Franco in the first weeks of the war in transporting Moors and Spanish Foreign Legionnaires from Spanish Morocco to the mainland and in bombing operations. According to the official German account, the first armored car detachment was dispatched in October 1936. In addition to taking part in the fighting, the detachment formed a school of instruction for Spaniards in the use of armored cars, guns, and flame throwers. In November the first elements of the German Condor Legion arrived in Spain, consisting of a complete air force corps (combat, pursuit, and reconnaissance planes) and also intelligence and anti-aircraft detachments, and approximately 6,500 "volunteers."[87]

Under international law, a foreign nation has no duty to prevent the participation by its individual subjects in an insurrection, whether belligerency has been recognized or not. Prior to the recognition of belligerency, the foreign state itself may not aid the rebels or permit hostile military expeditions to leave its territory to aid the rebels. Once belligerency is recognized, certain rules of law which have been embodied in the Hague conventions become applicable, among them one that declares: "Corps of combatants cannot be formed nor recruiting offices opened on the territory of a neutral power in the interests of the belligerents."[88]

Germany and Italy sent in regular military and air units which were definitely organized as corps of combatants before departing for Spain. Even so, they were euphemistically called "volunteers." Since neither nation had recognized the belligerency of the Nationalists prior to such aid, there is little doubt that the sending of the corps of combatants constituted an international wrong. On November 18, 1936, they extended recognition to the Nationalist government, and there can also be little doubt that recognition of legitimacy at that stage of the conflict constituted another international wrong against Spain because it was premature. Even if recognition were viewed as equivalent to recognition of belligerency, the law of neutrality would still have required that no corps of combatants be formed on German or Italian soil to fight in Spain. The fact that corps were formed amounted to more than mere intervention—it amounted to armed aggression or war.[89]

[87] On this aid rendered by the Germans and Italians, see Bolloten, *The Grand Camouflage*, pp. 95, 96, 134; U.S. Department of State, *Documents on German Foreign Policy, 1918–1945*, doc. no. 158.

[88] See relevences in nn. 51 and 52.

[89] This, of course, was always the view taken by Mexico. L. E. Smith, *Mexico and the Spanish Republicans*, p. 185.

IV. THE ROLE OF INTERNATIONAL INSTITUTIONS

Regional

At the time of the Spanish Civil War, no formal regional organization existed that could concern itself with the threat to peace posed by the conflict. There was an informal European organization, however, that was formed for the purpose of localizing the civil war and preventing it from spreading outside Spanish borders and leading to a general conflagration.[1]

Within a few weeks of the rebellion's commencement in Spain, it became evident that large quantities of material aid in the form of men and supplies were flooding into Spain from abroad. Aid from Portugal, Italy, and Germany went to the rebels. Charges were made that Russia was providing assistance to the Republican government. This foreign intervention caused considerable alarm to the French premier, who envisioned a clash between competing interests and ideologies over Spain which would lead to international war and involve France. He thereupon prohibited the sending of war material to either Spanish faction and, with British support, sought a joint agreement with other states to observe strict principles of nonintervention in Spain. Agreement was eventually forthcoming from some twenty-seven European states. The accord was informal and consisted of a series of unilateral declarations that nonintervention in varying degrees would be observed. The great majority of the states pledged themselves

1) to prohibit the direct or indirect export or re-export of arms, munitions, materials of war, aircraft (assembled or dismantled), and vessels of war;
2) to make the prohibition applicable to contracts in process of execution; and
3) to keep the other participating governments informed of measures taken to effectuate the application of the agreement.

Some seventeen states, including Britain and France but not Germany and Italy, assumed an even stricter duty "to abstain rigorously from all interference, direct or indirect, in the internal affairs" of Spain.[2]

This agreement could be considered a regional attempt at international cooperation for a limited purpose. It was primarily a declaration

---

[1] For a detailed discussion of the nonintervention system, see Norman J. Padelford, *International Law and Diplomacy in the Spanish Civil Strife* (New York: Macmillan, 1939), chap. 3. A briefer exposé is that of Francis O. Wilcox, "The Localization of the Spanish War," *American Political Science Review* 32 (1938): 237.

[2] Padelford, *International Law and Diplomacy in the Spanish Civil Strife*, p. 205.

of policy to be followed by the adhering states, the policy to be effected by national measures of each state. Observance of the accord was dependent solely upon the good faith of each state, for no sanctions or enforcement measures against states failing to live up to their word were created. An international organ was set up, the Nonintervention Committee, with its seat in London. This committee was instructed to gather information concerning the measures taken by each state to comply with the accord and to examine and resolve the difficulties arising from the application of these measures.[3] The membership of the committee consisted of representatives of the European states participating in the nonintervention agreement. The committee agreed to entertain complaints concerning violations of the agreement. Charges of violations began to flow in almost immediately. The complaints were directed primarily against Italy, Germany, and Portugal, which were charged with intervention in the form of arms shipments to the rebels, and against the Soviet Union, which was charged with intervention on the side of the government. Despite the fact that detailed complaints were presented and occasioned much wrangling in the committee, no censure or other definite action was forthcoming. The committee was hamstrung. It had no investigative machinery to corroborate the facts. After charge and flat denial by the accused, the committee could only find that sufficient evidence had not been presented to lead to condemnation. Recognizing that the committee had no way to check the facts, the parties agreed toward the end of November to submit no more complaints to the committee. Instead they decided to establish a control plan of reliable observers to report violations.[4]

At this time, the nonintervention accord proved ineffective and large amounts of contraband war material continued to enter Spain destined for both sides. Soviet officers and specialists were aiding and even commanding Loyalist forces. Thousands of volunteers were entering Loyalist territory to fight. The rebels were also receiving enforcements from the armed forces of Germany and Italy.[5] Since the nonintervention agreement did not apply to volunteers entering Spain, a proposal was made for collaboration among the powers to prevent their entry. On February 16, 1937, the powers decided that from midnight, February 20–21, the nonintervention agreement would be extended "to cover recruitment in and transit through or departure from their respective countries of persons of non-Spanish nationality proposing to proceed to Spain or Spanish dependencies for the purpose of taking service in the present

[3] Wilcox, "Localization of the Spanish War," p. 242.
[4] This stage of the Committee's life is well explained in David T. Cattell, *Soviet Diplomacy and the Spanish Civil War* (Berkeley: University of California Press, 1957), chap. 5.
[5] See the section on "Military Assistance" in pt. 3 above.

war." It was further agreed to adopt a system of supervision for the nonintervention agreement and its extension.[6] Originally a corps of observers inside Spain at various strategic points, had been planned, but the two factions in Spain reacted unfavorably to this proposal. Therefore, it became necessary to attempt to achieve the same results by stationing observers outside Spain. As finally adopted, the control plan provided for the supervision of Spanish land frontiers by an international force of observers stationed along the Gibraltar-Spanish border, the Portuguese-Spanish border, and the Franco-Spanish border. These observers were empowered to examine passports, to call for verification of the consignments of goods, and to enter railroad stations and similar places to determine whether war materials were being transported to Spain and whether foreign volunteers were attempting to enter. Infractions were to be reported to an official of the country in which the observer was stationed and also to the International Board for Nonintervention, an organ created to administer the observation scheme.[7]

The plan also provided for supervision of access to Spain by sea as well as by land. Officers were to be stationed at certain observation ports. Ships were to stop at these ports to be boarded by the observers, who would search for possible violations of the nonintervention accord. To fulfill their task, the observers were to be given all necessary facilities on the vessel; they were to be permitted to question passengers, officers, and crew and to examine their passports and identify papers; and they were to supervise the unloading of the cargo and the debarkation of passengers. If an observer discovered a violation, he was to report in confidence to the international board for transmission to the Nonintervention Committee.

To ensure that the supervision of access by sea was effective, a system of naval observation was also established around the Spanish coast. The coast was divided into eight zones, which were to be patrolled by warships of Britain, France, Germany, and Italy.[8] The zones were distributed so that the British and French patrolled access to the Nationalists, and Germany and Italy supervised those portions of the coast under Republican control. The patrol was conducted within ten miles of the Spanish coast but not within the three-mile limit. The patrol vessels were authorized to approach ships of participating countries to ascertain

[6] Agreement to Prohibit the Departure of Volunteers for Spain, and Scheme of Observation of the Spanish Frontiers by Land and Sea is contained in Padelford, *International Law and Diplomacy in the Spanish Civil Strife*, pp. 311 (n. 1), 369 ff.

[7] Wilcox, "Localization of the Spanish War," p. 247.

[8] The Soviet Union refused a part in the patrol, for she had been assigned a zone on the Bay of Biscay but wanted a zone on the Mediterranean coast. The other parties refused this request. See Cattell, *Soviet Diplomacy and the Spanish Civil War*, pp. 67–68.

their identity and, if necessary, to stop and board them, to examine their papers, and to discover whether the vessel had stopped at a designated observation port before approaching Spanish waters. When an offense against nonintervention was discovered, it was reported and the participating governments were called upon to take appropriate legal action against the owners or master of the vessel involved. Report of the penalties inflicted was to be given to the board. The control and direction of the patrol vessels were left solely in the hands of the state furnishing the vessels. The nonintervention committee in London received no instructions about the conduct or whereabouts of the warships within the zones.

The observation plan contained many weaknesses. It did not cover Spanish ships, either Nationalist or Republican, or ships of other nations not members of the committee. There was no air patrol; hence planes could be flown directly to Spain. No sanctions were provided for violations by governments.[9]

The naval patrol was not to be of long duration, for Germany and Italy withdrew from it on June 23, 1937, and France and Great Britain abandoned it upon initiation of an antipiracy patrol in September 1937. The facts behind the breakdown of the naval patrol system are as follows. On May 29, 1937, a Loyalist attack on a German patrol vessel occurred in the rebel-held port of Ibiza. The Spanish government claimed that it could not guarantee the safety of patrol vessels if they entered known ports of rebel activity. The Germans retaliated with a naval attack on the Spanish port of Almería and then refused to take part in the control scheme or in the Nonintervention Committee until guarantees against the recurrence of such events were received.[10] Thereafter, the Four-Power Agreement of June 12, 1937, was drafted, whereby Germany, Italy, France, and Great Britain agreed to act in concert if future attacks were made upon patrol vessels and further agreed to request the two contending Spanish parties to establish certain safety zones where the ships would be free from attack.[11] The Spanish government rejected the guarantee of safety zones. When the German cruiser, *Leipzig*, suffered a torpedo attack, consultation among the four parties occurred but failed to result in a line of action to be taken. Soon afterward, Germany and Italy withdrew from the naval patrol plan.[12]

Indiscriminate attacks on shipping in the Mediterranean by unidenti-

[9] *Ibid.*

[10] On the ending of the naval patrol, see *ibid.,* pp. 79 ff.; Padelford, *International Law and Diplomacy in the Spanish Civil Strife*, pp. 93 ff.

[11] Padelford, *International Law and Diplomacy in the Spanish Civil Strife*, pp. 32–33.

[12] On the *Leipzig* incident, see Cattell, *Soviet Diplomacy and the Spanish Civil War*, p. 82.

fied warships, aircraft, and submarines reached a high point in August 1937. Most of the targets were merchantmen of the Spanish Republic, the Soviet Union, and the democratic powers, although there were reports that two Italian ships were fired upon. When on August 31, 1937, a British cruiser reported an attack by an unidentified submarine, the British and French called a conference at Nyon to deal with the problem. Bulgaria, Egypt, Great Britain, France, Greece, Rumania, the Soviet Union, Turkey, and Yugoslavia were represented. Italy and Germany refused to attend, declaring that the matter should be referred to the Nonintervention Committee. Their absence did not deter the other powers, who drew up an agreement declaring the attacks by submarines not belonging to either of the Spanish contenders violative of international law as defined in part 4 of the London Naval Treaty of 1922 and identifying them as acts against humanity which should be treated as piracy. To protect ships not belonging to either of the Spanish factions, it was agreed that the Mediterranean should be patrolled primarily by the British and French navies. This patrol would engage any submarine that was guilty of piratical attack on non-Spanish vessels. The Nyon agreement was later extended to include attacks by surface vessels and aircraft against non-Spanish vessels. On September 21, Italy joined the arrangement and participated in the naval patrol. There was an immediate cessation of attacks, although a few were to occur again after a period of time.[13]

When the Germans withdrew from the naval patrol, the British and French proposed to fill the gaps with their own vessels with neutral, impartial observers aboard. The Germans and Italians refused and instead submitted their own proposals for the granting of belligerent rights to the two contending factions in Spain, the termination of the naval patrol (which they called ineffective), and the retention of the previously existing land and ship observation plans. A recognition of belligerency would confer on both sides the right of search and seizure on the high seas, confiscation of contraband goods, and maintenance of blockade. The two countries contended that such recognition would strengthen nonintervention. The conflicting parties themselves would be able to stop illegitimate arms traffic by a rigorous exercise of belligerent rights. Moreover, whereas the nonintervention scheme could control traffic only on ships of the participants, the conflicting parties, as belligerents, would and could extend their control to all ships. The German and Italian scheme, of course, would have redounded to the benefit of the Nationalists. They possessed greater naval strength than the Republicans and could, by means of search and seizure at sea and blockade, legiti-

[13] On the Nyon conference and agreement, see Padelford, *International Law and Diplomacy in the Spanish Civil Strife*, pp. 41 ff., 603 ff.

mately and effectively prevent the Republicans from acquiring outside help by sea.[14]

On May 29, 1937, the Council of the League of Nations had passed a resolution declaring that the most effective means of assuring non-intervention in Spain would be the withdrawal of all non-Spanish combatants.[15] The British, in an effort to work out an acceptable plan of continued nonintervention, submitted a program which combined the German-Italian proposals with the withdrawal of non-Spanish combatants. The British program envisioned the establishment of nonintervention officers in Spanish ports and the withdrawal of the naval patrol; the establishment of commissions to arrange and supervise the withdrawal of foreign nationals; and the recognition of belligerent rights as soon as the Nonintervention Committee determined that substantial progress had been made toward the withdrawal of foreign nationals. This program served as a basis for discussion, but basic disagreement could not be overcome. The Germans and Italians demanded that recognition of belligerent rights precede the withdrawal of non-Spanish combatants, while the Russians, who objected to a grant of belligerent rights in the existing circumstances, believed that a complete withdrawal of foreign troops would have to be accomplished first. Deadlock ensued. The question was reopened, however, and the Nonintervention Committee once again considered the matter, adopting a new plan on July 5, 1938. This plan provided for the withdrawal of the foreign volunteers, for the grant of certain belligerent rights at sea to the two Spanish parties, and for the observation of the Spanish land and sea frontiers. An elaborate scheme was worked out which set forth a timetable for the withdrawal of foreign combatants, defined the term "foreign volunteer," and created methods of financing and supervising the plan. The supervision was entrusted to the International Board for Nonintervention. Duties that had to be exercised in Spain were to be entrusted to two commissions attached to the two headquarters of the contenders.

The new plan received the approval of the Nonintervention Committee. It was then placed before the two parties in Spain for acceptance. The Republicans made a generally favorable reply, although they raised certain questions. The Nationalists accepted withdrawal in principle but demanded recognition of belligerency before the start of withdrawals and equal numbers of withdrawals from both sides. They also raised objection that the plan would not affect volunteers from states not participating in the nonintervention agreement. Consequently, 50 percent of the volunteers on the Republican side would be excluded from withdrawals. Finally, the scheme of observers on Spanish soil would, according to the

[14] *Ibid.*, pp. 96 ff.
[15] League of Nations, *Official Journal*, May-June 1937, p. 333.

Nationalists, usurp Spanish sovereign rights.[16] Stalemate existed once again.

In September 1938, the Republican government announced before the League of Nations its proposal unilaterally to withdraw foreign volunteers fighting on its side. This was not to be done under the Nonintervention Committee's auspices but under an international commission appointed by the League. A commission was appointed, and evacuation of foreign forces from Loyalist Spain began.[17] Thereafter Franco agreed to discuss the removal of foreign forces with the secretary of the Nonintervention Committee. On October 15, they arranged for the embarkation of ten thousand Italians. Thousands of foreign troops remained in Nationalist Spain, however, after the evacuation of all foreign soldiers from the Republican side.[18]

With the failure of the European powers to obtain acceptance of a withdrawal plan, the nonintervention system quietly died.

Global—the League of Nations

The Spanish Civil War and its threat to world peace intruded into the councils of the League of Nations in that unfortunate organization's dying years, although the question was not placed on the agenda of the Assembly when it met in September 1936 after the outbreak of the war.[19] The British and French had persuaded the Spanish delegate to refrain from formal presentation of the question. They favored the nonintervention approach and wanted the matter left to the Nonintervention Committee. The Spanish delegate did, however, insist on speaking on the question in the general debate, which could include matters not formally on the agenda, for the League was the only international body open to the Spanish government. It was not represented on the Nonintervention Committee. In his remarks, the Spanish representative declared that the conflict was more than civil strife, that "the blood-stained soil of Spain is already in fact, the battlefield of a world war."[20]

He went on to point out that a system of collective security, such as the League, was supposed to protect states against internal rebellion supported and fomented from outside, and he attacked the nonintervention agreement as actually an intervention in the internal affairs of the Spanish government on the side of the rebels.

[16] All of the documents about the proposed modification of the system are contained in Padelford, *International Law and Diplomacy in the Spanish Civil Strife*, p. 511.

[17] League of Nations, *Official Journal*, February 1939, p. 139.

[18] Cattell, *Soviet Diplomacy and the Spanish Civil War*, pp. 123–26.

[19] On the League of Nations and the Spanish strife, see Francis Paul Walters, *A History of the League of Nations* (London: Oxford University Press, 1952), 2: 721 ff., 789 ff.

[20] League of Nations, *Official Journal*, 1936, Special Supplement No. 155, p. 48.

No resolution was forthcoming from the Assembly. Only four other members made remarks concerning Spain. Three of these defended the nonintervention agreement as vital to European peace.[21] Mexico, on the other hand, objected strongly to the nonintervention policy, declaring that in effect it denied the government of Spain a legitimate means of defense against a military uprising and that it was not only unjust but contrary to international legal principles. Mexico also urged that the Spanish problem be placed before the League and that it not be handled by an outside agency, the Nonintervention Committee.[22]

In November 1936, the Spanish government did charge Germany and Italy with armed intervention against Spain, formally asking for a meeting of the Council of the League under Article 11 of the Covenant, which called upon the League to take action to safeguard the peace of nations in event of war or threat of war. The Council, by a resolution adopted on December 12, 1936, contented itself with an affirmation of the obligations of states not to intervene in the internal affairs of other states and a call for strict enforcement of the nonintervention agreement. The secretary-general was authorized to make the technical services of the League available for humanitarian needs during the reconstruction of Spain. The Spanish appeal was effectively shelved.[23]

Chile, early in 1937, brought before the Council of the League the problem of asylum of refugees in the embassies and legations in Madrid. It proposed that a League commission be sent to Spain to supervise the evacuation of the refugees. The Republican government rejected such intervention by the League. It did, however, indicate that it would negotiate directly with the states concerned.[24]

The Spanish government appealed its case to the Council under article 11 again in May 1937. It again charged Italian and German intervention and aggression in Spain. A white book was presented containing documentary evidence that contingents of the regular Italian army were operating in Spain, amounting, in its view, to an invasion of Spain by Italy. The bombing of Guernica was also detailed. Again the Council refused to act and simply supported the activities of the Nonintervention Committee, urging the withdrawal of foreign combatants and condemning the bombardment of open towns.[25]

The government appealed a third time to the League Council in August 1937, this time in the face of the bombing and torpedoing of Span-

---

[21] *Ibid.*, pp. 51–52 (France), p. 64 (Soviet Union), pp. 83–84 (Portugal).

[22] *Ibid.*, pp. 100–101.

[23] League of Nations, *Official Journal*, January 1937, pp. 18–19, 35.

[24] *Ibid.*, pp. 19–20; League of Nations, *Official Journal*, February 1937, pp. 130–31, 134.

[25] League of Nations, *Official Journal*, 1937, Special Supplement, No. 165; and *ibid.*, May-June 1937, pp. 333, 572.

ish vessels by unidentified submarines and aircraft. Aggression by the Italian government and navy was charged.[26] The president of the Council postponed the appeal and also the regular session of the Council until after the Nyon conference, which had been called to deal with such attacks.[27] The agreements that emerged from the conference, however, related only to the protection of foreign merchant ships and not those of Spain. Republican Spain was most indignant that collective security did not extend to her ships. In an attempt to placate the Spanish Government, the Council resolved that "all attacks of this kind against any merchant vessel are repugnant to the conscience of the civilized nations which now finds expression through the Council."[28]

The Assembly had had occasion to consider the Spanish conflict in September 1937, when the Spanish representative asked the Assembly to recognize

(1) That the aggression of Germany and Italy in Spain be recognized as such. (2) That, in consequence of this recognition, the League examine as rapidly as possible the means by which that agression may be brought to an end. (3) That full rights once more be given to the Spanish Government freely to acquire all the war material it may consider necessary. (4) That the non-Spanish combatants be withdrawn from Spanish territory. (5) That the measures to be adopted for security in the Mediterranean be extended to Spain, and that Spain be granted her legitimate share in them.[29]

A less innocuous resolution than in the past was finally negotiated in committee, recognizing that there were "veritable foreign army corps on Spanish soil, which [represented] foreign intervention in Spanish Affairs." The resolution accepted in principle the Spanish government's contention that if an immediate and complete withdrawal of foreign combatants could not be effected in the near future the members of the League should consider ending the policy of nonintervention. A large majority of states voted for this resolution, but since unanimity was required, it failed to pass.[30] However, the resolution may at least be said to constitute a moral confirmation of the Spanish Republican position. Despite the possible moral force of the large vote, months passed without any withdrawal of foreign military personnel. On May 13, 1938, the Spanish government, undeterred by its former defeats, again brought its troubles to the League, specifically requesting an end to the noninter-

[26] League of Nations, *Official Journal*, December 1937, pp. 1161–63.
[27] Padelford, *International Law and Diplomacy in the Spanish Civil Strife*, p. 131.
[28] League of Nations, *Official Journal*, December 1937, pp. 944–45.
[29] League of Nations, *Official Journal*, 1937, Special Supplement No. 169, pp. 55–59.
[30] *Ibid.*, pp. 99–100. See also Cattell, *Soviet Diplomacy and the Spanish Civil War*, p. 99.

vention system. Britain and France were opposed and sought to end the debate quickly by pushing a vote on Spain's resolution within a few hours of its presentation. Since this did not permit sufficient time for the delegates to receive their governments' instructions, a large number of abstentions permitted the resolution's defeat. Only Spain and the Soviet Union voted in favor.[31]

The Republican government made its final appeal to the League in September 1938. It had decided unilaterally to withdraw all foreign combatants fighting on its side. The League Assembly was therefore asked to request the Council to send impartial observers to assure that the withdrawal was carried out absolutely and completely.[32] The League delegates expressed approval of the decision of withdrawal, but many believed that the Nonintervention Committee should perform the task of supervision. The Spanish Republicans adamantly opposed any such referral of the matter to the committee on the ground that although Spain was not represented in its membership Germany and Italy, aggressors against Spain, were.[33] The Council then, on October 1, adopted a resolution which authorized the creation and dispatch to Spain of a commission.[34] Three months later after careful investigation this commission reported the complete withdrawal of the foreign combatants from Republican Spain.[35]

Explanation of the Role of International Institutions

The role of the ad hoc regional international organization, the European nonintervention system, and the global organization, the League of Nations, in solving problems arising from the Spanish Civil War proved to be very small.

A factor which no doubt limited the effectiveness of the nonintervention system was the controversy over its legality under international law. The Spanish Republican government, for example, called the nonintervention agreement a "legal monstrosity."[36] Mexico was of the opinion that it was a violation of customary international law.[37] Even some of the participating states in the nonintervention agreement seemed to have some doubts, for the plan was identified as a policy for this exceptional circumstance only.[38]

---

[31] League of Nations, *Official Journal,* May-June 1938, p. 356; Padelford, *International Law and Diplomacy in the Spanish Civil Strife,* p. 138.

[32] League of Nations, *Official Journal,* February 1939, p. 139.

[33] Walters, *A History of the League of Nations,* 2: 789-90.

[34] League of Nations, *Official Journal,* February 1939, p. 126.

[35] Walters, *A History of the League of Nations,* 2: 790.

[36] League of Nations, *Official Journal,* 1936, Special Supplement No. 155, p. 49.

[37] *Ibid.,* p. 101.

[38] See the Declaration by the Rumanian government, for example, in Padelford, *International Law and Diplomacy in the Spanish Civil Strife,* pp. 226-27.

This, then, was the legal difficulty. Although agreement is not universal, it is widely maintained that a status of insurgency favors the legitimate government, since the shipment of arms and war materials to that government is not forbidden whereas aid by other governments to the insurgents is. As long as a status of insurgency existed in Spain, which admittedly was not long, it has been contended that the nonintervention accord, by repeatedly denying aid to both sides, actually aided the insurgents, who benefited from the denial of aid to the government. Hence, nonintervention became intervention in the affairs of Spain. When the Spanish conflict reached the magnitude of war, which probably occurred within a very few months of the rebellion's outbreak, belligerency should have been recognized and neutrality observed. In failing to recognize belligerency and to grant full belligerent rights when all necessary conditions were present, the several European powers appear to have violated international law and to have intervened in Spanish affairs.[39]

It should be noted further that the nonintervention system imposed neutrality, as required by a status of belligerency, but refused to recognize belligerency. Neutrality bans the delivery of war supplies and the granting of loans by a *state* to the belligerents. It also requires the exercise of due diligence by a *state* to prevent corps of combatants from forming within its territory to fight on either belligerent side. It does not, however, forbid the traffic in war materials or the granting of loans by *private individuals* or the crossing of borders singly by persons going to fight for the belligerents. Once belligerency has been recognized the conflicting parties are accorded the right of search and seizure on the high seas.[40]

The nonintervention system placed a collective ban on the export of war materials by the state or by private individuals and also on the departure of troops or volunteers. Loans by governments were also proscribed by those states which subscribed to rigorous nonintervention. Moreover, the belligerent right of search and seizure was denied the two Spanish belligerents. The nonintervention system, then, insofar as traditional international law was concerned, was an aberration.

The composition of the nonintervention system and its committee also reduced its chances of effectiveness. The organization was regional, that is, confined to European participants. States outside the European community were free to ignore the prohibitions against the exportation of arms to Spain and later the departure of volunteers. As a result, there

---

[39] On insurgency and belligerency, see the section on "International Law, Civil Strife, and Foreign Governments" in pt. 3 above.

[40] See Lassa Oppenheim, *International Law* (7th ed.; London: Longmans Green, 1948), vol. 2, secs. 321, 322, 331, 332, 349, 350, 351, 352, 414.

were serious gaps in the system. Even more serious was the fact that the two contending factions were not participants in the nonintervention accord. This created special consultative problems and excluded land observers from Spanish soil and Spanish ships from the ship-observer scheme or naval patrol. Shipments of arms from participating states could easily be made to a consignee in a nonparticipating state and thus to Spain, perhaps even on a Spanish vessel. Such shipments would not be observed by the officers of the Nonintervention Committee. Shippers in participating states could also, with some connivance of the master and Spanish authorities, divert their vessels into Spanish waters and discharge their cargoes without formal entry or clearance.

The procedure of the Nonintervention Committee was most cumbersome and conducive to delay. Complaints could be received only from members. This, of course, precluded direct complaints from the two most interested parties, the Spanish Republican and Nationalist authorities. When a complaint was received concerning a violation of the agreement, the rules required its submission to the alleged violator for refutation. When a reply was received, it was distributed among all the members who in turn required time for examination before committee consideration. The committee had no authority to carry out on-the-spot investigations. As a result, sufficient evidence was never presented to condemn any state.[41]

The factor that limited the role of the nonintervention system most substantially was its dependence on the good faith of its members to prevent certain foreign intervention in Spain. Unfortunately, good faith was not extended by certain of its members, the most powerful ones. Hence the system was violated on a grand scale. The principal protagonists, Britain and France, admitted that the nonintervention system was a "leaky dam," but defended it on the ground that the war had been confined to Spain.[42] This was true for the immediate years of Spain's travail, but some five months after the end of the Spanish Civil War, World War II saw its inception.

As we have seen, the League of Nations played a very limited role in the crisis caused by the Spanish Civil War. Only at intervals was its forum utilized. There was no legal reason why the collective security and sanction machinery of the League should not have been applied in the Spanish situation. As long as the civil conflict was purely internal in nature, it would probably have been considered a domestic matter and

[41] For a discussion of these weaknesses, see Wilcox, "Localization of the Spanish War," pp. 242–44; Padelford, *International Law and Diplomacy in the Civil Strife*, p. 140.

[42] On the motivations of the various powers, see Cattell, *Soviet Diplomacy and the Spanish Civil War*, chap. 5; Wilcox, "Localization of the Spanish Civil War," pp. 258–60; Walters, *A History of the League of Nations*, 2: 721 ff., 789 ff.

outside the competence of the League. But when there was evidence of massive foreign intervention, the issue should no longer have been avoided.[43] Article 10 of the Covenant pledged the members to preserve against external aggression the territorial integrity and political independence of states and empowered the League Council, in case of such aggression, to advise the members on the fulfillment of their obligations. Article 11 made war and the threat thereof a matter of League concern, authorizing the League to take action to safeguard the peace of nations. Thus it would seem clear that collective action could have been taken against the foreign intervention and aggression in Spain.

Political facts of life, however, precluded League action. As discussed before, the British and French opposed consideration of the matter by the League and preferred to deal through the Nonintervention Committee. Their motivations have been explained in various ways. It has been said that they wanted no open break with the Axis powers and, hence, wanted no consideration of the war in Spain in the League, where the issue might have gotten out of hand. It has also been said that they wanted to prevent further weakening and embarrassment of the League, which had just suffered great loss of prestige by Italy's conquest of Ethiopia and the German occupation of the Rhineland. Any serious action by the League in the Spanish situation would have led to Italian withdrawal therefrom. In fact she did give notice of her withdrawal in December 1937, even though the League had never taken any serious action concerning Spain.[44] Germany had withdrawn several years previously. It was generally believed that more cooperation could be had outside the League. In any event, in view of previous League failures in the field of collective security, it would have been too much to hope that it could have dealt successfully with the ideological powder house and power politics of the Spanish strife.

[43] See Georg Schwarzenberger, *Power Politics* (3d ed.; New York: Praeger, 1964,) p. 282; Ann V. W. Thomas and A. J. Thomas, Jr., *Non-Intervention—the Law and Its Import in the Americas* (Dallas: S.M.U. Press, 1956), chap. 11.

[44] On these matters, see Walters, *A History of the League of Nations*, 2: 721, 768; Cattell, *Soviet Diplomacy and the Spanish Civil War*, p. 38.

Arnold Fraleigh

THE ALGERIAN REVOLUTION AS A CASE STUDY IN INTERNATIONAL LAW

I. THE RESORT TO FORCE

For a period of more than seven years—from November 1, 1954, to March 18, 1962—the forces of the Algerian National Liberation Front (FLN) fought the military forces of France. The casualties on the Algerian side have been estimated at 250,000, or 1,000,000 if all deaths of Moslem civilians are included.[1] On the French side, the casualties amounted to 20,000 military personnel and 25,000 civilians.[2] The nature of the warfare produced special categories of victims: refugees who sought exile in adjoining countries, regroupees who were resettled within Algeria, and detainees held in internment camps. Before the war ended, these war victims aggregated about 2,500,000: one-fourth of the population of Algeria.[3]

This human catastrophe was man's way of deciding the question whether Algeria and France should be two states or one—whether the people of Algeria should be given an opportunity to establish their own governmental system free of the political, economic, social, and cultural discrimination practiced against them by the French. How much of this catastrophe was due to the weakness of human nature and how much to the inadequacy of human institutions it is not possible to say. In this study, we shall limit ourselves to the role played in the catastrophe by the international legal system.

At the historical moment when the Algerian war broke out, that part of the international legal system having to do with the control of the use of military force attributed decisive significance to the distinction between international and internal wars. There was almost universal

[1] William H. Lewis, "The Decline of Algeria's FLN," *Middle East Journal*, Spring 1966, p. 164; Richard M. Brace, *Morocco, Algeria, and Tunisia* (Englewood Cliffs, N. J.: Prentice-Hall, 1964), p. 124; Arslan Humbaraci, *Algeria, a Revolution That Failed* (New York: Praeger, 1966), p. 2.

[2] *Le Monde*, March 9, 1962, p. 3; *New York Times*, Sept. 4, 1956, p. 1:8; Humbaraci, *Algeria*, p. 55. The estimate of French military casualties was drawn from *Le Monde* and includes both combat and accidental deaths and also deaths among paramilitary formations. The estimate of civilian deaths on the French side was obtained by adding a figure of 3,000 reported by the *Times* for the first two years of the war to a figure of 22,000, which Humbaraci gives for the period from 1956 to 1962 and which includes deaths of civilians in France.

[3] See the references cited in n. 1.

179

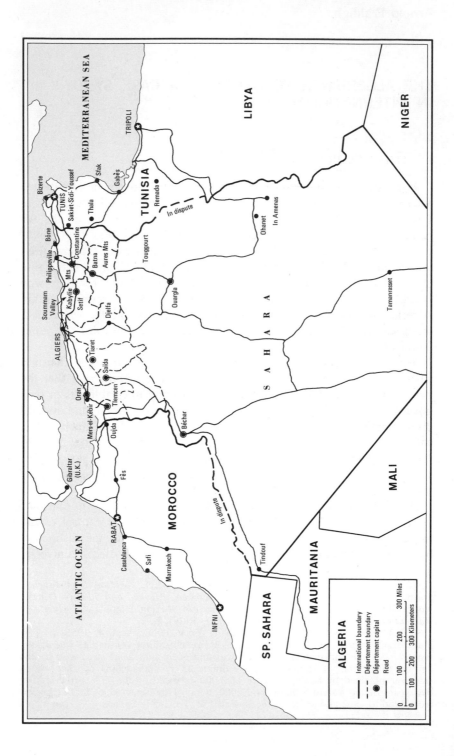

agreement among states that an international war—a war by one state against the political independence or territorial integrity of another state—was a violation of international law. One of the principal purposes for which the United Nations had been established was to organize a collective effort to enforce the prohibition against international wars. But there was then, and still is, no prohibition in the United Nations Charter against the use of military force within a state in an insurrection, a revolution, or a power struggle. Intervention in such internal wars by the United Nations was considered to be prohibited by article 2(7) of the Charter on the ground that internal wars are matters essentially within domestic jurisdiction.

There were, of course, even in 1954, the beginnings of an awareness of the inconsistency between a doctrine that the United Nations had no authority to intervene in a domestic insurrection, revolution, or power struggle, and the commitment of the United Nations to promote fundamental human rights. What if the internal war was fought to realize rights proclaimed by the United Nations in the Declaration of Human Rights to belong to every man? Or even if the internal war was merely a power struggle, was the slaughter of thousands of people a matter of no concern to the international community just because it occurred in an internal rather than an international war? The basic inconsistency between the dedication of the United Nations to the promotion of human rights and its preclusion from intervening in internal wars was especially evident during the period of the Algerian conflict, but it was still generally accepted that the international community acting through the United Nations could intervene in an international war but could not intervene in an internal war.

For the purpose of analyzing the application of the international legal system to the Algerian conflict, therefore, international lawyers had to face the question, Was the Algerian conflict an international or an internal war? The French claimed that the war was internal; in fact, they usually avoided calling it a war at all. To them it was a matter of using the force necessary to maintain domestic order. The FLN, on the other hand, repeatedly characterized the war as international and in 1958 formalized its view of the war by setting up a provisional government for Algeria.

It proved difficult even for an impartial observer to apply to the Algerian conflict the distinction which the legal system sought to draw between international and internal wars. Was the distinction to be based on the nature of the issue over which the war was fought? If so, there was some justification for saying that, as a war for political separation, the Algerian conflict should be classified as an international war. It was a war fought to decide whether there should be two states or one within a given area, a war between an existing state and a state struggling to be born.

Was the distinction between an international war and an internal war to be based on the extent of participation by outside states or by the spread of military operations beyond the confines of a single state? If so, the distinction was still difficult to apply to the Algerian conflict. The men who fired the guns were all nationals of the French Union, including soldiers on the French side from the French territories in Africa south of the Sahara and of course all those on the FLN side, assuming that Algeria was to be regarded as an integral part of France. Outside states did not send military forces to assist the FLN; but some states provided military and economic aid to France, and other states provided military and economic aid to the FLN. As for the territorial extent of military operations, the fighting took place for the most part in the territory of Algeria, with some guerrilla attacks within Metropolitan France, but there was a significant spillover of military action into Tunisia and Morocco.

There remained the possibility that the same war could be both international and internal, that its external and internal aspects could be regarded as severable, to be dealt with in different legal frameworks. This was essentially the position of the French government. In submitting its complaint against Egypt to the Security Council, the French government asserted that external aspects of the Algerian conflict were appropriately within the jurisdiction of the Security Council. At the same time, the French government contended that the struggle between the French and Algerian military forces was essentially an internal war, a domestic matter in which the political organs of the United Nations had no authority to intervene.

During the course of the Algerian conflict, there was no clear-cut resolution of the question whether the conflict was an international or an internal war. It remained a point of dispute between the French and the FLN until the cease-fire in 1962. In fact, the dispute persists even today. French authors and French sympathizers speak of the conflict as an insurrection or civil war, while Algerian authors and sympathizers with the Algerian side call it a revolution, a war for independence, or a war for the restoration of Algerian sovereignty.

It became apparent during the war that the distinction between international and internal wars, which was so significant under traditional international law, was not accorded much weight in the calculations of statesmen formulating policy regarding the Algerian conflict. Other distinctions were controlling. The question was not whether the conflict was international or internal. It was whether the conflict was a decolonization war or a secession. And there was a subsidiary question: Did the rebels aim to bring about a change of the basic economic and political system?

The Conflict as a War for Political Separation

From the first attacks of the war to the day of the cease-fire, the FLN proclaimed its objective to be national independence or self-determination for the people of Algeria. Self-determination implied the holding of a referendum in which the people of Algeria could express their preference for or against political separation from France. The FLN had no doubt that the vote would be for independence, and so it used the terms "self-determination" and "independence" as meaning practically the same thing.

For the first five years of the conflict, the French government flatly opposed independence or self-determination. It maintained that Algeria was an integral part of France, just like Provence or Brittany. The people of Algeria were French and should remain so. Other countries had populations of mixed race, culture, and language. Such differences did not prevent the integration of a people into a single nation.

The turning point of the war came in September 1959, when de Gaulle went on French television to address the French people on the future of Algeria. The people of Algeria, said de Gaulle, must be placed in a position to decide their own destiny.

> . . . I deem it necessary that recourse to self-determination be here and now proclaimed. In the name of France . . . I pledge myself to ask the Algerians, on the one hand, in their twelve Departments, what, when all is said and done, they wish to be; and, on the other hand, all Frenchmen, to endorse that choice.[4]

It appeared at first that the war for independence had been won; but there were qualifications to the endorsement of self-determination by de Gaulle, qualifications the FLN refused to accept. And it took two and a half more years of war to remove the qualifications.

One qualification was the refusal of de Gaulle to allow any participation by the FLN in the arrangements for the referendum on self-determination—a refusal even to discuss the political future of Algeria with the representatives of the FLN. The FLN was unwilling to accept a vote organized and supervised by the French Army. It insisted that the self-determination referendum be conducted either by the United Nations or by some authority mutually acceptable to both the French and the FLN,

[4] Speech of de Gaulle on Sept. 16, 1959, French Embassy, New York, *Major Addresses, Statements and Press Conferences of General Charles de Gaulle: May 19, 1958–Jan. 31, 1964* (New York: French Embassy, n.d.), p. 54.

an authority which could be counted upon to be impartial. It was not until the final negotiation at Evian in March 1962 that the French and the FLN agreed upon a formula for a joint French-FLN administration of Algeria to supervise the holding of the referendum.

The other qualifications of the principle of self-determination were dropped, one by one, by the French government. A nationwide vote was taken in January 1961, in which all of the people of France, including those in Algeria, voted in favor of self-determination for the Algerians. This removed the threat implied in de Gaulle's 1959 speech of a possible veto by the French people of the results of an Algerian vote for independence. Then, in September 1961, de Gaulle conceded that France would recognize that self-determination applied to the whole of Algeria, including the Saharan territory, instead of being limited to "the twelve departments of Algeria."[5]

Finally, as the French settlers in Algeria cut the ground from under their own feet by resorting to counterterrorism in an effort to stave off the transfer of political authority from the French to the Algerians, the French government abandoned its effort to obtain a privileged status for the French residents of Algeria. Conditions then were ripe for the political settlement which led to the separation of Algeria from France.

During the course of the long struggle of the Algerians for independence, they attached themselves to, and claimed to be the most aggressive leaders of, the drive of the peoples of Asia and Africa for independence. One of the consequences of this drive has been the development throughout the world of almost universal political support for a particular kind of war of political separation: the decolonization war. By their actions as well as by their votes in the political organs of the United Nations, the member states of the United Nations during the period of the Algerian conflict established the legitimacy of the decolonization war.

The important question raised by this legitimization is whether there should now be some adjustment of international law doctrines with regard to other wars of political separation. There is, of course, little political support for noncolonial wars of political separation, such as the abortive effort of the Katangans in 1960 and of the Biafrans during 1967–70. If international lawyers are concerned only with freezing into legal principle the widespread or uniform practice of states, then they must wait until there has been a sufficient record of successful or unsuccessful noncolonial wars of political separation to affirm what the legal status of such a war is or whether such wars are to be divided into subcategories, some legitimate because usually successful, others illegitimate because usually unsuccessful. But if international lawyers have the

---

[5] Press conference of de Gaulle on Sept. 5, 1961, *ibid*., pp. 144–45.

function of charting a course for the development of legal principles in the field of international relations, they should ask themselves whether the Algerian precedent is not more than a precedent to support the legitimacy of decolonization wars. Is it not also a precedent for the legitimacy of any war of political separation (even a noncolonial war) if the war is fought by a group with a territorial base for the same basic objective as a decolonization war—the protection of fundamental human rights, such as freedom from persecution, or the right to participate in the government of one's country on a basis of equality with fellow nationals?

The Conflict as an Internal Revolution

The Algerian conflict can also be described as an internal revolution— a revolution internal to Algeria. It was not the classic type of revolution such as the one in France in 1789 or the one in the Soviet Union in 1917, in which the struggle was intended to bring about a sweeping change of system for the government of an entire country. The Algerian rebels were not seeking to revolutionize the governmental system of France. They were aiming only to bring about a change within Algeria. But the change they contemplated for Algeria was of a revolutionary character.

In the handbills distributed at the outset of the revolution, the FLN listed as objectives (1) the restoration of the Algerian state, sovereign, democratic, and social, within the framework of the principles of Islam, and (2) the preservation of all fundamental freedoms without distinction of race or religion.[6] Almost two years later, when goals were reformulated by new leaders speaking for an expanded rebel organization, the FLN seemed to concentrate on the measures necessary for winning independence, without elaborating plans for the governmental system of the future state of Algeria.[7] It pledged, however, that after the cease-fire it would make arrangements for general elections to a constituent assembly which would form a government. Although it did not have in mind a revision of the governmental system in Algeria so radical as to preclude cooperative arrangements with France, the FLN did contemplate sweeping changes in landownership, voting rights, control over natural resources, and access to educational services.

[6] André Mandouze, *La Révolution Algérienne par les Textes* (Paris: François Maspero, 1961), pp. 157–61. An English translation of the handbill appears in FLN, *The Algerian People and Their Revolution* (Résistance Algérienne, 1967), pp. 17–18.
[7] Organe Central du Front de Libération Nationale, *El Moudjahid*, Special Issue No. 4, Nov. 1, 1956. A compilation in three volumes of the issues of *El Moudjahid* was made in 1962 by a publishing company in Yugoslavia and has been available at the Algerian mission in Washington, D.C.

During the period since World War II, international political scientists have found it necessary, in analyzing the practice of states, to divide internal revolutions into two categories: (1) those fought to change a governmental system from a noncommunist to a communist system, or vice versa, and (2) all other internal revolutions. The distinction is meaningful because many states consider that there is justification for intervention in the first type of internal revolution but few states justify intervention in the second type. Yet traditional international law has no room for distinctions between internal revolutions. It treats all internal revolutions in the same way as all other internal wars, as matters of domestic jurisdiction of the concerned state, matters in which neither other states nor the United Nations should intervene.

It seems clear that the Algerian Revolution was not a communist revolution.[8] There was a Communist party in Algeria, but it was dominated by French or European settlers. Neither it nor its members gave significant help to the rebel forces. Probably more convincing and definitive is the judgment of two strongly anticommunist organizations—the AFL-CIO and NATO. The AFL-CIO, working independently and also through the International Confederation of Free Trade Unions (ICFTU), gave support to the rebel forces throughout the conflict.[9] The North Atlantic Treaty Organization (NATO), which had included the three French departments in Algeria within the area covered by the treaty, never gave the French military operations in Algeria its formal endorsement.

In trying to cope with the new political developments concerning internal revolution, international lawyers face many questions: What should be the objective of the international community in dealing with internal revolutions—to try to discourage the involvement of outside states; to encourage the international community to assist the revolutionists if they are seeking to realize fundamental human rights; to assist the incumbent government to establish conditions of public order; or to bring about a cease-fire on existing battle lines? Should international law acknowledge that a different legal framework is applicable to communizing and decommunizing revolutions from that applicable to other revolutions? What is to be done about a war which is both an internal revolution and a war for political separation?

[8] Edward Behr, *The Algerian Problem* (New York: Norton, 1962), pp. 233–41; Michael Clark, *Algeria in Turmoil: A History of the Rebellion* (New York: Praeger, 1959), pp. 139, 320–29; Humbaraci, *Algeria*, pp. 170–76.

[9] International Confederation of Free Trade Unions, press communique of July 27, 1963, as summarized in ICFTU, *Report of the Eighth World Congress, 1965* (Brussels: ICFTU, 1965), p. 48.

Power-Struggle Elements of Conflict

Some military contests occurred during the Algerian conflict which can be separated from the main aspects of the conflict as a war of political separation and as an internal revolution. These contests fall into the category of the power-struggle type of internal war, in which leaders are fighting for control of the government of an existing state or for control of a revolutionary movement. The aim of the parties in such contests does not involve a political separation of one part of the country from the rest of the country, nor does the outcome of such contests mean a sweeping change in the political, social, or economic system of the country or in the objectives of the revolutionary movement. Such contests merely serve to decide who should preside over the government or who should form the leadership of the revolutionary movement.

There were power struggles on both the FLN side and the French side. Partisans of the FLN and of a rival nationalist movement fought each other during the period from 1954 to 1956.[10] After the fighting between the FLN and the French had ended and a peaceful settlement of the main conflict had been achieved, Ben Bella fought off other claimants for the leadership of the government of independent Algeria. And for three brief periods, the French settlers of Algeria rose to challenge the authority of the French government. The settlers did not attempt to set themselves up as the government of an independent Algeria; their insurrections were aimed at forcing the French government to make more strenuous efforts to repress the independence movement and to maintain Algeria as an integral part of France.

The power-struggle elements of the Algerian conflict never reached the stage where the question was posed of preventing outside states from assisting either one faction or the other. Each of the rival Algerian nationalist movements drew support, both verbal and material, from sympathizers in other states. But there never developed a situation comparable to that in the Congo in 1960 and 1961, when the United States and the Soviet Union championed different factions which were seeking control of the government. The ineffectiveness of the revolts of the French settlers indicated that they received little, if any, help from outside.

Nor was the question posed of United Nations intervention to bring about cease-fires and to promote peaceful methods of resolving the power contests. The United Nations was too absorbed with the main conflict, that between the FLN and France, to worry about the sub-

[10] Richard M. Brace and Joan Brace, *Ordeal in Algeria* (Princeton, N. J.: Van Nostrand, 1960), p. 103; Lorna Hahn, *North Africa: Nationalism to Nationhood* (Washington, D. C.: Public Affairs Press, 1960), p. 158.

sidiary contests. The struggle between the rival Algerian nationalist movements was in large part clandestine. The fratricidal warfare in Algeria in 1962 was stopped principally by nonpartisan Algerians who interposed themselves between the factions, crying "Seven years are enough!"[11] The intra-French struggles were resolved in favor of the French government before they could deteriorate into widespread attacks by Frenchmen against Frenchmen.

The Representative Character of the FLN

The FLN was an outgrowth of a secret organization formed in 1947 by a group of young Algerian nationalists, of whom Ben Bella is the best known.[12] Although most of the group started out with one or the other of the two publicly identified nationalist movements—those headed by Messali Hadj and by Ferhat Abbas—they became dissatisfied with the inability of the established nationalist movements to get anywhere. In the fall of 1954, the nine leaders of the group formed a club for the purpose of launching the revolution. The club maintained strict secrecy; and for some time after the initial rebel attacks, its composition was still unknown to the French. But while the names of the leaders were concealed, the formation of the Front was announced by handbills distributed throughout Algeria on November 1, 1954, the night of the first rebel attacks. All freedom-loving Algerians were urged to join.

Membership in the Front was on an individual basis and open to all. Mohammed Bedjaoui, minister of justice in the Algerian government for eight years and formerly legal adviser to the FLN, called it a "nation-party" to distinguish if from a political party which purports to represent the interests of only a portion of the people of a country.[13] By the middle of 1956, there was in Algeria no serious challenge to the leadership of the FLN. Moslem intellectuals, political and religious leaders, and the dominant labor and student unions all accepted it as the chosen instrument of Algerian nationalism.

The FLN took two courses of action to strengthen its qualifications to represent the people of Algeria in their claim for independence. One was to set up Algeria-wide institutions of a governmental character. It summoned delegates from the various districts of Algeria to a congress in the Soummam Valley in August 1956. The Soummam Congress, in turn, chose members of the National Council of the Algerian Revolution (CNRA), a policymaking or legislative body, and the Committee of

[11] Humbaraci, *Algeria*, pp. 79–80.

[12] Robert Merle, *Ben Bella* (London: Michael Joseph, 1967), pp. 11–12 and chap. 4.

[13] Mohammed Bedjaoui, *Law and the Algerian Revolution* (Brussels: International Association of Democratic Lawyers, 1961), p. 87.

Coordination and Execution (CCE), an executive organ. The latter institution was supplanted in September 1958 by the Provisional Government of the Algerian Republic (GPRA). The GPRA maintained its headquarters in Tunis and was in continuous operation from September 1958 to the end of the revolution. After its formation in 1956, and while the conflict was going on, the CNRA met four times for brief sessions—once in Cairo and three times in Tripoli.

The other course of action pursued by the FLN was to use strikes and demonstrations as evidence of popular support. There were general strikes in 1955 and 1956 on the fifth of July, the anniversary of the French invasion of Algeria in 1830. The General Union of Algerian Workers and the General Union of Algerian Moslem Students called a strike from January 28 to February 4, 1957, to coincide with consideration of the Algerian situation by the General Assembly of the United Nations. Elections held by the French administration in Algeria were boycotted. Bedjaoui has asserted that the manifestations of support for the FLN provided in the strikes and demonstrations constituted a "mandate of the people."

France relied upon the aloofness of traditional international law with respect to "domestic affairs" in refusing to deal with the FLN as the representative of the Algerian people in the prosecution of the claim for independence. The FLN argued for the development of a new pattern of international law, which would take account of the sanction to the principle of self-determination given by the United Nations Charter, United Nations resolutions, and the practice followed by many colonial states after World War II. How could a people prosecute a claim to self-determination if no one could assert authority to represent them?

The failure of the existing international legal system to provide any procedure for identifying an organization with the capacity to speak for a people seeking independence tends, of course, to encourage rival groups to enter into military struggles to decide the issue of who will represent that people. Since even the presentation of a demand for independence can be regarded as a treasonous act, the selection of a leader or group of leaders to make the demand is entirely extralegal and is frequently conducted in as brutal a fashion as the war of independence itself. It seems obvious that international lawyers need to give consideration to the development of orderly procedures whereby a people can prosecute a claim to self-determination.

Legality of the Use of Force by the FLN

It was the FLN that first resorted to the use of force in the Algerian conflict. It launched a series of guerrilla attacks, principally on French outposts in the rural areas of Algeria, on the night of November 1, 1954.

Of course, the FLN could not hope to establish the legitimacy of its military actions under the internal law of France. It could establish their legitimacy, if at all, only under international law. Yet traditional international law provided for the legitimization of a use of force by rebels only if the use resulted in the establishment of control over territory. Traditional international law required a rebel force to stake its legitimacy upon its success.

The two procedural methods under traditional international law by which a separatist group could seek legitimization of its use of force were (1) recognition of its belligerent status by outside states, and (2) recognition of its status as a government by outside states. The second method had an advantage over the first in that it not only conferred legitimacy upon the use of force by the rebel organization but could also be interpreted as legitimizing aid by outside governments to the rebel organization. Halfway through the Algerian conflict, the FLN employed the second method with limited success. It never gave the first method a serious try.

Acting on the assumption that the traditional rules and procedures needed to be changed, the FLN asserted the flat proposition that a people suffering from colonial oppression had the right to use force against their oppressors, that to establish the legitimacy of their use of force they did not have to wait until they achieved sufficient military success to qualify as a belligerent or until they set up a government, and that from the inception of their revolution to the moment of their ultimate victory their exercise of force was legitimate.

To cast its justification in currently fashionable phraseology, the FLN said it was fighting a war of self-defense, a delayed reaction but nevertheless a reaction to the French invasion of 1830. With such a justification, the FLN considered it unnecessary to obtain the approval of the United Nations before resorting to force against the French government.

The supporters of the FLN did not go so far as to try to secure from the General Assembly a blessing upon the military operations of the rebels. They sought only a blessing upon the right of the people of Algeria to independence. But it is a small jump from declaring that a people are entitled to independence to declaring that they may use force if independence is denied. In any event, neither France nor any other state sought to obtain from the United Nations a formal condemnation of the use of force by the FLN.

Though the Afro-Asian states did not choose during the Algerian conflict to push for a specific assembly resolution approving the use of force by the rebels, in 1966 at meetings of the Special Committee on Friendly Relations, they tried to insert in the formulation of the principle expressed in article 2(4) of the Charter (the general prohibition against the use of force) a specific exemption for force used in decolonization. Algeria was one of the states that proposed the following paragraph as an interpretation of article 2(4) of the United Nations Charter: "The prohibition of the use of force shall not affect . . . the use of force pursuant to . . . the right of peoples to self-defense against colonial domination, in the exercise of their right to self-determination."[14] The Australian representative objected to the proposed exemption because "under international law the right of self-defence applied not to peoples but to states," and the United Kingdom representative objected because the "so-called right of self-defence of peoples against colonial domination had no warranty whatsoever either under international law or under the Charter." The Algerian representative spoke for the proposed exemption, saying that, if colonized peoples were being kept in a state of subordination and exploitation, their only recourse was self-defense. The special committee was unable to agree upon a formulation of the principle expressed in article 2(4).

Legality of the Use of Force by France

The French government responded to the guerrilla attacks by dispatching parachute battalions to Algeria. French military forces were soon engaged in clearing and sweeping operations in the mountain areas. To the offer of the FLN for negotiations, François Mitterand, the French minister of the interior, replied: "The only form of negotiation is war."[15]

The French position was that there could be no question of the right of a government to put down an insurrection, using whatever military force appeared to it to be required. The maintenance of order in Algeria was an internal affair of France. Outside states had no business involving themselves either directly or indirectly through the political organs of the United Nations.

The FLN and its supporters did not succeed in persuading the international community to brand, in specific terms, the use of military force by the French against the FLN as illegal; but they achieved virtually the same result by persuading the Fifteenth General Assembly to adopt within a period of five days in December 1960 a Declaration against Colonialism and a resolution on Algeria. When the declaration and resolution are read together, they seem to point the finger at France. Paragraph 4 of the declaration says: "All armed action or repressive measures of all kinds directed against dependent peoples shall cease in order to enable them to exercise peacefully and freely their right to complete independence. . . ." The first operative paragraph of the resolution

---

[14] United Nations, General Assembly, *Report of the 1966 Special Committee* (A/6230), June 27, 1966, par. 26.

[15] Bedjaoui, *Law and the Algerian Revolution*, p. 150.

on Algeria says: "The General Assembly ... recognizes the right of the Algerian people to self-determination and independence." Ergo, in the view of the sixty-three states which voted for the resolution on Algeria and also for the Declaration against Colonialism, the use by France of military force to deny independence to Algeria was impermissible.

The Afro-Asian states and the communist states have been trying since the end of the Algerian conflict to embody a prohibition of the use of force to repress an independence movement in a document of more widely acknowledged obligatory effect than a unanimous declaration of the General Assembly. In the Sixth [Legal] Committee of the United Nations, in December 1966, they stated that they believed any formulation of restraints on the use of force should include a prohibition against the use of force for repression of liberation movements and for denial of the right of self-determination.[16]

The Military Stalemate

The war was mainly a guerrilla war. There were no set battles or fixed military fronts except those that developed along the Tunisian and Moroccan borders during the latter part of the war. It was even difficult while the war was going on to be sure which areas were held by FLN forces and which by French forces. Speckled maps of Algeria were prepared by the French military command from time to time to show concentrations of FLN forces or sympathizers, but no one appears to have had much faith in them.

At the beginning of the war, the FLN forces, including regulars and auxiliaries, numbered about 3,000 and the French forces 50,000.[17] By 1957, estimates of the size of the FLN forces ranged from 65,000 to 100,000, while French forces were approaching 500,000, the maximum strength of the French forces during the war.[18] The highest figure mentioned by the FLN for its forces during the war was 130,000, but after independence 250,000 claimed to have been fighters for the FLN.[19]

Aside from the casualty rate, the French measured the severity of the conflict by the number of exactions, that is, the number of wrongs or offenses committed against military forces, civilians, or property for

[16] United Nations, General Assembly, *Report of the Sixth Committee* (A/6547), Dec. 7, 1966, par. 41.

[17] Algerian Office of FLN, New York, *White Paper on the Application of the Geneva Conventions of 1949 to the French-Algerian Conflict* (New York, 1960), p. 6; Jean-Paul Benoit, "Chronologie de la Guerre en Algérie," *La Nef*, Nos. 12–13, October 1962–January 1963, p. 6. A collection of publications of the Algerian Office can be found in the library of American Friends of the Middle East, Washington, D.C.

[18] *New York Times*, Oct. 20, 1957, p. 33:1; Oct. 30, 1957, p. 14:3.

[19] Algerian Office of FLN, New York, *White Paper*, p. 6; Humbaraci, *Algeria*, pp. 62–63.

political reasons, ranging from murder to simple sabotage, theft, or destruction of crops.[20] According to the French count, the number of exactions rose gradually during the first two years of the war to about 2,500 a month. It then declined in 1957 to about 2,000 and for the rest of the war fluctuated between 1,000 and 2,000 per month.

In the beginning, the FLN forces carried out their guerrilla attacks and sabotage operations in the rural mountainous areas of Algeria. The Aurès and Kabylie Mountains remained rebel strongholds throughout the war, as did areas adjoining both the Tunisian and the Moroccan frontiers. But during the years 1956–57, the FLN brought terrorist tactics to the city of Algiers. The French retaliated by cordoning off the Casbah and conducting a systematic search for the rebel ringleaders. The "Battle of Algiers," as it was called, has been graphically portrayed in a semidocumentary film of that name by the French producer Jean Luc Godard.

The FLN relied heavily on support from both Tunisia and Morocco and used both countries as training grounds, as supply depots, as bases from which to launch attacks, and as sanctuaries from pursuit by French forces. The French tried by both diplomatic and military means to deny the use of Tunisian and Moroccan territory to the FLN forces. They placed their principal reliance on an electrified barrier constructed on the Algerian side of the borders with the two Arab countries. As a consequence, a considerable part of the FLN forces remained in Tunisia and Morocco, and the electrified barriers became static battle lines dividing French forces and the exterior forces of the FLN.

The military operations of the Algerian war ended in a stalemate, although each side claimed a military victory. The FLN proved incapable of driving the French forces out of Algeria; the French could not destroy the FLN forces facing them across the borders of Tunisia and Morocco. The French succeeded in reducing the incidence of guerrilla attacks within Algeria but remained unable to exercise authority over rural areas or to restore normal peacetime conditions to the cities.

The Algerian conflict resulted in a political victory for the FLN. The FLN gradually won the support of the Algerian population, partly by intimidation and the assassination of Moslems serving under the French administration, partly by an elaborate political organization at the local level which gave sympathetic consideration to the needs of the people. The French helped to insure their own defeat by adopting methods of warfare and of the treatment of civilians which turned the population against them. The measure of the political victory was the ultimate recognition by the French of the right of the Algerian people to choose independence for Algeria.

[20] Benoit, "Chronologie de la Guerre en Algérie," pp. 14–15.

II. CONDUCT OF THE BELLIGERENTS

For about a hundred years, efforts have been made to secure formal acceptance of restraints upon the actions of combatants for the sake of making war less inhumane. Some people regard the efforts as both misdirected and futile. Wars should be prevented or stopped, they say, not rendered a little less intolerable. Yet in the course of the Algerian conflict, public agitation over such inhumane practices as the execution of prisoners and the use of torture in interrogating suspects seems to have contributed significantly to the building of pressures for negotiations to end the war.

Treatment of Prisoners and Internees

The principal agreements for the protection of prisoners of war and civilian internees in effect at the time of the Algerian Revolution were the two Geneva Conventions of 1949. France had become a party to these conventions in 1951. In the agreements, the international community established comprehensive standards to be applicable in international wars and, for the first time, limited standards to be applicable in "armed conflicts not of an international character." The most significant of the limited standards was the prohibition of "violence to life and persons, in particular, murder of all kinds, mutilation, cruel treatment and torture."

Article 3 of each of the conventions, which prescribed the limited standards, purported to impose an obligation on both parties to any internal conflict occurring on the territory of a signatory state, although, of course, there was no way in which the rebel side could be made to agree in advance to such an obligation. The same article stated that the parties to an internal conflict "should endeavor to bring into force, by means of special agreements, all or part of the other provisions of the present Convention."

Throughout the conflict the FLN sought to arrive at an understanding with the French on the applicability of the Geneva Conventions. In the initial stage of the conflict, it invoked the limited standard prescribed for internal conflict. Midway in the conflict, it urged that the French enter into a "special agreement" to grant a more extended application of the safeguards of the conventions and even to deal with humanitarian problems not regulated by the conventions.[1] In the final stages of the war, the FLN attempted to obtain the full coverage of the conventions by executing the formalities necessary to become a party to the conven-

---

[1] Mohammed Bedjaoui, *Law and the Algerian Revolution* (Brussels: International Association of Democratic Lawyers, 1961), pp. 216–17.

tions; that is, by depositing an instrument of ratification with the Swiss government.[2]

In May 1960, the GPRA published, through the Algerian Office of the FLN in New York City, a *White Paper on the Application of the Geneva Conventions of 1949 to the French-Algerian Conflict.* A pamphlet of eighty-five pages, the *White Paper* was designed as an appeal for international support of the application of the Geneva Conventions to the Algerian conflict. It quoted extensively from various governmental and nongovernmental reports to demonstrate the failure of France to comply with the standards prescribed in the conventions. The GPRA once more announced its willingness to accept the full applicability of the conventions or, at a minimum, the provisions of article 3 of the four conventions and article 4 of the Convention on Prisoners of War. It called upon the other signatories to the conventions to urge France "to recognize its solemn engagement to the Conventions."

The French failed to respond to any efforts of the FLN to reach a formal understanding regarding the applicability of the conventions. Initially the French maintained that the FLN had no right to take any prisoners, since it had no right to institute an armed attack against the French government in Algeria. There was, therefore, in the French view, no reason for considering the mutual applicability of even the limited safeguards provided in the conventions. By the time the French gave some indications of a willingness to accept the limited standards of article 3, the FLN regarded such standards as inadequate. As for the presumption of the FLN to adhere to the Geneva Conventions, the French government issued the following notification to the other signatories to the conventions:

The French Government recalls that the self-styled "provisional government of the Algerian Republic," set up on foreign territory by the leaders of the rebellion in the French departments of Algeria, cannot, on any grounds, claim the capacity of "State" or that of "Power." Consequently, it does not possess the requisite competence to "adhere" to the said conventions, according to the text itself of those conventions.[3]

The International Committee of the Red Cross (ICRC) took the position that the Algerian conflict was "an internal conflict in which one of the parties does not recognize the opposing party," and hence it founded its actions not on the conventions as a whole but on article 3.[4]

[2] *Ibid.*, pp. 189–99.
[3] Note of July 25, 1960, from the French Ministry of Foreign Affairs to the Swiss Federal Political Department, Department of State Treaty Files.
[4] International Committee of the Red Cross, *The ICRC and the Algerian Conflict* (Geneva, 1962), p. 3.

It tried on several occasions to bring both sides to accept the limited standards of article 3 by mutual agreement, but these efforts, too, were in vain.

Despite the lack of a formal agreement on the standards to be applied to the protection of prisoners and internees, the FLN and the French conducted themselves in certain respects in accordance with provisions of the conventions. The FLN insisted throughout the conflict that it had conferred upon captured French soldiers the status of prisoners of war. Detailed directives were given to members of the FLN forces about procedures to be followed in forwarding prisoners from places of capture to places of imprisonment. While the ICRC did not send missions to inspect FLN prison camps, it appeared that this was due to the refusal of the French to authorize such missions rather than to the unwillingness of the FLN to receive them. In 1957, when the French charged that the FLN was holding certain captured French officers in Tunisia, an official of the ICRC did visit the FLN camp in which the officers were held to verify that it was actually in Algeria. The French prisoners who were later released by the FLN registered no complaints against their treatment.

The French, on their part, recognized a certain degree of responsibility regarding the handling of their prisoners and internees. They permitted the ICRC to send inspection missions to French prison and detention camps in Algeria. Ten missions were sent by the ICRC during the period from February 1955 to June 1962. In March 1958, according to the ICRC, the French government decided to give up the systematic prosecution of FLN militants in French courts. At the same time, General Salan ordered that military prisoners be held in special camps rather than in prisons with ordinary criminals. The ICRC construed these actions to mean that the French government intended to accord to FLN militants treatment "closely related" to that governing prisoners of war in international conflicts. Reports indicate, however, that the French resumed prosecutions of FLN militants and that courts continued to hand down sentences.

About midway through the war, the FLN apparently became convinced that it might do more to ameliorate the condition of FLN militants who had fallen into the hands of the French by seeking to qualify them as political prisoners rather than as full-fledged prisoners of war. While it was by no means clear what the status of political prisoners entailed, agitation began as early as June 1957 to obtain such status for all FLN militants. In a Paris prison, 700 Algerians went on a thirteen-day hunger strike in June 1959. Thousands of Algerians in prisons all over France went on a longer strike in November 1961. In explanation of the latter strike, the FLN argued that international support for the objectives of the Algerian Revolution and recognition by de Gaulle of the legitimacy of the objectives entitled the militant supporters of the revolution to be treated as political prisoners rather than as ordinary criminals.

States supporting the FLN succeeded in obtaining a General Assembly resolution in November 1961 appealing to the French government to grant the Algerians imprisoned in France the status of political prisoners "in accordance with established international practice and humanitarian principles."[5] A few days after passage of the resolution, the prisoners, satisfied that the French had substantially complied with its terms, called off the hunger strike; and the FLN announced that the ICRC had assumed responsibility for guaranteeing the prisoners treatment appropriate to their status.

Throughout the conflict, the ICRC was active in promoting and arranging for the release of prisoners by both sides in the conflict. It carried on its traditional functions of assistance in the search for missing persons and in establishing communications between prisoners and their families. It extended its humanitarian activities to the Algerian refugees in Morocco and Tunisia and to the Algerians assigned by the French to resettlement camps within Algeria, organizing and distributing relief supplies.

One aspect of the work of the ICRC deserves further examination by international lawyers concerned with the implementation of the conventions for the protection of prisoners of war and civilian internees. During the Algerian conflict, the ICRC continued to follow its policy of not revealing to the public the contents of the reports of its missions to the prisons and internment camps. The ICRC reports were submitted only to the government running the camps. In January 1960, the report of the visit of an ICRC mission to French prison camps in Algeria was leaked to the press,[6] and its contents contributed to the public pressure against the French government not only for amelioration of conditions in the camps but also for bringing an end to the war. Can the international community hope for implementation of humanitarian conventions if the impartial agency charged with the duty of investigating compliance with the conventions does not disclose to the public the results of its investigations? If it does not call upon the sanction of public opinion, on what sanction can the international community rely to force compliance with the conventions?

[5] United Nations, GA Res. 1650 (XVI), Nov. 15, 1961.
[6] *Le Monde* of Jan. 5, 1960, reprinted in Algerian Office of FLN, New York, *White Paper on the Application of the Geneva Conventions of 1949 to the French-Algerian Conflict* (New York, 1960), App. 5.

Executions: The Sanction of Reprisals

Each of the parties to the Algerian conflict executed some of the enemy military personnel whom it had captured. In August 1960, the FLN claimed that several hundred Algerian combatants had been condemned by French tribunals and executed during the war. On its part, the FLN deliberately executed five captured French military personnel—three in May 1958 and two in August 1960. On both occasions, the FLN said the prisoners had been tried and convicted by FLN military tribunals.

Each side denied that it had sentenced or executed military prisoners simply for the offense of bearing arms or for having engaged in a military attack. The strongest French denial came after the first executions by the FLN. The French government insisted that no rebel prisoner taken in combat had ever—even if condemned to death—been executed for the sole reason that he had borne arms against France.[7] The executions by the French were, presumably, for acts of assassination or other terrorist actions constituting crimes under French law. The FLN explained that its first executions, in 1958, were for torture, rape, and murder of civilians, acts which it described as "war crimes," and that the executions in 1960 were for "crimes and exactions."[8] Neither side accepted the explanation offered by the other.

As early as March 1956, the FLN claimed that two Algerian nationals were executed for the offense of bearing arms against France.[9] On the next day, in reprisal, Moslems killed or wounded 47 European civilians. This did not stop the executions. French authorities executed 104 rebels during the period from June 1956 to January 1958 and 30 more by the end of April 1958. Nor did the executions stop the terrorism. This was the period of the most intense terrorist activity in the city of Algiers: the Battle of Algiers.

Finding that terrorism was inadequate as a reprisal, the FLN, after threatening to execute members of the French armed forces in its custody if the French continued to execute captured members of the FLN, carried out three executions on May 11, 1958. It explained that simple justice required it to withhold the status of prisoner of war from soldiers whom it could not consider to be authentic combatants because they had violated the most elementary laws of war and had rendered themselves guilty of actions falling under the common law.[10]

[7] Communiqué issued by Office of the President of the French Council on May 11, 1958, printed in French Embassy, New York, *French Affairs*, No. 57, May 13, 1958.

[8] *New York Times*, May 10, 1958, p. 3:3,5; Aug. 12, 1960, p. 4:8.

[9] Edward Behr, *The Algerian Problem* (New York: Norton, 1962), pp. 99–100.

[10] *El Moudjahid*, No. 24, May 29, 1958.

Although the French condemned the executions, called the alleged trials of the prisoners by military tribunals of the FLN a parody of justice, and said they could not recognize "the jurisdiction of a rebellious act," there were few executions by the French during the remainder of 1958 or during 1959. Terrorism also subsided. In March 1960, the FLN charged that the French had resumed the cycle of executions and again threatened reprisals for "each assassination of an Algerian patriot." There was a short lull in executions; but in August the FLN once more charged that the French government had resumed its policy of executing FLN militants. It appealed to international standards for the protection of prisoners.

The Algerians thus brutally executed are combatants, taken prisoner by the enemy in time of war. Their legal defense is based upon their adherence to the Algerian Front of National Liberation, on their status as combatants who are members of an underground resistance movement, in conformity with the universally recognized laws of war and the terms of international conventions on this subject (of which France is a signatory).[11]

Two more Algerian nationalists went to the guillotine in Lyons, France, on August 5, 1960. A week later, the FLN carried out executions of two French soldiers over French protests.

Executions ceased to be an issue after that, as the two parties moved toward peace negotiations.

Torture and Other Inhumane Practices

While the account of executions of military personnel provides an example of the workings of the sanction of reprisals, the record of the handling of the problem of the use of torture is a case history of the workings of the sanction of public opinion. Significantly, it was the public opinion of the people of France, rather than world public opinion, which brought pressure to bear to stop the use of torture by French military authorities in Algeria. The pressure generated was so intense that it contributed to the ultimate decision by the French government to move toward recognition of the right of the Algerian people to independence. The fact that French military officers had to resort to torture and other despicable practices reminiscent of the Nazi Gestapo convinced many people that Algeria neither should nor could be held any longer as a part of France.

In 1956, French newspapers began to publish stories on the use by French military personnel of torture during investigations of suspects. The newspaper accounts were followed by articles and books written by

[11] Algerian Office of the FLN, New York, *Review of Developments, Aug. 1960* (New York, 1960), p. 5.

those who had undergone torture and survived to tell about it, by others who had witnessed the application of torture, and even by some who had been obliged to apply torture. Foreign Minister Pineau was forced to acknowledge the widespread accusations, although he denied their accuracy, in a speech to the General Assembly of the United Nations in February 1957.[12]

The first nongovernmental organization to take up the charges was the International Commission against Concentration Camp Practices (CICRC). The commission had been founded in 1950 by the concerted action of groups of former political deportees in countries which had been occupied by the Nazis during World War II. In April 1957, it sought and obtained from the French prime minister authorization to send a mission to Algeria to investigate conditions of arrest, detention, and policy interrogation. The mission was composed of a Belgian, a Norwegian, and a Dutchman and was accompanied by two French experts. It spent two weeks in Algeria and made public its report on July 26, 1957.[13]

The commission found evidence that the use of torture in the conduct of interrogations of suspects was a deliberate policy adopted by the French military authorities "to save lives" and to assist in ferreting out those responsible for the terrorism in the city of Algiers. The commission also concluded that, although the French had not established a concentration camp regime in Algeria, they had placed civilians under detention or "assigned residence" without providing them with any opportunity to know the charges against them, to prepare a defense, or to carry an appeal to a competent judicial body.

In April 1957, the same month that it authorized the CICRC to send a mission to Algeria, the French government appointed a national commission to make an investigation—the Commission for the Safeguard of Individual Rights and Liberties. As a consequence of the reluctance of the French government to publish the report of the commission, a summary of the report was first published by *Le Monde* on December 14, 1957. The commission found that the French forces in Algeria had committed "acts of violence" against the native population. The French Command had itself published a list of 274 cases of crimes in which the military disciplinary authority had imposed sanctions. There were several particularly serious cases in which groups of natives held for questioning had been locked up in wine caves and had been asphyxiated by the

[12] United Nations, General Assembly, *Official Records*, 11th sess., 1st Cte., 831st mtg., Feb. 4, 1957, par. 4–7.
[13] International Commission against Concentration Camp Practices (CICRC), *Saturn* 3 (August-September 1957).

fumes during the night. The commission also found evidence of the widespread use of torture to extract confessions.

In the section of its report on the subject of torture, the French national commission cited various authorities accepted in France that made it strictly forbidden to use torture to obtain confessions. It was forbidden by article 5 of the Universal Declaration of Human Rights, by article 31 of the Geneva Convention on the Protection of Civilians, and by article 186 of the French Penal Code. Reference to both international and domestic law served, apparently, to make it unnecessary for the commission to concern itself with the question of which of the two systems of law was applicable to the Algerian conflict.

Le Monde brought to public attention two additional reports: one concerning French treatment of Algerian prisoners of war, and the other concerning French treatment of civilians in regroupment camps. In January 1960, without authorization from the ICRC, *Le Monde* published the complete text of the report of the seventh mission of the ICRC to Algeria, which had taken place in October and November of 1959.[14] The report contained evidence of the use of torture on prisoners and of "miserable conditions" in certain internment camps. In April 1959, presumably without authorization from the French government, *Le Monde* published extracts from a report on the regroupment centers which had been prepared within the French government and submitted confidentially to the French delegate general in Algiers at the end of December 1958.[15] The government then published the text in full. This report described sanitary conditions in the centers as "generally deplorable" and their inmates as "menaced by famine."

Total War: Unanswered Complaints and Unasked Questions

There was no attempt by either of the parties or by any organization, governmental or nongovernmental, to invoke the provisions of the only international treaty extant during the period of the Algerian conflict that purported to prescribe rules of warfare: the Hague Convention No. IV of 1907. That treaty was so outdated as to be virtually forgotten. The rapidity of change in techniques of warfare discouraged long ago any ideas of a new international conference or a new convention on methods of warfare.

In spite of the lack of agreements imposing pertinent restraints on methods of warfare, the two belligerents professed to be trying to avoid killing and injuring civilians. When it became obvious that they were not trying hard enough, they attempted to justify their attacks on civilians by

[14] Cited in n. 6 above.

[15] Vidal-Naquet, *La Raison d'État* (Paris: Les Éditions de Minuit, 1962), pp 204–34, in *Le Monde*, April 18, 1959, p. 4.

explaining that the other side had resorted to unjustifiable attacks on civilians. It is probably impossible to determine which side was responsible for each successive widening of the conflict to encompass the civilian inhabitants of Algeria and also, to a limited extent, of France. But it is clear that by 1957 no civilian in Algeria, Moslem or French, could expect to be immune from either direct or indiscriminate attack.

In the first night of attacks launching the rebellion, the FLN rebels shot two civilians who were passengers on a bus. They soon embarked on a deliberate policy of assassination of civilians, both French and Moslem, who were part of the French administration of Algeria. They tried to invest these killings with a kind of judicial aura by attaching to the bodies of the slain civilians notes stating that they had been convicted by the FLN of treason, spying, or collaboration with the enemy. In August 1955, they deliberately stirred up a mass riot in the Constantine area, resulting in large numbers of civilian deaths. In the years 1956–57, they conducted a campaign of terrorism in the city of Algiers, exploding time bombs in cafes, sports stadiums, and at bus stops where Europeans congregated.

On their part, the French conducted aerial bombardments of rural areas where rebel forces were concentrated, and in the later years of the war, they used napalm. They gave warnings to inhabitants to move out of areas to be bombed but assumed that those who remained were FLN sympathizers. They made mass arrests and, with a greater claim to legitimacy but perhaps no greater claim to be enforcing justice, tried civilians in military courts, sentenced them to death, and executed them for treason, spying, or collaboration with the enemy. The French also gave arms to French and European civilians and, in the last years of the conflict, proved unable to control the use of plastic bombs by counterterrorists.

The French felt compelled to resort to stringent measures against the civilian population to counteract the willingness of the people to shelter and supply the guerrilla fighters. They employed such doctrines as collective responsibility, holding all the inhabitants of a village responsible for a terrorist attack believed to have emanated from the village. They assigned civilians to places of residence to facilitate military operations. In 1960, the number of Algerians who had been assigned residences amounted to over two million people. The GPRA in its *White Paper* of 1960 charged that this regroupment of civilians was in essence the creation of concentration camps and a violation of article 3 of the Geneva Convention on the Protection of Civilians. Raphael Lemkin declared that the practice was also in violation of the Genocide Convention, as it was accompanied by large losses of life resulting from disease and starvation. France had become a party to the Genocide Convention in 1950.

The GPRA on several occasions during the last three years of the war proposed to the ICRC that a special agreement be concluded on humanitarian problems, which would contain among other things a ban on such inhuman methods of warfare as the use of napalm; but nothing came of its proposals. In its comprehensive complaint based on the Geneva Conventions, the GPRA presented descriptions of the wiping out of villages for past or prospective support of the FLN, the creation of large numbers of refugees, and the regroupment of Moslems within Algeria. There was, however, no forum in which the GPRA could obtain serious consideration of its complaint.

"Peacetime" Interference with Shipping

In the Algerian conflict, the French undertook to intercept ships on the high seas and to seize contraband; but at the same time, they denied that the FLN had belligerent status. By virtue of the characterization they chose to place upon their efforts to maintain order in Algeria, the French were technically in violation of the prohibition against interference with shipping in peacetime. But states sympathetic to the French effort to maintain control of Algeria were not inclined to raise any objection to the interception of ships by the French; and states sympathetic to the FLN, while issuing verbal protests against interception, concentrated their attention on avoiding future interceptions. It was an obvious fact—even though the French chose not to admit it—that a full-scale war was in progress between the French and the FLN.

The French activity in the Mediterranean was brought into the glare of world publicity when a French warship intercepted the *Athos* on October 19, 1956. The *Athos* was of British registry but was owned by a Moslem who, according to the French, had been working for the intelligence services of the Egyptian government. The captain of the ship was a Greek national. The French government claimed that the cargo of arms aboard the *Athos* was being shipped by the Egyptian government to the FLN. It presented to the Security Council of the United Nations a complaint against Egypt for supplying arms to the FLN.[16]

The French contended that the Egyptian government had intervened in the rebellion in Algeria "in flagrant violation of the rules of international law." The Egyptian government refused to admit any complicity in the shipment of arms and later claimed that the interception of the *Athos* had taken place on the high seas and was, consequently, contrary to the rules of international law on freedom of the seas. Although the Security Council put the matter on its agenda at the request of the French government, the matter was never formally considered by the

[16] United Nations, Security Council, *Letter of October 25, 1956, from the French Representative to the Secretary-General* (S/3689).

council because it became engrossed, on the next day, with the British and French threats to invade Egypt in the area of the Suez Canal.

As the war progressed, several states—particularly communist states —protested against the interception of ships flying their flags. The protesting states denied that any arms found aboard the ships were destined for the Algerian rebels and contended that the interceptions had taken place on the high seas in violation of the doctrine of freedom of the seas. Yugoslavia protested against the seizure of the *Slovenija* on January 19, 1958, and demanded immediate restitution of the seized cargo and compensation for losses arising out of the incident. The Czech government sent two notes of protest to the French government over the seizure of arms aboard the freighter *Lidice* in April 1959. The West German government also protested the seizure of several cases of "war material" aboard the *Bilbao* in the English Channel, claiming that the material was not "war material" and in any event was destined for Morocco. The French rejected the Yugoslav and Czech protests but formally apologized to the West Germans.

Since the French government could not set up a prize court to handle complaints by shipowners without acknowledging the belligerent status of the rebels, it left shipowners no effective judicial recourse. Several months after the Algerian conflict had ended, an Italian shipowner brought a complaint against the French government in a French court, alleging that the interception of his ship in January 1959 on the high seas was a violation of international law. The French court rejected the complaint on the ground that it had no competence to pass upon the validity of acts which the French government considered necessary to the national defense.[17]

The FLN, the real object of the "peacetime" interference with shipping, had theoretical grounds for charging the French with violating the freedom of the seas but no practical means of pressing such charges. Besides, if the FLN had pressed such charges, it would have undercut its own position that the Algerian conflict was a full-fledged war. So rather than label the interceptions as violations of international law, the FLN cited them as evidence that the French actually recognized the FLN as a belligerent. This tactic, too, proved to be only an exercise in the ritual of traditional international law, with no practical consequences.

Aerial Hijacking

There was one significant incident which took place in the air over the high seas of the Mediterranean. On October 22, 1956, the French

[17] *Société Ignazio Messina et Cie.* v. *the State* [Minister of the Armed Forces "Marine"], Administrative Tribunal of Paris, Oct. 22, 1962; *Annuaire Française du Droit International*, vol. 8 (1962), pp. 920–22.

intercepted a plane chartered by the king of Morocco on which five rebel leaders were flying from Rabat to Tunis via the Balearic Islands. The plane was listed on the French registry, but the Moroccans claimed that it should be regarded as Moroccan since Morocco had attained independence only a few months earlier and arrangements were being made to set up a Moroccan registry. The plane was owned by a Moroccan airline company. The pilot and crew were French citizens in the employ of the Moroccan government. While the plane was flying over the high seas, French military authorities ordered the crew to land the plane at Algiers. The crew obeyed, and as soon as the plane landed, the five rebel leaders were arrested.

The incident provoked a variety of questions concerning the legality of the interception and arrest. There was, primarily, the dispute over the nationality of the plane. The king of Morocco injected another question by maintaining that the French government had approved the arrangements for the conference in Tunis with the rebel leaders and that the rebel leaders, as his guests, were clothed with his immunity. André Philip, professor of the faculty of law of the Sorbonne, argued that the French pilot was obligated to follow the instructions of the airline company as to the flight course.

Early in 1957, the Moroccan and French governments agreed to set up a commission of inquiry and conciliation to investigate the plane incident. The commission was composed of a French, a Moroccan, a Belgian, an Italian, and a neutral Lebanese member. There was never full agreement on the jurisdiction of the commission. The French maintained it was limited to issues arising over the disposition of the plane and could not consider the fate of the five FLN leaders. When the commission upheld French objections to the hearing of certain witnesses, the Moroccan and Lebanese members of the commission withdrew, and the commission held no further sessions.[18]

Extensions of the Conflict into Bordering States

The right of a state to protect itself against involvement in hostilities in an adjacent state by requiring the withdrawal of the forces of the belligerents from its territory proved meaningless in the situation in which Tunisia and Morocco found themselves. Neither of them had sufficient military strength to compel either the French forces or the FLN forces to leave its territory. French forces had freely entered Tunisia and Morocco while the peoples of those countries were still under French administration. Immediately after the two countries achieved independence in 1956, both countries demanded that the French give

[18] *New York Times*, March 1, 1958, p. 4: 5.

up their military bases and withdraw their troops. The French were reluctant to do so without assurances that Tunisia and Morocco would refuse to give sanctuary to FLN forces. These assurances Tunisia and Morocco were either unwilling or unable to give. As a consequence, the withdrawal of French forces was delayed. It was not until December 1960 that the last French forces left Rabat and not until 1963—after the Algerian conflict had ended—that French forces left Bizerte.

While insisting upon the withdrawal of French forces, the Tunisian and Moroccan governments, either because of their sympathy for the struggle being waged by their Moslem brothers in Algeria or because they were incapable of preventing the use of their territory by FLN forces, allowed the FLN to maintain large forces in bases on their territory and to launch attacks from those bases. In a speech at Thala, Tunisia, on August 13, 1957, President Bourguiba declared that "a state should not permit attacks from its own soil on a neighboring country."[19] But his general attitude was more clearly reflected in a statement he made in 1960—that Tunisia had no responsibility for military engagements taking place on Algerian territory, even though the FLN forces had used Tunisian territory as a staging area.[20]

The French employed a variety of tactics to try to counteract the advantage which the FLN had in its freedom to use adjacent Tunisian and Moroccan territory. One tactic was the invocation of a "right of pursuit" of fleeing Algerian rebels into the bordering states. On August 24, 1957, the French defense minister formally announced that French forces would exercise the right; and one week later, the pursuit of some guerrillas across the frontier was justified as an application of the right. The Tunisian government refused to acknowledge that any such right existed and announced that it would exercise its "right of legitimate defense" to prevent any future invasions of its territory by the French.

A second tactic which the French employed was to invoke a "right of riposte." This was the justification for firing into Tunisian territory, either from Algerian territory or from Algerian air space, in answer to fire coming from Tunisian territory. On May 28, 1957, for example, the French explained a bombardment of Tunisian territory by asserting that their planes had riposted after having been struck by bullets from machine guns fired from Tunisian territory. Again, on October 1, 1957, French planes bombed a customs building in a Tunisian village, presumably because it was from the building or its neighborhood that guns had fired upon the French planes. Bourguiba reacted as strongly against

[19] *Le Monde*, Aug. 15/16, 1957, p. 4.
[20] *Le Monde*, April 26, 1960.

the assertion of this right as he had against the assertion of the right of pursuit.

Neither the right of pursuit nor the right of riposte was adequate for French purposes; and on February 8, 1958, French military forces abandoned such nice distinctions and carried out a full-scale daylight air raid against the Tunisian town of Sakiet-Sidi-Youssef, killing 79 persons and wounding 130 others. This extension of the war, and a more limited attack three months later, provoked Tunisia to file complaints in the Security Council and stimulated the Americans and the British to mediate the dispute. The French refrained thereafter from large-scale attacks on Tunisian territory.

It was on a mechanical device that the French finally came to place their principal reliance in trying to nullify the advantages the FLN derived from use of Tunisian and Moroccan territory. By the end of 1957, the French had succeeded in constructing two electrified barrages within Algeria, close to and paralleling the frontiers with Tunisia and Morocco. The barrages were strengthened and extended in 1958. From 1958 to the end of the Algerian conflict, the barrages were, in effect, battle lines between French and FLN forces. The FLN forces were divided into interior and exterior forces. The latter maintained themselves in bases in Tunisia and Morocco and spent their time trying to devise means for breaking through the barrages.

During the last four years of the war, the Tunisian and French governments contented themselves with compiling lists of attacks carried out across the barrages. The Tunisians complained of attacks upon Tunisian territory, and the French of attacks launched from Tunisian territory.[21] But the complaints were for the record, and neither side moved to have them considered by the Security Council.

III. THE ROLE OF OUTSIDE STATES

Even had outside states wished to abide by international law principles in dealing with the Algerian conflict, they would have had considerable difficulty in trying to figure out what those principles were and how they should be applied. For the principles themselves were, and still are, in a state of flux. Traditionally, outside states had been expected to refrain from aiding forces rebelling against an established government, either before or after such forces attained the status of belligerents; and outside states had also been expected to refrain from aiding the estab-

---

[21] United Nations, Security Council, *Letters from the Tunisian Representative to the President of the Security Council* (S/4163), Feb. 16, 1959, (S/4307), April 28, 1960, and (S/5000), Nov. 24, 1961; *Letter from the French Representative to the President of the Security Council* (S/4309), May 2, 1960.

lished government after the level of belligerency was reached.[1] But the members of the international community had endorsed the principle of self-determination in the United Nations Charter and had also created international organizations in which opinions could be expressed on the validity of objectives sought by revolutionists. Consequently, outside states appealing to the developing law of decolonization could assert with considerable persuasiveness the right to guide their policy in a revolutionary situation by their judgment of the legitimacy of the objectives of the protagonists.

The Reliance of the Rebels on Outside Help

Whatever system of restraints the international community presumed to be applicable to the extension of outside help to revolutionists, it was apparent that the system was not strong enough to exercise a significant deterrent effect upon the launching of the Algerian Revolution. The Algerian nationalist leaders could not, at the outset of the revolution, expect to obtain open pledges of support from foreign governments. But they had reasons to expect that they could obtain outside help either clandestinely or through commercial or other nongovernmental channels.

The FLN leaders knew they could rely upon the cooperation of other Arab governments, particularly those of Egypt and Libya. The Egyptian government allowed the FLN leaders to set up an office in Cairo and to use Egyptian passports for travel to other countries to make arrangements to purchase arms. Nasser promised to help in the transmission of military supplies to the rebels by way of Egypt. King Idris of Libya secretly agreed to allow the transportation of these supplies through Libya.[2] The Tunisians could be counted upon to facilitate the passage of supplies, since they were fighting for their own independence from France. There was a possible alternate route for supplies through Morocco, which in 1954 was also demanding independence from France.

The Algerian rebel leaders also felt confident of their ability to make the necessary arrangements for the purchase of arms. They knew they could rely on the secrecy policies of Swiss banks, and it became evident during the conflict that Swiss banks were handling accounts for the FLN. Whether the rebel leaders sounded out manufacturers of munitions beforehand or not, soon after the revolution began FLN agents were

[1] The continuing confusion over the rules of international law on intervention in internal conflicts is illustrated by Evan Luard in *Conflict and Peace in the Modern International System* (Boston: Little, Brown, 1968), p. 154. Luard says once belligerency has been recognized, outside states have "an obligation either to become a party to the war or to adopt a position of strict neutrality." According to Luard, there is no restraint under international law against unilateral intervention on either side in an internal war.

[2] Majid Khadduri, *Modern Libya* (Baltimore: Johns Hopkins Press, 1963), pp. 268–69.

making purchases of arms in Europe. They bought small arms and ammunition from Belgium, Italy, and West Germany and from the communist countries of eastern Europe as well.[3] France ultimately tried to persuade the governments of the western European countries to stop the sales; but it could not, of course, invoke any principle of international law against the conduct of business as usual. To the extent that it succeeded in shutting off arms from western Europe, France merely turned over to the communists the business of selling arms to the FLN.

A most significant assurance of outside help that the Algerian rebels received before they resorted to force came from the international labor movement, including both free world and communist labor unions. In July 1952, the General Council of the International Confederation of Free Trade Unions (ICFTU) announced that it was prepared to support political campaigns for self-determination.[4] At its third world congress in July 1953, the ICFTU adopted a resolution supporting the struggle against colonial oppression which was then going on in Tunisia and Morocco. It did not at the time mention Algeria; but as early as 1950, Irving Brown, international representative of the American Federation of Labor, had visited four cities in Algeria, meeting with representatives of the nationalist movements in Algeria and encouraging the development of free trade unionism.[5]

The communist-dominated World Federation of Trade Unions (WFTU) had also given strong indications of support for any movements toward independence throughout the world. At its third world congress in Vienna in 1953, the WFTU called upon the workers of the world "to increase their solidarity and support for the peoples who were fighting for national independence, against imperialism, and for an end to the colonial system wherever it exists." The WFTU was considerably hampered in Algeria because its affiliate in Algeria was a regional federation of the French Confédération Générale du Travail (CGT), which, being composed of both European and Moslem members, had been unable to formulate a policy on the question of independence for Algeria. But the FLN could hope that the WFTU eventually might be able to exert an influence on the policy of its powerful French affiliate and perhaps, through its affiliate, upon the French government itself.

As a consequence of the various encouragements and assurances it had received, the FLN on November 1, 1954, embarked on its revolution. The traditional international law of neutrality had not been concerned sufficiently with the involvement of outside nongovernmental

[3] Edward Behr, *The Algerian Problem* (New York: Norton, 1962), p. 108.

[4] John Riddell, *Free Trade Unions in the Fight for African Freedom* (Brussels: ICFTU, 1961), pp. 6–7.

[5] International Confederation of Free Trade Unions, *Report of the Second World Congress, 1951* (Brussels: ICFTU, 1951), p. 36.

209

organizations, with the relative ease of acquiring arms on the commercial markets, or with the difficulties of preventing the transportation of arms to serve as any brake upon the resort to force. The developing international law of decolonization served as a positive incitement to revolution. The main question now had to be faced: Would international law of either the traditional or the developing variety have any impact upon the provision of outside aid during the revolution?

The International Status of the FLN

Among the first questions which outside states faced in dealing with the Algerian Revolution was whether to permit the entry of representatives of the FLN into their countries, whether to honor passports issued to such representatives by sympathetic Arab governments, and whether to allow such representatives to conduct commercial transactions and to dispense propaganda. In February 1957, the French foreign minister condemned the issuance of passports by Arab states to FLN representatives on false identification data as "outright interference in the domestic affairs of a state."[6] But no instance has been found in which a state refused to honor a passport issued by an Arab state to a member of the FLN. Presumably international law forbade any questioning of the "act of state" involved in the issuance of a passport.

While, theoretically, outside states had the capacity to refuse to permit FLN representatives to open offices within their territory, most states made no objection. The United States was perhaps a special case. FLN representatives could ask to be permitted to enter the United States to observe sessions of the United Nations at which the question of Algeria was being discussed. But the United States government imposed no significant restrictions on the activities of FLN representatives.

FLN representatives first came to New York City in September 1955. In 1957, the FLN established an Algerian Office in New York, which was maintained until independence was won. The man in charge of the office, Abdelkader Chanderli, in registering with the United States Department of Justice, gave the following description of his activities as a foreign agent:

Campaigning for the liberation of Algeria in the United States. Representing the principal (the Algerian Front of National Liberation) in the Afro-Asian group in the United Nations. Lecturing. Publishing news bulletins and press releases including an information sheet under the title "Free Algeria." Establishing contacts with all mass media, including press, radio and TV to provide a better knowledge of the Algerian question.[7]

[6] Speech by Pineau on Feb. 4, 1957, *Speeches and Press Conferences* (French Embassy, New York), No. 87, February 1957, p. 31.
[7] Registration No. 1007, filed with the Department of Justice on March 12, 1957.

At international conferences of states sympathetic to the Algerian cause, FLN representatives were accorded the status of observers or petitioners, as at the Bandung Conference in April 1955 and at the First Conference of Independent African States at Accra in April 1958. FLN representatives also maintained a variety of unofficial contacts with foreigners through international associations of labor and students, and through Pan-African conferences. The absence of official recognition of the FLN as a government did not hamper the FLN significantly either in its conduct of commercial business throughout the world or in its campaign to rally world support.

On September 19, 1958, the FLN established the Provisional Government of the Republic of Algeria (GPRA), which appealed for international recognition. The headquarters of the GPRA were set up in Tunis; but since some of its officials claimed to maintain offices within Algeria and since the FLN exerted control over some sections of Algeria, the GPRA denied that it was a government-in-exile and asserted its right to recognition on the basis of actual control and administration of part of the territory of Algeria.

The French government immediately stated that it would consider recognition of the GPRA by any government to be an unfriendly act. It made formal protests to Tunisia, Morocco, and Libya when they extended recognition to the GPRA. But it asserted no legal ground of complaint against any government, since, as *Le Monde* explained, it considered recognition to be a political act.[8] In the opinion of jurists, said *Le Monde*, recognition is not governed by any precise rule, not even by the effective exercise of authority over territory. The French did not break diplomatic relations with any country over recognition of the GPRA, even though fifteen countries had granted recognition by the end of 1958 and fourteen more granted recognition during the next three years.[9]

The manner in which states responded to the appeal by the GPRA for recognition revealed that most of them were acting on political and not on legal considerations. As K. P. Misra, a leading Indian scholar, has said, most states granting recognition made no reference to principles of international law but stressed instead their support for the Algerian cause.[10]

States indicating that they were aware of legal criteria for the granting of recognition disagreed over the application of the criteria to the GPRA. During the debate in the thirteenth and sixteenth sessions of the

[8] *Le Monde*, Sept. 24, 1958, p. 1.

[9] Mohammed Bedjaoui, *Law and the Algerian Revolution* (Brussels: International Association of Democratic Lawyers, 1961, pp. 137(n), 138.

[10] K. P. Misra, "Recognition of the Provisional Government of the Algerian Republic: A Study of the Policy of the Government of India," *Political Studies* [United Kingdom], 10 (June 1962), p. 142.

United Nations General Assembly on Afro-Asian draft resolutions mentioning the GPRA, delegates contending that the GPRA was not entitled to recognition gave as the reason that it was "a provisional government on foreign territory" or "a group of political leaders selected by processes which were far from clear and functioning outside the territory over which they claimed authority." Delegates from states which had recognized the GPRA maintained that it "was exercising all the attributes of national sovereignty over vast areas of Algerian territory." The governments of India and the United States, both professing to apply legal criteria, came up with different conclusions. India kept the matter of recognition under constant review and finally, in November 1961, extended de facto recognition. The United States appears to have made up its mind once and for all in September 1958 not to grant recognition.[11]

Whatever the reasons were which influenced states to grant or to deny recognition to the GPRA, it was apparent that the legal consequences of granting or withholding recognition were negligible. The French government protested against the grant of visas by the United States government to representatives of the FLN for entry into the United States to observe the fourteenth session of the United Nations General Assembly in 1959. Secretary of State Herter explained that traditionally the United States government had not withheld visas from persons with whom it disagreed politically.[12] The FLN replaced its offices in countries granting recognition with diplomatic missions, but the functions of the diplomatic missions differed little from the functions of the offices in countries that had not granted recognition.

The process of unilateral recognition of the GPRA by individual states may be compared with the process of collective endorsement by the United Nations General Assembly of the right of the Algerian people to self-determination. Both processes served the basic purpose of enabling the members of the international community to give formal expression to their view that Algeria was entitled to come into existence as a new state. But the process of unilateral recognition of the GPRA, unlike collective endorsement of the right of self-determination, had the effect of identifying the GPRA as the organization believed to be entitled to function provisionally as the governing authority in Algeria and entitled to enter into diplomatic relations with the recognizing state. Further, and also unlike collective endorsement of the right of self-determination, unilateral recognition of the GPRA appeared to obviate the necessity for a referendum to determine whether the people of Algeria really

---

[11] U.S. Department of State, Office of News, Transcript of Press and Radio Briefing on Sept. 25, 1958, *Daily News Conferences*, 18 (July–December 1958).
[12] U.S. Department of State, *American Foreign Policy: Current Documents, 1959*, p. 1102.

wanted independence. Consequently, it is not surprising that many more states were willing to go on record as favoring self-determination for Algeria than were willing to extend unilateral recognition to the GPRA. Forty-three of the sixty-three states which voted in the fifteenth session of the General Assembly to recognize the right of the Algerian people to self-determination had not recognized the GPRA.

The Legitimacy of Aid to the FLN

The states which supplied aid to the FLN appeared to be unconcerned that they were violating a precept of traditional international law—that aid is not to be given to the rebel side in a revolution either before or after the rebels attain the status of belligerents. They were acting under what they considered to be a developing principle of international law— that a people are entitled to outside assistance in a struggle to obtain independence from colonial rule. Even under the traditional rule, of course, it was by no means certain just where the line would have to be drawn between types of aid. Financial donations might be permitted, for example, while contributions of troops would not. But the states supporting Algerian independence considered that there were no limitations on the type of aid that could be extended to the FLN.

The French made various efforts during the Algerian conflict to bring to bear the traditional prohibition against aid to rebels. They made an official protest against a resolution in which the Arab League in March 1956 offered full support to the rebellion. In February 1957, French Foreign Minister Christian Pineau claimed that the Arab League maintained a fund on which the FLN could draw and that Colonel Nasser had admitted supplying money to the rebels for arms purchases. Pineau contended that assistance to encourage subversive activities "was considered inadmissible by international jurisprudence."[13] In November 1957, he repeated his charges of financial aid by the Arab states to the FLN and characterized such aid as in violation of the "most established principles" of the Charter of the United Nations.[14]

The Arab states disregarded the French complaints. The more the French complained, the more openly the Arab states provided aid. In 1957, Arab leaders informed the press of amounts contributed to the FLN. They conducted fund drives for the cause of Algerian independence. In October 1958, the council of the Arab League announced a decision to provide an annual subsidy to the FLN in the amount of $34 million. Proffers of aid to the FLN came from Communist China and later from the independent African states. Rather than conceal aid

[13] Cited in n. 6 above.
[14] Speech by Pineau on Nov. 27, 1957, *Speeches and Press Conferences* (French Embassy, New York), No. 103, Nov. 27, 1957.

in deference to traditional international law principles, states boasted of it in reliance upon their conception of the developing law of decolonization.

The French were most insistent that outside states should not provide military aid or facilitate the delivery of arms to the FLN. After their capture of arms shipped by Egypt aboard the *Athos* in October 1956, the French complained to the Security Council of the United Nations but did not press for council consideration. They decided instead, by joining with the British in an invasion of Egypt, to take into their own hands the enforcement of the principle for which they were contending. But they had so little confidence in obtaining international support for their position that they did not use it in the United Nations as even a partial justification for their participation in the attack upon Egypt.

Premier Guy Mollet renewed the charges against Egypt in a speech on January 9, 1957:

> The capture of the "Athos" has established, in an irrefutable manner, the military aid given by the Egyptian State itself to the armed groups in Algeria. It is not a matter of a little smuggling, more or less winked at. It is the Egyptian Government which furnishes arms taken from its arsenals and arranges for their transportation. It is the Egyptian Government which is systematically carrying on, in its centers of military instruction and its schools for commandos and sabotage, the training of cadres for the Algerian armed groups. It is the Egyptian public power which is furnishing administrative facilities and financial aid to the rebel organizations.
>
> There is no ambiguity about it. It is the Egyptian State which is interfering, which is giving its support to an insurrectional movement unleashed on our territory; France denounces this violation of international law and of the very principles of the United Nations Charter.[15]

It was obvious, however, that most of the other members of the United Nations were focusing upon a set of principles in the Charter different from those which seemed determinative to the French.

In November 1957, the French singled out Tunisia as responsible for the supply of military aid to the rebels in various forms, such as the provision of logistic bases and the use of military vehicles. When haled before the Security Council by Tunisia for the bombing of the Tunisian town of Sakiet, the French requested that the council condemn Tunisia for military aid to the rebels. The French apparently had no illusions that any condemnation would be forthcoming and so agreed to the reference of the dispute to the Anglo-American Good Offices Mission. When brought before the Security Council again in May 1958 for a second attack on Tunisian territory, the French representative again

[15] Speech by Mollet on Jan. 9, 1957, *French Affairs* (French Embassy, New York), No. 41, January 1957.

charged that the support afforded by Tunisia to the Algerian rebels constituted aggression. But France again consented to a settlement of the dispute outside the council. And when the settlement was concluded, it was found that, instead of obtaining any admission by Tunisia of wrongful conduct, the French had virtually admitted their own fault by agreeing to the evacuation of French troops from Tunisia.

The Legitimacy of Aid to France

Under the traditional theory of international law, outside states were free to aid the French government up to the point when a status of belligerency was reached, after which they were required to maintain a neutral position, refraining from aiding either party to the conflict. Under the developing theory as envisaged by the supporters of the principle of decolonization, outside states were obliged to refrain from aiding the French government at any time during the course of hostilities—whether before or after the existence of a state of belligerency.

The Arab states were the ringleaders in trying to persuade other states that they should not give aid of any kind to France. They concentrated their attention on the United States. In August 1955, spokesmen for eight Arab states requested the United States government to take action to prevent the use by France in North Africa of American equipment provided to France under North Atlantic Treaty Organization agreements.[16] United States officials revealed that they had made representations to France about the use of American military equipment against North Africans. On August 26, presumably in response to prompting from the United States, the French foreign minister issued a statement saying that, in accordance with assurances previously given to the United States, the French government was not using any United States materials for the "maintenance of order" in North Africa.

The Arab states were not convinced that any effective action was being taken to keep the French from using in North Africa military equipment supplied by the United States government. In June 1956 and May 1957, Arab states protested that the assistance given by the United States was being used to suppress the liberties of the Algerian people.[17] At this time, when there was greater justification, if not an obligation, under traditional international law for the United States to deny aid to France—since the Algerian conflict had clearly reached the dimensions of a war—the United States government said it was not willing to attach any conditions regarding Algeria to the use of military equipment provided to France. At the same time, Secretary of State Dulles said that

[16] New York Times, Aug. 26, 1955, p. 1:2.
[17] New York Times, June 16, 1956, p. 1:1; American Foreign Policy, Current Documents, 1957, pp. 1067–69.

the United States was seeking to avoid intervening or interfering in the Franco-Algerian dispute in any way. Although this was the language of neutrality, the secretary avoided use of the word; and certainly, unrestricted military aid to France could scarcely be reconciled with a policy of nonintervention or noninterference.

In February 1958, the use by the French of American-built planes in the bombardment of Sakiet prompted newsmen to ask Secretary Dulles at a news conference about the problem of French use of American military equipment in Algeria. This time Dulles reverted to the position taken in 1955 and 1956, implying that there were still restrictions upon French use of the equipment.[18] He said that it was extremely difficult to identify the source of any particular piece of equipment and how it came to be used in Algeria but that it was of interest and concern to the United States that the engagements of the French in regard to that equipment should be scrupulously observed.

In trying to attach restrictions to the military aid it supplied to France during the Algerian conflict, the United States government failed to satisfy either the requirements of the traditional international law of neutrality or the requirements of the developing international law of decolonization. Handing over arms to a government engaged in a military conflict with a request that that government not use the arms in the conflict makes about as much sense as the advice of mother to daughter in the nursery rhyme: "Hang your clothes on a hickory limb but don't go near the water." Surely the traditional law of neutrality does not excuse the supply of arms to a belligerent if the arms are marked "Not for use in the current conflict." And the developing rule, which would deny the use of arms to repress a movement for independence from colonialism, was interpreted by its sponsors as prohibiting outside states from supplying any arms to a government engaging in such repression.

No record has been found of complaints by the Arab states against the commercial, as distinguished from the governmental, provision of financial aid to France. The extent to which France was granted credit for the purchase of arms in the United States or in western Europe is not known. Commercial loans usually are not publicized, particularly loans by Swiss banks. According to a Swiss newspaper, Switzerland was making loans of Swiss francs to France as late as 1959, but these loans apparently were on a government-to-government basis.[19] It remains difficult to understand, however, why international law should attempt to regulate the provision of financial aid by governments to belligerents, if it places no obligation on governments to control loans to belligerents through commercial channels.

[18] *American Foreign Policy, Current Documents, 1958*, pp. 1086–87.
[19] *Le Monde*, June 20, 1959, p. 6.

The inadequacy—one might even say the insincerity—of efforts by either the traditionalists or the modernists to deal with arms aid is revealed also in their failure to place governments under any responsibility to regulate commercial sales of arms. A large part of the arms supplied to the FLN were supplied commercially. In the case of France, military equipment of United States manufacture flowed to the French through commercial channels more freely than through government channels. In 1955, the French government bought helicopters directly from the Sikorsky Company in Connecticut. In 1957, a Kansas City firm sold 350 army surplus M-8 combat cars to France for use in Algeria. It was only occasionally, and accidentally, that commercial sales were publicized; but there appears no doubt that no ban on the supply of arms from outside to either of the parties to the Algerian conflict could have been effective without control of commercially supplied as well as government-supplied arms.

There was never any indication at any point that the United States government determined its policy on the supply of military equipment to France on the basis of its assessment of whether the conflict in Algeria had reached the stage of belligerency. The United States supplied half a billion dollars' worth of military aid to France in 1955 and about half a billion in 1956.[20] The amount was cut in half in 1957 and reduced each year thereafter until, by 1962, only $40 million in military aid was being furnished. But neither the provision of the aid nor the attempt to impose restrictions on its use in Algeria revealed any evidence that relevance had been attached to the belligerent status of the combatants.

The Arab states protested against economic, as well as military, aid to France. Again they concentrated their attention on aid provided by the United States government. During the years 1955 and 1956, the economic aid provided by the United States to France was negligible. But by the end of 1957, the exigencies of its campaign in Algeria had placed France in a precarious financial position. To extricate itself, the French government negotiated with the United States government, with the International Monetary Fund, and with the European Payments Union for various forms of financial aid, with an aggregate value of $655 million.[21] The United States contribution—in the form, principally, of deferment of payments on previous loans—amounted to $274 million. When the GPRA, in September 1960, submitted to the NATO powers its condemnation of governmental aid to France, the chief item of financial aid was the $655 million of assistance extended in January 1958.

The FLN usually relied upon the Arab states to make diplomatic pro-

---

[20] Agency for International Development, *U.S. Overseas Loans and Grants, 1945–1965,* and related work papers.
[21] *American Foreign Policy, Current Documents, 1958,* pp. 572–78.

tests to the North Atlantic powers; but in September 1960, the GPRA prepared a comprehensive statement of the various forms of financial and military aid which the NATO powers had supplied to France.[22] In addition to items previously mentioned by the Arab states in their protests, the GPRA listed the support given to France by the American Sixth Fleet in the Mediterranean. The GPRA addressed the memorandum to the NATO powers and included a denunciation of the North Atlantic Treaty as far as its application to Algeria was concerned. How it attempted to deliver the memorandum to the NATO powers is not known; nor has any record been found of a reply.

In December 1960, the GPRA made an attempt to amalgamate the traditional law of neutrality with the developing law of decolonization, revealing clearly that the two could not be made to mesh. It submitted to the NATO powers a *Memorandum on the Recognition of Belligerency in the Franco-Algerian Conflict.*[23] In the *Memorandum*, the GPRA listed various actions of the French government, such as interception of shipping on the high seas, which were consistent only with recognition of the belligerent status of the FLN. Every recognition of belligerency, it said, carried with it an obligation to comply with the "rules of strict neutrality." According to these rules, the Atlantic powers were obliged to refrain from giving military aid to France. While this argument was consistent with the traditional law of neutrality, the GPRA in the same memorandum implied that the traditional law of neutrality had no application to the provision of military aid to the FLN. The FLN, it said, was struggling for the liberty of the Algerian people from an inhuman colonialism. Consequently, the GPRA made no pledge in its memorandum that the FLN would forego military aid from states willing to assist it in its fight against colonialism.

IV. THE ROLE OF INTERNATIONAL ORGANIZATIONS

The Algerian conflict revealed the limitations of regional organizations and the potentialities of the United Nations in dealing with an anticolonial revolution and, by implication, with other types of internal conflict. Regional organizations served mainly as vehicles for the coordination of the policies of groups of nations with respect to the Algerian

[22] Gouvernement Provisoire de la République Algérienne (GPRA), *Memorandum on the Denunciation of the North Atlantic Treaty by the Provisional Government of the Algerian Republic, September 19, 1960* (New York: Algerian Office of the FLN, 1960); also published in Bedjaoui, *Law and the Algerian Revolution*, pp. 200–206.

[23] GPRA, *Memorandum sur la Reconnaissance de Belligérance dans le Conflit Franco-Algérien* (n.d.), enclosure No. 1 to dispatch No. 259 of Dec. 5, 1960, from Embassy in Tunis to the Department of State, held in the Department of State Library.

conflict. They either supported one of the parties or tried to avoid involvement. The global organization sought to muster the opinion of the international community on the objectives of the parties and on recommendations appropriate for a peaceful settlement.

Regional Organizations: The Arab League and NATO

Two regional organizations were closely identified with the Algerian conflict: the League of Arab States and the North Atlantic Treaty Organization (NATO). The Arab League was active in the support of the FLN, especially during the first two years of the conflict. NATO was passive as an organization. During the early years of the conflict, the member states of NATO voted as a bloc in support of France in the United Nations General Assembly; but during the later years they split their votes.

Several legal questions were raised by implication, though not directly, by the active role of the Arab League and the passive role of NATO. One question was whether the endorsement which the Arab League gave to the use of force by the FLN against France tended in any way to sanction that use of force or to legitimize aid to the FLN by the members of the league or by other countries. Another question was whether a regional organization, such as NATO, which brings into being a military force and places it under a regional command, can be held responsible in any way for the uses made of portions of that force by a member of the regional organization.

From the inception of the Arab League in 1945, its members contemplated its sphere of interest as not only the territories of the initial members but also areas of Arab countries which should subsequently become independent. It was an objective of the league to assist Arab peoples in other countries to achieve independence. Representatives of the North African countries attended the meetings leading to the formation of the Arab League. Shortly after taking office, the secretary of the league established formal contacts with the nationalist political leaders in North Africa. In its early years, the league gave no indication that it intended to urge military moves for independence, but it committed itself to use fully the political means at its disposal.

Once the Algerian Revolution had been launched, the league gave its full backing to the rebels. The assistant secretary-general of the league spoke of the "solemn obligation" of the member states to support the FLN.[1] The secretary-general arranged for participation of North African nationalists at the Bandung Conference in 1955. Officials of the league helped to organize the successful campaign, in September 1955, to place

[1] *New York Times*, Nov. 13, 1954, p. 4:8.

the Algerian question on the agenda of the General Assembly of the United Nations. At a meeting in October 1955, the council of the league urged the members to use their political influence to secure recognition of the right of the Algerian people to self-determination.[2]

The support of the Arab League became even more open and specific during the later years of the war, although a rift between Tunisia and the United Arab Republic prevented full cooperation of the Arab states through the league. The league assessed its members $34 million yearly, beginning in 1958, for the support of the FLN.[3] The GPRA was permitted to send representatives to all league conferences after 1960, although Algeria was not formally admitted to membership until it achieved independence.

On several occasions, the league council discussed the possibility of recommending to all its members that they break diplomatic and economic ties with France or conduct a commercial boycott. The principal league members severed their relations with France immediately after the French participation in the invasion of Suez in 1956. The other league members were unwilling to take such drastic action. In 1960, the league approved a resolution calling upon its members to send "volunteers" to join the FLN forces.[4] However, no record has been found that "volunteers" were actually sent.

The French government found itself unable to make any effective protest against the actions taken by the league. French participation in the invasion of Suez was the most forceful effort by the French, but even that backfired. French officials objected to the "enormous lies" spread by the information outlets of the league and claimed that the league office in New York City had a budget of several hundred million dollars;[5] but the propaganda continued to flow. The ultimate French strategy appears to have been to ignore the league officially and unofficially to provoke divisions among its members.

Neither in the publications of the league, nor in the speeches of representatives of its members at meetings of the political organs of the United Nations, nor in the outpouring of material from the Algerian Office of the FLN in New York City can any trace be found of the contention that the endorsement by the league served to legitimize the use of force by the FLN or the giving of aid to the FLN. Neither the

[2] Muhammad Khalil, *The Arab States and the Arab League: A Documentary Record* (Beirut: Khayat's, 1962), vol. 2, p. 156.

[3] Robert W. MacDonald, *The League of Arab States* (Princeton, N. J.: Princeton University Press, 1965), pp. 140, 363–64.

[4] Resolution of Council of League of Aug. 24, 1960, in Algerian Office of FLN, New York, "The Latest Resolutions on Algeria by International Bodies" (New York, August 1960).

[5] *New York Times*, Dec. 7, 1956, p. 10:3,4.

Arab states nor the FLN was under any illusion about the reception which such a contention would have in the international community. Many states were not ready to accept the proposition that the Arab League could, by endorsing a particular military action, legitimize that action.

Since the end of the Algerian conflict, there have been frequent invocations of resolutions of regional organizations or of commitments to agreements in regional military security pacts to justify military operations. No government has been willing to state, however, that *any* regional organization may legitimize the use of force by its members. A government using force has been willing to say only that the regional organizations to which *it* belongs may justify *its* use of force.

The unwillingness of the NATO powers to pledge support openly for French actions in Algeria was due to the absence of any satisfactory evidence that the rebellion in Algeria was communist-instigated. NATO showed no reluctance to giving its blessing to the French campaign in Indochina in 1952. The NATO Council adopted a resolution stating that the "campaign waged by the French Union forces in Indochina deserves continuing support from the NATO governments."[6] Indochina was as far away from the North Atlantic as any country could be. In contrast, Algeria was in an area of vital concern to the North Atlantic powers, and the North Atlantic Treaty expressly included the Algerian departments of France within the area covered by the treaty. French officials made some half-hearted attempts to pin responsibility for the rebellion on the communists; but the most they could say was that there was a danger that the communists might take over the rebellion or that an independent Algeria might fall into the hands of the communists. Such a possibility might well exist, but it did not, in the eyes of most of the NATO governments, justify NATO endorsement of the denial of independence to Algeria.

There remains the claim of the league that NATO bore responsibility for having brought into being, financed, and equipped a military force, part of which the French deployed in Algeria. The responsibility for acts of this force fell upon all of the members of NATO, said the league. It was difficult, however, for the league to establish that NATO exercised any actual control over its members or could object to the withdrawal by a member of its NATO contingents for a non-NATO use. The complaint by the league was ignored by NATO; but a brief description of it seems worthwhile, as the question of the responsibility of a regional organization or of its members for actions of the organization may acquire

[6] U.S. Department of State, *American Foreign Policy, 1950–1955: Basic Documents*, 2 : 2368–2369.

221

greater significance as more and more authority is conferred upon such organizations.

When, in 1955, the French first notified the supreme commander of the NATO forces that France was withdrawing forces from the NATO Command for use in Algeria, the North Atlantic Council announced that it planned neither to approve nor to disapprove the withdrawal.[7] It is not clear from the announcement whether NATO was taking the position that it had no control over the contingents supplied by a member state or whether it chose not to exert any control in the circumstances. In March 1956, NATO headquarters issued a communique which supporters of the FLN later characterized as an official blessing by NATO upon the French operations in Algeria:

The North Atlantic Council has been consistently kept informed of the forces taken by France from the French troops put at NATO's disposal. It has examined the position in Europe resulting from these troop movements. It has noted that France has considered it necessary, in the interests of her own security, to increase French forces in Algeria, which forms part of the zone covered by the North Atlantic Treaty. The Council recognizes the importance for NATO of the maintenance of security in this area.[8]

Thereafter, principally in debates in the General Assembly, the Arab states in particular repeatedly referred to the use of "NATO arms" and "NATO troops" in Algeria and to the giving of aid by NATO.

The most complete expression of the complaint against NATO was the memorandum that the GPRA prepared on September 19, 1960, in which it denounced the inclusion of Algeria in the coverage of the treaty and listed the various forms of military, financial, and diplomatic aid which NATO had given to France during the Algerian conflict.[9] In the memorandum, the GPRA argued that the expenditures for military operations against the FLN were legally NATO expenditures because they were counted by NATO in the French contribution to the joint defense of the NATO area, and that each of the NATO members was responsible for the French "aggression" in Algeria because the organization tacitly approved of the use of NATO contingents in Algeria. But the GPRA failed to indicate any method by which a regional organization, such as NATO, could be held responsible for its acts.

The ICFTU, which was a champion of the FLN, stated in 1955 that it considered any activities by regional defense organizations in support of colonialism by the supply of arms or other means to be a violation of

[7] *New York Times*, June 3, 1955, p. 4:1.

[8] North Atlantic Treaty Organization, Council, Communique of March 27, 1956.

[9] Gouvernement Provisoire de la République Algérienne (GPRA), *Memorandum on the Denunciation of the North Atlantic Treaty . . .* (New York: Algerian Office of the FLN, 1960).

the proper functions of the organizations.[10] But it had no suggestions to offer at that time on what could be done about such a violation of functions. In February 1961, an ICFTU delegation met with the secretary-general of NATO to ask whether the organization could not put a stop to the aid being given by the North Atlantic powers to the French.[11] The secretary-general maintained that all aid had been provided exclusively by individual governments, none by NATO. The ICFTU delegation refused to accept this explanation, calling it a technical rather than a real distinction. But it had no proposals of ways to bring a regional organization to account.

The Security Council and External Aspects of the Conflict

It must have been apparent to the supporters of the FLN that they could not expect to obtain favorable action in the Security Council, where France itself had a veto and where France and its supporters would have enough votes to block inscription of the Algerian question on the agenda. But the supporters of the FLN nevertheless made several approaches to the Security Council. Saudi Arabia, a member of the council in 1955, brought the Algerian conflict to the attention of the council only a few months after it broke out but did not request a meeting of the council. In April 1956, sixteen Afro-Asian states sent a letter to the council on the situation in Algeria and two months later requested the calling of a meeting of the council. The council rejected the request for a meeting by a vote of 7-2-2. Twenty-one Afro-Asian states sent another letter to the council in July 1959 but did not follow it up with a request for a council meeting.

Tunisia, of course, did make an effort to bring before the council the problem of the extension of the Algerian conflict into Tunisia. It gave ample warning of its intention to do so if France did not cease to carry out military actions on Tunisian territory in a series of letters which the Tunisian representative addressed to the secretary-general during the period from May to October 1957. In February 1958, Tunisia submitted a formal complaint to the council over the French bombing of the Tunisian town of Sakiet. Again in May, Tunisia presented a formal complaint against France to the Security Council over the French bombing of the Remada area of Tunisia. After the first complaint the United States and Britain offered to mediate the dispute, and Security Council debate was avoided by the referral of the matter to the Anglo-American Good Offices Mission. After the second complaint, a brief discussion took

[10] NATO Information Division, *The Trade Unions and NATO* (Paris: 1957), App. IV.
[11] International Confederation of Free Trade Unions, *Report of the Seventh World Congress, 1962* (Brussels: ICFTU, 1962), p. 134.

place in the council but was soon adjourned to permit France and Tunisia to resolve the dispute in bilateral discussions. Although Tunisia did not force a full-scale Security Council debate, its recourse to the council did prompt France's allies to bring pressure on France to stop taking actions which threatened to extend the war into Tunisia.

France, with one exception, sought to avoid any consideration, by either the Security Council or the General Assembly, of the situation in Algeria. The exception was the French submission of a complaint to the council over Egyptian aid to the FLN, as evidenced by the shipment of arms aboard the *Athos*. France requested an immediate meeting of the council, and the item was placed on the agenda. But the council's attention was preempted the next day by the letter from the Egyptian government reporting the joint British-French threat to invade the Suez Canal. What the French government had hoped to accomplish by the submission of its complaint has not been revealed. Perhaps it really had hoped for favorable action by the council. Perhaps it had hoped merely to tie up the council so that the council could not take effective action to stop the British-French invasion of Egypt. Whatever its motive, it did not press for consideration of its complaint.

Throughout the period of the Algerian conflict, the French government held consistently to the position that neither of the political organs of the United Nations had competence to consider the internal aspects of the Algerian Revolution. To the extent that there were questions concerning external support for the rebellion, the French maintained that only the Security Council could consider such questions. That was their rationale for submitting the complaint against Egypt to the Security Council in October 1956. In several speeches in the General Assembly, French Foreign Minister Pineau referred to external aid supplied by Egypt and Tunisia to the FLN; but he did not claim that the foreign interference was such as to constitute a threat to international peace and security.[12] If foreign interference should develop to such proportions, it would be the Security Council and not the General Assembly which should consider the matter.

The Record of the General Assembly

It was in the General Assembly that the supporters of the FLN pressed their case for recognition by the international community of the right of the Algerian people to self-determination.[13] They succeeded in placing the question of Algeria on the agenda of the tenth session of the assembly in 1955, but the French delegation walked out in protest. To

[12] United Nations, General Assembly, *Official Records*, 11th sess., 1st Cte., 830th mtg., Feb. 4, 1957, and GAOR, 12th sess., 1st Cte., 913th mtg., Nov. 27, 1957.
[13] Mohamed Alwan, *Algeria before the United Nations* (New York: Robert Speller & Sons, 1959).

pacify the French, the assembly later deleted the item from its agenda. In the eleventh and twelfth assemblies, the Afro-Asian states succeeded in forcing the French representative to join in extended debates on the Algerian question, but they were able to obtain only innocuous resolutions expressing hope for "a peaceful, democratic and just solution" and a wish that *pourparlers* be entered into—without saying by whom. In the thirteenth assembly in 1958, the Afro-Asian states obtained an endorsement of the right of the Algerian people to independence by more than a two-thirds majority in the First Committee, but they fell one vote short of translating this endorsement into the adoption of a comprehensive resolution on Algeria by the assembly.

The Afro-Asian bloc had clearly demonstrated in 1958 in the General Assembly that the states of the international community supported the right of the Algerian people to independence by a ratio of two to one; but they continued to push for confirmation of this endorsement in a formal resolution. The debate in the fourteenth General Assembly in 1959 was intense, and the parliamentary maneuvering and vote-switching curious. Once again, though securing an overwhelming majority of 61 to 1 with 19 abstentions in the First Committee on a paragraph recognizing the right of the Algerian people to self-determination, the Afro-Asian states failed to obtain the requisite two-thirds for the adoption of a resolution by the General Assembly.

The day of glory finally came in December 1960 in the fifteenth General Assembly. By that time, the bitterness over the refusal of the Western states to allow the assembly to go on record in favor of Algerian independence had been built up into support for a sweeping resolution on anticolonialism. The assembly on December 14, 1960, adopted by a vote of 90-0-9 its famous declaration on the granting of independence to colonial countries and peoples. Five days later, the assembly adopted its first substantive resolution on the Algerian question by a vote of 63-8-27.[14] In this resolution, the assembly recognized (1) the right of the Algerian people to self-determination and independence, (2) the need for effective guarantees to ensure implementation of the right on the basis of respect for the unity and territorial integrity of Algeria, and (3) the responsibility of the United Nations to contribute toward the successful and just implementation of the right.

Competence of the General Assembly to Consider
a Nationalist Revolution

During the consideration of the question of Algeria in the seven consecutive sessions of the General Assembly from 1955 to 1962, the representatives of the member states discussed a wide range of issues regard-

[14] United Nations, GA Res. 1573 (XV), Dec. 19, 1960.

ing the competence of the General Assembly and the implications of its resolutions. The first issue was whether the General Assembly had the competence to consider a situation involving the use of force by a people against an existing government to achieve self-determination. The supporters of the FLN based their appeal to the General Assembly on two grounds: (1) the threat to international peace, and (2) the violation of human rights. They referred to article 11(2) of the United Nations Charter, which authorizes the assembly to discuss and make recommendations with regard to any question relating to the maintenance of international peace and security. They referred also to articles 10 and 14, which authorize the assembly to discuss and make recommendations concerning any matter within the scope of the Charter or concerning any situation resulting from a violation of the purposes and principles of the United Nations as set forth in the Charter. One of the purposes in article 1 of the Charter, the supporters of the FLN pointed out, was to develop friendly relations among nations based on respect for the principle of the self-determination of peoples.

The supporters of the FLN could not complain of intervention or the threat of intervention by an outside power to strengthen their case that the conflict was a threat to international peace. They relied almost entirely on the scale of the fighting. In 1958, they pointed to the French bombardment of a Tunisian village as an indication that the hostilities might spread beyond the frontiers of Algeria. The international tensions generated by the conflict, they said, created a threat to the peace.

The French position and that of its supporters was that there was no threat to international peace. It was a matter of the maintenance of internal order. Algeria was an integral part of France. Article 2(7) of the Charter acknowledged that the United Nations had no authority to intervene in a matter within the domestic jurisdiction of any state. A civil war, regardless of the issue over which it was fought, whether it was a power struggle or a fight for independence, should not be regarded as a threat to international peace.

The Afro-Asian states, however, revealed by the action they requested of the General Assembly that the threat to peace was not the principal basis for bringing the Algerian question to the assembly. They made no request that the assembly adopt a resolution calling for a cease-fire. No other state came forward in the assembly with such a request. The French representative stated that a cease-fire must be the first step in any effort to arrive at a peaceful solution of the conflict; but since France and its supporters maintained that the assembly had no competence to take any action in the Algerian situation, they could not consistently ask it to call for a cease-fire.

It was on the ground that the French action in Algeria constituted a denial of human rights—and particularly the right of the people of Algeria to self-determination—that the supporters of the FLN built their requests for action by the assembly. In the first letter which they addressed to the assembly in July 1955, they mentioned mass arrests, the outlawing of national political parties, the banning of newspapers, and the seizures of homes, as well as the fundamental denial of the right of self-determination. In their second letter, July 1956, they added the charge that France was violating the Genocide Convention. In their first draft resolution, submitted to the eleventh session of the assembly in February 1957, they asked the assembly (1) to recognize the right of the people of Algeria to self-determination, and (2) to request France to respond to the desire of the Algerian people by entering into negotiations.

Although this draft resolution and subsequent draft resolutions acknowledged that negotiations should include arrangements for a cease-fire, each draft resolution made clear that negotiations must be premised on a recognition of the right of the Algerian people to self-determination. When the assembly finally, in December 1960, adopted a resolution granting such recognition, the resolution made no mention of a cease-fire. Its operative paragraphs were concerned solely with the implementation of the right of self-determination.

Collective Recognition of the Right of Self-Determination

The adoption by the assembly of a resolution recognizing the right of the Algerian people to self-determination was an affirmation of the competence and authority of the assembly to pass upon a self-determination issue—upon the right of a people to choose political separation from an existing state. Previously, under traditional international law, individual states had made unilateral judgments on issues of political separation by either granting or denying recognition to the rebel government. Now, the member states of the United Nations, acting simultaneously, had registered their collective judgment on an issue of self-determination. The judgment had not been made in the traditional framework of ignoring the reasons why a people should be accorded the right and concentrating on whether they had successfully asserted control over territory. It had been made in the framework of examining criteria under which a people should be entitled to self-determination.

In their letters to the General Assembly and in the assembly debates, the supporters of the FLN offered the following criteria: prior conquest, colonial rule, current suppression of human rights, and the geographical separation of Algeria from France. They did not urge the existence of racial and religious differences as alone justification for the separation of Algeria from France; but they did present a catalogue of forms of

227

discrimination against Moslems in their exercise of political, economic, and social and cultural rights.

The FLN itself talked a great deal about a right of reconquest—the right of a people to throw out a conqueror, even though the conquest had occurred over a hundred years earlier.[15] In its elaboration of this justification for political separation from France, the FLN came close to shifting its case from one of self-determination to one of self-defense. It was fighting, it said, a war of reconquest, since Algeria had been a state before the French invasion of 1830. The people of Algeria were now reasserting a sovereignty they had never lost. Afro-Asian states gave some support to this thesis in their speeches in the General Assembly. Mongi Slim of Tunisia said that the Algerian people had never freely voted to become a part of France and so their sovereignty remained in spite of the French military conquest.[16] Krishna Menon of India said flatly that conquest was not a legal act.[17]

But in most of the statements to the assembly, the representatives of the Afro-Asian states linked the criterion of prior conquest to that of colonial rule. It was a prior *colonial* conquest that the Algerian people were now overcoming. It must have been obvious to the FLN and its supporters that advocacy of a simple right to reverse any prior conquest would not attract widespread international support to the Algerian cause. A wholesale right of reconquest would be too disturbing to the international order. The communist states could not support such a right without encouraging uprisings of conquered peoples within their borders —the peoples of Latvia, Lithuania, and Estonia, for example. If it were argued that the passage of hundreds of years did not erase a right of reconquest, what about the passage of a thousand years or more? Would not an unrestricted right of reconquest justify the people of Israel in driving the Arabs out of Palestine?

It was not an unrestricted right of reconquest that the Afro-Asian states were advocating but an unrestricted right to overthrow colonialism, to drive out the colonial power. Whenever a European power had imposed by military force its domination over an Asiatic, African, or Latin-American people, that people had the right to reassert their independence. Thus, as the Afro-Asian states used the term "self-determination," it meant "decolonization." And it was easy for them to obtain

[15] Algerian delegation to the Tenth General Assembly, "Memorandum to the Delegations of the Tenth General Assembly of the United Nations: The Peaceful Settlement of the Algerian Question," Oct. 13, 1955; and FLN delegation to the United Nations, "White Paper submitted by the Delegation of the Front of National Liberation to the United Nations Organization on the Franco-Algerian Conflict," April 12, 1956.
[16] UN GAOR, 11th sess., 1st Cte., 836th mtg., Feb. 7, 1957.
[17] UN GAOR, 13th sess., 1st Cte., 1022d mtg., Dec. 13, 1958.

228

ringing declarations of support for decolonization from all states except the colonial powers. The Latin-American representatives who had difficulty mustering enthusiasm for self-determination regained their customary fluency in speeches attacking colonialism. And when the communist countries led the drive in the General Assembly in 1960 for the adoption of the Declaration against Colonialism, there was no dissenting vote.

Underneath the glib speeches, there were indications that what the Afro-Asian states meant by colonialism was, in particular, the continued deprivation of human rights which characterized the colonial system. Along with descriptions of past colonial conquests went graphic and detailed accounts of existing injustices—denials of political, social, economic, and cultural rights. It was not so much for past sins as for current crimes that the people of Algeria were seeking political separation from France.

The point is important because what we are trying to determine is whether the General Assembly of the United Nations confirmed the right of the Algerian people to independence because French military forces invaded Algeria in 1830 and Abd-el-Kader was forced to surrender to General Bugeaud in 1847 or because the French government in 1954 and throughout the Algerian conflict was, by its system of administration and government in Algeria, violating the basic human rights of the people of Algeria. If the latter reason was the real one, then it is possible to say that the action of the General Assembly is a precedent for the authorization of political separation in any case where a people with a territorial base are being denied basic human rights.

The French representative in the General Assembly walked into a bear trap when he presented a detailed account of the benefits bestowed upon the people of Algeria by the French administration, implying that such benefits would justify the continuance of colonial rule.[18] The supporters of the FLN rose one after another in the General Assembly to paint a sharply different picture of conditions in Algeria.

From the welter of accusations and counteraccusations in the Assembly debates, there can be isolated at least some of the French acts or omissions which were claimed to be violations of the rights of the people of Algeria. First: the denial of political rights. In the debate in the eleventh General Assembly, the Greek, Moroccan, Saudi Arabian, and Tunisian representatives all called attention to the political discrimination against the Moslems of Algeria.[19] Under the electoral system estab-

[18] UN GAOR, 11th sess., 1st Cte., 830th mtg., Feb. 4, 1957, and GAOR, 12th sess., 1st Cte., 913th mtg., Nov. 27, 1957.
[19] UN GAOR, 11th sess., 1st Cte., 840th mtg., Feb. 9, 1957, Stratos (Greece); 834th mtg., Feb. 6, 1957, Ben-Aboud (Morocco); 837th mtg., Feb. 7, 1957, Dejany (Saudi Arabia); 845th mtg., Feb. 13, 1957, Slim (Tunisia).

lished by the French in Algeria, the vote of a Frenchman was equal to the vote of nine or ten Moslems. In the French National Assembly, the 9.5 million inhabitants of Algeria were represented by only fifteen deputies, while the 43 million inhabitants of France were represented by more than six hundred deputies. When de Gaulle described his electoral reforms, which reduced the discrimination by about one-half, as opening the way of "equal and universal suffrage" to the Algerians for the first time, Mongi Slim noted that Moslems were still permitted to elect only two-thirds of the Algerian deputies in the French National Assembly, although they constituted eight-ninths of the population of Algeria.

Second: the denial of economic rights. In the eleventh General Assembly, the Syrian and Moroccan representatives charged—and the French representative admitted—that the Europeans owned about one-third of the land in Algeria, including the areas which were most fertile.[20] Although the share of the tenant farmer in his crop had been increased from one-fifth to one-half, the Syrian representative claimed that in Syria the share of the tenant farmer was three-fourths. The few French agricultural workers received higher wages for a shorter workday than the Moslem agricultural workers. Though the French had an industrial program for Algeria, the profits from industry went almost entirely to French residents. The Arab spokesmen cited reports by committees of the French parliament on extensive unemployment and low wages in Algeria. The catalogue of economic discrimination went on and on.

Third: the denial of social rights. French representatives claimed that the increase in population in Algeria was due to the "civilizing mission of France."[21] New housing programs had been undertaken, as had new health services. Discrimination in education had been eliminated. But the Arab spokesmen claimed that Algeria had an illiteracy rate of 86 percent; that, although discrimination in the schoolhouse had been prohibited, 2.4 million Arab children still did not attend school at all.[22] Arab public schools had been suppressed by the French. The study of Algerian history had been made a criminal act. As for health conditions, about 50 percent of the Algerians died before reaching the age of five.

Fourth: the denial of cultural rights. French had become the only official language in Algeria. Arabic could not be used even in day-to-day dealings with administrative officials. The French representative, Jacques Soustelle, vainly pointed to contributions the French had made for instruction in Koranic schools, for the upkeep of mosques, and for salaries

[20] UN GAOR, 11th sess., 1st Cte., 840th mtg., Feb. 9, 1957, Tarazi (Syria); 834th mtg., Feb. 6, 1957, Ben Aboud (Morocco).
[21] UN GAOR, 11th sess., 1st Cte., 830th mtg., Feb. 4, 1957, Pineau (France).
[22] UN GAOR, 11th sess., 1st Cte., 832d mtg., Feb. 5, 1957, Zeineddine (Syria); and 840th mtg., Feb. 9, 1957, Tarazi (Syria).

of religious leaders.[23] The Arab spokesmen charged the French with undermining the Islamic religion.[24]

Another criterion given significance in the consideration of justifications for political separation was the factor of geographical separation. There were occasional references in the debates in the General Assembly to the geographical separation of Algeria from France. Statements were made both ways—that the salt-water separation of France from Algeria was a "distinguishing characteristic" of the situation, and on the other hand, that it could in no way alter the juridical position of the parties.[25]

It was not the existence of racial and religious differences but rather the fact that "fundamental human rights had been trampled underfoot," as Mongi Slim argued, that provided the justification for the political separation of Algeria from France.[26] It was not the circumstance that the denial of human rights took place in a framework of colonialism nor the coincidence that the oppressed people were living across salt water from their oppressors. It was the denial of human rights—the oppression itself—which justified political separation.

V. THE SETTLEMENT

Traditional international law, which has spawned many international agreements to provide peaceful alternatives to the initial resort to military force, seems to have given little attention to procedures and techniques for bringing the combatants in an actual conflict to a negotiated settlement. The combatants generally are left to their own devices. Once strong popular feeling has been aroused on both sides, it is extremely difficult for them even to propose meaningful negotiations. This is particularly true during a war for political separation. For even after an incumbent government has resigned itself to the fact that political separation must come about, it is reluctant to play into the hands of its opponent on the battlefield by acknowledging the authority of that opponent to exercise governmental power in the soon-to-be-created new state.

Negotiations between the French and the FLN

There were several series of negotiations between the French and the FLN before the final settlement was achieved in March 1962. Some of these negotiations were secret, and even the fact that they had occurred

[23] UN GAOR, 11th sess., 1st Cte., 835th mtg., Feb. 6, 1957, Soustelle (France).
[24] UN GAOR, 11th sess., 1st Cte., 832d mtg., Feb. 5, 1957, Zeineddine (Syria).
[25] UN GAOR, 12th sess., 1st Cte., 922d mtg., Dec. 4, 1957, Haikal (Jordan); GAOR, 13th sess., 1st Cte., 1016th mtg., Dec. 10, 1958, Amadeo (Argentina); GAOR, 13th sess., 1st Cte., 1018th mtg., Dec. 11, 1958, De Lequerica (Spain).
[26] UN GAOR, 11th sess., 1st Cte., 836th mtg., Feb. 7, 1957, Slim (Tunisia).

was kept from public knowledge, at least for a period. Other negotiations in the last two years of the war were conducted with full awareness on the part of the public that they were taking place and with considerable disclosure by one side or the other of the issues being discussed and the positions being taken.

The first series of negotiations was during the period from April to September 1956.[1] Members of the French Socialist party—to which the French premier belonged—held secret meetings with FLN leaders in Cairo, then in Belgrade, and finally in Rome. The French asked for an agreement on a cease-fire without prior conditions; the FLN refused to agree to a cease-fire without recognition of the right of the Algerian people to self-determination.

De Gaulle announced to the world at large in September 1959 his qualified acceptance of self-determination for Algeria.[2] For several months, both sides alternately stated in public their positions on a basis for negotiations. Then exchanges were cut off, ostensibly because the French government would not accept the designation by the FLN of the rebel leaders held in French prisons as the spokesmen for the FLN in negotiations.

There was an abortive meeting between the French and the FLN in Melun, a suburb of Paris, in June 1960.[3] The FLN sent two emissaries who discussed with French military leaders the possibility of arranging high-level talks. But the meeting broke up without agreement on arrangements. The FLN complained that its emissaries had been asked to agree to a predetermined agenda for the talks and had been denied the status and freedom of communication usually accorded to diplomatic negotiators.[4]

It became clear that, while de Gaulle in 1959 was ready to *bestow* self-determination upon Algeria under his own terms, he was not ready to *negotiate* the implementation of self-determination with the FLN, the only organization with any serious claim to speak for the people of Algeria. He opposed negotiation with the rebel organization because it would build up that organization as the only valid spokesman of the people of Algeria and would elevate it in advance to the status of government of the country. In September 1960, he expressed doubt that anyone could believe that France "would go so far as to discuss only with the external organization of the rebellion, with the insurgents, the

---

[1] Charles-Henri Favrod, "L'Histoire des 'Négociations Secrètes,' " *La Nef*, October 1962–January 1963, pp. 106–7.

[2] Speech of de Gaulle of Sept. 16, 1959, French Embassy, New York, *Major Addresses, Statements, and Press Conferences of General Charles de Gaulle: May 19, 1958–Jan. 31, 1964* (New York: French Embassy, n.d.), p. 54.

[3] *New York Times*, June 30, 1960, p. 2: 2, 3.

[4] Algerian Office of the FLN, New York, GPRA Communiqué of July 4, 1960.

whole political future of Algeria."[5] In November 1960, he ridiculed the idea that the rebel chiefs could determine with the French government the terms of the future referendum "as if they had been appointed beforehand, and appointed by me, as the rulers of Algeria."[6]

In spite of his previous statements of unwillingness to hold political negotiations with the FLN, de Gaulle on December 20, 1960, offered to hold talks with the rebels if he succeeded in obtaining endorsement of his policies on Algeria in a referendum to be held throughout France, including Algeria.[7] He did not explain the reasons for his change of mind; but two factors may account for it: (1) the readiness of the FLN to seek more help from the Soviet bloc, and (2) the reluctance of the French-speaking African countries to support French policy in Algeria. On January 8, 1961, the referendum was held throughout France and Algeria and recorded approval of the exercise of self-determination by Algeria "as soon as peace reigns."

For a brief period, President Bourguiba of Tunisia served as an intermediary. Then it was announced by both sides that peace talks would open on April 7, 1961; but the GPRA backed out when the French government revealed that it was not proposing to deal exclusively with the FLN but had plans to hold discussions also with the rival nationalist organization, the Mouvement National Algérien.[8] The FLN insisted on being recognized as the sole agent of the Algerian people in negotiations for self-determination.

Preliminary negotiations on substantive issues were finally held from May to July, 1961, first at Evian and then at Lugrin.[9] Although de Gaulle had conceded that he would deal exclusively with the FLN, the negotiations broke down over the French proposal to split off the Saharan portion of Algeria, allowing self-determination only for the rest of Algeria, and also over French proposals for protections to be accorded to the European minority for the postindependence period.

In September, de Gaulle withdrew the proposal for the separation of the Sahara. From then on, secret and informal discussions intensified until both sides were ready to hold the final negotiations at Evian in March 1962.

[5] Press Conference of Sept. 5, 1960, French Embassy, New York, *Major Addresses . . .*, p. 91.
[6] Television speech on Nov. 4, 1960, French Embassy, New York, *Major Addresses . . .*, p. 101.
[7] Address of Dec. 20, 1960, French Embassy, New York, *Major Addresses . . .*, pp. 104–7.
[8] *New York Times*, April 1, 1961, p. 1:8.
[9] Algerian Office of the FLN, New York, *Documents: The Franco-Algerian Negotiations at Evian and Lugrin, May 20, 1961–July 31, 1961*, Nos. 61–17, -18, -21, and -26.

Competence of the General Assembly to Call for Negotiations

The chief forum for public discussion of the problem of drawing the French and the FLN into peace negotiations was the General Assembly of the United Nations. The first question to arise in the debates was whether the assembly could even recommend negotiations for a settlement. In the draft resolutions which the Afro-Asian states submitted to the eleventh and twelfth assemblies, they included a call for negotiations; but both assemblies were unable to swallow that word. No mention was made of negotiations in the resolution ultimately adopted in the eleventh assembly.[10] In the twelfth assembly, the French saved themselves from being called upon to negotiate by securing the substitution of the word *pourparlers* for the word "negotiations."[11]

The second question to arise in the debates was whether the General Assembly had the competence to identify the parties to conduct negotiations. During the debate in the eleventh assembly, the Israeli representative said that to recommend negotiations with the FLN would tend "to give the impression that the Moslems alone constituted the legitimate population of Algeria" and would confirm the authority of the FLN leaders without any assurance that they were acting with the support even of the Moslem population.[12] The delegate from the Batista government of Cuba said that such a recommendation would amount to recognition of the belligerency of the FLN and would, by placing the FLN on an equal footing with the French government, amount to intervention by the United Nations between an official government of a member state and those who were rebelling against it.[13]

In the thirteenth and fourteenth sessions of the General Assembly, supporters of France prevented the adoption of resolutions on Algeria which either mentioned the GPRA or spoke of negotiations between "two parties." Mention of the GPRA was opposed on the ground that it would amount to recognition of the GPRA by the United Nations. The Peruvian delegate said that the United Nations had no authority to give revolutionary factions the right to represent groups or individuals.[14] Use of the phrase "two parties" was objected to as an implied identification of the FLN as the other side in peace negotiations. Although the supporters of the FLN deleted the mention of the GPRA in their proposed resolution as a concession to the supporters of France, the reso-

[10] United Nations, GA Res. 1012 (XI), Feb. 15, 1957.

[11] United Nations, GA Res. 1184 (XII), Dec. 10, 1957.

[12] United Nations, General Assembly, *Official Records*, 11th sess., 1st Cte., 841st mtg., Feb. 11, 1957, Najar (Israel).

[13] UN GAOR, 11th sess., 1st Cte., 844th mtg., Feb. 12, 1957, Nuñez Portuondo (Cuba).

[14] UN GAOR, 14th sess., 1st Cte., 1070th mtg., Dec. 2, 1959, Ulloa (Peru).

lution, which also urged negotiations between the "two parties," failed by one vote to win the required two-thirds majority in the fourteenth assembly.

The Afro-Asian states made heroic efforts to establish the competence of the General Assembly to identify the parties to peace negotiations and to obtain an exercise of this competence with respect to the Algerian conflict, but they failed. It is easy to understand why, at the fifteenth assembly in 1960, they abandoned attempts to secure a resolution calling for negotiations and moved instead to ask the United Nations itself to conduct a referendum on self-determination in Algeria. The only time the General Assembly passed a resolution using the word "negotiations" in connection with the Algerian conflict was in December 1961, after political negotiations had actually taken place.[15] By that time, the assembly had mustered enough confidence to "call upon the two parties to resume negotiations."

But in another respect the assembly had already asserted its competence with regard to negotiations for a settlement. In its resolution of December 1960, it prescribed the basis for negotiations on self-determination for Algeria.[16] Before de Gaulle was prepared to abandon the French proposal that the Algerian Sahara be exempted from the application of the self-determination principle and while he was still insisting that the European settlers should be accorded special privileges, the assembly resolved that self-determination should be accorded to the Algerian people "on the basis of respect for the unity and territorial integrity of Algeria."

The Evian Agreements

After all the storm and strife of the seven and one-half years of the Algerian conflict, the settlement which was concluded at Evian in March 1962 seems deceptively simple. It set up the procedures for an orderly exercise by the Algerian people of their right to self-determination. It prescribed a timetable for the withdrawal of French military forces from Algeria. It provided assurances for the protection of French lives and property in Algeria and certain guarantees for the preservation of French culture and customs. And it sketched the framework for future cooperative relations between Algeria and France.[17]

The French and the FLN agreed to create a transitional government to administer Algeria until the referendum on self-determination could

[15] UN GA Res. 1724 (XVI), Dec. 20, 1961.
[16] UN GA Res. 1573 (XV), Dec. 19, 1960.
[17] French Embassy, New York, *Texts of Declarations Drawn Up in Common Agreement at Evian, March 18, 1962 by the Delegations of the Government of the French Republic and the Algerian National Liberation Front* (New York: French Embassy, n.d.).

be held. It would be a joint FLN-French administration. A French-appointed high commissioner would exercise responsibility for foreign policy, defense, currency, and economic relations with other countries. A Provisional Executive, presumably selected by the FLN with French approval—although the settlement documents do not so specify—would exercise authority over all internal matters. The Provisional Executive would be a collective body: a president, vice-president, and ten members to serve as a cabinet. The Provisional Executive was charged with responsibility for preparing and implementing the referendum on self-determination.

Most of the French military forces, and particularly those stationed on the frontier, were to remain in Algeria until the proclamation of the results of the referendum on self-determination; but contact between FLN and French forces was to be avoided. The cease-fire was to apply not only to official military operations but also to acts of collective or individual violence by partisans of either side. A joint cease-fire commission would be set up to deal with any violations of the cease-fire. Within one year after self-determination—which was assumed to mean independence—French forces were to be reduced to 80,000 troops, and within three years they were to be completely repatriated. There were, however, specific arrangements for the retention by the French of certain military and air communication facilities for five years and for the lease by France of the base at Mers-el-Kebir for fifteen years.

There were provisions, typical of agreements for the stationing of military forces by one country in the territory of another, to regulate such sensitive matters as criminal jurisdiction. Crimes committed by members of the French armed forces, either while on duty or inside French bases, and crimes not involving Algerian interests were to fall under French military jurisdiction. All other crimes would come within the jurisdiction of the Algerian courts. Those members of the French forces whose detention was determined to be necessary by Algerian courts would not be held in Algerian but in French jails. French military personnel tried in Algerian courts would be accorded the "guarantees of fair legal proceedings sanctioned by the Universal Declaration of Human Rights and by the practice of democratic states."

The assurances for the protection of lives and property in Algeria were divided into three sets: those applicable to anyone, those applicable to Algerians of civil status, and those applicable to French persons residing as aliens in Algeria. The first set consisted of an exemption from prosecution or harassment for political acts committed before the cease-fire or for words or opinions on political matters expressed before the referendum on self-determination, and of an assurance of freedom of movement for Algerians wishing to leave Algeria. The protections granted to Algerians of civil status—that is, Frenchmen electing to become Algerian nationals—were freedom from discrimination and possession of the rights and liberties defined by the Universal Declaration of Human Rights. French persons residing in Algeria as aliens would receive treatment as nationals on most matters but would have only such political rights as the Algerian government chose to accord.

To give Europeans in Algeria time to decide whether they wanted to become Algerian nationals, they were divided into two groups: long-term residents and short-term residents. The former were to be accorded all the rights of Algerian nationals for a period of three years and at the end of three years could decide whether to choose Algerian nationality. Short-term residents had no right to become Algerian nationals but could, presumably, apply for naturalization. The division of Europeans in this fashion was intended as a kind of procedure for instant nationality on independence.

Certain assurances for the protection of cultural rights were granted to all people of French background in recognition of the difference between civil and Koranic law and to take into account their desire to use the French language. Those French nationals who elected to become Algerian nationals would be known as "Algerian nationals of ordinary civil status"; and they, as well as French nationals, would be subject to a special civil code or to French law in matters of personal status. In court proceedings concerned exclusively with personal status, a majority of the judges would be required to be of civil status, and in ordinary litigation either one-third of the jury or at least one judge of the court. French as well as Arabic was to be an official language; students could obtain education in French; and Algerian radio and television were to grant appropriate allotments of time for broadcasting in French.

The Declaration of Principles concerning Economic and Financial Cooperation stated in a preamble reciprocal commitments on the part of France and Algeria. Algeria agreed to "guarantee French interests and the vested rights of individuals and entities." France undertook "in return" to grant technical assistance to Algeria and "to make to its economic and social development a preferential contribution that is justified by the extent of French interests existing in Algeria." These commitments are spelled out in the articles of the declaration and in subsidiary declarations, in particular the Declaration of Principles on Cooperation for the Exploitation of the Wealth of the Saharan Subsoil.

The French commitment was to continue technical assistance and financial aid at existing levels for a period of three years after independence. France also agreed, within the framework of agrarian reform, to grant Algeria specific aid to cover "the repurchase in whole or in part of property rights held by French nationals." The terms and conditions of this aid were to be determined by agreement between the two parties "so as to reconcile the execution of the Algerian social and economic policy with the normal spreading out of the financial assistance provided by France." This vague formulation was later interpreted by France as an authorization to deduct from the amount of aid pledged to Algeria those amounts which France paid to the settlers in Algeria to compensate them for land nationalized under the Algerian land reform program.

The Algerian commitment consisted of a confirmation of all rights previously granted by the French Republic for the exploitation of the oil, gas, and other mineral resources of the Sahara and of other areas of Algeria as well. Algeria also was placed under an obligation to give a preference to French companies for six years after independence in the granting of research and exploitation permits for mining or transport in Algeria. And it was agreed that the exploitation of the wealth of the Saharan subsoil should be entrusted to a Franco-Algerian agency administered by a board composed of an equal number of French and Algerians. Recommendations of the agency concerning the regulation of mining or petroleum or concerning applications for mining titles were to be given legal effect by the Algerian government. In addition, Algeria was to ensure respect for patrimonial rights and other property rights and to deprive no one of these rights without fair compensation.

The Evian settlement prescribed various procedures to assure compliance with its terms. In the event of differences—not limited to differences arising from interpretation of the terms of the settlement—the two countries were to have recourse to conciliation or to arbitration and, as a last resort, to the International Court of Justice. A court of guarantees composed of two Algerian judges of civil status, two of Koranic status, and a fifth chosen by the four would decide disputes with respect to the grant of rights and liberties to Algerians of civil status. A special international court of arbitration composed of one arbitrator appointed by each of the parties and a third chosen by these two would decide all disputes arising over vested rights and interests in the exploitation of the mineral resources of the Sahara.

One of the key provisions of the final settlement at Evian in March 1962 was the sentence: "The FLN will be considered a legal body." The FLN was identified as the party with which the French government held the final negotiations; but the agreements at Evian were not signed, and so the French avoided the final humiliation of having the signatures of officials of the French government affixed to a document bearing the signatures of the leaders of the FLN. The French refrained from making any agreement to transfer governmental authority to the FLN either during the interim period or at the time of independence. While in this fashion the French kept from exerting direct influence on the choice of a government for the new state of Algeria, they doomed the Algerian people to a military struggle for power in Algeria immediately after independence.

The persistent issue of the representative character of the FLN was presented in a crucial form at the time of the peace settlement. The issue then was whether the FLN was the organization to which the French government should turn over governmental authority in Algeria. The extent to which this issue was discussed in the negotiation of the peace settlement at Evian is still shrouded in secrecy; but in the settlement there is a conspicuous absence of any designation of the organization entitled to exercise governmental authority in Algeria after independence. By the terms of the settlement, an interim joint French-FLN administration was set up in Algeria to exercise governmental authority from the time the settlement came into effect until the results of the self-determination referendum were known. It was assumed that the Algerians would vote for independence in the referendum, but nothing was agreed as to what was to happen to governmental authority after independence. When the day of independence arrived, the French government attempted formally to transfer governmental authority, not to the FLN or to the GPRA, but to the Provisional Executive, which the French and the FLN had jointly appointed presumably to exercise authority only during the interim period.

Even if the French had wanted to transfer governmental authority to the FLN on the granting of independence to Algeria, they would have had difficulty in doing so. For during the interim period—between the peace settlement and the self-determination referendum—the FLN split into two factions. After independence it split into several more factions. Liberation organizations that have held together surprisingly well during the winning of independence are notoriously susceptible to coming apart at the seams once independence is won. In the last years of the war, the FLN consisted of a collection of power centers: the original leaders in prison in France, the Provisional Government in Tunis, army commanders of one external army in Tunisia and of another in Morocco, and the commanders of the rebel forces in the districts of Algeria, who had been operating with considerable autonomy because of the nature of the war. Yet the difficulty of arranging for an orderly transfer of governmental authority is scarcely an excuse for abandoning the effort.

The question posed by the failure of the French to arrange for an orderly transfer of governmental authority in Algeria is whether the international community should not bear some responsibility for easing the birth pains of a new state. If the mother country is either unwilling or unable to make the necessary arrangements for a peaceful transfer of governmental authority, then should it not be obliged to appeal to an international authority for assistance? Perhaps even if the mother country is willing to make arrangements, the international community ought to have a chance to pass upon their adequacy.

The Consequences of the Algerian Revolution

If the objective of the FLN is regarded simply to have been the political separation of Algeria from France, that objective was realized by the Algerian Revolution. The joint French-FLN transitional administration was set up in Algeria as contemplated in the Evian settlement. The Provisional Executive organized the referendum on self-determination in accordance with the terms of a French decree promulgated by de Gaulle on March 19, 1962, as an integral part of the settlement. The decree was carefully drawn to assure that the referendum was conducted with all the safeguards, inspections, and supervision desired by either side. The question was put to the voters in a way which left no doubt as to the outcome. On July 1, over six million voters went to the polls in Algeria, and all except 16,534 voted in favor of independence.[18] On July 3, de Gaulle recognized the independence of Algeria.[19]

If the objective of the FLN is regarded as the decolonization of Algeria—and this is the form in which the FLN and its supporters most frequently stated the objective—then presumably political separation is not all that is required. Decolonization has come to mean freedom from all forms of control by the mother country, including indirect control through the continued presence of military forces, continued insistence on special privileges and preferences, and the application of economic power to influence governmental policy. Most if not all of these forms of control over Algeria by France were eliminated on paper by the Evian settlement. It remained to be seen whether they would disappear in actual practice.

The military provisions of the Evian settlement were strictly observed by France. The last contingents of French troops evacuated Algeria in June 1964, a year ahead of schedule.[20] In July 1967, the French relinquished their missile and space centers in Algeria.[21] Early in 1968, France completely withdrew from the base at Mers-el-Kebir, although it was entitled to retain the base until 1977.[22]

There could be no complaint on the part of the Algerian government

---

[18] *Journal Officiel de l'État Algérien, Ordonnances et Décrets*, No. 1, July 6, 1962.

[19] French Embassy, New York, *French Affairs*, No. 140 (July 3, 1962).

[20] David C. Gordon, *The Passing of French Algeria* (New York: Oxford University Press, 1966), p. 233.

[21] *New York Times*, July 1, 1967, p. 7:5; July 2, 1967, p. 9:2.

[22] *New York Times*, Feb. 1, 1968, p. 3:6.

that the French were seeking to preserve special privileges for French nationals in Algeria. The Evian agreements did not give French nationals in Algeria protection significantly more extensive than that accorded any man in the Universal Declaration of Human Rights. In fact, within two years after the Evian settlement, the number of Europeans in Algeria had dropped from about a million to a hundred thousand.[23] The exodus was an obvious demonstration that French authority no longer was able to preserve a special status for Frenchmen in Algeria.

The implementation of the economic provisions of the Evian settlement appeared to remove most of the traces of French domination of the Algerian economy. The Algerian government could scarcely complain about the retention by the French of their mining and transportation rights because the French had in effect repurchased these rights with the pledge to continue economic aid to Algeria. The French carried out their pledge, granting aid for the first three years at the level of about $200 million per year, subject to the deduction of sums applied by France to indemnify Frenchmen for the nationalization of their lands.[24] In 1965, as part of a new petroleum agreement assuring the continued protection of French interests in the Sahara, France committed itself to contribute $80 million yearly over a five-year period toward the industrial development of Algeria.[25]

It is not intended to imply that all relations have been smooth between the French and Algerian governments since independence. The Algerian resort to nationalizations of commercial as well as agricultural property early in 1963 provoked a charge by the French government of a violation of the Evian settlement.[26] But the French government held in reserve a power to offset losses of its citizens due to nationalizations by corresponding cuts in the aid furnished to Algeria. There appeared to be no indication that the Algerians would provide any compensation. In December 1966, Algeria exhumed a previously neglected body of claims against France: claims for compensation for the destruction of Algerian villages by France during the war.[27] Presumably these claims were introduced as a talking point to discourage the French from pursuing their claims for compensation for nationalized property.

The problems surrounding an equitable distribution of the wealth realized from the exploitation of the Sahara also have been continuous

---

[23] William Zartman, "Les Relations entre la France et l'Algérie depuis les Accords d'Evian," *Revue Française de Science Politique* 14 (December 1964): 1088.

[24] Gordon, *The Passing of French Algeria*, p. 224; *New York Times*, June 27, 1963, p. 8 : 4.

[25] *New York Times*, July 30, 1965, p. 1:7; French Embassy, New York, *French Aid to Developing Countries in 1968* (May 17, 1970).

[26] *New York Times*, April 6, 1963, p. 3:4.

[27] *Le Monde*, Dec. 20, 1966.

irritants in Franco-Algerian relations. The Algerians have kept pushing for a greater share. They succeeded in 1965 in raising from 40 to 50 percent their ownership of stock in one of the companies operating in the Sahara. In 1965 also, there were adjustments in the taxes and royalties payable by the companies which were expected to increase Algeria's annual oil revenues from $80 million to $240 million within a five-year period.[28] When the Algerian government permitted a British company to construct a five-hundred-mile oil pipeline in Algeria, companies already operating in Algeria filed a complaint with the special joint arbitration court; but the pipeline was built and the dispute settled out of court.[29] It can be presumed that Algeria will use all possible means to assure that its share of the profits from the exploitation of Saharan oil is comparable to the shares realized by other oil-producing countries; otherwise, Algeria would have to consider itself still under the economic domination of France.

The foregoing analysis indicates that, insofar as the goal of the FLN was the elimination of the colonial domination of France, that goal has been realized. But what about the internal revolution—the effort to realize political and economic rights for the people of Algeria?

The Evian settlements were silent on the kind of government which would be set up in Algeria after independence. That was a matter for determination solely by the Algerian people, not by joint agreement of the two countries. The same was true of the economic system to be established in Algeria after independence. That, too, was considered to be beyond the scope of the settlement.

The people of Algeria, like those in many newly independent countries, were given little opportunity to assert their preferences for a new governmental system. Elections for the first Algerian National Assembly, held on September 20, 1962, were a mere formality. The voters were presented with only one slate of candidates nominated by the political bureau of the FLN. The political bureau was instrumental also in the drafting of the Algerian constitution. Although the draft constitution was submitted to the National Assembly for debate, the debate did not have a significant impact on its provisions. The people of Algeria had no alternative but to endorse the constitution when it was submitted to them for a vote on September 8, 1963.

The constitution of Algeria recognized the supremacy of the National Liberation Front in the structure of the government.[30] Ben Bella became the sole candidate for president and, not surprisingly, received the over-

[28] *New York Times*, July 30, 1965, p. 1:7; Aug. 22, 1965, sec. 3, p. 1:2.

[29] *New York Times*, April 11, 1964, p. 29:2.

[30] For the text of the Algerian constitution, see *Journal Officiel de la République Algérienne*, Sept. 10, 1963. An English translation appears in Amos J. Peaslee, *Constitutions of Nations* (3d ed., rev.; The Hague: Martinus Nijhoff, 1965), vol. 1: *Africa*, pp. 6–15.

whelming approval of the Algerian people in the first presidential election. The first National Assembly was largely ineffective.

When elections for the second National Assembly were held in April 1964, again only one slate of candidates was presented.[31] The only way to show opposition was by abstention. Estimates of the abstentions ran from 15 to 41 percent. After the coup by Boumedienne in June 1965, the National Assembly was "all but dissolved."[32] The conclusion appears unavoidable that the people of Algeria have been denied political rights —first under the dictatorial leadership of Ben Bella and, more recently, under the military government of Colonel Boumedienne.

In the matter of economic rights, the people of Algeria appear to have been equally unfortunate. The takeover of the property of the departing Europeans has been largely unregulated. As a consequence, a small minority of Algerians has realized windfall benefits. Positions have been opened to Algerians, but unemployment remains at a level higher than that prior to the revolution. In June 1968 it was estimated to exceed 50 percent.[33] Arslan Humbaraci, looking at the Algerian conflict primarily as a struggle to bring socialism to Algeria, has called it "the Revolution that failed."

It is sometimes argued that the international community should not endorse political separation as a technique by which a people can seek relief from an oppressive government, because there is no assurance that the new government will not be equally oppressive. It does seem that, if the international community intends to be effective in the promotion of human rights, it will have to concern itself not only with oppressions that provoke wars for political separation but also with oppressions that provoke only internal struggles. But one crime against humanity cannot be condoned because another may take its place. Colonial regimes cannot seek to justify themselves on the ground that other governments are equally oppressive.

The failure of the Algerian Revolution to realize basic political and economic rights for the people of Algeria cannot be urged as proof that the rebels had no justification for seeking the political separation of Algeria from France. The French government denied political and economic rights to the people of Algeria. In their struggle to realize these rights, the Algerian people had to oppose the French government. It now remains for them to make the Algerian government respond to their wishes.[34]

[31] Gordon, *The Passing of French Algeria*, pp. 152–53.
[32] *New York Times*, July 30, 1965, p. 1:7.
[33] *New York Times*, June 10, 1968, p. 69:6. Unemployment continues at the 50 percent level, according to William B. Quandt in "Algeria: The Revolution Turns Inward," *Mid East* August 1970, p. 12.
[34] For a description by the Algerian government of recent progress, see *Algeria 65/69*, published by the Algerian Ministry of Information, March 1970.

Donald W. McNemar

THE POSTINDEPENDENCE WAR IN THE CONGO

I. CONFLICT IN THE CONGO

The mutiny of the Congolese *Force publique* against their Belgian officers on July 5, 1960, touched off the longest and most complex post-independence struggle in Africa. The Republic of the Congo, which had been free from Belgian colonial rule for only five days when the violence began, faced all of the administrative and political problems of a new state trying to develop rapidly. During the struggle, the parties continually disputed control of the Congo's national government, two provinces seceded from the republic, Belgian paratroopers became involved in the violence, superpowers threatened to intervene, and the United Nations mounted the largest peacekeeping operation in its history. The country was finally united after two and a half years of strife.

A study of the Congo case is particularly significant for two reasons. First, it is representative of civil wars occurring in newly independent states.[1] These wars do not often have a single rebel force challenging an established government but rather a number of factions struggling to fill the political void left by the withdrawal of the colonial power. The conflict over control of the central government in the Congo was a war of this type. Second, in the Congo, an attempt was made to limit and control a civil war's effects on the rest of the international system through the involvement of an international organization.[2] (Cyprus is the only other case in which the United Nations established large field operations in a civil-war situation.[3]) The experience in the Congo permits us to evaluate the effectiveness of international legal prescriptions relating to civil wars when they are strengthened by the presence of a UN operation.[4]

[1] A civil war is defined here as a violent struggle over political control of a state occurring entirely within the geographic boundaries of that state. The Postindependence War in the Congo fulfills these requirements and is here analyzed as an example of a civil war.

[2] A case for UN involvement in civil strife is made in Richard A. Falk and Saul H. Mendlovitz, "Towards a Warless World: One Legal Formula To Achieve Transition," *Yale Law Journal* 73 (January 1964): 399–424.

[3] For discussion of the comparable peacekeeping effort in Cyprus, see James A. Stegenga, *The United Nations Force in Cyprus* (Columbus: Ohio State University Press, 1968); and Linda B. Miller, *Cyprus: The Law and Politics of Civil Strife*, Occasional Papers in International Affairs, No. 19 (Cambridge, Mass.: Harvard University, Center for International Affairs, 1968).

[4] It is frequently argued that the weakness of international law is its lack of institutions to develop and enforce international norms. The UN action in the

244

The Congo civil war represents an extremely important event in international politics of the early 1960s. As the Congo happenings recede into history, relations between the East and West improve, and African conflicts no longer produce grave international concern, people may wonder why the Congo civil war produced such a tempest. To understand the crisis, it must be viewed in the international context of 1960. At that time cold war tensions remained severe. The Berlin crisis was touched off by the Warsaw Pact nations' declaration in February 1960 that they were prepared to sign separate peace treaties with East Germany unless the Western powers agreed to make West Berlin a free city. China took over Tibet, fighting broke out in Laos, the United States pledged to defend Quemoy, a border dispute raged between China and India, and relations deteriorated rapidly between the United States and the Castro regime in Cuba. Immediately preceding Congolese independence, Premier Khrushchev refused to participate in a summit conference in Paris because of a U-2 flight by the United States over his country, and the Soviet delegation walked out of the East-West disarmament talks. The Congo crisis, therefore, came at a time of accelerated cold war tensions; and fear that the crisis might become a part of the cold war is not difficult to understand.

The Congo crisis began during 1960 at the height of a decolonization period; in that year sixteen newly independent African states joined the United Nations.[5] The fervor for ending colonialism was so strong among African states that no major power could afford to oppose this sentiment. In fact, there was a shift in political power toward the third world because of the increasing number of Afro-Asian states in the United Nations. Both the United States and the Soviet Union were concentrating their efforts on winning the support of the African states. Thus, the Postindependence War in the Congo was an important event in the continuing East-West conflict.

Issues Raised in the Congo

The Congo civil war was not simply a struggle to decide who would rule in Leopoldville but rather a conflict that involved the more fundamental issues of decolonization, unification, and political control. The relationship between the former colonizer and the newly independent state is the first factor of significance. When the Belgian government sent

---

Congo represents a step toward such institutions since representatives of the secretary-general were active in the Congo, the Security Council and General Assembly debated and passed resolutions, and a UN force carried out operations in the field.

[5] For a discussion of the decolonization movement, see Richard P. Stebbins, *The United States in World Affairs, 1960* (New York: Harper & Bros., for the Council on Foreign Relations, 1961), pp. 152–212.

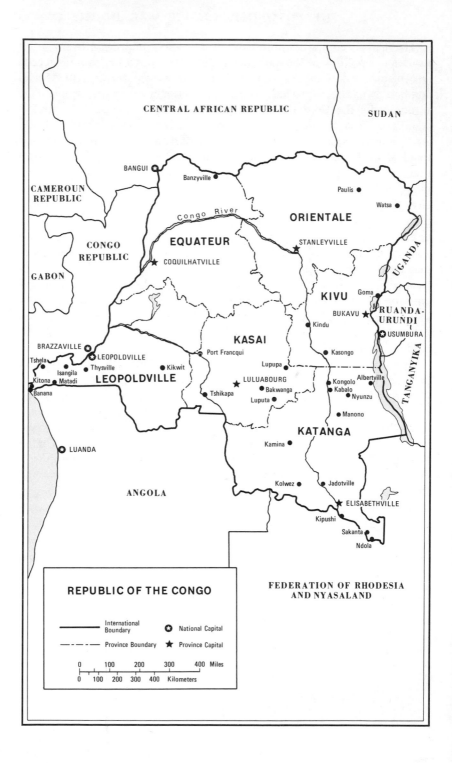

REPUBLIC OF THE CONGO

paratroopers into the Congo on July 10, 1960, the Belgians believed they were taking action to produce order; the Congolese leaders, on the other hand, perceived the move as an attempt to reestablish a colonial regime. Throughout this period, the Congolese government needed aid, and the Belgian government was best prepared to grant it; but the tenuousness of the relationship between the two prevented the former colony from making a request. The Congo civil war was seen in colonial terms by the other African states and the great powers as well. Because there was widespread consensus on the justice of decolonization, none of the great powers dared veto proposals for establishing a UN force; and the Afro-Asian states gave the UN effort strong support.

The degree of unification in the government of the Congo was also at stake in this war. Prior to independence agreement had been reached on a strong national government,[6] but just eleven days after independence Moise Tshombe declared Katanga independent, and Albert Kalonji subsequently declared independence for South Kasai. In spite of innumerable negotiations between provincial and national government officials, Katanga remained outside the state until January 1963. Whether the Congo was to be a single state was very much in question throughout the struggle.

The political control of the country was also disputed in the civil war. At the outset Joseph Kasavubu and Patrice Lumumba jointly headed the central government. The September constitutional crisis, in which Kasavubu dismissed Lumumba, marked the beginning of the struggle for control of the central government. With each leader refusing to relinquish power, Joseph Mobutu, the military chief of staff, took over the running of the country. The followers of Lumumba, who had been captured by troops of the Leopoldville government, set up a rival government in Stanleyville under Antoine Gizenga and claimed to be the legitimate authority of the country. In August 1961, another government was formed under Cyrille Adoula; but this government, too, was eventually challenged in 1964 by rebel forces called the Conseil National de Liberation (CNL). This rise and fall of factions resulted in a continual struggle for control of the Congolese government.

Preparation for Independence

Belgian colonial policies had set the stage on which the struggle was enacted. The Belgians had not expected to grant independence in the

---

[6] Various positions had been represented in the Congo on the question whether the government should be federalist or centralist, but at the Brussels Round Table, the idea of a centralized government was accepted. For the position of parties on this issue, see Herbert F. Weiss, *Political Protest in the Congo: The Parti Solidaire Africain During the Independence Struggle* (Princeton: Princeton University Press, 1967), pp. 70–72.

near future and had done very little to develop Congolese capabilities. Their relation to the Congo can best be described as gradually lessening paternalism.[7] The inability of the Congolese government to maintain order and public safety can be traced directly to the lack of preparation by Belgian administrators for independent rule.

The Belgians pursued a horizontal rather than a vertical system of development in the sense that they insisted on raising the living standard and the education of the entire Congolese population rather than rapidly developing a ruling elite.[8] The colonial administration was highly centralized, with power running from the king and parliament to the local level. All positions of responsibility were held by Belgians, and the Congolese were permitted to participate only in minimal capacities. The development of political parties was prevented by restrictions on the right of association. In the field of education there were 1,460,000 children in primary school and 28,961 in secondary school in the Congo in the period 1959–60, but that year only 136 completed a secondary education.[9] In the economic sphere, the management of businesses was firmly in the hands of the Europeans, and the colony's budget had to be approved by the Belgian parliament since the Congolese had no political institutions of their own. Likewise in the professions, all of the doctors, dentists, and lawyers were Belgians, while the nurses, midwives, and medical assistants were Congolese. The policies pursued by the Belgian government were clearly not designed to prepare the Congolese to administer their own country.

When independence for the colony was considered at all, it was as a very slow, evolutionary process, as indicated by the first plan proposed by Professor A. A. J. Van Bilsen of the Institute for Colonial Studies in Antwerp, which called for a period of transition of thirty years.[10] Even this plan was considered too radical by most Belgians since it implied eventual full independence for the Congolese. Most Belgians continued to assume that their task was to work for economic and social advancement rather than political development of the Africans, that the state would be a combined rule of Europeans and Africans, that a black

[7] The best descriptions of this colonial development are provided in Crawford Young, *Politics in the Congo: Decolonization and Independence* (Princeton: Princeton University Press, 1965), pp. 33–72; and Alan P. Merriam, *Congo: Background of Conflict* (Evanston: Northwestern University Press, 1961), pp. 3–113.

[8] Catherine Hoskyns, *The Congo since Independence: January 1960–December 1961* (London: Oxford University Press, 1965), p. 8.

[9] Ministry of Education, *L'Education au Congo*, November, 1961, as found in Hoskyns, *Congo since Independence*, pp. 12–13.

[10] A. A. J. Van Bilsen, *Vers l'Indépendance du Congo et du Ruanda-Urundi: Réflexions sur les Devoirs et l'Avenir de la Belgique en Afrique Centrale* (Kraainem: By the author, 1958), pp. 164–202, quoted in Marriam, *Congo: Background*, pp. 68–71.

middle class would emerge, that the king of Belgium would also be the king of the Congo, and finally, that there was still a great deal of time before independence.[11] With these views as a background, the Belgian administrators organized Congolese elections in three cities during 1957. These were the first elections ever held for the Congolese, and they put into practice the Belgians' idea that political education should begin at the local level.

Several factors converged in 1958 to ignite interest in independence on the part of the Congolese. Their leaders were not immune to the sudden rush toward decolonization throughout Africa, and they were quick to note President de Gaulle's statement at Brazzaville in 1958: "Whoever wishes independence can have it as soon as he wishes."[12] Another factor was a side effect of the elections held at the close of 1957—the development of political parties.[13] The Congolese leaders were now emerging as African nationalists and party leaders. This process was facilitated by the attendance of Lumumba at the Pan-African Conference held in Accra, Ghana, in December 1958, and the presence of large Congolese delegations at the World's Fair in Brussels, which contributed to the stature of the Congolese leaders and their acquaintanceship. The climax of this year of political awareness was the Leopoldville riot of January 4–6, 1959. Police intervention at a political rally touched off a riot which resulted in 49 African deaths by official count, with unofficial estimates running as high as 500 killed.[14] The immediate results of this event were a reevaluation of the Belgian policy, the arrest of political leaders, which made them national heroes, and the repatriation of unemployed youths to the countryside, which helped to politicize the rural area.[15]

Following the Leopoldville riot, the Belgian government committed itself to Congolese independence for the first time.[16] A round table of Belgian and Congolese leaders was called for January 1960 to determine the Congo's future. Confronted by unity on the part of the African leaders and a demand for immediate independence, the Belgian government agreed to leave by June 30, 1960. This sudden end of colonial

[11] Young, *Politics in the Congo*, pp. 33–58.

[12] Quoted in Merriam, *Congo: Background*, p. 81.

[13] For discussion of the political parties in the Congo, see Weiss, *Political Protest*, or René Lemarchand, *Political Awakening in the Belgian Congo* (Berkeley: University of California Press, 1964), pp. 167–300.

[14] Weiss, *Political Protest*, p. 17.

[15] *Ibid.*, pp. 17–18.

[16] The government declaration of Jan. 13, 1959, which states the goal of independence without setting a time table, may be found in Centre de Recherche et d'Information Socio-Politique, *Congo: 1959: Documents belges et africains* (Brussels: Les Dossiers du CRISP, 1962), pp. 45–49 (hereinafter cited as CRISP, *Congo: 1959*, *Congo: 1960*, and so on). CRISP has published a yearly collection of documents on politics of the Congo since 1959.

administration with only a six-month period of preparation was necessitated by a number of factors. The Belgian government was unable to generate internal support for a policy of controlling the Congo through force. The Algerian model was uppermost in the minds of government officials, and they were intent on avoiding such a fiasco. The government was politically unable to commit Belgian draftees to duty in the Congo.[17] French success in the establishment of a "community" with its former colonies inspired the Belgians to attempt the same. At the time of the round table, whole provinces were totally out of control, and an agreement of some kind had to be secured with the Congolese.[18] The success of the moderate Parti National du Progrès (PNP) in the elections of December 1959 had led the Belgians to assume—falsely, as it turned out in the May 1960 elections—that a moderate party would form the first Congolese government and that the country would continue to rely on Belgians in running the government after independence. They envisioned continued Belgian sovereignty over such important policy areas as defense, foreign affairs, currency, and telecommunications.[19] The six months of preparation for independence permitted the writing of the *Loi Fondamentale*, the holding of a meeting to work out financial arrangements between the two countries, and the signing of the Treaty of Friendship to formalize relations between the two countries. The Belgians assumed that the real transfer of power would take place over a long period following June 30.

Congolese expectations concerning independence were distinctly different. The masses of people assumed that independence would answer all their problems and that they would begin immediately to live like Belgians.[20] But after the gala independence ceremony, all of the problems remained: the breakdown in administrative control, unemployment, taxes, and the presence of many Belgian clerks and army officers. The only people obviously benefiting from independence were the politicians who now rode in new Cadillacs.[21] The discontent was particularly great among the members of the *Force publique*, which was called upon to do the bidding of the politicians and which still had an officer corps composed entirely of Belgians.[22] When the Belgian commander, General Janssens, called the African noncommissioned officers together and

---

[17] Weiss, *Political Protest*, p. 38.

[18] Young, *Politics in the Congo*, pp. 152–54.

[19] *Ibid.*, p. 160.

[20] For a description of attitudes toward independence in both a city and a small village, see Merriam, *Congo: Background*, pp. 173–204.

[21] Hoskyns, *Congo since Independence*, p. 87.

[22] Smith Hempstone lists the pay of a private in the *Force publique* at $72 a year as opposed to $10,000 a year for Congolese national assemblymen. Hempstone, *Rebels, Mercenaries, and Dividends: The Katanga Story* (New York: Frederick A. Praeger, Inc., 1962), p. 105.

wrote on the blackboard, "After Independence=Before Independence,"[23] the Congolese soldiers mutinied against their Belgian officers. The mutiny, which began July 5, 1960, spread quickly throughout the country; and as the troops began attacking Belgians, the Postindependence War in the Congo began.

Primary Actors

Although many parties were involved in the Congo, the three primary actors were the central government in Leopoldville, the Katanga government in Elisabethville, and the Organisation des Nations Unies au Congo (ONUC), the UN force which was distributed throughout the country. The central government, established under the *Loi Fondamentale*, was the government to which the Belgians had turned over power on June 30, 1960. This government, headed by Lumumba and Kasavubu, incorporated most of the major tribes and political groups in the Congo and controlled the entire Congo.

The dismissal of Lumumba by Kasavubu on September 5, 1960, marked the breakup of the Leopoldville government. Mobutu declared that he was neutralizing the politicians and, on September 14, 1960, established a college of commissioners to run the country. The followers of Lumumba then fled to Stanleyville, where they consolidated their power and claimed the right to rule the entire Congo. The Mobutu government appointed Joseph Ileo prime minister in February 1961; but it was not until the Lovanium parliament of August 1961 that all factions were united in the central government. All dissidents except Katanga were joined in this government under Adoula, with Gizenga, a follower of Lumumba, serving as the first vice-premier. The Adoula government remained in power until July 9, 1964, when Tshombe, who had previously headed the secessionist regime in Katanga, came back from exile to lead the national government in its fight against the rebel forces under Pierre Mulele and Christophe Gbenye. Following the removal of this threat, a Mobutu coup replaced the Tshombe government on November 25, 1965.

Despite the frequent and rapid change in personnel of the central government during the conflict, and a period of great division in which both the Leopoldville and Stanleyville governments claimed to be the national government of the Congo, the objectives of the government in Leopoldville remained constant. It consistently favored a unified national government; it opposed all efforts at secession and used its resources to insure the continuance of the Republic of the Congo as a single state under a central authority.

[23] CRISP, *Congo: 1960*, vol. 1, prepared by J. Gérard-Libois and Benoit Verhaegen, p. 372.

The Katanga government, on the other hand, claimed independence for its territory on the basis of self-determination.[24] On July 11, 1960, shortly after the mutiny of the *Force publique*, Tshombe declared the independence of the province of Katanga. When Lumumba refused to call in the Belgian troops, the Belgian government granted Tshombe's request for assistance. Tshombe, with aid from the Belgians for retraining his army and with control of the 45 percent of the Congo state revenues coming from Katanga,[25] was able to maintain independence until January 21, 1963.

The third actor was the UN peacekeeping force (ONUC) which went into the Congo at the request of the Kasavubu-Lumumba government.[26] ONUC was established by a Security Council resolution of July 14, 1960, which was passed with abstentions by former colonial powers Britain and France and also by Nationalist China.[27] The force eventually involved 93,000 men from 34 countries, with an average strength of about 15,000 troops. The total cost of the military operation from July 1960 through June 1964 was $411 million.[28] In addition to the troops deployed throughout the Congo, the United Nations was involved in technical assistance programs and in reconciliation efforts.

Although the focus of ONUC at the outset was to restore law and order and to facilitate the withdrawal of Belgian troops, in the course of the Congo operation the following four functions evolved. ONUC attempted to maintain the territorial integrity and political independence of the Congo; assist the central government in maintaining law and order; prevent a breakdown into an extended civil war; and secure the withdrawal of foreign military, paramilitary, and political advisers and mercenaries.[29] Secretary-General Dag Hammarskjold originally envisioned the UN force as refraining from any involvement in internal affairs,[30] but the mere presence of ONUC throughout the Congo made it one of the primary actors in the civil war.

[24] For a discussion of the self-determination issue, see René Lemarchand, "The Limits of Self-Determination: The Case of the Katanga Secession," *American Political Science Review* 56 (June 1962): 404–16.

[25] Crawford Young, "The Politics of Separatism: Katanga, 1960–63," in *Politics in Africa: 7 Cases,* ed. Gwendolen Margaret Carter (New York: Harcourt, Brace & World, 1966), p. 170.

[26] For the texts of the cables to the United Nations, see UN Doc. S/4382, July 13, 1960, pp. 11–12.

[27] UN Doc. S/4387, July 14, 1960, p. 16; and United Nations, Security Council, *Official Records*, 15th year, 879th mtg. (July 13/14, 1960), p. 42.

[28] Ernest W. Lefever, *Uncertain Mandate: Politics of the U.N. Congo Operation* (Baltimore: Johns Hopkins Press, 1967), p. 89.

[29] U Thant, "The Congo: an Account of United Nations Action . . . and a Look Ahead," *United Nations Review* 10 (February 1963): 6–13.

[30] Hammarskjold's first report on implementation of the Security Council resolution is contained in UN Doc. S/4389, July 18, 1960, pp. 16–24.

Phases of the Struggle

Events in the Congo can best be understood in a framework which divides the fighting into three periods on the basis of the issues involved and the nature of the central government. The first phase was carried out under a unified central government headed by Kasavubu and Lumumba. This phase lasted from independence on June 30, 1960, to the constitutional crisis on September 5, 1960. The primary issue was anti-colonialism, as indicated by the Congolese desire to remove the Belgian paratroopers, whose presence confirmed, at least to their minds, Belgium's interest in reasserting control.

A few days after the mutiny of the Congolese troops, on July 10, 1960, the Belgian government sent paratroopers into the country without the consent of the Congolese as required by the Treaty of Friendship.[31] The move was justified by the Belgians as necessary to protect their nationals, but the Congolese leaders viewed the act as aggression and requested military aid from the United Nations "to protect the national territory of the Congo against the present external aggression which is a threat to international peace."[32] The Security Council authorized the establishment of such a force, and within twenty-four hours Hammarskjold had UN troops in the Congo. ONUC took responsibility for maintaining order in the Congo and for administering certain areas. By September 1960, the regular Belgian troops withdrew.

The colonial question took a different form in the province of Katanga. Tshombe invited the Belgian troops to maintain order and then took advantage of their assistance to declare independence for his province. Both Europeans living there and investors in the mining concerns were happy to assist a moderate leader who was willing to accept their support. The central government, on the other hand, was anxious to end the secession of Katanga since it was the richest province. Lumumba urged the United Nations to end the secession, but Hammarskjold refused to involve the international organization in this internal matter. Lumumba then requested and received Soviet assistance. Although his armies failed to regain Katanga, the Armée Nationale Congolaise (ANC) did end the secession of South Kasai in what turned out to be a virtual blood bath of the Baluba tribesmen by the undisciplined Lumumba soldiers.[33] These military efforts ended when the strained political relations among Congolese leaders erupted in the constitutional

[31] This treaty to govern the relations between the new republic and the former colonial power was signed on June 29, 1960, but was not yet ratified at independence. The text is found in CRISP, *Congo: 1960*, 1:312–14.

[32] UN, SCOR, 15th year, 879th mtg. (July 21, 1960), p. 28; UN Doc. S/4382, July 13, 1960, pp. 11–12.

[33] Hoskyns, *Congo since Independence*, p. 194.

crisis of September, marking the end of the unified Leopoldville government.[34]

The second phase of the war lasted from September 1960 until the formation of a new government under Adoula at the Lovanium parliament in August 1961. Throughout this period the government of the country was divided. The Kasavubu and Mobutu factions in Leopoldville and the Gizenga government in Stanleyville each claimed to be the legitimate national government, while the governments of Kalonji and Tshombe declared their independence. There were thus four separate regimes in the Congo, making the primary struggle during this period the establishment of a central government.

An impasse developed between Kasavubu and Lumumba over who had the authority to fire whom, which led to the army takeover on September 14, 1960.[35] Lumumba remained at his official residence in Leopoldville under UN protection, while his supporters established a government in Stanleyville. On November 27, 1960, he left UN protection to join his supporters but was captured by Leopoldville troops on December 1, 1960. He was subsequently transferred to Katanga on January 17, 1961, where he was murdered.[36] The execution of the most popular nationalist leader in the Congo was met with outrage in the states which favored Lumumba.

During this internal breakdown, ONUC was forced to keep peace in a political vacuum. In the absence of a clearly recognized government, ONUC itself made decisions and administered policies. UN officials refused to recognize any faction as legitimate and at the same time worked toward the establishment of a new government. The UN conciliation commission was active during this period in gaining agreement among the factions to reconvene parliament on June 25, 1961, at the University of Lovanium, with security guaranteed by ONUC.[37] Although Tshombe

[34] Throughout this study the names of Leopoldville, Elisabethville, and Stanleyville have been used since these were the names of the cities at the time of these events. All of them were Africanized on June 30, 1966, Leopoldville becoming Kinshasa, Elisabethville Lubumbashi, and Stanleyville Kisangani.

[35] For discussion of the constitutional crisis, see Hoskyns, *Congo since Independence*, pp. 197–246.

[36] Much attention has been focused on the killing of Lumumba and particularly on the reason it was done in Katanga, which at the time had seceded from the republic which held him captive. It seems that even an imprisoned Lumumba continued to threaten the government in Leopoldville; therefore he was shipped to his bitterest enemies in Katanga on the expectation that he would be killed. For a discussion of his transfer, see Hempstone, *Rebels*, pp. 125–33. The UN commission on the death of Lumumba concluded that Lumumba and his companions were killed on Jan. 17, 1961, "in the presence of high officials of the government of Katanga province, namely Mr. Tshombe, Mr. Munongo, and Mr. Kibwe. . . ." UN Doc. S/4976, Nov. 11, 1961, p. 117.

[37] The report of the UN conciliation commission is contained in UN Doc. A/4711, March 20, 1961, pp. 69–112.

refused to attend, all other groups participated, and the period of internal breakdown was ended by the formation of the Adoula government on August 2, 1961.

The third stage focused on ending the secession of Katanga. As soon as the central government was united, it began pursuing a policy designed to reintegrate Katanga. The Security Council requested ONUC to remove foreign mercenaries from the Congo, and since many of them were located in Katanga, this action weakened the province's position.[38]

During this period ONUC and the Katanga gendarmerie clashed in three rounds of fighting in that province.[39] On August 28, 1961, the UN forces in Elisabethville moved swiftly and repatriated 338 non-Congolese personnel from the Katanga gendarmerie. This did not finish the task, but further efforts to remove non-Congolese personnel were unsuccessful and produced fighting. In the view of Hammarskjold's representative in the Congo, Conor Cruise O'Brien, the UN effort was designed not to remove foreigners but rather to end the independence of Katanga.[40] In this first clash, UN and Katanga forces fought at Elisabethville, Jadotville, and Kamina. The gendarmerie claimed victory over ONUC, and the fighting ended in a cease-fire. While traveling to negotiate a settlement, Dag Hammarskjold died in a plane crash on September 18, 1961.[41] For its participation in this first round of fighting, the United Nations was severely criticized by many states.

In December 1961, a new round of fighting broke out when the UN forces took steps to insure freedom of movement and to restore law and order. This fighting ended when Adoula and Tshombe met at Kitona and finally reached an agreement to reintegrate Katanga into the Republic of the Congo. Their negotiations dragged on throughout the next year. Since the two leaders were unable to implement reunification, the new secretary-general, U Thant, proposed a "Plan of National Recon-

[38] UN Doc. S/4741, Feb. 21, 1961, p. 147.

[39] The three rounds of fighting between ONUC and the Katangese gendarmerie are described in Ernest W. Lefever, *Crisis in the Congo: A United Nations Force in Action* (Washington: Brookings Institution, 1965), pp. 72–121.

[40] The official version of these events reports that the UN soldiers returned fire in a defensive action. See UN Doc. S/4940, Feb. 21, 1961, p. 103. O'Brien reports in his account of the incident that Operation Morthor had been undertaken with the objective being the "ending of the secession of Katanga by the use of force" but that, when the operation went badly and a great deal of violence resulted, Hammarskjold redefined the operation as a defensive one. Conor Cruise O'Brien, *To Katanga and Back: A UN Case History* (New York: Simon & Schuster, 1962), pp. 261–67.

[41] For the most complete account of this plane crash, see Arthur L. Gavshon, *The Mysterious Death of Dag Hammarskjold* (New York: Walker & Company, 1962).

ciliation."[42] Both leaders accepted this plan as the basis for establishing a new constitution, integrating the armies, and unifying the economies. But Katanga continued its independence, and U Thant requested economic sanctions on December 14, 1962. Before these restrictions could be put into effect, a final round of fighting between ONUC and the gendarmerie broke out. The UN forces occupied strategic points in Elisabethville, Jadotville, and Kolwezi; and Tshombe announced on January 14, 1963, that

we are ready to proclaim to the world that the Katangese secession is ended. We are ready to allow United Nations troops freedom of movement throughout Katanga. We are also ready to return to Elisabethville to arrange for the complete implementation of the Thant Plan.[43]

This announcement marked the unification of the country and the end of the Postindependence War.

Although this particular war was ended, the country still faced continuing conflict and the tremendous task of developing a state which would be economically and politically stable. When the UN troops withdrew on June 30, 1964, a third of the country was under control of the CNL rebels. On July 9, 1964, Tshombe returned from exile to accept the post as prime minister of the central government. He proceeded to hire mercenaries to deal with the rebel threat. The continued interest of the great powers in the Congo was demonstrated by the United States–Belgian airdrop on Stanleyville on November 24, 1964, to free rebel-held hostages.[44] A year later, on November 25, 1965, Mobutu once again took control, bringing to an end, at least for a time, the internal division of the Republic of the Congo.

The political and legal questions involved in the Congo case are extremely complex as is evident from this brief review of events. The civil war involved not only control of the government but also relations with a former colonial power and the right of parts of a country to secede. Since the superpowers wanted to establish influence in this developing nation, outside countries played a vital role in the civil war. The presence of an international peacekeeping force also introduced a new dimension into an internal conflict. The combination of all these factors presented unique and important legal considerations.

[42] UN Doc. S/5053/Add. 13/Annex I, Nov. 26, 1962, pp. 37–42.
[43] UN Doc. S/5053/Add. 15/Annex V, Jan. 30, 1963, p. 82.
[44] For discussion of the Stanleyville operation, see Kenneth W. Grundy, "The Stanleyville Rescue: American Policy in the Congo," *Yale Review* 56 (Winter 1967): 242–55; and Richard A. Falk, *Legal Order in a Violent World* (Princeton: Princeton University Press, 1968), pp. 324–35.

II. LAW AND THE CONDUCT OF CIVIL WAR

During war the aim of the parties is not total destruction of the enemy but rather the achievement of certain goals. Both sides have a common interest in using force economically in pursuance of these aims and not in intentionally destroying civilians or prisoners.[1] Therefore, specific restraints on the conduct of war have been developed to promote humanitarianism and to prevent wanton destruction. Many of these laws of war have been codified in a series of treaties, the most recent general formulation being the Geneva Conventions of 1949.[2] While the law of war was developed in the context of international wars, there is now new interest in its application to civil wars. In recent years, wars fought within states have become more prevalent as states have been deterred by the nuclear threat from initiating international wars. With the increased destruction and personal suffering occurring in civil wars, the application of laws of war to these types of conflicts has become urgent.

With the codification of the laws of war in the four Geneva Conventions after World War II, their application to civil wars was considered for the first time.[3] Article 3 of each of the four conventions introduces a minimum standard to be applied "in case of armed conflict not of an international character."[4] Formerly it had been necessary for a state to recognize the existence of a state of belligerency before conventions on

---

[1] For further discussion of the common interest which is the basis of the law of war, see Myres S. McDougal and Florentino P. Feliciano, "International Coercion and World Public Order: The General Principles of the Law of War," in *Studies in World Public Order*, by Myres S. McDougal and associates (New Haven: Yale University Press, 1960), pp. 237–334.

[2] Earlier conventions relating to warfare included Laws of War on Land, enacted at the First Peace Conference at the Hague in 1899; conventions of the Second Peace Conference at the Hague in 1907 on sea warfare, opening hostilities, and rights and duties of neutral powers; protocol of 1925 on gas warfare; Geneva Conventions of 1929 on the treatment of sick and wounded and prisoners of war; and the London Protocol of 1936 on submarine warfare.

[3] General works on the question of the laws of war and civil war include G. I. A. D. Draper, "The Geneva Conventions of 1949," *Recueil des Cours, 1965: I*, 144 (Hague: Hague Academy of International Law, 1965): 82–100; Jean S. Pictet, "La Croix-Rouge et les Conventions de Genève," *Recueil des Cours, 1950: I*, 76 (Hague: Hague Academy of International Law, 1950): 5–117; Roger Pinto, "Les Règles du Droit International Concernant la Guerre Civile," *Recueil des Cours, 1965: I*, 114 (Hague: Hague Academy of International Law, 1965): 455–548; Jean Siotis, *Le Droit de la Guerre et les Conflits armés d'un Caractère non-international* (Paris: Librairie générale de droit et de jurisprudence, 1958); and Erik Castrén, "Civil War," in *Annales Academiae Scientiarum Fennicae* (Helsinki: Suomalainen Tiedeakatemia, 1966), vol. 142.

[4] This and all future references in the text to articles of the Geneva Conventions are quoted from and refer to International Committee of the Red Cross, *The Geneva Conventions of August 12, 1949* (2d rev. ed.; Geneva: 1950).

the laws of war came into effect.[5] Article 3, however, made the provisions applicable irrespective of recognition by outside states and permitted the involvement of groups like the Red Cross without predetermining the issue of recognition.

Difficulty arose in trying to determine the cases to which article 3 would be applicable. After considerable debate as to the inclusion of civil wars in the Geneva Conventions, the framers adopted the phrase "armed conflict not of an international character." This wording indicates the framers' intention to extend rules of humane treatment to struggles within states, without defining exactly which events would be covered. G. I. A. D. Draper suggests

that the current tendency is to consider an "Article 3 conflict" to be in existence whenever sustained troop action is undertaken against rebels, even though the rebel organization and control of any area is minimal, and the situation is such that the police are not able to enforce the criminal law in a particular area by reason of rebel action.[6]

In the case of the Congo, the existence of armed conflict between organized armies that held territory certainly produced the conditions for an application of article 3.

Among the provisions of this article is protection for people not involved in the hostilities. Such persons include civilians or members of the "armed forces who have laid down their arms and those placed *hors de combat* by sickness, wounds, detention, or any other cause." Specific actions prohibited are violence to life and person, such as mutilation, murder, or torture; the taking of hostages; outrages upon personal dignity; and the passing of sentences without judicial guarantees. After these specific acts, which form a basic bill of rights, the second section of article 3 provides that the wounded and sick shall be collected and cared for and that humanitarian bodies may offer their services. The article concludes by urging parties to a conflict "to bring into force, by means of special agreements, all or part of the other provisions of the present Convention."

The Geneva Conventions of 1949, therefore, took a new step in making laws of war applicable to strife which had previously been subject only to domestic regulations. While difficulties remain in application and enforcement, article 3 of the conventions demonstrates the intention of the parties to provide some minimum humanitarian standards for the

---

[5] L. Oppenheim, *International Law: A Treatise, II: Disputes, War, and Neutrality*, ed. H. Lauterpacht (7th ed.; London: Longmans, Green and Co., 1952), pp. 210–12; and Hans Kelsen, *Principles of International Law*, rev. and ed. Robert W. Tucker (2d ed.; New York: Holt, Rinehart & Winston, 1966), pp. 412–14.

[6] Draper, "The Geneva Conventions of 1949," p. 94.

conduct of civil wars. This intention was strengthened by the inclusion of similar provisions in the Hague Conventions of 1954.[7] By signing these conventions, states accept restraints on their reaction to rebellion within their territory—in other words, they accept a significant limit on their domestic jurisdiction.

Application of the Laws of War

In analyzing the relevance of the laws of war to the Congo crisis, it is evident that the criteria for armed conflict were met in the material sense. The next question becomes, then, Were the participants bound in any way by the Geneva Conventions? At the outset none of the parties to the conflict had signed the conventions; yet for the norms to be operative in a conflict, it must occur "in the territory of one of the High Contracting Parties." The Republic of the Congo had existed only five days when the violence began and had not become a signatory to the conventions. According to the interpretation of the International Committee of the Red Cross (ICRC), however, the Republic of the Congo, as a former colony, was a party to the conventions in spite of the fact that it had taken no formal action.

Participation of newly independent States in the Geneva Conventions can therefore be admitted as implied by virtue of the signature of the former Colonial Power. It is considered advisable, however, that they officially confirm their participation in the Conventions by notifying the administering State, that is to say the Federal Council at Berne. This is a question neither of accession nor of ratification, but of confirmation of participation or of declaration of continuity.[8]

Thus, since Belgium had ratified the conventions in 1952, the Republic of the Congo was considered bound by them from the start of the violence. Furthermore, the ministry of foreign affairs of the Congolese government sent a declaration to Berne on February 20, 1961, reaffirming the participation of the Congo in the conventions.[9] The stated position of the ICRC and the declaration of the Congolese government in the midst of the conflict make it clear that the Congo should be considered a party to the conventions.

There were complicating circumstances, however, in regard to other actors in the conflict, notably Katanga. After issuing an appeal on Feb-

[7] Hague Conventions of 1954 on the Protection of Cultural Property in the Event of Armed Conflict, *United Nations Treaty Series,* 249: 240–90.

[8] International Committee of the Red Cross, *International Review of the Red Cross* 2 (April 1962): 208.

[9] "The Red Cross Action in the Congo," *International Review of the Red Cross* 2 (January 1962): 7–8.

ruary 22, 1961, to all authorities in the Congo to uphold the human-itarian principles of the conventions, the ICRC reported that

Tshombe has now informed Geneva that he is adhering to the principles mentioned in that appeal. President Tshombe has also noted the offer made by the ICRC to come to the aid of victims of the present events and he has accordingly given authorization for a delegate of the ICRC to visit places of detention in Katanga.[10]

Although Katanga had declared its independence, it had not received recognition as an independent state, and it had not formally acceded to the conventions. Nevertheless, its leader responded affirmatively to the appeal to uphold the principles of the conventions.

Application of the Laws of War to the United Nations

The question of the relationship of the laws of war to troops under UN auspices requires special attention. It had been discussed previously during the Korean War, but the fighting between ONUC and the gen-darmerie in Katanga added a new perspective.[11] Because the Katanga experience represents the first case in which a UN force became involved in regular combat, the applicability of the laws of war to such a force is a particularly important question to resolve.

Three specific arguments have been advanced to demonstrate that the forces of the United Nations are not bound by the laws of war. The simplest contention is that the United Nations is not a signatory to the Geneva Conventions; therefore it is not bound by them. Julius Stone has succinctly summarized this position: "In the technical legal sense United Nations forces *stricto sensu* would not be bound by *treaty* rules of war,

---

[10] "The ICRC in the Congo," *Revue Internationale de la Croix-Rouge, Supplement* 14 (March 1961): 43–45.

[11] The Korean case and the Congolese case are treated here as two distinct, and not really comparable, forms of UN action. The former consisted of asking the United States to carry out the military measures, and it is doubtful that such a delegating of responsibility to a major power will ever be repeated. The Congo and Cyprus cases represent establishment of a UN force consisting of troops seconded to the organization and directly under UN command.

Studies on the application of the laws of war in Korea include Howard J. Taubenfeld, "International Armed Forces and the Rules of War," *American Journal of International Law* 45 (October 1951): 671–79; and "Should the Laws of War Apply to United Nations Enforcement Action?" Report of Committee on Study of Legal Problems of the United Nations, *Proceedings of the American Society of International Law, 1952* (Washington: ASIL, 1952), pp. 216–20.

Similar analyses of the Congo are Finn Seyersted, *United Nations Forces in the Law of Peace and War* (Leyden: A. W. Sijthoff, 1966), pp. 314–98; D. W. Bowett, *United Nations Forces: A Legal Study* (New York: Frederick A. Prae-ger, 1964), pp. 484–516; and R. Simmonds, *Legal Problems Arising from the United Nations Military Operations in the Congo* (Hague: Martinus Nijhoff, 1968), pp. 168–96.

even if it could be argued that (on the analogy of newly created States) they were bound by *customary* rules. Rules for such forces were simply not created by the treaties concerned."[12] The 1949 conventions were drawn up four years after the UN Charter, which provided for a military force under UN command; yet there was absolutely no consideration given by the framers to the relationship of an international force to the conventions. This omission may have resulted from the fact that the conventions were drafted after the breakup of the UN Military Staff Committee and prior to the organization of the force for Korea, making the likelihood of a UN force seem remote. The *travaux préparatoires* of the Geneva Conventions evidence no attempt to exclude international forces; rather, the question simply was not considered.[13] Article 2 of the conventions does provide for an application of the provisions to a conflict between a party and a nonparty when both accept and undertake to apply them. Presumably, then, a UN contingent in conflict with a party to the conventions would also become subject to them through article 2. In addition, the contention is made that the United Nations could and should accede to the conventions so as to remove whatever doubt might remain as to the relevance of the regulations to an international body.[14]

The second argument against the binding nature of the laws of war on the United Nations relates to the ability of the organization to ensure the observance of the provisions of the conventions. The troops in the Congo were national contingents seconded to the United Nations for that particular operation. While the troops were placed directly under the orders of the UN commander and were not to obey orders from their own government, they continued, as national units, to be subject to military rules and regulations of their own states.[15] From this evidence of equivocal status, Draper concludes that the United Nations does not have the means of enforcing the laws of war.[16] Yet, in the case of the Congo, the United Nations did assume international responsibility for

---

[12] Julius Stone, *Legal Controls of International Conflict: A Treatise on the Dynamics of Disputes-and-War Law* (New York: Rinehart & Company, 1954), p. 315.

[13] The United Nations was represented by an observer at the diplomatic conference at Geneva in 1949, but the only mention of the United Nations in the *travaux préparatoires* is in relation to registration. See Seyersted, *United Nations Forces*, p. 346.

[14] Seyersted builds a strong case for the possibility and desirability of United Nations accession to the conventions. Seyersted, *United Nations Forces*, pp. 330–99. Bowett suggests that a General Assembly resolution would be sufficient. Bowett, *United Nations Forces*, pp. 510–11.

[15] Bowett, *United Nations Forces*, p. 211.

[16] G. I. A. D. Draper, "The Legal Limitations upon the Employment of Weapons by the United Nations Force in the Congo," *International and Comparative Law Quarterly* 12 (April 1963): 409.

enforcement in the sense that all claims against ONUC were lodged with the United Nations and the organization, in turn, presented demands and protests on behalf of the soldiers to the Congolese governments. Since the Geneva Conventions do not specify an agency for trying persons who have committed war crimes, there seems to be no reason the United Nations could not rely on the states providing contingents to try their own participants.[17] Thus, although a UN force is composed of national soldiers, the United Nations has assumed international responsibility for these troops in the past and could further assume the duty of enforcing the laws of war through the troops' states.

The third argument suggests that, since war is now outlawed, any conflict in which the United Nations became involved would be a war of aggression. Those holding this position propose that the same restraints should not be imposed on both the United Nations and the aggressor. Georg Schwarzenberger contends that the United Nations should not be limited by the laws of war in suppressing an "illegal" war.[18] This particular question was considered during the Korean War by a panel of the American Society of International Law. The panel concluded that the legal character of an international enforcement action is different from that of a war between two states and that the principles of sovereignty which underlie the laws of war do not apply to a situation in which the United Nations faces an aggressor.

The United Nations should not feel bound by all the laws of war, but should select such of the laws of war as may seem to fit its purposes (e.g., prisoners of war, belligerent occupation), adding such others as may be needed, and rejecting those which seem incompatible with its purposes.[19]

This argument fails to make a distinction between the manner in which a war is conducted and the purposes of the parties to the war. Once a de facto war exists, there is always a need for certain limits and restraints in regard to the victims of the strife, and the United Nations should not be exempt from these limits.[20] The rationale for the Geneva Conventions does not rest on the nature of a particular war. Some of the laws of war, such as those relating to occupation or economic settle-

---

[17] This is the position taken by Seyersted, *United Nations Forces*, p. 373; and Simmonds, *Legal Problems*, pp. 195–96.

[18] Georg Schwarzenberger, *International Law as Applied by International Courts and Tribunals,* vol. 2: *The Law of Armed Conflict* (London: Steven & Sons, 1968), pp. 96–106.

[19] Should the Laws of War Apply to United Nations Enforcement Action?" p. 220.

[20] It is notable that most authors writing after the involvement of the United Nations in combat situations in Katanga have taken the position that the United Nations is bound by the laws of war when a de facto state of war exists.

ment, may not apply in all types of conflicts, but the humanitarian norms are just as necessary and applicable whether the suffering is caused by hostility between states or between an international organization and an aggressor.[21]

In the case of the Congo, U Thant considered ONUC bound by laws of war. Article 43 of the "Regulations for the United Nations Force in the Congo" states that "the Force shall observe the principles and spirit of the general international conventions applicable to the conduct of military personnel."[22] The acting secretary-general emphasized this in writing to the president of the ICRC:

I am in entire agreement with you in considering that the Geneva Conventions of 1949 constitute the most complete standards granting to the human person indispensable guarantees for his protection in time of war or in case of armed conflict whatever form it may take. I also wish to confirm that UNO insists on its armed forces in the field applying the principles of these Conventions as scrupulously as possible.[23]

It must be noted that U Thant did not specify whether he was referring only to the minimal provisions of article 3 or to the entire Geneva Conventions.[24]

Treatment of Prisoners

Whatever the answer to the question concerning the application of the laws of war in the Congo, there was adherence to these principles in several areas. With regard to the treatment of prisoners, article 3 of the Geneva Conventions states that prisoners "shall in all circumstances

[21] Those who support the applicability of the laws of war include Bowett, *United Nations Forces*, pp. 498–99; Richard R. Baxter, "The Role of Law in Modern War," *Proceedings of the American Society of International Law, 1953*, pp. 90–98; McDougal and Feliciano, "International Coercion," p. 310; and Seyersted, *United Nations Forces*, p. 242.

[22] *Regulations for the United Nations Force in the Congo*, UN Doc. ST/SGB/ONUC/1, July 15, 1963. (Although these were not published until 1963, they were in effect throughout the operation.)

[23] "The United Nations and the Application of the Geneva Conventions," *International Review of the Red Cross* 2 (January 1962): 29.

[24] This uncertainty has been answered differently by various legal scholars. Draper suggests that only the provisions of article 3 might be applicable and even that is doubtful. Draper, "Legal Limitations," p. 410. Simmonds suggests that the mere presence of the United Nations transforms the conflict into one of an international character with the result that the entire conventions are applicable. Simmonds, *Legal Problems*, p. 183. Seyersted holds that certainly the customary laws of war apply but not the conventional ones; however, this contention is not supported by a delineation of the content of the two sets of international law. Seyersted, *United Nations Forces*, p. 315. Richard A. Falk suggests that the conventions are in fact declaratory of customary law. Clergy and Laymen Concerned about Vietnam, *In the Name of America* (Annandale, Va.: Turnpike Press, 1968), p. 25.

be treated humanely" and explicitly prohibits "violence to life and person, in particular murder of all kinds, mutilation, cruel treatment, and torture." Most captives in the Congo civil war were detained under acceptable conditions and exchanged or released in the course of hostilities. The International Committee of the Red Cross visited prisons representing all factions during the crisis in an effort to ensure that prisoners received treatment in accordance with the Geneva Conventions. After these inspections, the ICRC reported directly to the detaining power, and according to the inspectors, improvements resulted in a number of prisons.[25] Since the reports remain secret, it is impossible to determine the exact conditions of prisoners, but the absence of major complaints suggests that adequate prison standards were maintained.

The ICRC was also active in efforts to release prisoners. In Katanga many of the prisoners taken by both sides were quickly exchanged. On October 25, 1961, as provided by the September cease-fire agreement, 190 ONUC prisoners and 240 Katangese prisoners were exchanged.[26] Captives were again transferred at the close of 1961, when ONUC released the Katangese troops it held and the Katangese reciprocated by freeing 1,500 men of the UN force.[27]

Despite efforts to treat prisoners humanely and to provide for their exchange, violations occurred and received widespread publicity. In one instance, forty-seven ONUC soldiers, mostly Ghanians, lost their lives after being taken prisoner in Port Francqui on April 28, 1961. The Armée Nationale Congolaise (ANC) had disarmed the Ghanian troops and arrested their two British officers. When shots were heard outside the city the next day, the disarmed ONUC troops were herded together by the Congolese and executed.[28] A second violation occurred on November 11, 1961, with the murder of thirteen Italian airmen at Kindu. Two-hundred and sixty soldiers of the ANC attacked the UN mess, arrested the Italians, immediately shot them, and dismembered their bodies, giving pieces to the crowd that had gathered.[29] Colonel Pakassa, who was in charge of the ANC troops, could only report that he had had no control over his troops. When it became clear what had occurred, he was turned over to the central government. Another instance of disre-

[25] International Committee of the Red Cross, *Annual Report, 1962* (Geneva, 1963), p. 15.

[26] *Yearbook of the United Nations, 1961* (New York: United Nations, 1963), p. 64.

[27] International Committee of the Red Cross, *Annual Report, 1962*, p. 15.

[28] Ernest W. Lefever, *Uncertain Mandate: Politics of the U.N. Congo Operation* (Baltimore: Johns Hopkins Press, 1967), pp. 233–34; Kwame Nkrumah, *Challenge of the Congo* (London: Nelson, 1967), p. 161. H. T. Alexander sets the number killed at 120. Alexander, *African Tightrope: My Two Years as Nkrumah's Chief of Staff* (New York: Frederick A. Praeger, 1966), p. 66.

[29] *Yearbook of the United Nations, 1961* (New York, 1963), pp. 66–67.

gard for the proper treatment of prisoners involved ninety-two Baluba tribesmen who were taken prisoner by the Liberian battalion of ONUC in Kasai Province in September 1960. Although the reason for their arrest has never been clarified, it is known that they were loaded into unventilated railroad cars, where they suffocated.[30] These examples of violations of the laws of war represent exceptions, for the majority of captives received adequate treatment and were promptly exchanged.

Protection of Civilians

Protection for civilians under the Geneva Conventions is based on the distinction between those who actively engage in combat and those who do not. "The High Contracting Parties specifically agree that each of them is prohibited from taking any measure of such a character as to cause the physical suffering or extermination of protected persons in their hands."[31] Inevitably, civilians were killed in the Congo, but their numbers never reached such proportions as to obliterate the distinction between soldiers and civilians. During the three clashes between ONUC and the Katanga gendarmerie in densely populated areas, Ernest Lefever has calculated that only fifty civilians lost their lives.[32]

Most civilian deaths in the Congo civil war occurred in tribal struggles. Lefever has estimated the number of men killed in ONUC-Congolese clashes as less than one thousand for all sides but in tribal fighting and from starvation as tens of thousands.[33] These figures give an indication of the suffering of civilians, since most of these tribal deaths were not soldiers but civilian victims of massacres.

Lumumba's attack on the secessionist states of South Kasai and Katanga in August 1960 was followed by one such civilian massacre. When Lumumba's ANC recaptured the capital of South Kasai on August 26, 1960, the conquest turned into a slaughter of the Baluba tribe. Hammarskjold gave this description of the events:

Information which has reached us from the United Nations and International Red Cross personnel in the Kasai region indicates that the personnel of the Armée nationale congolaise have engaged in slaughter not only of combatants but also of defenceless civilians. In the Bakwanga region, for

[30] Carl von Horn, *Soldiering for Peace* (New York: David McKay Co., 1967), p. 238; and Philippa Schuyler, *Who Killed the Congo?* (New York: Devin-Adair, 1962), p. 234.

[31] Geneva Convention Relative to the Protection of Civilian Persons in Time of War, 12 August 1949, Article 32.

[32] Ernest W. Lefever, "The U.N. as a Foreign Policy Instrument: The Congo Crisis," in *Foreign Policy in the Sixties*, ed. Roger Hilsman and Robert C. Good (Baltimore: Johns Hopkins Press, 1965), p. 153.

[33] Ernest W. Lefever, "The Costs of Intervention: Five Examples from Africa," paper delivered at conference on "Intervention and the Developing States," Princeton, New Jersey, November 11, 1967.

example, hundreds of Balubas were reported killed on 29 and 30 August, according to World Health Organization and Red Cross officials who visited the area at that time. One shocking incident that was widely reported is that of the massacre on 31 August 1960 by troops from the Armée nationale congolaise, using machetes, of 70 Balubas including women and children who had taken refuge in a mission school. Other reports indicate that villages have been pillaged and burnt and their inhabitants, men, women and children, killed. United Nations officials were informed that unarmed persons were deliberately killed simply on the ground that they were Balubas.[34]

The secretary-general conveyed the seriousness of these incidents by saying "they involve a most flagrant violation of elementary human rights and have the characteristics of the crime of genocide since they appear to be directed toward the extermination of a specific ethnic group, the Balubas."[35]

Another instance of civilian abuse occurred in northern Katanga at the close of 1960. Tshombe did not have control of the area and there were no forces to preserve law and order; Balubakat Jeunesse roamed the territory murdering traditional chiefs and terrorizing the public.[36] When Tshombe did send his gendarmerie to establish control over this area, they advanced into the hostile Baluba areas burning villages and killing civilians as they went.[37]

Political prisoners constitute a special class of civilians under the laws of war. According to the Geneva Conventions, such prisoners may be executed for treason by the state, but they must be given a trial before a court with judicial guarantees. Patrice Lumumba was the most notorious political prisoner in the Congo. After his capture by ANC soldiers, he was manhandled and severely injured. The secretary-general called upon the Congolese government to treat Lumumba humanely, and an ICRC representative managed to visit him at Thysville in December 1960.[38] On January 17, 1961, Lumumba was transferred from the prison at Thysville to Katanga, where he was executed.[39] Although some details surrounding his death remain speculative, it is clear that not even the minimal standards of justice were applied in his case.

Lumumba's death triggered a series of killings of political prisoners.

[34] United Nations, Security Council, *Official Records*, 15th year, 896th mtg. (Sept. 9, 1960), p. 18.

[35] *Ibid.*

[36] Smith Hempstone, *Rebels, Mercenaries, and Dividends: The Katanga Story* (New York: Frederick A. Praeger, 1962), pp. 114–21.

[37] *Yearbook of the United Nations, 1960* (New York, 1961), p. 87.

[38] UN Doc. S/4571, Annexes I and II (Dec. 5, 1960), pp. 71–73; "The Red Cross Action in the Congo," p. 5.

[39] For accounts of Lumumba's fate, see UN Doc. S/4976, Nov. 11, 1961, pp. 67–129; Hempstone, *Rebels*, pp. 125–33; or Jules Gérard-Libois, *Katanga Secession*, trans. Rebecca Young (Madison: University of Wisconsin Press, 1966), p. 142.

On February 9, 1961, seven Lumumbist prisoners were transferred from Leopoldville to Bakwanga, where they were tried for "crimes against the Baluba nation" by a "traditional court" of Baluba chiefs and six were executed and one imprisoned. In retaliation, on February 20, fifteen political prisoners, including five of Mobutu's officers, were shot by an army firing squad in Stanleyville.[40] These killings took place without trials and as reprisals, in spite of the prohibition of such actions by the laws of war.[41] As the Lumumba case and its aftermath illustrate, political prisoners are a special class of civilians, and restraints on their treatment are difficult to enforce. In order to eliminate political enemies, the various factions in the Congo frequently denied the basic right of a trial.

Civilians as hostages present another important class of noncombatants. Article 34 of the Geneva Convention on civilian persons states simply that "the taking of hostages is prohibited." In November 1964, Gbenye's rebel headquarters in Stanleyville held 1,700 persons as hostages and threatened to kill them if the ANC advanced. When negotiations for their release were unsuccessful, the United States and Belgium undertook an air drop.[42] The rebels began killing the hostages as Belgian paratroopers approached; 27 people died, but the remainder were evacuated safely. While the rebels' use of hostages was clearly illegal, the debate at the United Nations centered instead on the operation as a colonialist move. The Africans viewed the incident in racial terms, since the United States and Belgium had acted to release predominately white hostages whereas previously they had done nothing to save an estimated 18,000 black Congolese killed by the rebels.[43]

Avoidance of Nonmilitary Targets

Protection of nonmilitary targets provoked controversy in the Congo.[44] Article 19 of the Geneva Convention on the wounded and sick provides that "fixed establishments and mobile medical units of the Medical

---

[40] Crawford Young, *Politics in the Congo: Decolonization and Independence* (Princeton: Princeton University Press, 1965), p. 331; Catherine Hoskyns, *The Congo since Independence: January 1960–December 1961* (London: Oxford University Press, 1965), p. 317; UN Doc. S/4727, Feb. 18, 1961, pp. 136–37.

[41] Geneva Convention Relative to the Protection of Civilian Persons in Time of War, 12 August 1949, articles 3 and 33; Morris Greenspan, *The Modern Law of Land Warfare* (Berkeley: University of California Press, 1959), p. 170.

[42] Details of the OAU negotiations prior to the air drop are included in William Attwood, *The Reds and the Blacks: A Personal Adventure* (New York: Harper & Row, 1967), pp. 196–236.

[43] See Kenneth W. Grundy, "The Stanleyville Rescue: American Policy in the Congo," *Yale Review* 56 (Winter 1967): 242–55; and Richard A. Falk, *Legal Order in a Violent World* (Princeton: Princeton University Press, 1968), pp. 324–35.

[44] In regard to material damages of nonmilitary targets, it should be noted that the United Nations did assume financial responsibility for material damages caused by

Service may in no circumstances be attacked, but shall at all times be respected and protected by the Parties to the conflict." In telegrams to the secretary-general on December 8 and 9, 1961, the Belgian government charged that "hospitals have been hit, not by isolated shells, but by mortar fire apparently aimed at them, resulting in the wounding of hospital staff and in heavy damage."[45] The secretary-general replied that one of the "hospitals" shelled had a mercenary observation post on its roof and that the other hospital had been hit by some shells aimed at the main base of the Katangese gendarmerie two hundred meters away.[46] In another incident, on December 12, 1961, Indian-piloted Canberra jets flying for the United Nations shot up a hospital at Shinkolobwe.

Perhaps the most publicized violation of the laws of war in regard to nonmilitary targets was the killing of three Red Cross workers on the outskirts of Elisabethville. The bodies of Georges Olivet, chief delegate of the ICRC, and two voluntary aides were found on December 23, 1961, buried a few yards from their burnt-out ambulance. The ambulance, marked with the protective emblem of the Red Cross, had been destroyed by bazooka fire, and the passengers had been wounded by machine gun or light automatic weapons.[47] A joint commission for the United Nations and the ICRC was established to investigate the incident. Although the commission report was not made public, Finn Seyersted reveals that conflicting evidence made it impossible for the commission to establish all the facts but that they did find that the bullets which killed the Red Cross workers were not the type used by the Katangese troops.[48] The outcome of the investigation was that "the United Nations, without admitting any legal or financial obligation, paid to the *Comité international de la Croix-Rouge* a *'somme forfaitaire'* for the injury it had suffered. The *Comité* distributed the entire sum among the dependents of the victims."[49]

ONUC, which were not directly related to military necessity. At the completion of the operation in the Congo, the United Nations agreed to compensate individuals who had suffered damages for which the organization was legally liable. Claims boards were established and approximately 2,000 claims were made by Congo residents. After excluding damage resulting from the normal course of military operations and damage caused by third parties, the United Nations accepted 581 Belgian claims. In February 1965, an agreement was reached whereby the United Nations was to pay Belgium a lump sum of $1.5 million as a final settlement of all claims by Belgian nationals. See UN Doc. S/6597, Aug. 6, 1965, pp. 156–59; and UN Doc. S/6589, Aug. 3, 1965, pp. 151–52.

[45] UN Doc. S/5025, Dec. 15, 1961, p. 192.

[46] *Ibid.*, pp. 195–96.

[47] International Committee of the Red Cross, *Annual Report, 1962*, pp. 14–15; and Draper, "Legal Limitations," p. 410.

[48] Seyersted, *United Nations Forces*, p. 195.

[49] This information is presented in Seyersted, *United Nations Forces*, p. 195. He secured the information from a "letter of 23 October 1962 from the *Comité international* to M. A. Vroonen, husband of one of the victims, published, together with the latters' reply, in *Essor du Katanga*, 13 November 1962."

Misuse of the Red Cross symbol introduced another complication in relation to the protection of nonmilitary targets. The laws of war provide that protection ceases if the medical units are "used to commit, outside their humanitarian duties, acts harmful to the enemy."[50] The United Nations made the accusation that the Katanga forces "regularly abused the Red Cross symbol, employing vehicles painted with red crosses to transport gendarmes and to snipe at United Nations personnel."[51] Once medical units have been used in this manner, they lose their protection, but it is frequently difficult to determine whether protection has been forfeited.

A heavy air attack against the Union Minière in Elisabethville in December 1961 raised the question whether the works could be considered a nonmilitary target. Katangese officials claimed that it was civilian property and should not have been bombarded. It was suspected, however, that the Union Minière was supplying the Katanga authorities with arms and equipment and was providing working papers for the mercenaries. Substantiation of military involvement came when UN troops occupied the factory after having been under mortar attack from the grounds.[52] Therefore, although the factory was not formally a part of the Katangese military base, it forfeited its claim to protection as a nonmilitary target, according to international law, when the grounds of the company were used to fire upon ONUC.[53]

Conclusions

This analysis of the Congo case reveals the factors in civil wars both for and against the application of the laws of war. The first pressure toward observance of these laws was the agreement of *all* parties to adhere to the Geneva Conventions. Had one party maintained that the conventions were inapplicable, their relevance would have been in doubt. The ICRC was a second influence toward observance since it secured commitments to the Geneva Conventions from the parties and was active in the field in visiting prisoners, arranging prisoner releases, supplying

[50] Geneva Convention for the Amelioration of the Condition of the Wounded and Sick in Armed Forces in the Field, 12 August 1949, article 21.

[51] *Yearbook of the United Nations, 1961*, pp. 72–73.

[52] *Ibid.*, pp. 73–74.

[53] Forfeiture of immunity from attack in the case of the Union Minière could be based on the following reasoning: (1) by using the factory to make materials for the Katangese army, the factory could be considered a military works under article 2 of the Hague Conventions IX, 1907, and therefore open to bombardment; (2) once fire came from the plant, it could no longer be considered undefended under article 25, Hague Regulations, 1907, but rather would become open to bombardment out of military necessity; and (3) even such protected places as hospitals lose their immunity when they are used for military purposes. Greenspan, *Modern Law of Land Warfare*, pp. 332–41.

medical relief, and educating the parties to the conflict in the laws of war. A third pressure toward restraint was ONUC, which operated under a limited mandate and whose use of force was restricted to self-defense. The UN presence also ensured publicity for all actions in the Congo. Because a world organization involves continual reports and debates, information on the Congo was always readily available, and this publicity was an important support for the laws of war. The UN force itself was under great pressure to maintain the highest standards of conduct; member states felt that any misconduct detracted from the reputation of the United Nations. The behavior of the UN force had a spill-over effect on the other parties to the conflict. Since ONUC had to adhere rigidly to the laws relating to the conduct of war, the other parties had less need to fear deviations from the laws and thus could more easily perceive the common interest in adopting them. The Congo experience suggests that a UN presence contributes to the effectiveness of the laws of war.

Despite the strong influences favoring the laws of war, there were also several factors working against their application in the Congo. First, the very nature of civil war worked against the laws. The issues involved ranged from strictly domestic to primarily international problems. Strife in the Congo varied from mass demonstrations to clashes between ONUC and the Katangese gendarmerie. The impossibility of ascertaining precisely which actions were part of the civil war and which were not made it difficult to apply the laws of war. This inability to distinguish normal domestic actions and warfare will hinder future applications of these laws to civil wars.

The second reason for many violations of the laws of war in the Congo was the inability of civil and military authorities to control their soldiers. Many of the attacks on civilians followed rebellions of Congolese troops against their officers. If the observance of the laws of war is predicated on the discipline of a military unit, the lack of military discipline, which may prove common to civil wars in developing countries, will be a significant hindrance to the future success of international law. Finally, ignorance of the laws of war may result in their violation. Many of the persons fighting in the Congo had little or no knowledge of any rules of war, and this pattern will undoubtedly repeat itself in other emerging nations.[54]

Pressures both for and against application of the laws of war are inherent in civil war situations, and it is impossible to balance precisely compliance against violation. Although illegal acts can be cited in the

---

[54] The Red Cross produced and distributed illustrated booklets about the Geneva Conventions in Congolese languages. International Committee of the Red Cross, *International Review of the Red Cross* 1 (December 1961): 501.

Congo conflict, they cannot be interpreted as denying the relevance of law. There is other, strong evidence that the actors in the Congo considered the laws of war relevant to the conflict and made *no* attempt to sabotage or deny the existence of such norms. The relevance of the laws of war in the Congo was demonstrated by the circumstances that all parties considered themselves bound by these laws; they based claims and counterclaims on these laws; and they restricted their actions in accordance with these laws.

III. THE ROLE OF FOREIGN COUNTRIES

The relationships of foreign countries to the parties involved in any civil war raise extremely important questions. The granting or withholding of assistance by other states can be decisive in determining the outcome of the struggle. There is also the possibility that intervention and counterintervention will escalate a domestic conflict into an international war. At the outset of the Congo struggle, outside states were not committed to any of the Congolese factions, leaving the situation fluid. When the Belgians disqualified themselves from the role of ally by sending paratroopers into the Congo, other states concluded they no longer had to remain aloof. Since the Congo was viewed as an especially important African country, numerous foreign states were anxious to play a role in its civil war.

These unilateral efforts must be considered in conjunction with the multilateral operation of the United Nations. The Congo case presents a special model of the use of UN action to control the effects of a civil war on the international system. Both of the superpowers had interests in the Congo, but each had an even greater interest in avoiding a confrontation. By involving the United Nations, each state hoped to prevent gains by the other while avoiding the necessity of a unilateral commitment. Thus, the United Nations was to insulate an internal war from the rest of the international system.[1] The effectiveness of the organization in this role can be assessed only after the specific instances of involvement by foreign countries in the Congo civil war are examined. This analysis of outside assistance will be concerned with the nature of the aid, the recipient, and the connection between the multilateral and unilateral acts to determine which kinds of aid are or are not permissible in a civil war.

[1] For the presentation of a different interpretation of the UN role which suggests that the UN presence introduced international politics into the Congo, see Ernest W. Lefever, *Uncertain Mandate: Politics of the U.N. Congo Operation* (Baltimore: Johns Hopkins Press, 1967), pp. 207–22.

Belgian Use of Troops

Shortly after receiving independence, the Congolese army mutinied against its Belgian officers. The hostile acts of the mutinous soldiers were directed primarily at Europeans remaining in the Congo; therefore, pressure was placed on Belgium to reestablish order in the Congo. The Belgian government sent paratroopers into the country on July 10, 1960. During the next eight days Belgian troops were deployed in twenty-six areas throughout the Congo.[2] This introduction of foreign military personnel (especially those of the former colonial power) entirely changed the nature of the issues in the Congo and crystallized the positions of the actors in the conflict.

The troops had been dispatched without any request from the Congolese government. A specific provision of the Treaty of Friendship between the two countries provided that "all military intervention by Belgian forces stationed in Congo bases can take place only on the express command of the Congolese Minister of National Defense."[3] The Belgians had acted without the required command of Lumumba; yet the two governments might still have reached agreement on maintaining law and order. The death of a dozen Congolese, however, in the Belgian bombardment of Matadi, from which most Europeans had been evacuated, and the declaration of Katangese independence convinced the Congolese that Belgium was attempting to take control of the country once more.[4]

Congolese officials claimed that the Belgian actions constituted aggression against the sovereign government of the Congo. They requested military assistance from the United States, but President Dwight Eisenhower suggested that they seek aid from the United Nations.[5] Lumumba and Kasavubu then requested UN military assistance, interpreting the Congo situation as follows:

---

[2] W. J. Ganshof Van Der Meersch, *Fin de la Souveraineté Belge au Congo: Documents et Réflexions* (Brussels: Institut Royal des Relations Internationales, 1963), p. 460.

[3] "Treaty of Friendship between Belgium and the Congo" is available in English as Appendix D of Ernest W. Lefever, *Crisis in the Congo: A United Nations Force in Action* (Washington: Brookings Institution, 1965), pp. 199–200.

[4] Catherine Hoskyns, *The Congo since Independence: January 1960–December 1961* (London: Oxford University Press, 1965), pp. 98–100.

[5] Lefever suggests that the US refusal to grant direct military assistance was based on a fear of Soviet counterintervention, a desire to share the responsibility for African security, an effort to maintain the friendship of leaders of emerging states, and an interest in UN peacekeeping. Lefever, *Uncertain Mandate*, p. 77. Arthur Larson proposes that Eisenhower, as an expert administrator, had a channel for everything and that he simply assumed that the United Nations was the channel for international problems like the Congo. Larson, *Eisenhower: The President Nobody Knew* (New York: Charles Scribner's Sons, 1968), pp. 57–58.

The real cause of most of the disturbances can be found in colonialist machinations. We accuse the Belgian Government of having carefully prepared the secession of Katanga with a view to maintaining a hold on our country. The Government, supported by the Congolese people, refuses to accept a *fait accompli* resulting from a conspiracy between Belgian imperialists and a small group of Katanga leaders. The overwhelming majority of the Katanga population is opposed to secession which means the disguised perpetuation of the colonialist régime. The essential purpose of the requested military aid is to protect the national territory of the Congo against the present external aggression which is a threat to international peace.[6]

The Belgian government, on the other hand, justified its military action as the fulfillment of a duty to protect its nationals. In justifying the action, Prime Minister Gaston Eyskens argued that

the Belgian troops intervened when there was imminent danger and the government found itself in a situation of absolute necessity. The Belgian government like any government has a duty to observe a rule of international ethics and international law which imposes upon a country the protection of its nationals. The Belgian government intervened solely to prevent bloodshed and to offer the protection which was necessary for the preservation of human lives.[7]

Although the protection of nationals is a responsibility of states, the Belgian case was weak on two grounds. The failure to seek Congolese consent was a violation of a specific treaty commitment and the aggravation of an extremely sensitive colonial issue. Second, the Belgian actions in Katanga were more extensive than necessary for the protection of nationals and significantly contributed to the province's ability to remain independent.

The introduction of foreign military forces into the Congo shifted the character of the struggle from a mutiny to a conflict over Katanga's secession and the removal of Belgian troops. The move also compromised Belgian relations with the national government and committed the Belgians to aiding Katanga. The Congolese were spurred to seek UN assistance and thus to involve the United Nations in what had been a strictly domestic matter. The introduction of Belgian troops permitted characterization of the struggle as a threat to international peace and provided justification for a UN operation.

Relations with the Leopoldville Government

The first major recipient of aid in the Congo was the Leopoldville government. Its leaders had assumed national control at the outset, al-

---

[6] UN Doc. S/4382, July 13, 1960, p. 11.

[7] Speech before the Belgian Senate by Prime Minister Eyskens on July 12, 1960, reported in Ganshof Van Der Meersch, *Fin de la Souveraineté*, p. 457 (author's translation).

though they were later challenged by the seceded provinces and the Stanleyville government and their government itself was changed from the Kasavubu-Lumumba coalition, to Mobutu's college of commissioners, and finally to unified rule under Adoula. Since the Belgians had relinquished control to the central government, it was recognized by other states whose embassies were located in Leopoldville. The Leopoldville government thus had a special advantage in communicating with other countries through diplomatic channels.

The national leaders were quick to use the instruments of diplomacy to register disapproval of policies. Kasavubu and Lumumba broke diplomatic relations with Belgium immediately after the sending of paratroopers. On two occasions the Congolese expelled the Soviet embassy from the country. When Mobutu took over the government, he announced that the Soviet and Czech diplomats and technicians had forty-eight hours to leave the country because of their aid to Lumumba.[8] And again, on November 21, 1963, the entire Soviet embassy staff was ordered out of the country, when a plot against the government was discovered. The central government also broke relations with Ghana and the UAR in November 1960 because of suspected assistance to Lumumba, who was then being held in prison. The central government did not hesitate to sever diplomatic relations as a means of eliminating its opponent's support and registering public disapproval.

After the constitutional crisis, there was a shift of diplomatic support away from the central government. Some of the communist countries and the more radical African states recognized the Lumumbist regime at Stanleyville as the national government. The United Nations recognized no government in the Congo during this period as none was established in accordance with the *Loi Fondamentale*. ONUC dealt with any officials that were available until the government established at the Lovanium parliament was recognized.

UN members favoring the Mobutu group did provide this government with assistance at UN headquarters. Following the admission of the Congo to the United Nations on September 20, 1960, the seat was contested by two delegations—one appointed by Kasavubu, the other by Lumumba. In November the Western bloc succeeded in seating the Kasavubu delegation.[9] The United States further assisted Kasavubu and Mobutu by denying Lumumba and Tshombe visas to enter the country and present their cases to the United Nations.

Ideological aid, such as statements of support and provision of propaganda facilities, from both the East and the West were directed to the

[8] Hoskyns, *Congo since Independence*, pp. 214–17.
[9] See report of the Credentials Committee, UN Doc. A/4578, Nov. 17, 1960, pp. 1–6.

central government as long as Kasavubu and Lumumba ruled jointly. After the constitutional crisis, support was divided—the West continued to aid the Kasavubu-Mobutu government, which took a stance compatible with that of the capitalist states, while the East gave support to the Gizenga government. Ideological aid was extremely important to Kasavubu in the struggle for power immediately after his dismissal of Lumumba. When the United Nations closed down the Leopoldville radio station to prevent inflammatory broadcasts, Fulbert Youlou, president of Congo (Brazzaville), permitted Kasavubu to continue his propaganda campaign from the Brazzaville radio station just across the river. Since Lumumba had no similar means of appealing to the Congolese people, this assistance contributed significantly to Kasavubu's continued control of the Leopoldville government.

While it is difficult to determine precisely how much economic assistance the central government received, it is clear that the United States and Belgium were the major contributors. The total flow of economic assistance to the Congo for the period 1960–64 shows $305 million contributed by Belgium and $141 million by the United States.[10]

Military aid to the Leopoldville government was sharply circumscribed in the early stages of the struggle, and the Security Council requested all states to refrain from unilateral intervention in the Congo.[11] One major exception was the Soviet aid given Lumumba in his attack on Katanga in August 1960. The Russians delivered 100 military trucks, 14 Ilyushin transport planes, and 200 technicians, without which Lumumba could not have launched his attack.[12] Since this help was given outside the UN framework, it raised the question whether unilateral military aid might be granted once a multilateral operation had been undertaken. The Soviet Union's assistance was given at the request of Lumumba, who planned his own military campaign after he was unsuccessful in getting ONUC to

[10] Organisation for Economic Co-operation and Development, *Geographical Distribution of Financial Flows to Less Developed Countries: 1960–1964* (Paris: OECD, 1966), pp. 80–81.

[11] UN Doc. S/4405, July 22, 1960, p. 34; and United Nations, Security Council, *Official Records*, 15th year, 879th mtg. (July 21/22, 1960), pp. 19–22.

[12] The precise amount of Soviet military assistance cannot be determined, but it was on the order suggested here. Hammarskjold notes that "a certain number of planes, type IL-14, have been put directly at the disposal of the Government of the Republic of the Congo by the Government of the USSR, presumably with crews, technicians, ground personnel, etc." and asks about the 100 Soviet trucks promised to the United Nations but never delivered. UN Doc. S/4503, Sept. 11, 1960, pp. 154–55. Catherine Hoskyns reports the Russians put 16 Ilyushin transport planes at Lumumba's disposal and gave him an additional one for his own use. Hoskyns, *Congo since Independence*, p. 190. Colin Legum reports that "the Russians delivered 100 military trucks and 29 Ilyushin transport planes, together with 200 technicians." Legum, *Congo Disaster* (Baltimore: Penguin Books, 1961), p. 141.

end the secession of Katanga. The Soviet Union argued that UN resolutions "do not contain any provisions restricting in any way the right of the Congolese Government to request assistance directly from the Governments of other countries and to receive such assistance, just as they do not and cannot restrict the rights of states to render assistance to the Republic of the Congo."[13]

Hammarskjold did not accept the Soviet's claim and took the position that such aid interfered with the multilateral operation. A Tunisian-Ceylonese resolution introduced in the Security Council stipulated that "no assistance for military purposes be sent to the Congo except as part of the United Nations action."[14] The Soviets exercised their veto over this resolution and for the first time split with the Afro-Asian states. On September 20, 1960, a similar resolution was passed in the General Assembly by a vote of 70 to 0, with France, the Union of South Africa, and the communist countries abstaining. The resolution called "upon all States to refrain from the direct and indirect provision of arms or other materials of war and military personnel and other assistance for military purposes in the Congo during the temporary period of military assistance through the United Nations. . . ."[15] Many of the members of the United Nations favored ending the Katangese secession, which was the purpose of Soviet aid, but they did not support the right of a country to give aid to any of the parties to a civil war if the United Nations was also active in the war. The Soviets continued to defend their right to grant aid and launched a bitter attack on the United Nations, but they refrained from sending any more military assistance.

The Belgian government was active throughout in providing military assistance to the Leopoldville government. Belgian military advisers continued to serve in Leopoldville after the break in diplomatic relations, and more advisers and equipment were supplied at the request of the Kasavubu-Mobutu government. In December 1960, Belgium assisted the troops of this government in moving through Ruanda-Urundi to attack Bukavu, the capital of Kivu Province. Although a resolution condemning Belgium failed in the Security Council, Hammarskjold viewed their military support as a violation of the prohibition against direct unilateral military aid.[16]

Subversive activities are difficult to identify since governments do not claim that such activities are legal but simply deny them. The Central

[13] UN Doc. S/4503, Sept. 10, 1960, p. 156.
[14] UN Doc. S/4523, Sept. 16, 1960, p. 173.
[15] UN Doc. A/RES/1474 (E.S. IV), Sept. 20, 1960, p. 1; United Nations, General Assembly, *Official Records,* Fourth Emergency Special Session, 863rd mtg. (Sept. 19, 1960), p. 102.
[16] UN Doc. S/4606, Jan. 1, 1961, p. 6; and UN Doc. S/4606/Add. 1, Jan. 6, 1961, pp. 12–15.

Intelligence Agency (CIA) was active in the Congo in selecting and supporting Mobutu. The CIA also had a key part in establishing the Adoula government. Other countries were equally active in supporting factions and trying to manipulate events in the Congo, but the United States was particularly adept in insuring that the men it backed came to power.[17]

Relations with the Stanleyville Government

When the Kasavubu-Lumumba government dissolved, many of the leaders of Lumumba's Mouvement National Congolais (MNC) returned to Stanleyville. Gizenga established a government on December 12, 1960, following Lumumba's arrest, and declared Stanleyville the capital of the entire Congo. The primary form of support granted this regime by outside states was diplomatic recognition. After the death of Lumumba in February 1961, several countries recognized the Stanleyville government. These included the USSR, Communist China, Mongolia, Albania, Poland, Bulgaria, Hungary, Czechoslovakia, Rumania, East Germany, Yugoslavia, Cuba, Indonesia, Iraq, the UAR, Guinea, Mali, Morocco, Ghana, and the Algerian Provisional Government.[18] Many of these countries had already supported the Lumumba delegation to the United Nations in the debate over the seating of the Congolese representative. When Lumumba was arrested, these states effectively demonstrated their support for him and his regime by withdrawing their troops from the UN operation. Over six thousand soldiers left the Congo at the beginning of 1961, when Morocco, Guinea, the UAR, Mali, Sudan, and Indonesia recalled their troops.[19]

Although the communist states and the militant African countries recognized the Gizenga regime, they granted it very little economic and military support. Pierre Mulele established an office in Cairo to represent this government and coordinate aid from outside countries. The UAR sent technicians and set up a radio station in Stanleyville.[20] The communist countries supplied financial assistance with which Gizenga paid his troops.[21] For a time, small arms and other military equipment reached Stanleyville through the UAR. But in February 1961, the Sudan

---

[17] "How C.I.A. Put 'Instant Air Force' into Congo," *New York Times*, April 26, 1966, pp. 1, 30. This article discusses the extensive involvement of the CIA in the Congo situation.

[18] Centre de Recherche et d'Information Socio-Politique, *Congo: 1961*, ed. Benoit Verhaegen (Brussels: Les Dossiers du CRISP, n.d.), pp. 183–86 (hereinafter cited as CRISP, *Congo: 1961, Congo: 1960*, and so on).

[19] For a chart showing the terms of service of contingents with ONUC, see Lefever, *Uncertain Mandate*, p. 228.

[20] Hoskyns, *Congo since Independence*, p. 292.

[21] Carl von Horn, *Soldiering for Peace* (New York: David McKay Co., 1967), p. 228.

announced that it would not permit transit across its territory by air or land unless authorized by the secretary-general.[22] This move effectively denied outside states access to Stanleyville and confined their assistance to diplomatic recognition and extensive propaganda at the United Nations.

Relations with Katanga

The role of outside countries was most extensive in the secession of Katanga. In declaring Katanga independent, Tshombe called upon all states to recognize its right of self-determination. No state responded, however, at any time. Belgium refused to grant such recognition and sent telegrams to other states urging them to do likewise.[23] The Katangese officials continued to press for diplomatic recognition, since this would have given the province legal stature as a state.[24] They based their claim to independence on the right of self-determination, but even this right was not accepted by other states. Their case was weakened by several facts: Katangese leaders had previously accepted a unified state; large areas of Katanga were controlled by the *Balubakat*, not by the Elisabethville government; and Katanga was dependent on extensive outside support. In previous cases, the right of self-determination had been recognized only for areas coinciding with former colonial boundaries and not for parts of these areas, especially if foreign assistance was involved.[25]

While no state granted diplomatic recognition, several states, including former colonial powers, South Africa, Rhodesia, and former French colonies, viewed Tshombe's government as the one Congolese authority in effective control of its territory. These friendly countries assisted the province by keeping communication routes open, protecting its borders, serving as places of refuge, and permitting the recruiting of mercenaries. Katanga launched a major campaign for support abroad by establishing offices in New York, Brussels, Paris, and several African countries. The propaganda effort in the United States was headed by Michel Struelens, a Belgian public relations man, who organized "The American Committee for Aid to Katanga Freedom Fighters," took advertisements in eighteen important American newspapers, and organized a mass meeting

[22] Hoskyns, *Congo since Independence*, p. 328.

[23] Text of the message from minister of foreign affairs Pierre Wigny to other states is found in CRISP, *Congo: 1960*, 2:721.

[24] Young reports that "Katanga emissaries offered to pay Costa Rica $2,500,000 for diplomatic recognition." Crawford Young, "The Politics of Separatism: Katanga, 1960–63," in *Politics in Africa: 7 Cases*, ed. Gwendolen Margaret Carter (New York: Harcourt, Brace & World, 1966), pp. 167–68.

[25] René Lemarchand, "The Limits of Self-Determination: The Case of the Katanga Secession," *American Political Science Review* 56 (June 1962): 404–16.

at Madison Square Garden. Because of the vocal support of officials like Senator Thomas J. Dodd, the Katanga publicity program was able to bring pressure on the American government.[26] The effectiveness of this campaign suggests the importance of public relations work in winning support for unrecognized parties to internal wars.

Katanga faced no economic difficulties, as the government received revenue from taxes, dividends, and duties paid by the Union Minière.[27] The mining concern took the position that its taxes on revenue must be paid to the provincial government as the de facto legal authority. Since the company provided Tshombe with 80 percent of the $100 million in revenue he received during the first year of independence, its decision to pay the money to Katanga rather than to the Leopoldville government was extremely important in helping the province maintain independence. The Belgian government also assisted the Elisabethville regime by urging Belgians to stay at their jobs, providing Belgian advisers for political officials, and establishing a Belgian technical mission in Katanga immediately after it declared independence.

Belgium extended extremely important military assistance to Katanga. When the Belgian paratropers went into Katanga, they went far beyond the protection of their own nationals by occupying key posts in the province, disarming and expelling troops unfriendly to Tshombe, retraining the gendarmerie, providing military leadership, and generally maintaining order in the province. When the Belgian regulars withdrew from the Congo, they left men and equipment for the Tshombe troops. It was estimated that these materials and personnel included 25 airplanes, 100 tons of arms and munitions, 89 officers from the *Force publique*, 326 Belgian junior officers and soldiers, and 70 agents of the Belgian gendarmerie.[28] After withdrawal, the Belgians continued to supply arms to Elisabethville, flying in several tons of weapons in September 1960.[29] Belgian assistance permitted Katanga to form an effective military force, which maintained internal order and could defend itself against external challenges.

Mercenaries were an important part of Katanga's fighting units and

[26] Roger Hilsman reveals the pressures within the government resulting from Struelens' efforts. Hilsman, *To Move a Nation: The Politics of Foreign Policy in the Administration of John F. Kennedy* (New York: Dell Publishing Co., 1967), pp. 252–62.

[27] Jules Gérard-Libois reports that contributions from Union Minière to the Katanga treasury were "2,617 million Belgian francs in 1960; 2,096 million in 1961; and 1,485 million in 1962 (declaration by Henry Fortemps of the UMHK, July 24, 1963)." Gérard-Libois, *Katanga Secession*, trans. by Rebecca Young (Madison: University of Wisconsin Press, 1966), p. 206 (n.).

[28] Crawford Young, *Politics in the Congo: Decolonization and Independence* (Princeton: Princeton University Press, 1965), p. 452.

[29] UN Doc. S/4482/Add. 2, Sept. 10, 1960, p. 140.

proved a source of continual international contention. Tshombe recruited five hundred white mercenaries in South Africa and European countries to bolster his fighting force. The United Nations attempted to remove these foreign fighters, and a Security Council resolution of February 21, 1961, urged "that measures be taken for the immediate withdrawal and evacuation from the Congo of all Belgian and other foreign military and paramilitary personnel and political advisers not under the United Nations Command, and mercenaries."[30] A subsequent resolution went even further in authorizing for this purpose "the use of a requisite measure of force, if necessary."[31] ONUC repatriated 273 non-Congolese personnel in August 1961 in "Operation Rumpunch," but later efforts were less successful, and in November 1961, 237 such persons remained in Katanga.[32]

Control of foreigners who were supporting the Katangese government proved extremely difficult. The Security Council called for their removal, but efforts by ONUC to remove them resulted in fierce fighting between the UN force and the gendarmerie. Tshombe was not willing to end their services voluntarily since his power was largely dependent on them. Immediately after the passing of the February 21, 1961, resolution, Belgium took the position that it had no control over its citizens in the Congo or other foreigners. Later, however, both Belgium and France offered to withdraw the passports of citizens continuing to serve in Katanga.[33] Thus, the United Nations was not able to remove all mercenaries from the civil war, but it did restrict their participation by bringing pressure on Tshombe and the countries from which the mercenaries held citizenship.

Postwar Assistance

With the ending of Katangese secession, the pattern of external involvement shifted drastically. The unification of the country marked the end of the Postindependence War, and the United Nations took the position that its mandate had been fulfilled. Any further rebel activity was considered strictly an internal matter in which ONUC should not be involved. As the UN operation was ending in 1963, Adoula concluded a series of pacts for bilateral military assistance with Western states. The United States had proposed in the Greene Plan that aid in retraining and reorganizing the ANC be coordinated by the United Nations, but U Thant rejected this proposal when the militant Afro-Asian bloc ob-

[30] UN Doc. S/4741, Feb. 21, 1961, p. 147.
[31] UN Doc. S/5002, Nov. 24, 1961, p. 149.
[32] *Yearbook of the United Nations, 1961* (New York, 1963), pp. 62–64.
[33] Lefever, *Uncertain Mandate*, pp. 119, 143.

jected. Adoula then signed agreements with Belgium, Canada, Italy, Israel, Nigeria, Norway, and the United States.

When the Congolese government was challenged in 1964 by rebel activity throughout large areas of the country, military aid increased sharply. Belgium sent 75 advisers to the Congo, and about 300 Congolese went to Europe for training.[34] During the fiscal year 1964 the United States provided $6.6 million of military aid including vehicles, aircraft, communications material, a 100-man training mission, and the schooling of twelve Congolese officers in the United States.[35] The United States also supplied Tshombe with an air force consisting of 6 T-28 fighters, 4 C-130 transports, and 5 B-26 bombers. CIA agents flew combat missions in June 1964 until the Department of State learned of it, at which time they were replaced by Cuban refugees.[36]

During the fighting in 1964 the rebels received support from the communist and militant African states. The Chinese were particularly active in training Africans in guerrilla techniques and supplying money to leaders. Weapons made in the Soviet Union and eastern Europe, which reached the rebels from the UAR and Algeria, constituted an important part of their arsenal (the Sudan was then permitting overflights).[37]

A pattern of bilateral assistance quickly emerged after the withdrawal of ONUC. The struggle in 1964 demonstrated that the UN operation had been mainly a holding action, since once the multilateral force was withdrawn, the role of foreign countries expanded tremendously. The UN operation did freeze the situation in 1960, however, when cold war tensions were highest and the Congo situation so fluid that explosive interventions were likely.

Norms on Foreign Assistance

Permissible foreign assistance in the Congo was determined by the type of aid and the presence of the United Nations rather than by the recipient's position as incumbent or insurgent. Once the United Nations undertook the operation to maintain peace and security, foreign coun-

---

[34] *Ibid.*, p. 70.

[35] Ernest W. Lefever, "The U.N. as a Foreign Policy Instrument: The Congo Crisis," in *Foreign Policy in the Sixties: The Issues and the Instruments*, ed. Roger Hilsman and Robert C. Good (Baltimore: Johns Hopkins Press, 1965), p. 147; and Lefever, *Uncertain Mandate*, pp. 88–89.

[36] "How the C.I.A. Put 'Instant Air Force' into Congo," pp. 1, 30.

[37] For discussions of the Russian and Chinese support for the rebels, see William Attwood, *The Reds and the Blacks: A Personal Adventure* (New York: Harper & Row, 1967), p. 204; Brian Crozier, *The Struggle for the Third World: A Background Book* (Chester Springs, Pa.: Dufour Editions, 1966), pp. 57–80; and John K. Cooley, *East Wind over Africa: Red China's African Offensive* (New York: Walker and Co., 1965), pp. 106–22.

tries were precluded from granting military assistance on a unilateral basis. The Security Council left no doubt that Belgian paratroopers were to be withdrawn and Belgian military aid terminated. Likewise Soviet provision of equipment for Lumumba was condemned. Many countries claimed the right to grant assistance at the request of a government, as the Soviets were doing, but the presence of a multilateral force altered the situation, making unilateral action unacceptable. The General Assembly resolution of September was a rebuke to the Russians and specifically prohibited the granting of direct or indirect military assistance while ONUC was in the Congo. Likewise, Belgian assistance to Kasavubu in attacking Bukavu was regarded as a violation. These incidents demonstrate the development of a norm that a UN multilateral operation preempts the right of any foreign country to grant military assistance on a unilateral basis.

The United Nations urged that economic and technical assistance be channeled through the UN Civilian Operation, but the organization was not able to regulate the sending of all of these kinds of assistance to the Congo. Whereas military aid was clearly impermissible, the case in relation to economic assistance was not as definite. The United Nations provided a multilateral channel for such aid and urged states to act collectively, but the resolutions did not go so far as to prohibit all unilateral economic aid, although such action was not precluded for the future.[38]

No norms limiting diplomatic or ideological support emerged in the Congo. Although the United Nations did recognize the Kasavubu-Lumumba and Adoula governments, while withholding recognition from the Mobutu and Tshombe regimes, individual states remained free to grant recognition to whichever authority they favored. Likewise, each country could grant ideological support in the form of worldwide propaganda and vocal praise or condemnation at the United Nations to serve its own best interests.

The norm for excluding unilateral military assistance is basic to the success of a UN attempt to limit the effects of a civil war. The United Nations' effectiveness in dealing with the difficult problem of intervention and counterintervention rests on its ability to control the source of military assistance, thereby eliminating confrontations between major powers in internal conflicts. The limits on unilateral military aid are essential since the United Nations is not competing with states but rather attempting to monopolize military intervention in civil war to prevent a domestic conflict from expanding into an international conflict.

---

[38] A similar view of the norms in the Congo is presented in Alan Karabus, "United Nations Activities in the Congo," *Proceedings of the American Society of International Law, 1961* (Washington: ASIL, 1961), pp. 30–40.

IV. THE ROLE OF INTERNATIONAL INSTITUTIONS

As states become more interdependent, and the prospect of great power confrontations arising from internal wars increases, international institutions become relevant to wars within countries. The Congo civil war is a notable example of an internal struggle in which an international organization was an important actor. The actual operation of the UN force and the related legal questions are examined in this section. What was the relationship between regional and global organizations in the Congo civil war? What was the basis of the UN action, the principles governing the organization's participation? How did the UN force actually operate? Answers to these questions should permit an evaluation of the UN's potential and limits in civil wars.

Regional Actions

Since Congolese independence was an important event in the continent-wide revolt against colonialism, there was extremely high regional interest in the Congo case. Although they did not have a region-wide organization in 1960, the nations of the continent came together in a series of meetings for African leaders. Lumumba organized the first meeting to deal specifically with the Congo for leaders of thirteen independent African states.[1] These leaders met in August 1960 at Leopoldville, and Lumumba urged them to support his plan for a military attack on Katanga. The regional leaders, however, with only Guinea dissenting, endorsed the UN effort and opposed unilateral aid for Lumumba's campaign.

This unity was not permanent, and with the collapse of the Congolese central government, the African countries polarized (into groups later known as the "Casablanca powers" and the "Monrovia states") over the question whether to back Kasavubu or Lumumba. Both groups opposed the secession of Tshombe and supported the UN operation, but they differed over who should rule as the national government and how aggressive the UN force should be against Katanga. The militant African states met at Casablanca in January 1961, and it was only the vigorous opposition of Kwame Nkrumah that kept them from endorsing direct military aid for the Gizenga government.[2] These states, with the exception of Ghana, withdrew their troops from ONUC at this time to protest

[1] Independent states attending were Cameroun, Congo (Brazzaville), Ethiopia, Ghana, Guinea, Liberia, Mali, Morocco, the Somali Republic, Sudan, Togoland, Tunisia, and the UAR. Representatives were also present from nationalist movements in Algeria, Northern Rhodesia, Tanganyika, Ruanda-Urundi, and Angola.

[2] States represented at Casablanca included Morocco, the UAR, Guinea, Ghana, Mali, Libya, Ceylon, and the Algerian Provisional Government.

283

the UN's failure to prevent Lumumba's arrest and to endorse the Stanleyville government. The more moderate African states, including the former French colonies, which inclined toward sympathy for Tshombe, met in May 1961 at Monrovia.[3] This meeting passed resolutions supporting the central government and reaffirming "its faith in the United Nations as the only organisation which, in spite of past weaknesses and mistakes in its work, is best adapted to achieve a real solution of the Congo problem."[4]

Both groups of African states were able to unite in establishing the Organization of African Unity (OAU) at Addis Ababa in May 1963. Once this regional institution was set up, its members played a larger role in the conflict between Tshombe's government and the rebels which occurred after UN withdrawal in 1964. A Congo conciliation commission was established by the OAU to deal with the Congo question, and its leader, Jomo Kenyatta, viewed the commission's task as one of removing all outside assistance to both factions and then reconciling the parties. Tshombe felt the main purpose of the OAU should be to prevent other African countries from assisting the rebels, while his opponents felt it should concentrate on eliminating American support for Tshombe. The Leopoldville government and the United States took the position that the OAU could not interfere with a bilateral agreement between established governments and refused to deal with the OAU commission.[5] The OAU's efforts at negotiation were overtaken by the recapture of Stanleyville, and thus the war ended before any agreements had been reached through the commission.

In assessing the role of the regional group, it must be remembered that no continent-wide organization existed until after Katanga was retaken but that African officials had already demonstrated their intense concern through the series of meetings. While the resolutions of these meetings evidenced disunity because of the split over support for Kasavubu and Lumumba, the Africans were united in supporting a UN role and condemning the secession of Katanga. Even when the Casablanca

[3] States at Monrovia were Cameroun, Central African Republic, Chad, Congo (Brazzaville), Dahomey, Ethiopia, Gabon, Ivory Coast, Liberia, Libya, Malagasy Republic, Mauritania, Niger, Nigeria, Senegal, Sierra Leone, Somalia, Togo, Tunisia, and Upper Volta.

[4] "Resolution on Threats to Peace and Stability in Africa and the World," Monrovia Conference, May 8–12, 1961, reproduced in Colin Legum, *Pan-Africanism: A Short Political Guide* (rev. ed.; New York: Frederick A. Praeger, 1965), p. 217.

[5] For Tshombe's position, see Moise Tshombe, *My Fifteen Months in Government*, trans. Lewis Bernays (Plano, Tex.: University of Plano Press, 1967), pp. 53–54. The American attitude is described in William Attwood, *The Reds and the Blacks: A Personal Adventure* (New York: Harper & Row, 1967), pp. 199–203.

powers withdrew their troops from ONUC, they did not demand dis-solution of the operation but rather a return to its original purpose, which they interpreted to be support of the Gizenga government. With the establishment of the OAU and withdrawal of the UN force, regional efforts increased. Proposals were made for introducing an African force into the Congo and even for making the Congo a trusteeship of the OAU.[6] Regional attempts at limiting outside intervention and negotiat-ing among the parties were overtaken by Tshombe's military success, but the Security Council resolution in December 1964 called upon the OAU to continue its efforts.[7]

Regional action was restricted by the divisions among the African states and by their limited capabilities in terms of organizational struc-ture, financial resources, and military strength. Given their intense con-cern and yet meager resources, it was natural that the African states should want to operate through the United Nations. The unity of African representatives in that body on colonial questions gave them enough in-fluence to mobilize the resources of richer states for their own purposes. Thus, much of the regional effort in the Congo actually originated within the context of the global organization. By caucusing and presenting group positions on issues, the Africans had leverage on the superpowers, who wanted to avoid alienating the nonaligned states.[8] African repre-sentatives such as Mongi Slim of Tunisia, who was on the Security Council at the time, also played significant roles as compromisers in securing the passage of resolutions on the Congo. And the Afro-Asians were indispensable to the field operations of ONUC since they provided 82.4 percent of the manpower.[9] Afro-Asian representatives also consti-tuted the UN's conciliation commission and the secretary-general's ad-visory committee on the Congo.

Basis for UN Involvement

The UN action in the Congo was launched on the initiative of the secretary-general when he informed the Security Council of the request for military assistance from Kasavubu and Lumumba. Hammarskjold acted for the first time under article 99 of the UN Charter, which pro-vides that "the Secretary-General may bring to the attention of the Security Council any matter which in his opinion may threaten the main-

[6] Legum, *Pan-Africanism,* pp. 142–43; and Kwame Nkrumah, *Challenge of the Congo* (London: Nelson, 1967), p. 228.

[7] UN Doc. S/6129, Dec. 30, 1964, p. 329.

[8] For discussion of the African groups at the United Nations, see Thomas Hovet, Jr., *Africa in the United Nations* (Evanston, Ill.: Northwestern University Press, 1963).

[9] Ernest W. Lefever, *Uncertain Mandate: Politics of the U.N. Congo Operation* (Baltimore: Johns Hopkins Press, 1967), p. 159.

tenance of international peace and security." Following Hammarskjold's recommendation, Slim introduced a resolution calling for the withdrawal of Belgian troops and authorizing the secretary-general to provide military assistance to the Congolese government. Debate in the council centered on the issue of withdrawal, with the Soviet Union identifying Belgium as the aggressor and demanding the immediate and unconditional removal of troops, and the United States recommending the coordination of the recall of Belgian troops and the deployment of UN forces. The superpowers both supported the resolution, and Slim's proposal was adopted with eight votes in its favor and abstentions by the United Kingdom, France, and Nationalist China.

This original resolution made no reference to the Charter section under which the United Nations was acting. Subsequent discussion of the legal basis for the action has concluded that it was not an enforcement action against a state under article 41 or 42 but rather a "provisional measure" under article 40. In December 1960, Hammarskjold pointed out that "the Council did not invoke Articles 41 and 42 of Chapter VII, which provide for enforcement measures and which would override the domestic jurisdiction limitation of Article 2(7). . . . The resolutions may be considered as implicitly taken under Article 40 and, in that sense, as based on an implicit finding under Article 39. . . ."[10] Likewise, Oscar Schachter, director of the UN general legal division, suggested that "an analysis of the language used in the resolutions and of relevant statements in the Council indicate that Article 40 could appropriately be considered as the applicable provision."[11] Article 40 states that "in order to prevent an aggravation of the situation," the Council may "call upon the parties concerned to comply with such provisional measures as it deems necessary or desirable."

The operation falls between a coercive international enforcement action under article 42 and a strictly contractual assistance arrangement with an independent government.[12] ONUC was not established as a means of taking sanctions against Belgium as an aggressor but rather as an effort to maintain law and order. Yet the use of article 99 and debate in the council indicate that the situation was considered a threat to international peace and security. Therefore, the legal basis of the action is

[10] United Nations, Security Council, *Official Records*, 15th yr., 920th mtg. (Dec. 13/14, 1960), pp. 18–19.

[11] E. M. Miller [Oscar Schachter], "Legal Aspects of United Nations Action in the Congo," *American Journal of International Law 55* (January 1961): 5.

[12] For presentation of this position, see Oscar Schachter, "Legal Issues at the United Nations," in *Annual Review of United Nations Affairs, 1960–1961*, ed. Richard N. Swift (New York: Oceana Publications by arrangement with New York University Press, 1960), pp. 142–48. See also John W. Halderman, "Legal Basis for United Nations Armed Forces," *American Journal of International Law 56* (October 1962): 971–96.

best regarded as article 40, which permits "provisional measures" for dealing with threats to international peace.[13]

Since ONUC was not an enforcement action, the suspension of the domestic jurisdiction limitation in article 2(7) was not operative. In fact article 40 specifically states that the UN action "shall be without prejudice to the rights, claims, or position of the parties concerned." By continually emphasizing that ONUC was not to intervene in internal politics, Hammarskjold demonstrated his belief that the domestic jurisdiction restraints on ONUC had not been removed by the Security Council resolutions.[14]

The question also arose whether or not the Security Council resolutions were binding on members, since an enforcement action was not involved. The council left no doubt that the provisions were binding by specifically referring to articles 25 and 40 in the resolution of August 9, 1960.[15] These articles state that members have agreed to "accept and carry out decisions of the Security Council" and to afford "mutual as-

---

[13] The author interprets the Security Council's actions as being taken under article 40 of chapter VII of the Charter. This is the position taken by Hammarskjold (UN, SCOR, 15th year, 920th mtg. [Dec. 13/14, 1960], pp. 18–19) and Schachter ("Legal Issues at the United Nations," p. 146), but there have been several alternative interpretations.

Halderman suggests that the action was taken under article I (1) ("Legal Basis for United Nations Armed Forces," pp. 972–74); D. W. Bowett relies on article 39 (*United Nations Forces: A Legal Study* [New York: Frederick A. Praeger, 1964], p. 178); G. I. A. D. Draper sees the action as taken under article 29 ("The Legal Limitations upon the Employment of Weapons by the United Nations Force in the Congo," *International and Comparative Law Quarterly* 12 [April 1963]: 392); and Finn Seyersted proposes that the Charter basis shifted from article 40 to article 42 with the passage of the Feb. 21, 1961 resolution authorizing the use of force (*United Nations Forces in the Law of Peace and War* [Leyden: A. W. Sijthoff, 1966], p. 140). Nathaniel L. Nathanson also suggests that the Charter basis may have shifted during the action. He notes that the secretary-general emphasized the mandatory nature of Security Council decisions under chapter VII early in the operation to reduce Belgian and Katangese resistance but later emphasized chapter VI to preclude coercion of Katanga ("Constitutional Crisis at the United Nations: The Price of Peace-Keeping, I," *University of Chicago Law Review* 32 [Summer 1965]: 657).

The International Court of Justice in its opinion of July 20, 1962, on "Certain Expenses of the United Nations" did not see the need for determining which articles of the Charter were applicable, but it did state that the resolution "was clearly adopted with a view to maintaining international peace and security," although it "did not involve 'preventive or enforcement measures' against any state under Chapter VII." "Certain Expenses of the United Nations" (article 17, paragraph 2 of the Charter), Advisory Opinion of 20 July 1962, *I.C.J. Reports 1962*, pp. 175, 177.

[14] The importance of noninvolvement in internal issues was made explicit in the resolution of Aug. 9, 1960, by stating that the Security Council reaffirms that "the United Nations Force in the Congo will not be a party to or in any way intervene in or be used to influence the outcome of any internal conflict, constitutional or otherwise." UN Doc. S/4426, Aug. 9, 1960, p. 92.

[15] UN Doc. S/4426, Aug. 9, 1960, pp. 91–92.

sistance in carrying out the measures decided upon by the Security Council."

Functions of ONUC

The original resolution of July 14, 1960, only called for the withdrawal of Belgian troops and authorized the secretary-general to provide military and technical assistance to the Congolese government. In response to the changing situation, however, five Security Council and five General Assembly resolutions later expanded and clarified the mandate. The preamble to the final Security Council resolution on the Congo summarized the general tasks of the UN force as follows:

1) "To maintain the territorial integrity and the political independence of the Republic of the Congo."[16] The original threat to international peace resulted from the Belgian use of troops, and the UN resolutions and actions were designed to secure withdrawal and to prevent intervention by other states. The principle of territorial integrity also committed the United Nations to supporting the country as a unit and opposing secessionist movements.

2) "To assist the Central Government of the Congo in the restoration and maintenance of law and order." A major part of the threat to international peace was the disorder within the Congo. ONUC was to assist in reestablishing law and order so that the incentive for outside intervention would decrease. The UN force met this responsibility by protecting citizens and property from unlawful acts, disarming law breakers, and retraining the ANC. Protection for Lumumba's residence and for those of all other political leaders who requested it was an example of ONUC's policing action. One extremely difficult question that arose was whether ONUC should disarm the ANC, which had been involved in the mutiny. Major-General H. T. Alexander, the chief of staff with the troops from Ghana, made a strong case for taking the arms, but Undersecretary Ralph Bunche, who was acting officer in charge in Leopoldville, took the position that the United Nations had no authority to disarm the military of a government that the organization was assisting.[17] The ANC was never disarmed, an act which undoubtedly would have contributed to law and order.

3) "To prevent the occurrence of civil war in the Congo." Following the death of Lumumba, the council adopted a resolution which provided for "the use of force, if necessary, in the last resort," to prevent civil

[16] UN Doc. S/5002, Nov. 24, 1961, p. 148. For discussion of these functions, see Bowett, *United Nations Forces*, pp. 186–96; or R. Simmonds, *Legal Problems Arising from the United Nations Military Operations in the Congo* (Hague: Martinus Nijhoff, 1968), pp. 79–95.

[17] Alexander's report is found in UN Doc. S/4445/Annex II, August 19, 1960, pp. 101–2, and Bunche's reply in UN Doc. S/4451, Aug 21, 1960, pp. 113–15.

war in the Congo.[18] While the original question had not been one of internal hostilities, by this time the relations among the Leopoldville, Stanleyville, and Elisabethville governments had deteriorated to such an extent that large-scale civil war seemed likely. Therefore, the resolution authorized ONUC to take all measures, including the use of force (which had never before been authorized for any purpose other than self-defense), to prevent civil war. This was a mandate, not to employ force to end the secession of Katanga, but rather to keep all of the parties from engaging in civil war.

4) "To secure the immediate withdrawal and evacuation from the Congo of all foreign military, paramilitary and advisory personnel not under the United Nations Command, and all mercenaries." As the UN operation continued, its attention focused on the foreign military personnel and mercenaries who were still taking part in the struggle. At the start, Security Council resolutions had concentrated on removal of Belgian troops, but later they emphasized the ejection of the other outsiders who were active in Katanga. In August 1961, ONUC undertook an operation in Katanga to remove the foreign nationals who were supporting the military effort there. This was done in accordance with the February 21, 1961, resolution and at the request of the reunited central government. The operation was initially partially successful, but renewed efforts resulted in fighting between ONUC and the gendarmerie in Katanga. Another Security Council resolution of November 24, 1961, strongly deprecated the secessionist activities of Katanga, and went even farther in authorizing "the use of a requisite measure of force, if necessary," for detaining and deporting these foreigners.[19] ONUC continued its efforts to remove the outside military people until the end of Katanga's secession.

5) "To render technical assistance." From the outset, the resolutions called upon ONUC to assist in the running of the country and the reestablishment of effective administration throughout its territory. The civilian part of the UN operation was extremely important in stabilizing and rebuilding the country.

The functions fulfilled by the UN force evolved in the course of the operation and in response to the changes in the Congo. While efforts to maintain territorial integrity and political independence were aimed at the removal of Belgian troops at the time of the original mutiny, UN functions also came to include the continuation of the territory under a single government. Likewise, the provision for preventing civil war was clearly not envisioned at the outset but rather developed when ONUC found itself in the midst of a variety of factions and the council called

18 UN Doc. S/4741, Feb. 21, 1961, p. 147.
19 UN Doc. S/5002, Nov. 24, 1961, p. 149.

upon it to see that these factions resolved their issues peacefully and not through civil war. Finally, the function of securing the withdrawal of foreign military personnel and mercenaries was not a problem in the beginning, but as Belgian troops were replaced by mercenaries in Katanga, the council called for their removal under the same rationale as that used to remove Belgian troops. The council at no point gave ONUC a specific mandate to end the secession of Katanga through the use of force, but by attempting to maintain territorial integrity, prevent civil war, and remove mercenaries, ONUC did in effect secure the end of secession. As the UN force's mandate was expanded to encompass these functions, which eventually led to the end of secession, it definitely had an increased impact on the internal events of the country, but the council never instructed ONUC to impose a specific solution in the Congo.

Principles Governing ONUC

In fulfilling these functions, ONUC followed general principles governing the operation of UN peacekeeping forces. These rules of operation had been set forth by Hammarskjold in his study of the United Nations Emergency Force (UNEF), which was established in the Middle East in 1958;[20] and when he proposed the Congo operation, the secretary-general suggested that the UNEF precedents would be followed. In the Congo, however, where the UN force was dispersed throughout a society racked by conflict, conditions proved to be quite different from the UNEF case where the United Nations had patrolled borders between Israel and the Arab states. Therefore, rules governing the force had to be reinterpreted for application in a different context, but both secretary-generals upheld them as the norms governing the operation and acted accordingly.[21]

1) *Nature of the force.* The Security Council resolution established ONUC as a subsidiary organ of the council under the command of the secretary-general; the selection and organization of the force was left to Hammarskjold. He chose national contingents to make up the force, and on the basis of the UNEF precedent, he excluded troops from any of the permanent members of the council. He did not rule out the use of African troops as interested parties but in fact based the force largely

[20] UN Doc. A/3943, Oct. 9, 1958, pp. 8–33.

[21] For more detailed discussion of these principles, see Bowett, *United Nations Forces*, pp. 196–224; Miller [Schachter], "Legal Aspects," pp. 9–20; Oscar Schachter, "The Relation of Law, Politics and Action in the United Nations," *Recueil des Cours, 1963: II*, 109 (Hague: Hague Academy of International Law, 1964): 200–32; Nathaniel L. Nathanson, "Constituional Crisis at the United Nations: The Price of Peace Keeping, II," *University of Chicago Law Review* 33 (Winter 1966): 249–313; and Simmonds, *Legal Problems*, pp. 96–133, 197–228.

on the contributions of African countries. The secretary-general rejected suggestions for an all-African force, maintaining that the operation must be more representative. Although national units were involved, the soldiers were strictly under international command and were not free to follow instructions from their national governments.

2) *Consent of host state.* ONUC entered the Congo with the consent of the Congolese government, and the United Nations and the host government signed agreements covering the rights and conditions of operation of the force.[22] Nevertheless, a question quickly arose as to the nature and degree of Congolese control over ONUC. Lumumba took the position that he had invited the United Nations into the country and that the United Nations should cooperate with him in ending the secession of Katanga. Hammarskjold, on the other hand, felt strongly that "the United Nations operation must be separate and distinct from activities by any national authorities" and must not be subject to the direction of the Congolese government.[23] ONUC therefore refused to enter forcibly into Katanga, support the attack on Katanga, remove UN officials, give up positions, or arrest Congolese—all of which were requested by the Congolese government.

Lumumba's split with Hammarskjold over these issues led him to request the withdrawal of ONUC, which raised the primary question of whether the operation was dependent on the continuing consent of the host country. The original resolution suggests that such on-going consent was necessary by stating that UN assistance was to be given until "the national security forces may be able, in the opinion of the Government, to meet fully their tasks," but subsequent resolutions and the basic agreement between the Republic of the Congo and the secretary-general emphasize the responsibility of the Security Council for terminating the operation.[24] Schachter explains that

since members of the Council considered that the situation in the Congo (particularly the breakdown of law and order) involved a threat to international peace and security, and since the Council adopted measures of a mandatory character pursuant to Chapter VII of the Charter, the territorial government could not by unilateral action decide that the threat was over or that measures taken by the Council should be terminated.[25]

[22] The basic agreement between the Republic of the Congo and the United Nations is UN Doc. S/4389/Add. 5, July 29, 1960, pp. 27–28, and the status of forces agreement, which was considered retroactive to the arrival of the troops, is UN Doc. A/4986, Nov. 27, 1961, pp. 1–14.

[23] UN Doc. S/4389, July 18, 1960, p. 19.

[24] UN Doc. S/4387, July 14, 1960, p. 16; UN Doc. S/4389/Add. 5, July 29, 1960, pp. 27–28.

[25] Miller [Schachter], "Legal Aspects," p. 15.

3) *Freedom of movement.* The right to freedom of movement within the entire area for the UN force was established as UNEF precedent and in the basic agreement with the Congolese government. In order to fulfill its functions, the organization had to have this right, but it was quickly challenged in relation to entry into Katanga. To insure freedom of movement, ONUC took control of airports and other means of transportation and communication.

4) *Force only in self-defense.* Hammarskjold made it clear in his first report on the operation in the Congo that ONUC was to use armed force only in self-defense and that the initiation of force was prohibited.[26] Even though later resolutions provided for the use of force in preventing civil war and in expelling foreign personnel, the United Nations never claimed the authorization to initiate armed conflict.[27] Rather, it maintained that it could only defend positions already held. The United Nations was not free to assume any position it wished but could only defend positions taken in pursuit of its mandate.[28] However, ONUC retained considerable latitude in selecting and defending positions. The questions relating to the use of force were most prominent in the fighting between ONUC and the Katanga gendarmerie. The United Nations acted only after being attacked and then only to insure its freedom of movement. While this use of armed force was, strictly speaking, self-defense, the action had the effect of ending the secession of Katanga.

5) *Noninvolvement in internal questions.* The secretary-general insisted from the beginning that ONUC must remain impartial in relation to the outcome of the internal struggle. The resolution of August 9, 1960, specifically stated that the force "will not be a party to or in any way intervene in or be used to influence the outcome of any internal conflict."[29] This principle was designed to protect domestic jurisdiction and to maintain support for the operation. The United Nations had not undertaken to impose a political solution but rather to control a threat to international peace. Its nonintervention stance was quickly challenged first by the desire of Lumumba to end Katanga's secession and then by the constitutional crisis. The United Nations said it would not assist in ending the secession or recognize any faction as the government of the whole country. Following the establishment of the Adoula government, however, the Security Council denounced the province's independence, and U Thant actively supported the unification of the country. The extensive UN action inevitably affected the outcome of the Congo issues in spite of efforts to remain noninvolved in internal matters.

[26] UN Doc. S/4389, July 18, 1960, pp. 19–20.
[27] UN Doc. S/4741, Feb. 21, 1961, p. 147; and UN Doc. S/5002, Nov. 24, 1961, pp. 148–50.
[28] Schachter, "The Relation of Law, Politics, and Action," pp. 225–28.
[29] UN Doc. S/4426, Aug. 9, 1960, p. 92.

UN Mediation and Assistance Operations

Discussion of ONUC has focused on its peacekeeping efforts to maintain law and order, prevent civil war, and remove foreign military personnel. This aspect of the operation has raised the most legal questions and inspired more political debate, but there were also other important attempts in the area of reconciliation and state-building. These operations were just as necessary in the civil war context as the presence of a military force.

The peacemaking effort was aimed first at reestablishing a central government and later at reuniting the central government and Katanga. After the constitutional crisis, a UN conciliation commission was established by the secretary-general's advisory committee on the Congo. The commission, which included representatives of all African states and the four Asian nations that were supplying troops, was directed to prepare a study of the means of reconstituting a parliamentary government for the entire Congo.[30] The conciliation commission visited the Congo in January and February of 1961 and then issued a report calling for efforts to expand parliamentary support for the Ileo government in Leopoldville.[31] Although the death of Lumumba and the February 21, 1961, resolution authorizing ONUC to use force to prevent civil war, overshadowed the report, UN officials in the Congo continued to work for reconciliation along these lines. When the Lovanium parliament convened, the United Nations helped to ensure the safety of participants, and officials of the organization facilitated negotiations among the political leaders who were present.

Representatives of the United Nations in the Congo were also active in attempting to negotiate a settlement between Adoula and Tshombe for reintegrating Katanga into the Congo. Following the fighting in Katanga in December 1961, Tshombe and Adoula met at the UN military base at Kitona with Ralph Bunche as the representative of the secretary-general. Although an agreement was reached, little progress was made toward implementation and the secession continued. Therefore, U Thant proposed his plan for national reconciliation on August 20, 1962, as a basis for reunification. Throughout the crisis, the United Nations was active in efforts to resolve the issues through negotiation.

The UN civilian operation provided a major portion of the finances, personnel, and supplies necessary to keep the Congolese state operat-

[30] The instructions given to the conciliation commission are found in UN Doc. A/4592, Nov. 24, 1960, pp. 1–2.

[31] The final report of the conciliation commission is UN Doc. A/4711, March 20, 1961, pp. 1–99.

ing.[32] When the civil war began and the Belgian technicians fled, the organization was called upon to provide emergency relief services, to aid in administering the country, and to educate the Congolese to fulfill these tasks. By July 1963, the civilian operation had recruited 1,149 full-time specialists from 47 countries to meet the needs of the Congo.[33] This multilateral effort was organized with the support of the special agencies and closely coordinated with the political and military activities of the United Nations in the Congo. Financing for the program came at first through the *Ad Hoc* Account for the United Nations Operation in the Congo, which was part of the regular assessments, but was later switched to the United Nations Fund for the Congo. Between September 1960 and the beginning of 1963, members donated almost $40 million to this fund.[34] The prior consent of the Congolese government was necessary for the civilian operations, and this requirement sometimes hindered their effectiveness. The massive action in the Congo was a burden on the resources and personnel of the United Nations, but such efforts to build a state through technical assistance may, in the long run, prove to be its most important role in a civil war.

Role of the United Nations

Given the experience of the United Nations in the Congo, is it possible to say whether the involvement of international organizations in civil wars is an adequate means of controlling their effects on the international system? The roles played by the United Nations and the norms governing its operation in the Congo have been discussed, and an evaluation of the overall results must be made. The problems and difficulties of ONUC must be taken into account in determining the future usefulness of international participation in internal wars.

The first difficulty is the very involvement of the United Nations. Domestic jurisdiction and state sovereignty normally shield internal strife from international scrutiny. States are hesitant to sanction international intervention for fear of establishing precedents for future actions within their own territories. In addition, by the time an internal war is clearly an international threat, outside countries are frequently so committed to factions in the struggle that international action is not feasible. In the Congo case, the actions of the Belgian paratroopers produced an early

[32] Further discussions of the technical assistance operations may be found in Harold Karen Jacobson, "ONUC's Civilian Operations: State-Preserving and State-Building," *World Politics* 17 (October 1964): 75–107; Robert L. West, "The United Nations and the Congo Financial Crisis: Lessons of the First Year," *International Organization* 15 (Autumn 1961): 603–17; and Garry Fullerton, *UNESCO in the Congo* (Paris: UNESCO, 1964).

[33] "Civilian Assistance to the Congo," *United Nations Review* 10 (August-September 1963): 27.

[34] "Congo Aid Program," *United Nations Review* 10 (January 1963): 2.

definition of the struggle as a threat to peace before outside states had aligned themselves with internal factions. Such an early characterization is necessary for the involvement of the United Nations. Although international intervention may be justifiable in many civil wars on the grounds of a potential threat to international peace and security or on the grounds of protection of basic human rights, the methods for making such a determination remain undeveloped.[35]

The impossibility of total impartiality for a UN operation presents a second problem. There can be no agreement within the United Nations on any blanket political solution to be imposed in civil wars. ONUC attempted to remain entirely neutral in relation to internal questions, but this proved to be impossible. The very act of establishing and maintaining peace affected the outcome of the internal power struggle. The dilemma of the United Nations in civil war situations is that it is committed to respect domestic jurisdiction and not to affect internal questions and yet any action it takes is in fact an interference.

A very closely related problem arising from UN involvement in civil wars is the unintended prevention of any solution to the conflict. The heart of a civil war is a power struggle over the authority to govern the country, and an enforced stand-off may prevent resolution of the issue. This may necessitate an extended international operation since there is likely to be a new eruption of violence once the UN force leaves. While the threat to peace may justify UN action, the organization is not equipped to deal with the resolution of internal problems.

Any UN action must be undertaken with the consent and support of its members. States do have common interests which permit involvement of an international force. The difficulty of continuing support, however, throughout a prolonged civil war may prove formidable. As it becomes evident that a UN operation is working in the interests of some countries and against those of others, the support for the organization's action may disappear. This was indeed the case in the Congo when the Soviet Union turned against the operation and bitterly attacked the secretary-general. Fortunately, Hammarskjold had enough support and exercised enough initiative to continue the operation, but only at considerable cost to the United Nations. The necessity of maintaining support among diverse members throughout the course of a civil war is a severe restraint in initiating such operations.

A practical restraint on the UN's ability to act in internal conflicts is the organization's meager resources. Since the military force envisioned in the Charter has never materialized, the United Nations has no standing force prepared to go into new struggles. International armies must

---

[35] For discussion of a legal basis for UN involvement in what was basically an internal matter, see Simmonds, *Legal Problems*, pp. 58–78.

be put together on an ad hoc basis for each particular conflict. The availability of financial resources for such operations is also an important limitation. The refusal of members to pay for ONUC precipitated a budget and constitutional crisis within the organization.[36] Later peace-keeping operations have been dependent on the willingness of the involved countries to finance the operations, further circumscribing support for peacekeeping. The Congo incident heavily drained UN resources and emphasized the necessity of ensuring financial support before launching another peacekeeping operation.

In spite of these limitations, the United Nations and ONUC did effectively insulate the Congo's civil struggles from competitive intervention. First, the introduction and passage of several resolutions on the Congo encouraged states to agree upon and enumerate their expectations with regard to the situation, thus centralizing the formation of norms about permissible and impermissible behavior. Second, ONUC constituted an ever present observation corps for detection of outside involvement in the conflict. Finally, the operation provided a multilateral channel through which aid could be given for preventing violence, facilitating negotiations, and granting technical assistance. All of these functions contributed to preventing a confrontation between outside states in the Congo.

The United Nations offers no easy solution to international problems raised by civil wars. The organization is not an independent actor but rather an instrument which can give interested states leverage in confronting international problems. Furthermore, the United Nations is not equipped to solve any country's internal problems. Despite these limitations, however, the Congo case does suggest that the United Nations can be an important means of regulating foreign participation in civil wars.

V. END OF THE POSTINDEPENDENCE WAR

The Postindependence War ended with the reunification of Katanga into the Congo state on January 14, 1963. With the fall of Tshombe's regime, the foreign troops were removed from the country, the entire territory came under the central government in Leopoldville, and Adoula was recognized as the legitimate ruler. The issues touched off by the mutiny following independence were settled.

Prior to the defeat of Tshombe, relations between the central government and Katanga had been the subject of numerous negotiations among the Congolese leaders. Agreement was reached at Kitona in December

---

[36] The legal questions relating to the financing of ONUC have been taken up in Norman J. Padelford, "Financing Peacekeeping: Politics and Crisis," *International Organization* 19 (Summer 1965): 444–62; and John G. Stoessinger, *Financing the United Nations System* (Washington: Brookings Institution, 1964), pp. 100–90.

1961; but this agreement was never implemented. During 1962, pressures within the United Nations mounted for ending the operation, Belgium and the United States offered increased support to the central government in dealing with Tshombe, and emphasis was placed on ending the secession peacefully. On August 20, 1962, U Thant proposed a plan for national reconciliation.

Plan for National Reconciliation

U Thant's plan was proposed as a basis for bringing the two governments together. Among the steps anticipated by the plan were preparation of a federal constitution, division of basic revenue with half going to the central government and half to the Katanga government until definitive arrangements could be reached, currency unification, integration of the armies, foreign representation only by the central government, a general amnesty, and inclusion of all political groups in the central government.[1] Many of these ideas had been discussed previously, but the secretary-general presented them in a concrete, nonnegotiable form for acceptance or rejection by Adoula and Tshombe. Two of the most important provisions of the plan were the establishment of deadlines for making the terms operative and U Thant's call for sanctions to ensure that the plan was carried out: "I have in mind economic pressure upon the Katangese authorities of a kind that will bring home to them the realities of their situation and the fact that Katanga is not a sovereign State and is not recognized by any Government in the world as such . . . this could justifiably go to the extent of barring all trade and financial relations."[2]

By the introduction of this plan, U Thant took an active role in the settlement of the civil war. The secretary-general's threat of sanctions considerably increased pressure on the Tshombe government since it reflected increased support for a negotiated settlement in the Kennedy administration (which had originated the reconciliation plan) and in the Spaak government, which was willing to pledge Belgian cooperation in applying economic pressures on Katanga.[3] Both Congolese governments agreed to the proposal, but it was not implemented. On December 10, 1962, U Thant notified Elisabethville that it had not taken serious steps in this direction.[4] Adoula then requested foreign governments to em-

[1] The text of the plan for national reconciliation is published in UN Doc. S/5053/Add. 13/Annex I, Nov. 26, 1962, pp. 37–42. For a discussion of the plan, see Jules Gérard-Libois, *Katanga Secession*, trans. Rebecca Young (Madison: University of Wisconsin Press, 1966), pp. 253–71.

[2] UN Doc. S/5053/Add. 11, Aug. 20, 1962, pp. 12–18.

[3] For a discussion of the US role in the plan and the pressures within the US government, see Roger Hilsman, *To Move a Nation: The Politics of Foreign Policy in the Administration of John F. Kennedy* (New York: Dell Publishing Co., 1967), pp. 249–62.

[4] UN Doc. S/5053/Add. 14/Annex XII, Jan. 11, 1963, pp. 30–32.

bargo imports of Katangese copper and cobalt.[5] This was followed by U Thant's announcement that such economic sanctions were in accord with his plan and a request for Belgium to exert pressure on the Union Minière to cease payment of revenues to the provincial government.[6] However, before the legal questions involved in the authorization of economic sanctions under the UN Charter or the practical aspects involved in the limitation of the import of ores could be raised, the final fighting began between ONUC and the gendarmerie.

In this third round of fighting between the two forces, ONUC had the greater strength in terms of military personnel and equipment and also in terms of support among members of the United Nations. The Katangese refusal to make a beginning toward reintegration and its continued reliance on foreign mercenaries had weakened its position. Once the military operation began, ONUC again acted to guarantee its freedom of movement, this time throughout the entire province. Jadotville, a major mining center, was taken with little fighting, and Kolwezi, the last stronghold of Tshombe's government, was entered peacefully on January 21, 1963. Although this military operation began only after ONUC had come under fire and was justified as self-defense and as necessary for the establishment of freedom of movement, the UN force pursued the gendarmerie until it held the important centers throughout the province. With the United Nations in control of Katanga, the mercenaries fled to Angola and Tshombe announced the end of secession.

With the end of the civil war, the Congo still faced the tasks of unifying the country, producing a viable governmental structure, and modernizing the society, as evidenced by the subsequent economic problems, rebel activities, and military coup. However, the threat to international peace and security caused by the presence of foreign troops had been removed and the withdrawal of UN troops could begin. The last member of ONUC did not leave the Congo until June 30, 1964, but the force's activities during the last year were restricted to assisting in maintaining law and order and in training the Armée Nationale Congolaise (ANC) to take over. ONUC did not stay on to deal with rebel activities in 1964, since there were financial and political pressures within the United Nations for the withdrawal of the force and strong feelings that ONUC could not, and probably should not, solve these Congolese problems. U Thant observed that the United Nations "cannot permanently protect the Congo, or any other country, from the internal tensions and disturbances created by its own organic growth toward unity and nationhood."[7] Although the problems of nation-building remained, Belgian

[5] UN Doc. S/5053/Add. 14/Annex XVI, Jan. 11, 1963, p. 39.

[6] UN Doc. S/5053/Add. 14/Annex XVII, Jan. 11, 1963, pp. 39–40; and UN Doc. S/5053/Add. 14/Annex XIII, Jan. 11, 1963, pp. 32–34.

[7] The report of the secretary-general on the withdrawal of the UN force in the Congo is contained in UN Doc. S/5784, June 29, 1964, p. 293.

troops had been removed, the secession of Katanga had ended, and a unified government had been established in Leopoldville.

VI. INTERNATIONAL LAW AND THE CONGO CIVIL WAR

Limited knowledge of the Postindependence War in the Congo might lead to the conclusion that the traditional rules of international law had had very little influence on the outcome. During the conflict, there was no discussion of whether the status of Katanga was one of belligerency or insurgency; all states simply refused it recognition and treated the Katangese officials as provincial officers. The terms incumbent and insurgent were not used in relation to the struggle, and references to de jure or de facto governments are difficult to find. The role of foreign countries was not discussed in terms of the duties of neutrals or the rights due incumbent authorities. Such terms have played an important part in other civil wars, and the lack of consideration in the Congo conflict of the status of participants and the duties of nonparticipants might be interpreted as an absence of such norms.

A more extensive understanding of the Congo situation and the legal issues involved, however, would suggest that international law did have great importance for the course of events. The legal questions were not raised in the traditional manner, but rather new expectations emerged as international norms for dealing with civil war situations. Traditional international law was designed to isolate conflicts through nonintervention. The shifts in the international system resulting from the cold war have reduced the likelihood of nonintervention.[1] Since the emergence of a stalemate between the superpowers, and the attempt of the UN Charter to outlaw international wars, intervention in internal wars has become important as a means of expanding spheres of influence. Yet the superpowers recognize that their intervention and counterintervention in civil war situations may escalate into an international war with its ever present threat of nuclear confrontation. Faced with the tremendous potential for increased influence in the Congo, but also with the threat of confrontation, the superpowers chose to involve the United Nations in an attempt to prevent gains by either bloc and to avoid unilateral participation. The incentives for intervention were so great that the traditional rules of nonintervention would not have been effective. An international buffer was introduced to insulate the civil war and to limit the disruptive effects on the international system. Different legal issues were raised by this international approach to civil wars.

[1] For a general discussion of the concept of nonintervention in various periods and the international law relating to it, see Richard A. Falk, *Legal Order in a Violent World* (Princeton: Princeton University Press, 1968), pp. 109–55.

Laws on Conduct of War

The need for the application of humanitarian principles to the conduct of war is as great, if not greater, in a civil war as in an international conflict. Inhumane treatment of prisoners, the massacre of civilians, and destruction of nonmilitary targets are found in all kinds of war. The Geneva Conventions of 1949 took note of this fact by including article 3 in all four conventions to extend the basic humanitarian principles to struggles of other than international character.

To suggest the need for application of such principles is not sufficient to ensure that they will be observed, and civil war situations present a number of special difficulties. The principle of domestic jurisdiction makes other actors hesitant to interfere. The boundary between what is civil war and subject to the Geneva Conventions and what is not and governed only by the domestic authorities is difficult to determine. The fighting itself is much less regularized because of untrained fighters, indefinite command of the forces, and guerrilla warfare.

In the Congo hostilities, the International Committee of the Red Cross attempted to ensure the observance of rules of warfare by spreading information, visiting prisoners, and providing assistance to wounded fighters. All three of the participants voiced their commitment to the principles of the Geneva Conventions; yet some violations did occur. The question of the applicability of the Geneva Conventions to an international force was raised; and even though the United Nations had never signed these conventions, the secretary-general made it clear that the organization was prepared to respect them. While such a declaration from the United Nations on the principles binding it in such action might be helpful in clarifying and updating the laws of war, the important issue was not who had or had not signed a particular convention but rather who was following humanitarian principles in military operations. Evidence concerning UN military operations indicated not only that they were conducted in accord with humanitarian principles but also that there was an emphasis on limiting the use of force itself. Of course, the United Nations is especially sensitive to the importance of observing such laws of warfare since its actions are open to criticism by member states. But since there is common interest in limiting the suffering of people caught up in a civil war situation, UN observance of the laws of war induces similar observance on the part of other participants.

Limiting Intervention

The question of the extent of intervention permitted in a civil war situation was answered in the Congo case by a resolution stating that, as long as the United Nations was giving military assistance, individual states must refrain from granting such aid. Rather than defining who could give aid to whom in what manner, the members of the United Nations took the position that the United Nations should have a monopoly on the granting of military aid. Most countries have accepted the view that there should be no interference in conflicts which are strictly domestic in nature, but they have carefully maintained their right to grant assistance to governments in combating foreign aggression. The Soviets justified their aid to the central government as a grant to the established regime to combat a rebellion which was inspired and supported by outside (Belgian) military forces. Other nations refused to recognize such a right while the United Nations was involved and condemned the Russian actions.[2] The Congo case established the precedent that unilateral military aid to either party in a civil war is prohibited while the United Nations is deploying an international force in the war.

The United Nations also called upon all states to refrain from providing unilateral economic assistance and set up the UN civilian operation as an international channel for economic, financial, and technical support. The United Nations did not, however, censure countries that provided such assistance on a bilateral basis. While the intention to restrict economic involvement of outside countries is clear, the UN efforts at enforcement did not go so far as in the case of military assistance. And in the case of unilateral diplomatic or ideological support, no attempt was made at regulation. The United Nations did grant and withhold recognition to the various governments set up in the Congo, but no effort was made to force these views on individual countries, leaving each free to pursue its national policies through diplomatic and ideological instruments.

Role of the United Nations

The relevance of international law in the Congo situation has been seen to be tied to the manner in which the UN force carried out its mandate. The one remaining question is whether the U.N. is capable in the future of fulfilling the role of insulating a civil struggle from the international system. The United Nations lacks its own base of power and authority and therefore must rely on the consent and support of its members for action. An important limit on the functioning of the body is the right of members to withdraw their support and resources from any international operation at any time. Another important limit is the radical division of its members on many issues, which prevents agreement on what solutions to internal wars should be.

[2] UN Doc. A/RES/1474 (E.S. IV), Sept. 20, 1960, p. 1.

Recognition of these weaknesses does not preclude the possibility of a similar type of action in the future but rather assures a realistic evaluation of the United Nations' capabilities. The United Nations did survive the Congo crisis, which involved the largest peacekeeping activity ever undertaken by the organization, and its action there prevented the projection of the cold war onto the African continent, forestalling a confrontation between the East and West that might have led to a nuclear war. United Nations members would again support a UN operation if any other course seemed to threaten world war.

The effects of civil wars upon the nations of the world may be controlled through a number of different approaches: strict nonintervention, action by a single state, action by a regional organization, or action by an international body. In the case of the Congo the international approach was used, and the instrument was an international force established by the United Nations. The characteristics of the present international system have altered so drastically that this approach may prove the only effective means of dealing with internal wars, making the Congo a model for the future.

Kathryn Boals

THE RELEVANCE OF INTERNATIONAL LAW TO THE INTERNAL WAR IN YEMEN

One purpose of this study is to describe, analyze, and evaluate the role played by international law in the internal war in Yemen. That is not, however, its only purpose. Rather, after first demonstrating that international law played almost no role in the Yemen conflict, the study goes on to assess critically the usefulness of international law both as a determinant of behavior and as an analytical perspective from which to view global politics. A concluding section then discusses how international law can be made relevant to internal war situations.

I. INTERNATIONAL LAW AS A METHOD FOR SHAPING THE BEHAVIOR OF ACTORS IN A CONFLICT

An evaluation of the efficacy of international law as a determinant of international actors' behavior naturally requires some set of desired functions against which the operation of international law can be checked and measured. While from the point of view of the parties to international disputes the major function of international law is to legitimize the course of action they have undertaken on other grounds, from the Olympian viewpoint of the international lawyer or political analyst concerned with the international system as a whole, the basic function of international law in dealing with conflict situations is to restrain the behavior of the parties to the conflict and also that of outsiders responding to the conflict. In addition to this restraint function, some writers, notably Richard A. Falk, have argued that international law can serve a communication function by providing a precise, unemotional legal language in which opposing claims may be stated, thereby reducing emotionalism, exaggerated claims, and overreactions.[1] Third, one might mention a conflict-resolution function in which established procedures provide a framework for seeking compromise and peaceful settlement of disputes.

The actual application of international law, however, occurs largely through the claims and counterclaims of the parties and the reactions to

Written under the auspices of the Center of International Studies, Princeton University.
[1] Richard A. Falk, "New Approaches to the Study of International Law," *American Journal of International Law* 61 (April 1967): 481.

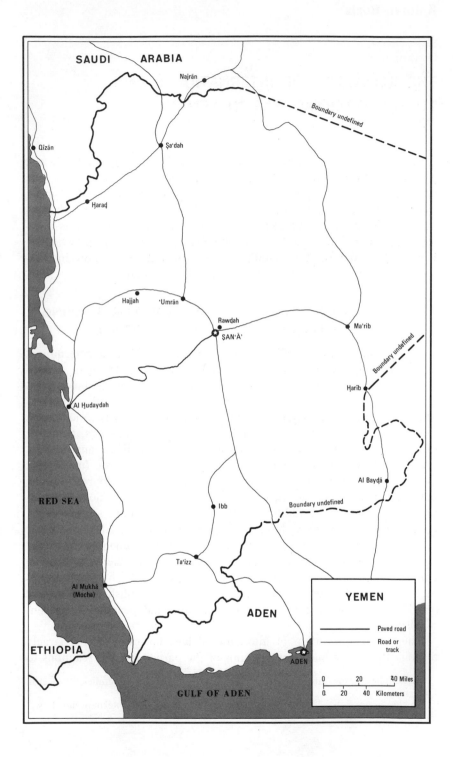

SAUDI ARABIA

Najrān

Boundary undefined

Qīzān

Ṣaʻdah

Ḥaraḍ

Hajjah   ʻUmrān

Rawḍah   Maʼrib

ŞANʻĀ'

Boundary undefined

Ḥarīb

Al Ḥudaydah

Al Baydā

RED SEA

Ibb   Boundary undefined

Taʻizz

Al Mukhā
(Mocha)

ADEN

ETHIOPIA

ADEN

GULF OF ADEN

YEMEN

——————— Paved road

——————— Road or
track

0   20   40 Miles

0   20   40 Kilometers

them of other states and of international organizations, not through Olympian legal pronouncements. Consequently, we must begin our examination of the role of international law in the internal war in Yemen by considering the legal norms actually invoked by the participants in the Yemen conflict, the way in which those norms were used, and the extent to which their invocation influenced the course and conduct of the war.

Before doing so, however, it is perhaps worth pausing briefly to consider why international law deals with the problem of internal war at all, since internal war takes place largely within the territorial confines of a single state and is a struggle over the locus of political power and authority within that state. The major reason for international law's concern with the problem of internal war both in the past and in the present international system has been the need to define the rights and obligations of outside states vis-à-vis the parties to an internal war. This has taken the form of legal norms concerning, *inter alia*, the recognition of states and governments, legal characterization of the parties to an internal war (as either rebels, insurgents, or belligerents), intervention, and aggression. The primary purpose of all of these norms has been to restrict interference on the part of outside states. Particularly in the contemporary international system, the focus of international legal norms relating to internal war is on preventing or ending intervention by outside states or at least limiting the scope, duration, and methods of such intervention.

Consequently, the problem of the role of international law in internal war must be seen in the context of the larger problem of the role and effectiveness of international law with respect to intervention. This larger problem, in turn, has far-reaching consequences for the nature and structure of the international system as a whole. We shall thus be led—after describing and analyzing the role of international law in the internal war in Yemen—to expand our inquiry in order to account for the difficulties encountered by existing international law in coping with internal war.

The Role of International Law in the Internal War in Yemen

Since it is possible to talk about the role of international law in the internal war in Yemen without going into detail about the causes, course, and outcome of the struggle, only a brief outline will be presented at this point. Additional information will be provided in a later section in connection with a discussion of the relationship between modernization and intervention in the contemporary international system.

The internal war in Yemen began in September 1962, when a group of army officers carried out a palace coup against the ruling imam and proclaimed the Yemen Arab Republic in place of a kingdom. The ousted imam and his supporters immediately began organizing a counterrevolution, recruiting northern Yemeni tribesmen and requesting help from Saudi Arabia in the form of training bases, arms, money, and supplies. Meanwhile, the Republicans asked the United Arab Republic for technical and military assistance.

With Saudi Arabia helping the Royalists and the United Arab Republic aiding the Republicans, fighting between the two sides began in October 1962 and continued sporadically despite attempts by outside states, international organizations, and the parties themselves to reach a settlement. Although the United Arab Republic withdrew its forces from Yemen after the June 1967 war with Israel, the conflict within Yemen itself remained unresolved until 1969.

In discussing the role of international law in the internal war in Yemen we shall consider three major problem areas: the responses of outside states to the Yemen conflict, the conduct of that conflict, and the process of attempted conflict resolution. For each of these areas we will examine the legal norms invoked by the parties to the conflict, and also by other states and international organizations, and the extent to which these norms served the community-oriented functions of international law discussed above.

The role of international law in regulating the responses of outside states to the conflict. The norms of international law dealing with recognition of governments will remain of central importance in internal war situations as long as international law distinguishes between insurgents and incumbents in defining the acceptable limits within which foreign states may aid one or the other faction. Unless it can be unambiguously determined who the incumbents and the insurgents are, norms differentiating between the two will have no practical application. How, then, is the distinction between incumbents and insurgents made? To oversimplify a bit, the general presumption of traditional international law has been that a government remains the government until conclusively proved to have been supplanted. Recognition of a new government, therefore, rests on effective control and administration of the major part of a country's territory and also on general support by its people. If these conditions are not met, recognition is considered premature and an offense against the old government if that government succeeds in putting down the opposition forces. In the contemporary international system, however, recognition depends less on territorial control or popular support than on the preferences of outside states as to which side should prevail. The political character of recognition is clearly predominant in the case of Yemen.

The Yemeni Republicans were recognized as the legitimate government by the United Arab Republic and the Soviet Union on September 29, 1962, two days after the proclamation of the Yemen Arab Republic.[2] This recognition came at a time when the situation in Yemen was still unclear and reliable information on the extent of Republican territorial control and popular support was lacking.[3]

The "progressive" and republican governments in the Middle East also quickly recognized the Republicans. One exception was the republican government of Iraq, which hesitated until October 9, 1962, before recognizing the Yemeni Republicans, reportedly because it awaited information on the Republicans' position concerning Iraq's claim to Kuwait rather than because it was applying traditional legal criteria for recognition.[4]

Further evidence of the contemporary standards governing recognition is provided by the pattern of recognition in the Yemeni case: of the twenty-nine states that had recognized the Yemen Arab Republic by November 10, 1962, most were either Eastern bloc countries or radical Afro-Asian states.[5] United States recognition was eventually granted as a *quid pro quo* for Egyptian promises to withdraw and Republican promises to honor previous Yemeni international obligations.[6]

Nonetheless, principles of international law concerning popular support and effective territorial control were invoked both by Yemeni Republicans seeking recognition and by Royalists seeking to prevent recognition of the Republicans and also by states wishing for other reasons to delay Republican recognition. Thus, the Republicans sought recognition from the United States in October 1962 on the ground that they had secured popular support and control of territory, while the Royalists argued that the Republicans were only a small, unrepresentative group

[2] "Chronology," *Middle East Journal* 17 (Winter-Spring 1963): 141.

[3] In the days immediately following the coup, foreign newsmen were not permitted in Yemen, and contact was even broken between the Republican capital at San'a' and the sympathetic Aden Trade Union Congress in the neighboring Federation of South Arabia. (*Economist* [London], Oct. 6, 1962, p. 42.) In addition, there were few foreigners in Yemen at the time, and few states had legations there.

[4] *Economist*, Oct. 13, 1962, p. 130.

[5] Jane Smiley Hart, "Basic Chronology for a History of the Yemen," *Middle East Journal* 17 (Winter-Spring 1963): 150. One exception was West Germany, which recognized the Republicans on Oct. 23, 1962, the first major Western state to do so. (*Ibid.*)

[6] US recognition came on Dec. 19, 1962, the day after the Republicans declared "the firm policy of the Republic to honor its international obligations, including all treaties concluded by previous governments...." The UAR confirmed the statement and "signified its willingness to undertake a reciprocal expeditious disengagement and phased removal of its troops from Yemen...as external support ... of the Yemen royalists is terminated...." In announcing its recognition of the Yemen Arab Republic the United States welcomed both statements in the belief "that these declarations provide a basis for terminating the conflict over Yemen...." (Hart, "Basic Chronology," p. 151.) All the above quotations are from the US statement.

of army officers who had no popular support and who held only the three major cities.[7] The United States and the United Kingdom also initially invoked the traditional criteria of international law, largely in order to delay recognition. The United Kingdom did so because it feared that a republican government in Yemen would have undesirable repercussions on the British position in the Federation of South Arabia, while the United States sought to avoid offending the United Kingdom and Saudi Arabia and to use the granting of recognition as a bargaining counter. Thus, while the decisions by outside states to grant or withhold recognition were not made on the basis of traditional principles of international law, these principles were invoked by the parties and by outside states both to justify their own position and to convince others to adopt similar policies.

Similarly, the recommendation of the Credentials Committee of the United Nations General Assembly that the Republican delegation be seated as the representative of Yemen and the approval of that recommendation by the General Assembly hinged on factors other than the traditional legal criteria for recognition.[8] It is surely not irrelevant, for example, that the Assembly's decision was made on the day following US recognition of the Yemeni Republicans.

Once the political decision to seat the Republican delegation—and thus to recognize the Republicans as the legitimate government of Yemen in the eyes of the United Nations as an institution—had been made, however, the United Nations proceeded to draw legal consequences from it. Having recognized the Republicans, the United Nations tried in effect to pretend that the Royalists no longer existed. Thus, when Dr. Ralph Bunche was sent by the secretary-general on a mediation mission in connection with the Yemen internal war, he was instructed not to talk with the Yemeni Royalists but only with the Republicans, the Saudis, and the Egyptians. Consequently, the Saudis refused to talk with him, and his role as a mediator was totally undercut.[9] When an agreement on disengagement was finally worked out through US mediation, only the Republicans, the Saudis, and the Egyptians were parties to it. It was only at the very end of 1963 that the United Nations

---

[7] *New York Times*, Oct. 7, 1962; "Chronology," p. 141; United Nations, General Assembly, *Official Records*, 17th sess., 1201st mtg., Dec. 20, 1962, pars. 96–98, 109–11. Additional Republican arguments were that delay in recognition might jeopardize US interests in Yemen and that Yemen might have to turn to the Soviet bloc for aid if recognition were not granted.

[8] See UN Doc. A/5395, Report of the Credentials Committee, which contains the draft resolution proposed by Guinea and adopted by the Credentials Committee on Dec. 20, 1962, by six votes to zero, with three abstentions. The report was approved by GA Res. 1971 (XVIII), adopted on Dec. 20, 1962, by 73 votes to 4, with 23 abstentions.

[9] *New York Times*, March 8, 1968.

adapted its attitude to the actual circumstances in Yemen and began talking with the Royalists as well, even though it had long been apparent that Royalist actions would have an important influence on the implementation of any disengagement agreement between Saudi Arabia and the United Arab Republic.[10]

To summarize, while there was agreement on what the relevant legal criteria for recognition were, these criteria were used by states with respect to the Yemen internal war simply as slogans for legitimizing policies adopted for other reasons and not as objective standards for policy formulation. Since even the seating of the Yemeni Republican delegation by the General Assembly left individual states free to continue to recognize the Royalists as the legitimate government, the application of legal principles differentiating between incumbents and insurgents in internal war situations could not help to restrain intervention. Furthermore, the way in which the United Nations itself chose to interpret the consequences of its seating of the Yemeni Republicans severely limited the organization's usefulness. Thus, the way in which legal norms about recognition were invoked and applied in the Yemen case fostered neither restraint nor communication and, indeed, hindered rather than helped conflict resolution. The extent to which these norms might be useful as analytic concepts for the impartial observer will be discussed in a later section.

Because of the way in which the concepts of aggression and intervention were used by participants in the Yemen conflict, they will be considered together, although as legal concepts their meaning and connotations are quite different. While "aggression" has never been precisely defined in existing international law and is therefore commonly used to cover a multitude of factual situations, its basic form may be taken to be an armed attack by one state against another. "Intervention," on the other hand, usually refers to interference by one state in the internal affairs of another, whether by supporting one faction in an internal war or by subversion or by pressure on a government to shape its domestic policies in a particular direction.

Yet in general political usage, there is a tendency to use "aggression" rather than "intervention" in characterizing the actions of one's opponents in order to make their policies seem as reprehensible as possible. A further reason for doing this is to broaden the range of acceptable responses to their actions, since the measures which can legally be taken against aggression are more severe than those against intervention.

Both the United Arab Republic and Saudi Arabia initially justified their support of different Yemeni factions on the basis of the Jiddah Pact of 1956, a military assistance agreement concluded between Egypt,

[10] *New York Times*, Nov. 10, 1963.

Saudi Arabia, and Yemen pledging mutual aid in case of aggression against any of the parties.[11] Since that treaty was concerned with aggression rather than intervention, the United Arab Republic and Saudi Arabia sought to justify their actions under the former.[12] Thus, the United Arab Republic argued that its forces were in Yemen "with the sole purpose of enabling the Yemeni people to practice their inherent right of self-defence in a war launched against them from outside Yemeni territory by the enemies of the Revolution."[13] The UAR justified its air attacks on Saudi border settlements as "punishment to the aggressor" at his "base of aggression" and as part of the "legal right of self-defense," since they had taken place while "chasing remnants of an abortive invasion" launched on Yemen from Saudi Arabia.[14]

The Yemeni Republicans used similar arguments. For example, on October 11, 1962, one Republican spokesman was quoted as saying that Saudi Arabia was massing troops on the Saudi-Yemeni border and sending arms into Yemen, that the Republicans considered those actions "an attack on the Yemeni Republic," and that Yemen was, consequently, "at war with Saudi Arabia."[15] On the other side, the representative of the Kingdom of Yemen in the General Assembly debate over the rival delegations charged the United Arab Republic with "an act of aggression against the people of Yemen which was an act of war," since in the Royalist view the Republicans were "only a front for the expansionist moves of the United Arab Republic."[16]

Thus, on both sides there was an attempt to portray the conflict in terms of aggression by a foreign state against the people of Yemen, who loyally supported their legitimate (Republican or Royalist) government. In addition, however, both sides also used the term "intervention" to describe and denounce the actions of outside states. Both apparently used "intervention" to signify reprehensible and illegal interference by

[11] *Economist*, Oct. 20, 1962, p. 213. In a note sent on Oct. 5, 1962, to the Yemeni Republicans, President Gamal Abdul Nasser assured them that Egyptian troops and arms would be provided if Yemen were attacked and said that he considered the Jiddah Pact in full force. (*New York Times*, Oct. 7, 1962.)

[12] For the UAR and the Republicans, the Jiddah Pact of 1956 was superseded by the UAR-Yemeni Defense Pact of November 10, 1962, which stipulated that any armed aggression against either state or its forces would be considered aggression against both of them and in such a case each state was committed to aiding the other. (Hart, "Basic Chronology," p. 151.)

[13] GAOR, 17th sess., 1202d mtg., Dec. 20, 1962, par. 44. The UAR viewed the struggle as a defense of the Yemen Arab Republic's sovereignty and territorial integrity. (*Ibid.*, par. 45.)

[14] Hart, "Basic Chronology," p. 152; *New York Times*, Nov. 9, 1962.

[15] *New York Times*, Oct. 11, 1962.

[16] GAOR, 17th sess., 1201st mtg., Dec. 20, 1962, par. 98. Similar views have been expressed by others, including Stanko Guldescu, "Yemen: The War and the Haradh Conference," *Review of Politics* 28 (July 1966): 322–23.

one state in another's internal affairs. Saudi Arabia referred to the United Arab Republic as "the interventionist Government" and denied that it was itself engaged in intervening in Yemen "militarily or otherwise."[17] Later, in acknowledging its involvement in Yemen, Saudi Arabia argued that both customary law and international law required Saudi Arabia to aid the Yemeni imam "as the legal ruler" against "a military group revolting against him."[18] Similarly, the United Arab Republic denied that the presence of Egyptian troops in Yemen constituted intervention because they were there to defend Yemen against Saudi aggression and also because they were there at the request of the legitimate government.[19] Thus, both Saudi Arabia and the United Arab Republic invoked the traditional international law principle that aid to incumbents does not fall under the scope of international legal norms prohibiting intervention.

At other times, Saudi Arabia and the United Arab Republic employed an alternative argument about intervention: that their own actions, though possibly interventionary, could be justified on the principle that prior foreign intervention in support of one faction in an internal war legitimizes proportional counterintervention, in support of the other side.[20] Thus, Saudi Arabia argued that the United Arab Republic had intervened first by sending forces to Yemen and that "aid to the royalists in food, clothing and rifles in the face of Egyptian intervention by warships, planes and tanks" was thus justified to redress the balance.[21] In response, Egypt argued that the Saudi Arabian "pretext" for intervening "to the effect that other countries had interfered in Yemen" was invalid because such prior intervention had not occurred.[22] By implication, both accepted the principle of proportional counterintervention.

Again, as in the case of norms affecting recognition, both sides in the conflict invoked the same principles of international law concerning aggression and intervention to justify their actions, including self-defense against aggression, the legitimacy of aid to incumbents, and the acceptability of proportional counterintervention. Also again, however, each side applied these principles in diametrically opposed ways. Furthermore, it is clear that the concepts "aggression" and "intervention" were

[17] GAOR, 17th sess., 1201st mtg., Dec. 20, 1962, pars. 81–82, 197.

[18] Hart, "Basic Chronology," p. 152.

[19] United Nations, *Yearbook 1962,* p. 149.

[20] This principle is discussed in Richard A. Falk, "International Law and the United States Role in the Viet Nam War," *Yale Law Journal* 75 (1966): 1123; Manfred Halpern, "The Morality and Politics of Intervention," in James N. Rosenau (ed.), *International Aspects of Civil Strife* (Princeton: Princeton University Press, 1964), p. 269.

[21] Hart, "Basic Chronology," p. 152.

[22] GAOR, 17th sess., 1201st mtg., Dec. 20, 1962, pars. 81–82.

used as highly charged, emotional and political terms, not as precise legal concepts that might have fostered exact communication of claims and counterclaims. From the perspective of an impartial analyst, it seems clear that the vocabulary of aggression is inapplicable to the Yemen conflict, while that of intervention does apply, although somewhat problematically.

As for "aggression," as it was used in the Egyptian and Republican arguments, while it is true that the war was "launched . . . from outside Yemeni territory by the enemies of the Revolution," it is also the case that those enemies were Yemeni Royalists, not Saudis. As far as is known, the aid provided by Saudi Arabia to the Royalists was limited to arms, money, supplies, and asylum. While such aid to one faction in an internal war does constitute intervention, it is not aggression in the usual meaning of that term. Thus, the Republican argument that such actions were equivalent to "an attack on the Yemen Republic" does not seem solidly grounded.

Similarly, the Royalist and Saudi argument that the United Arab Republic committed "an act of aggression against the people of Yemen" because the Republicans were only puppets of Cairo is weak. The 1962 revolution was in fact part of a larger revolutionary process that had been going on in Yemen for over twenty years. Furthermore, the actual coup was planned and executed by Yemenis inside Yemen, and Yemenis in Cairo (and elsewhere) learned of the coup only afterward. Thus, there appears to be no basis for this argument about Egyptian aggression.

The vocabulary of intervention does appear applicable to Egyptian and Saudi participation in the Yemen internal war, since the conflict was essentially between two Yemeni factions, each of which received support from outside states. The impartial analyst still encounters difficulty in applying international legal norms concerning intervention to the Yemen conflict, however. For example the principle that aid to the incumbents is legitimate while aid to the insurgents is not is of little help because the Egyptians had recognized the Republicans as the legitimate government, while the Saudis continued to recognize the Royalists. In addition, given the speed of events after the September 1962 coup and the initial concern of both the United Arab Republic and Saudi Arabia to deny their involvement in Yemen, it is extremely difficult to apply the principle of counterintervention, since it is difficult to establish an exact chronology.[23] Furthermore, if proportionality of

[23] Thus, at a news conference in early October, a Yemeni Republican spokesman said that Egyptian "experts" were in Yemen but denied that the UAR was supplying arms to the Republicans. (*New York Times*, Oct. 8, 1962.) On Oct. 20, 1962, however, San'a' Radio announced that "new Egyptian troops" had arrived. ("Chronology," p. 142.) On Oct. 10, 1962, Mecca Radio denied reports of Saudi

response is included as a criterion of justifiable counterintervention, the matter becomes even more complex because of wide differences in types of aid provided to each faction and the vagueness of the concept of proportionality.

Before we go on to consider the distinction in international law between rebellion, insurgency, and belligerency, it is worth noting another point argued by Saudi Arabia against Egyptian intervention; Saudi Arabia denied that intervention in support of the Republicans could be justified on the ground that the Republicans would promote progress and development in Yemen, since the imam had himself instituted a policy of reforms.[24] This argument is interesting, since it implies that intervention would have been justified in the absence of such a reform policy. The fact that Saudi Arabia found it necessary or advisable to argue along these lines is evidence of the growing concern in the international community with the social goals and policies of both incumbents and insurgents in internal war situations. We shall consider the relevance of such criterion in a later section.

In traditional international law, the rights and obligations of states toward the parties in an internal war are determined by whether the nonincumbents are considered rebels, insurgents, or belligerents. The term "rebels" is supposed to be applied to a group that can be easily dealt with by police measures of the legitimate government; other states are free to aid the incumbents but must refrain from aiding the rebels. If the internal struggle attains wider scope, duration, and intensity, it is classified as either insurgency or belligerency. If belligerency, the appropriate legal principles are similar to those applicable to war between states; the two participants are placed on a footing of equality, and both may be aided by outside states. The category of insurgency is a residual category without clearly defined rights and obligations.[25]

The participants in the Yemen conflict did not attempt to make use of these traditional legal categories of internal war and, indeed, used

---

intervention in Yemen, and on Oct. 23, 1962, Crown Prince Faysal said that military aid to the Yemeni imam depended on a request from him, thereby implicitly suggesting that no such aid was yet being given. ("Chronology," pp. 132–33.) In addition, in a speech on Jan. 25, 1963, Crown Prince Faysal stated that Saudi Arabia had originally refrained from intervening in Yemen. (Hart, "Basic Chronology," p. 152.) The first open declaration from Yemen of participation by Egyptian troops in the fighting was on Oct. 29, 1962, when San'a radio announced that a "large infiltration force" from Beihan had been repulsed by Yemeni troops "reinforced by UAR troops." (*New York Times*, Oct. 30, 1962.)

[24] GAOR, 17th sess., 1202d mtg., Dec. 20, 1962, pars. 81–82.

[25] For an exposition and critique of traditional international law in the area of internal war, see Richard A. Falk, "Janus Tormented: The International Law of Internal War," in Rosenau (ed.), *International Aspects of Civil Strife*, pp. 185–248.

"rebels" and "insurgents" interchangeably. Thus, one Saudi spokesman used in the same sentence the words "rebellion" in Yemen and "the Yemeni insurgents."[26] Furthermore, the vocabulary of rebellion continued to be used even after the conflict had attained a much wider scope, duration, and intensity. Thus, in January 1963, Saudi Arabia still spoke of "the legal ruler" and "the military group revolting against him."[27] This use of the vocabulary of rebellion was in fact political and was intended to enhance one faction's legitimacy so that aid could be given to that faction as the incumbent government.

The vocabulary of belligerency was not used by the participants, although the consequences of recognizing a status of belligerency were echoed by the argument of both Yemeni factions that support given to one by outside states constituted an act of war against the other. The significant difference between the viewpoint of traditional international law and that of the Yemeni factions, however, is that both factions spoke of an act of war not against one of two parties in an internal conflict but against the people of Yemen as a whole.

Thus, the distinction in traditional international law between rebels, insurgents, and belligerents was not applied in the Yemen conflict. Instead, the whole focus of discussion was on which faction was the "legitimate government," and both sides in the struggle held that aid to the legitimate government was permissible. This shift of focus in the contemporary international system away from the traditional distinctions and toward the recognition of one side or the other as the legitimate government is perhaps a reflection of the all-or-nothing character that internal wars now have.

The role of international law in regulating the conduct of the conflict. Having considered the role of international law in regulating the responses of outside states to the internal war in Yemen, we shall now discuss the role of legal norms in regulating the actual conduct of the conflict. The subject of the conduct of the conflict can be divided into the following areas: treatment of prisoners, protection of civilians and avoidance of nonmilitary targets, use of weapons proscribed under international law, and extension of the territorial scope of the conflict beyond Yemeni territory.

The laws of war applicable to internal war are set forth in article 3 of the Geneva Conventions of 1949, which deals with minimum standards of behavior in "armed conflict not of an international character."[28] Even in the absence of specific statements by the parties to the Yemen

[26] GAOR, 17th sess., 1202d mtg., Dec. 20, 1962, par. 81.

[27] Hart, "Basic Chronology," p. 152.

[28] For the text of the conventions, see *American Journal of International Law,* Supplement, 47 (October 1963): 119–20.

conflict, these minimum standards could be taken as the basis for evaluating the actions of the parties, since they are representative of international community expectations. In fact, however, such specific statements were made, and by January 1963, both the Royalists and Republicans had agreed to "respect the principles" of the Geneva Conventions of 1949.[29] Indeed, these pledges appear to go beyond acceptance of the provisions of article 3 and to support a more far-reaching interpretation of the obligations of the parties with respect to the laws of war than might otherwise be the case in an internal war. In spite of these pledges, however, it is difficult to identify ways in which international law played any role in regulating the conduct of the conflict in the substantive areas mentioned above.

The treatment of prisoners varied a great deal during the course of the war. Initially, Royalist tribesmen killed all captured enemies, since they considered it "honourable to use their swords against the 'cowards' who had let themselves be captured."[30] Their state of mind was described by the imam in a November 1962 news conference: he would not display any Egyptian prisoners, he said, "because my people are so outraged that they kill all the Egyptians."[31] In addition to killing captured Egyptians and Republicans, Royalist tribesmen engaged in multilation of the dead, often cutting off ears and noses.

In an effort to prevent the killing of prisoners, the imam ordered in early 1963 that all prisoners be brought alive to him personally, and he offered a monetary reward for doing so.[32] This measure was apparently of some help in reducing the killing of prisoners, since eventually the Royalists established five prisoner-of-war camps. It would appear that most of the men in these camps were Egyptians rather than Yemeni Republicans, perhaps because some of the men captured from the Republican National Guard agreed to serve the Royalists as clerks and secretaries.[33] Although the conditions under which Egyptian prisoners were kept in detention were uncomfortable, they were in many respects no worse than the conditions of life of their guards.[34]

The most important factor in alleviating the conditions of prisoners during the war was the presence of International Red Cross personnel, who visited the prisoners, arranged exchanges, and protested hardships

[29] International Committee of the Red Cross, *Annual Report, 1963* (Geneva: ICRC, 1963), pp. 16–17.

[30] *Ibid.*

[31] *New York Times*, Nov. 11, 1962. See also *New York Times*, Dec. 12, 1962.

[32] International Committee of the Red Cross, *Annual Report, 1963*, p. 17.

[33] Dana Adams Schmidt, *Yemen: The Unknown War* (New York: Holt, Rinehart and Winston, 1968), p. 122.

[34] International Committee of the Red Cross, *Annual Report, 1964* (Geneva: ICRC, 1964), p. 8.

like the use of leg irons.[35] Their presence and role are closely linked to international law in the sense that they are primarily concerned with humanitarian standards of treatment of human beings regardless of faction. Indeed, in practice the Red Cross personnel were living representatives of international law in Yemen, and without them it is likely that conditions would have been a good deal worse.

This is not to say that the relevant norms of international law played a direct role in alleviating the prisoners' lot but rather that the threat of disapproval by the rest of the international community may have had some effect on the behavior of the parties.

The treatment of civilians, avoidance of nonmilitary targets, and use of poison gas can be treated together, since all concern the general subject of the kind of war fought in Yemen. Even more than in other guerrilla wars being fought today, the distinction between military and civilian personnel practically did not exist in Yemen. Those fighting on the Royalist side were tribesmen who, in the tradition of Arabian tribal fighters, came and went between Royalist camps and their home villages with great frequency and irregularity. Furthermore, tribesmen were recruited not as individuals but as members of a tribe whose allegiance had been given to one side or the other in the internal war.

The war itself was basically a guerrilla war of ambushes and sieges rather than a conventional armed conflict between regular, uniformed opposing armies. The similarities with Vietnam are all too apparent, both in terms of the basic structure of the conflict and in terms of the parties' disregard for the laws of war.

This disregard was particularly visible on the Republican side, since it was the Republicans who had planes and modern weapons. Throughout the war, Royalist villages were indiscriminately bombed by Egyptian planes and pilots fighting for the Republicans. Even more serious was the use of poison gas in some of the bombings, which resulted in the burning, blinding, and death of Royalist villagers.[36]

Article 3 of the Geneva Convention of 1949 forbids violence to the life and person of anyone "taking no active part in the hostilities"; in addition, use of poison gas has been outlawed in a number of international treaties, including the Geneva Protocol of 1925, ratified by Egypt in 1928.[37] The problem, then, was not the lack of relevant principles but rather the ignoring of them by the parties to the conflict.

The major attempt to expand the territorial scope of the conflict in Yemen was the bombing by Egyptian pilots of Saudi villages near the

[35] For reports of these activities, see the annual reports of the International Committee of the Red Cross for 1963 through 1966.

[36] For a more detailed discussion, see Schmidt, *Yemen*, pp. 257–73.

[37] Schmidt, *Yemen*, p. 272.

Saudi-Yemen border.[38] The Egyptian justification for the bombings was that they constituted "punishment to the aggressor" at his "base of aggression,"[39] a justification which requires that the Saudi involvement be classified as "aggression." As we have seen in the section on aggression, however, use of the vocabulary of aggression in connection with the involvement of either Saudi Arabia or the United Arab Republic is not appropriate in the Yemen case. The appropriate legal principle would seem to be that the territorial scope of an internal war ought not to be expanded beyond the confines of a single state, even when there is intervention by a neighboring state.[40]

Thus, international law was extremely ineffective in regulating the conduct of the parties in the Yemen internal war, and hostilities went forward largely without reference to applicable standards of conduct embodied in existing or evolving legal norms.

The role of international law in attempts at conflict resolution. Having examined the role of international law in regulating the conduct of hostilities and the responses of outside states, we turn now to a consideration of the role played by international law in attempts to resolve the Yemen conflict. If one takes a very broad view of the potential contribution of international law, it can be said that international law played a role in the Yemen conflict by providing a set of procedural mechanisms, including negotiation, mediation, and large formal conferences, and also by providing institutional mechanisms—the United Nations, peacekeeping forces, the League of Arab States—through which such procedures could be carried out or reinforced.

These mechanisms were fairly extensively utilized in the Yemen conflict. Attempts at mediation included the letters written by President John F. Kennedy to Saudi Arabia and the United Arab Republic in late 1962, Dr. Ralph Bunche's mediation mission for the United Nations in March 1963, US presidential emissary Ellsworth Bunker's mediation mission in April 1963, mediation attempts by Algeria and Iraq in 1964, mediation by the Sudan at the Khartoum meetings during the summer of 1967, and also efforts by the UN representative in Yemen during the period of the United Nations Yemen Observation Mission

[38] Egyptian bombings of Najran and Qizan took place primarily in late 1962 and early 1963.

[39] Hart, "Basic Chronology," p. 152.

[40] On the impermissibility of expanding the territorial scope of an internal war and on the importance of "objective" limits on conflict like international boundaries and the threat of recourse to nuclear weapons, see Richard A. Falk, "International Law and the United States' Role in the Viet Nam War," pp. 1123, 1125–26, 1132, 1136, and "Janus Tormented: The International Law of Internal War," pp. 221 (n. 55), 222 (n. 58).

(UNYOM). Direct negotiations also took place between Saudi Arabia and the United Arab Republic and between Royalist and Republican representatives.[41]

As a result, a series of agreements was concluded between the United Arab Republic and Saudi Arabia, including a disengagement agreement in the spring of 1963 which provided for UN peacekeeping forces to supervise phased Egyptian troop withdrawals and Saudi cessation of aid to the Royalists, the Saudi-Egyptian agreement of September 1964, and the Jiddah Agreement of August 1965, which sketched the outlines of a political settlement within Yemen and established machinery for its implementation.[42] Thus, at least on the question of disengagement, the parties who had intervened in Yemen used established procedures of international interaction to create specific conventions applicable to their actions in the Yemen conflict. Their resort to established procedures of negotiation and mediation kept open channels of communication as well.

The history of the disengagement agreement of 1963, however, only serves to point up the overall ineffectiveness of international law as a restraint on states' behavior in the Yemen conflict.[43] Even as a means of communication the disengagement agreement was of little help, since each side interpreted its provision quite differently.[44] And the same problems arose with respect to later agreements as well, including the Jiddah Agreement, which was supposed to serve as the basis for a political settlement within Yemen.

Indeed, it might even be argued that recourse to the international legal procedures of concluding formal agreements on disengagement and related questions hindered rather than helped conflict resolutions, since it papered over deep rifts in goals with a façade of agreement on general principles which had little chance of implementation. It is true that taken as a whole, the various agreements on disengagement and resolu-

---

[41] For a brief descriptive account of mediation efforts and negotiations among the states directly involved in the Yemen conflict, see Manfred W. Wenner, *Modern Yemen, 1918–1966* (Baltimore: The Johns Hopkins Press, 1967), pp. 197–228.

[42] For the disengagement agreement, see *New York Times*, May 30, 1963; for the text of the Jiddah agreement, see "Saudi-UAR Agreement on Yemen," *Middle East Journal* 20 (Winter 1966): 93–94.

[43] On implementation of the disengagement agreement and the role of UNYOM, see the following Reports of the Secretary-General to the UN Security Council: S/5412 of Sept. 4, 1963; S/5447 of Oct. 28, 1963; S/5501 of Jan. 2, 1964; S/5572 of March 3, 1964; S/5927 of Sept. 2, 1964.

[44] Saudi Arabia maintained that Saudi cessation of aid to the Royalists was contingent on Egyptian troop withdrawals, while in the Egyptian view UAR troop withdrawals were contingent upon both prior cessation of all Saudi aid to the Royalists and the effective suppression of the Royalist counterrevolution. (*Ibid.*, S/5412, pars. 7, 13, 18.)

tion of the conflict defined the general outlines for any negotiated ending of the internal war. Yet much of the "agreement" reflected in the documents was illusory, since efforts to implement any of the formal agreements always revealed serious divergences of view.

To repeat, the role played by international law in attempts at resolving the conflict in Yemen was at best ambiguous. While it is true that mediation by the United Nations and outside states helped keep channels of communication between Saudi Arabia and the United Arab Republic open, thereby facilitating the conclusion of agreements on disengagement, it is also true that the actual results of these agreements were negligible.

II. INTERNATIONAL LAW AS A METHOD OF POLITICAL ANALYSIS

In addition to its role in shaping the behavior of participants in conflict situations, international law can also serve as an analytic framework or perspective for describing, evaluating, and understanding world politics. It can be viewed and judged, in other words, as an aid to understanding and conceptualizing complex global political processes. As we have seen, the role of international law in Yemen in shaping the behavior of the participants was negligible indeed. It remains for us to examine its usefulness as a conceptual framework within which to view the Yemeni situation.

The Conceptual Framework of International Law

The basic unit of analysis from the perspective of international law is usually the state, and the focus of analysis is relationships between states. This approach suffices well enough for the study of diplomatic history, including topics like international conferences, the interpretation of treaties, and the development of customary international law through state practice, since for these purposes there is no need to distinguish between the state and the government or to understand or investigate domestic politics. Since in fact the study of international politics was until very recently the study of diplomatic history, it is not surprising that the state remains the basic unit of analysis for most students of international politics, including international lawyers. The concern of international law for "domestic jurisdiction," "nonintervention," "territorial integrity and political independence," and the like, reinforces the idea of the state as the relevant unit of analysis. This emphasis on the nature and capabilities of states also focuses attention on relationships between rather than within states.

This perspective carries over into the area of internal war. As noted above, there are in international law three categories of intrastate violence: rebellion, insurgency, and belligerency. In rebellion, the essential identity between state and government remains unchanged. (This may be one reason why it has been so easy for Walt W. Rostow and others interested in counterinsurgency to see armed uprisings against particular governments only as external aggression or subversion perpetrated against the state; that is, because the traditional perspective of international law—which is also that of conventional international politics—does not distinguish between the state and the government.) In belligerency, on the other hand, the state in which the internal war is taking place becomes, in effect, two states, each with its own government.

The contemporary abandonment of these traditional categories in favor of recognition of one side or the other in an internal war as "the legitimate government" only reinforces the tendency toward identification of the state with a particular government, as can be seen from the statements of both sides in the Yemen conflict. Thus, as already noted, both the Royalists and the Republicans identified themselves with the Yemeni people and their opponents with those outside Yemen; the Egyptians and the Saudis accused one another of aggression against the Yemeni people when each chose to support opposing factions; and the United Nations refused even to talk with the Royalists once the General Assembly had decided to seat the Yemeni Republican delegation as the legitimate representative of the country. In this respect, of course, the Yemen case is typical.

Even the attempt of some theorists to develop another terminology and to speak, for example, of "incumbents" and "insurgents" without incorporating notions of normative governmental legitimacy does not get us very far beyond the basic state perspective of international law, since the focus is still on the opposition between two well-defined groups, on their struggle to seize power and the state apparatus.

Thus, in analyzing the Yemen case from the conceptual perspective of international law one necessarily speaks primarily in terms of "Saudi Arabia," "the United Arab Republic," "the Republicans," "the Royalists," and so on, a vocabulary which implies that there are in fact enduring, cohesive groups to which these labels can rightfully be applied. As we shall see, such a perspective misses the most crucial aspect of the Yemeni situation. It misses both the ways in which Yemen is unique and the ways in which it is representative of a worldwide process of societal upheaval and transformation. Let us therefore return at this point to the Yemen case in order to see just how much we have missed by applying the traditional analytical perspective of international law.

Yemen as a Political System

Let us see first to what extent the concept of the state is applicable to Yemen, remembering that this concept implies a territorially defined geographic area in which a central government exercises effective control. At the same time let us see to what degree Yemen qualifies as a nation—that is, a self-conscious political community which is the prime focus of the individual citizen's political allegiance. In order to do this, we must review certain aspects of traditional Yemeni society.

Traditional Yemeni society. The basic characteristic of traditional Yemeni society—as, indeed, of traditional Arab society generally—is that active conflict with outsiders is required in order for individuals to form themselves into groups.[1] Groups are thus temporary, conflict-oriented, and exceedingly susceptible to dissolution and internal factionalism, as epitomized in this typical Arab proverb: I against my brother; my brother and I against my cousin; my cousin and I against the stranger. Solidarity exists, consequently, only in the face of threats from outside and is quick to give way when the outside threat has passed. The individual therefore must worry not only about his effectiveness in dealing with the external threat (whether extrafamilial, extratribal, or whatever) but also about his position vis-à-vis his allies of convenience, who will soon again become his rivals. Thus, there are rather severe limits on what degree and kinds of collaboration can take place and also on what forms of conflict can occur.[2]

Given this ever-changing pattern of conflict-generated groups in every sphere of life, it is somewhat misleading to analyze traditional Yemeni society in terms of social classes, since the kind of solidarity and group consciousness usually thought to be properties of social classes or even of interest groups are largely lacking. If we keep this caveat in mind, however, it is useful to view traditional Yemeni society as a network of social divisions, most of which continue to be of importance in under-

[1] The factual material on Yemen which appears in this and succeeding sections is drawn from a variety of sources, among which the following are the most important: Mohamed Said El Attar, *Le Sous-Développement Economique et Social du Yémen: Perspectives de la Révolution Yéménite* (Algiers, 1964); Manfred Wenner, *Modern Yemen, 1918–1966* (Baltimore: The Johns Hopkins Press, 1967); and William R. Brown "The Yemeni Dilemma," *Middle East Journal* 17 (Autumn 1963): 349–67.

[2] This style of interaction is one variant of a behavioral pattern (polarity) which Manfred Halpern calls "direct bargaining" and classifies as one of eight possible behavioral patterns open to man in his individual and group relationships. Stressing only this pattern in discussing Yemeni society is an oversimplification, since Yemenis had recourse to other behavioral patterns in traditional society as well, but exploration at this level is sufficient for the purposes of this study. For a brief exposition of the eight polarities, see Manfred Halpern, "A Redefinition of the Revolutionary Situation," *Journal of International Affairs* 23 (1969): 58–65.

standing the configuration of social forces in contemporary Yemen. A brief description of these divisions is therefore in order.

One of the most basic traditional divisions within Yemeni society is that between two Muslim sects, the Zaydi ("heretical" Shi'i) and the Shaf'i ("orthodox" Sunni), with about half the population belonging to each group. The fact that until 1962 Yemen was ruled by a succession of Zaydi imams who favored their Zaydi subjects over the Shaf'is heightened social tensions between the two groups. Moreover, these tensions are reinforced by geographic and urban-tribal divisions within the society. While the population in the north and northeast is over-whelmingly Zaydi, that of the south and the coastal region is predominantly Shaf'i. More important, some four-fifths of the Yemeni tribes are Zaydi, while only about one-fifth are Shaf'i. Thus, in broad outline one can speak of a geographical and cultural division in Yemen between an Arab, Zaydi, and tribal north and northeast and an Arabized, Shaf'i, and urban (or at least less strongly tribal) south and coastal region. Military power and economic wealth in Yemen are also split along religious lines. Under the Zaydi imams only Zaydis were allowed to become army officers, since the imams did not trust the loyalty of the Shaf'i population. And since most of the fighting men were obtained through tribal levies, they were Zaydis as well. By contrast, most Yemeni businessmen and merchants are Shaf'i. Thus, the Zaydi-Shaf'i cleavage was reinforced by the division of military and economic power within the society.

Cutting across these divisions within the traditional Yemeni social system was the division between the common people and the sayyid, or aristocratic, class composed of those who claimed descent from the Prophet Muhammad. As the executor of the often oppressive policies of the imam, this class was generally hated. Further, the sayyids, including the imamic Hamid al-Din family, were of Adnani (north Arabian nomadic) rather than Qahtani (south Arabian sedentary) descent and were therefore looked down upon by the racially proud tribesmen, almost all of whom are Qahtanis. Indeed, some Zaydi northerners still consider the sayyids foreigners in Yemen even after almost one thousand years. There were also persistent tensions between the imam and the sayyid class from which he came and between the imam and the tribes, on which he depended for military support, since they held the balance of military power in the society. In addition to all these tensions, there were also significant tensions within each segment of Yemeni society, particularly within the imamic family, the sayyid class, and the various tribes.

The combination of all these tensions in the traditional Yemeni system resulted in strong rivalries, frequent rebellions, and continuous attempts by all parties to shift the balance of forces in their favor. Yet the fact that no group was either internally united or independent of the other groups meant that none was able to secure a decisive victory and could at most gain a temporary advantage. This was as true for the imam as for any other individual or group within the traditional system. Every imam had to assert what power and authority he could muster literally from day to day in order to engage in the never ending struggle against tribal autonomy. Medieval chronicles tell of imams who went from place to place putting down revolts and collecting taxes, "pacifying" one locale only to have to return to it immediately to confront renewed dissidence. More recent imams faced the same challenge and struggle, although by the mid-1930s internal security was finally reasonably well established. No decisive victory of central authority over tribal autonomy was achieved, however.

Moreover, the Yemeni political system was not territorially defined in two important senses. First of all, the whole conceptual basis of the polity was nonterritorial—in contrast to the modern concept of the state. Moreover, boundaries continually expanded and contracted as a ruler's power rose or declined. Even the signing of treaties with Saudi Arabia and Great Britain in 1934 left Yemen's eastern boundary completely undemarcated, and the southern boundary with what is today Southern Yemen is still a subject for disputation.

Thus, Yemen hardly qualified as a state, being neither a territorial entity nor a polity in which a central government exercised effective authority in the Western sense. Nor was Yemen a nation, since the primary allegiance of practically all individuals was to tribes if they were tribesmen, as more than 80 percent were, or to the particularistic interests of a family, ruling house, or religious sect.

In the 1930s a qualitatively new kind of struggle was added to those in existence for centuries, a struggle between those who sought to continue the traditional political system of conflict and collaboration and those who sought its transformation.

The rise of modernizing elements. As had been the case elsewhere, in Yemen the desire for additional military power to deal with other states was the Trojan horse that undermined the traditional system. In an attempt to acquire modern military technology in order to enforce his claim to territory in the Aden Protectorates, the imam sent a small training mission to Baghdad Military College in 1936. Shortly after the return of this first group, one of its members was imprisoned for "spreading modern ideas."[3] This incident is of great symbolic significance as an indication not only of the still traditional nature of Yemeni society

[3] Wenner, *Modern Yemen*, p. 84, citing Sharaf al-Din, *Al-Yaman*.

at that time but also of the fragility of that society when confronted by new—and in the Yemeni context, revolutionary—ideas. Indeed, the imam's perception of danger led him to stop sending students to Iraq, and he instead invited an Iraq military mission to Yemen. The result was the same, however, since the Iraqi officers brought with them those dangerous "modern ideas" and spread them among the officers they trained.

The 1930s also saw the beginning of a new kind of political opposition to the imam from Yemeni emigrants in Aden. By the early forties these men had formed the Free Yemeni party and were demanding a constitutional assembly and the creation of a modern bureaucracy staffed by capable men with a relevant modern education. Their demands were supported by the small number of Yemenis who received university educations abroad. In the Yemeni context these demands were clearly revolutionary, since in order to meet them the imam would have had to transform his whole relationship with his bureaucracy and the tribes. The composition of the bureaucracy would have had to be radically altered, thereby fundamentally changing the relationship between the sayyid class and the rest of the society. And such a bureaucracy would have wanted to make changes that would have called into question the basic structure of Yemeni society. A modern bureaucracy staffed by men trained in public administration and law and with competence in various technical fields—economics, banking, management, and so forth—could not have functioned on the basis of abrupt and arbitrary shifts in the political context and in their support and instructions from the ruler. Moreover, the members of the sayyid class who staffed the imam's traditional bureaucracy would have lacked the education, skills, and technical competence needed to perform in a modern bureaucracy and therefore either would have tried to subvert it or would have had to be deprived of their traditional positions of status and wealth gained from bureaucratic corruption. A modern bureaucracy would have wanted to find more efficient ways of doing things, to engage in economic development, to lay down fixed rules to cover particular classes of situations, to redistribute land, to start factories, to allow contact with the outside world, and so forth.

Yet the military officers, intellectuals, and businessmen spoke at first only in terms of reform and modification of the traditional system and attempted to carry out their program by linking themselves to conservative opposition elements in order to overthrow and replace particular imams. An attempt to do so was made in 1948 but failed because of lack of funds to pay tribesmen and army and government employees, Zaydi-Shaf'i tensions and other friction among the insurgents, the lack of military force to resist counterinsurgencies, the wait-and-see policy of many provincial governors and tribal leaders, and a lack of organization. After the failure of a second and less well-organized attempt in 1955, the focus shifted from reformism to revolution and to the belief that nothing short of the abolition of the imamate as a political institution would be sufficient to carry out the desired societal transformation. Thus, when another coup was carried out in September 1962, the revolutionaries immediately proclaimed a republic.

Within a few days, fighting between Royalists and Republicans broke out in Yemen, and Saudi Arabia and the United Arab Republic intervened in support of opposing factions. Thus began the long and bloody internal war in Yemen. With its beginning, both the ongoing conflict over the ends and structure of Yemeni society and the process of disintegration of traditional forms of relationship entered a new phase.

In 1962 Yemen was not yet either a state or a nation; moreover, as we shall see in examining the makeup of the Republican and Royalist coalitions, even to speak of "incumbents" and "insurgents" as though each was a cohesive group united in its opposition to the other misleads us analytically about the nature, causes, and consequences of the struggle taking place.

The Republican coalition. Although the actual coup was carried out by a small number of young army officers led by the head of the Palace Guard, Abdullah al-Sallal, plans for such a coup had been formulated by a broader group including intellectuals and businessmen. While the businessmen generally favored Arab unity and the reform of traditional Islam but feared socialism and were suspicious of Nasserism, the views of the military officers and intellectuals covered an ideological spectrum ranging from simple reformists to Marxist revolutionaries and including Nasserites, Ba'athists, and Muslim Brothers, with the most radical elements being in the military. There was general agreement only on overthrowing the imamate, modernizing the country, and raising the general standard of living but no agreement on a program to accomplish the latter two goals and, indeed, no clear notion of what modernization might entail. Thus, there were built-in contradictions and antagonisms within the core group of Republicans on the level of ideology.

Further, in addition to the core group, the Republican coalition included a number of tribes whose leaders had supported the revolutionaries after the 1962 coup, not because of a positive commitment to republican ideology but rather because of grievances against a specific imam. Consequently, tribal support was limited and not necessarily permament, since many were not opposed to the imamate as an institution but were opposed to the kind of societal transformation that some core group Republicans sought. Zaydi tribesmen were natural opponents

325

of republicanism since "in any open competition for official positions or for control of the country's wealth in which only individual skills and competence were considered, the Shaf'is would almost certainly gain a dominant role in Yemen."[4]

The support which the Republicans received from some other tribes was even more limited, since it was based not on grievances against an imam but rather on traditional intertribal feuds. If a tribe's traditional enemy joined the Royalists, then that tribe might join the Republicans and continue to pursue the ancient quarrel. Still more tenuous was the tribal support gained through payment of large subsidies, since such support would be lost as soon as subsidies stopped or a higher subsidy was offered by the Royalists.

In summary, then, the Republican coalition was composed of a core group of middle-class elements divided within itself in terms of both modern ideology and traditional social tensions, and of tribal supporters of varying degrees of allegiance based on particular grievances, traditional tribal enmities, or subsidies. Overlapping Zaydi-Shaf'i, military-civilian, and urban-tribal tensions were thus present within the Republican group.

The Royalist coalition. Similar tensions and contradictions were present from the outset in the Royalist group as well. The backbone of Royalist strength were the northern Zaydi tribesmen who opposed the republic on a variety of grounds. First, they attached great importance to the imam's religious role, a factor which the Republicans neglected. Consequently, in several Zaydi regions local imams were proclaimed by those who saw the republic as a symbol of atheism. This led to fighting in Zaydi regions between local tribesmen and Republican forces. Second, many northern Zaydi tribes saw the Republic as the triumph of the Shaf'is, many of whom participated actively in the first Republican government. These attitudes were played upon by the sayyids, whose social position depended upon overthrowing the Republicans, and by members of the Hamid al-Din imamic family, who had immediately begun to recruit support for a Royalist counterrevolution. As a result of the stressing of these religious factors, even some Zaydi tribesmen who realized that the Republicans would improve their socioeconomic lot fought with the Royalists.

The presence of Egyptian troops also aroused tribal opposition to the republic. The fact that the Egyptians are Shaf'is reinforced Zaydi fears of Shaf'i domination. In addition, their presence led some tribes to identify the republic with foreign domination and, consequently, to fight determinedly against it. Other tribes, which had at first remained neu-

[4] Brown, "The Yemeni Dilemma," p. 365.

tral, were moved to join the Royalists by Egyptian and Republican errors in dealing with them. And, as was the case with some tribes who supported the Republicans, some tribes joined the Royalists as a result of traditional intertribal enmities and the offer of subsidies.

Thus, like the Republicans, the Royalists were a heterogeneous coalition, with a nucleus composed of the Hamid al-Din family and other sayyids who drew support almost entirely from northern Zaydi tribes. Preexisting social tensions within and among these various elements continued during the internal war. The Hamid al-Din family, and particularly Imam Muhammad al-Badr, had been very much disliked by the tribes before the revolution of 1962, and this dislike continued. An earlier rivalry between the reformist Imam al-Badr and his conservative uncle, Prince Hassan, did not decrease, although the imam was forced to ally himself with Prince Hassan and the sayyid oligarchy against the republic. The opposition between Qahtani tribesmen and Adnani sayyids also remained a factor in the Royalist equation and perhaps even increased in importance. In addition to these tensions, there were divergent views on the kind of political system which should replace the republic once it was overthrown.

The Internal War in Yemen and the Conceptual Framework of International Law

Given the persistent social tensions within Yemeni society, it is clear that the internal war cannot be viewed simply as the opposition of Royalists and Republicans and that these groups were not well-defined, ideologically cohesive political movements. Rather, both were heterogeneous coalitions within which high levels of friction and ideological diversity existed, and both underwent significant change and fragmentation in the course of the internal war. Even the core group of Republicans, drawn from various elements of the middle class, had by the beginning of 1965 split into a number of opposing factions. As for Royalist cohesiveness, there is something ludicrous about the whole notion of a "Royalist tribesman" in view of the historical tensions between the imam and the tribes. Thus, the usual vocabulary and conceptual framework of international law cannot be applied to the war between Yemeni Royalists and Republicans.

In addition, using the legal vocabulary of "incumbents" and "insurgents" focuses attention on the internal war between Royalists and Republicans as a struggle for control of the state apparatus and of political authority as the "legitimate government." But Yemen has never been a state in the sense of a territorial entity having defined boundaries within which a central government exercised strong authority. Indeed, as noted above, the whole concept of territoriality which is central to the modern idea of the state is inappropriate in the Yemeni context. Prior to the mid-1930s, governmental authority in Yemen diminished rapidly as geographical distance from the central government increased. Tribal rebellions were frequent, and the possibility of tribal dissidence was always present. Tribal dissidence continued to threaten internal security even after the mid-1930s, and a tribal rebellion in the 1950s was only narrowly averted. In addition, prior to the 1962 revolution, the "state apparatus" consisted largely of the imam himself and a few of his ministers who personally saw to many of the smallest administrative details. Thus, there was really no state organization for the Republicans to take over when they proclaimed the Yemen Arab Republic.

Moreover, to speak of either Royalists or Republicans as the "legitimate government" ignores the fact that neither Royalists nor Republicans are in fact "governing." To the degree that order existed at all in Yemen during the internal war, it existed not because of the efforts of either group to provide it but rather because social life persisted even in the absence of all government by a central authority.[5] Thus, neither side fighting in Yemen satisfied the traditional international law criteria for recognition as the legitimate government. Neither controlled and administered a majority of the country's territory. Similarly, neither side could count on the support of the majority of the population; even those who joined one side or the other did so for reasons unrelated to the ideological issue of theocracy versus republicanism. Many Yemenis have, in fact, tried, albeit unsuccessfully, to remain aloof from the conflict. Essentially, the conflict remains one between a new elite with a new social background and new social goals and an old elite whose claim to status, wealth, and power rests on traditional bases; and each has recruited allies wherever it could within the society.

Thus, the traditional terminology of international law can be seen to be irrelevant and misleading when applied to the Yemen situation. Its misleading character is even more clear from a consideration of the Egyptian intervention in Yemen—an intervention which was conducted on the basis of the same *Weltanschauung* that underlies contemporary international law.

The Egyptians apparently saw the internal war as a military conflict between two organized groups and therefore as a situation to be dealt with by conventional military means, including bombing villages, holding isolated garrisons, and so forth. This conceptualization proved to be politically disastrous. Bombing villages, while quite ineffectual from a military viewpoint, stiffened opposition to the Republicans and made

---

[5] This insight was suggested in passing in a manuscript on Yemen by Manfred W. Wenner, who then goes on to deal at length with the various committees, councils, and decrees created by the Republican "government."

eventual resolution of the conflict more difficult. Treating tribes that had originally remained neutral in the internal war as enemies rather than as potential allies alienated them, thereby swelling opposition to the Republicans. Even more important, this stress on military strategy led to the neglect of the political struggle—the effort to build active support for needed social change in those areas of Yemen that were more or less under Republican administration. Neither the Egyptians nor the Republicans realized that the basic political struggle was not against the Royalists as an organized, structured opponent but rather against the forces of fragmentation and cleavage inherent in the structure of Yemeni society.

The kinds of questions on which international law focuses are also irrelevant to the sources, nature, and consequences of the Yemeni conflict. Who is the incumbent and who the insurgent? Is one group's intervention "proportional counterintervention"? Is intervention to support "the legitimate government" permitted? Does the external involvement that has occurred come under the rubric of aggression and self-defense, intervention and counterintervention, or what? None of these questions, I would argue, gets to the heart of the matter. Even questions like "How can peace be established?" "How can intervention be ended?" and "How can stability be promoted?" which go well beyond the usual focus of international legal analysis, require treatment in fundamentally different conceptual perspectives.

Thus, as a conceptual framework no less than as a restraint on and molder of the behavior of participants in international conflicts, international law can be seen in the Yemeni case to be not only irrelevant but positively misleading. Might it not be true, however, that Yemen is an anomalous and aberrant example? How representative is the case of Yemen and to what degree can conclusions about the usefulness of international law drawn from consideration of it be generalized to other cases?

Yemen in Comparative Perspective

Perhaps the most illuminating, as well as the most topical and interesting, comparison is that between Yemen and Vietnam. The fact that it would be possible to apply almost everything said above about the effects of Egyptian intervention on modernization in Yemen to United States intervention in Vietnam demonstrates a strong underlying similarity between the two cases despite their obvious differences of history, culture, and international position. This close similarity alone makes Yemen representative of an important class of cases. In addition, however, Yemen is typical of a very broad range of international war situations in which the basic problem is how to create linkages among individuals and groups that will be capable of transcending traditional ethnic, tribal, and class conflicts and will make possible societal cohesion to meet the demands of the modern age.

The similarities between Yemen and Vietnam are especially striking. In both Yemen and Vietnam the traditional society had broken down, but a state in the modern sense had not yet been created. In both cases the struggle was one between ideologically opposed elites neither of which could count on majority support, and the major problem to be faced was the creation of new linkages relevant to the tasks of modernization. Just as the Egyptians committed fundamental errors in the way they conducted their intervention in Yemen, so, too, the Americans in Vietnam fell prey to similar fundamental failures of conceptualization. In particular, both tended to see their major task as the military suppression of an organized opponent rather than the creation of new linkages between individuals and groups.[6]

The failure of both the Americans and Egyptians to conceptualize the internal wars in which they intervened as revolutions of modernization, stems, I think, from two common causes: first, the inadequacy of most existing theories of modernization to throw light on the nature of the fundamental changes now taking place in the world; and second, the analytic gap which traditional concepts create between domestic and international politics. Both policymakers and social scientists have, it is true, long been aware that

old societies are changing their ways. . . . This process is truly revolutionary. It touches every aspect of the traditional life: economic, social and political. . . . Like all revolutions, the revolution of modernization is disturbing. . . . Men and women in the villages and the cities, feeling that the old ways of life are shaken and that new possibilities are open to them, express old resentments and new hopes.[7]

But they have also tended to assume that

the introduction of modern technology brings about not merely new methods of production but a new style of family life, new links between the villages and the cities, the beginnings of national politics, and a new relationship to the world outside.[8]

[6] On Vietnam, see John T. McAlister, Jr., *Viet Nam: The Origins of Revolution* (New York: Alfred A. Knopf, 1969).

[7] Walt W. Rostow, "Countering Guerrilla Attack," an article drawn from an address by its author to the graduating class of the Counter Guerrilla course of the Army's Special Warfare Center at Fort Bragg, printed in *Army Magazine* (September 1961), and reproduced in Richard A. Falk (ed.), *The Vietnam War and International Law* (Princeton: Princeton University Press, 1968), pp. 127–28.

[8] *Ibid.*

That is, they have tended to see modern technology as the primary causal factor in the breakdown of traditional societies as coherent social systems and have, in addition, either seen the breakdown as coincident with the forging of new connections or have assumed that somehow, given enough time and economic development, new linkages would inevitably emerge to take the place of old.

Such a view, since it relies on the mysterious workings of an autonomous, technologically based process, naturally leads to the neglect of politics and of the crucial need for building active support for programs designed to create new connections. This neglect has far-reaching consequences, for if what is involved in coping with the revolution of modernization is just hanging on until problems get solved "as momentum takes hold in an underdeveloped area,"[9] then intervention for modernization becomes simply a question of staving off perceived enemies, whether "communists" in Vietnam or "Royalists" in Yemen, until the difficult "transitional" stage has passed. Thus, the focus tends to become "winning the war," and "defeating the enemy" militarily rather than intervening "not merely [as] a manipulation of power, but [as] a sharing in the historical trials of others" through participation in creative attempts to fashion new connections.[10]

From this position, it is just a very small step to the assumption that all armed opposition to a government one perceives as "modernizing" is outside agitation rather than authentic internal political conflict. This peculiar train of thought is exemplified by the following passage:

A guerrilla war is an intimate affair, fought not merely with weapons but fought in the minds of the men who live in the villages and in the hills; fought by the spirit and policy of those who run the local government. . . . We are determined to help destroy this international disease; that is, guerrilla war designed, initiated, and supplied, and led from outside an independent nation.[11]

What begins in this passage as a sensitive realization of the true stakes in an internal war fought over the ends and structure of a society deeply affected by the revolution of modernization ends with the characterization of such internal war as an "international disease."

In the first instance, then, inadequate theories of modernization implicitly or explicitly held by most policymakers and many scholars are

---

[9] *Ibid.*

[10] Manfred Halpern, "The Morality and Politics of Intervention," in James N. Rosenau (ed.), *International Aspects of Civil Strife* (Princeton: Princeton University Press, 1964), p. 269.

[11] Rostow, "Countering Guerrilla Attack," p. 131.

responsible for our faulty perception of internal wars. There is, however, also a second major reason why such conceptualizations of guerrilla war are so tenaciously held. Despite the currency of clichés about the shrinking globe, increasing world interdependence, and so forth, social scientists have barely begun to bridge the analytic gap that traditional conceptualizations create between national and international society. This gap causes particularly serious problems in analyses of intervention in internal war, since once intervention is thought to have taken place the analyst tends to shift from the set of concepts now used in comparative politics to those current in international relations.

How this substitution of sets of concepts operates is illustrated by such statements as the following, in which the ambiguous use of the term "outside" serves as the springboard for jumping from internal to international politics:

The truth is that guerrilla warfare, mounted from external bases—with rights of sanctuary—is a terrible burden to carry for any government in a society making its way towards modernization. . . . A guerrilla war mounted from outside a transitional nation is a crude act of international vandalism. . . . The sending of men and arms across international boundaries and the direction of guerrilla war from outside a sovereign nation is aggression. . . .[12]

While this particular statement was made by an American thinking primarily about Vietnam, it could equally well have been made by an Egyptian thinking about Yemen. Indeed, as we have seen, Egyptian spokesmen have argued that Egyptian forces were in Yemen "with the sole purpose of enabling the Yemeni people to practice their inherent right of self-defence in a war launched against them from outside Yemeni territory by the enemies of the Revolution."[13] That such statements are accurate reflections of the thought processes of those who make them rather than rhetorical declarations issued for effect is clear from the policies actually pursued by those intervening in Yemen and in Vietnam.

We have already seen how the concepts and principles of existing international law mislead us in our analysis of international war, intervention, and the relationship between internal and international politics. Having now seen also that Yemen is in this respect representative of an important class of internal war situations, we need finally to ask whether international law can be made relevant to internal war situations.

[12] *Ibid.,* p. 132.
[13] United Nations, General Assembly, *Official Records*, 17th sess., 1202d mtg., Dec. 20, 1962, par. 44.

III. ON MAKING INTERNATIONAL LAW RELEVANT TO INTERNAL WAR SITUATIONS

The question of whether international law can be made relevant to internal war situations has two quite separate aspects, as indicated by our discussion up to this point: Can international law shape international actors' behavior? And can international law supply a conceptual framework for understanding the nature of international politics? Two distinct answers must be given to these questions. Let us begin by considering its relevance as a shaper of behavior.

Making Law Relevant to the Behavior of Participants

We must first consider the reasons for the ineffectiveness of international law in shaping the behavior of participants in international conflicts like the Yemen internal war. It would be possible to list an assortment of reasons, such as the freedom of actors to choose for themselves which legal norms to invoke in particular cases and how to apply them to the facts of the case, the vagueness of some of the legal norms in the realm of aggression and intervention, and the tendency of actors to use legal language as emotional rhetoric rather than as a technique for communication. What is really needed at this point is a more systematic framework within which to analyze and evaluate the functioning of international law, however, since the effects of factors like those listed cannot be meaningfully evaluated in isolation.

Such a systematic framework can be constructed using the interrelated concepts of structure, behavior, and performance. It is surely a common assumption which need not be argued here that the structure of a system influences the behavior of the units in that system and that the behavior, in turn, shapes the system's performance with respect to specified goals. Theoretical models, whether of economic, social, or political systems, often postulate a one-to-one correlation among structure, conduct, and performance such that a certain structure will cause certain kinds of behavior that will result in the achievement of specified performance goals. This is the case, for example, in the economist's theoretical model of competition, in some political scientists' models of democracy, and in some highly abstract models of the international system.

It is also the case, I would argue, in the ideological model of the international system that gradually took shape in the nineteenth century and is still the primary basis of the provisions of the Charter of the United Nations, the rhetoric of much diplomatic discourse, and almost all of the substantive norms and procedural mechanisms of contemporary, and of course of traditional, international law. In that model the structure of the international system is one of autonomous, sovereign, and independent nation-states capable of enforcing rights and fulfilling obligations. The performance goals are variously stated in terms of "international peace and security," international justice, sovereign equality, independence, and so forth. While recent developments in international law, including the renunciation of force and violence in the Charter and the attempt to shift at least some of the focus from individual states to the organized international community, undeniably create important differences between contemporary and traditional international law, the basic assumption on which the system depends, sovereign and independent states, remains. It is this fact rather than the differences between traditional international law and "the law of the Charter" on which I wish to concentrate.

I think it is at least arguable that traditional international law grew up in response to the structural realities of the pre-twentieth century international system and in many ways is therefore a reflection of those structural realities. The problems with which international law dealt were in fact the problems which confronted societies in their interactions with one another, and the solutions which it developed were usually the result of the evolution of actual practice among states. Indeed, to the extent that the international system in the nineteenth century was fundamentally stable, international law served—as law does in any stable political system, whether domestic or international—largely to mirror structural realities, endowing them in the process with a normative patina and emotional legitimacy that in turn reinforced the system's stability.

At the same time these legal principles gained an emotional legitimacy independent of structural realities through a process that one author has called "vivification," that is, the endowment of concepts "with the power of a firmly fixed life force."[1] They gained thereby a certain quasi autonomy and thus could be used at least in a limited way to effect further changes in the empirical system. But such reforms took place within the basic structure of the empirical system and thus enhanced its long-run stability. The ideal model of international interaction on which the substantive and procedural norms of international law rested was close enough to the actual structure to permit fruitful dialogue between the two. The performance goals specified by the ideal model were, by and large, those of the units in the empirical system as well, and these goals were relevant to the historical problems that the system

[1] Manfred Halpern, "A Redefinition of the Revolutionary Situation," *Journal of International Affairs* 23 (1969): 60–61.

had to confront. Thus, there was a close and mutually supportive relationship between structural realities and legal norms.

The structural situation is very different in the contemporary international system, but the nineteenth-century model of sovereign and independent states interacting autonomously with one another has been carried over and applied to it. We are very far indeed from the ideal of sovereign and equal nation-states functioning as autonomous, independent, and internally cohesive units capable of carrying out obligations and securing rights. It is clear, for example, that most present-day states are not in any sense nations, if to be a nation is to be a community united by past culture and history or by present aspirations. In some cases, like the Arab countries, the boundaries of a nation may extend well beyond the confines of a single state; in others, like Nigeria, they do not begin to encompass an entire state. Thus, even the achievement of internal cohesion on the basis of national communities would involve substantial transformation of existing political boundaries or— even more fundamentally—radically new conceptualizations of the national community.

Furthermore, even if the problem of the nation versus the state could be resolved, it seems obvious that the "mini-states" now being created— and, for that matter, most existing states of whatever size—cannot begin to cope with the tasks of economic development, education, social services, and the like, not to mention defense against outside aggression or subversion. Indeed, the reality for most contemporary societies is a powerlessness to control or even significantly affect their own destinies in crucial respects, a vulnerability to subversion and external control, and an even greater vulnerability to internal fragmentation, factionalism, and violence. Not only is there an entirely different structure from that postulated in the nineteenth-century ideal model, but there are also fundamentally new and different historical challenges to be met.

This state of affairs naturally has consequences for the effectiveness of existing norms of international law concerned with intervention, since those norms reflect the structural characteristics and performance goals of an earlier international system in which intervention was a threat and a challenge to its very foundations—that is, to those behavioral rules which *in fact* served to maintain order among states in their interactions with one another. It is a continuation of that earlier outlook that causes uninvolved states and international organizations to seek to prevent, curtail, or end intervention as quickly and completely as possible. This, indeed, has often been the only goal of UN action.[2]

---

[2] Thus, for example, US and UN mediation efforts in Yemen focused on securing a Saudi-Egyptian agreement on disengagement and neglected the internal situation in Yemen that had caused the original conflict. In addition, insufficient

This focus on preventing intervention is bound to be ineffective in the contemporary international system, since under conditions of increasing interdependence states often have too much at stake in the outcome of one another's domestic struggles over the ends and structure of society not to become involved in them. If it is in fact true that many of the problems confronting domestic societies can only be dealt with in a framework larger than that of the individual society, such concern with the success or failure of other states in confronting common problems is both understandable and rational. Furthermore, the weakness and vulnerability of most contemporary societies to penetration from outside is great and increases the temptations to, and likelihood of, intervention.

Thus, the basic reason for the ineffectiveness of international law in shaping the behavior of international actors is the existing cleavage between normative ideology and rhetoric, on the one hand, and the actors' interests and structural realities, on the other. Such a divergence between structure and ideology is of even greater import in the international system than it would be in domestic society, since in the international system the conflict between the interests of the individual (state) and those of the community as a whole is not smoothed over and partially transcended, as it is in at least some domestic societies, by overarching bonds of community.[3] Law has a limited role in any system, and it is especially limited in the international system. Thus, if international law is to function at all effectively in shaping states' behavior, its norms must be realistically related to the structure of the international system. In the absence of structural sanctions against deviation,

---

attention was paid to the ways in which the evolution of that internal situation would influence implementation of the disengagement agreement. Thus, in his report to the Security Council of Sept. 4, 1963, the secretary-general states: "It bears emphasis also that the agreement on disengagement involves only Saudi Arabia and the United Arab Republic. . . . UNYOM, therefore, is not concerned with Yemen's internal affairs." (S/5412, par. 7.) Saudi Arabia and the UAR, however, were very much concerned with Yemen's internal affairs, and the following statement from the secretary-general's report of Oct. 28, 1963, shows the effects on UN effectiveness of neglecting the internal situation: "That mandate, set forth in the disengagement agreement, is so limiting and restrictive as to make it virtually impossible for UNYOM to play a really helpful and constructive role in Yemen." (S/5447, par. 29.)

[3] In the first volume of his tetralogy on the masks of God, Joseph Campbell argues that one essential function of myth is to reinforce the social order by providing a transcendent fourth principle by which the brutality of the conflict among the three principles of love and pleasure, power and success, and duty can be softened and their interactions infused with a larger meaning. (Joseph Campbell, *Primitive Mythology* [Princeton: Princeton University Press, 1959].) The lack of such a unifying myth in the international system is thus of great importance in understanding that system.

its norms are unlikely to receive compliance from states whose interests would thereby be impaired.

Only when there is again a close correspondence between structural realities and the ideological underpinnings of international law will it be possible for international law to bring a normative perspective effectively to bear on political interactions in the realm of intervention. As long as legal norms on intervention continue to stress nonintervention as the basic formative perspective, their disregard is all but guaranteed.

It can, of course, be argued that the existence of a normative perspective stressing nonintervention serves to limit, moderate, and modify the interventions that do take place and that for this reason it ought not to be abandoned. It is true that the rules we now have do have some influence on behavior, at least to the extent that states feel they must justify their interventions by citing one of the traditional principles— defense against external aggression, aid to the "legitimate government" against insurgents, and the like—and therefore may be discouraged from intervening overtly when such pretexts are not available. Indeed, embarrassment before the world community may cause states to terminate particular interventions, as, for example, when the United States ended its organization of Nationalist Chinese guerrilla units to function within mainland China in the 1950s.[4]

Since there are very few cases in which conventional pretexts for intervention are unavailable, however, the restraining force of existing norms is limited and marginal. Moreover, it is likely to get even smaller. In a world in which some men are becoming more and more conscious of alternatives to existing modes of life while others grow ever more fearful of change and cling to known ways, internal struggles over the ends and structure of society are likely to increase in number and intensity. Given the potential for political violence inherent in such conflicts and in the very process of the breakdown of traditional connections among individuals and groups, it seems likely that states will be moved to intervene in other states' affairs and that they will have little trouble finding a justification in international law. If no other justification is available, it is usually possible, if not always plausible, for a state to assert that another state intervened first and, thus, to claim that its own intervention is merely proportional counterintervention. While such a pretext is not available in cases like U-2 flights over Soviet territory or preparation of guerrilla units to be sent into mainland China, it is usually available in connection with interventions in most new states. Therefore, we have little to lose from a shift of focus to qualitatively

[4] I owe this example to a conversation with Manfred Halpern on May 17, 1969.

different norms and little to gain by reiteration of historically outmoded principles.[5]

Thus, the first thing to be said about whether international law can be made relevant to the behavior of participants in internal war situations is that it cannot, as long as it is based on a paradigm of nonintervention, no matter how refined its principles and how often and passionately it is reiterated.[6]

The second thing to be said is that, whatever the paradigm on which it is based, international law is unlikely to have very much influence on international actors' behavior in the contemporary world. This is not primarily because of a lack of international institutions with the power of sanctions but rather because of the factors which the absence of such institutions reflects—namely, the unbridgeable ideological gaps which divide men from one another. As long as such fundamental differences about long-term goals exist, there will almost certainly be contradictory and self-serving interpretations of whatever norms exist, since these differences prevent agreement on what terms mean, how to apply them to particular cases, and what conclusions to draw from such application. As we have seen, in order to be effective, law requires some minimal consensus on social policies and goals and some basic sense of community among those whose behavior it is to regulate. Neither of these obtains in the contemporary international system, and the law itself has become a tool in the conflict rather than a regulatory force above the conflict.

It would therefore be highly unrealistic, in my opinion, to expect principles proposed by scholars and lawyers to have much effect on behavior. Why, then, does it make any difference what principles are proposed? There are, in my view, two answers to this important question. On the level of behavior, it can be argued that there are some positive effects, albeit marginal ones, that flow from use of one rhetoric as opposed to another, and that one therefore might as well try to replace the current historically irrelevant legal rhetoric with one that at least has the virtue of being potentially relevant, should international actors ever decide to try seriously to translate it into practice. Law cannot stop the movement of history—cannot, for example, return the world to a Eurocentric system. Those who apply law can, however, if they understand the direction in which history is moving, use that appli-

[5] Cf. Manfred Halpern, "The Morality and Politics of Intervention," in James N. Rosenau (ed.), *International Aspects of Civil Strife* (Princeton: Princeton University Press, 1964).

[6] For a recent example of such historically irrelevant reiteration, see John Norton Moore, "The Control of Foreign Intervention in Internal Conflict," *Virginia Journal of International Law* 9 (May 1969): 205–342.

cation to channel, shape, and ease events[7]—or at least avoid the kind of legal ineffectiveness that springs from historical irrelevance. And scholars can play a role in generating discussion on how to use law to create patterns of interaction relevant to historically new and unique problems and demands. Moreover, there appears to be no alternative course of actions for scholars to take that would more rapidly increase the potential relevance of international law.

The second answer that can be given to the question of why it matters which paradigm is the basis for legal principles lies, I think, in the realm of analysis rather than behavior and is perhaps the more immediately important of the two. As we have seen, the basic concepts of traditional international law distract us from the real problems in actual cases. The present use of the categories and the basic outlook of international law by international lawyers and political analysts, no less than by UN officials, US congressmen, and third world diplomats, makes it impossible to come to grips practically or analytically with the problems of powerlessness and the breakdown of traditional connections, which are the essence of the revolution now upon us. To speak of "states," "nations," "incumbents," "insurgents," "legitimate governments," and the like, without stopping to ask whether they exist in the reality one is analyzing risks making international law ineffective and irrelevant conceptually, as well as practically.

Thus, a shift of analytic focus might make it possible to conceptualize empirical reality much more accurately. This shift may not lead to agreement on a basic framework in which to carry on conflict and collaboration, and perhaps no system of legal norms can at present be very effective in shaping states' behavior. This is not true only of international law; law in domestic societies is in the same beleaguered situation, as it attempts to cope with incoherent racial, ethnic, and ideological conflicts.[8] Yet even if international law is ineffective in large areas of international life, it can at least supply an analytic perspective relevant to the fundamental transformations now taking place in both national and international society.

[7] In the United States the Supreme Court has recently served this function by channeling basic historical trends in many areas of national life, including civil rights and reapportionment. An example of the effects on both law and society of attempts to stem the tides of change is provided by the Court's decisions on socioeconomic issues and labor questions during the 1930s.

[8] This suggests the importance of comparing the functioning of law in domestic and international settings. Useful comparison is hindered, however, by the assumption of most international lawyers that the relevant comparison is between the state as the subject of international law and the individual as the subject of municipal law. It would seem instead that the relevant comparison is between the state—that is, a society as a political entity—and politicized domestic groups, whether ethnic, racial, linguistic, ideological, class, or caste, since such groups are

339

Making Law Conceptually Relevant to Internal War Situations

In order to become conceptually relevant and effective, legal principles must be related to the movement of history. What, then, is the nature and direction of that historical movement? In an article redefining the revolutionary situation, Manfred Halpern characterizes our age as historically unique in terms of the quality of change now underway. He argues that the continuous breaking of connections in all systems by which human life is organized results in the destruction of man's capacity to cope with the most basic issues of social life, and that it is this very breaking of connections which constitutes "history's first common, world-wide revolution," the revolution of modernization. In his view, traditional forms of connection among individuals, groups, and societies are inadequate to handle the new problems and demands which arise in the modern age and, consequently, will continue to break when confronted by those problems and demands. Thus mankind must either develop the capacity to overcome this dissolution of traditional, established connections or else continue to suffer the consequences of their unintended and uncontrolled breakdown.[9]

From this point of view, intervention may foster rather than hinder the creation of new and modernizing connections among individuals, groups, and societies.[10] Thus, we have potentially much to gain from shifting the focus of law from prevention or curtailment of all kinds of intervention toward distinctions between those interventions which do and those which do not help to create a more freely interdependent world. One of the bases of the paradigm of nonintervention was the implicit assumption that entities labelled "states" were in fact capable of fulfilling the role assigned to states in the international system as a legal order—that is, that they were in fact autonomous units capable of assuming international rights and obligations. On this assumption, intervention would naturally be a violation of a state's rights and would prevent it from fulfilling its proper role in the international system. Today, as we have seen, this assumption is clearly invalid for most states.

---

the foci of men's allegiance and act as political units. This perspective allows for comparison between domestic and international situations in which law must function, not as the supposedly impartial and Olympian arbiter of disputes among isolated, apolitical individual units, but rather as one factor shaping a political conflict among consciously politicized groups. The advantages of this perspective include the possibility of heightened sensitivity to the interrelationship of law and politics and a more realistic expectation about what international law can accomplish. It would, furthermore, focus attention, not on the somewhat illusory issue of centralization versus decentralization of legal systems, but rather on law's function in creating, maintaining, and transforming political connections among groups, including societies.

[9] Halpern, "A Redefinition of the Revolutionary Situation," pp. 57–58.

[10] Halpern, "The Morality and Politics of Intervention," p. 250.

Nor can the matter of intervention be decided on the basis of principle rather than on the basis of careful empirical investigation. For in an age in which the fashioning of new connections between individuals, groups, and societies has become the worldwide revolutionary challenge, there may well be cases in which conscious and creative intervention can in fact help to forge such connections both within the society in which intervention takes place and between that society and the larger international community.

An additional reason for viewing the problem of intervention from the perspective of modernization is that the historical challenge of modernization is already assuming a more and more prominent place in the rhetoric used to justify interventions, if not yet in a serious way in the formulation of policy by those who intervene. Indeed, intervention and modernization have for quite some time been linked together in the practice and minds of policymakers, and men and societies with quite divergent social philosophies have decided that "modern societies must be built" and have in one way or another declared themselves "prepared to help build them."[11] Recent cases in which intervention has been justified at least in part on the grounds of its contribution to modernization include US intervention in Vietnam and Soviet intervention in Czechoslovakia, as well as Egyptian intervention in Yemen.[12] Thus, the task of clarifying the dynamics of the relationship between modernization and intervention is of immediate importance, since we must first know what kinds of intervention can in fact contribute to modernization before we can assess in particular cases an intervener's justification of his intervention on the ground of its contribution to modernization.[13] In any case, if it is man's success or failure in responding to the revolution of modernization which is crucial for both the present and the future, then the central criterion for evaluating interventions should be their effects on modernization.

---

[11] Walt W. Rostow, "Countering Guerrilla Attack," reproduced in Richard A. Falk (ed.), *The Vietnam War and International Law* (Princeton: Princeton University Press, 1968), p. 131.

[12] On the Vietnam case, see *ibid.* For the justification of intervention in terms of modernization used by the Soviet Union in connection with the invasion of Czechoslovakia, which is representative of the general Soviet approach to the issue, see the condensed text of an Aug. 14, 1968, *Pravda* article by I. Pomelov, which appears in *Current Digest of the Soviet Press* 20 (Sept. 4, 1968): 3–5, under the title "Common Principles and National Characteristics in the Development of Socialism." Justification of intervention in terms of modernization was also used by the United Arab Republic in connection with Egyptian intervention in Yemen; see p. 313 above.

[13] I have tried to do this at greater length than is possible here in my doctoral dissertation, "Modernization and Intervention: Yemen as a Theoretical Case Study," as well as more briefly in a paper presented to the Middle East Studies Association's Second Annual Convention in November 1968 on "Yemen: Modernization and Intervention."

The focus of concern from the point of view of the revolution of modernization is not the state but the society, not the government but the organization of men in fundamentally new relationships, not incumbents and insurgents but modernizing elites, not the prevention of intervention as such but the prevention of interventions that do not foster modernization, not internal wars as such but struggles between contending elites over the ends and structure of society. Thus, making international law on intervention relevant to the revolution of modernization requires a thoroughgoing transformation of the key concepts of international law and also of the questions with which it typically deals. Furthermore, it implies development of specific legal principles related to the revolution of modernization. In order to give some idea of the kind of principles I have in mind, I shall attempt below to sketch two such principles. They are intended as a subsidiary part of my general argument about the nature and role of contemporary international law rather than as the main point of this study.

The Principles of Modernizing Legitimacy and of Modernizing Intervention

As we have seen, one of the crucial aspects of traditional international law in the area of internal war and intervention is the differentiation between opposing elites. How can this differentiation be made in a way relevant to the revolution of modernization? I would suggest that a basis for differentiation could be provided by *a principle of modernizing legitimacy,* that is, legitimacy measured in terms of the relative capacity of the contending groups to develop the consciousness, creativity, institutionalized power, and justice necessary for coping with the revolution of modernization.[14]

The argument for using this criterion of modernizing legitimacy in internal war situations can be stated as follows: everywhere in the world the traditional society has already broken down as a coherent social system as a result of the rise of new social classes and new kinds of men who want to deal with their societies' social, political, and economic problems. Achievement of this goal is not possible under traditional forms of interaction. Long-run stability in any society depends upon the creation of new linkages among individuals and groups which allow sustained collaboration for new goals, since only on this basis can stability be achieved in the modern age. Therefore, it is crucial to distinguish between competing elites on the basis of their modernizing capacity.

[14] For a discussion of each of these components of the capacity for modernization, see Halpern, "A Redefinition of the Revolutionary Situation," pp. 69–74. The theory of modernization on which this study is based is that expounded by Halpern in this article.

There are at least two reasons why the principle of modernizing legitimacy would not represent a radical departure from current policies on recognition in internal war situations. First, the traditional legal criteria of territorial control and popular support are themselves political criteria—that is, they embody particular philosophical ideas about governmental legitimacy. Thus, shifting from the traditional principle of recognition to the principle of modernizing legitimacy would simply involve a shift from one political principle to another, not from an "objective" legal principle to a political one.

Second, as we saw earlier, in the contemporary international system, the decision to recognize or not to recognize is usually taken for reasons that have nothing to do with an objective assessment of territorial control and popular support. An outside state commonly evaluates the ideological differences between the two competing factions and recognizes the group whose policies are most congenial to its own interests and social philosophy. As we have also seen, there is a growing concern within the international community with the social goals and policies of both sides in an internal war, even when such policies do not directly affect outside states' interests. Thus, for example, the General Assembly's decision to seat the Republican delegation as the representatives of Yemen clearly was taken in part because of widespread dislike of the social, political, and economic policies pursued by the imams.

Since it is already the case that decisions about recognition are commonly made on grounds which involve consideration of the social policies of the factions contending for recognition, there is much to be said for making this evaluative process explicit and subject to discussion and also for relating the evaluative process to the general problem of modernization. This suggested shift in focus is of importance primarily in relation to the problem of intervention. In that connection the main effect of adopting a principle of modernizing legitimacy would be to call into question most current justifications for intervention, including those which rely on the traditional principle of aid to the "legitimate government," as that principle is normally formulated. The criteria of governmental legitimacy would be altered in such a way that it would no longer be possible, for example, for a state to justify its intervention in favor of incumbents simply on the ground that they had been in power prior to the outbreak of internal war. Rather, the intervening state would have to argue that the incumbents' modernizing capacity was greater than that of the insurgents *and* that its own intervention would help increase that modernizing capacity.

Further, a state could no longer justify its intervention solely on the ground that it constituted counterintervention, however proportional. Nor, on the other hand, would a state have to wait until it could plausibly allege that another state had already intervened in order to justify its own intervention. Thus, for example, Saudi Arabia would not have been able to justify its intervention in Yemen as counterintervention even if in fact Egypt had intervened first, nor would the United Arab Republic have had to justify its own intervention in support of the Republicans as counterintervention. It would, however, have had to justify it on grounds more solidly related to the problem of modernization—that is, on the basis of Republican potential as modernizers in Yemen.

Differentiation among interveners in terms of the goals of their interventions and the nature of the groups they intervene to support already takes place in the international legal order to some degree. It occurs notably in connection with anticolonial movements and wars of national liberation. While intervention in support of an anticolonial movement is generally thought of as permissible, aid to the colonial power usually is not. Indeed, differentiation in terms of modernizing capacity may already exist in embryonic form; in Yemen, for example, Saudi Arabia found it expedient to argue that Egyptian intervention in Yemen could not be justified by a desire to foster progress and development in Yemen because the imam himself had instituted a policy of reforms. The implication of this argument is that in the absence of such a policy of reforms intervention would have been justified. Thus, differentiation among internal factions in terms of their modernizing capacity would not be an unheard-of innovation.

Substantial innovation would nonetheless be required to make international law fully relevant to the revolution of modernization, since it would be necessary to develop an additional principle by which the contributions of outside interventions to modernization could be judged. It would not be enough that intervention take place in support of the faction that had more modernizing potential; intervention would also have to be likely to contribute to the development of modernizing capacity. Thus, the second principle, which might be called *the principle of modernizing intervention*, would require that, in order for a state's intervention to be permissible, there would have to be a reasonable expectation that it would contribute to the modernization of the society in which it took place. This is admittedly a vague standard, although no vaguer perhaps than a concept like "proportional counterintervention" or even "popular support," and it comes closer than they do to the actual reasons why intervention takes place in the contemporary world.

The principle could be applied in a number of ways. For example, in cases like Yemen, where the whole notion of "military victory" is simply inapplicable, intervention in the form of large-scale military operations might be judged as clearly unable to contribute to modernization, in particular because such large-scale military intervention would be likely to shift political support away from the side who received it. In fact, in a case like Yemen where there are such staggering problems to be confronted and so few Yemenis able to begin to deal with them, any kind of intervention, however well-intentioned, might not be able to accomplish very much in terms of modernization and, consequently, could perhaps not be justified under this principle. The primary focus of the principle, however, would be on distinguishing among different kinds of intervention in terms of their effects on modernization in each particular case and not on judging a priori whether or not intervention in any form could possibly be helpful for modernization.

This new way of conceptualizing the legality of intervention could be applied not only to intervention in internal wars but also to intervention by one society in the internal affairs of another, whatever the form and circumstances of that intervention. Indeed, such a broadening of focus would be essential in order to make international law relevant to the revolution of modernization, since much of what is usually seen as "normal" interaction between states is in fact interventionary in terms of its consequences for a society's development of modernizing capacity. Just as claims to governmental legitimacy in internal war situations can be examined in the light of the principle of modernizing legitimacy, so the legitimacy of any incumbent regime can be investigated in terms of its modernizing capacity and intervention on its behalf evaluated even in the absence of an internal war.

Making the principles of modernizing legitimacy and modernizing intervention the central criteria for evaluating intervention would not have the effect of legitimizing more interventions than can be justified under existing norms of international law; indeed, it would make intervention much harder to justify. It would no longer be enough, for example, for a state to justify its intervention on the ground that it was aiding the "legitimate government." For in evaluating that state's intervention in terms of its effects on modernization, it would be appropriate and necessary to ask whether that "legitimate government" was in fact either legitimate or capable of governing anything, was engaged in deliberate efforts to modernize, and (in internal war situations) was likely to be more capable than the opposing group of undertaking the task of modernization successfully. Only if all these questions could be answered affirmatively would intervention in support of the "legitimate government" be permissible—and even then only if the state wishing to intervene could make a case for the contributions of its intervention to modernization.

This would be a stringent standard indeed and one not likely to legitimize very many interventions—certainly not most of those now underway in the world. Consequently, if it were seriously applied, its effects in reshaping patterns of interaction among states would be very great. One need not go beyond some of the factors already mentioned as reasons for international law's behavioral ineffectiveness, however, to realize that the same factors would probably prevent the application of these new norms. There are too many short-term, specific interests that lead potential interveners to intervene against rather than for modernization. Even more important, there are mutually incompatible, competing conceptions of what modernization really involves, whether American or Soviet, Egyptian or Cuban. Thus, there would inevitably be contradictory conclusions drawn from the application of these norms to particular cases like Vietnam or Czechoslovakia. At least, though, it would then be possible to discuss those competing conceptions rather than to conduct the normative discussion on the basis of outmoded principles.

Another obvious possibility is that these principles could easily be twisted to suit the desire of an actor for justification of an intervention decided upon on more traditional grounds. However, to the extent that use of a particular rhetoric has any influence at all on the way its users behave, there would be marginal benefits from use of a rhetoric linked to the revolution of modernization, however self-serving and biased its application. Even under the most pessimistic assessment, it is difficult to see that things would be any worse than they are at present, and they might perhaps be somewhat better.

There would be other problems as well in the application of these principles to particular cases—problems of lack of information, of criteria for detecting modernizing capacity, of the inherent uncertainty of predictions about the future performance of competing elite groups, of the difficulty of judging the potential benefits of particular forms of foreign intervention, and so forth.[15] It is certainly true that we have not yet developed operational criteria for easily identifying modernizing capacity, nor has intervention been extensively studied from the point of view of its impact on modernization. Indeed, the development of such criteria and of probabilistic hypotheses about the costs and benefits of various kinds of intervention in terms of modernization would be one of the first tasks of scholarly research. It is likely that a good deal of room for disagreement in particular cases would remain, but at least scholars would be disagreeing about the central issues rather than refining historical irrelevancies.

---

[15] A number of these problems were called to my attention in a paper prepared by Jim Miller, a University Scholar at Princeton University.

IV. CONCLUDING SUMMARY

The actual task of developing operational criteria and trying to classify kinds of intervention from the point of view of modernization is one that goes well beyond the scope of this study. I have tried, rather, to demonstrate the ineffectiveness and irrelevance of existing norms of international law in the area of internal wars and intervention and to suggest the direction in which international law would have to be transformed in order to restore its relevance to international needs and problems. As I have tried to show, such a transformation could in principle take place, and norms relevant to the revolution of modernization could be developed. It is clear that such a transformation is unlikely. That it is nonetheless necessary if international law is to be relevant and effective either in shaping states' behavior or in providing a conceptual framework for analysis of contemporary problems is, I hope, equally clear.

P. E. Corbett

THE VIETNAM STRUGGLE AND INTERNATIONAL LAW

I. THE CONFLICT: A FACTUAL INTRODUCTION

However the present struggle in Vietnam is envisaged—whether as a civil war to determine what leadership is to govern the country as a whole, or as an international war between two sovereign states—the foreign participation far exceeds that in any previous conflict of a comparable nature. This would be true even if we left out of account the assistance from the Soviet Union, the People's Republic of China, and other communist states to Ho Chi Minh's Democratic Republic of Vietnam;[1] for more than five hundred thousand American and allied men are engaged on the side of South Vietnam and approximately twenty-four billion dollars a year are being spent by the United States in its cause. The civil or international war between two segments of the same state or between two minor states in Southeast Asia has become the focus of a vast competition for regional power, involving the constant risk of a world war *à l'outrance*.

We shall later have occasion to compare various aspects of this ominous struggle with the Spanish Civil War of 1936–39, which is in many ways its nearest precedent. For the moment, the comparative scale can be indicated by the figures for foreign personnel involved. According to the painstaking effort of Ann Van Wynen Thomas and A. J. Thomas, Jr., to reconcile conflicting statistics, roughly one hundred and sixty thousand foreigners were engaged on the Nationalist and fifty-two thousand on the Loyalist side, as compared with the more than half-million assisting one side alone in Vietnam.[2] The conflict is also unique in that it is not only for strategic control of a region deemed vital to the security of the powers involved but also to determine which of two alien political ideologies and systems is to replace an age-old native culture sustaining its own traditional values.

In any attempt to assess the issues involved in the internal and external struggle for Vietnam and the possible form of a durable settlement, it is essential to realize that for a thousand years or more the

---

[1] By Secretary of Defense Robert S. McNamara's estimates, the total of this assistance shrinks to material, if not moral, insignificance when compared with American and allied aid to South Vietnam. See below, pp. 364–65.

[2] Ann Van Wynen Thomas and A. J. Thomas, Jr., "International Legal Aspects of the Civil War in Spain, 1936–39," in this book, pp. 164–65.

nearest thing to a consistent thread in Vietnamese history has been a struggle to achieve and hold independence from foreign domination. Internal violence was endemic between feudal families competing for actual control under a formal monarchy or setting up new dynasties to govern an expanding country; but the continued resistance to renewed subjugation by China expressed something of that sense of identity and unity which is the basis of all nationhood. Against this long background of tenuous community, the present war between North and South Vietnam cannot fairly be regarded, either from the northern or from the southern point of view, as an enterprise of mere nationalistic or imperialistic expansionism. Even at the height of her power in Indochina, France was quite unable to extinguish the urge for independent statehood throughout the area of predominantly Vietnamese population.[3]

Between 1859 and 1883, France made a colony of Cochin-China and established protectorates over Annam and Tonkin. In 1887 she united them, together with Cambodia and Laos, in the Indochinese Union, the title under which she exercised power over the peninsula east of Siam from the frontier with China at 23°25′ N to the South China Sea at 8°30′ N.

Annam retained its emperor who, however, was subject to exile if the French found him too difficult to manage. Tonkin had a viceroy representing the emperor. Everywhere, final decision rested with French or French-trained officials. A French judicial system controlled the administration of justice. The old Confucian curriculum of literary, moral, and administrative instruction was replaced by a French system of education featuring the study of French and of the Western arts, sciences, and philosophy. The traditional mandarin officials were reduced to minor positions and the lowest salary scales. The disoriented victims of this remodeling of civic and instructional institutions helped to man and lead underground associations dedicated to the struggle for independent nationhood.[4]

Of these associations the most effective was the noncommunist Viet Nam Quock Dan Dang (VNQDD), the Vietnam Nationalist party, which in February 1930 led an abortive attempt to start a general uprising against the French. It was broken up by the French and only resumed operations in World War II. At a conference organized in 1941 by Nguyen Ai Quoc, now known everywhere as Ho Chi Minh, some remnants of it joined other revolutionary groups to form the Viet-Nam

[3] Joseph Buttinger, *Vietnam, A Dragon Embattled* (New York: Praeger, 1967), chaps. 2 and 3.
[4] For a history of the colonial period, see Virginia Thompson, *French Indo-China* (New York: Macmillan, 1942).

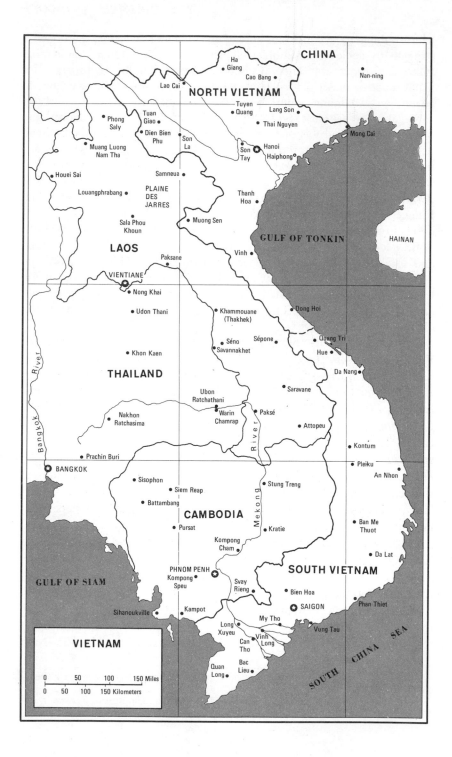

Doc Lap Dong Minh Hoi, the league for Vietnam Independence, abbreviated in the familiar form, Vietminh.[5]

The groups forming the Vietminh in 1941 varied in political coloring from democratic through socialist to communist, their one common aim being the expulsion of all foreign government from Indochina. They had been engaged in scattered revolts which up to that time had been put down with heavy immediate casualties and a long series of trials by French courts-martial. United in the Vietminh, they still had defeats in store; but as the Japanese displaced the French, finally taking over in March 1945, the Vietminh, under Ho Chi Minh's skilled guidance, gathered strength. In the last months of the war, it was even assisted by the American OSS in its guerrilla activities against the Japanese.[6] Within three weeks of Japan's surrender, it took over the government in Hanoi and proclaimed the Democratic Republic of Vietnam (DRV). Bao Dai, who had served as formal head of state in Annam under both the French and the Japanese, abdicated with enthusiastic salutations to the new republic and was named supreme councillor to Ho Chi Minh's government. Even in Cochin-China, the Vietminh, in the flush of what looked like a nationalist victory, was able temporarily to reconcile competing groups and to set about the task of organizing administration from Saigon.[7]

The Communist party of Indochina was formed at a conference assembled in February 1930 at Hong Kong by Ho Chi Minh as a delegate of the Comintern and attended by communists from Tonkin, Annam, and Cochin-China. The first two of the ten slogans drafted by Ho Chi Minh and adopted by the conference laid down its essential program:

1. To overthrow French imperialism, feudalism, and the reactionary bourgeoisie of Vietnam.

2. To win complete independence for Indochina.[8]

The party, despite repeated near annihilation by the French for its incitement of strikes and peasant revolts, managed to survive and to become first the solid core of the nationalist movement throughout the Indochinese Union, then creator of the Democratic Republic of Vietnam, and finally the commanding organizer (though now under the name of Vietnamese Workers party) of the war against the United

[5] Bernard Fall, *Le Viet-Minh, La République Démocratique du Vietnam, 1945–1960* (Paris: A. Colin, 1960), p. 17.

[6] See *ibid.*, pp. 33–34.

[7] Text of the declaration of independence and of the abdication in Marvin E. Gettleman (ed.), *Vietnam: History, Documents and Opinions* (Greenwich, Conn.: Fawcett Publications, 1965), pp. 57–61.

[8] Ho Chi Minh, *Oeuvres Choisies* (Paris: F. Maspero, 1967), p. 84 (my translation).

States and its allies in Southeast Asia.[9] For this the revolutionary genius of Ho Chi Minh was largely responsible. Those who have most studied his life and work are agreed that his lifelong dedication to the liberation of Vietnam equaled or predominated over his devotion to communism and that this fact, inspiring his national-front tactics, explained the extent of his following in South Vietnam.[10]

The Vietminh's exuberant march in 1945 toward national independence for Vietnam as a whole was interrupted by execution of the Potsdam agreements about Southeast Asia. The United Kingdom, given responsibility for the restoration of peace in that part of the world, handed over to the Kuomintang the role of disarming and repatriating the Japanese forces north of the sixteenth parallel. South of that dividing line, the occupying British force, interpreting its mission as the restoration of the country to France, actively opposed the Vietminh and the whole nationalist movement. Facilitating the reentry and reequipment of French troops, and even assisted by rearmed Japanese units, the British Command broke up the provisional government in Saigon and, early in 1946, after bitter fighting, handed over the southern zone to France. Bringing in new forces and using lend-lease equipment, the French, though they never succeeded in stamping out resistance in the south, were able to occupy Hanoi. There the Chinese had already insisted on the incorporation of rightist elements in the government, and Ho Chi Minh, under this pressure and confronted with growing French power, was obliged in March 1946 to form a coalition nationalist administration with the noncommunist groups assembled in the revived VNQDD.

As a momentary compromise, the French on March 2, 1946, entered into an agreement with this coalition recognizing the Republic of Vietnam as a free state, member of the Federation of Indochina and the French Union. A referendum was promised to determine whether Annam and Cochin-China should be united with Tonkin. The quid pro quo for France was to be a friendly reception for the French army as it relieved the Chinese troops.[11]

During the spring and summer, negotiations went on in Fontainebleau in France and at Dalat in Annam to settle the details of the allocation of territory and authority between the Federation of Indochina, the French Union, and the various parts of Indochina. No referendum was

[9] For tactical reasons, such as getting on with the Kuomintang, which was replacing the Japanese north of the sixteenth parallel, and to disarm anticommunist opposition generally, the Indochinese Communist party was formally dissolved in November 1945. Its members continued to be the leading element in the Vietminh, and it reemerged in Vietnam in March 1951 as the Vietnamese Workers party. See Fall, *Le Viet-Minh*, pp. 43–44, and the Preface by Paul Mus, p. ix).

[10] See *ibid.*, especially the biographical study of Ho on pp. 20–37.

[11] Harold Isaacs (ed.), *New Cycle in Asia* (New York: Institute of Pacific Relations, 1947), p. 169.

held, the French demanding delay until peaceful conditions could be established but in fact setting up a puppet government in Saigon opposed to the Vietminh and ready to accept separation of Cochin-China under French protection. This would have secured for France that part of the peninsula in which her heaviest and most profitable investments lay. In November the National Assembly in Hanoi adopted a constitution uniting Cochin-China, Annam, and Tonkin.[12] On November 23, French forces bombarded Haiphong by way of putting a stop to the DRV's violent reaction to the establishment of a French customs office at that port. In December Vietnamese troops attacked the French in Hanoi, and the war began which was to end with the annihilation of the French defenders of Dienbienphu on May 8, 1954.

We have seen that the OSS had rendered personal and material aid to the Vietminh as an ally in the task of driving Japan back out of Southeast Asia at the end of World War II.[13] But after Japan's surrender, it was only in the years 1949–50 that Washington again became actively concerned in the turmoil of Vietnam. This time it entered the arena as a foe of the Vietminh, which it had come to regard as an essentially communist organization dedicated to the militant expansion of communism. As for the Democratic Republic of Vietnam under Ho Chi Minh, what had been considered the rallying point of the forces struggling to liberate Indochina as a whole from France's colonial empire—an objective evoking general American sympathy—now appeared as the spearhead of the communist thrust.[14] The communist victory in China in 1949, followed in January 1950 by the recognition of the DRV by the USSR and the new-born People's Republic of China, had put a different light upon events in Southeast Asia. Bounding Vietnam on the north was now the open frontier of a communist power credited with a fanatical determination to expand and certain to use Ho Chi Minh and his following as means to that end. To build up a regional defense against the spread of an ideology and mode of government which Washington now held a threat to the vital interests of the United States, the Truman administration, along with Great Britain, in February 1950 recognized Bao Dai as head of a government of all Vietnam.[15]

[12] Fall, *Le Viet-Minh*, pp. 51–54.

[13] See above, p. 351.

[14] *Department of State Bulletin* (hereinafter cited as *DSB*), Feb. 13, 1950, p. 244.

[15] More than thirty states had recognized the state of Vietnam before the Geneva Agreements of 1954, while the DRV had been recognized by the USSR, People's Republic of China, and several eastern European states (John Norton Moore, "International Law and the United States Role in Viet Nam: A Reply," *Yale Law Journal* 6 (May 1967): 1056, n. 20).

Even before the end of 1946, the French had begun to cultivate Bao Dai as a figure around which Vietnamese groups hostile to Ho Chi Minh might be organized in active opposition to the Democratic Republic. The former emperor, having been sent by Ho Chi Minh on a mission to China, had chosen to take up residence in Hong Kong rather than return—a fact which had not increased his far from strong following in Vietnam. Weak as he was, the French chose him as the best available instrument and after three years of sporadic negotiations offered the minimum concession that would induce him to work with them. That was the independence of Vietnam, including Cochin-China, as an associated state in the French Union. Promised this in the Elysee Agreements of March 1949, Bao Dai resumed the imperial title and formed a cabinet that purported to be the legitimate government of Cochin-China, Annam, and Tonkin as one united state. For their various purposes the claim was recognized by France, the United States, and Great Britain.

In Paris, on May 8, 1950, Secretary of State Dean Acheson issued a statement including the following paragraph:

The United States Government, convinced that neither national independence nor democratic evolution exist in any area dominated by Soviet imperialism, considers the situation to be such as to warrant its according economic aid and military equipment to the Associated States of Indochina and to France in order to assist them in restoring stability and permitting these states to pursue their peaceful and democratic development.[16]

How utterly unsuccessful this policy was, though American aid soon exceeded a level of $500 million a year and included the provision of American military and political advisers and instructors, was demonstrated by the French debacle of 1954, by which time the French and noncommunist nationalist forces were in retreat before the Vietminh's People's Army from Hanoi to Saigon.

It was the grave view of these events taken by the Eisenhower administration, and the possibility of a direct clash between the United States and the People's Republic of China, that led to the Geneva Conference of April-July, 1954. In a speech to the Overseas Press Club in New York on March 29, 1954, Secretary of State John Foster Dulles put the administration's position in these words:

Under the conditions of to-day, the imposition in Southeast Asia of the political system of Communist Russia and its Chinese Communist ally, by whatever means, must be a grave threat to the whole free community. The

[16] *DSB*, May 22, 1950, p. 821.

United States feels that that possibility must not be passively accepted but should be met by united action. This might involve serious risks. But these risks are far less than those that will face us a few years from now if we dare not be resolute to-day.[17]

The Geneva Conference was attended by representatives of Cambodia, the Democratic Republic of Vietnam, France, Laos, the People's Republic of China, the state of Vietnam, the USSR, the United Kingdom, and the United States. The foreign ministers of the United Kingdom and the USSR were joint chairmen. On July 20 the conference reached Agreements for the Cessation of Hostilities between the People's Army of the DRV and the French Union forces and their allies in Vietnam, Cambodia, and Laos. It provided for an International Commission for Supervision and Control (ICSC), consisting of one commissioner each from Canada, India, and Poland, to supervise and control the application of the agreements. A provisional military demarcation line, with a demilitarized zone of not more than five kilometers on each side of it, was established along the seventeenth parallel of north latitude. The French Union and the DRV were given three hundred days to withdraw military forces, equipment, and supplies into the regroupment zones to the south and north, respectively, of the demarcation line. No troop reinforcements were to be introduced on either side, no new military bases established, and no military alliance adhered to for either the northern or the southern regrouping zone. The final declaration of the conference, dated July 21, 1954, emphasized that "the military demarcation is provisional and should not in any way be interpreted as constituting a political or territorial boundary."[18] It also stipulated that the general elections, called for by article 14 of the Agreement on the Cessation of Hostilities in Vietnam to "bring about the unification of Vietnam," "should be held in July 1956 under the supervision of an international commission" and that "consultations will be held on this subject between the competent representative authorities of the two zones from July 20, 1955, onward."

From the beginning, the United States had considered the conference too willing to compromise with communism for the sake of immediate peace. At one time it seemed that Washington would withdraw all high-level participation in the meeting. In the end, however, it took note, through its representative, General Walter Bedell Smith, of the agree-

---

[17] *DSB*, April 12, 1954, pp. 539–40.
[18] Par. 6. The texts of the Agreement on the Cessation of Hostilities in Vietnam and of the Final Declaration are printed in Great Britain, House of Commons, *Sessional Papers*, vol. 31 (1953/54), Cmd. 9239.

355

ments and of paragraphs 1 to 12 of the final declaration, declaring that it would "refrain from the threat or use of force to disturb them, in accordance with Article 2 (Section 4) of the Charter of the United Nations . . ." and "would view any renewal of the aggression in violation of the aforesaid Agreements with grave concern and as seriously threatening international peace and security." The omission of the thirteenth and final paragraph of the declaration in this "taking note" was clear notice that "grave concern" implied no obligation to consult with the other members of the conference on any measures that might prove necessary to ensure that the Agreements on the Cessation of Hostilities in Cambodia, Laos, and Vietnam were respected. Secretary of State Dulles had already drafted *his* plan for an overwhelming response to any renewal of communist aggression. This was to take form in the Southeast Asia Collective Defense Treaty (SACDT) concluded at Manila in September 1954 between Australia, France, New Zealand, Pakistan, the Republic of the Philippines, Thailand, the United Kingdom, and the United States, with the protocol extending its protective provisions to Cambodia, Laos, "and the free territory under the jurisdiction of the State of Vietnam."

As for Bao Dai's "State of Vietnam," it representatives were not admitted to negotiate formally at Geneva. France would have had them participate directly, but the DRV refused to negotiate with the Bao Dai government and insisted on bilateral negotiation with France. B. S. N. Murti, a former member of the staff of the ICSC, suggests that the DRV "probably wanted to show the world that they were the only Vietnamese party which fought against France for freedom and at the same time to impress upon the Vietnamese that Bao Dai's Government was only a puppet of France."[19] Bao Dai's representatives nevertheless insisted from the sidelines, though to no avail, that they alone were legally competent to speak for Vietnam as a whole and refused to enter into any agreement stipulating, however temporarily, a division of the country. Nor has Saigon from that day to this ceased to protest the demarcation line fixed by the conference at the seventeenth parallel. Yet in spite of its general rejection of the agreements, Bao Dai's government, like that of the United States, undertook not to use force to resist the procedures for carrying the cease-fire into effect.[20]

---

[19] B. S. N. Murti, *Vietnam Divided* (New York: Asia Publishing House, 1964), p. 16.

[20] Great Britain, House of Commons, *Sessional Papers*, vol. 31 (1953/54), "Record of the Closing Session," Cmd. 9239, pp. 5–9.

Two weeks before the end of the Geneva Conference, Bao Dai had appointed Ngo Dinh Diem prime minister. In October 1955 this choice of the emperor was to depose him and to declare the territory south of the seventeenth parallel "the Republic of Vietnam." Diem was a leading figure among the two million Roman Catholic Vietnamese. Spending several years in the United States, he had won the enthusiastic support of important personages in the Roman Catholic hierarchy there and rapidly became Washington's main hope for the production of a united, powerful, and democratic Vietnam. In a letter of October 23, 1954, offering to plan with Diem a greater and more effective American "contribution to the welfare and stability of the Government of Vietnam," President Eisenhower explained that the purpose of his offer was "to assist the Government of Vietnam in developing and maintaining a strong, viable state, capable of resisting attempted subversion or aggression through military means."[21]

For some years the United States was persuaded that Diem was making firm progress toward these ends. Four main knots of opposition and misrule confronted him when he took office. These were the two religious sects, the Cao Dai and the Hoa Hao, the former practicing a native but recent conglomerate creed, the latter Buddhist, each with its own army and both resisting the monopoly of power in Diem and his Roman Catholic appointees. A third disruptive "sect" was the Bin Xuyen, controlling prostitution, organized crime, *and the police* in and about Saigon. Vigorous measures against all three brought them under control. For a time Diem was also able to neutralize the seditious activities of the cadres left in the southern zone to keep alive and organize support for the Vietminh in preparation for the promised elections and the confidently expected return of the communist leadership. Best of all, his productive cooperation with governmental and private American agencies facilitated the migration and eventual settlement of nearly a million refugees (more than two-thirds of them Catholics fleeing communism) from the northern zone. In April 1956 France, under the strain of revolt in Algeria and disposed to liquidate her costly interests in Asia, withdrew her High Command from Vietnam, leaving the obligations assumed in the Geneva Agreements to their chances under Diem.

As for the 1956 elections stipulated in the Geneva Agreements, Diem ignored repeated proposals from the DRV to begin the organizing consultations that the final declaration had called for between the competent

[21] *DSB*, Nov. 15, 1954, pp. 735–36.

representative authorities of the two zones from July 20, 1955 onward.[22] His explanation was the very plausible one that the DRV would never permit a free vote in the north and, along with the American authorities, he was convinced that elections in 1956 would result in an overwhelming victory for the Vietminh. His policy was to eradicate all forms of cooperation with that body.

Diem's early successes were enough to persuade public and government in the United States that Vietnam was well on the way to the stable Western-style democracy that would stem the advance of communism in Southeast Asia. He was enthusiastically received in Washington and given renewed assurance of the economic and political aid needed for his impressive program of reform. He returned home to confront a rising tide of troubles that were to result in his assassination in 1963 along with a brother, Ngo Dinh Nhu, who had directed the ruthless police measures that brought on the military coup of that year.[23]

Sporadic revolt in the villages against the brutal and haphazard measures adopted by Diem's forces in hunting down suspected communist collaborators had expanded in the years 1958–59 into widespread guerrilla warfare organized by the Vietminh cadres and conducted by the communist and noncommunist nationalists associated in what was now known as the Vietcong. An attempted military coup d'etat on November 11, 1960, was easily subdued; but the next month saw the formation of the National Liberation Front of South Vietnam (NLF), which has ever since been the command organization for the combined communist and noncommunist warfare against the Saigon regime.[24]

The general deterioration in Diem's control over events in South Vietnam, culminating in his assassination in 1963, continued to be regarded in the United States as the work of resurgent communism stimulated and reinforced by increasing infiltration of men, munitions, and supplies from the DRV, assisted by the USSR and the People's Republic of China. The American response was to multiply economic and military aid to Diem. A report issued by the U.S. Department of State in February 1965 asserts that "from 1959 to 1960, when Hanoi was establishing its infiltration pipeline, at least 1,800 men, and possibly 2,700 more, moved into South Vietnam from the North. The flow increased to

[22] Par. 7. For printed source, see n. 18.
[23] Cf. Roger Hilsman, *To Move a Nation* (Garden City, N.Y.: Doubleday, 1967), pp. 416–18.
[24] Phillipe Devillers, "The Struggle for Unification of Vietnam," *China Quarterly*, January-March 1962, pp. 16–20.

a minimum of 3,700 in 1961 and at least 5,400 in 1962." The figure given for 1963 is 4,200, and for 1964 an established minimum of 4,400, with an estimated 3,000 more.[25] The total up to the end of 1964 was raised in a more recent calculation issued by the Department of State to 40,000. This later report goes on to say that "most of these men were infiltrated through the territory of Laos in plain violation of the 1962 Geneva Agreement on the Neutrality of Laos. Native North Vietnamese began to appear in large numbers in early 1964, and in December 1964 full units of the regular North Vietnamese Army began to enter the South."[26]

In a joint statement by Vice-President Lyndon B. Johnson and Ngo Dinh Diem, dated Saigon, May 13, 1961, we find the acknowledgment that "free Vietnam cannot alone withstand the pressure which this Communist empire is exerting against it" and a statement of "the need of free Vietnam for increased emergency assistance and the will and determination of the United States to provide such assistance." This was followed on December 14 of the same year by a letter from President John F. Kennedy assuring Diem that "we shall promptly increase our assistance to your defense effort."[27] This announced the beginning of an expansion of the military personnel in South Vietnam from about one thousand in 1961 to twelve thousand in 1962. In addition to increased economic aid, American military support now included advisers, technicians, helicopters, and propellor aircraft with pilots and mechanics.[28] Under President Johnson, the total had risen to 23,000 in January 1965, and in the spring of that year, after the bombing of North Vietnam had begun, combat units were dispatched from the United States to join in ground, air, and naval action against the Vietcong in South Vietnam. By 1967, American forces there numbered nearly half a million. Since the inauguration of the air offensive against North Vietnamese targets with the object immediately of cutting down the flow of men and supplies and ultimately of reducing the military potential of the DRV to the point where Ho Chi Minh would be glad to negotiate a settlement, the struggle has assumed the proportions of major war.[29]

[25] "Aggression from the North: The Record of North Viet-Nam's Campaign to Conquer South Viet-Nam," *DSB*, March 22, 1965, p. 407.

[26] U.S. Department of State, "The Basis for United States Action in Vietnam under International Law," 5 (mimeographed), quoted by John Norton Moore, "The Lawfulness of Military Assistance to Vietnam," *American Journal of International Law* 61 (1967): 10–11.

[27] *DSB*, June 19, 1961, pp. 956–57, and Jan. 1, 1962, pp. 13–14.

[28] Hilsman, *To Move a Nation*, p. 424.

[29] For the evolution of American policy and strategy, see especially *ibid.*, pp. 413–537. For details of troops engaged and casualties, see the article by R. W. Apple, Jr., in the *New York Times*, Aug. 7, 1967, pp. 1, 14.

II.   THE INTERNATIONAL SETTING

The war in Vietnam is part of the general power struggle between the communist countries and the Western democracies. On both sides there are serious differences both as to the general conflict and as to its particular focus in Vietnam, and these differences go far to explain why neither the world organization for the pacific settlement of disputes nor the special machinery set up to establish and maintain peace in Indochina has been able to control events there. Though we are as yet far from a clear and generally accepted law to govern external participation in civil strife, an effective application of the United Nations Charter or of the Geneva Agreements of 1954 would have saved not only Vietnam but the United States as well from much, if not all, of a long and tragic ordeal. What have been the principal great-power interests that have worked against such collective action?

The Soviet Union

The story of the Geneva Conference of 1954 leaves no doubt of Moscow's essential contribution to the agreements reached there on a cessation of hostilities in Vietnam, Laos, and Cambodia. The first representative of the DRV, Pham Van Dong, came with demands that were unacceptable to France, to Cambodia, and to Laos. These included French recognition of the sovereignty of Khmer in Cambodia and Pathet Lao in Laos and their representation at the conference. All foreign troops were to be withdrawn from these sovereign states. V. M. Molotov, Soviet foreign minister and, with Foreign Secretary Anthony Eden, co-chairman of the conference, was able, with the assistance of Chou En-lai of the People's Republic of China, to persuade the DRV to drop these demands and accept an agreement between the French and Viet-minh commands on the conditions of a cease-fire and the details of withdrawal and regroupment of forces. With Eden, moreover, he was responsible for agreement to set up a commission of neutrals (the ICSC) to secure observance of the cease-fire and regroupment provisions. Moscow was content with the de facto recognition of the military authorities of the DRV as competent to make a binding agreement with the French High Command for Laos, Cambodia, and Vietnam. This concession to Ho Chi Minh's communist regime explains the refusal of the United States fully to endorse the Geneva Agreements and Secretary of State Dulles' zeal to organize in the Southeast Asia Treaty Organization (SEATO) a defensive alliance against communist imperialism in the Far Eastern and Pacific areas. The Kremlin's assistance in an arrangement that saved French face is said to have been the quid pro quo for France's rejection of the plan for a European Defense Community.[1]

The Soviet Union was an active participant in the second Geneva Conference which, in a year of sporadic and difficult negotiation from 1961 to 1962, produced the Declaration and Protocol on the Neutrality of Laos. Charges of violation of this excellent arrangement by the DRV, the RVN and the USA led Moscow in July 1965 to call for a reassembly of the conference on Laos, with the later suggestion that the agenda might be extended to cover the whole conflict in Indochina. In this it was energetically supported by France, and for some time the People's Republic of China and the DRV seemed willing to participate. Later, however, outbursts from Peking and Hanoi reviled Moscow's conciliatory efforts as a sellout to American imperialism. The French and Russian proposals had not mentioned conditions preliminary to conferring, whereas the public pronouncements emanating from Peking and Hanoi demanded an immediate and complete withdrawal of American and allied troops. What this appeared to amount to was an insistence upon acceptance, prior to any renewed conference, of their terms of final settlement. If the two capitals had at any time been willing to contemplate neutralization as proposed by France, they now appeared determined to resist any settlement that might lead to a neutral coalition in Saigon, weakening the NLF, which they regarded as the sole legal government in South Vietnam, with a mixture of rightist and American-supported "cliques."[2]

By March 1965, the Russian position had hardened to the same point. On the nineteenth of that month Moscow published a document calling upon the United States to withdraw all troops and weapons from South Vietnam and leave the people there to decide their internal affairs without external interference.[3]

This position was confirmed by the Goldberg-Gromyko dialogue in the General Assembly of the United Nations in September 1966. When Ambassador Arthur J. Goldberg declared on September 22,

For our part, we have long been and remain to-day ready to negotiate without any prior conditions. . . . The United States is willing once again to take the first step. We are prepared to order a cessation of all bombing of North Vietnam the moment we are assured, privately or otherwise, that this step

[1] Donald Lancaster, *The Emancipation of French Indochina* (New York: Oxford University Press, 1961), pp. 336–37.

[2] Cf. Franz Schurmann, Peter Dale Scott and Reginald Zelnick, *The Politics of Escalation in Vietnam* (Greenwich, Conn.: Fawcett Publications, 1966), pp. 37, 66–67, 72–73.

[3] *Ibid.*, pp. 71–72.

will be answered promptly by a corresponding and appropriate de-escalation on the other side.

Foreign Minister Andrei Gromyko treated the offer with disdain. Citing, on September 23, what he called "the indisputable fact . . . that each so called 'peace offensive' of Washington is followed by a further escalation of aggressive actions," he went on to describe Goldberg's statement as a mere defense of American aggression and to assert "that there are still no signs testifying to the seriousness of the intention of Washington to seek a settlement." The solution of the Vietnam problem, he said, was simple. The United States had merely to accept the program proposed by the DRV and the NLF:

unconditional cessation of the bombing of the territory of the D.R.V., withdrawal of all armed forces of the United States and their allies from South Vietnam, removal of foreign armaments, the granting to the Vietnamese people of a chance to settle their internal problems themselves. The aggressor came to Vietnam, the aggressor must depart.[4]

The dialogue was resumed a year later, again in the opening meetings of the General Assembly of the United Nations. No apparent progress toward peace had occurred in the interval. On the contrary, the year had been marked by a steady intensification and extension of hostilities. Only a few miles now separated American bombing targets from the Chinese border, and an occasional bomber inevitably strayed over that line. Opposition to the war among the American people and around the world had become increasingly vocal. The earnestness of Ambassador Goldberg's appeal to the United Nations and all its members to assist in the search for peace could hardly be doubted by any unprejudiced listener. It made no visible impression upon Soviet Foreign Minister Gromyko. For him there was nothing new in this restatement of the American position. He insisted that it showed no intention of "getting out" of Vietnam and that it continued to make cessation of the bombing of North Vietnam conditional upon concessions from the other side.

It is true that Ambassador Goldberg, after declaring that the search for peace in Vietnam should be the major concern of the whole community of nations and asking the active participation of the United Nations in the quest, had made it quite clear that the United States would not contemplate any unilateral and unconditional retreat. He said, "We do not seek to impose a military solution on North Vietnam or on its adherents. By the same token, in fidelity to a political solution, we will

[4] United Nations, General Assembly, *Official Records*, 21st sess., 1413th plen. mtg., Sept. 23, 1966, p. 12.

not permit North Vietnam or its adherents to impose a military solution upon South Vietnam." But he repeated the offer of the United States to seek a political solution either at the conference table or in private negotiation. If either of these courses could be facilitated by mutual military restraint, scaling down with or without a formal cease-fire, the United States would be prepared to take this path. He noted that there had never been any assurance from Hanoi that negotiations would follow a cessation of the bombing of North Vietnam, and he asked what Hanoi and its supporters would do or refrain from doing if the bombing stopped. Then, in case the way to negotiation could be eased by indicating, without prejudice or precondition to that interchange, the principles his government considered the basis of an honorable settlement, he in effect set out a summary of the Geneva Agreements under five heads:

1. Cease fire and disengagement.
2. "No military forces, armed personnel or bases to be maintained in North or South Vietnam except those under the control of the respective governments."
3. "Full respect for the international frontiers of the states bordering on North and South Vietnam, as well as for the demarcation line and demilitarized zone."
4. "Peaceful settlement by the people in both North and South Vietnam of the question of reunification without foreign interference."
5. "Finally, supervision of all the foregoing by agreed upon international machinery."[5]

Elaborating his rejection of this approach, Foreign Minister Gromyko observed that "the wall of moral and political isolation around the aggressor is growing" and appealed to "every honest man in the world" to condemn the aggression of the United States.[6] By way of conclusion he repeated his warning of the previous year that the Soviet Union and other socialist countries would go on supplying "the fraternal people of Vietnam" with the support and assistance necessary to repel aggression. The NLF was, he declared, the only genuine representative of the people of South Vietnam: its program was in conformity with the Geneva Agreements and had the full support of the Soviet Union as a just basis for settlement. For any assistance that the Soviet Union and its allies might give, the Kremlin could plead the same justification as the United States, namely, collective self-defense.

There is much in this to suggest that the USSR was now less inter-

---

[5] *Department of State Bulletin* (hereinafter cited as *DSB*), October 16, 1967, pp. 483–86.
[6] *New York Times*, Sept. 23, 1967, p. 2.

ested in a peace settlement in Vietnam than in the continuing discomfiture of the United States. The suggestion is reinforced by the fact that recently it has been Great Britain, not the Soviet Union, that has been pressing for a new Geneva conference. The British effort to persuade the Russian cochairman to join in summoning such a meeting has apparently been met by insistence on the prior condition that the United States unconditionally halt all its military operations in Vietnam.[7] If, for all its tragic magnitude, the war in Vietnam is essentially part of a general power struggle between the world's greatest states, it is easy to understand that the Soviet estimate of its continuing cost to the United States in human and material resources, in international moral and political influence, and in the capacity for effective action in other critical areas may have become a dominant factor in determining Moscow's policy.

The People's Republic of China (PRC)

As we have seen, the PRC was an active participant in the Geneva Conference of 1954. The same is true of the 1962 conference on Laos. On the latter occasion it even agreed to pay 17.6 percent (the same quota as France, the USSR, the United Kingdom, and the United States) of the expenses incurred by the International Commission for Supervision and Control in Laos, over and above pay and allowances, which are borne by Canada, India, and Poland.[8]

When France and the Soviet Union began to press for another conference on Indochina that might neutralize the country, they reported that the PRC and the DRV were prepared to attend such a meeting. But since the end of 1964, with the military escalation of the conflict, Peking rejects the idea of neutralization and refuses to attend any conference until all foreign forces have been withdrawn from South Vietnam and what it regards as the provisions of the Geneva Agréements of 1954 have been reaffirmed. In a speech of April 8, 1965, Hanoi's Premier Pham Van Dong takes the same position. The engagement of a large American and allied army and the bombing of North Vietnam had apparently stiffened the communist resistance.[9]

I have described the USSR and the PRC as noncombatant allies of the DRV. It must be pointed out, however, that their economic and

[7] For a later British-Russian interchange on this subject, see the report on conversations between Foreign Minister Andrei Gromyko and Foreign Secretary George Brown on Sept. 23, 1967, in *New York Times*, Sept. 24, 1967, p. 5.

[8] Article 18. *DSB*, Aug. 13, 1962, p. 263.

[9] See, for example, Schurmann, Scott, and Zelnik, *The Politics of Escalation*, pp. 65, 67, 150–51.

military aid shrinks to insignificance in comparison with that given to the RVN by the United States. In a statement before the Senate Preparedness Investigation Subcommittee, Secretary of Defense McNamara put North Vietnam's total imports at 5,800 tons per day, and of this only 550 tons per day consisted of military equipment. Supplies required by communist forces in South Vietnam at their present level of operations were substantially less than 100 tons a day. They "could be transported by only a few trucks." For these reasons, and in view of the increased risk of war with the PRC, the Secretary of Defense strongly advised against the sharp increases in the air offensive in North Vietnam that the subcommittee, yielding entirely to its military witnesses, saw fit to recommend.[10]

The United Kingdom

For what they have been worth, the Geneva Agreements of 1954 must be credited in large part to the patient diplomacy of Britain's Foreign Minister, Sir Anthony Eden, now Earl of Avon. And it may be that the conference over which he and V. M. Molotov jointly presided was the alternative to a large-scale intervention by the United States in aid of a not overenthusiastic France—an intervention which at that moment might have touched off a war with the Soviet Union and the People's Republic of China. It was the refusal of the British government to take part in such an intervention that caused the Eisenhower administration to drop a plan upon which Mr. Dulles seems to have set his heart. The United Kingdom was determined to try the conference method of preventing the Vietnam conflict from expanding into general war.[11]

The foreign ministers of Great Britain and the Soviet Union continue to be cochairmen of a Geneva Conference that is, as it were, in indefinite recess. In 1962 they called it back into session for the neutralization of Laos. They have also acted as recipients of complaints from either side about violations of the agreements and declarations made at these conferences and of reports from the ICSC. Naturally, any action they may take depends upon the decisions of their respective governments, which have not always seen eye-to-eye on the possible value of

[10] *New York Times*, Aug. 26, 1967, p. 5; and Sept. 1, 1967, p. 10.

[11] Secretary of State Dulles' speech of March 29, 1954, in New York, *DSB*, April 12, 1954, pp. 539–40; Chalmers M. Roberts, "The Day We Didn't Go to War," *Reporter*, Sept. 14, reprinted in Marvin E. Gettleman (ed.), *Vietnam, History, Documents, and Opinions* (Greenwich, Conn.: Fawcett Publications, 1965), pp. 96–105; Lancaster, *The Emancipation of French Indochina*, pp. 313–26; 332–37; Dwight D. Eisenhower, *Mandate for Change, 1953–56* (New York: New American Library, 1965), pp. 424–25.

a further meeting of the conference. Up to 1965, Moscow more than once proposed such a meeting; since that time Britain has taken over the role of promoter.[12] Generally, the British government has taken no stand against American military action in Vietnam, though it takes no part in it. Prime Minister Harold Wilson, however, publicly deplored the bombing of Hanoi and Haiphong and is reported, after his visits to Moscow in 1966, to have warned President Johnson of the danger of general war if such escalation continued.

In the Twenty-second General Assembly, British Foreign Secretary George Brown strongly supported Ambassador Goldberg's appeal for negotiations leading to peaceful settlement and condemned Hanoi's intransigent attitude. He repeated the American delegate's statement that the DRV had never said what it would do or refrain from doing if the bombing ceased.[13] Within a week, on the other hand, the annual Labour Party Conference passed somewhat inconsistent resolutions asking the Labour government "to dissociate itself completely" from U.S. policy in Vietnam and "to try to persuade the United States to end the bombing immediately, permanently and unconditionally." This did not alter the official British position. Mr. Brown was on hand to defend the Labour government and, to some extent, the United States, citing, as he did, five halts in the bombing with no sign of response from Hanoi.[14]

France

In 1956 France withdrew from Vietnam and since that time has given no material aid to either side, though President Charles de Gaulle hardly concealed his disapproval of the American enterprise there. Drawing upon his predecessors' disastrous failure in Indochina and his own experience in liquidating the French attempt to hold Algeria, he predicted that if the United States persisted in its military undertaking to make South Vietnam a bastion against the spread of communism and the expansion of Chinese power over Southeast Asia the result would be a general war with all its nuclear consequences. From time to time after 1964, often in consultation with Moscow, he therefore urged a cessation of the bombing of North Vietnam, unconditional negotiations, another Geneva conference, and a settlement calling for the withdrawal of all foreign forces and a neutralization of Indochina. These proposals were accompanied by an offer to assist the Vietnamese people to unite their country and establish its independence of external influence.[15]

[12] See the report on the conversations between Foreign Secretary George Brown and Foreign Minister Andrei Gromyko, *New York Times*, Sept. 24, 1967, p. 5.

[13] *New York Times*, Sept. 27, 1967, p. 1.

[14] *New York Times*, Oct. 5, 1967, pp. 1 and 5.

[15] *New York Times*, Aug. 30, 1963, p. 1.

Moreover, the French president, not content with press interviews and telecommunication, sent at least one mission via Peking to Hanoi to sound out attitudes in regard to negotiation. This was carried out by M. Jean Sainteny, a senior diplomat with much Far Eastern experience, in June and July 1966.

Those months were a busy period of third-party intercession, including in addition to M. Sainteny's mission the visit of the Canadian diplomat, Chester Ronning, to Hanoi and one of U Thant's appeals to stop the bombing of North Vietnam, move toward a cease-fire, and open negotiations among all the combatants.[16] The failure of all such approaches has been attributed in official American statements to out-of-hand rejection by Hanoi, abetted by Peking. Some observers, however, not excluding members of Congress, have attributed it to an alleged unwillingness of the United States government to contemplate any compromise settlement.[17]

Sharply indicative of the divergence of French and American policy is France's refusal to join in the resolutions of the SEATO Council and of the Manila Conference (1966) declaring the determination of the participants to go on furnishing such military and economic aid as may be necessary to stop what is termed the communist aggression in South Vietnam. This accentuates the posture assumed by France under President de Gaulle as a hard-bitten former combatant who now, being neutral, seeks to persuade the belligerents to settle their differences at the conference table and thus avert the grave danger of world war.

This does not mean support for the United States in its repeated attempts to persuade the United Nations to deal with the conflict. As recently as September 1967, the French foreign minister, M. Couve de Murville, saw no hope that the Security Council or General Assembly could bring peace to Vietnam and continued to press, as he had in the previous year, for a renewal of independent negotiations along the lines of the Geneva Conferences of 1954 and 1962.[18] In this, the United States, "perhaps the world's greatest Power," would have to take the initiative, since its massive military action in Indochina was the chief threat to peace in the Far East and in the world. As a final settlement he followed President de Gaulle in advocating neutralization by international treaty to be concluded by the great powers and others directly concerned. The question of reunification and of the kind of government

---

[16] *New York Times*, June 21, 1966, p. 1.

[17] See Senator Vance Hartke, "Where Are the Peacemakers?" in *Progressive*, Sept. 1966, pp. 12–14, and Schurmann, Scott, and Zelink, *The Politics of Escalation, passim.*

[18] *New York Times*, Sept. 29, 1967, pp. 1 and 6.

was to be left to the people of North and South Vietnam to settle entirely by themselves.

The Final American Position

In the United Nations many members joined in the plea for a cessation of the bombing of North Vietnam as a necessary step toward negotiation.[19] The pressure there, reinforced by the growing strength of American opinion to the same effect, was a factor in determining a gradual relaxation of the conditions attached to Washington's offer. In a speech at San Antonio on September 28, 1967, President Johnson toned down upon a reciprocal reduction of military activity by Hanoi. "The United States," he said, "is willing to stop all aerial and naval bombardment of North Vietnam where this will lead promptly to productive discussion. We, of course, assume that while discussions proceed, North Vietnam would not take advantage of the bombing cessation or limitation."[20] The DRV scornfully rejected this overture as the same old conditional offer.

Six months later, on March 31, 1968, President Johnson went a step farther toward meeting Hanoi's conditions. He announced a substantial and unconditional reduction in the level of hostilities. All attacks on North Vietnam were stopped "except in the area north of the demilitarized zone where the continuing enemy build-up directly threatens allied forward positions. . . ."[21] In response, the DRV government declared "its readiness to appoint its representative to contact the U.S. representative with a view to determining with the American side the unconditional cessation of the U.S. bombing raids and all other acts of war against the Democratic Republic of Vietnam so that talks may start."[22] This carefully limited acceptance opened the way for that curious diplomatic phenomenon, talks to determine the conditions of talks. Beginning in early May 1968 these talks were still in progress when on Thursday, October 31, President Johnson, in the hope of moving from preliminaries to substantive negotiations, ordered "that all air, naval and artillery bombardment of North Vietnam cease as of 8 A.M., Washington time, Friday morning."[23] This went some way to convince neutral governments that the US administration was doing everything politically feasible to move from the battlefield to the conference table.

[19] See note of Secretary-General U Thant to Ambassador Goldberg, Dec. 20, 1966, *DSB*, Jan. 23, 1967, p. 139.
[20] *DSB*, Oct. 23, 1967, p. 521.
[21] *DSB*, April 15, 1968, p. 482.
[22] *DSB*, April 22, 1968, p. 513.
[23] *DSB*, Nov. 18, 1968, p. 517.

III. INTERNATIONAL LAW AND CIVIL STRIFE

It has often been assumed that international law recognizes a right of revolution.[1] In what entities this assumed right vests, whether in the individual or in politically disaffected groups, is a question that has not been adequately explored. It would seem, however, sharply out of character for the positive international law to which the practice of states has in some degree conformed in the last three centuries to have penetrated so far into the internal order of the state as either to confer or to deny a right of revolution while still refusing to recognize the personality of individuals or groups not organized as states. The right could indeed only be logically asserted by an identification of international with natural or moral law, which, of course, posited duties of the sovereign to his subjects. When in the nineteenth century great powers were moved to intervene for the protection of ethnic or religious minorities or for the liberation of revolting colonies, they relied for justification upon general moral principles rather than any norm of positive international law.

The points upon which most theoretical arguments turned in the traditional literature were (a) whether foreign states were legally entitled to intervene only on the side of the incumbent government, (b) whether they must observe a strict neutrality between the opposing sides, or (c) whether they were free to assist whichever side they considered just. If there was any distinction in the position actually taken by governments, it was, I think, that they confidently asserted an international-law right to assist an established and recognized regime but appealed, rather, to dictates of humanity and the conscience of mankind when they espoused a rebel cause. But under one formula or the other, governments in the nineteenth century, as now, gave aid to incumbent or opposition, or adopted a neutral stance, as their notions of national interest dictated.

The thesis of a right of revolution, remote though it is from the practice of states before and after 1945, has found new adherents since the United Nations Charter was ratified, especially among groups dedicated to eradicating the colonial relationships that survived World War II. These groups, refusing to acknowledge any distinction between *principle* and *right*, insist that articles 1 and 55 establish a *right* of self-determination in the undefined entity "people" and at the same time, since revolution is a normal mode of self-determination, a right of revolution. There would probably have been fewer converts to this doctrine in the noncommunist world if it had been observed that it goes a long way to support the disruptive Soviet assertion that it is entirely legal to assist

---

[1] Quincy Wright, "United States Intervention in the Lebanon," *American Journal of International Law* 53 (1959): 122; Wright, "Subversive Intervention," *ibid.*, 54 (1960): 529.

in "wars of liberation" and illegal to assist an established government in repressing attempts at "liberation," "liberation" being defined as the overthrow of a capitalist government and its replacement by a socialist regime. For, if there is an international-law right of revolution—that is, of recourse to violence to overthrow an established government or to achieve independence as a new state—there must be some question as to whether the existing government has any right to resort to force to suppress the exercise of such a right. If it has not, there can *a fortiori* be no right on the part of foreign states (and this is the principal point of the doctrine as it is now invoked) to come to the aid of the incumbent, irrespective of any request to do so.

My contention is that the Charter in its recognition of a principle of self-determination does not purport to confer a legal right upon undefined entities—something that law cannot do without at least establishing a defining authority. Rather, it records one of the general objectives to be sought by cooperative political action on the part of the United Nations and its state members, the merits of each claim to be determined by collective political evaluation, not by judicial decision. It is significant that no claim based upon an alleged right of self-determination has yet been brought before the International Court of Justice. The tumultuous application of the principle, doubling the number of formally sovereign states and the membership of the United Nations, has been a process of hasty political adaptation to the postwar revulsion from imperialism, stimulated and expedited by the Soviet Union's policy of eroding the power of the principal states of the West.

The liquidation of empires had begun soberly enough under the League of Nations. In the successor organization it gathered speed, unrestrained by any legal norm of qualification for statehood. But if self-determination was ever expected to immunize the political community from external interference, these expectations have been frustrated. It has been repeatedly demonstrated—in Vietnam (1950——), Guatemala (1954), Hungary (1956), Lebanon and Jordan (1958), East and West Africa (1964), the Dominican Republic (1965)—that states continue to lend active aid either to established government or to insurgent opposition as they deem expedient. We must probably regard the present frequency and scope of such enterprises as a normal offshoot of the change in method that appears to have taken place in the struggle for power—a change in which the contestants have tried to substitute for direct war, with its incalculable nuclear costs, active participation in civil strife with a view to aligning a given country on their side.[2] What-

---

[2] Cf. G. Schwarzenberger, "From the Laws of War to the Law of Armed Conflict," in *Current Legal Problems* (London: Stevens, 1968), pp. 239–58; Richard A. Falk, "The International Law of Internal War," in James N. Rosenau (ed.), *International Aspects of Civil Strife* (Princeton: Princeton University Press, 1964), pp. 218–19.

ever the rationale, the frailty of any restraints imposed upon intervention by the existing law of nations has become deplorably clear.

For a long time before the Covenant of the League of Nations and the United Nations Charter laid down their statutory prescriptions on the international use of force, much doctrinal effort, with some assistance from governmental proposals and agreements, has been expended in elaborating a code for the conduct of states in relation to foreign insurrection. The general starting point was the position that rebellion, insurgency, and civil war were stages in a factual situation to which foreign states might legally accommodate themselves by certain steps designed to protect public and private interests. Thus, foreign states were held to be at liberty, when rebels had won control of some considerable territory, especially coastal territory, to recognize insurgency. This meant conceding to the insurgents the right to take military action on the land and in the ports under their control, as well as in the corresponding territorial waters, though not on the high seas, that might damage interests of the recognizing state. In return, that state expected observance of the laws of war insofar as it and its nationals were concerned.[3]

Further, if the rebels had gained sufficient following and mobilized sufficient military strength to win control over a large part of the country, making the issue of the conflict seriously doubtful, a foreign state might find it expedient, for the better protection or advancement of strategic, economic, or political interests, to recognize them as belligerents. The recognition might take the form of, or be accompanied by, a declaration of neutrality; and while it conceded all belligerent rights to both sides, even on the high seas, it entitled the recognizing state and its nationals to the treatment, from both sides, prescribed by international law for neutrals. It also eventually exempted the winning side from any responsibility for injuries inflicted by its opponent upon nationals of recognizing states in the course of hostilities, as well as from any liability for debts incurred by that opponent for the purpose of carrying on the war. The calculation of gain or loss in this equation depended upon the circumstances of each case, and the decision was one within the political discretion of the foreign state concerned,[4] with this reservation, however, that a recognition either of insurgency or of belligerency before the conflict had reached the proportions suggested above might be treated by the government in power as an illegal intervention designed to assist in its overthrow.

[3] See Norman J. Padelford, *International Law and Diplomacy in the Spanish Civil Strife* (New York: Macmillan, 1939), p. 4.
[4] See "The Three Friends," 166 U.S. 1 (1896), cited by Quincy Wright above, p. 48.

Recognition of belligerency by the government under attack gave all foreign states the rights of neutrality, if they desired to claim them, with the attendant duties. They were under no obligation to accept the recognition, but insofar as they did so, it legalized acts outside the territorial limits of jurisdiction, such as visit and search, seizure of contraband, and blockade, that would otherwise have constituted violations of international law, and it exempted the government from responsibility for acts of the rebels.

That the calculation of profit and loss might well result in refusal to recognize belligerency was demonstrated in connection with the Cuban revolt of 1875, when President Ulysses S. Grant decided against recognizing the rebels as belligerents because of the rights that act would give both parties on the high seas and the exoneration of the Spanish government from responsibility for damage done by the rebels.[5] For similar reasons, the twenty-seven parties to the Nonintervention Accord of 1936 insisted that their signature implied no recognition of the belligerency of either side in the Spanish Civil War, though, with the exception of the Soviet Union, they all, like President Grant in the Cuban case, recognized insurgency.[6] By that time, however, the new factors already suggested had begun to enter into the determination of the positions taken by the principal powers in relation to civil strife.

The rough pattern of theory and practice sketched above was worked out in the nineteenth century, mainly in connection with the revolt of the Spanish-American colonies and the Civil War in the United States. By the time the latter conflict had come to an end and the ensuing international liabilities had been resolved by negotiation and arbitration, writers felt able to formulate with some confidence rules of international law with regard at least to the most advanced type of civil strife. The lesser type or stage, called insurgency, continued to be a matter of debate, though there was a trend toward postulating at the very least subjection to "the laws of humanity" and prohibition of acts "shocking the conscience of mankind."

The range of discretion left to states in deciding whether the point had been reached for recognition of insurgency or belligerency was not at all peculiar in a legal order, if such it may be called, where subjective interpretation is the rule. What was under way was an advance toward clarity of prescription that could be useful for purposes of arbitral decision where states agreed upon that mode of settlement. Some uncertainty, in other words, was being removed from the law in the books.

[5] Quoted by Quincy Wright above, pp. 48–49.
[6] Padelford, *International Law and Diplomacy*, pp. 4–5; Ann Van Wynen Thomas and A. J. Thomas, Jr., "International Legal Aspects of the Civil War in Spain, 1936–39," pp. 143–46 in this book.

But a large area of controversy still surrounded the question of foreign participation in conflicts between governments and opposing groups, and it remained for the Latin-American states, with their anti-intervention passion, to initiate intergovernmental attempts at clarification.

In 1928, the Conference of American States at Havana adopted a Convention on the Rights and Duties of States in the Event of Civil Strife. The contracting parties, of which the United States was one, undertook, *inter alia*, the following obligations:

To use all means at their disposal to prevent the inhabitants of their territory, nationals or aliens, from participating in, gathering elements, crossing the boundary or sailing from their territory for the purpose of starting or promoting civil strife.

To forbid the traffic in arms and war material, except when intended for the government, while the belligerency of the rebels has not been recognized, in which latter case the rules of neutrality shall be applied.

To prevent that within their jurisdiction there be equipped, armed or adapted for warlike purposes any vessel intended to operate in favor of the rebellion.[7]

It is to be noted that in this instrument the parties adopted the position that before recognition of belligerency the supply of military equipment to the established government was permissible, while similar aid to the rebels was illegal, and that neutrality became obligatory only on recognition of belligerency. The last paragraph quoted also provides evidence that the rules adopted in the Anglo-American Treaty of Washington (1871) for the Alabama arbitration were being accepted as part of the general law of nations.

The duty of the state to refrain from fomenting civil strife abroad, and to prevent activities in its territory calculated to foment such strife, appears again in the Draft Declaration on the Rights and Duties of States prepared by the International Law Commission of the United Nations and submitted to the General Assembly in 1950. The General Assembly adopted a laudatory resolution commending the draft "to the continuing attention of member States and of jurists of all nations," thus politely shelving the subject *sine die*. How far this has influenced the conduct of states may be judged from the Soviet Union's intervention in Hungary in 1956 and from the Bay of Pigs adventure of 1961, in which the United States ignored not only this and later resolutions of the General Assembly but also the formally binding Havana convention of 1928.

There is no lack of evidence of a broad abstract consensus in the contemporary aggregate of states against foreign participation in civil

[7] 46 U.S. Stat. at Large, 2749.

strife. In 1948, the General Assembly condemned external assistance to the guerrillas in Greece.[8] In 1954, the Draft Code of Offenses against the Peace and Security of Mankind, prepared on the General Assembly's request by the International Law Commission, listed prominently among such offenses the organization or toleration of armed bands and participation in or support of their incursions in foreign territory.[9] In 1956, the Soviet Union's intervention in Hungary was condemned at the Second Emergency Session of the General Assembly.[10] The Declaration on the Inadmissibility of Intervention in the Domestic Affairs of States and the Protection of Their Independence and Sovereignty, adopted by the General Assembly on December 21, 1965, Res. 2131 (XX), was emphasized the next year in Res. 2225 (XXI), adopted by the same body by a vote of 114 to 0 with only two abstentions. The latter urged observation of Res. 2131 and appealed to all states to refrain from armed intervention or the promotion or organization of subversion, terrorism, or other indirect forms of intervention for the purpose of changing by violence the existing system of another state or interfering in civil strife in another state. The reader can hardly fail to be struck by the irony in the contrast between the unanimity of this formal position and the reasons given for the resolution, namely, the General Assembly's deep concern at the evidence of increasing armed intervention of certain states in the domestic affairs of other states in different parts of the world.

It may be conceded that resolutions of the General Assembly are not binding commands and therefore of themselves impose no legal obligation. Yet on the face of them, especially when they approach unanimity, they express a world-community consensus, if not as to what the law is, then as to what it ought to be. It is to be observed also that these resolutions appear to place intervention on behalf of an existing government on the same footing as aid to its rebel opposition, for surely any assistance to the former designed to promote its victory is interference in civil strife and may well, in any particular case, arrest the process of self-determination. Neutrality from the earliest stages of insurrection would therefore seem to be the prescribed policy. This makes all the more obvious the gap between prescription and the practice even of states professing greatest devotion to the development of an effective law of nations.

For what it is worth, the application of the laws of war to civil strife is no longer a matter of doctrinal recommendation or special agreement.

[8] United Nations, G.A.Res. 193 (III), Nov. 27, 1948.

[9] United Nations, General Assembly, *International Law Commission Report,* Suppl. 9 (A/2693), 1954, p. 10.

[10] United Nations, General Assembly, *Official Records,* 2d emergency sess., 564th mtg., Nov. 4, 1956, p. 20.

For the more than sixty-five parties to the Geneva Conventions of 1949, of whom the United States has been one since 1955, it is a matter of solemn obligation. Both the RVN and the DVR have acceded to these conventions; but the latter did so with the reservation that it would not apply them to war criminals. Since there is nothing to limit the classification, this reservation reduces the conventions, for the North Vietnamese, to practically nothing, as is demonstrated by Hanoi's arbitrary assertion that all its American prisoners belong in this category.

In a most moderately expressed statement of its grave concern about the treatment of the more than one hundred sixty American military personnel confined in North Vietnam and the several hundred more considered missing because the National Liberation Front and North Vietnam withheld the names and forbade letters, the United States appealed to both the NLF and the DRV to permit impartial inspection of prisoners, like that conducted by the International Committee of the Red Cross in South Vietnam, and to arrange repatriation of the sick and wounded.[11]

The two greatest changes introduced by the Geneva Conventions of 1949, as compared with those drawn up at the Hague in 1899 and 1907 and at Geneva in 1929, are that they apply to noncombatants and in hostilities that do not rank as international war. Humane treatment is still the general principle, but this is spelled out as care for the civilian sick and wounded and prohibition of murder, mutilation, torture, and the taking of civilian hostages. Nor is anyone to be punished without regular trial meeting civilized standards.[12]

Against the Vietcong the United States charges assassination of more than 6,900 civilians, including 436 officials, and the kidnapping of nearly 30,000, including 1,131 officials, between 1962 and 1965.[13]

Against the United States, Hanoi of course records the destruction and death inflicted by the bombing of North Vietnam, together with the demolition of villages and the laying waste of crop lands in the South, with the resultant casualties.[14]

Acts of terrorism by the Vietcong in South Vietnam soon became a regular feature of its guerrilla warfare there. On the other side, the downfall and assassination of Ngo Dinh Diem in 1963 was the result

---

[11] White House statement on prisoners of war, *New York Times*, July 18, 1967, pp. 1, 2.

[12] Prisoners of War Convention, arts. 3 and 4; Convention on the Protection of Civilian Persons in Time of War, art. 3; Convention for the Amelioration of the Condition of the Wounded and Sick in Armed Forces in the Field, art. 3; Convention for the Amelioration of Forces at Sea, art. 3.

[13] *Hearings before the Senate Committee on Foreign Relations on S.2793*, Annexes 1, 2, 3, 89th Cong., 2d sess. (1966), pt. 1, pp. 114–115.

[14] See Ho Chi Minh's letter on peace conditions, *New York Times*, Jan. 29, 1966, p. 2.

of his government's brutal methods of control. On the whole, the record shows little regard for the laws of war as set forth in the Geneva Conventions of 1949.

In Africa, Asia, and Latin America, guerrilla warfare threatens to become endemic. Given the constant increase of foreign interest and foreign personnel, together with the national and international enterprises of economic, social, cultural, and technical assistance in progress in those parts of the world, the effects of such warfare cannot be confined to their peoples, and foreign intervention becomes practically inevitable. How are the interests of the world community to be advanced and the danger of international war through the adherence of foreign powers to one side or the other to be averted? Nonintervention agreements, even if enforced, are not enough. The broad community of the United Nations has demonstrated by declarations, resolutions, draft conventions, and missions its concern with human rights to security, welfare, and dignity in the world as a whole. For the protection of these rights, collective intervention must be developed, albeit with the caution exhibited in the European international communities. To be effective in preserving peace and promoting the security, welfare, and dignity of the individual, the prohibitilon of unilateral intervention must be combined with provisions for collective action and means of enforcement devised for both. This is no short-term task; but the possibility of progress has been demonstrated in specific cases, and its advancement should be constantly on the agenda of regional and universal organizations.

How Vietnam, hitherto an object lesson in the inadequacy of the law of nations regarding civil strife, might serve as a pilot project in this development is the subject of the final chapter in this study.

IV. THE LEGAL ISSUES IN VIETNAM

Discussion of the legal questions raised by the war in Vietnam inevitably focuses upon the action of the United States as the great foreign power employing massive military force in an attempt to determine the outcome of the struggle. That is why the charges against the United States, followed by its defense and countercharges and by the reply to these, have been chosen as the sharpest way of formulating the legal issues involved.

The Charges

a) The struggle in Vietnam is a civil war between the people of Vietnam operating under the banner of the National Liberation Front, on the one side, and, on the other, a succession of puppet administrations raised to power and kept there by the economic and military assistance of the United States. The NLF is fighting for self-determination by the Vietnamese people, and the armed intervention of the United States is a violation at once of what articles 1 and 55 of the United Nations Charter recognize as one of the main principles and purposes of the United Nations and of article 2, which prohibits any use of force "inconsistent with the purposes of the United Nations."[1]

b) The Geneva Agreement of 1954 on the Cessation of Hostilities in Vietnam was violated in essential provisions by the collusive refusal of the Bao Dai regime and the United States to join in arranging and holding the general election fixed by the agreement for 1956 to determine the government of all Vietnam. It was violated, further, by the establishment of American bases, increase in equipment and military personnel from the United States, and the extension by protocol of the defensive arrangements of SACDT to South Vietnam.[2] These violations justified the DRV, Vietminh, and Vietcong in resuming the struggle to ensure national self-determination in Vietnam as a whole.

c) The sinking of DRV torpedo boats and the naval bombardment of DRV ports in the Gulf of Tonkin, August 2–4, 1964, were acts of aggression. They were also violations of the United States' undertaking at the close of the Geneva Conference of 1954 "to refrain from the threat or the use of force to disturb" the arrangements made there.

d) The bombing of North Vietnam, beginning on February 5, 1965, and carrying the attack beyond the area of civil strife, is flagrant aggression by any definition of that term and has been carried out without regard for civilian casualties and with the destruction of nonmilitary property in violation of the Geneva Conventions of 1949. These attacks are again violations of the pledge given by the United States not to use force to disturb the Geneva Agreements.

e) Since the middle of 1964, the United States has been carrying out air missions in Laos for reconnaisance and attack in direct violation not

---

[1] See Quincy Wright, "Legal Aspects of the Viet-Nam Situation," *American Journal of International Law* 60 (1966): 750–69; Consultative Council of the Lawyers Committee on American Policy towards Vietnam, *Vietnam and International Law* (Flanders, N. J.: O'Hare, 1967) (hereinafter cited as *Vietnam and International Law*), pp. 63–66; Ho Chi Minh's letter on peace conditions, *New York Times*, Jan. 29, 1966, p. 2; Richard A. Falk, "International Law and the United States Role in Vietnam: A Response to Professor Moore, *Yale Law Journal* 6 (May 1967): 1095–1158; Falk, *The Six Legal Dimensions of the Vietnam War* (Princeton: Center of International Studies, Princeton University, October 1968); Senator Ernest Gruening and Herbert W. Beaser, *Vietnam Folly* (Washington: National Press, 1968).

[2] See arts. 17(a), 18, and 19 of the agreement and paras. 4 to 8 of the final declaration, printed in Great Britain, House of Commons, *Sessional Papers*, vol. 31 (1953/54), Cmd. 9239. See below, p. 394, for the ICSC's finding that there was a de facto military alliance between the United States and South Vietnam in violation of art. 19 of the agreement.

only of section 1 of the Declaration on the Neutrality of Laos signed at Geneva on July 23, 1962, by which the parties undertook to respect in every way that neutrality, but also of section 2(*g*), which reads as follows: "They will not introduce into the Kingdom of Laos foreign troops or military personnel in any form whatsoever, nor will they in any way facilitate or connive at the introduction of any foreign troops or military personnel."

American Defense and Countercharges

a) International practice since 1954 clearly shows that, whether or not the parties to the Geneva Agreements regarded the dividing line as purely temporary, North Vietnam and South Vietnam are distinct and independent political entities. South Vietnam has been recognized as the Republic of Vietnam by some sixty states, North Vietnam as the Democratic Republic of Vietnam by twenty-four. The Republic of Vietnam has been three times (first, as the state of Vietnam) recommended by the General Assembly for admission to the United Nations. Its membership was prevented by the veto of the Soviet Union in the Security Council, but it belongs to a number of the technical agencies and to international associations independent of the United Nations. It is a party to numerous treaties. The armed attack initiated by the North against the South is therefore of the nature of international war, and the assistance of the United States is participation in the collective self-defense recognized by customary international law and by article 51 of the United Nations Charter.[3]

b) The general election mentioned in article 14 of the Geneva Agreements of 1954 and in paragraph 7 of the final declaration of the conference did not constitute an essential condition of the undertaking to cease fire and withdraw forces, and the failure to arrange and hold such an election therefore provides no legal justification for the resumption by the DRV of activities designed to overthrow the regime in the South, even if that regime had been a party to the agreement, which it was not. The DRV did not believe in the possibility of election but accepted the formula because they expected the collapse of the Bao Dai and Diem regime. Moreover, even if the election provision had been

---

[3] "The Legality of United States Participation in the Defense of Vietnam," memorandum submitted by Leonard C. Meeker, Legal Adviser to the Department of State, to the Senate Committee on Foreign Relations (hereinafter cited as Meeker Memorandum), *Department of State Bulletin* (*DSB*) March 28, 1966, pp. 474–89. This defense is supported by professors of international law in thirty-one universities in a statement reproduced in the *Congressional Record*, 89th Cong., 2d sess., for Jan. 27, 1966, vol. 112, pt. 1, pp. 1408–09. See also the comprehensive defense by John Norton Moore and James L. Underwood in collaboration with Myres S. McDougal, reproduced in *Congressional Record*, 89th Cong., 2d sess., for July 13, 1966, vol. 112, pt. 12, pp. 15519–67.

binding on Saigon, it would have been justified in refusing to join in preparatory consultations since conditions in the North would have made a free vote impossible.[4]

The Democratic Republic of Vietnam violated the Geneva Agreements of 1954 by maintaining and reinforcing cadres in South Vietnam after the establishment of the military demarcation line. The Legal Committee of ICSC held (the Polish Member dissenting) that

there is evidence to show that armed and unarmed personnel, arms munitions and other supplies had been sent from the zone in the North to the zone in the South with the object of supporting, organizing, and carrying out hostile activities, including armed attacks directed against the Armed Forces and Administration of the zone in the South.

These acts are in violation of articles 10, 19, 24, and 27 of the agreement.

The same committee found evidence that the People's Army of Vietnam (PAV) had

allowed the zone in the North to be used for inciting, encouraging and supporting hostile activities in the zone in the South, aimed at the overthrow of the Administration in the South. The use of the zone in the North for such purposes is in violation of Articles 19, 24 and 27 of the Agreement.[5]

c) Neither the United States nor South Vietnam was a party to the Geneva Agreements of 1954. Both merely declared, at the closing session of the conference, that they would not resort to force to prevent the cease-fire from being carried into effect. Neither had resorted to force until after the aid from the North to the Vietcong, in violation of the agreement, had released them from this obligation and had amounted to an armed attack justifying collective defense.

d) The action taken by the US destroyers in the Gulf of Tonkin in August 1964 was in reprisal for the attack by DRV gunboats on those destroyers outside territorial waters.[6]

---

[4] John Norton Moore, "International Law and the United States Role in Vietnam: A Reply," *Yale Law Journal* (May 1967): 1061–64; P. J. Honey, "Hanoi and the War," *Mizan*, January-February 1967, pp. 1–2; Meeker Memorandum, pp. 483–89.

[5] Special Report of ICSC, 1962, Sec. 9, Subsects. 2–3; Meeker Memorandum, pp. 475, 482.

[6] This incident provided the occasion for the joint resolution passed by Congress on Aug. 7, 1964, which "approves and supports the determination of the President as Commander-in-Chief to take all necessary measures to repel armed attack against the forces of the United States and to prevent further aggression. . . . The United States is therefore prepared, as the President determines, to take all necessary steps, including the use of armed forces, to assist any member or protocol State of the S.A.C.D.T. requesting assistance in defense of its free-

e) Similarly, the bombing of North Vietnam began in February 1965 as reprisal for North Vietnamese attacks on Pleiku and Tuy Hoa and continued as a means of checking the invasion of South Vietnam by units of the PAV, as well as by irregular forces infiltrating from the North, and of impeding the supply of arms and munitions to the forces illegally operating in the South.

f) North Vietnam has aided and abetted the Vietcong in attacks on hospitals and schools, the murder of teachers and village leaders, and other acts of terrorism, all in violation of the Geneva Conventions of 1949.[7]

g) By the end of 1964, North Vietnam had infiltrated more than 40,000 men, mostly through Laos, into South Vietnam in violation of section 2(*a*, *g*) of the 1962 Geneva agreement guaranteeing the neutrality of Laos. In December 1964, full units of the regular army of the DRV had begun to invade the South.[8]

h) The air strikes in Laos have been limited to the infiltration routes used by the DRV for the supply and reinforcement of the Pathet Lao forces in Laos and of the Vietcong and the regular DRV army units in South Vietnam. This use of Laotian territory is a direct and prior violation of the declaration and protocol adopted at Geneva in 1962 and absolves the United States of the obligation undertaken in those instruments.[9]

Reply to American Defense and Countercharges

a) The dividing line of the seventeenth parallel is constantly described in the 1954 agreement as a "provisional military demarcation line"[10] and the divided parts are designated simply "regroupment zones," not states or political units. The final declaration reemphasizes this essential point in paragraph 6— ". . . the military demarcation line is provisional and should not in any way be interpreted as constituting

---

dom" (*American Journal of International Law* 60 [1966]: 580–81). This is the resolution cited by the president, especially the phrase "and to prevent further aggression," as authorizing the bombing of North Vietnam, though Under-Secretary of State Katzenbach, appearing before the Senate's Foreign Relations Committee on Aug. 17, 1967, argued that the resolution was unnecessary, since the president has ample powers under the Constitution for action of this kind. *Hearings before the Senate Committee on Foreign Relations*, 90th Cong., 1st sess. (Aug. 16, 17, and 21 and Sept. 19, 1967), pp. 77–78; cf. Wright, "Legal Aspects of the Viet-Nam Situation," p. 768.

[7] *New York Times*, Feb. 28, 1965, pp. 30–32.

[8] "The Basis for United States Actions in Vietnam Under International Law," Department of State Mimeograph 5, quoted by John Norton Moore, "The Lawfulness of Military Assistance to Vietnam," *American Journal of International Law* 61 (1967): 10–1.

[9] *New York Times*, Jan. 16, 1965, pp. 1, 3.

[10] Arts. 1–4, 6, 8, 14, 16, 17. See n. 2 for printed source.

a political or territorial boundary." The fact that the zones have in the interval been treated as distinct political entities is the result of the maintenance by the United States of a puppet government in the South and in no way alters the fact that the population of North and South regards itself as one people, engaged, after years of colonial servitude, in winning independence for all Vietnam and in working out a consensus upon its government. Only the intervention of the United States has raised the struggle of contending factions to the level of civil war.

South Vietnam was never recommended by the General Assembly for membership in the United Nations as a distinct entity. The assembly's recommendation has always been to admit Vietnam, and it was Vietnam, not South Vietnam, that was admitted to six of the technical agencies years before the provisional division of 1954. Similarly, it was to Vietnam or the Republic of Vietnam that recognition has been granted by some sixty states. Nor has North Vietnam been recognized as a state by twenty-four others. It has been recognized as the Democratic Republic of Vietnam. In a word, the recognitions granted have been to what the recognizing states considered the one legal state in the whole of Vietnam.[11]

b) From the moment when France withdrew her High Command from Saigon on April 28, 1956, and disowned any further obligations under the decisions of the Geneva Conference of 1954, the administration of South Vietnam succeeded to those obligations. Article 27 of the 1954 Agreement on Vietnam reads in part as follows: "The signatories of the present Agreement and their successors in their functions shall be responsible for ensuring the observance and enforcement of the terms and provisions thereof."

c) The United States destroyers in the Gulf of Tonkin entered the twelve-mile area that the DRV, like many other countries, claims as territorial waters. The torpedo boats were patrolling those waters to prevent repetition of a naval attack on July 31 by the RVN. The plea of reprisals has no beginning of justification. No damage had been done to the destroyers, no complaint had been lodged with the DRV, and no effort had been made to reach a pacific settlement. The sinking of gunboats and bombardment of ports was out of all proportion to any injury suffered by the United States.

Similarly, the plea of reprisals in the bombing of North Vietnam had no legal leg to stand on. No proof had been produced that the attacks on Pleiku and Tuy Hoa had been carried out by North Vietnamese forces, no formal complaint had been addressed to the Government of the DRV, and no effort at peaceful settlement had been made. The

[11] *Vietnam and International Law*, pp. 37–39.

bombardment, with its slaughter and destruction, was out of all proportion to the alleged injury.

Customary international law permits reprisals only for damage inflicted in violation of the law and only after complaint and the demand for peaceful compensation has failed to obtain redress. It further requires that the punitive action taken should be proportional to the illegal damage suffered.

Neither in the Gulf of Tonkin incident nor in the bombing of North Vietnam had these requirements been met.

Further, the Charter of the United Nations had now (article 2[4]) prohibited reprisals, since they do not constitute self-defense or execution of a mandate from the United Nations and, as a unilateral use of force unjustified by the customary law of nations, are inconsistent with the purposes of the organization.[12]

The Tone of Legal (and Quasi-Legal) Discussion

It is not the purpose of this paper to pass judgment in favor of one party or another. What is being attempted here is an analysis of a particular case of internal conflict, complicated by massive foreign participation, with a view to assessing the present state of the relevant international law and suggesting clarification and development that might enable us to bring such conflicts under collective control. The task does, however, call for an examination of legal opinion on the rights and wrongs of what is going on in Vietnam, for that opinion will go some way to determine the direction of any changes that may be attempted in the existing law.

The first three parts of this chapter are essentially a summary of legal arguments heard in the United States for and against the intervention in Vietnam and the way in which it is being conducted.[13] The debate is not confined to lawyers. Such publications as that of the Office of the General Assembly of the United Presbyterian Church in the United States of America, under the title *Vietnam—the Christian, the Gospel, the Church* (1967), and that of Clergy and Laymen Concerned about Vietnam, *In the Name of America* (1968), testify to a general concern about the moral and legal aspects of the United States' part in the struggle. The sharpness with which the case against intervention is stated demonstrates the freedom of expression enjoyed by Americans, while the research in the customary and treaty law of nations by which the

---

[12] *Vietnam and International Law*, pp. 53–57.

[13] American legal writing for and against the legality of the action of the United States in Vietnam has been collected by Richard A. Falk, himself a sharp critic of the government's policy, in *The Vietnam War and International Law* (Princeton: Princeton University Press, 1968).

nonprofessional as well as the professional statements are supported reflects a widespread conviction of the importance of law as a determinant of policy.

Abroad, the most voluminous commentary emanating from juristic sources is Russian. There is, however, a marked difference between Soviet and American discussion of Vietnam. In the United States it is a debate, for the most part sober and conscientiously documented. In the USSR it is a chorus of condemnation of the United States and its "lackeys." The tone is vituperative, not juristic. For wide circulation, this quasi-legal attack has now been made available in English. The brochure, *U.S. Aggression in Vietnam and International Law*, by the Novosti Press Agency, was published in 1968 in Moscow. It is of course approved Soviet doctrine that law is an instrument of policy, and the use as political propaganda of an ex parte version of the norms relevant in any particular case—a practice not wholly confined to communist jurists—is an everyday occurrence. What is more revealing is that the same tone should prevail in professional symposiums and in legal articles aimed at domestic readers. A few examples, involving some of the most eminent Russian international lawyers, will be enough to convey the general style.

In *Sovetskoe Gosudarstvo i Pravo* (No. 6, 1965, pp. 134–36), an article by M. E. Volosov, entitled "The Aggression of American Imperialism against the Vietnamese People, Crime against Peace and International Security," gives an account of a joint meeting of the Government and Law Institute of the Soviet Academy of Sciences, the Soviet Association of Political Scientists, and the Soviet Association of International Law, convened for the purpose indicated by the title. N. A. Yshakov, director of the International Law Section of the institute, declared that the United States, having taken note of the Geneva Agreements of 1954 and the first twelve paragraphs of the final declaration and having declared that it would not use or threaten force to disturb their application, was bound by these instruments. It had systematically violated their provisions by sabotaging the promised elections and by creating a separate state in South Vietnam, under a government of marionettes, which was to be an American colony and a base of aggression against the peoples of Southeast Asia. In addition, it had violated the laws and customs of war, especially by the use of napalm.

These charges were reiterated by M. A. Krutogolov, general secretary of the Soviet Association of Political Scientists, by F. I. Kozhevinikov, professor of international law in the Institute of International Relations, by S. V. Molodtsov, and by O. V. Bogdanov, the last of whom attacked the US government's thesis that it was not bound by any prohibition of poison gases. Professor G. I. Tunkin, best known of Soviet jurists in the

West and a member and one-time president of the UN International Law Commission, asserted that the United States had excused its aggression by ascribing the popular movement in South Vietnam to the infiltration of forces from the North and, by bombing the sovereign and peace-loving DRV, had committed the worst possible violations of the general law of nations.

Pravda for May 5, 1967 (p. 4), has an article by I. Karpets, vice-president of the International Association of Democratic Jurists (which, it is stated, has members from more than fifty countries), castigating the U.S. "imperialists" and their "hirelings" for their war crimes. The association had sent a delegation to Hanoi in 1965 to collect evidence and documents and has now formed a permanent research commission, drawing in representatives of other organizations and distinguished individual jurists "from all continents and different political systems, for the study of the criminal acts of American imperialism."

The same newspaper published on July 19, 1967 (p. 4), an article by V. M. Chkhickvadze, a corresponding member of the Soviet Academy, entitled "The Self-Appointed Gendarme, the Aggression in Vietnam and International Law." This is a gloating summary, with liberal quotations, of the book, *Vietnam and International Law*, published here in 1967 by the Consultative Council of the Lawyers Committee on American Policy towards Vietnam.

This account of Soviet legal writing on Vietnam could be extended indefinitely. For the present purpose, it will be sufficient to add that the same unqualified indictments appear in current textbooks. Thus the *Mezhdunarodnoe Pravo*, published by the Ministry of Higher and Secondary Specialist Education of the RSFSR in Moscow in 1964 as a manual for legal institutes and faculties, accuses the colonial powers, including of course the United States, of stifling the struggle for self-determination and waging war against the peoples of Indonesia, Indochina, Malaya, Algeria, and other countries. The authors compare alleged violations of the laws of war, including the Geneva Conventions of 1949, by these "imperialists" with those of Hitler's Germany.[14]

Turning now to the less politically dedicated legal writing of western Europe, we find some searching studies of the conflict in Vietnam by French and German jurists.

Roger Pinto of the Faculty of Law, University of Paris, has represented France in many organs and agencies of the United Nations and has, moreover, had more than seven years of varied academic and advisory service in Indochina. Underlying his legal competence, then, is an unusual knowledge of the land and people. In his course on "Les Règles du Droit International concernant la Guerre Civile," given at

[14] See esp. pp. 131–32, 398–99, 403–4.

the Hague Academy in 1965, Vietnam inevitably had a prominent place, and the opinions sustained there are repeated in his report on "The Principle of Non-Intervention" to the Helsinki Conference of the International Law Association in 1966.

Pinto rejects the American contention that the war is not a local and spontaneous rebellion against the established government but an armed attack initiated, directed, and supplied by the communist regime in Hanoi. The uprising began before any military assistance came from the DRV, and the NLF, he insists, is not a screen for a communist program of conquest but an organization which, though clearly under the influence of the communist parties and the DRV, is independent in its composition and in its aims. The war took on an international character only with the American and South Vietnamese attacks upon the territory of North Vietnam. It remains in form and substance a civil war undertaken with the purpose of establishing a new political regime that could not be achieved by constitutional methods.

The duty of respect for established power yields to the principle of effectivity and ceases when that power totters. At that point the general international law of the present permits third states to assist the party of their choice. Declarations of war and recognitions of belligerency have become irrelevant. But in Vietnam the Geneva Agreements of 1954 prohibit the introduction of new forces, establishment of bases, and formation of alliances. The undertaking of the United States not to threaten or use force to disturb the agreements implies an obligation to respect them. Its military assistance violates this obligation. The same obligation has been violated by the DRV, but the infiltration of forces to assist one side in civil war is not armed aggression and gives no right of attack upon the territory of the state from which they come. If it did, the same right would justify the DRV in attacking bases in the United States from which supplies and reinforcements are dispatched to Vietnam.

Nor can the aerial bombardment of the North be justified as reprisals. Reprisals were condemned by the Security Council, with the emphatic approval of the United States, in the resolution of April 9, 1964, and the attacks upon targets in the DRV constitute armed aggression in violation of the United Nations Charter.

Annuaire Français de Droit International Public for 1966 (pp. 50–88) publishes an article by Paul Isoart of the Faculty of Law and Economics in the University of Nice. The author modestly refrains from taking an explicit position on the nature of the conflict in Vietnam; but the context makes it pretty clear that he approves the statement made by Prime Minister Harold Wilson in the House of Commons on February 8, 1966, to the effect that we are witnessing there a war that is both civil and international. He appears also to accept the view so sharply put by Roger Pinto that the National Liberation Front is an independent organization dedicated to the establishment of a new regime and, like Pinto, holds that reprisals, even if proportionate, are no longer legal. Thus, though far from dogmatic in tone, Isoart's study clearly finds little law to support the official American position. The author believes that the essential objective of the United States is peace; but he is soberly critical of its methods.

Gerard Lyon-Caen, in *Le Monde* of August 15, 1967, is personally noncommittal, making no case for one side or the other. What he offers his readers is an account of the lively argument over Vietnam in American legal circles and between lawyers and the State Department. The chief interest of the note from our point of view is its evidence of the immediate attention attracted in France, as it was in Russia, by the lawyers committee publication, *Vietnam and International Law*. Obviously, the argument set forth in that study, leading, as it does, to the conclusion that "the United States course of action in Vietnam violates fundamental rules of international law in several serious respects," makes a strong appeal to the many audiences throughout the world that are predisposed to condemn American policy in Southeast Asia.

The *Annuaire Français* for 1967 (pp. 153–201) publishes "Le Droit de la Guerre dans le Conflit Vietnamien," by Henri Meyrowitz, doctor of law, advocate at the court of Paris, and author of a number of earlier studies on the law of war. This is an analytical tour de force. As the title indicates, it is not a general examination of the legal aspects of the war. It begins with a discriminating enquiry by a master hand into the relevance of customary and treaty rules of war to the conduct of the various parties to this extraordinarily complex struggle. This is followed by a delicately balanced assessment of the observation by the parties of relevant prescriptions. Revealing as it does all the possibilities of contradictory interpretation in the application of the law in the books to known facts, the work may well stand as a handbook for the jurists who may eventually be called upon to draft a clear and consistent code for the control of civil strife.

In order to determine how much of the law of war is relevant, Meyrowitz found it necessary to define the nature of the conflict. Here his conclusion supports the official American position. By 1965, with multiplied American participation augmented by five allied contingents, any remaining civil features of the conflict had been overshadowed by its dominantly international character. This means that the customary and conventional laws of war apply in their entirety,[15] and the writer finds

[15] Cf. "The Geneva Convention and the Treatment of Prisoners of War in Vietnam," *Harvard Law Review* 80 (1967): 858.

that they have been violated on both sides. The attacks upon the North have often, he holds, exceeded the legal bounds set by customary law and by the Geneva Conventions of 1949. The use of napalm is lawful only against purely military targets, and the destruction of crops and devastation of areas to prevent reoccupation is not justified either by military necessity or by the peculiar character of guerrilla warfare. As for the DRV, its refusal to treat captives as prisoners of war on the ground that the destruction of civilian life and property made them war criminals is entirely unjustified in the absence of judicial trial and conviction. In regard to the National Liberation front, the reader will find especially interesting this study of the extent to which a group that is not a state and not a party to the Geneva Conventions is bound by the rules of war and entitled to their protection.

Next to Meyrowitz's work, the most sharply analytical study that I have found in the foreign-language legal literature is that of Jochen Abr. Frowein, lecturer in the University of Bonn, published under the title "Völkerrechtliche Aspekte des Vietnam-Konfliktes" as the leading article in the *Zeitschrift für ausländisches öffentliches Recht und Völkerrecht* for July, 1967.

Frowein questions the view, taken for instance by Quincy Wright (*American Journal of International Law* [1966]: 762), that South Vietnam is bound, as successor to France, by the Geneva Agreements as a whole. But by a qualified principle of succession, he holds that when the French departed in 1956 the Republic of Vietnam took over a territory divided in the manner accepted by France through its High Command[16] and that Saigon is therefore bound at least by the territorial provisions of the agreements.

In the old debate about intervention at the request of an incumbent government, Frowein takes the position that this is still lawful. He also accepts, after careful consideration, the American thesis of collective self-defense, arguing that article 51 of the United Nations Charter should not be narrowly construed. But does collective self-defense justify the bombing of the North? Frowein leaves this question in a state of delicate balance.

Equally discriminating is the treatment here of the application of the Geneva Conventions of 1949 to the various entities engaged in the Vietnam war. Like Meyrowitz's work, the whole article is marked by a scientific detachment and a scholarly thoroughness that make it a distinguished contribution to the clarification and further development of a vitally important part of the law of nations.

[16] It is to be noticed here that Frowein does not rely upon the Treaty of Independence of June 4, 1954, cited by Hull and Novogrod below, p. 393, n. 11.

V. INTERNATIONAL ORGANIZATION AND
THE WAR IN VIETNAM

SEATO

There was no regional organization in Asia to which the issues at stake in the long tragedy of Vietnam might have been referred before they reached the battlefield. The South East Asia Collective Defense Treaty (SACDT), with its council and secretariat (SEATO), was Secretary of State Dulles' device for recouping the losses to communism represented by the 1954 Geneva Agreements and for organizing the Asian sector of the United States' worldwide crusade against that enemy. It dates only from September 8, 1954, is essentially, for all its promotion of economic, medical, and cultural activities, an alliance against communism, establishes no machinery for pacific settlement, and includes neither the DRV nor the RVN among its parties. The protocol of the same date does indeed extend its defensive cover to "the States of Cambodia and Laos and the free territory under the jurisdiction of the State of Vietnam"; but this instrument, far from advancing peaceful settlement in the area, has brought fresh combatants from Australia, New Zealand, the Philippines, South Korea, and Thailand to reinforce one side in the struggle there. Among the parties to SACDT, only France and Pakistan refuse to join in the use of SEATO to determine the political color of government in Vietnam.

Asia is indeed beginning to organize regionally, and SEATO is assisting in this movement, while reinforcing its anticommunist orientaton. The council at its last meeting in April 1967, with France conspicuously absent and Pakistan refusing to join in the communiqué, noted that "the Asian Development Bank is now a reality, the Asian and Pacific Council has been established and is soon to hold its second ministerial meeting in Bangkok; the Association of Southeast Asian States has taken on renewed life; the Southeast Asian Ministers of Education Secretariat is pursuing an active program; and there have been several regional or subregional conferences devoted to economic development and other matters of mutual concern."[1] How far this movement is from aiming at an inclusive regional organization is indicated by the next paragraph of the communiqué: "The Council observed with gratification these developments, in which SEATO members are working towards common ends with other countries."[2]

From SEATO's point of view, these economic and cultural services

[1] *Department of State Bulletin (DSB)*, May 15, 1967, p. 745.
[2] *Ibid.*

are means rather than ends. Among those peoples where they operate, they "strengthen further their capacity to resist Communist blandishments and alien domination."[3] That the defeat or containment of communism is the prime objective of SEATO is made clear by the dominance of this motif in the communiqué. The following paragraph is typical of the general tone.

The Council again recalled that various Communist leaders have declared their belief that the assault on the Republic of Vietnam is a critical test of the concept of what they call a "war of national liberation" but which is in reality a technique of aggression to impose Communist domination. It reaffirmed its conclusion at Manila in 1954, at London in 1965 and at Canberra in 1966 that the defeat of this aggression is essential to the security of Southeast Asia and would provide convincing proof that Communist expansion by such tactics will not be permitted.

The Manila Conference, 1966

Not content with SEATO as the sole mechanism of collective resistance to communism in its area, the states actively assisting South Vietnam inaugurated in 1966 another procedure of consultation and decision. A summit conference of "the leaders of seven nations in the Asian and Pacific region" met in Manila on October 24 and 25 of that year. The Republic of China (Taiwan) took no part. The countries represented were Australia, New Zealand, the Philippines, the Republic of Korea, Thailand, the Republic of Vietnam, and the United States. Three members of SEATO were not present, namely, the United Kingdom, France, and Pakistan, none of which has participated in the present war in Vietnam. The conference decided that regular meetings of ambassadors would be held in Saigon and further meetings of foreign ministers or heads of government would be convened as required.[4]

The 1966 conference heard a long and optimistic report from the government of South Vietnam, represented by Chairman Nguyen Van Thieu and Prime Minister Nguyen Cao Ky, on its plans of pacification, democratization, and economic development. This involved acknowledgment of internal differences and a statement of the people's readiness "to engage in a program of national reconciliation." Not all its troubles, then, infiltrate from the North. Full confidence was expressed, however, that "when the aggression has stopped, the people of South Vietnam will move more rapidly toward reconciliation of all elements in the society and will move forward, through the democratic process, towards human dignity, prosperity and lasting peace." Hope that these blessings would be shared with the North was expressed in a statement deploring the

[3] *DSB*, May 15, 1967, p. 746.
[4] Text of the communiqué in *DSB*, Nov. 14, 1966, pp. 730–35.

partition of 1954 but undertaking to respect it "until, by the free choice of all Vietnamese, reunification is achieved."

For the rest, the communiqué reads much like the reports of SEATO's council. There is the same assertion that "allied forces are in the Republic of Vietnam because that country is the object of aggression and its Government requested support. . . . They shall be withdrawn, after close consultation, as the other side withdraws its forces to the North, ceases infiltration, and the level of violence thus subsides." This provided allied approval of the conditions appended to President Johnson's offers to negotiate—conditions of a reciprocal reduction of military initiative repeatedly attached to his offers to stop bombing the North.

As for observance of the laws of war, "the participants observed that Hanoi has consistently refused to cooperate with the International Committee of the Red Cross in the application of the Geneva Conventions [with respect to prisoners of war] and called on Hanoi to do so." At the same time, "they reaffirmed their determination to comply fully with the Geneva Conventions of 1949 for the protection of war victims." This was followed up by President Johnson on July 17, 1967, with a statement of concern about the treatment of prisoners of war and an appeal to the National Liberation Front and North Vietnam "to permit impartial inspection of all prisoners" and to repatriate sick and wounded prisoners as stipulated by the Geneva Conventions.[5] Hanoi, though like South Vietnam a party to the conventions, has hitherto refused to admit that its captives are entitled to the stipulated protection because, it insists, they are war criminals. Neither the DRV nor the National Liberation Front permits the International Committee of the Red Cross (ICRC) to inspect the living conditions and general treatment of prisoners. Inspection is permitted in South Vietnam, sick and wounded have been repatriated, and the seven heads of government meeting in Manila pledged full cooperation with the ICRC.

Terrorism and the taking of hostages, both contrary to the Geneva Conventions, have been constant features of the war. How to prevent them in the hit-and-run tactics of guerrilla warfare is an unsolved problem. Both sides are accused, though the United States Command appears to be doing what it can to impose some humanitarian limits on the conduct of hostilities.

The ICSC

The Geneva Agreements on the Cessation of Hostilities in Vietnam set up machinery to organize, supervise, and control their application. Part of this was a joint commission, consisting of an equal number of

[5] *DSB*, Aug. 7, 1967, p. 170.

representatives of the commanders of the two parties, France and the Democratic Republic of Vietnam, to ensure:

a) A simultaneous and general cease-fire in Vietnam for all regular and irregular forces of the two parties.
b) A regroupment of the armed forces of the two parties.
c) Observance of the demarcation lines between the regroupment zones and of the demilitarized sectors.[6]

To assist in these tasks, joint groups were to be set up by the commission at agreed points on the demarcation line. Overall supervision and control were, however, vested in an International Commission for Supervision and Control (ICSC), to be made up, on the "troika principle," of representatives of Canada, India, and Poland and presided over by the Indian member. This commission was to be informed and assisted by fixed and mobile inspection teams manned by equal numbers of officers appointed by Canada, India, and Poland. Recommendations by the ICSC for amendment of the Geneva Agreements on the Cessation of Hostilities in Vietnam required a unanimous vote, and the same rule applied in the decision of "questions concerning violations, which might lead to a resumption of hostilities." Other business was to be transacted by majority.[7]

No powers or means of enforcement were assigned to the ICSC.[8] Its essential method was one of mediation. Failures to get agreement between the parties or to induce them to adopt remedial measures were referred to the joint chairmen of the 1954 conference. No collective action was ever taken on such reports. The joint initiation of coercive action by the United Kingdom and the Soviet Union became increasingly unlikely as the issues at stake in Vietnam merged with those of the general conflict between the United States and communism.

In spite of these weaknesses, the ICSC was remarkably useful in the first years of its operation. In its interim reports up to the end of 1955, it was able to record that the provisions of the Geneva agreement regarding withdrawal of forces into their respective regroupment zones and the exchange of prisoners of war and interned civilians were being

[6] Arts. 30–33, printed in Great Britain, House of Commons, *Sessional Papers*, vol. 31 (1953/54), Cmd. 9239.
[7] Arts. 29, 34–45, in *ibid.*
[8] Article 27 of the Agreement on Vietnam placed the responsibility for observance upon the signatories, who represented the commanders-in-chief, respectively, of the French Union Forces in Indochina and the People's Army of Vietnam (PAV) and their successors, while article 22 laid down that the commanders should ensure suitable punishment of violators; but in its fourth interim report (1955) the ICSC notes that the French High Command "could not take adequate remedial action" in its zone. It was prevented from doing so by the independent attitude of the Saigon regime.

carried out with a tolerable approximation to the preestablished time-tables. The extent to which this success was due to the conciliatory work of the ICSC was gratefully acknowledged by the commanders on both sides. General Paul Ely ended his letter to the chairman of ICSC with an especially warm tribute. "Above all," he said, "in the course of an experiment which I am sure will constitute a remarkable precedent on the international plane, you have succeeded in creating, in particularly difficult circumstances, a climate of *détente*."[9]

There had been difficulties on both sides of the demarcation line, and these increased from early 1956 on. North and South, inspection teams were obstructed in their attempts to inspect air fields, docks, and other positions for observation of the clauses in the Geneva agreement prohibiting the introduction of fresh troops, military personnel, arms, and munitions and the establishment of new bases. The same was true of their efforts to ensure application of article 14(c), in which each party undertook "to refrain from any reprisals or discrimination against persons or organizations on account of their activities during the hostilities and to guarantee their democratic liberties." In a statement attached to the commission's fourth interim report, the Canadian representative dissented from the finding that this part of article 14 had been satisfactorily observed and pointed out further that the DRV had obstructed the departure of civilians desiring to move to the southern zone, thus violating article 14(d).

A marked difference in cooperation is recorded, however, as between North and South. In Hanoi the commission was usually able, after patient and sometimes protracted negotiation, to obtain compliance with the agreement. Even in its more successful years it found the going much harder in Saigon. The reason suggested for the difference reappears again and again in the documentation. In its fourth interim report (1955) the commission complained that

in the case of the Zone of the French High Command . . . the independent attitude of the Government of the State of Vietnam, which controlled the civil administration and which had not signed the Geneva Agreements, made the obstruction and difficulties progressively more serious. . . .

Some of the "obstruction" took the most concrete form. B. S. N. Murti, who spent three years with the ICSC, gives an account of demonstrations against it in various parts of South Vietnam, culminating on July 20, 1955, in the looting of the Saigon hotels in which its personnel were lodged. His narrative includes evidence that this attack, like the

---

[9] Great Britain, House of Commons, *Sessional Papers*, vol. 45 (1955/56), "Fourth Interim Report," Vietnam No. 3, 1955, Cmd. 964, pp. 6–7.

other demonstrations, had the warm approval of Ngo Dinh Diem's government.[10] The commission itself reported to the joint chairmen that the French High Command and the government had failed to make any serious provision for the safety of its members and staff.

When the French withdrew in 1956, the joint commission of the two commands fell apart, leaving the ICSC without an essential piece of the machinery for applying the agreements. Saigon would do nothing to fill the gap. It has never been impressed with the argument that, having taken over the last remnant of French authority in Vietnam, it had succeeded to the obligations of the French High Command. Article 27 of the Agreement on Vietnam reads as follows: "The signatories of the present Agreement and their successors in their functions shall be responsible for ensuring the observance and enforcement of the terms and provisions thereof." Saigon argues that the "successors" were nothing more than the officers who might take over the respective commands from those who held them at the time of the agreement. This is of course arguable. It is noticeable, however, that the successive governments of South Vietnam have not avoided the inconsistency of complaining of violation of an agreement to which, they insist, their country was not a party.[11]

Argument has never ceased on the question whether the protocol to SACDT extending its defensive provisions to Cambodia, Laos, and South Vietnam constituted a violation of article 19 of the Geneva Agreement:

---

[10] B. S. N. Murti, *Vietnam Divided* (New York: Asia Publishing House, 1964), pp. 157–62.

[11] For an unqualified assertion that the RVN succeeded to the obligations of the French Command, see Quincy Wright, "Legal Aspects of the Viet-Nam Situation," *American Journal of International Law* 60 (1966): 762. Cf. Consultative Council of the Lawyers Committee on American Policy towards Vietnam, *Vietnam and International Law* (Flanders, N. J.: O'Hare, 1967), p. 45, and Roger Hull and John Novogrod, *Law and Vietnam* (Dobbs Ferry, N. Y.: Oceana, 1968), p. 50. The authors last named rely upon the Treaty of Independence of June 4, 1954, between France and Bao Dai's state of Vietnam. But this treaty preceded the Geneva Agreements of July 20, 1954, and while it covered obligations contracted by France up to the date of signature, it can hardly be interpreted as binding the newly independent state to future obligations assumed by any French authority, military or civil. At the Geneva Conference of 1954 both the Saigon delegation and the French foreign minister, M. Bidault, emphasized the complete and independent sovereignty which this treaty conferred upon the state of Vietnam and upon the government of His Majesty Bao Dai as sole authority competent to commit it. See Great Britain, House of Commons, *Sessional Papers*, vol. 31 (1953/54), Cmd. 9186, pp. 123, 134. It is to be noted that the obligations assumed by the state of Vietnam are those resulting from treaties and conventions *"contractés,"* and the past connotation is emphasized by the limitation that these are binding on it only "dans la mesure ou ces actes *concernaient* (not *concernent*) le Vietnam." The text as a whole is reproduced in *British and Foreign State Papers* 161: (London: Her Majesty's Stationery Office, 1963), 649.

With effect from the date of entry into force of the present Agreement, no military base under the control of a foreign State may be established in the regrouping zone of either party; the two parties shall ensure that the zones assigned to them do not adhere to any military alliance and are not used for the resumption of hostilities or to further an aggressive policy.

In the seventh and eighth interim reports, the ICSC mentions complaints from Hanoi that a de facto military alliance had been established between the Republic of Vietnam and the members of SEATO, evidenced by the presence of a South Vietnamese observer at the SEATO conference held in Manila in March 1958 *inter alia*. In its special report of 1962, the commission states its view that "though there may not be any formal military alliance between the Governments of the United States of America and the Republic of Vietnam, the establishment of a U.S. Military Assistance Command in Vietnam, as well as the introduction of a large number of U.S. military personnel beyond the stated strength of the MAAG (Military Assistance Advisory Group), amounts to a factual military alliance, which is prohibited under Article 19 of the Geneva Agreement. . . ."

The same special report also records the conclusion of the Legal Committee of ICSC that "there is evidence to show that armed and unarmed personnel, arms, munitions, and other supplies have been sent from the zone in the North to the zone in the South with the object of supporting, organizing, and carrying out hostile activities, including armed attacks, directed against the Armed Forces and Administration of the zone in the South. These acts are in violation of Articles 10, 19, 24, and 27 of the Agreement on the Cessation of Hostilities in Vietnam."[12]

From this finding of the Legal Committee, the Polish member of ICSC dissented, as he had dissented from the commission's dismissal of a complaint from Hanoi against Law 10/59 passed by the South Vietnamese General Assembly. This law imposed sentence of death or hard labor for life for a list of crimes committed with a view to sabotage and set up military courts to try the offenders. Belonging to an organization promoting such crimes was to be punished in the same way. The commission's decision was based upon the narrow but correct legal grounds that because the law did not specifically discriminate against, or subject to reprisals, persons or organizations on account of their activities during the hostilities, it did not infringe article 14(c) or any other part of the Geneva Agreement on Vietnam. But the extraordinary severity of the law not only testified to the multiplicity and pertinacity of anti-government groups in the country but revealed the government's readi-

---

[12] Great Britain, House of Commons, *Sessional Papers*, vol. 39 (1961/62), "Special Report," Vietnam No. 1, 1962, Cmd. 1755, secs. 20, 9.

ness to resort to the most extreme methods of repression. This was indirectly admitted in the rider, a masterpiece of understatement, attached by the commission to its decision—"certain provisions of this Law are of such a nature that they may in specific cases be applied in a manner which may be incompatible with Article 14(c). . . ."[13]

From this point on the troika character of the ICSC, and the ascendancy in it of motives transcending local objectives in Vietnam, became increasingly clear. When two members found the Democratic Republic of Vietnam lacking, the Polish member dissented, while complaints against South Vietnam and American activity there were apt to be vetoed by the Canadian member, sometimes with the support of the Indian chairman. The fact that no reports were made between 1962 and 1965 is eloquent evidence of a permanent division and resulting paralysis of the commission. When, in February 1965 the representatives of Poland and of India were moved to make a special report, the Canadian dissent found the commission incapable of formally condemning the United States bombing of North Vietnamese targets, with the result that the other two members, after reviewing statements from Saigon and Hanoi about these attacks, were able only to conclude that "these documents point to the seriousness of the situation and indicate violations of the Geneva Agreements."

The United Nations

Why has every means of persuasion or coercion at the command of the United Nations not been brought to bear upon the war in Vietnam? Surely this is an obvious case for urgent action in the cause of world peace. The Hanoi-Peking argument that the machinery set up at Geneva in 1954 is exclusively competent to deal with the issues at stake is legally irrelevant.[14] The Geneva Agreements have signally failed to achieve their objectives, have indeed, to all practical intents and purposes, been nullified by multiple violations on both sides. The United Nations is not rendered incompetent, when breach of the peace or threats to the peace occur, by the existence of other arrangements that have not succeeded in preventing them. Nor, as Hanoi has conceded by the negotiations that began in Paris in May 1968, does the existence of one set of arrangements legally prevent interested states from making others.

The argument of UN incompetence was a transparent cover for Hanoi's insistence that its conditions of settlement be met before ne-

---

[13] Great Britain, House of Commons, *Sessional Papers*, vol. 39 (1961/62), "Eleventh Interim Report," Vietnam No. 1, 1961, Cmd. 1551, sec. 17.

[14] Submission of the Vietnam Conflict to the United Nations, Hearings before the Senate Committee on Foreign Relations, 90th Cong., 1st sess. (Oct. 26, 27, and Nov. 2, 1967) (hereinafter cited as Hearings), p. 152.

gotiations began. So, also, the argument endorsed even by Secretary-General U Thant, that the United Nations cannot act because two or more of the parties concerned are not members, is a political, not a legal, argument.[15] Article 2(6) of the Charter imperatively directs the organization to "ensure that states which are not members of the United Nations act in accordance with these principles so far as may be necessary for the maintenance of international peace and security." This is not to say that the secretary-general's argument is less potent for lack of a legal base. Its political base is clear enough. It is Moscow's stubborn resistance to all proposals of UN action and the resulting certainty of a veto. Though, on February 2, 1966, the United States did succeed in getting the nine votes necessary to place Vietnam on the Security Council's agenda—a procedural matter not subject to veto—subsequent discussions with members of that body convinced the president, Ambassador Akira Matsui of Japan, that there was "a general feeling that it would be inopportune for the Council to hold further debate at this time."[16]

This opinion was accepted. It may explain why no attempt was made to have the Security Council refer the matter to the General Assembly. The United States has declared itself quite willing to discuss it there.[17] This was the course taken in the Korean War in 1950 after the Soviet Union had resumed attendance in the Security Council and again in the Suez crisis of 1956, when the council was prevented by the United Kingdom and France from taking action. The General Assembly has of course taken full advantage of the liberty given it by article 11 of the Charter to discuss Vietnam. Not to have done so would have been to display an inexcusable indifference to a cause of worldwide anxiety. But the assembly is precluded by article 12 from making any recommendation with regard to a dispute or situation with which the Security Council is dealing unless the council requests it to do so. In his letter to the secretary-general on February 26, 1966, Ambassador Matsui wrote:

It is my understanding that the Council, having decided on 2 February to place on its agenda the item contained in the letter dated 31 January by the Permanent Representative of the United States of America (S/7105), remains seized of the Viet-Nam problem.[18]

The frustration of the United Nations machinery in a conflict now in its twenty-fifth year makes an instructive study in the clash of politics

[15] *United Nations Monthly Chronicle*, March 1965, p. 33 and April 1967, p. 68.
[16] Hearings, pp. 154–56; and UN Docs. S/6575, Aug. 1, 1965; S/7106, Jan. 31, 1966; S/7168, Feb. 26, 1966.
[17] *New York Times*, Sept. 23, 1966, p. 12.
[18] Hearings, p. 156.

and law. The law in the books is clear, its influence upon events hardly perceptible.

Not only does the Charter impose upon members the obligation to submit to the organization disputes that they fail to settle by other peaceful means; it also imposes upon the organization the obligation to "determine the existence of any threat to the peace, breach of the peace, or act of aggression" and to "make recommendations, or decide what measures shall be taken" (article 39). Both obligations were emphasized by Ambassador Goldberg as well as by Quincy Wright in hearings before the Senate Committee on Foreign Relations in late 1967.[19] If the United States had referred the conflict to the United Nations at an earlier stage in its development, before it had brought about the present deep division among the member states, action as effective as that taken in Korea in 1950 and in the Suez crisis in 1956 might have been possible.[20] There were, however, special features in those cases not present in the case of Vietnam. In the Korean case, there was a sudden invasion in force, which the Security Council, rather dubiously equating absence with an affirmative vote, was able to respond to because of the Soviet Union's temporary boycott of that body. Subsequent direction of operations, after the return of the protesting Soviet Union to the council, was referred, by a procedural vote not open to veto, to the General Assembly. The strong interest of the United States and the weight of membership approval made the assembly's recommendations effective. In the Suez crisis, when the dispute was referred to the General Assembly in order to by-pass the negative votes of France and the United Kingdom, the general disapproval of the Anglo-French assault and the momentary concurrence of American and Soviet policy had a similar result. Ambassador Matsui's report, supported as it is by the secretary-general's repeated statements, makes it doubtful whether reference to the assembly today, even with the added authority of the 1950 Uniting for Peace Resolution, could mobilize the two-thirds majority necessary for a recommendation of collective action.

On two marginal questions, the United Nations did adopt tentative measures. In 1959, Laos, a member since 1955, appealed to the Security Council for a peace-keeping force to stop aggression from North Viet-

[19] Hearings, pp. 113, 150–51. The relevant parts of the Charter are arts. 1(2), 2(3), 24(1), 25 and 39 and chaps. VI and VII generally.

[20] As early as May 12, 1953, however, Clement Attlee, then leader of the opposition, had expressed the fear in the House of Commons that reference to the United Nations would divide the organization between the Western democracies and the Soviet bloc and cause "what is even more serious for us, a split in the Commonwealth." He had in mind, obviously, the interest of Australia and New Zealand, later to be manifested by contingents fighting on the side of South Vietnam. Great Britain, *Parliamentary Debates* (Commons), vol. 515 (May 12, 1953), pp. 1067–68.

nam. Over protests from the Soviet Union, which argued that the matter was substantive rather than procedural, the council set up by resolution, jointly sponsored by France, the United States, and the United Kingdom, a subcommittee consisting of representatives of Argentina, Italy, Japan, and Tunisia. This body spent a month in Laos and reported guerrilla operations there that "must have had a centralized coordination." On January 1 and 2, 1961, again, Laos reported that Soviet airplanes were supplying rebel forces and that DRV units had occupied points in its northern territory. Such were the preliminaries leading to the Geneva Conference of 1962 that agreed to neutralize Laos.[21]

Sixteen states, all of them except Trinidad and Tobago Asian or African, succeeded in having the General Assembly consider charges of violations of human rights in Vietnam, affecting especially the Buddhists. Saigon invited a mission, and the president of the General Assembly appointed representatives of seven states to respond to this invitation. The mission spent ten days in Saigon and sent a delegation for one day to Hue. It heard fifty-four witnesses in all, seven of them for the government side, its last three days coinciding with the beginning of the coup against Diem. On its return to New York, it submitted a detailed report, which the assassination of Diem rendered somewhat irrelevant. The General Assembly decided that further consideration of the complaint was not necessary.[22]

In April and May 1964, Cambodia, also a member of the United Nations since 1955, complained to the Security Council of repeated attacks by armed forces of the United States and South Vietnam upon its territory and population. Pointing out that its request for a meeting of the Geneva Conference to guarantee its neutrality had been opposed by the United Kingdom and the United States, the Cambodian government asked that a mission of inquiry be sent to examine on the spot accusations of complicity with South Vietnamese rebels that the United States had lodged in justification of the attacks.

In the debate that followed, the Soviet representative accused the United States of having taken a leading part in the alleged aggressions and urged the council to condemn this action and take measures to prevent its recurrence. The only participation admitted by the United States was that American advisers had accompanied the Vietnamese troops and that it had apologized for the one occasion when the adviser had crossed the border into Cambodia. The American representative in the Security Council said that his government would not oppose a commission of enquiry, which should make recommendations on means of protecting the ill-marked frontier from further violations. The French

[21] *United Nations Yearbook*, 1959, pp. 63–67.
[22] *United Nations Yearbook*, 1963, pp. 47–50; "Report of the Mission," UN Doc. A/5630.

representative urged a new Geneva conference as the only way to secure Cambodian neutrality and territorial integrity. The Security Council adopted resolution 189 (1964), Doc. S/5741, deploring the incidents, requesting fair compensation, and inviting measures to prevent recurrence. The president of the council named Brazil, the Ivory Coast, and Morocco for the mission.

This trio submitted its report on July 27, 1964. Its principal recommendations were that Cambodia and the RVN should resume political relations broken off in August 1963 and agree upon marking their frontier and that UN observers should be sent to report upon the operation of the arrangements adopted. The Security Council was asked to take note of Saigon's undertaking to respect Cambodian neutrality and territorial integrity.

The Saigon government thought the observer group inadequate for a task that would require an international police force, but it was willing to continue the attempt to devise agreed methods of control. Cambodia, on the other hand, rejected the mission's recommendation out of hand. It was indignant that the three members should merely have recorded incidents without assigning responsibility for them, and it characterized their recommendation of a resumption of political relations and a settlement of the dispute with Saigon as outside the mission's mandate and an intervention in internal affairs. It continued to charge the United States and the RVN with further incursions, consistently denied by Washington and Saigon. No further action was taken by the United Nations. Prince Sihanouk broke off relations with the United States in 1965 by way of protest and refused to resume them until agreement was reached on the border.[23]

The Vietcong's practice of raiding South Vietnam from Cambodian territory and then retreating to sanctuary there has raised the question of hot pursuit across a land frontier, and the United States has tried to reach agreement with Prince Sihanouk on the matter, just as, between 1911 and 1916, it tried to persuade the de facto government of Mexico to accept a mutual right to pursue raiding parties across the border.

Hague Convention II of 1899, annex, article 57, and Hague Convention V of 1907, article 11, require a neutral into whose territory troops of a belligerent have penetrated to intern them. That these provisions, which the Hague conventions took verbatim from the unratified Declaration of Brussels of 1874, would be taken by an impartial international authority as binding upon Cambodia, either because their content has become part of the customary law of nations[24] or because Cambodia has

---

[23] *New York Times*, Nov. 5, 1967, pp. 1, 6.
[24] For the opinion that the Hague Rules of Land Warfare were part of customary international law, see the judgments of the Nuremberg and Far Eastern War Crimes Tribunals.

succeeded to the obligations of France, seems highly probable. While there is no evidence that the draftsmen of 1874, 1899, or 1907 had civil war in mind, grounds for applying the norm can be found in the fact that the war in Vietnam has an international as well as a civil aspect or in the fact that there has been implied recognition of the belligerency of the contending parties.

Even if it be granted, however, that the provisions of the Hague conventions are applicable, it is to be noted that they contain no sanction against a neutral failing in its obligation. When the conventions were concluded, the offended belligerent was of course at liberty to make the failure a *casus belli*, but there was no established right to pursue enemy troops across a neutral border without committing what the neutral was free to regard as an act of war, unless such a right could be found under the rubric of self-defense.

The old *Caroline* doctrine, which justified a defensive invasion of sovereignty when the occasion was one of "instant and overwhelming necessity, leaving no choice of means and no moment for deliberation," would hardly be adequate in a situation where raid and retreat to sanctuary are frequent occurrences calling for deliberate and standing protective arrangements. Since neither North nor South Vietnam is a member of the United Nations, article 51 of the Charter is not clearly relevant. Yet, given the reality of recurrent international violence, often taking the form of competing interventions in civil strife rather than traditional war, much can be said for general recognition of the right to take effective measures when a neighboring state is unable or unwilling to prevent the abuse of its neutrality.

"Hot pursuit" is the term for the well-established norm that permits the chase out of territorial waters on to the high sea and the arrest there of a foreign ship reasonably suspected of breaking the law of a riparian state. This legalizes an exercise of jurisdiction which would otherwise be illegal on the high sea; but the right of pursuit comes to an end the moment the pursued ship enters the territorial waters of its own or a third state. The analogy thus does little to support any claim to send armed forces into neutral territory. The claim is more cogently based upon the obligation of a neutral not to permit the use of its territory for belligerent purposes. Sanctuary after armed invasion is a flagrant instance of such use, and in the claim to prevent it by armed force, the immediacy of pursuit may well be regarded as irrelevant. A belligerent may of course limit its claim of right to cases where the invader has been actually driven across the neutral border, and a strong case can be made for this minimum exception to the sovereignty of a sanctuary state that fails to take effective action to prevent such abuse of its neutrality. But where repeated sorties are mounted from bases established in neutral territory, it would seem difficult to justify prohibition, in the name of neutral sovereignty, of deliberate remedial operations by the offended belligerent. It should be clear, however, that these are matters in regard to which the law needs at the very least clarification, if not amplification.[25]

VI. CONCLUSIONS AND PROPOSALS

Thirty years ago the civil war in Spain displayed the naked weakness of international law and institutions as means of protecting the interests of either the troubled state itself or the aggregate of states in cases of major internal conflict. The day had long passed when the web of inter-state relations had been loose enough to leave the external problems incidental to such strife to direct arrangements between foreign govern-ments and the contestants. In 1936 the general complex of economic, political, and strategic interests was so close-knit that foreign interven-tion was inevitable in the absence of effective international controls. From the point of view of the "family of nations," the great problem was how to prevent such intervention not merely from taking decision out of the hands of the divided people but from so exacerbating and lengthening the conflict as to lay waste the country, multiply human casualties, and possibly, expand into general war.

The twenty-seven governmental declarations elicited by Great Britain and France and forming the Nonintervention Agreement of August 1936 expressed a genuine desire on the part of most of the signatories to avert just such consequences. To Nazi Germany and Fascist Italy, who were among the signatories and who made a mockery of the im-plementing arrangements, the struggle in Spain presented a precious opportunity to expand their power and to gain experience for the greater conflict soon to follow. In the early stages another signatory, the Soviet Union, also made an attempt, through material and technical aid to the Loyalist government, to gain profit for itself and the Comintern from the catastrophe of Spain.

The Nonintervention Committee set up in London was able to or-ganize a naval patrol that substantially limited losses to international shipping. Neither it nor the League of Nations was able to check the

---

[25] The operations of American forces in Cambodia in the spring of 1970 appear to have been undertaken, if not by invitation of the newly established government at Pnompenh, at least with its tacit consent and subsequent cooperation. The targets were North Vietnamese supply bases and forces whose activities were in breach of Cambodia neutrality. Leaving aside the question how far the new government owed its existence to American support, actual or prospective, there is no obvious basis for any charge that the action taken was in violation of existing international law.

flow of military forces and supplies from Germany or Italy to the Nationalists or, despite many national statutes prohibiting enlistment on either side, to prevent the influx of volunteers. The failure of the league to respond to the Spanish government's repeated appeals for assistance against flagrant aggression, coming so soon after the failure of sanctions in Mussolini's conquest of Ethiopia, emphasized the bankruptcy of the first general organization of collective security.[1]

Vietnam has made it clear that despite all the conventions, resolutions, and international organizations that have been contrived since 1939, the interstate system is still incapable of quarantining civil strife. The fact is a challenge to all lawyers concerned about the preservation of world peace. The first need is the clearest possible code, then improved methods of interpretation and enforcement.

It was pointed out in the section on International Law and Civil Strife (pp. 369–76) that General Assembly resolutions 2131 (XX) and 2225 (XXI) seem to prohibit intervention at the request of a recognized government as well as at the request of its rebelling opposition. If this was the intention, the demand for so radical a change in the actual practice of states should be made explicit beyond all question. For in spite of the unanimity with which the second of these resolutions was adopted, the doubt remains whether they represent any serious intent of reform. The long-established powers still cite the request of a recognized government as full legal justification for every kind of assistance. Even the Soviet Union, which asserts the legality of assistance in "wars of liberation" as a mode of self-determination, defended its military interventions in Hungary and in Czechoslovakia on that ground. The newer African and Asian states urge intervention against any established government that they regard as preventing self-determination. No fault could be found with this, if it were limited to pressure for collective intervention by the United Nations in conformity with the principle of self-determination recognized in articles 1 and 55 of the Charter. Insofar as it encourages unilateral action based upon subjective judgment, it is to be condemned as an inexhaustible source of international conflict.

The fact that states resort to the practice of getting the invitation to intervene from a government of their own making is one symptom of the change that has made intervention on one side or the other in foreign civil strife a substitute for formal war as a mode of preserving or expanding national power. What is needed is a clear-cut, explicit

---

[1] Norman J. Padelford, *International Law and Diplomacy in the Spanish Civil War* (New York: Macmillan, 1939), *passim*; F. P. Walters, *A History of the League of Nations* (London: Oxford University Press, 1952), chaps. 57 and 65; Ann Van Wynen Thomas and A. J. Thomas, Jr., "International Legal Aspects of the Civil War in Spain, 1936–39," pt. 1.

prohibition of unilateral intervention on the side either of a government in power or of its rebelling opposition.

What now of collective intervention? If, as some would have it, civil strife is a matter "essentially within the domestic jurisdiction," intervention by the United Nations is prohibited by article 2(7) of the Charter except as incidental to enforcement measures taken under chapter VII. But this limitation would not apply to cases where civil strife, probably because foreign states are participating, threatens international peace. Chapters VI and VII of the Charter clearly take that type of situation out of the exclusive domestic jurisdiction of members of the United Nations by authorizing the Security Council to deal with them.

If and when they come into force, the Draft Covenants on Human Rights unanimously adopted by the twenty-first session of the General Assembly will create another opening for collective intervention in civil strife. Where the cause of insurrection is denial of the rights stipulated in these covenants, the Economic and Social Council or the Human Rights Committee may recommend remedial action. The intervention here is of the mildest possible type, consisting essentially in bringing to bear a kind of general censure and a collective behest to observe the covenants. But clearly, it would not be open to a party to argue that civil strife in such circumstances is a matter essentially within its domestic jurisdiction.

The two types of cases mentioned are instances where specific international agreements make the doctrine of domestic jurisdiction inapplicable. The fact is, however, that the inclusion of civil strife in this reserved category is becoming generally untenable. The intensification of economic, social, cultural, and political relations among the peoples of the world in the last half-century makes anything approaching a civil war in any state a matter of grave international concern. Foreign investments are lost; aliens are in peril of their lives; foreign embassies are attacked; the work of official and unofficial international agencies is disrupted. Failing adequate international protection of the complex of threatened interests, unilateral intervention is a matter of course. Add to this the current practice of rival states fishing for national advantage in the troubled waters, and the case for world-community control becomes invincible.

This does not mean that any supranational organization should attempt to determine the issue of the struggle. Its function would be to prevent foreign intervention on either side, to see that the laws of war are observed, that the safety of alien lives and property is as far as possible preserved, and that equitable compensation is made to the victims of illegal attack. This will of course call not only for strong supranational organization but for clear formulation of appropriate norms.

Supranational organization of such authority and actual power can only be approached by degrees, but it should be clearly portrayed as the ultimate objective. Official work upon the code can begin at once. That is largely a matter of completing and consolidating in one convention the relevant parts of the conventions, declarations, and draft codes on the rights and duties of states, on crimes against the peace and security of mankind, and on peaceful relations among states that have been elaborated, and many of them shelved, in recent years. Most important—the final convention must contain an article obliging the parties to submit to the International Court of Justice disputes, not otherwise peaceably settled, as to the interpretation and application of its terms. Of all professions, lawyers should most readily appreciate the importance of judicial decision as the essential alternative to the subjective interpretation that at present reduces the most formally established norms to conformity with the policy of the governments that they purport to bind. Within the last five years the bar associations of more than a hundred countries have joined in a crusade for Peace through World Law. They should concentrate their collective effort first of all upon persuading governments to accept the jurisdiction of the ICJ under the optional clause of its statute or to withdraw the crippling reservations attached to acceptances already declared.

The best agency for carrying the work of codification through to the point of submission to the General Assembly for its approval and reference to governments for ratification, or to a diplomatic conference such as that which at Geneva in 1958 gave final form to the four Conventions on the Law of the Sea, is probably the International Law Commission of the United Nations. But an inevitably long and arduous task can be expedited by worldwide discussion in the organization of the legal professions mentioned above. The enterprise as a whole should not shun a teleological approach or be intimidated by charges of idealism. Its object, after all, is law for a new world community.

The most essential principle of the world community that the Charter of the United Nations sought to organize was to be that no state should be free to use force in its international relations for self-determined purposes or to impose self-defined values. This was an approach on a supranational level to that internal monopoly of force that has characterized the well-ordered state. The principle has been repeatedly ignored by governments professing the greatest devotion to peace. Until it is seriously accepted in practice and collectively enforced, the chance of man's survival in the nuclear age must depend upon an increasingly precarious balance of terror.

Edwin Brown Firmage

SUMMARY AND INTERPRETATION

Those civil wars which have provoked intervention by foreign states differ from each other in many respects. They do, however, reveal certain common characteristics which underlie the unsatisfactory condition of this increasingly important aspect of international law.

Classic international law has been only marginally concerned with the application of international rules of conduct to internal conflict. Such rules as exist are few, tentative, and to a considerable extent contradictory. Norms governing intervention in civil wars generally veer between two opposite approaches: one stresses the legitimacy of outside support for the incumbent government against either internal political rebellion or secession—an approach that has been described by one author as "Metternich legitimacy."[1] The other stresses that "international law developed a stronger emphasis upon anti-intervention doctrine than upon doctrine favoring constitutional legitimacy."[2] The former approach favors one-sided intervention, the latter neutrality. The case studies, however, show clearly that neither principle has been consistently observed and that the same outside power has applied one or the other, depending upon the circumstances and its political strategy. Continental powers, in particular the United States and the Soviet Union, have in the postwar period tended to practice one-sided intervention in the exercise of a hegemonial interest in the political and social structure of states considered to be within their "sphere of influence."

Interventions in civil wars have increased in scope as the worldwide struggle of conflicting ideologies has become enmeshed with the global strategic confrontations of superpowers who avoid more direct battle with each other because of limitations imposed by the nature of nuclear weaponry. Considerations of national security and foreign policy have increasingly prevailed over such restraints as international law imposes upon intervention. The primary objective of the case studies has been to examine individual civil wars in depth, to analyze both their individual particularities and the general legal problems raised by them. On the whole, the case studies reveal the lack of a broad consensus on prin-

The summary chapter was prepared for the Panel on the Role of International Law in Civil Wars by one of its members, Edwin Brown Firmage, Professor of Law, University of Utah College of Law.

[1] Wolfgang Friedmann, "Law and Politics in the Vietnamese War: A Comment," *American Journal of International Law* 61 (1967): 776, 782.

[2] Richard A. Falk, *Legal Order in a Violent World* (Princeton: Princeton University Press, 1968), p. 134.

ciples to be applied. This underlines the importance of developing a coherent and generally applicable international structure to govern intervention in internal conflict.

The solutions proposed by the different authors indicate a wide spectrum of approaches to a problem area that, in view of the growing international importance of internal conflicts, poses a major challenge to contemporary international law. Among the principal proposals is the quest for a stronger community role as a substitute for individual state intervention. While the primary organ of the international community is the United Nations, regional organizations, such as the OAS, may, in certain civil war situations, be the more appropriate international authorities for intervention. It has also been suggested that a United Nations' sponsored code of intervention should replace the practices of the individual states. The author of the Yemen study has suggested the criterion of "modernization" as the standard by which intervention should be judged.

The following summary will seek to indicate the areas of agreement and disagreement revealed by the various case studies. The organization will be that of the case studies—foreign state participation, conduct of hostilities, and the role of international organizations in internal conflict. Finally, directions for further inquiry will be noted from the perspective of this summation.

I. THE ROLE OF INTERNATIONAL LAW IN REGULATING FOREIGN PARTICIPATION IN INTERNAL CONFLICT

Customary rules of international law and civil strife—the categories of rebellion, insurgency, and belligerency with their corresponding rights and duties—grew out of nineteenth-century experience, primarily the revolt of the Spanish-American colonies and the American Civil War.

Quincy Wright's study of the American Civil War demonstrates that the traditional rules worked reasonably well during that conflict.[3] The conclusion of Wright is that there was no plan on the part of Palmerston, Russell, and Gladstone to recognize the Confederacy or intervene on its behalf.

Though the Lincoln administration vigorously protested the recognition of belligerent status for the Confederacy by Britain and Britain's consequent neutrality, the same action was taken by almost all commercial nations and was justified by the Union blockade of Confederate

---

[3] It should be noted, however, that the traditional rules of international law were ineffective in other situations of civil conflict in the nineteenth century. United States intervention in Latin American civil strife is but one example of this.

ports. Following Lincoln's partial Emancipation Proclamation and Union military victories, Britain withheld any offer of mediation. Most European states did not permit their territory to be used for belligerent purposes, though Britain permitted the *Alabama* and other vessels to leave British ports and had to pay reparations consequent to arbitration following the war. Britain recognized belligerent rights of visit, search, capture, and condemnation of commercial vessels as defined by international law. Wright concludes that the "position of foreign states during the war, wholeheartedly accepted by the Confederacy and half-heartedly by the Union, was that civil strife recognized as civil war should be identified with international war and the international law of war and neutrality should be applied so long as the war lasted."[4]

The customary rules of international law regarding outside participation in civil strife—of inconsistent effectiveness during the nineteenth century, as we have said—have subsequently diminished in influence. Whatever the cause—changes in the state system, technological revolution, increased regional hegemonial influence by major powers, dogmatic and strategic conflict between superpowers—it is apparent that rules purporting to govern intervention in internal conflict are now relatively impotent.[5]

New rules, based upon state practice, treaties, resolutions of the United Nations, and proposals of scholars, are emerging. There seems to be consensus among the Panel upon the outer limits of rules delimiting intervention. At one extreme, the sweeping prohibition upon intervention of any kind illustrated by the language of article 18 of the Revised Charter of the OAS, and repeated by the UN General Assembly, is at the same time undesirable and impossible of accomplishment, whether or not a state is experiencing civil strife:

No state or group of States has the right to intervene, directly or indirectly, for any reason whatsoever, in the internal or external affairs of any other State. The foregoing principle prohibits not only armed force but also any other form of interference or attempted threat against the personality of the State or against its political, economic, and cultural elements.

The unintended influence of the United States within the Western Hemisphere—taken alone—insures that such a proscription will be continually violated. The cultural and economic impact of any great power upon smaller states within the region will be massive without any conscious effort on the part of the great power to have it so. Aspects of the

---

[4] Wright, pp. 93–94. All references to case studies within this volume will be by author and page number.

[5] See Boals, pp. 306–12; Tom Farer, "Intervention in Civil Wars: A Modest Proposal," *Columbia Law Review* 67 (1967): 266.

influence may be either helpful or destructive. It has been noted that the intentional refusal of a great power to act—for example, the decision by the United States to refuse to build the Aswan Dam—has profound influence upon a society.[6] Again, the very existence of the United States or other major powers, with their particular patterns of government, may influence the ideals of other systems and may itself be a causative factor of civil strife. Any norms circumscribing intervention in civil strife by outside states must be established with the realization that there will be preexisting and continuing economic, cultural, and political forces emanating from those states which may directly, though not necessarily intentionally, affect the outcome of civil strife.

There is also agreement at the opposite end of the spectrum of intervention that a frenetic policy of indiscriminate intervention in support of the status quo or in support of revolution—whether the civil tumult be caused by palace coup or social revolution, subversive activity by a foreign power, military revolt, or a war of decolonization—may be counterproductive for the goals sought by the intervener and is unquestionably violative of international law. Potential interveners must avoid a "Metternich doctrine of legitimacy" in opposition to any revolutionary change or a crusading subscription to revolution in support of a particular political ideology.[7]

One basic prerequisite for nonintervention by states in foreign civil strife is that such a rule be uniformly observed. As seen from the perspective of the Thomas and Thomas study in this volume, this is the most powerful of the many lessons of the Spanish Civil War. Though there is no evidence that Germany and Italy precipitated the revolt of the army officers, within ten days of its initiation and before Franco had assumed leadership, both states were providing substantial aid to the Nationalist forces. Salazar had allowed activity preliminary to the revolt to take place in Portugal. By the time Britain and France were attempting to establish a generally accepted policy of neutrality, massive aid, including troops and the machinery of war, was already being supplied the Nationalist forces. Even if the refusal of Britain, France, and the United States to provide supplies to the incumbent government was justified under international law by an actual though unrecognized status of belligerency following the Loyalist imposition of blockade upon Nationalist ports and the territorial control exercised by the Nationalist forces, the unequal adherence by other states to the doctrine of neu-

---

[6] Manfred Halpern, "The Morality and Politics of Intervention," in Richard A. Falk (ed.), *The Vietnam War and International Law* (Princeton, N. J.: Princeton University Press, 1968), 1: 41.

[7] Friedmann, "Law and Politics," p. 782; Farer, "Intervention in Civil War"; Richard Barnet, *Intervention and Revolution* (Cleveland: World Publishing Co., 1968).

trality destroyed its objective. Although the private commercial sale of weapons to both sides was permitted for some time by Britain, and Mexico and the Soviet Union actively supported the constituted government, the nature of foreign intervention supporting both sides was so disproportionately in favor of the Nationalist forces that such intervention probably decided the outcome of the war. Without uniform adherence to the doctrine of nonintervention in civil strife, an exception to the doctrine must be allowed to permit limited counterintervention.

The attempts by France and Britain to establish a workable nonintervention agreement provide guidelines for those who would propose new norms to circumscribe intervention in civil strife. Its initial failure to proscribe the participation of foreign manpower permitted the use of "volunteers" in the form of organized military units from Germany and Italy as well as irregular forces organized by the Soviet Union and other states. The later prohibition on volunteers accomplished by a broadening of the nonintervention agreement had a negative impact, as the observation system established by the Nonintervention Committee was unevenly effective. German, Portugese, and Italian volunteers entered Spain in undiminished numbers, while support for the Loyalist forces dropped precipitously. From that point, the war continued to an inevitable end.

There would seem to be consensus among Panel members and participants that a system permitting unilateral intervention by big states in civil strife within smaller states will often be undesirable—even when not destablizing—when judged by other criteria such as diversity or justice. Intervention beyond the area generally acknowledged as the sphere of interest of the intervening power will be inherently destablizing. But before states can be expected to adhere to rules delimiting intervention, provision must be made to insure that there will be greater probability of uniform adherence to such a system. Roger Fisher has made this point:

> Simply to refrain from intervention ourselves is not likely to produce restraint in other governments. Our bad example will surely be followed; our good example, by itself, will not. A successful policy must not only avoid providing an excuse for forceful intervention; it must tend to induce other nations to lessen their subversive activities. It must decrease the possibility of gain from subversion and increase the cost of the gamble. In such a policy, international law can play a central role.[8]

[8] Fisher, "Intervention: Three Problems of Policy and Law," in Falk (ed.), *The Vietnam War and International Law*, 1: 140. Falk's book also contains a relevant quotation from J. S. Mill:
"The doctrine of non-intervention, to be a legitimate principle of morality, must be accepted by all governments. The despots must consent to be bound by it as well as the free states. Unless they do, the profession of it by free countries comes but to this miserable issue, that the wrong side may help the wrong, but the right must not help the right" (p. 38).

Percy Corbett has proposed that one way in which international law could aid in such a quest would be the negotiation of a treaty code under UN aegis specifying the precise conditions under which foreign intervention in civil strife would be permitted, the nature and extent of such intervention, and the role of regional and universal international organizations in civil strife.[9] The philosophical and tangible support several groups of states give to wars of national liberation would be only one of the multitude of seemingly insurmountable problems standing between us and the realization of such a goal.[10]

While there would seem to be consensus as to the need for agreement defining the role of foreign states and international organizations in civil strife, there is no unanimity as to its basis, even among the contributors to this and past volumes on civil strife. Corbett, Falk, and Barnet have all proposed severe restriction if not complete prohibition upon foreign state intervention in civil strife in favor of regional or UN intervention under certain restrictive conditions.[11]

For Corbett, unilateral intervention by foreign states in civil strife would be prohibited on behalf of either the incumbent government or the rebels or insurgents, and broad interventionary authority would be granted the United Nations. Foreign states have used the traditional rule permitting aid to a widely recognized incumbent government prior to recognition of belligerency as the basis for intervention in Czechoslovakia, Hungary, the Dominican Republic, and Vietnam, to name only the most recent. (In the case of Czechoslovakia, at least, the Soviet intervention was clearly in violation of any rule of international law, as there was no request for aid from the Czech government. The powerful intimidation employed by the Soviet Union upon the new Czech government to manufacture such a request months after the intervention by Soviet and Warsaw Pact troops is some indication of the Soviet desire to legitimate an act of invasion. An additional impediment to the impossible task of legitimating the Soviet intervention was, of course, the absence of any internal tumult that might have precipitated a request for aid or intervention.) Mrs. Boals has noted that both the United Arab Republic and Saudi Arabia justified their support of the contending factions in Yemen on the basis of the Jiddah Pact of 1956, which obligated those three states to provide mutual assistance in case of aggres-

[9] Corbett, pp. 401–4.

[10] See, for example, George Ginsburg, "Wars of Liberation and the Modern Law of Nations—the Soviet Thesis," *Law and Contemporary Problems* 29 (1964): 910.

[11] Corbett, p. 401; Falk, "International Law and the United States Role in the Viet Nam War," in *The Vietnam War and International Law*, 1: 362; Barnet, *Intervention and Revolution*, pp. 257–85.

sion against any one of them. Each outside state identified the other as the aggressor and announced its support for the "legitimate" government, that is, the faction supported by it. Both Saudi Arabia and the UAR justified their action under norms of traditional international law allowing complete national control over the act of recognition and the determination of incumbency.

Others would attempt to reach the same goal as Corbett, but by another route—that of allowing approximately the traditional consequences to follow from the act of recognition, namely, a bias in favor of the incumbent government over contending factions—but would delimit the authority of the nation state over the act of recognition.[12] The United Nations would receive increased jurisdiction to pronounce the benediction of incumbency.

For others, the propensity and capacity of a faction to accomplish certain identified values would determine the legality of foreign state or international organization intervention in their support. From his study of the Algerian revolution, Fraleigh suggests that there is an international consensus in support of wars of decolonization and that this support should be broadened to other forms of wars of political separation which also have as their goal the protection of fundamental human rights.

. . . If international lawyers have the function of charting a course for the development of legal principles in the field of international relations, they should ask themselves whether the Algerian precedent is not more than a precedent to support the legitimacy of decolonization wars. Is it not also a precedent for the legitimacy of any war of political separation (even a non-colonial war) if the war is fought by a group with a territorial base for the same basic objective as a decolonization war—the protection of fundamental human rights, such as freedom from persecution or the right to participate in the government of one's country on a basis of equality with fellow nationals?[13]

Of course, the Marxian classification of the war of national liberation as a just war is another variant of the identification of direct (and subjective) values with contending factions, with legal consequences following such identification. Certain Asian and African states have argued in favor of a similar international legal norm legitimating wars of self-determination.

Mrs. Boals has concluded from her study of the Yemen civil war that the major criterion determining legitimacy and hence a favored position

---

[12] For example, see Fisher, "Intervention."
[13] Fraleigh, pp. 184–85.

regarding foreign intervention should be the capacity and willingness of the faction to accomplish modernization. On this basis she would accord the right of foreign support to the Republican forces, though she suggests that Egypt, had it correctly interpreted the nature of the struggle in Yemen as one pitting the forces of modernization against those of the status quo, should have eschewed military intervention on the side of the Republicans for other forms of support. Both the Egyptians in Yemen and the Americans in Vietnam erred, says Mrs. Boals, in believing that a predominantly military intervention could hold off an opposing force until a new society took the place of a traditional one that was in the process of disintegrating. Intervention, therefore, should take place on behalf of the modernizing faction in the form of political and economic aid aimed at system transformation:

> The focus of concern from the point of view of the revolution of modernization is not the state but the society, not the government but the organization of men in fundamtntally new relationships, not incumbents and insurgents but modernizing elites, not prevention of intervention as such but the prevention of interventions that do not foster modernization. . . .[14]

Some obvious problems exist with an approach that would determine the permissibility of intervention on behalf of a regime by an identification of subjective values with it. By what means does a nation or an international institution determine the capacity and commitment of a faction to self-determination? to modernization? to fundamental human rights? Perhaps it may be presumed that an organization such as the FLN in Algeria is supporting decolonization and its opponents the political status quo. But what does the potential intervener do when certain of these subjective values are in conflict? And has the practice of states in the past given any hope that intervention in the future will be based upon such altruistic and ambiguous factors?

Such questions are raised by those who would determine the legitimacy of foreign intervention upon objective categorical rules. Most, if not all, of the Panel and the majority of the participants (with the possible exceptions of Mrs. Boals and Arnold Fraleigh) would reject the application of subjective values as legal norms governing intervention. This is not to say, however, that value-free rules either could or should be devised. Those favoring the application of objective nonintervention rules are not proposing a Wechslerian search for "neutral principles." They recognize that community values will—and should—have an impact upon norms governing intervention.

[14] Boals, p. 342.

Tom Farer would permit foreign intervention in support of insurgents or the incumbent government, without distinction, as long as such support did not intrude upon tactical operations or a zone of combat. Economic aid, military training in noncombat zones, the supplying of military hardware, all would be permitted outside a tactical combat zone. No "advisers" or "volunteers" would be allowed in a combat zone.[15]

Richard Falk would also reject subjective values as norms in favor of the application of rules determined by an identification of the nature and the scope of the conflict.[16] "Direct and massive" use of force across a frontier, as in Korea, could precipitate unilateral or collective neutralizing counterintervention by outside states; substantial military intervention by outside states in a predominantly internal struggle for control could be met by proportionate counterintervention confined to the internal area if a prior attempt at a peaceful solution through regional or universal international systems was unsuccessful. An internal war for control of a society which could be determined independent of foreign participation would be largely removed from foreign state intervention. The discretion of both the victim state and the potential intervening third state to characterize covert aggression as "armed attack" would be limited by the necessity of acquiring prior "organized international community" assent.[17]

Others have noted the problem of attempting to formulate universal norms governing intervention in civil strife of profoundly differing types and locations. An impressive attempt to respond to this problem was accomplished by a panel member, John Norton Moore.[18] Another panel member stated that

one norm purporting to govern all types of civil strife regardless of purposes, origin, or geographical location—from colonial revolt and social revolution to palace coup, in nonaligned countries or within the security zones of the major powers—is drastically insufficient.[19]

Rules that ignore the basic security interests of states, especially those interests of the major powers, have little chance of acceptance.

[15] Farer, "Intervention in Civil Wars," p. 67, and "Harnessing Rogue Elephants: A Short Discourse on Foreign Intervention in Civil Strife," *Harvard Law Review* 82 (1969): 511.

[16] Falk, *Legal Order in a Violent World*, pp. 227–28.

[17] Falk, "International Law and the United States Role in Viet Nam: A Response to Professor Moore," Yale *Law Journal* 76 (1967): 1095, 1142–50.

[18] Moore, "The Control of Foreign Intervention in Internal Conflict," *Virginia Journal of International Law* 9 (1969): 205.

[19] Firmage, review of Falk (ed.), *The Vietnam War and International Law*, in *Utah Law Review*, 1970, p. 174.

II. THE ROLE OF INTERNATIONAL LAW IN CONTROLLING THE CONDUCT OF HOSTILITIES IN INTERNAL CONFLICTS

There has been a degradation of the observance of the laws of war from the time of the American Civil War to that of the Spanish Civil War as the strategy of total war has had its influence upon civil as well as international war.[20] The initial attempts of the Lincoln administration to treat the crews of southern privateers operating under letters of marque and reprisal issued by the Confederate government as pirates were reversed under pressure from Supreme Court decisions holding contrarily and from Confederate threats of retaliation upon Union prisoners. After the publication of Dr. Francis Lieber's code by the War Department in 1863 as general orders governing the conduct of the Union armies, Quincy Wright has concluded, both sides generally attempted to apply the laws of war to the hostilities. While Lieber's Code did not specify that international law required that the laws of war be applied to civil strife, it did stress that such laws be applied as principles of humanity.

Wright found that prisoners of war were generally treated according to the laws of war. Most of the hardship experienced by the prisoners resulted from the lack of medical knowledge of the time and the scarcity of food in the Confederacy rather than intentional mistreatment. Further, the persons and property of enemy civilians were protected under the provisions of Lieber's Code and these provisions were generally observed by both sides at least until the concepts of total war began to emerge in Sherman's march to the sea.

The general observance of principles of international law and humanity in the conduct of the American Civil War is in complete contrast with the savage disregard of such restraints in the Spanish Civil War. Both of the Nationalist and Loyalist forces engaged in the systematic murder of civilians and prisoners of war; civilian property was seized and destroyed as part of the method of war; political prisoners were tortured and killed on a massive scale; hostages were kept in areas of likely air attack and naval bombardment; thousands of Republican prisoners died of malnutrition, disease, and abuse following the Nationalist victory. The general rules of international law concerning the conduct of war—the humane treatment of prisoners of war, the protection of

---

[20] The term "total war" is used here to refer to the failure to distinguish between civilian and soldier and between military targets and the property of noncombatants; it is not used in the sense of indicating a total use of weaponry or a geographical escalation of hostilities.

414

civilians and their property, the avoidance of nonmilitary targets—had been upheld with a considerable degree of consensus for half a century preceding the Spanish Civil War. These had been codified in the Hague Conventions of 1907 and the Geneva Convention of 1929. Although these conventions were generally held to be inapplicable to civil strife, the scope and territorial nature of the Nationalist revolt resulted in a status of de facto belligerency which would be hard to distinguish from the status of de jure belligerency enjoyed by the Confederacy in the American Civil War. The rules of war would seem to have been as binding upon the conduct of the Spanish Civil War as upon the American.

The failure of international law to moderate the viciousness of the Spanish Civil War is another testimony to the increased need in an age of total war (without clear distinctions between civilian and military personnel and property) for regional or international institutions of control. The self-restraint exercised upon the conduct of civil war in an earlier era is insufficient to control the conduct of hostilities in this century.

The contrast between two instances of civil strife which have taken place since the Geneva Conventions of 1949 presents a different manifestation of the same problem. Article 3 of each of the four Geneva Conventions of 1949 deals with "armed conflict not of an international character" and was purposely drafted to obviate any necessity for defining civil war or of requiring that any status of belligerency be reached or recognized before the general laws of international war as stipulated in article 3 were made applicable to internal war. These provisions of the Geneva Conventions apply whenever sustained military response beyond normal police action is taken against organized rebel armies holding substantial territory. The traditional rules of humane conduct toward prisoners of war, civilians and their property, the wounded, and so on, as found in the laws of war are thereby made applicable to internal wars.

The major participants in the civil war in the Congo acknowledged the applicability of the principles of the Geneva Conventions. The central government of the Congo, Tshombe in Katanga, and the secretary-general of the United Nations considered that the actions of their respective forces were circumscribed by the Geneva Conventions. And in Yemen Mrs. Boals reports that both Royalists and Republicans in the civil conflict agreed to "respect the principles" of the Geneva Conventions of 1949. But McNemar and Mrs. Boals reach opposite conclusions regarding the effectiveness of the Geneva Conventions in moderating the conduct of hostilities in these two instances of internal war. The tribal nature of both conflicts limited the effectiveness of international restraints, but the degree to which international law was effective in the Congo is remarkable when contrasted with the conclusion of Mrs. Boals that it had no modifying effect on the conduct of the war in Yemen. The lack of distinction between civilians and combatants by both Republicans and Royalists, the systematic killing of prisoners by the Royalists, and the use of gas by the Egyptians are testimony to the lack of effect of international law upon the contending factions in Yemen.

In contrast to this, McNemar reported that the provisions of the Geneva Conventions of 1949 were generally observed in the Congo civil war. Most prisoners of war were well treated. Isolated violations occurred—most notably in the murder by Congolese troops of forty-seven Ghananian soldiers of the UN forces—but this was the exception. The protection of civilians and their property as provided in the Geneva Conventions was also observed by both Katangese and UN forces. The ill-trained Congolese army was responsible for many violations of the Geneva Conventions relating to the protection of civilians, but the major cause of civilian casualties was fierce tribal fighting. Even then, most tribal deaths did not occur in battle but in massacre, as the slaughter of the Baluba tribesmen by Lumumba's troops after the capture of the capital of South Kasai.

McNemar concluded that the "Congo experience suggests that a United Nations presence contributes to the effectiveness of the laws of war."[21] The publicity attendant on the UN presence and the effective functioning of the International Committee of Red Cross, made possible by its close working relationship with UN forces, both helped to enforce the integrity of international normative restraints.[22]

One significant point for further inquiry is raised by Fraleigh's study of the Algerian conflict. To what degree are the Geneva Conventions of 1949 appropriate and effective regarding wars of national liberation? Several factors which are often present in a war of national liberation would seem to make this type of conflict unique. The modern form of the war of national liberation has been fashioned after the civil war in China, which was just reaching its end at the time of the Geneva Conventions of 1949. That it was to become the model for many anti-colonial conflicts, among others, could not have been foreseen. As a consequence, certain aspects of this variant form of guerrilla war were not taken into account at Geneva. The absence of fixed territorial positions in several types of internal conflict could be used by the constituted government to deny the applicability of the Geneva Conventions. Even

[21] McNemar, p. 270.

[22] The contrast between Yemen and the Congo, though striking, is not as marked as that between the Congo and Nigeria-Biafra, where over a million deaths occurred in civil strife.

416

though they were drafted to avoid the necessity of the recognition of belligerency or the definition of civil war, the nonterritorial nature of the war of national liberation may frustrate the purpose of the Geneva Conventions. In Algeria, for example, though the Red Cross considered article 3 of the Geneva Conventions to be applicable and the FLN attempted to ratify the conventions, France never recognized the capacity of the FLN to do so.

Another factor often present in the war of national liberation—the calculated use of terror against elements of the civilian population loyal to the incumbent government—makes it likely that certain provisions of the Geneva Conventions will be unheeded. French trial and execution of some prisoners for terrorist activities is directly related to this problem of defining the status of calculated terror in internal conflicts.

Other forms of violence proscribed by the Geneva Conventions but indulged in by one or both sides in the Algerian war—torture, mutilation, and execution of prisoners, aerial bombing of rural villages allegedly containing rebels on the rationale of collective responsibility—do not present problems unique to the war of national liberation.

III.   THE ROLE OF INTERNATIONAL ORGANIZATIONS IN INSULATING AND RESOLVING CIVIL STRIFE

The Regional Approach

The basic strengths and weaknesses of regional control over internal violence are in some respects the same as those which have been claimed for and against the concert of Europe of Metternich and Castlereagh. They are summed up by one question: What price—at the expense of human diversity and sometimes of justice—will the international community be willing to pay to effect a possible lessening of friction within regions of the world?

It is obvious from the studies of this volume that regional approaches to controlling internal strife are partial at best. Corbett concluded that no regional organizations existed through which peace could have been achieved in Vietnam. The Southeast Asia Treaty Organization was created primarily in reaction to the internal wars in what was then French Indochina and was a defensive alignment aimed at one side of that conflict. The International Commission for Supervision and Control (ICSC), established by the Geneva accords to supervise adherence to the terms of the truce, had no power or means of enforcement. Its usefulness further atrophied at the departure of the French and the refusal of the Republic of Vietnam to consider itself the successor of the French in regard to the activities of the ICSC.

This absence of cohesive and appropriate regional organizations is not limited to Asia. No regional African organization existed when civil strife in the Congo began. Lumumba initiated a meeting of the leaders of thirteen independent African states to consider joint action against Katanga. This was rejected. After the collapse of the Kasavubu-Lumumba government, the African states divided into groups supporting Lumumba (and later the regime at Stanleyville) and those backing Kasavubu. Since the establishment of the Organization of African Unity in 1963, the regional organization has been more effective in furthering bloc politics at the United Nations than in preventing or controlling internal war, as has been tragically demonstrated in Nigeria-Biafra.

Fraleigh concludes that the Algerian war demonstrated the weaknesses of the regional approach to international control over internal war and the potential strength of the United Nations. In Algeria the two major participants were members of different regional organizations. A possible escalation (rather than containment) of domestic conflict through the involvement of regional organizations was avoided by the refusal of the North Atlantic Treaty Organization to give its blessings to French activity in Algeria, even though NATO had supported the French cause in Indochina. NATO tacitly branded the Algerian war as a colonial enterprise lacking communist initiation or leadership and therefore remained aloof. Though the Arab League actively supported its cause, the FLN never used this endorsement as an argument in support of its legitimacy. Instead, the usual arguments based upon decolonization and self-determination were employed with significant success in the United Nations.

Two regional organizations—or more accurately the two major powers behind those organizations—have made arguments which dramatically affect traditional rules of recognition, incumbency, and sovereignty. In 1962 the Castro government of Cuba was read out of the inter-American system by members of the Organization of American States meeting at Punta del Este. Although it would require a not inconsiderable (and potentially damaging) leap, it has been argued from this that the adoption of a Marxist social and economic order permits the inter-American regional organization to remove the status of legitimacy from an incumbent government within this hemisphere. Further consequences could then be drawn regarding the permissibility of aid to insurgent groups in Cuba.[23]

The possibility of US intervention in Latin America if OAS collective action was not taken in response to "outside" communist penetration was alluded to by President John F. Kennedy in 1961:

[23] Falk, *Legal Order in a Violent World*, pp. 150–51.

. . . Let the record show that our restraint is not inexhaustible. Should it ever appear that the inter-American doctrine of non-interference merely conceals or excuses a policy of nonaction—if the nations of this hemisphere should fail to meet their commitments against outside Communist penetration—then I want it clearly understood that this Government will not hesitate in meeting its primary obligations, which are to the security of our Nation.[24]

That the words "outside Communist penetration" could be loosely interpreted was demonstrated by United States intervention in the Dominican Republic in 1965.

On August 3, 1968, Czechoslovakia, the Soviet Union, and four other members of the Warsaw Pact pledged cooperation "on the basis of the principles of equality, respect for sovereignty and national independence [and] territorial integrity. . . ."[25] Seventeen days later Czechoslovakia was invaded by those same members of the Warsaw Pact. This was done without the prior existence of internal strife or an invitation from any major faction. That internal strife would be a sufficient provocation to produce intervention had been established in Hungary the decade before. The Soviet defense of the invasion of Czechoslovakia led to the pronouncement of the Brezhnev doctrine of limited sovereignty.[26] Brezhnev declared that communist countries' sovereignty is limited to the extent that armed intervention by the Soviet Union and other socialist countries will be precipitated and justified whenever, in the judgment of the Soviet Union, Marxist principles of social development are

[24] Kennedy, "The Lesson of Cuba," *U.S. State Department Bulletin*, No. 44 (1961), p. 659, as quoted in Falk, *ibid.*, p. 187.

[25] As quoted in *Czechoslovakia and the Brezhnev Doctrine*, prepared by the Subcommittee on National Security and International Operations, Senate Committee on Government Operations, 90th Cong., 1st sess. (1969), p. 3.

[26] The first intimation of the emerging Brezhnev doctrine came in an article by Sergei Kovalev in *Pravda* on September 25: "There is no doubt that the peoples of the socialist countries and the Communist Parties have and must have freedom to determine their country's path of development. However, any decision of theirs must damage neither socialism in their own country nor the fundamental interests of the other socialist countries nor the worldwide workers' movement, which is waging a struggle for socialism. This means that every Communist Party is responsible not only to its own people but also to all the socialist countries and to the entire Communist movement. Whoever forgets this in placing sole emphasis on the autonomy and independence of Communist Parties lapses into one-sidedness, shirking his internationalist obligations. . . . The sovereignty of individual socialist countries cannot be counterposed to the interests of world socialism and the world revolutionary movement" (*ibid*).

And it was announced in a speech by Leonid Brezhnev, general secretary of the Soviet Communist party before the Polish Communist party, Nov. 12, 1968:

". . . The CPSU (Communist Party of the Soviet Union) has always advocated that each socialist country determine the specific forms of its development along the road to socialism with consideration for its specific national conditions.

"However, it is known, comrades, that there also are common laws governing socialist construction, a deviation from which might lead to a deviation from

threatened by internal forces. Immediate opposition to this assertion of unilateral and regional control over internal matters of socialist states was voiced by the majority of communist parties around the world.[27]

A regional centralization of authority over presently unilateral state decisions regarding recognition and incumbency, possibly followed by an assertion of exclusive regional prerogatives of intervention, could at least lessen the number of potential interveners in civil strife. In addition, such centralized control might insure that internal war could be limited in geographical scope, time, and level of destruction. But the potential cost in terms of human values, diversity, national self-determination, and justice would be great. The specter of Israeli domestic conflict leading to a legitimized intervention by the Arab League, or emerging liberalism in eastern Europe being destroyed with the sanction of international law places metes and bounds upon the prospects for regionalism, taken alone.

It has been proposed that a protection against aberrant regional norms could be secured by requiring Security Council approval under article 53(1) prior to any drastic coercion by a region to enforce homogeneity.[28] Presumably, a regional organization could employ cultural and

---

socialism as such. And when the internal and external forces hostile to socialism seek to revert the development of any socialist country toward the restoration of the capitalist order, when a threat to the cause of socialism in that country, a threat to the security of the socialist community as a whole, emerges, this is no longer only a problem of the people of that country but also a common problem, concern for all socialist states.

"It goes without saying that such an action as military aid to a fraternal country to cut short the threat to the socialist order is an extraordinary enforced step, it *can be sparked off only by direct actions of the enemies of socialism inside the country and beyond its boundaries, actions, creating a threat to the common interests of the camp of socialism*" (*ibid.*, p. 4 [emphasis added]).

[27] Almost all communist parties outside eastern Europe attacked both the Soviet assault upon Czechoslovakia and the Brezhnev doctrine of limited sovereignty offered in its defense. Within eastern Europe, General Secretary Ceausescu of Rumania and President Tito of Yugoslavia immediately objected to the doctrine. An example of the reaction consistent with the general expressions of the communist parties throughout Europe is that of a member of the Central Committee of the Austrian Communist party writing in *Volksstimme* October 9: "... No norm exists or has existed anywhere giving a socialist country or a group of such countries the right to intervene in a fraternal socialist country. Incidentally, such a right of intervention is in conflict with all existing norms of relations among fraternal socialist countries and among Communist parties.... On any basis other than ... the basis of autonomy, a world Communist movement is not possible" (*ibid.*, p. 6).

[28] See Falk, *Legal Order in a Violent World*, pp. 150–51; and compare Barnet, *Intervention and Revolution*: "A rehabilitation of the rule in the United Nations Charter prohibiting foreign intervention in a civil war, as opposed to collective defense against a foreign invasion, would mean that a government would have to handle its own insurgency problems unless it could get assistance, including the help of an international police force, from either the Security Council or the General Assembly" (p. 279).

perhaps economic sanctions against an alien state but could not use military force without prior Security Council approval. Only when the approval of the universal international organization indicated that a state was in violation of international as well as regional norms could regional coercion of a forceful nature be taken. It may be seriously questioned whether this proposal is within the range of possible adoption as state practice.

The United Nations

If one basic theme emerges from all of the case studies, it would be that there is an increasing need for more centralized control over outside intervention in civil strife. It is generally recognized that some *purposes* of intervention—for example, self-protection or the fulfilling of humanitarian goals—may be acceptable and desirable goals. But the *decision* to intervene and the identity of the intervener may be abrasive to the international community if the actor is a nation-state. If, therefore, unilateral foreign state intervention in domestic strife is to be circumscribed by international law, something must be put in its place to perform the legitimate moral and security functions now met by such intervention.

Increased community decision to intervene and community selection of the intervener are necessary to accomplish the valid purposes of intervention and yet avoid the anarchy implicit in intervention by foreign states. It is recognized that—on the basis of cold war politics and spheres of interest, among other reasons—some types of civil strife may best be controlled by regional rather than universal international organizations. But in general, UN control over third party intervention would seem to be the most desirable eventual goal in that decisions to intervene would be based on a wider community consensus. This would lessen the chances of regional intervention against a government whose social order is acceptable in the world community but is an aberration in its region.

Certain writers stressed the present capacity and limitations of the United Nations, while others focused upon an ultimate goal of UN utilization in limiting the effects of civil strife upon the international community. Conclusions range from Corbett's suggested complete proscription of foreign state intervention on behalf of both incumbent and insurgent groups, coupled with a grant of limited power to the United Nations to permit intervention by the world community, to the much more restrictive view of possible United Nations effectiveness in dealing with civil wars as expressed by McNemar.[29]

[29] Corbett, pp. 401–4; McNemar, pp. 283–90, 301–2. Cf. the position of Wolfgang Friedmann: "In sum, international law has never been equipped to inter-

Substantial growth is seen by a comparison of the embryonic international institutional tools available at the time of the American Civil War, with its limited though effective use of postwar arbitration, and the functioning of the United Nations in the Congo. This is complemented by the increased commitment of the major powers to use existing international machinery, as demonstrated by contrasting the success of the UN force in the Congo with the complete failure of the major powers to use the League of Nations to limit intervention in the Spanish Civil War. But the factors which were present in the successful Congo operation of the United Nations also indicate its limitations. Both superpowers had an interest in the Congo. Yet it was not a traditional battlefield of the cold war or a geographical area of critical interest to the United States or the Soviet Union. Both wanted to minimize the influence of the other. Hostilities in the Congo began with events which provided the superpowers and a huge majority of the members of the United Nations with a unifying specter—the threat of a reintroduction of colonial influence into the newly independent African state. Without a confluence of some of these factors—the interest of the major powers, the isolated location of the civil strife away from strategic areas of the superpowers' major interests, and the presence of one of the few issues, colonialism, upon which all but a handful of states agree—the UN activity in the Congo would not have been possible. And yet it is demonstrable that an exact grouping of all of these factors is not a prerequisite to the performance of UN peacekeeping functions. The experience of the United Nations in Cyprus provides another illustration of major UN field operations.[30] There, the major actors and geographical area deeply involved NATO. No element of colonialism was present. And it should also be noted that the Cyprus force was not made possible by a procedural windfall not likely to be repeated, as in the case of Korea.

The limited basis of support and yet the degree of strength possessed by the United Nations once peacekeeping action has been commenced

---

vene in civil war situations. While today the United Nations does have some reserve function in this area where international peace is concerned, this is more than countered by the increased turbulence of a multitude of unsettled international conditions in an increasing number of countries. The powers granted to the United Nations, especially by Article 24 of the Charter, should, therefore, be used only in exceptional circumstances, generally in situations which imply *national* rather than *social* conflict and where the intervention of the United Nations can help in the cooling down of the national conflicts involved. Any intervention of the United Nations in essentially ideological and political conflicts is likely to split it beyond repair and to destroy the already fragile political and financial support on which it depends" ("Intervention, Civil War and the Role of International Law," in Falk [ed.], *The Vietnam War and International Law,* 1: 151, 158).

[30] L. B. Miller, *Cyprus: The Law and Politics of Civil Strife* (Harvard University, Cambridge Center for Internal Affairs, 1968).

are both revealed by one of the major precedents to come from the Congo experience. Lumumba, while still a member of the central government, appealed to the Soviet Union for military aid to be used against Katanga. The Soviet Union complied. With the division between East and West following the dissolution of the central government caused by the split between Kasavubu and Lumumba, the Security Council called upon all states to refrain from providing unilateral military aid to one or the other faction. The Soviets asserted that the Security Council resolution could not restrict the right of the Congo to request aid and the right of another nation to provide it. Hammarskjold took direct issue with this proposition. Following the veto by the Soviet Union of the Tunisian and Ceylonese resolution in the Security Council which would have forbidden any state to provide military aid to any party in the Congo except through the United Nations, the General Assembly passed by a 70 to 0 margin (with the abstention of the communist states) a resolution to the same effect. Though the Soviets launched a bitter campaign against the UN action in the Congo and against Hammarskjold personally, unilateral Soviet aid seems to have been terminated.

After Lumumba's arrest and the establishment of a government by Gizenga at Stanleyville, Sudan was able to make effective use of the General Assembly resolution by forbidding transport through its territory of economic and military aid to the rebels from the United Arab Republic and various communist states unless the secretary-general of the United Nations approved. As McNemar observed, this prohibition of unilateral military assistance while the UN force was operating in the Congo demonstrates "the development of a norm that a United Nations multilateral operation preempts the right of a foreign country to grant military assistance on a unilateral basis."[31] While no such norms developed from the Congo experience regarding economic and technical assistance, or diplomatic recognition, this must be considered as a development in the law of civil strife of high importance. Without this, events in the Congo could have paralleled—in direction if not in scope —the tragedy of the Spanish Civil War.

As it was, battlefield deaths were under one thousand, and though tribal massacres claimed many thousands, hostilities were brought to an end within a reasonable time. Peace was effected through the direct involvement of the United Nations. The conciliation commission, established by the secretary general's advisory committee on the Congo, was instrumental in establishing parliamentary government at Leopoldville. United Nations representatives also played key roles in negotiating a settlement between Adoula and Tshombe and reintegrating Katanga into

[31] McNemar, p. 282.

the Congo. Another important factor in the establishment of whatever degree of stability existed after the cessation of hostilities was the United Nations Civilian Operation. This organization provided technical support to the central government in administering its essential services and training Congolese to take them over later.

The growth of UN jurisdiction from the initial rationale of preventing the reimposition of colonial control to the final assertion of responsibility for the establishment of domestic peace in the Congo is impressive evidence of UN effectiveness under certain conditions. The influence of the United Nations, particularly the General Assembly, in the institution of negotiations between France and the FLN in the Algerian war is further indication of its potency when issues of nationalism and decolonization are present. A comparison between these successful experiences and the complete failure of the United Nations to effect a settlement in Vietnam is instructive in that similar issues of colonialism and nationalism are present. In addition, the country, while located in an area of some strategic significance, is outside the general spheres of influence of either the Soviet Union or the United States. Seemingly, then, the same factors are present which produced sufficient identity of interests between the two superpowers to permit effective UN action in the Congo. Why, then, the tragic disparity in result? One reason is that the issues of nationalism and decolonization (which enjoy US support) and the prevention of the expansion of communism by forceful, military means, both seemed to American decisionmakers to be present in Vietnam and dictated opposite reactions.[32] Whether the civil tumult in Vietnam was characterized as being predominantly a process of decolonization or communist aggression determined the direction of American foreign policy there.

The refusal of France, the Soviet Union, and the United States, at different times during the years of hostilities in Vietnam, to seek a solution through the United Nations again establishes the fact that the organization will be only as effective on any issue as the major powers want it to be. As was true in the failure of the League of Nations during the Spanish Civil War, there is no international legal reason why the collective security and sanctions provisions of the Charter cannot be used. Power still resides in the nation-states. Something approaching ultimate power is possessed by two. Constitutional and administrative reform of the United Nations, while desirable, is of peripheral importance as compared with the value of a decision by the major powers to make it work.

However, the accomplishment of certain reforms in the structure and

[32] See Firmage, "International Law and the Response of the United States to Internal War," in Falk (ed.), *The Vietnam War and International Law*, 2: 89, 106–7.

powers of the United Nations may be of some influence upon the major states in ceding to the world organization interventionary powers now possessed by them. Several important reforms have been suggested by the members of the Panel on the Role of International Law in Civil Wars and by the participants in the case studies. If implemented, these may be of some help in moving from the present limited utility of the United Nations in insulating civil tumult from the international community, as emphasized by McNemar, Friedmann, and others, to a position somewhat closer to that advocated by Falk, Corbett, and Barnet.

Two participants, Boals and Fraleigh, advocated a centralized institutionalization of the process of recognition to effect a uniform international policy of aid or its denial to incumbent and insurgent factions. A similar position has been taken by Roger Fisher.[33] Fisher has also noted a related problem of factual characterization and has suggested a centralization of this process.[34]

A plausible thesis could be suggested that, contrary to the revisionist writing on the origin of the cold war in the middle and late 1940s, the major mistakes of United States foreign policy did not come at that time but later, as lessons learned there were misapplied. Arab nationalism in the Middle East and Southeast Asian decolonization were equated, it could be argued, with European communism and its threat to Greece and Turkey in the 1940s. Perhaps such mistakes could be lessened by making increased provision for international fact-finding through the United Nations. The world body would probably not be effective in preventing conflicts involving intense intraregional tension such as surrounded events at Cuba in 1961 or Czechoslovakia in 1968. However, if sufficient information on Vietnam had been available to American decisionmakers from 1946 to 1965 to properly establish and characterize the facts, the relative strengths of various processes, movements, and historical trends might have been more clearly seen, and the subsequent choice between competing labels—decolonization, aggression, civil war —perhaps more accurately made.

Corbett has proposed the proscription of unilateral intervention by a foreign state on behalf of either the incumbent government or an insurgent group and suggests that General Assembly resolutions 2131(XX) and 2225(XXI) are sufficiently broadly phrased to accomplish this if accepted as binding by the international community. This prohibition would be coupled with a grant of power to the United Nations to permit its intervention. Article 2(7) would continue to delimit UN action from those aspects of civil strife which are truly internal. Civil strife

[33] Fisher, "Intervention: Three Problems of Policy and Law," in Falk (ed.), *The Vietnam War and International Law*, 1: 135, 144–45.
[34] *Ibid.*, p. 144.

below the level of actual or imminent civil war would continue to be beyond the United Nations' competence. Intervention in civil war by the United Nations would not be directed at a particular solution of substantive issues in dispute but rather at the insulation of the international community from the effects of civil war. Corbett has suggested that an explicit code be drafted by the International Law Commission detailing the precise conditions under which the United Nations would possess interventionary rights and the rules prescribing UN conduct as an intervener, including the process of termination.[35]

Falk has proposed an authorization of limited legislative competence to the United Nations to intervene "whenever civil strife threatens world peace or whenever gross abuses of fundamental human rights take place."[36] Others have suggested the implementation of article 43 with the creation of a standing UN police force and provision for its financing.[37] The chronology of reform and responsibility must be essentially simultaneous. Major states will resist grants of power to an administratively inadequate organization; a responsible and mature United Nations will not emerge until it shares significant prerogatives now possessed by the sovereign states.

IV. DIRECTIONS FOR FURTHER INQUIRY

One major theme emerges from these case studies of civil strife. There is a compelling necessity for increased community control over the international aspects of civil strife. There has also emerged, however, the essential inability of international and regional organizations to meet this need, caused not only by their structural deficiencies but more basically by the unwillingness of states to cede sufficient power to them to permit effective action. Moreover, traditional rules governing foreign state participation in civil strife have been shown to be impotent in influencing state action. Directions for further study follow from this confrontation between need and present capacity.

First, there must be agreement especially but not exclusively between

[35] *Cf.* Louis Sohn, "The Role of the United Nations in Civil Wars," *Proceedings of the American Society of International Law* 2 (1963): 208.

[36] Falk, *Legal Order in a Violent World*, pp. 336, 344.

[37] Louis Sohn, "The Authority of the United Nations to Establish and Maintain a Permanent United Nations Force, *American Journal of International Law* 52 (1958): 229; Edwin B. Firmage, "A United Nations Peace Force," *Wayne Law Review* 11 (1965): 717.

A panel named by the United Nations Association and including Charles Yost, Kingman Brewster, Jr., Cyrus Vance, and General Mathew Ridgeway recommended such a standing force. See "U.S. Panel Urges U.N. Peace Force," *New York Times*, April 27, 1969, p. 1; and Rosalyn Higgins (ed.), *United Nations Peacekeeping 1946–1967* (London: Oxford University Press, 1969).

the major powers on the circumstances permitting UN intervention in civil strife. This would include the degree to which UN action precluded intervention by foreign states. Preceding any such agreement, there must be continued scholarly dialogue on the role of the United Nations in civil strife. This must include investigation of necessary Charter reform or reinterpretation to make the organization adequate to its tasks, including fact-finding, peacekeeping, and decisionmaking. To establish an enlarged though carefully defined responsibility for international organizations in controlling civil strife, with a circumscribed role for foreign states, would require as a practical political prerequisite a broader area of international consensus on the utility and morality of various types of civil strife than exists at present on the permissibility (or perhaps more accurately a recognition of the probability) of conflict in the process of decolonization.

There is a substantial body of UN resolutions supporting General Assembly competence to authorize or proscribe assistance to national liberation movements.[38] These precedents—particularly the recent Portuguese Territories, Southern Rhodesian, South African, and South West African resolutions[39]—raise a set of issues which deserve further inquiry, since many states, including the great powers of the West, dispute such competence. Corresponding studies of the utility of regional organizations in civil strife should also be accomplished.

Second, a diminished role for foreign states in civil war must be defined. Such a definition would presumably not only provide for proportionate delimitation of unilateral state intervention through displacement by universal and regional organizations but would also create new norms for governing the conditions and extent of outside state intervention in civil strife regardless of involvement by international organizations.

Major internal wars with significant third-party participation have not been examined in this study. The civil war in Greece at the end and after World War II, the Bolshevik coup d'état and subsequent civil war in Russia, the Chinese civil war, and the Korean war of 1950–53 are four important examples. Additional case studies undertaken from the perspective of third-party intervention and the role of international law and international organizations in insulating the international community should be undertaken. Significant wars of political separation such as the American Revolutionary War and wars involving Latin America and Spain could profitably be examined from the same perspective.

One type of civil war—the war of national liberation—demands further study because of its peculiar dogmatic base, the degree of commit-

---

[38] For a listing and analysis of these resolutions, see Marjorie Whiteman, *Digest of International Law* 13 (1968): 679–768.

[39] *Ibid.*, pp. 721–33, 733–49, 756–68.

ment of East and West to its resolution, and the particular strategy and tactics of its insurgents and counterinsurgents.[40]

Finally, even if a significant degree of agreement on international legal rules regarding civil strife can be accomplished, the problem of achieving state adherence to those rules remains. Further study should be done on the relationship between foreign policy and international law. More specifically, the influence of law on the decisionmaking process might be examined from the perspective of foreign state involvement in civil war.

The conclusion that "policy, not law, determines the actions of states with regard to intervention in civil wars"[41] may come uncomfortably close to describing the present. (It may be more accurate to say that law plays an undetermined but probably a very subordinate role in the establishment of policy with regard to intervention in civil wars.) But, as Wolfgang Friedmann observed, such a condition is unacceptable if we are to meet the minimum requirements of world peace. To advocate an increasing role for law and its institutions of community organization in protecting the international community from the effects of civil strife is perhaps to risk being labelled an idealist. It has been noted, however, that the prerequisites of peace in a world possessing weapons of complete destruction include prescriptions which are at once realistic and idealistic. The present attainment of minimum world order realistically sufficient for survival demands the accomplishment of idealistic goals of utopian thinkers of the past. A "contemporary Machiavelli, perceiving this novel necessity for a community of mankind, might be dismissed by the best minds as recklessly utopian."[42] The displacement— or at least the circumspection—of the unilateral application of force, by law, is at once an idealistic goal and a realistic necessity.

[40] See Falk, "The International Law of Internal War: Problems and Prospects," in *Legal Order in a Violent World*, pp. 109, 143–45.

[41] Friedmann, "Intervention, Civil War and the Role of International Law," pp. 151, 158–59.

[42] Falk, "The International Law of Internal War," p. 115.

428

NOTES ON CONTRIBUTORS

RICHARD A. FALK is Albert G. Milbank Professor of International Law and Practice at Princeton University. He is acting as Research Director of the North American Section of the World Order Models Project and as Codirector with C. E. Black of a project to study the future of the international legal order. His books include *Legal Order in a Violent World* and *The Status of Law in International Society*. He has edited *Security in Disarmament* (with R. J. Barnet), *The Strategy of World Order* (with Saul H. Mendlovitz), *The Future of the International Legal Order* (with C. E. Black), and *The Vietnam War and International Law*.

QUINCY WRIGHT was Professor of International Law at the University of Chicago, 1923–56, and at the University of Virginia, 1958–61, and also visiting professor at numerous American and foreign universities. He was past president of the American Society of International Law, the American Political Science Association, the International Political Science Association, and the American Association of University Professors. He was a consultant to the US Department of State, 1943–45, and a technical adviser to the American judge on the Nuremberg Tribunal, 1945. His writings include *Control of American Foreign Relations* (1922), *Mandates under the League of Nations* (1930), *A Study of War* (1942; 2d ed., 1965), *The Study of International Relations* (1955), *International Law and the United Nations* (1959, 1960), *The Strengthening of International Law* (1959), *The Role of International Law in the Elimination of War* (1961), *On Predicting International Relations: The Year 2000* (1970), and numerous journal articles.

ANN VAN WYNEN THOMAS served with the US Department of State during and immediately after World War II, first as Vice Consul in Johannesburg and later in London and the Hague. Since her marriage to A. J. Thomas, Jr., she has devoted herself to legal research and writing and to teaching international law and constitutional law courses in the Department of Political Science of Southern Methodist University. She is the author of *Communism versus International Law*.

A. J. THOMAS, JR., was with the US Foreign Service for three years as Vice Consul in Costa Rica, Portugal, and the Netherlands. In 1947 he joined the faculty of Southern Methodist University School of Law, where he is a professor of international and constitutional law and has been for many years the Chairman of the Committee on Graduate Legal Studies. He is the author of *Economic Regulation of Scheduled Air Transport: National and International* and the co-author, with Ann Thomas, of many international legal studies, including *Non-Intervention: The Law and Its Import in the Americas*, *The Organization of American States*, and *Legal Limits on the Use of Chemical and Biological Weapons*.

ARNOLD FRALEIGH is a graduate of Cornell University and Cornell Law School. After a period of the private practice of law and a tour of duty in the United States Naval Reserve during World War II, he served for eighteen years, from 1946 to 1964, in the US Department of State and Foreign Service. More recently he has taught international law and international organization at George Washington University, where his major interests have been the control of the use of force and human rights.

DONALD W. MCNEMAR is Assistant Professor of Government at Dartmouth College. He graduated from Earlham College, Richmond, Indiana, and did his graduate work in politics at Princeton University, where he held Woodrow Wilson, Danforth and Corwin teaching fellowships. He was also a Research Fellow of the Center of International Studies at Princeton. He has served with the Quaker United Nations Office. His research is focused on the role and capabilities of the United Nations in controlling conflicts and the attitudes and interest of youth in the United Nations.

KATHRYN BOALS is Assistant Professor of Politics at Princeton University and has recently completed a dissertation on "Yemen as a Theoretical Case Study of the Relationship between Modernization and Intervention." She has published *Jordan Water Conflict* (*International Conciliation*, No. 533, May, 1965), as well as several articles on the Middle East, and is currently working on the politics of male-female relations.

PERCY E. CORBETT is Adjunct Professor of International Relations at Lehigh University. Formerly a Fellow of All Souls College, Oxford, and a member of the League of Nations Secretariat, he was successively Professor of Roman and International Law and Dean of the Law Faculty at McGill University, Professor of Law and Political Science and Chairman of the Department of Political Science at Yale University, and Research Associate in the Center of International Studies at Princeton University. His books include *The Settlement of Canadian-American Disputes, Law and Society in the Relations of States*, and *Law in Diplomacy*.

EDWIN BROWN FIRMAGE is Professor of Law at the University of Utah College of Law, where he has taught since 1966. He was graduated magna cum laude from Brigham Young University with a baccalaureate degree in political science and a master's degree in history. He was named National Honors Fellow by the University of Chicago Law School and was graduated with the J.D. degree in 1963. At Chicago he was an editor of the *University of Chicago Law Review*, and was awarded a graduate scholarship to pursue a course of study in international law and international relations, which led to the LL.M. and S.J.D. degrees, awarded in 1964. From 1964 to 1965 he taught international law and conflict of laws at the University of Missouri Law School. He was named White House Fellow for the years 1965–66 and in that capacity served on the staff of Vice-President Hubert Humphrey, with responsibility in the areas of civil rights and urban problems.

430

INDEX

Africa, recognition of liberation groups in, 14, 25, 427

African states: in Congo war, 283–85, 290–91, 418; Lusaka Manifesto of *1969*, 25 (n. 53). *See also* Organization of African Unity

Aggression: attack on intervening state as, 377; attack on nonintervening state as, 398–401; Confederate view of American Civil War as, 31, 78; defined, 309; guerrilla warfare as, 332; infiltration of military forces as, 332, 385; League Covenant provision on, 178; limitation on characterization of use of force as, 413; military aid as, 215, 310, 312; tendency to characterize military intervention as, 309–10, 312; UN Charter provision on, 190–91, 404; war of national liberation as, 389. *See also* Military intervention characterized as aggression

Aid, forms of, line between permissible and impermissible, 22–23, 213. *See also* Diplomatic aid; Economic aid; Ideological aid; Military aid; Military intervention

Aid, regulation of. *See* Collective action, forms of; Collective military intervention; Collective recognition; Regional action, forms of; Regional military aid; Regional military intervention; Regulation of intervention

Aid to either party: as actual practice, 14, 369, 370; if approved by global organization, 5; if approved by regional organization, 5, 220–21, 418–20; by dominant power within sphere of influence (*see* Spheres of influence); for ideological reasons, 186, 418–20; when incumbency disputable, 277–78, 311–14, 354, 358–59, 364–65, 410–11 (*see also* Incumbency); on invitation of puppet government, 402; as norm, 385; if party recognized as a government (*see* Aid to recognized government); preceding outbreak of war, 22; after recognition of belligerency, 208 (n. 1), 313; re-

stricted by judgment on goals of party, 208, 342–44, 370, 411–12

Aid to incumbent government: in Algerian war, 215–18, 222–23; bias of world system in favor of, 25; Central American states' policy of, 107 (n. 10); conflict with nonintervention norm, 405; in decolonization war, 215, 344; impermissible from inception of insurgency, 106–7, 141; when incumbency disputable, 311–12; as norm, 118, 311, 312, 369, 387; permissible before recognition of belligerency, 12, 31, 142, 155, 176, 373, 410; proposal to abolish norm of, 343, 345; recent interventions justified as, 410; refused in Spanish war, 143–46; as undesirable norm, 408; by UN, 25; in war of national liberation, 369–70. *See also* Incumbency

Aid to insurgent: in Algerian war, 213–15, 218–20; as banned under traditional international law, 213; as banned under UN Charter, 214; in Congo war, 278–79; covert, 5; for decolonization, 213–15, 344; under general moral principles, 369; while insurgent not recognized as government, 164–65, 213–15, 278–79; for "national liberation," 369–70, 427; in nineteenth century, 100, 369; in Spanish war, 164–65; treaty ban on, 373; as undesirable norm, 408

Aid to neither party. *See* Impartiality, duty of; Neutrality; Nonintervention

Aid to recognized government: considered permissible, 106–7, 379 (n. 6), 410; when incumbency disputable, 277–78, 311–12, 314, 354, 358–59, 364–65, 410–11; when insurgent recognized as government, 158, 160–61, 211–13; as premise for overt intervention, 5; when a puppet government, 402

Aircraft of intervening state, military: in Congo power struggle of *1964*, 281; in Congo war, 253, 272; in Spanish war, 115, 138, 165; in Vietnam war, 359, 362–63, 364, 367, 368,